ADVENT

CHRISTMAS

LENT

EASTER

PENTECOST

ORDINARY TIME

BIBLE DIARY 2014

Reflections

Fr. Jonathan A. Bitoy, CMF

Introduction to the Seasons of the
Liturgical Year by

Fr. Anscar J. Chupungco, OSB

Illustrations by

Fr. Antonino "Nick" Eucapor, CMF

CLARET
PUBLISHING GROUP

CLARETIAN PUBLICATIONS

BIBLE DIARY® 2014
Copyright © 2013 **Claretian Communications Foundation, Inc.**
U.P. P.O. Box 4, Diliman, 1101 Quezon City, Philippines
Tel: (6 32) 921-3984 • Fax: (6 32) 921-7429
Email: cci@claret.org / ccfi@claretphilippines.com
www.claretianpublications.com

The **Bible Diary®** is a product of the **Claretian Publications**, a division of the **Claretian Communications Foundation, Inc. (CCFI)**, is a pastoral endeavor of the Claretian Missionaries in the Philippines that brings the Word of God to people from all walks of life. CCFI aims to promote integral evangelization and renewed spirituality that is geared towards empowerment and total liberation in response to the needs and challenges of the Church today.

CCFI is a member of **Claret Publishing Group**, a consortium of the publishing houses of the Claretian Missionaries all over the world: Bangalore, Barcelona, Buenos Aires, Chennai, Macau, Madrid, Manila and São Paolo.

Biblical texts taken from **Christian Community Bible, Catholic Pastoral Edition (57ᵗʰ Edition)**

The New English Translation of the ROMAN MISSAL
With permission from the **EPISCOPAL COMMISSION ON LITURGY** of the Catholic Bishops' Conference of the Philippines

A Compilation of Reflections by *Fr. Jonathan A. Bitoy, CMF*
Introduction to the Seasons of the Liturgical Year by *Fr. Anscar J. Chupungco, OSB*

Cover by *Jayson Elvin Guevara*
Illustrations by *Fr. Antonino "Nick" Eucapor, CMF*
Creative design by *Novel Estillore*
Inside Front & Back Cover Illustrations by *Eleazar D. Solas*
Graphic Decorations, Images of saints and quotes: *With Permission from various public domains of the Internet*

ISSN: 1656-457X (Philippines)
ISBN: 971-501-332-5 (USA)
APC-FT197603

Personal Information

NAME:	
HOME ADDRESS:	
CITY/PROVINCE:	
TEL NO.: ( )	MOBILE NO.:
E-MAIL ADDRESS:	
BUSINESS ADDRESS:	
TEL NO.: ( )	FAX NO.: ( )
BUSINESS E-MAIL ADDRESS:	
TAX IDENTIFICATION NO.:	
SOCIAL SECURITY NO.:	
RESIDENCE CERTIFICATE NO.:	
DATE ISSUED:	PLACE ISSUED:
DRIVER'S LICENSE NO.:	
CAR REGISTRATION NO.:	
PASSPORT NO.:	VALID UNTIL:
DATE ISSUED:	PLACE ISSUED:
IN CASE OF EMERGENCY, PLEASE NOTIFY:	
ADDRESS:	
TEL.: ( )	MOBILE NO.: ( )

Dedication

ABOUT THE WRITER OF REFLECTIONS
Fr. Jonathan Advincula Bitoy, CMF

Fr. Jonathan Advincula Bitoy, CMF is a Claretian Missionary from, Iloilo City, Philippines. He holds a Licentiate Degree in Church History and its Cultural Patrimony from The Gregorian Pontifical University, Rome, Italy. At present he is a member of the Faculty of the Institute for Consecrated Life in Asia (ICLA) Philippines and has recently relinquished his post from the said Institute as Secretary and Registrar to move to his new assignment as Assistant Director of the Claretian Communications Foundation, Inc. (CCFI).

Born in Cotabato City, Fr. Jonathan loves to study the culture and heritage of different peoples. He is also into art appreciation and is an advocate for its preservation and proper documentation so that future generations could still enjoy the patrimony of the past. He has had missionary stints in Tumahubong, Basilan the home of "martyrs" and in Surabay, Tungawan and Zamboanga City – all in Mindanao. To date, he is enrolled in the Executive Doctorate for Education Leaders (EDEL) at the Development Academy of the Philippines, Ortigas, Pasig. He believes that missionaries should have exposures in leadership and management skills programs so that they have the necessary competencies to meet the challenges of the 21st century.

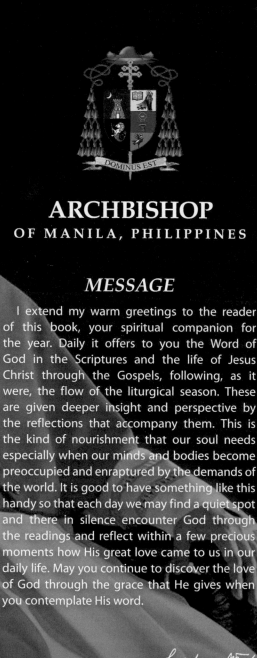

ARCHBISHOP
OF MANILA, PHILIPPINES

MESSAGE

I extend my warm greetings to the reader of this book, your spiritual companion for the year. Daily it offers to you the Word of God in the Scriptures and the life of Jesus Christ through the Gospels, following, as it were, the flow of the liturgical season. These are given deeper insight and perspective by the reflections that accompany them. This is the kind of nourishment that our soul needs especially when our minds and bodies become preoccupied and enraptured by the demands of the world. It is good to have something like this handy so that each day we may find a quiet spot and there in silence encounter God through the readings and reflect within a few precious moments how His great love came to us in our daily life. May you continue to discover the love of God through the grace that He gives when you contemplate His word.

+ Luis Antonio G. Tagle
Cardinal

Pope Francis

formerly Cardinal Jorge Mario Bergoglio, S.J.

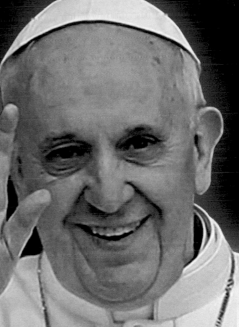

Early years
- born on 17 December 1936 in Buenos Aires.
- studied and holds a degree as a chemical technician
- chose the priesthood and entered the seminary of Villa Devoto.
- 11 March 1958: moved to the novitiate of the Company of Jesus where he finished studies in the humanities in Chile.
- 1963: upon returning to Buenos Aires, obtained a degree in philosophy at the St. Joseph major seminary of San Miguel.
- Between 1964 and 1965: taught literature and psychology at the Immacolata College in Santa Fe.
- In 1966: taught the same subjects at the University of El Salvador, in Buenos Aires.
- From 1967 to 1970: studied theology at the St. Joseph major seminary of San Miguel where he obtained a degree.
- On 13 December 1969: ordained a priest.
- From 1970 to 1971: completed the third probation at Alcala de Henares, Spain, and
- On 22 April 1973: pronounced his perpetual vows.

As A Religious
- novice master at Villa Varilari in San Miguel from 1972 to 1973, where he also taught theology.
- On 31 July 1973: elected as Provincial for Argentina, a role he served as for six years.
- From 1980 to 1986: rector of the Philosophical and Theological Faculty of San Miguel as well as pastor of the Patriarca San Jose parish in the Diocese of San Miguel.
- March of 1986: went to Germany to finish his doctoral thesis.
- The superiors then sent him to the University of El Salvador and then to Cordoba where he served as a confessor and spiritual director.

As A Bishop
- On 20 May 1992, John Paul II appointed him titular Bishop of Auca and Auxiliary of Buenos Aires.
- Received the episcopal consecration in the Cathedral of Buenos Aires from Cardinal Antonio Quarracino, Apostolic Nunzio Ubaldo Calabresi, and Bishop Emilio Ognenovich. of Mercedes-Lujan on 27 June of that year.
- On 3 June 1997: appointed Coadjutor Archbishop of Buenos Aires and succeeded Cardinal Antonio Quarracino on 28 February 1998.
- Adjunct Relator General of the 10th Ordinary General Assembly of the Synod of Bishops, October 2001.
- Served as President of the Bishops' Conference of Argentina from 8 November 2005 until 8 November 2011.

As A Cardinal
- created and proclaimed Cardinal by Blessed John Paul II in the consistory of 21 February 2001, of the Title of S. Roberto Bellarmino (St. Robert Bellarmine).
- a member of:
  The Congregations for Divine Worship and Discipline of the Sacraments; for the Clergy; and for Institutes of Consecrated Life and Societies of Apostolic Life; the Pontifical Council for the Family; and the Pontifical Commission for Latin America.
- Also the Ordinary for Eastern-rite faithful in Argentina who lack an Ordinary of their own rite,

Following the resignation of Pope Benedict XVI, on 13 March 2013 the papal conclave elected Bergoglio, who chose the papal name Francis in honor of Saint Francis of Assisi.
- the first Jesuit pope;
- the first pope from the Americas, and
- the first pope from the Southern Hemisphere.

Throughout his life, both as an individual and a religious leader, he has been known for his humility, his concern for the poor, and his commitment to dialogue as a way to build bridges between people of all backgrounds, beliefs, and faiths. Since his election to the papacy, he has displayed a simpler and less formal approach to the office, including a decision to reside in the Vatican guesthouse rather than the papal residence used by his predecessors since 1903.

Calendar 2014

JANUARY

Sun	Mon	Tue	Wed	Thu	Fri	Sat
			1	2	3	4
5	6	7	8	9	10	11
12	13	14	15	16	17	18
19	20	21	22	23	24	25
26	27	28	29	30	31	

FEBRUARY

Sun	Mon	Tue	Wed	Thu	Fri	Sat
						1
2	3	4	5	6	7	8
9	10	11	12	13	14	15
16	17	18	19	20	21	22
23	24	25	26	27	28	

MARCH

Sun	Mon	Tue	Wed	Thu	Fri	Sat
						1
2	3	4	5	6	7	8
9	10	11	12	13	14	15
16	17	18	19	20	21	22
23	24	25	26	27	28	29
30	31					

APRIL

Sun	Mon	Tue	Wed	Thu	Fri	Sat
		1	2	3	4	5
6	7	8	9	10	11	12
13	14	15	16	17	18	19
20	21	22	23	24	25	26
27	28	29	30			

MAY

Sun	Mon	Tue	Wed	Thu	Fri	Sat
				1	2	3
4	5	6	7	8	9	10
11	12	13	14	15	16	17
18	19	20	21	22	23	24
25	26	27	28	29	30	31

JUNE

Sun	Mon	Tue	Wed	Thu	Fri	Sat
1	2	3	4	5	6	7
8	9	10	11	12	13	14
15	16	17	18	19	20	21
22	23	24	25	26	27	28
29	30					

JULY

Sun	Mon	Tue	Wed	Thu	Fri	Sat
		1	2	3	4	5
6	7	8	9	10	11	12
13	14	15	16	17	18	19
20	21	22	23	24	25	26
27	28	29	30	31		

AUGUST

Sun	Mon	Tue	Wed	Thu	Fri	Sat
					1	2
3	4	5	6	7	8	9
10	11	12	13	14	15	16
17	18	19	20	21	22	23
24	25	26	27	28	29	30
31						

SEPTEMBER

Sun	Mon	Tue	Wed	Thu	Fri	Sat
	1	2	3	4	5	6
7	8	9	10	11	12	13
14	15	16	17	18	19	20
21	22	23	24	25	26	27
28	29	30				

OCTOBER

Sun	Mon	Tue	Wed	Thu	Fri	Sat
			1	2	3	4
5	6	7	8	9	10	11
12	13	14	15	16	17	18
19	20	21	22	23	24	25
26	27	28	29	30	31	

NOVEMBER

Sun	Mon	Tue	Wed	Thu	Fri	Sat
						1
2	3	4	5	6	7	8
9	10	11	12	13	14	15
16	17	18	19	20	21	22
23	24	25	26	27	28	29
30						

DECEMBER

Sun	Mon	Tue	Wed	Thu	Fri	Sat
	1	2	3	4	5	6
7	8	9	10	11	12	13
14	15	16	17	18	19	20
21	22	23	24	25	26	27
28	29	30	31			

Calendar 2015

JANUARY

Sun	Mon	Tue	Wed	Thu	Fri	Sat
				1	2	3
4	5	6	7	8	9	10
11	12	13	14	15	16	17
18	19	20	21	22	23	24
25	26	27	28	29	30	31

FEBRUARY

Sun	Mon	Tue	Wed	Thu	Fri	Sat
1	2	3	4	5	6	7
8	9	10	11	12	13	14
15	16	17	18	19	20	21
22	23	24	25	26	27	28

MARCH

Sun	Mon	Tue	Wed	Thu	Fri	Sat
1	2	3	4	5	6	7
8	9	10	11	12	13	14
15	16	17	18	19	20	21
22	23	24	25	26	27	28
29	30	31				

APRIL

Sun	Mon	Tue	Wed	Thu	Fri	Sat
			1	2	3	4
5	6	7	8	9	10	11
12	13	14	15	16	17	18
19	20	21	22	23	24	25
26	27	28	29	30		

MAY

Sun	Mon	Tue	Wed	Thu	Fri	Sat
					1	2
3	4	5	6	7	8	9
10	11	12	13	14	15	16
17	18	19	20	21	22	23
24	25	26	27	28	29	30
31						

JUNE

Sun	Mon	Tue	Wed	Thu	Fri	Sat
	1	2	3	4	5	6
7	8	9	10	11	12	13
14	15	16	17	18	19	20
21	22	23	24	25	26	27
28	29	30				

JULY

Sun	Mon	Tue	Wed	Thu	Fri	Sat
			1	2	3	4
5	6	7	8	9	10	11
12	13	14	15	16	17	18
19	20	21	22	23	24	25
26	27	28	29	30	31	

AUGUST

Sun	Mon	Tue	Wed	Thu	Fri	Sat
						1
2	3	4	5	6	7	8
9	10	11	12	13	14	15
16	17	18	19	20	21	22
23	24	25	26	27	28	29
30	31					

SEPTEMBER

Sun	Mon	Tue	Wed	Thu	Fri	Sat
		1	2	3	4	5
6	7	8	9	10	11	12
13	14	15	16	17	18	19
20	21	22	23	24	25	26
27	28	29	30			

OCTOBER

Sun	Mon	Tue	Wed	Thu	Fri	Sat
				1	2	3
4	5	6	7	8	9	10
11	12	13	14	15	16	17
18	19	20	21	22	23	24
25	26	27	28	29	30	31

NOVEMBER

Sun	Mon	Tue	Wed	Thu	Fri	Sat
1	2	3	4	5	6	7
8	9	10	11	12	13	14
15	16	17	18	19	20	21
22	23	24	25	26	27	28
29	30					

DECEMBER

Sun	Mon	Tue	Wed	Thu	Fri	Sat
		1	2	3	4	5
6	7	8	9	10	11	12
13	14	15	16	17	18	19
20	21	22	23	24	25	26
27	28	29	30	31		

Liturgical and Sanctoral Catholic Calendar

JANUARY	
1	Mary, Mother of God
2	Basil the Great / Gregory of Nazianzen
3	Most Holy Name of Jesus
4	Elizabeth Ann Seton
5	Epiphany of the Lord
6	
7	Raymond of Penyafort
8	
9	
10	
11	
12	Baptism of the Lord
13	*Psalter I, 1st Week in Ordinary Time*
14	
15	
16	
17	Anthony
18	
19	Feast of Sto. Niño
19	(USA) *2nd Sunday in Ordinary Time*
20	Fabian / Sebastian
21	Agnes
22	Vincent of Saragossa
23	
24	Francis de Sales
25	Conversion of St. Paul
26	*Psalter III, 3rd Sunday in Ordinary Time*
27	Angela Merici
28	Thomas Aquinas
29	
30	
31	John Bosco

FEBRUARY	
1	
2	Presentation of the Lord
3	Blaise / Ansgar
4	
5	Agatha
6	Paul Miki
7	
8	Jerome Emiliani / Josephine Bakhita
9	*Psalter I, 5th Sunday in Ordinary Time*
10	Scholastica
11	Our Lady of Lourdes
12	
13	
14	Cyril / Methodius
15	
16	*Psalter II, 6th Sunday in Ordinary Time*
17	The Seven Holy Founders of the Order of Servites
18	
19	
20	
21	Basil the Great
22	Chair of St, Peter
23	*Psalter III, 7th Sunday in Ordinary Time*
24	
25	
26	
27	
28	

Liturgical and Sanctoral Catholic Calendar

MARCH	
1	
2	*Psalter IV, 8th Sunday in Ordinary Time*
3	Katherine Drexel
4	Casimir
5	**Ash Wednesday**
6	
7	
8	
9	**Psalter I, 1st Sunday of Lent**
10	
11	
12	
13	
14	
15	
16	**Psalter II, 2nd Sunday of Lent**
17	
18	
19	Joseph, Husband of Mary
20	
21	
22	
23	**Psalter III, 3rd Sunday of Lent**
24	
25	**Annunciation of the Lord**
26	
27	
28	
29	
30	**Psalter IV, 4th Sunday of Lent**
31	

APRIL	
1	
2	
3	
4	
5	
6	*Psalter I, 5th Sunday of Easter*
7	
8	
9	
10	
11	
12	
13	*Palm Sunday of the Lord's Passion*
14	
15	
16	
17	Holy Thursday
18	Good Friday of the Lord's Passion
19	The Vigil in the Holy Night of Easter
20	*Easter Sunday / Our Lord's Ressurection*
21	Octave of Easter – Monday
22	Octave of Easter – Tuesday
23	Octave of Easter – Wednesday
24	Octave of Easter – Thursday
25	Octave of Easter – Friday
26	Octave of Easter – Saturday
27	*Psalter II, 2nd Sunday of Easter*
28	Peter Chanel / Louis Marie de Montfort
29	Catherine of Siena
30	Pius V

Liturgical and Sanctoral Catholic Calendar

MAY	
1	Joseph the Worker
2	Athanasius
3	Philip and James, Apostles
4	*Psalter III, 3rd Sunday of Easter*
5	
6	
7	
8	
9	
10	Damien Joseph de Veuster of Moloka'i
11	*Psalter IV, 4th Sunday of Easter*
12	Nareus and Achilleus / Pancras
13	Our Lady of Fatima
14	Matthias, Apostle
15	Isidore the Farmer
16	
17	
18	*Psalter I, 5th Sunday of Easter*
19	
20	Benardine of Siena
21	Christopher Magallanes
22	Rita of Cascia
23	
24	
25	*Psalter II, 6th Sunday of Easter*
26	Philip Neri
27	Augustine of Canterbury
28	
29	
30	
31	Visitation of the Blessed Virgin Mary

JUNE	
1	*Ascension of the Lord*
2	Marcellinus and Peter
3	Charles Lwanga
4	
5	Boniface
6	Norbert
7	
8	*Pentecost Sunday*
9	Ephrem of Syria
10	
11	Barnabas
12	
13	Anthony of Padua
14	
15	*Solemnity of the Most Holy Trinity*
16	
17	
18	
19	Romuald
20	
21	Aloysius Gonzaga
22	*The Blood and Body of Christ*
23	
24	Nativity of John the Baptist
25	
26	
27	*Sacred Heart of Jesus*
28	Immaculate Heart of Mary
29	Peter and Paul, Apostles
30	First Martyrs of the Church of Rome

Liturgical and Sanctoral Catholic Calendar

JULY

1	Juniperro Sera
2	
3	Thomas, Apostle
4	Elizabeth of Portugal
5	Anthony Mary Zaccaria
6	*Psalter II, 14th Sunday in Ordinary Time*
7	
8	
9	Augustine Zhao Rong
10	
11	Benedict
12	
13	*Psalter III, 15th Sunday in Ordinary Time*
14	Kateri Tekakwitha
15	Bonaventure
16	Our Lady of Mount Carmel
17	
18	Camillus de Lellis
19	
20	*Psalter IV, 16th Sunday in Ordinary Time*
21	Lawrence of Brisindi
22	Mary Magdalene
23	Bridget of Sweden
24	Sharbel Makhluf
25	James, Apostle
26	Joachim and Ann
27	*Psalter I, 17th Sunday in Ordinary Time*
28	
29	Martha
30	Peter Chrysologus
31	Ignatius of Loyola

AUGUST

1	Alphonsus Liguori
2	Eusebius of Vercelli / Peter Julian Eymard
3	*Psalter II, 18th Sunday in Ordinary Time*
4	John Mary Vianney
5	Dedication of St. Mary Major
6	Transfiguration of the Lord
7	Sixtus II and companions / Cajetan
8	Dominic
9	Teresa Benedicta of the Cross
10	*Psalter III, 19th Sunday in Ordinary Time*
11	Clare
12	Jane Frances de Chantal
13	Pontian / Hippolytus
14	Maximilian Mary Kolbe
15	Assumption of the Blessed Virgin Mary
16	Stephen of Hungary
17	*Psalter IV, 20th Sunday in Ordinary Time*
18	
19	John Eudes
20	Bernard of Clairvaux
21	Pius X
22	Queenship of Mary
23	Rose of Lima
24	*Psalter I, 21st Sunday in Ordinary Time*
25	Louis of France / Joseph Calasanz
26	
27	Monica
28	Augustine
29	Martyrdom of John the Baptist
30	
31	*Psalter II, 22nd Sunday in Ordinary Time*

Liturgical and Sanctoral Catholic Calendar

SEPTEMBER	
1	
2	
3	Gregory the Great
4	
5	
6	
7	*Psalter III, 23rd Sunday in Ordinary Time*
8	Nativity of the Blessed Virgin Mary
9	Peter Claver
10	
11	
12	Most Holy Name of the Blessed Virgin Mary
13	John Chrysostom
14	Triumph of the Cross
15	Our Lady of Sorrows
16	Cornelius / Cyprian
17	Robert Bellarmine
18	
19	Januarius
20	Andrew Kim Taegon / Paul Chong Hasang and Companions
21	*Psalter I, 25th Sunday in Ordinary Time*
22	
23	Pio of Pietrelcina
24	
25	
26	Cosmas and Damian
27	Vincent de Paul
28	*Psalter II, 26th Sunday in Ordinary Time*
29	Michael, Gabriel and Raphael
30	Jerome

OCTOBER	
1	Therese of the Child Jesus
2	Holy Guardian Angels
3	
4	Francis of Assisi
5	*Psalter III, 27th Sunday in Ordinary Time*
6	Bruno / Bl. Marie Rose Durocher
7	Our Lady of the Rosary
8	
9	Denis and companions / John Leonardi
10	
11	
12	*Psalter IV, 28th Sunday in Ordinary Time*
13	
14	Callistus I
15	Teresa of Avila
16	Hedwig / Margaret Mary Alacoque
17	Ignatius of Antioch
18	Luke, Evangelist
19	*Psalter I, 29th Sunday in Ordinary Time*
20	Paul of the Cross
21	
22	
23	John of Capistrano
24	Anthony Mary Claret
25	
26	*Psalter II, 30th Sunday in Ordinary Time*
27	
28	Simon and Jude, Apostles
29	
30	
31	

Liturgical and Sanctoral Catholic Calendar

NOVEMBER	
1	All Saints' Day
2	Commemoration of All Faithful Departed
3	Martin de Porres
4	Charles Borromeo
5	
6	
7	
8	
9	Dedication of the Lateran Basilica
10	Leo the Great
11	Martin of Tours
12	Josaphat
13	Frances Xavier Cabrini
14	
15	Albert the Great
16	*Psalter I, 33rd Sunday in Ordinary Time*
17	Elizabeth of Hungary
18	Rose Philippine Duchesne
19	
20	
21	Presentation of the Virgin Mary
22	Cecilia
23	*Solemnity of Christ the King*
24	Andrew Dung Lac
25	Caherine of Alexandria
26	
27	
28	
29	
30	*Psalter I, 1st Sunday of Advent*

DECEMBER	
1	
2	
3	Francis Xavier
4	John of Damascus
5	
6	Nicholas
7	*Psalter II, 2nd Sunday of Advent*
8	Immaculate Conception of Mary
9	Juan Diego
10	
11	Damasus I
12	Our Lady of Guadalupe
13	Lucy
14	*Psalter III, 3rd Sunday of Advent*
15	
16	
17	
18	
19	
20	
21	*Psalter IV, 4th Sunday of Advent*
22	
23	John of Kanty
24	
25	*Nativity of the Lord*
26	Stephen, First Martyr
27	John, Apostle and Evangelist
28	*Holy Family of Jesus, Mary & Joseph*
29	Thomas Beckett
30	
31	Sylvester I

Daily Prayers

Sign of the Cross

In the name of the Father,
and of the Son,
and of the Holy Spirit.
Amen.

The Lord's Prayer

Our Father, in heaven,
holy be your name;
your Kingdom come;
your will be done on earth
as it is in heaven.
Give us this day our daily bread;
and forgive us our sins
as we forgive those
who sin against us;
do not bring us to the test,
but deliver us from evil.
Amen.

Hail Mary

Hail Mary, full of grace,
the Lord is with you.
Blessed are you among women,
and blessed is the fruit of your womb,
Jesus.
Holy Mary, Mother of God, pray for us
sinners, now, and at the hour of our death.
Amen.

Glory to the Father

Glory to the Father, and to the Son,
and to the Holy Spirit;
as it was in the beginning,
is now, and will be,
forever.
Amen.

Come Holy Spirit

Come, Holy Spirit,
fill the hearts of your faithful
and enkindle in them the fire of your love.
Send forth your spirit
and they shall be created;
and you will renew the face of the earth.
Lord, by the light of the Holy Spirit,
you have taught the hearts of your faithful.
In the same Spirit help us to relish
what is right and always rejoice
in your consolation.
We ask this through Christ our Lord.
Amen.

The Benedictus

Blessed be the Lord, the God of Israel!
He has visited his people
and redeemed them.
He has raised up for us a mighty savior
in the house of David his servant,
as he promised by the lips of holy men,
those who were his prophets from of old.
A savior who would free us from our foes,
from the hands of all who hate us.
So his love for our fathers is fulfilled
and his holy covenant remembered.
He swore to Abraham our father
to grant us, that free from fear,
and saved from the hands of our foes,
we might serve him in holiness
and justice all the days of our life
in his presence.
As for you, little child,
you shall be called a prophet
of God, the Most High.
You shall go ahead of the Lord
to prepare his way before him.
To make known to his people
their salvation through forgiveness
of all their sins, the loving-kindness
of the heart of our God
who visits us like the dawn from on high.
He will give light to those in darkness,
those who dwell in the shadow of death,
and guide us into the way of peace.

The Magnificat

My soul magnifies the Lord,
and my spirit rejoices in God, my Savior;
because he has regarded
the lowliness of his handmaid;
for behold henceforth
all ages shall call me blessed.
Because he who is mighty
has done great things for me,
and holy is his name;
and his mercy is from generation
to generation on those who fear him.
He has shown might with his arm,
he has scattered the proud
in the conceit of their heart.
He has put down the mighty
from their thrones
and has exalted the lowly.
He has filled the hungry with good things,
and the rich he has sent away empty.
He has given help to Israel,
his servant, mindful of his mercy,
even as he spoke to our fathers,
to Abraham and to his posterity forever.
Amen.

Hail Holy Queen

Hail Holy Queen, Mother of mercy;
hail, our life, our sweetness, and our hope.
To you do we cry,
poor banished children of Eve;
to you do we send up our sighs,
mourning and weeping in this valley
of tears.
Turn, then, most gracious advocate,
your eyes of mercy toward us;
and after this, our exile,
show us the blessed fruit
of your womb, Jesus;
O clement, O loving, O sweet Virgin Mary.

Memorare

Remember, O most gracious Virgin Mary,
that never was it known
that anyone who fled to your protection,
implored your help,
or sought your intercession
was left unaided.

Inspired by this confidence, I fly to you,
O Virgin of Virgins, my Mother.
To you I come, before you I stand,
sinful and sorrowful.
O Mother of the Word Incarnate,
despise not my petitions
but in your mercy, hear and answer me.
Amen.

The Angelus

V. The angel of the Lord declared to Mary.
R. And she conceived by the Holy Spirit.
   Hail Mary…
V. Behold the handmaid of the Lord.
R. Be it done to me according
   to your Word.
   Hail Mary…
V. And the Word was made flesh.
R. And dwelt among us.
   Hail Mary…
V. Pray for us, holy Mother of God.
R. That we may be made worthy
   of the promises of Christ.

Let us Pray:
Pour forth, we beseech you, O Lord,
your grace into our hearts,
that we to whom the incarnation of
Christ your Son was made known by the
message of an angel, may, by his passion
and cross be brought to the glory
of his resurrection, through Christ our
Lord.
Amen.

Regina Coeli

Queen of heaven, rejoice, alleluia!
For Christ, your Son and Son of God,
has risen as he said, alleluia!
Pray to God for us, alleluia!
V. Rejoice and be glad, O Virgin Mary,
   alleluia!
R. For the Lord has truly risen, alleluia!
Let us Pray:
God of life, you have given joy to the world
by the resurrection of your Son,
our Lord Jesus Christ. Through the prayers
of his mother, the Virgin Mary,

bring us to the happiness
of eternal life.
We ask this through Christ our Lord.
Amen.

Apostles' Creed
I believe in God,
the Father almighty,
Creator of heaven and earth;
and in Jesus Christ,
His only son, our Lord:
Who was conceived
by the Holy Spirit
born of the Virgin Mary;
suffered under Pontius Pilate,
was crucified, died,
and was buried.
He descended into hell;
On the third day
he rose again form the dead;
He ascended into heaven,
is seated at the right hand
of God the Father Almighty;
From thence He shall come
to judge the living and the dead.
I believe in the Holy Spirit,
the Holy Catholic Church,
the communion of Saints,
the forgiveness of sins,
the resurrection of the body,
and life everlasting.
Amen.

Grace Before Meals
Bless us, O Lord,
and these your gifts
which we are about to receive
from your bounty,
through Christ our Lord.
Amen.

Grace After Meals
We give you thanks almighty God,
for all your gifts,
through Christ our Lord,
who live and reign,
now and forever.
Amen.

Act of Contrition
My God, I am sorry for my sins
with all my heart.
In choosing to do wrong
and failing to do good,
I have sinned against you
whom I should love
above all things.
I firmly intend, with your help,
to do penance, to sin no more,
and to avoid whatever
leads me to sin.
Our Savior Jesus Christ suffered
and died for us.
In his name, my God,
have mercy.

Prayer for Peace
(St. Francis of Assisi)
Lord, make me an instrument
of your peace.
Where there is hatred,
let me sow love;
Where there is injury, pardon;
Where there is doubt, faith;
Where there is despair, hope;
Where there is darkness, light;
Where there is sadness, joy.
O Divine Master,
grant that I may not so much
seek to be consoled,
as to console;
to be understood,
as to understand;
to be loved, as to love.
For it is in giving
that we receive;
it is in pardoning
that we are pardoned;
and it is in dying
that we are born to eternal life.

Morning Offering
O Jesus, through the Immaculate
Heart of Mary,
I offer you all of my prayers,
works, joys, and sufferings
of this day in union

with the Holy Sacrifice
of the Mass throughout the world.
I offer them for all the intentions
of your Sacred Heart:
the salvation of souls,
reparation for sin,
the reunion of all Christians.
I offer them for the intentions
of our bishops,
and of all Apostles of Prayer,
and in particular
for those recommended
by our Holy Father this month.
Amen.

Prayer for Generosity

O Lord, teach me to be generous.
Teach me to serve you
as you deserve;
To give and not to count the cost;
To fight and not
to heed the wounds;
To toil and not to seek for rest;
To labor and not to ask for reward
Save that of knowing
that I am doing your holy will.
Amen.

Soul of Christ

Soul of Christ, sanctify me.
Body of Christ, save me.
Blood of Christ, inebriate me.
Water from the side of Christ,
wash me.
Passion of Christ,
strengthen me.
O good Jesus, hear me.
Within your wounds,
shelter me.
Permit me not
to be separated from you.
From the evil one protect me.
At the hour of my death
call me and bid me come to you,
that I may praise you
with all your saints
for ever and ever.
Amen.

The Beatitudes

Fortunate are those
who have the spirit of the poor,
for theirs is the kingdom of heaven.
Fortunate are those who mourn,
they shall be comforted.
Fortunate are the gentle,
they shall possess the land.
Fortunate are those who hunger
and thirst for justice,
for they shall be satisfied.
Fortunate are the merciful,
for they shall find mercy.
Fortunate are those with pure heart,
for they shall see God.
Fortunate are those who work
for peace, they shall be called
children of God.
Fortunate are those persecuted
for the cause
of justice, for theirs
is the kingdom of heaven.
Fortunate are you,
when people insult you
and persecute you
and speak all kinds
of evil against you because you
are my followers.
Be glad and joyful,
for a great reward is kept
for you in God.

Oratio Imperata

Almighty God, our loving Father,
Creator and lover of all life,
You created us in Your own image and likeness.

Give us the strength and courage
to defend and protect marriage,
the family, and all human life:
from conception,
at the moment of fertilization,
to natural death.

We ask Your divine healing, comfort,
and peace for all those suffering
from marital and family problems.
Grant to them forgiveness,
understanding, and strength.

We pray for all our leaders and legislators.
Grant to them wisdom, fear of the Lord,
and steadfastness
to enable them
to reject all proposed measures opposed
to Life and the Family.

May Mary, our most loving Mother,
intercede for the Filipino people / your people.
We entrust to Her this cause for the protection of Life and the Family.
To You, O Lord, through Her, we consecrate the Filipino nation / our nation.

We ask all these through Christ, Our Lord.
Amen.

O Mary, Mediatrix of All-Grace and Queen of the Family, pray for us.
St. Joseph, Chaste Spouse of the Virgin Mary, pray for us.
Saints Lorenzo Ruiz and Pedro Calungsod, pray for us.
Blessed John Paul the Great, Defender and Promoter of the Culture of Life, pray for us.

Blessed John Paul the Great, defender and promoter of the Gospel of Life, pray for us.
(with permission from the Commission on Family and Life, Catholic Bishops' Conference of the Philippines)

Family Prayers

Prayer of Husband and Wife

Father, all-powerful and eternal God, we give you thanks and bless your holy name. You created mankind as man and woman and blessed their union, making them a help and support for each other.

Remember us today. Look kindly on us and grant that our love may be completely unselfish, a gift like that of Christ to his Church. May we live many years together in joy and peace, and may we always give you heartfelt praise through your Son and in the Holy Spirit. *Amen*

Prayer for the Gift of a Child

God our Father, all parenthood comes from you. Allow us to share in that power which is yours alone, and let us see in the child you send us a living sign of your presence in our home.

Bless our love and make it fruitful so that a new heart to love you, and a new life to bear witness to you. *Amen.*

When Expecting a Child

Father, we thank you for your marvelous gift; you have allowed us to share in your divine parenthood. During this time of waiting, we ask you to protect and nurture these first mysterious stirrings of life.

May our child come safely into the light of the world and to the new birth of baptism. Mother of God, we entrust our child to your loving heart. *Amen.*

Prayer of a Father or Mother

Father of mankind, you have given me these children, and entrusted them to my charge, to bring them up for you and to prepare them for everlasting life.

Help me with your heavenly grace to fulfill this sacred duty.

Teach me what to give, and what to withhold; when to reprove and when to forbear.

Make me gentle, yet firm; considerate and watchful. Through Christ our Lord. *Amen.*

Prayer for Renconciliation Between Spouses

Until now, Lord, seperation was something that happened to someone else, anyone else, except me. Yet here I am, my mind full of the details of separation, and my heart full of pain. If this separation is a mistake, guide me toward my spouse and the reconciliation which will allow us to work toward a successful marriage.

Although it seems difficult now, I know that we can work toward reconciliation if we remember the love that first brought us together. It will not be easy, but the home and life my spouse and I have built together might be able to be restored if we both are willing to try again. Guide us, Lord, with Your love and grace at this difficult time. *Amen.*

Prayer for Renconciliation with Family Members

Lord, Jesus, my family needs Your help today. We are searching for tranquility and peace and can end to the discord that keeps us apart. Give us strength and compassion to understand each other, wisdom and love to help one another, and the trust and patience we need to live peacefully together. I pray that our family might become a holy family that works, prays, and plays together, a family that embraces peace and love, a family whose members are dedicated in love to each other and to God. *Amen.*

Prayer for Easing of Financial Difficulties

Dear Lord, I have been taught that money is not what is most important, yet money Is often a problem in life. These latest financial difficulties are particularly hard. Help me to use money wisely—to resist buying what I do not need and to stop comparing my possessions with those of others. Grant me what I need in this life, so that I may care for myself and those dear to me, with enough to share with those less fortunate. *Amen.*

Prayer for a Loved one with Drug or Alcohol Problem

Dear Lord, watching someone I love being destroyed by drugs and alcohol seems more than I can bear. My threatening, arguing, rationalizing, and controlling have proved futile. The problem continues, and I am discouraged and frustrated. I realize I am powerless over this problem and powerless over anyone's life but my own.

Guide my words and actions so that I will say and do all I can to hasten recovery. Help me to also detach so that my loved one may admit the problem and seek help. May I take care of what is my responsibility and no more. Above all, Lord, help me let go and let You take care of everything in my life. May I never lose faith in Your power. *Amen.*

Prayer for an End to Domestic Violence

Dear God, when I think of a family, I think of a mother, father, and children—all living together and sharing mutual love, concern, and kindness. For some, however, family life is filled with pain, anger, and fear. The harsh reality of physical, verbal, and emotional abuse that is present among so many families is a problem that must not be ignored. Father, guide all people so they do not resort to abuse of any kind in their relationships.

Give those who have difficulty coping with their responsibilities the wisdom and courage to recognize their problems and, when needed, to seek counseling. I ask You also to protect the children raised in abusive families from continuing the harmful cycle of abuse as they mature and become parents themselves. *Amen.*

Prayer of Spouses for one another

Jesus, You saw so much value in the love between husband and wife that You elevated married life to a sacramental level. I know that marriage is a sign of the love and unity that exists between You and Your Church.

Continue to give Your help to us that our love may grow day by day. Help us to realize that our love must overflow into the world around us. Give us strength in times of trial and difficulty; give us happiness, security, and the joy of seeing our love expand beyond ourselves to others. I ask this through the intercession of Mary and her beloved spouse, St. Joseph. *Amen.*

Prayer of Parents for their Children

O God, make me a better parent. Help me to understand my children, to listen patiently to what they have to say, and to answer all their questions wisely and kindly. Keep me from criticizing them so that they can learn from their strengths and weaknesses. Keep me from making

all decisions so that they can develop responsibility. Yet, help me to have the courage to refuse giving in to what will harm them.

Help me to appreciate my children as they are, not as I would have them to be. When I grow discouraged, remind me that my child is Your child also. You abide in us always—sheltering us in Your care, surrounding us with Your goodness, and enfolding us in Your love. *Amen.*

Prayer of a Single Parent

It is late, Lord, and yet I sit here, trying to rally strength for tomorrow. I feel burdened as a single parent. The pressure of juggling work, home, school, and sitter schedules leaves little time. Somewhere in the middle I am lost, a wheel with a hundred spokes, each pulling me and demanding comfort, support, and attention. I am weighed down with guilt about the job I am doing. Refusing demands for material things is difficult, but refusing demands for my time is worse. Give me the courage to persist in this difficult task of parenting. Make me realistic in what I expect of myself and others. Nurture me and love me, Lord. Let me know You are with me in all my stumblings, in all my days. Bring me and my loved ones through these hard times so that we may find happiness and peace. *Amen.*

Prayer for One's Parents during difficult times

Lord, seeing my parents grow older has been hard for me. I struggle to retain my view of them as they were when I was young. They seemed so strong then, able to work endlessly, to love completely, to give selflessly. I made demands of them then, as does any child, sometimes being unreasonable, unappreciative, and selfish. Now the tables are turned. My parents seem set in their ways, unwilling to bend much, unable to give much. Their bodies are less strong, and their energy limited. This is my time to show love for them—to overlook their moods, to respect their independence.

I pray for my parents, my lifelong friends. May they be comforted with Your healing, solace, and strength. Help all of us to be patient and to love one another in the understanding, undemanding way that You love each of us. *Amen.*

Healing in the Family - Special Intention

I pray to you, O Lord, for a very special intention: (name concern). You promised us that whatever we ask for in Your name will be granted. I, for my part, will do what I can, Lord, but without Your help, I can accomplish nothing. Grant that my will may always be one with Yours. *Amen.*

Prayer of Thanksgiving

Dear Lord, I am grateful that my loved ones have had this day together, with ample food and shelter, and with the love of one another to lighten the day's burdens and magnify the day's of joys. May we truly forgive one another's failings—the unkind words or forgotten thank you—that are not so important in the long run. May we have the courage to discuss the things that are important to us.

I thank You for all the experiences this day has brought. May I remember these encouragement. Help me to grow past my mistakes and to develop strength for future challenges. I ask You to bless and protect my home and all who are dear to me. *Amen*

Visit this House

Visit this house, we beg you, Lord, and banish from it the deadly power of the evil one. May your holy angels dwell here to keep us in peace, and may your blessing be always upon us. We ask this through Christ our Lord. *Amen.*

Prayer before a Crucifix

Good and gentle Jesus, I kneel before you, I see and ponder your five wounds. My eyes behold what David prophesied about you: "They have pierced my hands and feet; they have numbered all my bones".

Imprint on me this image of yourself. Fulfill the deep desires of my heart. Give me faith, hope and love, repentance for my sins, and the strength to serve your people with respect and love. *Amen.*

Prayer for those Making a Journey

My holy Guardian Angel, ask the Lord to bless the journey which I undertake, that it may profit the health of my soul and body; that I may reach its end, and that, returning safe and sound, I may find my family in good health. Do thou guard, guide and preserve us. *Amen.*

Prayer for a Holy Death

O Christ, let me confess Your name with my last breath. In Your mercy receive me and do not dissapoint me in my hope. Open the gates of life for me, and let the prince of darkness have no power over me. Protect me by Your kindness, shield me with Your might, and lead me by Your right hand to the place of refreshment, the tabernacle You have prepared for Your servants and for those who revere You. *Amen.*

Prayer for Meetings

Opening

Lord, as we gather in your name,
we want to be in your presence.
Grant us a spirit of dialogue,
illumine our minds with the light of truth
and strengthen our fraternal spirit
that we may always seek and do your will.
Through Jesus Christ, our Lord.
Amen.

Closing

Father of goodness,
we thank you for this encounter
in which we have shared
our dreams and doubts,
our projects and our difficulties.
Make us always respond efficaciously
to our vision and our mission in the world.
Through Jesus Christ, our Lord.
Amen.

Sacrament of Penance

Prayer before Confession

I, a great sinner, come before you Lord, acknowledging my many sins and with an earnest desire to repent and to sin no more. Grant me perfect contrition for my sins, that I may detest them with deep sorrow. Send forth your light into my soul and reveal to me all those sins which I ought to confess at this time. Assist me with your grace that I may be sincere and humble in confessing them.

O Mary, my mother, be with me and help me to obtain remission of my sins with a contrite heart. *Amen.*

Examination of Conscience
Confession of Sins

In the confessional, humbly present yourself to the confessor saying *'Bless me, father, for I have sinned'*. Make the sign of the cross, then mention when you made your last confession. Then briefly and sincerely make your accusation.

Then say, *'For these and for all the sins of my past life, especially…* (here you confess your sins to the confessor)' *I ask pardon of God and penance and absolution from you father.*

Listen attentively to the advice and the penance the priest will give you. *Amen.*

Absolution

Confessor: God, the Father of mercies through the death and resurrection of his Son, has reconciled the world to himself and sent the Holy Spirit among us for the forgiveness of sins; through the ministry of the Church may God give you pardon and peace, and I absolve you from your sins in the name of the Father, and of the Son, and of the Holy Spirit. *Amen.*

The priest may add: May the passion of our Lord Jesus Christ, the intercession of the Blessed Virgin Mary and of all the saints, whatever good you do and suffering you endure, heal your sins, help you to grow in holiness, and reward you with eternal life. Go in peace. *Amen.*

Prayer after Confession

Almighty and merciful God, once again you have shown me your tender mercy by accepting me back even though I have gone on my own way. I renounce with my whole heart all the sins of my past life and resolve to commit them no more. I promise to hate sin and to avoid all the occasions that lead to it. Lord, without you I can do nothing; therefore, trusting in your grace I want to begin a new life. Mary, my mother, be at my side and assist me always. *Amen.*

Thanksgiving after Confession

I thank you Jesus for the blessing of this Sacrament of forgiveness and for Your pardon and peace. Immaculate Virgin, my Guardian Angel and all you Saints, by your powerful intercession obtain for me the grace never to sin again. *Amen.*

Scriptural Rosary

JOYFUL MYSTERIES
Monday and Saturday

The Annunciation
Then the angel said to her, "Do not be afraid, Mary, for you have found favor with God. Behold, you will conceive in your womb and bear a son, and you shall name him Jesus"… Mary said, "Behold, I am the handmaid of the Lord. May it be done to me according to your word." *Luke 1:26–38*

The Visitation
When Elizabeth heard Mary's greeting, the infant leaped in her womb, and Elizabeth, filled with the Holy Spirit, cried out in a loud voice and said, "Most blessed are you among women, and blessed is the fruit of your womb… Blessed are you who believed that what was spoken to you by the Lord would be fulfilled." *Luke 1:39–45*

The Birth of Jesus
While they were there, the time came for her to have her child, and she gave birth to her firstborn son. She wrapped him in swaddling clothes and laid him in a manger, because there was no room for them in the inn. *Luke 2:1–20*

The Presentation of Jesus in the Temple
When the days were completed for their purification according to the law of Moses, they took him up to Jerusalem to present him to the Lord, just as it is written in the law of the Lord. *Luke 2:22–38*

Finding of Jesus in the Temple
And [Jesus] said to them, "Why were you looking for me? Did you not know that I must be in my Father's house?" But they did not understand what he said to them. *Luke 2:41–50*

SORROWFUL MYSTERIES
Tuesday and Friday

Jesus' Agony in the Garden
My Father, if it is not possible that this cup pass without my drinking it, your will be done! *Matthew 26:36–42*

Jesus is Scourged
So Pilate, wishing to satisfy the crowd, released Barabbas to them and, after he had Jesus scourged, handed him over to be crucified. *Mark 15:1–16*

Jesus is Crowned with Thorns
Weaving a crown out of thorns, they placed it on his head, and a reed in his right hand. And kneeling before him, they mocked him, saying, "Hail, King of the Jews!" They spat upon him and took the reed and kept striking him on the head. *Matthew 27:27–31*

Jesus Carries His Cross
So they took Jesus, and carrying the cross himself he went out to what is called the Place of the Skull, in Hebrew, Golgotha. *John 19:16–22*

Jesus Dies on the Cross
When Jesus had taken the wine, he said, "It Is finished." And bowing his head, he handed over the spirit. *John 19:23–30*

GLORIOUS MYSTERIES
Wednesday and Sunday

The Resurrection of Jesus
Then the angel said to the women in reply, "Do not be afraid! I know that you are seeking Jesus the crucified. He is not here, for he has been raised just as he said. Come and see the place where he lay." *Matthew 28:1–10*

The Ascension of Jesus
Then he led them {out} as far as Bethany, raised his hands, and blessed them. As he blessed them he parted from them and was taken up to heaven. *Luke 24:44–53*

The Coming (or "Descent") of the Holy Spirit
And they were all filled with the Holy Spirit and began to speak in different tongues, as the Spirit enabled them to proclaim. *Acts 2:1–13*

The Assumption of Mary into Heaven
A great sign appeared in the sky, a woman clothed with the sun, with the moon under her feet, and on her head a crown of twelve stars. *Revelation 12:1–6*

Mary is Crowned Queen of Heaven
The Mighty One has done great things for me, and holy is his name… He has thrown down the rulers from their thrones but lifted up the lowly. Luke 1:46–55

LUMINOUS MYSTERIES
Thursday

The Baptism of Jesus in the Jordan River
After Jesus was baptized, he came up from the water and behold, the heavens were opened {for him}, and saw the Spirit of God descending like a dove {and} coming upon him. And a voice came from the heavens, saying, "This is my beloved Son, with whom I am well pleased." *Matthew 3:13–17*

The Miracle at the Wedding of Cana: Jesus Changes Water into Wine
Jesus did this as the beginning of his signs in Cana in Galilee and so revealed his glory, and his disciples began to believe in him. *John 2:1–11*

Jesus Proclaims the Kingdom of God
After John had been arrested, Jesus came to Galilee proclaiming the gospel of God: "This is the time of fulfillment. The kingdom of God is at hand. Repent, and believe in the gospel." *Mark 1:14–15*

The Transfiguration of Jesus
And [Jesus] was transfigured before them, and his clothes became dazzling white; such as no fuller on earth could bleach them… Then a cloud came, casting a shadow over them; then from the cloud came a voice, "This is my beloved Son. Listen to him." *Mark 9:2–10*

Institution of the Eucharist
While they were waiting, Jesus took bread, said the blessing, broke it, and giving it to his disciples said, "Take and eat; this is my body." Then he took a cup, gave thanks, and gave it to them, saying, "Drink from it, all of you, for this is my blood of the covenant, which will be shed on behalf of many for the forgiveness of sins." *Matthew 26:17–35*

The Way of the Cross

In the church or at home, this prayer will help you to meditate on the last moments of Jesus' life. To begin each one of the stations, pray:

    V.   We adore you, O Christ, and we bless you.

    R.   Because by your holy cross you have redeemed the world.

Then, you make a minute or two of silence, meditating on the content of the station. You can end praying Our Father.

1. The Last Supper
2. Jesus in the Garden of Gethsemane
3. Jesus Before the Sanhedrin
4. Jesus Before Pontius Pilate
5. The Whipping and Crowning with Thorns
6. The Carrying of the Cross
7. Simon of Cyrene Helps Jesus Carry His Cross
8. Jesus Comforts the Women of Jerusalem
9. The Stripping and Crucifixion of Jesus
10. The Repentant Thief
11. Mary and John Before the Cross of Jesus
12. The Death of Jesus on the Cross
13. The New Sepulchre
14. The Resurrection of Jesus

Praying with the Bible

PRAYING THE BIBLE IN GROUPS

First Step

Inviting the Lord and his Spirit. The coordinator asks a member of the group to invoke the presence of the Lord and his Spirit. The rest of the group may complete the prayer and share their own prayer.

Second Step

Reading the text. The coordinator points out the chapter and verses to be read. One member of the group reads the text aloud. After the reading, all observe a moment of silence.

Third Step

Abiding with the text. Let each participant say aloud a word or a sentence that is of special importance to him or her. After each participant says the word or sentence, there is a short moment of silence. Each one can repeat interiorly two or three times the words that were spoken, allowing them to sink in. Once all have spoken, the whole text is read again, aloud and slowly.

Fourth Step

Silence. After a second reading of the text, the coordinator invites everybody to keep silent letting them know how long the silence will be (3 to 5 minutes). This silence prepares the participants to reflect together on the text and to pray the text.

Fifth Step

Sharing what has touched their life. Participants are invited to share spontaneously from their hearts what has touched them. This is the time to put together the words reflected upon from Scripture and the individual feelings and experiences of each participant.

Sixth Step

Praying together. The coordinator invites the group to pray. Participants respond with spontaneous prayers to God who has spoken to them through the text. The meeting may conclude with a song.
Begin with this prayer:

PRAYING THE BIBLE ALONE

Father, you created me
and put me on earth for a purpose.
Jesus, you died for me
and called me to complete your work.
Holy Spirit, you help me to carry out
the work for which I was created
and called.
In your presence and name—Father, Son,
and Holy Spirit—I begin my meditation.

Follow these steps:

1. Read the meditation prayerfully. (About one minute.)
2. Think about what struck you most as you read the meditation. Why this? (About four minutes.)
3. Speak to God about your thoughts. (About one minute.)
4. Listen to God's response. Simply rest in God's presence with an open mind and an open heart. (About four minutes.)
5. End each meditation by praying the Lord's Prayer slowly and reverently.

SHORTLIST OF BIBLICAL PRAYERS

that can be used at any time or according to your personal situation.

Genesis 15:2-3
Supplication of Abraham for his son.

Exodus 5:22-23
Moses complains to God about the situation of his People.

Isaiah 12:1-6
Song of thanksgiving for the liberation of the People.

Daniel 3:26-49
Prayer of the Three Youths condemned to the furnace, interceding for the People.

Luke 1:45-55
Song of Mary, the Magnificat, for what God has made in her and history.

Luke 1:68-79
Zechariah's thanksgiving song for what God has made for his people.

Matthew 6:9-13
The Our Father.

John 11:41-42
Jesus' prayer of thanksgiving at Lazarus' resurrection.

Acts 4:24-30
Communitarian prayer asking for interior fortitude to announce the Word of God.

BIBLICAL PRAYERS FOR A PERSON IN DANGER OR VERY SICK

Read each supplication slowly, asking the sick person or the person in danger to repeat it, if possible, as a litany. Other supplications from the Bible can be added.

- The Lord is my light and my salvation. (Ps 27:1)
- My soul thirsts God, for the living God. (Ps 42:3)
- Although I walk through the valley of the shadow of death, I fear no evil, for you are beside me. (Ps 23:4)
- I stretch out my hands to you, and thirst for you like a parched land. (Ps1 43:6)
- To you, O Lord, I lift up my soul. (Ps 25:1)
- My loving God will come to help me. (Ps 59:11)
- Fill me with joy and gladness. (Ps 51:10)
- Send forth your light and your truth; let them be my guide. (Ps 43:3)
- Come, blessed of my Father! Take the possession of the kingdom prepared for you. (Mt 25:34)
- We will be with the Lord forever. (1 Thes 4:17)
- Who shall separate us from the love of Christ? (Rom 8:35)
- We love our brothers and sisters, and with this we know that we have passed from death to life. (1 Jn 3:14)
- Now has salvation come, with the power and the kingdom of our God. (Rev 12:10)
- Yes, I am coming soon. Amen. Come Lord Jesus. (Rev 22:20)

A SIMPLIFIED FORM OF LECTIO DIVINA

A simple form of Lectio Divina replaces the regular reflection on the readings of the day on Sundays.

Lectio Divina is Latin for divine reading, spiritual reading, or "holy reading," and represents a traditional Christian practice of prayer and scriptural reading intended to promote communion with God and to increase In the knowledge of God's Word. Pope Benedict XVI encourages the practice of Lectio Divina: "The diligent reading of Sacred Scripture accompanied by prayer brings about that intimate dialogue in which the person reading hears God who is speaking, and in praying, responds to him with trusting openness of heart (cf. Dei Verbum, n. 25). If it is effectively promoted, this practice will bring to the Church—I am convinced of it— a new spiritual springtime."

Using the archetypal rule of 3 where the human brain could process comfortably 3 concepts at a time, the Bible Diary 2014 tweaked the process of the Lectio Divina without sacrificing its essence into three simple steps of *READ, REFLECT, RESPONSE*. These corresponds to the Lectio, Meditatio, Actio steps. The Oratio was made as the reader's participation in this process; hence, a blank space is provided so that the reader can formulate his or her own prayer intention for that day. This enables a reader-text interaction and make the daily reading of the word participative. Hence, the process of doing Lectio Divina for this Bible Diary 2014 is:

The Four Simple Steps:
LECTIO (READ): is slow, reverent, and repeated reading of the suggested biblical text (careful reading). TASTE the words, understand the Text.   WHAT DOES THE TEXT SAY?

MEDITATIO (REFLECT): is "entering" into the truth of the text. CHEW the word; printed word becomes the Word of God. WHAT DOES THE TEXT TELL ME?

ORATIO (PRAY): is the first prayer which comes from meditation-adoration, thanksgiving, repentance, petition. TALK to Jesus, the Living Word. WHAT DO YOU WANT TO TELL GOD IN YOUR PRAYER?

ACTIO (ACT): is making fruitful in our lives what the Word has taught us, resolution on how you will live out God's message concrete plan of action: simple, doable; who, when, etc. RESPOND to the Word. WHAT DOES THE TEXT WANT ME TO DO?

How to use the
Bible Diary®

Some useful tips on how to make fruitful use of the Bible Diary®

- Reserve a particular time daily for reading the day's biblical texts and commentary. Allow some time for reflection and prayer. God speaks to you. Listen with your heart and you will discover and understand God's message.

- A simple form of Lectio Divina replaces the regular refection on the readings of the day on Sundays. See the preceeding page for a guide on how to use the Lectio Divina on Sundays.

- Make the Bible Diary® very personal to you so that you may have the freedom to write on it without reservations.

- Put into writing all the feelings you experience through the day: feelings of love, fear, guilt, or anger. Write down your reflections and realizations, your resolutions, little dialogues with yourself; your dreams, wishes, and hopes; your responses to events and to people.

- Be creative and compose your own prayers, verses, sayings and poems.

- When you look back and read them all over, you will begin to see and discover more about yourself. Then your Bible Diary® becomes a dialogue not only with yourself but with God who always speaks and is present through his Word.

---

*Important Note: Some portions of several Bible readings have been carefully condensed to enable the one-page per weekday and two-page per Sunday format. Condensed readings have been marked with an asterisk (*). Auto-hypenation is used to accommodate the texts in the layout. Thank you very much.*

Bible Diary 2014

"Daily it offers to you the Word of God in the Scriptures and the Life of Jesus Christ through the Gospel."

From the message of
His Eminence Luis Antonio Cardinal Tagle, DD,
Archbishop of Manila

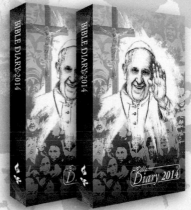

Hardbound (Available in Green and Yellow covers)
Full Color • 5.5 x 8.5 inches

Vinyl and Special Edition (Magnetic Locker)
Full Color • 5.5 x 8.5 inches

ALSO AVAILABLE IN FILIPINO

Daily Gospel 2014
(Pocket-size edition of the Bible Diary)
Softbound
2 Color • 3.875 x 5.75 inches

PANg Araw-araw 2014
Hardbound
2 Color • 5.5 x 8.5 inches

Pandesal 2014
Softbound
2 Color • 4.3125 x 5.5 inches

01
JANUARY

Wednesday

Ps 67:2–3, 5, 6, 8
May God bless us in his mercy.

SOLEMNITY OF MARY, MOTHER OF GOD
Psalter: Proper / (White)

1st Reading: Num 6:22–27

*Y*ahweh spoke to Moses saying, "Speak to Aaron and his sons and say to them: This is how you shall bless the people of Israel; you shall say:

May Yahweh bless you and keep you!

May Yahweh let his face shine on you, and be gracious to you!

May Yahweh look kindly on you, and give you his peace!

In that way shall they put my name on the people of Israel and I will bless them."

2nd Reading: Gal 4:4–7

*B*rothers and sisters: When the fullness of time came, God sent his Son. He came, born of woman, and subject to the law, in order to redeem the subjects of the law, that we might receive adoption, as children of God. And because you are children, God has sent into your hearts, the spirit of his Son, who cries out: Abba! that is, Father!

You, yourself, are no longer a slave, but a son or daughter, and yours is the inheritance, by God's grace.

Gospel: Lk 2:16–21

*T*he shepherds came hurriedly, and found Mary and Joseph, and the baby lying in the feeding trough. On seeing him, they related what they had been told about the child; and all were astonished on hearing the shepherds.

As for Mary, she treasured all these words, and pondered them in her heart.

The shepherds then returned, giving glory and praise to God for all they had heard and seen, just as the angels had told them.

On the eighth day, the circumcision of the baby had to be performed; he was named Jesus, the name the angel had given him before he was conceived.

Motherhood creates a sense of group spirit where anyone and everyone who knows that a child has been born somehow becomes part of the birthing process. Mary had only Joseph, the shepherds and the animals in the manger to witness the birth of her Son our Savior. Yet, these simple witnesses with no claim to power and honor never diminished the dignity of Mary becoming a mother to the Son of God. Her pre-eminent place among the creatures of God is assured. For she is a consistent witness to the elevation of the lowly through God's mercy. The simple girl-woman from Nazareth, Joseph, the silent man of the Gospels, the unnamed shepherds and the animals in the manger were privileged to have the first glimpse of the Messiah. It was a blessed night indeed for the lowly hearts.

THURSDAY BEFORE EPIPHANY
St. Basil the Great & St. Gregory
of Nazianzen, bishops & doctors
Psalter: Week 1 / (White)

Thursday

Ps 98:1, 2–3ab, 3cd–4
All the ends of the earth have
seen the saving power of God.

02
JANUARY

St. Basil the Great

Did you know that: Sts. Basil the Great and Gregory of Nazianzen are among the four great doctors of the Eastern Church.

1st Reading: 1 Jn 2:22–28

Beloved: Who is the liar? The one who denies that Jesus is the Christ. This is an antichrist, who denies both the Father and the Son. The one who denies the Son is without the Father, and those who acknowledge the Son also have the Father.

Let what you heard, from the beginning, remain in you. If what you heard from the beginning, remains in you, you too, will remain in the Son and in the Father. And this is the promise he, himself, gave us: eternal life.

I write this to you, thinking of those who try to lead you astray.

You received from him, an anointing, and it remains in you, so you do not need someone to teach you. His anointing teaches you all things. It speaks the truth and does not lie to you; so remain in him, and keep what he has taught you.

And now, my children, live, in him, so that when he appears in his glory, we may be confident, and not ashamed, before him when he comes.

Gospel: Jn 1:19–28

This was the testimony of John, when the Jews sent priests and Levites to ask him, "Who are you?" John recognized the truth, and did not deny it. He said, "I am not the Messiah."

And they asked him, "Then who are you? Elijah?" He answered, "I am not." They said, "Are you the Prophet?" And he answered, "No." Then they said to him, "Tell us who you are, so that we can give some answer to those who sent us. How do you see yourself?" And John said, quoting the prophet Isaiah, *"I am the voice of one crying out in the wilderness: Make straight the way of the Lord!"*

Those who had been sent were Pharisees; and they put a further question to John, "Then why are you baptizing, if you are not the Messiah, or Elijah, or the Prophet?" John answered, "I baptize you with water, but among you stands one whom you do not know; although he comes after me, I am not worthy to untie the strap of his sandal."

This happened in Bethabara beyond the Jordan, where John was baptizing.

People are not defined by what they do externally. It may be part of their being but it does not capture the whole mystery of a human's personhood. But there are some who demand that we define ourselves before them, making it easier for them to relate to us positively or in a hostile manner. They will now have a basis to judge us using their own criteria. However, John did not fall into this trap. His answer was vague enough to invite them to contemplate the mystery of his personhood, to get to know him better through time. This does not sit well with the priests and the Levites. They had no time and patience to know the real John. Thus they missed knowing the greater mystery of Whom John was working for.

03
JANUARY

Friday
Ps 98:1, 3cd–4, 5–6
All the ends of the earth have
seen the saving power of God.

FRIDAY BEFORE EPIPHANY
The Most Holy Name of Jesus
Psalter: Week 1 / (White)

1st Reading: 1 Jn 2:29 – 3:6

*Y*ou know, that he is the Just One: know, then, that anyone living justly is born of God.

See what singular love the Father has for us: we are called children of God, and we really are. This is why the world does not know us, because it did not know him.

Beloved, we are God's children, and what we shall be has not, yet, been shown. Yet, when he appears in his glory, we know, that we shall be like him, for, then, we shall see him as he is. All who have such a hope, try to be pure, as he is pure.

Anyone who commits a sin, acts as an enemy of the law of God; any sin acts wickedly, because all sin is wickedness. You know, that he came to take away our sins, and that there is no sin in him. Whoever remains in him, has no sin, whoever sins, has not seen, or known him.

Gospel: Jn 1:29–34

*T*he next day, John saw Jesus coming toward him, and said, "There is the Lamb of God, who takes away the sin of the world! It is he of whom I said: A man comes after me, who is already ahead of me, for he was before me. I myself did not know him, but I came baptizing to prepare for him, so that he might be revealed in Israel."

And John also gave this testimony, "I saw the Spirit coming down on him, like a dove from heaven, and resting on him. I myself did not know him, but God, who sent me to baptize, told me, 'You will see the Spirit coming down, and resting on the one who baptizes with the Holy Spirit.' Yes, I have seen! And I declare that this is the Chosen One of God!"

Names in ancient times were not selected randomly but with great care and a lot of thinking. Names have meanings that somehow direct one's future life. The name Jesus means "Yahweh saves." This gave Jesus his identity and mission which He fulfilled in His lifetime. Today we celebrate the Most Holy Name of Jesus. Let us pause for a while and contemplate on the meaning of our own name and see whether it somehow influenced our choices in life or if we have strayed far from the identity and mission that our name gives us. Perhaps, knowing the meaning of our personal name will help us redirect our steps into the right path.

Saturday

Ps 98:1, 7–8, 9
All the ends of the earth have
seen the saving power of God.

04
JANUARY

St. Elizabeth Ann Seton
Did you know that: Before becoming a Catholic, St Elizabeth Ann Seton founded an organization called the Society for the Relief of Poor Widows with Sick Children and she became known as "the Protestant Sister of Charity."

1st Reading: 1 Jn 3:7–10

My little children, do not be led astray; those who do what is right are upright, just as Jesus Christ is upright. But those who sin belong to the devil, for the devil sins from the beginning.

This is why the Son of God was shown to us, he was to undo the works of the devil.

Those born of God do not sin, for the seed of God remains in them; they cannot sin, because they are born of God.

What is the way to recognize the children of God, and those of the devil? The one, who does not do what is right, is not of God; so, too, the one who does not love his brother or sister.

Gospel: Jn 1:35–42

On the following day, John was standing there again, with two of his disciples. As Jesus walked by, John looked at him and said, "There is the Lamb of God." On hearing this, the two disciples followed Jesus. He turned and saw them following, and he said to them, "What are you looking for?" They answered, "Rabbi (which means *Master*), where are you staying?" Jesus said, "Come and see." So they went and saw where he stayed, and spent the rest of that day with him. It was about four o'clock in the afternoon.

Andrew, the brother of Simon Peter, was one of the two who heard what John had said, and followed Jesus. Early the next morning, he found his brother Simon and said to him, "We have found the Messiah" (which means the *Christ*), and he brought Simon to Jesus. Jesus looked at him and said, "You are Simon, son of John, but you shall be called Cephas" (which means *Rock*).

The greatness of John lies in his capacity to accept his role in the grand design of God, that is, he is not the main actor but the precursor of the Messiah in the plan of salvation. Thus, even at the expense of his own followers leaving him, he did not shrink from his role as the one pointing to the coming Savior. He did not feel poor even when his following diminished. How many of us are capable of such self-giving in the service of our mission in life? No wonder Jesus praised John as the man whom no man was born greater of a woman. His greatness did not lie with what he acquired but what he was willing to let go in fidelity to his call.

05
JANUARY

Sunday

Ps 72:1-2, 7-8, 10-11, 12-13
Lord, every nation on earth
will adore you.

1st Reading: Is 60:1-6

Arise, shine, for your light has come. The glory of Yahweh rises upon you. Night still covers the earth and gloomy clouds veil the peoples, but Yahweh now rises and over you his glory appears. Nations will come to your light and kings to the brightness of your dawn.

Lift up your eyes round about and see: they are all gathered and come to you, your sons from afar, your daughters tenderly carried.

This sight will make your face radiant, your heart throbbing and full; the riches of the sea will be turned to you, the wealth of the nations will come to you.

A multitude of camels will cover you, caravans from Midian and Ephah. Those from Sheba will come, bringing with them gold and incense, all singing in praise of Yahweh.

2nd Reading: Eph 3:2-3a, 5-6

Brothers and sisters: You may have heard of the graces God bestowed on me, for your sake. By a revelation, he gave me the knowledge of his mysterious design, as I have explained in a few words.

This mystery was not made known to past generations, but only now, through revelations, given to holy apostles and prophets, by the Spirit. Now, the non-Jews share the inheritance; in Christ Jesus, the non-Jews are incorporated, and are to enjoy the Promise.

Gospel: Mt 2:1-12

When Jesus was born in Bethlehem, in Judea, during the days of king Herod, wise men from the East arrived in Jerusalem. They asked, "Where is the newborn king of the Jews? We saw the rising of his star in the East and have come to honor him."

When Herod heard this he was greatly disturbed, and with him all Jerusalem. He immediately called a meeting of all high-ranking priests and teachers of the law, and asked them where the Messiah was to be born.

"In the town of Bethlehem in Judea," they told him, "for this is what the prophet wrote: *And you, Bethlehem, in the land of Judah, you are by no means the least among the clans of Judah, for from you will come a leader, one who is to shepherd my people Israel.*"

Then Herod secretly called the wise men and asked them the precise time the star appeared. He sent them to Bethlehem with these instructions, "Go and get accurate information about the child. As soon as you have found him, report to me, so that I, too, may go and honor him."

After the meeting with the king, they set out. The star that they had seen in the East went ahead of them and stopped over the place where the child was. The wise men were overjoyed on seeing the star again. They went into the house, and when they saw the child with Mary his mother, they knelt and worshiped him. They opened their bags and offered him their gifts of gold, incense and myrrh.

In a dream they were warned not to go back to Herod, so they returned to their home country by another way.

Reading: Wise men from a distant land came unannounced seeking the newborn King of the Jews signified by the rising of a bright star. This unsettled king Herod who took great pains to know the exact location of this new King's birthplace, gave direction to the wise men with an instruction to report to him once they found the Child-King. With joy, they saw the newborn King and presented their gifts and worshipped him. Then, they returned to their land by another route.

Reflection: Life surprises us with its sudden intrusion of our comfort zone. Like Herod who was jolted from his complacency when his being the only king of the Jews was challenged by the birth of a new King, we too are brought news that challenges our own settled ways, routine and old mentalities. Then, we feel insecure; we get into action; we spend tremendous amount of energy just to secure what we have. We even trick others and ourselves into thinking that we are ready for the change that will happen ahead. We miss the opportunity to grow.

Response: The only thing that doesn't change is change itself. Hitch onto the wagon and be ready for a new adventure that a changed life offers ahead.

06
JANUARY

Monday
Ps 2:7bc–8, 10–12a
I will give you all the nations
for an inheritance.

MONDAY AFTER EPIPHANY
St. André Bessette, religious
Psalter: Week 2 / (White)

1st Reading: 1 Jn 3:22 – 4:6*

Beloved: Whatever we ask, we shall receive, since we keep his commands and do what pleases him. His command is, that we believe in the name of his Son Jesus Christ, and that, we love one another, as he has commanded us. Whoever keeps his commands remains in God and God in him. It is by the Spirit God has given us, that we know he lives in us. My beloved, do not trust every inspiration. Test the spirits, to see, whether they come from God, because many false prophets are now in the world. How will you recognize the Spirit of God? Any spirit recognizing Jesus as the Christ, who has taken our flesh is of God. But any spirit that does not recognize Jesus, is not from God, it is the spirit of the antichrist. You have heard of his coming, and even, now, he is in the world. (…)

They are of the world and the world inspires them, and those of the world listen to them. We are of God, and those who know God, listen to us, but those who are not of God, ignore us. This is how we know the spirit of truth, and the spirit of falsehood as well.

Gospel: Mt 4:12–17, 23–25

When Jesus heard that John had been arrested, he withdrew into Galilee. He left Nazareth and went to live in Capernaum, a town by the lake of Galilee, at the border of Zebulun and Naphtali.

In this way, the word of the prophet Isaiah was fulfilled: *Land of Zebulun and land of Naphtali, crossed by the Road of the Sea; and you, who live beyond the Jordan, Galilee, land of pagans:*

The people who lived in darkness have seen a great light; on those who live in the land of the shadow of death, a light has shone. From that time on, Jesus began to proclaim his message, "Change your ways: the kingdom of heaven is near." Jesus went around all Galilee, teaching in their synagogues, proclaiming the good news of the kingdom, and curing all kinds of sickness and disease among the people.

The news about him spread through the whole of Syria; and the people brought all their sick to him, and all those who suffered: the possessed, the deranged, the paralyzed; and he healed them all. Large crowds followed him from Galilee and the Ten Cities, from Jerusalem, Judea, and from across the Jordan.

St. André Bessette
Did you know that: St. André Bessette worked as a porter at Notre Dame College in Côte-des-Neiges, Quebec, with additional duties as sacristan, laundry worker and messenger.

Sometimes, prudence is the greater part of valor. When the heat was turned up on John, Jesus knew that John's activities did not sit well with the powers that be. Jesus' work was somehow similar to John's. He therefore might have been the next potential target so He withdrew to Capernaum. There, far from the center of power, He would have more freedom to do what He needed to do without fear of arrest or persecution. This move netted good results. Jesus was able to create a base to strengthen the movement He was starting. Level-headedness made His initial works fruitful. It pays to be prudent in certain situations sometimes.

Tuesday

Ps 72:1–2, 3–4, 7–8
Lord, every nation on earth
will adore you.

07
JANUARY

St. Raymond of Penyafort

Did you know that: St. Raymond of Penyafort refused the Archbishopric of Tarragona, pleading that he preferred his life of solitude, study, and preaching.

_____

_____

_____

_____

_____

_____

_____

_____

_____

_____

_____

Genuine concern and care demands that sometimes we have to inconvenience ourselves willingly. True and genuine sharing at some point will hurt because it does not only come from our surplus but from our very poverty itself. Thus the apostles, wanting the easy way out, requested Jesus to tell the people to fend for themselves. Their Master had the numbers to show judging from the multitude that flocked to hear Him preach. Now they could rest and let go of these people. But Jesus showed them that service does not end when the praise and accolade subside. It continues relentlessly in good times and bad. This is the real miracle in this story: the capacity to give continuously without counting the cost and without reserve.

1st Reading: 1 Jn 4:7–10

*M*y dear friends, let us love one another, for love comes from God. Everyone who loves, is born of God and knows God.

Those who do not love have not known God, for God is love.

How did the love of God appear among us? God sent his only Son into this world, that we might have life, through him.

This is love: not that we loved God, but that, he first loved us and sent his Son, as an atoning sacrifice for our sins.

Gospel: Mk 6:34–44

*A*s Jesus went ashore, he saw a large crowd, and he had compassion on them, for they were like sheep without a shepherd. And he began to teach them many things.

It was now getting late, so his disciples came to him and said, "This is a lonely place and it is now late. You should send the people away, and let them go to the farms and villages around here, to buy themselves something to eat."

Jesus replied, "You, yourselves, give them something to eat." They answered, "If we are to feed them, we need two hundred silver coins to go and buy enough bread." But Jesus said, "You have some loaves; how many? Go and see." The disciples found out and said, "There are five loaves and two fish."

Then he told them to have the people sit down, together in groups, on the green grass. This they did, in groups of hundreds and fifties. And Jesus took the five loaves and the two fish and, raising his eyes to heaven, he pronounced a blessing, broke the loaves, and handed them to his disciples to distribute to the people. He also divided the two fish among them.

They all ate and everyone had enough. The disciples gathered up what was left, and filled twelve baskets with broken pieces of bread and fish. Five thousand men had eaten there.

Wednesday

Ps 72:1–2, 10, 12–13
Lord, every nation on earth
will adore you.

1st Reading: 1 Jn 4:11–18

*D*ear friends, if such has been the love of God, we, too, must love one another.

No one has ever seen God, but if we love one another, God lives in us, and his love comes to its perfection in us.

How may we know that we live in God and he in us? Because God has given us his Spirit.

We ourselves have seen, and declare, that the Father sent his Son to save the world. Those who confess that Jesus is the Son of God, God remains in them, and they in God.

We have known the love of God and have believed in it. God is love. The one who lives in love, lives in God, and God in him.

When do we know, that we have reached a perfect love? When, in this world, we are like him, in everything, and expect, with confidence, the Day of Judgment.

There is no fear in love. Perfect love drives away fear, for fear has to do with punishment; those who fear do not know perfect love.

Gospel: Mk 6:45–52

*A*fter the five thousand men were satisfied, immediately, Jesus obliged his disciples to get into the boat and go ahead of him to the other side, toward Bethsaida, while he himself sent the crowd away. And having sent the people off, he went by himself to the hillside to pray.

When evening came, the boat was far out on the lake, while he was alone on the land. Jesus saw his disciples straining at the oars, for the wind was against them; and before daybreak he came to them, walking on the lake, and he was going to pass them by.

When they saw him walking on the lake, they thought it was a ghost and cried out; for they all saw him and were terrified. But, at once, he called to them, "Courage! It is I; don't be afraid!" Then Jesus got into the boat with them, and the wind died down. They were completely astonished, for they had not really grasped the fact of the loaves; their minds were dull.

What was the secret of Jesus' strength and fortitude? Why was He so fruitful and successful in His initial ministry? This passage in Mark gives us a glimpse of Jesus' secret weapon: His prayer life. Perhaps the reason why this was recorded in the Gospels was because it was one of the striking memories the Apostles had of their Lord and Savior. Sometimes, we think that sitting for a time in prayer and meditation is a sterile time, unproductive and a waste of opportunity. We equate possibility of success with activity and doing. But prayer made Jesus walk calmly above the chaos of everyday life. He lorded it over the unruly passions of the heart and the wild imaginings of the mind. He stayed focused on what He needed to do because His prayer gave Him the center that kept Him steady through joy and sorrow, through life and death and new life. Prayer is what led Him to victory.

Thursday

Ps 72:1–2, 14 & 15bc, 17
Lord, every nation on earth
will adore you.

09 JANUARY

1st Reading: 1 Jn 4:19 – 5:4

*B*eloved, let us love one another, since he loved us first.

If you say, "I love God," while you hate your brother or sister, you are a liar. How can you love God, whom you do not see, if you do not love your brother, whom you see? We received from him, this commandment: let those who love God also love their brothers.

All those, who believe that Jesus is the Anointed, are born of God; whoever loves the Father, loves the Son. How may we know, that we love the children of God? If we love God and fulfill his commands, for God's love requires us to keep his commands. In fact, his commandments are not a burden because all those born of God overcome the world. And the victory, which overcomes the world, is our faith.

Gospel: Lk 4:14–22

*J*esus acted with the power of the Spirit; and on his return to Galilee, the news about him spread throughout all that territory. He began teaching in the synagogues of the Jews and everyone praised him.

When Jesus came to Nazareth, where he had been brought up, he entered the synagogue on the Sabbath, as he usually did. He stood up to read, and they handed him the book of the prophet Isaiah.

Jesus then unrolled the scroll and found the place where it is written: *"The Spirit of the Lord is upon me. He has anointed me, to bring good news to the poor; to proclaim liberty to captives; and new sight to the blind; to free the oppressed; and to announce the Lord's year of mercy."*

Jesus then rolled up the scroll, gave it to the attendant and sat down; and the eyes of all in the synagogue were fixed on him. Then he said to them, "Today, these prophetic words come true, even as you listen."

All agreed with him, and were lost in wonder, while he spoke of the grace of God.

Sometimes, the medium hinders the message to be effectively delivered. In some cases it is not the fault of the medium but of the receivers who, even though they are convinced of the message, nevertheless do not make the necessary adjustment to their appreciation of the medium. For there are mediums who are so self-assured that they don't need to spruce up their credentials by adjusting their outward appearances. Nor will they rewrite their life history in order to upgrade their lineage or social standing. Their message is such that those who will not accept it are the ones left shortchanged. How many times therefore has Jesus Christ come to us in a form we least expected and thus we rejected Him and His message?

10
JANUARY

Friday

Ps 147:12–13, 14–15, 19–20
Praise the Lord, Jerusalem.

FRIDAY AFTER EPIPHANY
Psalter: Week 2 / (White)

1st Reading: 1 Jn 5:5–13

Beloved: Who has overcome the world? The one who believes that Jesus is the Son of God.

Jesus Christ was acknowledged through water, but also through blood. Not only water, but water and blood. And the Spirit, too, witnesses to him, for the Spirit is truth.

There are, then, three testimonies: the Spirit, the water and the blood, and these three witnesses agree.

If we accept human testimony, with greater reason must we accept that of God, given in favor of his Son. If you believe in the Son of God, you have God's testimony in you.

But those who do not believe, make God a liar, since they do not believe his words when he witnesses to his Son.

What has God said? That he has granted us eternal life, and this life is in his Son. The one who has the Son has life, those who do not have the Son of God do not have life.

I write you, then, all these things, that you may know, that you have eternal life, all you, who believe in the name of the Son of God.

Gospel: Lk 5:12–16

One day, in another town, a man came to Jesus covered with leprosy. On seeing Jesus, the man bowed down to the ground, and said, "Lord, if you want to, you can make me clean."

Stretching out his hand, Jesus touched the man and said, "Yes, I want to. Be clean." In an instant, the leprosy left him. Then Jesus instructed him, "Tell this to no one. But go, and show yourself to the priest. Make an offering for your healing, as Moses prescribed; that will serve as evidence for them."

But the news about Jesus spread all the more; and large crowds came to him, to listen and to be healed of their sickness. As for Jesus, he would often withdraw to solitary places and pray.

Contagious diseases like leprosy divide the afflicted from the greater community. It makes the affected person a pariah even to those who know him or her. Thus they are apt metaphors for sin that isolates and sets apart the person from the group. Forgiveness restores one's standing in the community making one again a member rather than an outsider. And Jesus has infinite resources in forgiving those who ask. How many times have we tried to avail of this free and gratuitous mercy? Today I would like to end my isolation and enjoy again the warmth of community. I will muster the courage like the leper of the Gospel to ask Jesus to heal me of my sins.

Saturday

Ps 149:1–2, 3–4, 5–6a & 9b
The Lord takes delight
in his people.

11 JANUARY

1st Reading: 1 Jn 5:14–21

Beloved: Through him we are fully confident that whatever we ask, according to his will, he will grant us. If we know that he hears us whenever we ask, we know that we already have what we asked of him.

If you see your brother committing sin, a sin which does not lead to death, pray for him, and God will give life to your brother. I speak, of course, of the sin which does not lead to death. There is also a sin that leads to death; I do not speak of praying about this. Every kind of wrongdoing is sin, but not all sin leads to death.

We know that those born of God do not sin, but the one who was born of God protects them and the evil one does not touch them.

We know that we belong to God, while the whole world lies in evil.

We know that the Son of God has come and has given us power to know the truth. We are in him who is true, his Son Jesus Christ. He is the true God and eternal life.

My dear children, keep yourselves from idols.

Gospel: Jn 3:22–30

Jesus went into the territory of Judea with his disciples. He stayed there with them and baptized. John was also baptizing in Aenon near Salim where water was plentiful; people came to him and were baptized. This happened before John was put in prison.

Now John's disciples had been questioned by a Jew about spiritual cleansing, so they came to him and said, "Rabbi, the one who was with you across the Jordan, and about whom you spoke favorably, is now baptizing and all are going to him."

John answered, "No one can receive anything except what has been given him from heaven. You yourselves are my witnesses that I said: 'I am not the Christ but I have been sent before him.' Only the bridegroom has the bride; but the friend of the bridegroom stands by and listens, and rejoices to hear the bridegroom's voice. My joy is now full. It is necessary that he increase but that I decrease."

"It is necessary that He increase but that I decrease." With these words John affirmed his greatness. It may be a concession of an inferior status in the eyes of those driven to be at the top, but from the optics of the spirit acceptance of one's true worth affirms one's certainty of oneself. There are people who go through life trumpeting themselves and their achievements hoping to leave an impressive memory. Some succeed but in time, their greatness built on sand crumbles. There are those who fail miserably because their boasting about themselves, their ego and their shadow leave a bitter taste on the people tired of hearing about it. There is an Asian saying that captures quiet greatness, "silent water runs deep."

12

JANUARY

Sunday

Ps 29:1-2, 3-4, 9-10
The Lord will bless his people with peace.

1st Reading: Is 42:1-4, 6-7

Thus says Yahweh, "Here is my servant whom I uphold, my chosen one in whom I delight.

I have put my spirit upon him, and he will bring justice to the nations.

He does not shout or raise his voice, proclamations are not heard in the streets.

A broken reed he will not crush, nor will he snuff out the light of the wavering wick.

He will make justice appear in truth.

He will not waver or be broken until he has established justice on earth; the islands are waiting for his law.

I, Yahweh, have called you for the sake of justice; I will hold your hand to make you firm; I will make you as a covenant to the people, and as a light to the nations, to open eyes that do not see, to free captives from prison, to bring out to light those who sit in darkness.

2nd Reading: Acts 10:34-38

Peter then spoke to them, "Truly, I realize that God does not show partiality, but in all nations he listens to everyone who fears God and does good. And this is the message he has sent to the children of Israel, the good news of peace he has proclaimed through Jesus Christ, who is the Lord of all. No doubt you have heard of the event that occurred throughout the whole country of the Jews, beginning from Galilee, after the baptism John preached. You know how God anointed Jesus the Nazarean with Holy Spirit and power. He went about doing good and healing all who were under the devil's power, because God was with him."

Gospel: Mt 3:13-17

At that time Jesus arrived from Galilee and came to John at the Jordan to be baptized by him. But John tried to prevent him, and said, "How is it you come to me: I should be baptized by you!"

But Jesus answered him, "Let it be like that for now; so that we may fulfill the right order." John agreed.

As soon as he was baptized, Jesus came up out of the water. All at once, the heavens opened and he saw the Spirit of God come down like a dove, and rest upon him. At the same time, a voice from heaven was heard, "This is my Son, the Beloved; he is my Chosen One."

Reading: Jesus went to John for baptism amidst the latter's objection. Then God tore the heavens to declare that Jesus is His Beloved Son and sent the Spirit in the form of a dove as a sign of his fatherly affection.

Reflection: To be loved publicly is a tremendous boost to our own sense of self-worth, especially if such declaration requires an effort like tearing the heavens apart just to be heard. Now we know why

Jesus had the strength to carry on the will of the Father even unto death. He knew He was loved. Thus He staked His all for this loving Father who is not shy to show such love. God's power that kept Him going is the power of love.

Response: When was the last time you showed your love to someone spontaneously and without censorship? Give someone a boost today by reminding him or her that he or she is loved.

Ordinary Time

O rdinary Time consists of 33 or 34 weeks outside the seasons of Advent, Christmas, Lent, and Easter. The Sundays and weekdays in Ordinary Time unfold the other mysteries of Christ that are not explicitly commemorated by the seasons. During this time the Church calls attention to Our Lord's ministry of preaching, healing, and liberating. These, in some way, become present to us as we listen with faith to the biblical readings every Sunday and indeed every day.

Of great importance, therefore, are the biblical readings, especially the gospel, during the Masses in Ordinary Time. When we listen to them we are enabled to listen to the preaching of Christ and experience the saving and healing power of his word. It is useful to keep in mind that his words and actions, which the gospel proclaims, allow us to paint the picture of our Father in heaven. We obtain knowledge of the Father through what Christ preached and performed.

Likewise, the Prefaces during Ordinary Time are worthy of our attention. They proclaim the wonderful works of God in creation and salvation history through Jesus Christ.

Ordinary Time is called "ordinary", but its message Sunday after Sunday, day after day, is not ordinary: it is always extraordinary, because it is about the person of Jesus Christ who reveals to us by his words and action the person of the Father.

13
JANUARY

Monday

Ps 116:12–13, 14–17, 18–19
To you, Lord, I will offer
a sacrifice of praise.

1ST WEEK IN ORDINARY TIME
St. Hilary, bishop & doctor
Psalter: Week 1 / (Green / White)

1st Reading: 1 S 1:1–8

There was a man from Ramathaim, in the hills of Ephraim, whose name was Elkanah. He was son of Tohu, son of Jeroham, of the clan of Zuph. He had two wives, Hannah and Peninnah. Peninnah had children but Hannah had none.

Every year Elkanah went to worship and to sacrifice to Yahweh of hosts at Shiloh. The priests there were the two sons of Eli, Hophni and Phineas. Whenever Elkanah offered sacrifice, he gave portions to his wife, Peninnah and to all her sons and daughters. To Hannah, however, he gave the more delightful portion because he loved her more, although she had no child. Yet Hannah's rival used to tease her for being barren.

So it happened every year when they went to Yahweh's house. Peninnah irritated Hannah and she would weep and refuse to eat. Once Elkanah, her husband, asked her, "Hannah, why do you weep instead of eating? Why are you sad? Are you not better off with me than with many sons?"

Gospel: Mk 1:14–20

After John was arrested, Jesus went into Galilee and began preaching the Good News of God. He said, "The time has come; the kingdom of God is at hand. Change your ways and believe the Good News."

As Jesus was walking along the shore of Lake Galilee, he saw Simon and his brother Andrew casting a net in the lake, for they were fishermen. And Jesus said to them, "Follow me, and I will make you fish for people." At once, they left their nets and followed him. Jesus went a little farther on and saw James and John, the sons of Zebedee; they were in their boat mending their nets. Immediately, Jesus called them and they followed him, leaving their father Zebedee in the boat with the hired men.

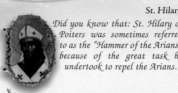

St. Hilary

Did you know that: St. Hilary of Poiters was sometimes referred to as the "Hammer of the Arians" because of the great task he undertook to repel the Arians.

It is good to labor, alone if you must, on certain convictions in life. But if this is too big for one person the natural thing to do is gather a group that will work with you. Jesus did not find it beneath His dignity to seek partners and collaborators to help in His task. He may be the Lord and King of the universe but He willingly entered our state. Thus He also embraced the finiteness of our possibilities. Jesus sanctified collaboration and shared mission when He called His first apostles. He who by His word can effect what He wills will now learn and understand in a human way how it is to need partners in the one task of proclaiming the kingdom of God. It would be days of mutual discovery between God and man. It would be an exciting journey of Master and follower in the days ahead.

Tuesday

1 S 2:1, 4–5, 6–7, 8abcd
My heart exults in the Lord,
my Savior.

14
JANUARY

1st Reading: 1 S 1:9–20

After they had eaten and drunk in Shiloh, Hannah stood up not far from Eli, the priest: his seat was beside the doorpost of Yahweh's house. Deeply distressed she wept and prayed to Yahweh and made this vow, "O Yahweh of hosts, if only you will have compassion on your maidservant and give me a son, I will put him in your service for as long as he lives and no razor shall touch his head." As she prayed before Yahweh, Eli observed the movement of her lips. Hannah was praying silently; she moved her lips but uttered no sound and Eli thought Hannah was drunk. He, therefore, said to her: "For how long will you be drunk? Let your drunkenness pass." But Hannah answered: "No, my lord, I am a woman in great distress, not drunk. I have not drunk wine or strong drink, but I am pouring out my soul before Yahweh. Do not take me for a bad woman. I was so afflicted that my prayer flowed continuously." Then Eli said, "Go in peace and may the God of Israel grant you what you asked for." Hannah answered, "Let your maidservant deserve your kindness." Then she left the temple and when she was at table, she seemed a different woman. Elkanah rose early in the morning and worshiped before Yahweh with his wives. Then they went back home to Ramah. When Elkanah slept with his wife, Hannah, Yahweh took compassion on her, and she became pregnant. She gave birth to a son and called him Samuel because she said: "I have asked Yahweh to give him to me."

Gospel: Mk 1:21–28

They went into the town of Capernaum and Jesus taught in the synagogue on the Sabbath day. The people were astonished at the way he taught, for he spoke as one having authority, and not like the teachers of the Law. It happened that, a man with an evil spirit was in their synagogue, and he shouted, "What do you want with us, Jesus of Nazareth? Have you come to destroy us? I know who you are: You are the Holy One of God." Then Jesus faced him and said with authority, "Be silent and come out of this man!" The evil spirit shook the man violently and, with a loud shriek, came out of him. All the people were astonished and they wondered, "What is this? With what authority he preaches! He even gives orders to evil spirits and they obey him!" And Jesus' fame spread throughout all the country of Galilee.

The synagogue is a sacred space and the Sabbath is a sacred day. Combine them with Jesus, the holy one of God and you have a space and time most holy. But then surprisingly there is a man with an evil spirit in this sacred space on a sacred time in the presence of Jesus. This tells us that evil can live side by side with all things sacred. Thus it is not surprising that evil deeds are done even in sacred offices, ministries and missions. It is not that God tolerates it or is impotent in the face of it. Jesus did show the evil spirit who is Lord and Master between them. But sometimes, evil tries to wear the mantle of holiness to test our resolve. Thus scandalizes us and sometimes robs us of our faith, hope and love. Faced with evil Jesus did not shrink but with authority commanded it to leave. Likewise we are enjoined to bring back the sacred in defiled spaces, time and offices. We can only do this if our love and zeal for the Lord is greater than our fear, disappointment and hate.

15
JANUARY

Wednesday

Ps 40:2 & 5, 7–8a, 8b–9, 10
Here am I, Lord;
I come to do your will.

1ST WEEK IN ORDINARY TIME
Psalter: Week 1 / (Green)

1st Reading: 1 S 3:1–10, 19–20

The boy Samuel ministered to Yahweh under Eli's care in a time in which the word of Yahweh was rarely heard; visions were not seen.

One night Eli was lying down in his room, half blind as he was. The lamp of God was still lighted and Samuel also lay in the house of Yahweh near the ark of God. Then Yahweh called, "Samuel! Samuel!" Samuel answered, "I am here!" and ran to Eli saying, "I am here, did you not call me?" But Eli said, "I did not call, go back to sleep." So he went and lay down.

Then Yahweh called again, "Samuel!" and Samuel stood up and went to Eli saying, "You called me; I am here." But Eli answered, "I did not call you, my son. Go back to sleep."

Samuel did not yet know Yahweh and the word of Yahweh had not yet been revealed to him. But Yahweh called Samuel for the third time and, as he went again to Eli saying, "I am here for you have called me," Eli realized that it was Yahweh calling the boy. So he said to Samuel, "Go, lie down, and if he calls you again, answer: "Speak, Yahweh, your servant listens."

Then Yahweh came and stood there calling as he did before, "Samuel! Samuel!" And Samuel answered, "Speak, for your servant listens."

Samuel grew; Yahweh was with him and made all his words become true. All Israel, from Dan to Beersheba, knew that Samuel was really Yahweh's prophet.

Gospel: Mk 1:29–39

On leaving the synagogue, Jesus went to the home of Simon and Andrew with James and John. As Simon's mother-in-law was sick in bed with fever, they immediately told him about her. Jesus went to her, and taking her by the hand, raised her up. The fever left her and she began to wait on them. That evening, at sundown, people brought to Jesus all the sick and those who had evil spirits: the whole town was pressing around the door. Jesus healed many who had various diseases, and drove out many demons; but he did not let them speak, for they knew who he was.

Very early in the morning, before daylight, Jesus went off to a lonely place where he prayed. Simon and the others went out, too, searching for him; and when they found him they said, "Everyone is looking for you." Then Jesus answered, "Let's go to the nearby villages so that I may preach there too; for that is why I came."

So Jesus set out to preach in all the synagogues throughout Galilee; he also cast out demons.

A strong prayer life may have been one salient feature of Jesus that remained in the memory of the apostles but it is always in function to His mission. Prayer does not take away the Lord from His work but it is the wellspring and springboard of His creativity. Thus when He was praying and His apostles sought Him because of the pressing need of people, Jesus did not linger but immediately invited them to go to nearby villages to preach and expel demons. His prayer did not take Him away from others. It prepared Him to encounter them meaningfully.

Thursday

Ps 44:10–11, 14–15, 24–25
Redeem us, Lord,
because of your mercy.

16
JANUARY

1st Reading: 1 S 4:1–11

At that time Samuel was a prophet of Israel. The Israelites went out to battle against the Philistines. They encamped at Ebenezer, while the Philistines encamped at Aphek. The Philistines then drew up in battle formation. They attacked Israel and after a fierce fighting, Israel was defeated, leaving about four thousand men dead on the battlefield. When the troops retreated to their camp, the elders of Israel asked, "Why has Yahweh allowed us to be defeated by the Philistines? Let us take the ark of God from Shiloh and bring it here so that Yahweh may be with us and save us from our enemies." So the people sent messengers to Shiloh to take the ark of Yahweh who is seated on the cherubim. Eli's two sons, Hophni and Phineas, accompanied the ark.

As soon as the ark of Yahweh entered the camp, the Israelites began to cheer so loudly that the earth resounded. The Philistines heard the shouting and asked, "What does this loud shout in the camp of the Hebrews mean?" And they were told that the ark of Yahweh had been brought to the camp.

The Philistines were overcome with fear. They exclaimed, "A god has come into the camp. Woe to us! For nothing like this has happened before. Woe to us! Who can save us from the power of these mighty gods? These are the gods who struck the Egyptians with all sorts of plagues—and in the desert. Take courage and conduct yourselves like men, O Philistines, lest you become slaves to the Hebrews the way they have been slaves to you. Be manly and fight."

So the Philistines fought and Israel was defeated. Everyone fled to his home. It was a disastrous defeat; thirty thousand foot soldiers of Israel were killed. The ark of God was captured and the two sons of Eli, Hophni and Phineas, were slain.

Gospel: Mk 1:40–45

A leper came to Jesus and begged him, "If you want to, you can make me clean." Moved with pity, Jesus stretched out his hand and touched him, saying, "I do want to be clean." The leprosy left the man at once and he was made clean. As Jesus sent the man away, he sternly warned him, "Don't tell anyone about this, but go and show yourself to the priest and for the cleansing bring the offering ordered by Moses; in this way you will make your declaration." However, as soon as the man went out, he began spreading the news everywhere, so that Jesus could no longer openly enter any town. But even though he stayed in the rural areas, people came to him from everywhere.

The leper in today's Gospel could teach us some aspects of a good prayer of petition. First, his prayer leaves all possibilities in the hand of God. "If you so will, you can make me clean." He does not dictate and coerce but asks humbly. He knows his place and lets the Lord be the Lord. Secondly, he did not keep it upon himself but proclaimed to others the goodness of Jesus once his petition was answered. Thus his blessing becomes the blessing of the community.

17
JANUARY

Friday
Ps 89:16–17, 18–19
For ever I will sing
the goodness of the Lord.

1ST WEEK IN ORDINARY TIME
St. Anthony, abbot
Psalter: Week 1 / (White)

1st Reading: 1 S 8:4–7, 10–22a*

All the chiefs of Israel gathered together and went to Samuel in Ramah. They said to him, "You are already old and your sons are not following your ways. Give us a king to rule over us as in all the other nations." (…) So Samuel answered those who were asking him for a king, and he told them all that Yahweh said to him, "Look, these will be the demands of your king: he will take your sons and assign them to his chariot and his horses and have them run before his chariot. Some he will assign as commanders over a thousand men and commanders over fifty. He will take your daughters as well to prepare perfumes, to cook and to bake for him. He will take the best of your fields, your vineyards and your olive orchards and give them to his officials. He will take a tenth portion of your grain and of your vineyards, and give it to his officers and to his servants. He will take your menservants and maidservants, the best of your cattle and your asses for his own work. He will take the tenth of your flocks and you yourselves will become his slaves. When these things happen, you will cry out because of the king whom you have chosen for yourselves. But by then, Yahweh will not answer you." (…)

Gospel: Mk 2:1–12

After some days, Jesus returned to Capernaum. As the news spread that he was at home, so many people gathered that there was no longer room even outside the door. While Jesus was preaching the word to them, some people brought to him a paralyzed man. The four men who carried him couldn't get near Jesus because of the crowd, so they opened the roof above the room where Jesus was and, through the hole, lowered the man on his mat. When Jesus saw the faith of these people, he said to the paralytic, "My son, your sins are forgiven." Now, some teachers of the Law who were sitting there wondered within themselves, "How can he speak like this insulting God? Who can forgive sins except God?" At once Jesus knew through his spirit what they were thinking and asked, "Why do you wonder? Is it easier to say to this paralyzed man: 'Your sins are forgiven,' or to say: 'Rise, take up your mat and walk?' But now you shall know that the Son of Man has authority on earth to forgive sins." And he said to the paralytic, "Stand up, take up your mat and go home." The man rose and, in the sight of all those people, he took up his mat and went out. All of them were astonished and praised God saying, "We have never seen anything like this!"

St. Anthony
Did you know that: St. Anthony of Egypt is revered as first master of the desert and pinnacle of holy monks in Eastern Churches.

The grind of daily life that crowds and obscures Jesus Christ in our life is sometimes daunting and seemingly insurmountable. It is in these situations that friends are indeed blessings from God. The paralytic himself could never go near the Lord. There were too many people like him wanting an audience with Jesus. But he was carried on the shoulders of his friends. On the strength of his friends' perseverance their efforts led him directly in front of the Lord who cured him. Let us thank God for friends who care enough to carry us towards the Lord when our own faith fails us. And may we too be their support when they in turn experience paralysis in their life.

1ST WEEK IN ORDINARY TIME
Psalter: Week 1 / (Green / White)

Saturday

Ps 21:2–3, 4–5, 6–7
Lord, in your strength
the king is glad.

18
JANUARY

1st Reading: 1 S 9:1–4, 17–19, 10:1

There was a man from the tribe of Benjamin whose name was Kish. He was the son of Abiel, son of Zeror, son of Becorath, son of Aphiah, a valiant Benjaminite. Kish had a son named Saul, a handsome young man who had no equal among the Israelites, for he was a head taller than any of them.

It happened that the asses of Kish were lost. So he said to his son Saul, "Take one of the boys with you and go look for the asses." They went all over the hill country of Ephraim and the land of Shalishah but did not find them. They passed through the land of Shaalim and the land of Benjamin, but the asses were nowhere to be found. So, when Samuel saw Saul, Yahweh told him, "Here is the man I spoke to you about! He shall rule over my people." Saul approached Samuel in the gateway and said, "Tell me, where is the house of the seer?" Samuel answered Saul, "I am the seer. Go up ahead of me to the high place, for today you shall eat with me. In the morning, before you leave, I will tell you all that is in your heart." Then Samuel took a vial of oil and poured it on Saul's head. And kissing Saul, Samuel said, "Yahweh has anointed you to rule over and to lead his people Israel. And this will be Yahweh's sign to you that he has anointed you."

Gospel: Mk 2:13–17

When Jesus went out again beside the lake, a crowd came to him and he taught them. As he walked along, he saw a tax collector sitting in his office. This was Levi, the son of Alpheus. Jesus said to him, "Follow me." And Levi got up and followed him.

And it so happened that while Jesus was eating in Levi's house, tax collectors and sinners were sitting with him and his disciples; there were a lot of them, and they used to follow Jesus.

But Pharisees, men educated in the Law, when they saw Jesus eating with sinners and tax collectors, said to his disciples, "Why does your master eat and drink with tax collectors and sinners?"

Jesus heard them and answered, "Healthy people don't need a doctor, but sick people do. I did not come to call the righteous, but sinners."

It was a simple and direct invitation. "Follow me," without frills or fanfare. Surprisingly, "Levi got up and followed Him." The invitation of a mature God found an astonishing response from a man who was numbered among the habitual sinners, "the small people," the *anawim* of God. It is perhaps to point to us that greatness is something ingrained in each and every one of us irrespective of our background and social attainments. The invitation to actualize it comes to us many times and in various ways, some not as obvious as the invitation of Jesus to Levi. It is whether we have the capacity to risk or not that makes the difference.

19

JANUARY

Ps 97:1, 2-3, 3-4, 5-6
All the ends of the earth
have seen the saving power of God.

1st Reading: Is 9:1–6

The people who walk in darkness have seen a great light. A light has dawned on those who live in the land of the shadow of death.

You have enlarged the nation; you have increased their joy. They rejoice before you, as people rejoice at harvest time as they rejoice in dividing the spoil.

For the yoke of their burden, the bar across their shoulders, the rod of their oppressors, you have broken it as on the day of Midian.

Every warrior's boot that tramped in war, every cloak rolled in blood, will be thrown out for burning, will serve as fuel for the fire.

For a child is born to us, a son is given us; the royal ornament is laid upon his shoulder, and his name is proclaimed: "Wonderful Counselor, Mighty God, Everlasting Father, Prince of Peace."

To the increase of his powerful rule in peace, there will be no end. Vast will be his dominion, he will reign on David's throne and over all his kingdom, to establish and uphold it with justice and righteousness from this time onward and forever.

The zealous love of Yahweh Sabaoth will do this.

2nd Reading: Eph 1:3–6, 15–18

Blessed be God, the Father of Christ Jesus our Lord, who in Christ has blessed us from heaven with every spiritual blessing.

God chose us in Christ before the creation of the world to be holy and without sin in his presence.

From eternity he destined us in love to be his adopted sons and daughters through Christ Jesus, thus fulfilling his free and generous will.

This goal suited him: that his loving-kindness which he granted us in his Beloved might finally receive all glory and praise.

I have been told of your faith and your affection towards all the believers, so I always give thanks to God, remembering you in my prayers.

May the God of Christ Jesus our Lord, the Father of Glory, reveal himself to you and give you a spirit of wisdom and revelation, that you may know him.

May he enlighten your inner vision, that you may appreciate the things we hope for, since we were called by God.

May you know how great is the inheritance, the glory, God sets apart for his saints.

Gospel: Mt 18: 1-5, 10

At that time the disciples came to Jesus and asked him, "Who is the greatest in the kingdom of heaven?"

Then Jesus called a little child, set the child in the midst of the disciples, and said, "I assure you that, unless you change and become like little children, you cannot enter the kingdom of heaven. Whoever becomes humble like this child is the greatest in the kingdom of heaven, and whoever receives such a child in my name receives me.

"See that you do not despise any of these little ones, for I tell you: their angels in heaven continually see the face of my heavenly Father."

Reading: The disciples became so preoccupied with greatness. They had to settle the question to prepare themselves. Little did they know that Jesus would surpise them greatly. Jesus presented to them the children as examples of greatness. They reflect the attitude needed to receive the Kingdom of God effectively. Thus these children who do not count in society became a pedagogical tool for the disciples to learn from in order to enter God's kingdom.

Reflection: Most in the world today will only pay attention if it is something big. The little things are despised as a waste of time. But all big things were once small. They got to their present stature not by leaps and bounds but by a slow painstaking process of growth. Jesus does not dismiss the little ones of this world. He sees the potential locked within them that with proper nurturance will someday unleash the greatness that is inside. It takes special eyes to see this potentiality hidden deep within; eyes that are continuously kept clear by a respectful love for all that are small.

Response: Have you paid attention lately to the little things in your life? Perhaps we need to be distracted from our present quest of *Citius* (Faster), *Altius* (Higher), *Fortius* (Stronger) in this lifetime and start our journey from something small and nurture it to grow as big as it can get. Perhaps we need to make an inventory of our life and see what small things are there that could be the start of an adventure towards growth.

20
JANUARY

Monday
Ps 50:8–9, 16bc–17, 21 & 23
To the upright I will show
the saving power of God.

2ND WEEK IN ORDINARY TIME
St. Fabian, pope & martyr
St. Sebastian, martyr
Psalter: Week 2 / (Green / Red)

1st Reading: 1 S 15:16–23

*S*amuel then told Saul, "Enough! Let me tell you what Yahweh said to me last night." Saul replied, "Please tell me. "So Samuel went on and said, "Though you had no confidence in yourself, you became chief of the tribes of Israel, for Yahweh wanted to anoint you king over Israel. Then he sent you with this command, 'Go. Completely crush the Amalekite offenders, engaging them in battle until they are destroyed.' Why then did you not obey the voice of Yahweh but instead swooped down on the spoil, doing what was evil in his sight?" To this, Saul replied, "I have obeyed the voice of Yahweh and have carried out the mission for which he sent me. I have captured Agag, king of Amalek and completely destroyed the Amalekites. If my men spared the best sheep and oxen from among those to be destroyed, it was in order to sacrifice them to Yahweh, your God, in Gilgal." Samuel then said, "Does Yahweh take as much delight in burnt offerings and sacrifices, as in obedience to his command? Obedience is better than sacrifice, and submission better than the fat of rams. Rebellion is like the sin of divination, and stubbornness like holding onto idols. Since you have rejected the word of Yahweh, he too has rejected you as king."

St. Fabian

Did you know that: St. Fabian was just on a pilgrimage in Rome and was suddenly elected pope because of a dove that descended on his head just like the descent of the Holy Spirit.

Gospel: Mk 2:18–22

*O*ne day, when the Pharisees and the disciples of John the Baptist were fasting, some people asked Jesus, "Why is it that both the Pharisees and the disciples of John fast, but yours do not?" Jesus answered, "How can the wedding guests fast while the bridegroom is with them? As long as they have the bridegroom with them, they cannot fast. But the day will come when the bridegroom will be taken from them, and on that day they will fast.

"No one sews a piece of new cloth on an old coat, because the new patch will shrink and tear away from the old cloth, making a worse tear. And no one puts new wine into old wineskins, for the wine would burst the skins, and then both the wine and the skins would be lost. But new wine, new skins!"

To try something new is risky. One needs a lot of adjustment to one's mindset as well as that of others. We are more comfortable with what is the usual, the old and familiar. They provide us with security; change always unsettles, provokes fear and anxiety and generates negative reactions. But no human convention is ever written in stones. Most of all, they are always subservient to the Law of Love. Jesus Christ the Word of God and the Author of law and order is divine love embodied. Thus before Him every human convention and law bend their knees. When we are before Him, we need to constantly adjust our perspectives until we put on the new man or the new woman. Then we will never again struggle with love because we have it within us forever.

2ND WEEK IN ORDINARY TIME
St. Agnes, virgin & martyr
Psalter: Week 2 / (Red)

Tuesday

Ps 89:20, 21–22, 27–28
I have found David, my servant.

21
JANUARY

St. Agnes

Did you know that: The wool used to make the pallium sent by popes to archbishops comes from the lambs offered to St. Agnes' church on her feast day.

_____
_____
_____
_____
_____
_____
_____
_____
_____
_____
_____
_____
_____
_____
_____
_____
_____

When we become too preoccupied with the externals to the point of obsession, we tend to miss the bigger picture of why the externals exist in the first place. They are meant to articulate deeper realities on the physical plane. In the case of the Sabbath, it is to give us the chance to rest, to recuperate and recreate ourselves so that we may go back again to our works renewed. It is not meant to impose more things to do but to ease our burden. Sabbaths are meant to be times of rejoicing and gladness. The Pharisees with their number of do's and don't's turned it into a burden instead of a blessing.

1st Reading: 1 S 16:1–13*

Samuel asked, "How can I go? If Saul hears of this, he will kill me!" Yahweh replied, "Take a heifer with you and say, 'I have come to sacrifice to Yahweh.' Invite Jesse to the sacrifice and I will let you know what to do next. You shall anoint for me the one I point out to you." Samuel did what Yahweh commanded and left for Bethlehem. When he appeared, the elders of the city came to him asking, fearfully, "Do you bring us peace?" Samuel replied, "I come in peace; I am here to sacrifice to Yahweh. Cleanse yourselves and join me in the sacrifice." He also had Jesse and his sons cleansed and invited them to the sacrifice. As they came, Samuel looked at Eliab the older and thought, "This must be Yahweh's anointed." But Yahweh told Samuel, "Do not judge by his looks or his stature for I have rejected him. Yahweh does not judge as man judges; humans see with the eyes; Yahweh sees the heart."

Jesse called his son Abinadab and presented him to Samuel who said, "Yahweh has not chosen this one either." Jesse presented Shammah and Samuel said, "Nor has Yahweh chosen this one." Jesse presented seven of his sons to Samuel who said, "Yahweh has chosen none of them. But are all your sons here?" Jesse replied, "There is still the youngest, tending the flock just now." Samuel said to him, "Send for him and bring him to me; we shall not sit down to eat until he arrives." So Jesse sent for his youngest son and brought him to Samuel. He was a handsome lad with ruddy complexion and beautiful eyes. And Yahweh spoke, "Go, anoint him for he is the one." Samuel then took the horn of oil and anointed him in his brothers' presence. From that day onwards, Yahweh's Spirit took hold of David. Then Samuel left for Ramah.

Gospel: Mk 2:23–28

One Sabbath Jesus was walking through grainfields. As his disciples walked along with him, they began to pick the heads of grain and crush them in their hands. Then the Pharisees said to Jesus, "Look! they are doing what is forbidden on the sabbath!" And he said to them, "Have you never read what David did in his time of need, when he and his men were very hungry? He went into the house of God when Abiathar was High Priest and ate the bread of offering, which only the priests are allowed to eat, and he also gave some to the men who were with him." Then Jesus said to them, "The Sabbath was made for man, not man for the Sabbath. So the Son of Man is master even of the Sabbath."

22
JANUARY

Wednesday
Ps 144:1b, 2, 9–10
Blessed be the Lord, my Rock!

2ND WEEK IN ORDINARY TIME
St. Vincent, deacon & martyr
Psalter: Week 2 / (Green / Red)

1st Reading: 1 S 17:32–33, 37, 40–51*

Saul told David, "You cannot fight with this Philistine for you are still young, whereas this man has been a warrior from his youth." David continued, "Yahweh who delivered me from the paws of lions and bears, will deliver me from the hands of the Philistines." Saul then told David, "Go and may Yahweh be with you!" David got rid of all this armor, took his staff, picked up five smooth stones from the brook and dropped them inside his shepherd's bag. And with his sling in hand, he drew near to the Philistine. The Philistine moved forward, closing in on David, his shield-bearer in front of him. When he saw that David was only a lad, (he was of fresh complexion and handsome) he despised him. Cursing David by his gods, he continued, "Come and I will give your flesh to the birds of the sky and the beasts of the field!"

David answered the Philistine, "You have come against me with sword, spear and javelin, but I come against you with Yahweh, the God of the armies of Israel whom you have defied. Yahweh will deliver you this day into my hands and I will strike you down and cut off your head. (…)" No sooner had the Philistine moved to attack him than David rushed to the battleground. Putting his hand into his bag, he took out a stone, slung it and struck the Philistine on the forehead; it penetrated his forehead and he fell on his face to the ground. David triumphed over the Philistine with a sling and a stone. He rushed forward, stood over him, took the Philistine's sword and slew him by cutting off his head. (...)

Gospel: Mk 3:1–6

Jesus entered the synagogue. A man, who had a paralyzed hand was there and some people watched Jesus: would he heal the man on the sabbath? If he did, they could accuse him.

Jesus said to the man with the paralyzed hand, "Stand here in the center." Then he asked them, "What does the Law allow us to do on the sabbath? To do good or to do harm? To save life or to kill?" But they were silent.

Then Jesus looked around at them with anger and deep sadness, because they had closed their minds. And he said to the man, "Stretch out your hand." He stretched it out, and his hand was healed. As soon as the Pharisees left, they met with Herod's supporters, looking for a way to destroy Jesus.

St. Vincent

Did you know that: St. Vincent, Patron of Vintners and Vinegar-makers, made his torturers wept with rage because of his faithfulness and courageousness despite the tortures he suffered.

One of the greatest tragedies that may befall us is to acquire a closed mind in the course of our life. We become enclosed, hindered and unfree. The real paralytic in the Gospel today may not be the man with paralyzed hands but those people whose minds had been paralyzed by routine, legalism and self-righteousness. Physical infirmities never presented any difficulties on the part of Jesus. He cured them easily. It was only when people stubbornly clung to their beliefs to the point of being blind to the miracle unfolding in front of them that even He could hardly perform any miracle. It is our spiritual paralysis that could dry up the spring of wonder flowing from God.

Thursday

Ps 56:2–3, 9–10a, 10b–11, 12–13
In God I trust; I shall not fear.

23
JANUARY

1st Reading: 1 S 18:6–9; 19:1–7

When they arrived after David had slain the Philistine, the women came out from the cities of Israel to meet King Saul singing and dancing with timbrels and musical instruments. They were merrily singing this song: "Saul has slain his thousands, and David, his tens of thousands."

Saul was very displeased with this song and said, "They have given tens of thousands to David but to me only thousands! By now he has everything but the kingdom!" From then on, Saul became very distrustful of David.

Saul told his son Jonathan and his servants of his intention to kill David. But Jonathan, who liked David very much, said to David, "My father Saul wants to kill you. Be on your guard tomorrow morning and hide yourself in a secret place. I will go out and keep my father company in the countryside where you are and I will speak to him about you. If I find out something, I will let you know." Jonathan spoke well of David to his father Saul and said, "Let not the king sin against his servant David for he has not sinned against you. On the contrary, what he has done has benefited you. He risked his life in killing the Philistine and Yahweh brought about a great victory for Israel. You yourself saw this and greatly rejoiced. Why then sin against innocent blood and kill David without cause?" Saul heeded Jonathan's plea and swore, "As Yahweh lives, he shall not be put to death." So Jonathan called David and told him all these things. He then brought him to Saul and David was back in Saul's service as before.

Gospel: Mk 3:7–12

Jesus and his disciples withdrew to the lakeside, and a large crowd from Galilee followed him. A great number of people also came from Judea, Jerusalem, Idumea, Transjordan and from the region of Tyre and Sidon, for they had heard of all that he was doing.

Because of the crowd, Jesus told his disciples to have a boat ready for him, to prevent the people from crushing him. He healed so many, that all who had diseases kept pressing towards him to touch him. Even the people who had evil spirits, whenever they saw him, would fall down before him and cry out, "You are the Son of God." But he warned them sternly not to tell anyone who he was.

Being at the service of God sometimes creates danger, a hazard of the trade known as fame. People cannot get enough of us. Since we are conduits of God's grace, just being near us or just by touching us makes them think that they have touched heaven itself. This might be a real incentive for some, but it does bring a lot of responsibilities. The challenge is not to think that it's because of us that all of these things happen and to redirect this attention to God who is the reason why people come to us in the first place. It is to fulfill the role with dignity while being detached from the perks that come with it. For we too are followers and are not meant to usurp the role of God whom we serve.

24
JANUARY

Friday

Ps 57:2, 3-4, 6, & 11
Have mercy on me,
God, have mercy.

2ND WEEK IN ORDINARY TIME
St. Francis de Sales,
bishop & doctor
Psalter: Week 2 / (White)

1st Reading: 1 S 24:3–21*

Now David and his men were far back in the cave. David's men said to him, "This is the day which Yahweh spoke of: look I will deliver your enemy into your hands and you will do with him as you see fit." So David moved up and stealthily cut off an end of Saul's robe. But afterward, David regretted having cut off an end of Saul's robe, and he said to his men, "Let me not lay my hands on my master, for he is Yahweh's anointed." (…)

Then David himself stepped out of the cave and called after Saul, "My master, the king!" When Saul looked back, David knelt and then bowed to the ground in homage and asked him, "Why do you listen to those who say that I want to harm you? Look, today you have seen that Yahweh delivered you into my hands in the cave, and I was told to kill you but I held myself back and I said: 'I will not lift my hands against my master who is Yahweh's anointed.' (…) May Yahweh be judge between you and me and may he exact justice from you in my case, but I shall do you no harm." (...)

After David had spoken these words, Saul asked, "Is that your voice, my son David?" He wept aloud and said to David, "You are right and I am wrong, for you have repaid with kindness the harm I have inflicted on you. This day you have shown your righteousness to me by not taking my life when Yahweh put me into your hands. For if a man finds his enemy, will he let him go unharmed? May Yahweh reward you for what you have done for me today. Now I know for certain that you shall reign and the kingdom of Israel will be firm in your hand.

Gospel: Mk 3:13–19

Jesus went up into the hill country, and called those he wanted, and they came to him. He appointed twelve to be with him; and he called them apostles. He wanted to send them out to preach, and he gave them authority to drive out demons.

These are the Twelve: Simon, to whom he gave the name Peter; James, son of Zebedee, and John his brother, to whom he gave the name Boanerges, which means "men of thunder"; Andrew, Philip, Bartholomew, Matthew, Thomas, James son of Alpheus, Thaddeus, Simon the Cananean and Judas Iscariot, the one who betrayed him.

St. Francis de Sales
Did you know that: St. Francis de Sales is the Patron Saint of Writers and Journalists.

Now is the test whether collaboration between God and man could flourish. After all, our faith history has been littered with hits and misses on this divine-human partnership. Jesus sends His appointed apostles to preach and heal, to teach and make whole, to show the way and liberate people. We have seen the journeys of these apostles, their struggles, their defeats and triumphs. They mirror who we are and what we could become if we but hold on to faith. The Eleven kept the faith while Judas Iscariot did not. To whose side do we belong?

Saturday

Ps 117:1bc, 2
Go out to all the world,
and tell the Good News.

25 JANUARY

1st Reading: Acts 22:3–16 (or Acts 9:1–22)

Paul said, "I am a Jew, born in Tarsus in Cilicia, but brought up here, in this city, where I was educated in the school of Gamaliel, according to the strict observance of our law. And I was dedicated to God's service, as are all of you today. As for this way, I persecuted it to the point of death and arrested its followers, both men and women, throwing them into prison.

"The High Priest and the whole Council of elders can bear witness to this. From them, I received letters for the Jewish brothers in Damascus; and I set out to arrest those who were there, and bring them back to Jerusalem for punishment. But, as I was traveling along, nearing Damascus, at about noon a great light from the sky suddenly flashed about me. I fell to the ground and heard a voice saying to me: 'Saul, Saul, why do you persecute me?' I answered: 'Who are you, Lord?' And he said to me: 'I am Jesus, the Nazorean, whom you persecute.' The men who were with me saw the light, but they did not understand the voice of the one who was speaking to me. I asked: 'What shall I do, Lord?' And the Lord replied: 'Get up and go to Damascus; there, you will be told all that you are destined to do.' Yet, the brightness of that light had blinded me; and, so, I was led by the hand into Damascus by my companions.

"There, a certain Ananias came to me. He was a devout observer of the law, and well spoken of by all the Jews who were living there. As he stood by me, he said: 'Brother Saul, recover your sight.' At that moment, I could see; and I looked at him. He, then, said, 'The God of our ancestors has chosen you to know his will, to see the Just One, and to hear the words from his mouth. From now on you shall be his witness before all the pagan people, and tell them all that you have seen and heard. And now, why delay? Get up and be baptized; and have your sins washed away, by calling upon his Name.'"

Gospel: Mk 16:15–18

Jesus told his disciples, "Go out to the whole world and proclaim the Good News to all creation. The one who believes and is baptized will be saved; the one who refuses to believe will be condemned. Signs like these will accompany those who have believed: in my name they will cast out demons and speak new languages; they will pick up snakes, and if they drink anything poisonous, they will be unharmed; they will lay their hands on the sick, and they will be healed."

Today, we celebrate the rebirth of a remarkable man, Paul of Tarsus who was a former persecutor of Jesus' followers but turned ardent and faithful apostle. His conversion on the road to Damascus was a turning point in our faith history. For here is an outsider being invited by the Lord to be one of His own. His outsider status might appear as a handicap but later developments showed that Paul was precisely needed in order to expand the notion of mission as being for the whole world and not only for Israel. Paul the Apostle to the Gentiles was God's instrument in unleashing His love to all.

26
JANUARY

Sunday

Ps 27:1, 4, 13–14
The Lord is my light
and my salvation.

1st Reading: Is 8:23 – 9:3

*Y*et, where there was but anguish, darkness will disappear.

He has just afflicted the land of Zebulun and the land of Naphtali; but in the future he will confer glory on the way of the sea, on the land beyond the Jordan— the pagans' Galilee.

The people who walk in darkness have seen a great light. A light has dawned on those who live in the land of the shadow of death.

You have enlarged the nation; you have increased their joy. They rejoice before you, as people rejoice at harvest time as they rejoice in dividing the spoil.

For the yoke of their burden, the bar across their shoulders, the rod of their oppressors, you have broken it as on the day of Midian.

2nd Reading: 1 Cor 1:10–13, 17

I beg of you, brothers, in the name of Christ Jesus, our Lord, to agree among yourselves, and do away with divisions; please be per fectly united, with one mind and one judgment.

For I heard from people, of Cloe's house, about your rivalries. What I mean is this: some say, "I am for Paul," and others: "I am for Apollos," or "I am for Peter," or "I am for Christ." Is Christ divided, or have I, Paul, been crucified for you? Have you been baptized in the name of Paul?

For Christ did not send me to baptize, but to proclaim his Gospel. And not with beautiful words! That would be like getting rid of the cross of Christ.

Gospel: Mt 4:12 – 23 (or Mt 4:12-17)

*W*hen Jesus heard that John had been arrested, he withdrew into Galilee. He left Nazareth and went to live in Capernaum, a town by the lake of Galilee, at the border of Zebulun and Naphtali.

In this way, the word of the prophet Isaiah was fulfilled: *Land of Zebulun and land of Naphtali, crossed by the Road of the Sea; and you, who live beyond the Jordan, Galilee, land of pagans:*

The people who lived in dark ness have seen a great light; on those who live in the land of the shadow of death, a light has shone.

From that time on, Jesus began to proclaim his message, "Change your ways: the kingdom of heaven is near."

As Jesus walked by the lake of Galilee, he saw two brothers, Simon called Peter, and Andrew his brother, casting a net into the lake, for they were fishermen. He said to them, "Come, follow me; and I will make you fish for people."

At once they left their nets and followed him.

He went on from there and saw two other brothers, James, the son of Zebedee, and his brother John, in a boat with their father Zebedee, mending their nets. Jesus called them.

At once, they left the boat, and their father, and followed him.

Jesus went around all Galilee, teaching in their synagogues, proclaiming the good news of the king dom, and curing all kinds of sickness and disease among the people.

Reading: John had been arrested. Jesus knew that the likes of him who preached the Kingdom of God would soon be rounded up by the civil authorities for disrupting peace and order. He prudently withdrew to the periphery to escape the heat of civil power concentrated in the center.

Reflection: Walking away when the heat becomes unbearable is sometimes the greater part of valor. We cannot stake our all at the initial stage of our work. To do this, we need a tremendous amount of self-awareness and control. We need to be aware of our strengths and deficiencies and control our desire to shortcut ourselves to success by engaging in risky ventures and behaviors. Jesus was fully aware and in control of Himself. He walked away from the short war in order to push His mission long enough to raise a band of brothers who would see to its completion. His calculations paid off. We are where we are because He did not call the fight when it was still premature.

Response: When was the last time you walked away from a useless fight, argument or struggle? Things that will not bear fruits are best left alone allowing us to redirect our energy to those that will. Our only payment would be our bruised ego that did not have the last word. Never mind, just go and walk away and you will be the wiser next time when a similar situation comes.

_____
_____
_____
_____
_____
_____
_____
_____
_____

27
JANUARY

Monday

Ps 89: 20, 21-22, 25-26
My faithfulness and my mercy
shall be with him.

3RD WEEK IN ORDINARY TIME
St. Angela Merici, virgin
Psalter: Week 3 / (Green / White)

1st Reading: 2 S 5:1–7, 10

All the tribes of Israel came to David at Hebron and said, "We are your bone and flesh. In the past, when Saul was king over us, it was you who led Israel. And Yahweh said to you, 'You shall be the shepherd of my people Israel and you shall be commander over Israel.'" Before Yahweh, king David made an agreement with the elders of Israel who came to him at Hebron, and they anointed him king of Israel.

David was thirty years old when he began to reign, and he reigned for forty years: he reigned over Judah, from Hebron, seven and a half years; and over Israel and Judah, from Jerusalem, for thirty-three years.

The king and his men set out for Jerusalem to fight the Jebusites who lived there. They said to David, "If you try to break in here, the blind and the lame will drive you away," which meant that David could not get in. Yet David captured the fortress of Zion that became the "city of David." And David grew more powerful, for Yahweh, the God of Hosts, was with him.

Gospel: Mk 3:22–30

The teachers of the law, who had come from Jerusalem, said, "He is in the power of Beelzebul: the chief of the demons helps him to drive out demons."

Jesus called them to him, and began teaching them by means of stories, or parables. "How can Satan drive out Satan? If a nation is divided by civil war, that nation cannot stand. If a family divides itself into groups, that family will not survive. In the same way, if Satan has risen against himself and is divided, he will not stand; he is finished. No one can break into the house of a strong man in order to plunder his goods, unless he first ties up the strong man. Then indeed, he can plunder his house.

"Truly, I say to you, every sin will be forgiven humankind, even insults to God, however numerous. But whoever slanders the Holy Spirit will never be forgiven. He carries the guilt of his sin forever."

"This was their sin whom they said, 'He has an unclean spirit in him.'"

St. Angela Merici

Did you know that: St. Angela Merici's Company of Saint Ursula, or the Ursulines, was the first group of religious women to work outside the cloister and the first teaching order of women.

Envy can blind us to the reality manifesting itself right in front of us. The teachers of the Law, waiting for the favorable time of the Lord missed the opportunity to recognize the signs wrought by Jesus as the prelude to the coming of the Kingdom of God. Their deepest aspiration happening right before them eluded their detection. Their eyes were green with envy. They had already decided how this Kingdom of God would come and Jesus did not fit into their vision. Thus rather than welcoming it with open hearts and minds, they battled against it.

3RD WEEK IN ORDINARY TIME
St. Thomas Aquinas, priest & doctor
Psalter: Week 3 / (White)

Tuesday
Ps 24:7, 8, 9, 10
Who is this king of glory?
It is the Lord!

28
JANUARY

St. Thomas Aquinas

Did you know that: St. Thomas Aquinas was called "The Dumb Ox" by his classmates when he was studying in Cologne under St. Albert the Great.

1st Reading: 2 S 6:12b–15, 17–19

King David was told that Yahweh had blessed the family of Obededom and all that belonged to him because of the Ark of God, so he went to bring up the Ark of God from the house of Obededom to the city of David, rejoicing. After those who carried the Ark of Yahweh had walked six paces, they sacrificed an ox and a fattened calf.

David whirled round dancing with all his heart before Yahweh, wearing a linen ephod, for he and all the Israelites brought up the Ark of Yahweh, shouting joyfully and sounding the horn.

They brought in the Ark of Yahweh and laid it in its place, in the tent which David had pitched for it. Then David offered burnt and peace offerings before Yahweh. Once the offerings had been made, David blessed the people in the name of Yahweh of Hosts, and distributed to each of them, to each man and woman of the entire assembly of Israel, a loaf of bread, a portion of meat and a raisin cake. With this, all the people left for their homes.

Gospel: Mk 3:31–35

Jesus' mother and brothers came. As they stood outside, they sent someone to call him. The crowd sitting around Jesus told him, "Your mother and your brothers are outside asking for you." He replied, "Who are my mother and my brothers?"

And looking around at those who sat there, he said, "Here are my mother and my brothers. Whoever does the will of God is brother and sister and mother to me."

Our significant relations extend our reach to other people. Their own network of relationships could be ours too especially if they facilitate our entry into them. Yet they also tend to limit our social space especially if they think they have the first right to our time and presence more than the others. And so Jesus situates the nature of His relationship with His family. It is not by blood relationship but by something deeper, kinship in a common obedience to the will of the one Father of all in heaven. And so, everyone has the right to His person and time. Nobody is above the rest because people of goodwill are mothers and brothers of Jesus and of one another.

29
JANUARY

Wednesday
Ps 89:4–5, 27–28, 29–30
For ever I will maintain my love
for my servant.

3RD WEEK IN ORDINARY TIME
Psalter: Week 3 / (Green)

1st Reading: 2 S 7:4–17

Gospel: Mk 4:1–20

Again, Jesus began to teach by the lake; but such a large crowd gathered about him, that he got into a boat and sat in it on the lake, while the crowd stood on the shore. He taught them many things through parables. In his teaching he said, "Listen! The sower went out to sow. As he sowed, some of the seed fell along a path; and the birds came and ate it up. Some of the seed fell on rocky ground, where it had little soil; it sprang up immediately, because it had no depth; but when the sun rose and burned it, it withered, because it had no roots. Other seed fell among thorn bushes; and the thorns grew and choked it; so it didn't produce any grain. But some seed fell on good soil, grew and increased and yielded grain; some seed produced thirty times as much, some sixty, and some one hundred times as much." And Jesus added, "Listen then, if you have ears."

When the crowd went away, some who were around him with the Twelve asked about the parables.

He answered them, "The mystery of the kingdom of God has been given to you. But for those outside, everything comes in parables, so, that, *the more they see, they don't perceive; the more they hear, they don't understand; otherwise they would be converted and pardoned.*"

Jesus said to them, "Don't you understand this parable? How, then, will you understand any of the parables? What the sower is sowing is the word. Those along the path, where the seed fell, are people who hear the word, but as soon as they hear it, Satan comes and takes away the word that was sown in them.

"Other people receive the word like rocky ground. As soon as they hear the word, they accept it with joy. But they have no roots, so it lasts only a little while. No sooner does trouble or persecution come because of the word, than they fall.

"Others receive the seed, as seed among thorns. After they hear the word, they are caught up in the worries of this life, false hopes of riches and other desires. All these come in and choke the word, so that finally it produces nothing.

"And there are others who receive the word as good soil. They hear the word, take it to heart and produce: some thirty, some sixty, and some one hundred times as much."

It is always good to ask and not to assume understanding especially if there is none in the first place. For asking the right question sets one on the path of knowledge and wisdom. This is what the Twelve and some who were around Jesus learned when He expounded on the parable of the seeds. And they received an answer that would give them the perspective to understand the succeeding teachings of the Lord. If they had not risked asking, they would have spent the greater part of their life wondering what Jesus meant by those words. Now they could move on and increase in knowledge and in wisdom simply because they had the courage to ask. What about us? Have we resolved our questions lately by asking the very person who could answer them?

3RD WEEK IN ORDINARY TIME
Psalter: Week 3 / (Green)

Thursday

Ps 132:1–2, 3–5, 11, 12, 13–14
The Lord God will give him
the throne of David, his father.

30
JANUARY

1st Reading: 2 S 7:18–19, 24–29

King David went in, sat before Yahweh and said, "Who am I, O Yahweh God, and who is my family that you have brought me so far? Yet this was not enough for you, O Yahweh God, for you have also spoken of your servant's house for a long time to come. Is this the way men act, O Yahweh God?

"You have set apart your people Israel to become your people forever; and you, Yahweh, have become their God.

"Now, O Yahweh God, keep forever the promise you made and have now revealed to me regarding myself and my family, that your name may be honored forever and people may say, 'Yahweh of Hosts is God over Israel.' The house of your servant David will be secure before you because you, O Yahweh of Hosts, God of Israel, have made it known to your servant and have said to him: 'Your family will last forever.' This is why I have dared to address this prayer to you.

"So now, O Yahweh God, since you are the faithful God, and have promised me this good thing, please bless my descendants, that they may continue forever before you. For you, O Yahweh God, have spoken and, with your blessing, my family shall be blessed forever."

Gospel: Mk 4:21–25

Jesus said to his disciples, "When the light comes, is it put under a basket or a bed? Surely it is put on a lamp stand. Whatever is hidden will be disclosed, and whatever is kept secret will be brought to light. Listen then, if you have ears!"

And he also said to them, "Pay attention to what you hear. In the measure you give, so shall you receive, and still more will be given to you. For to the one who produces something, more will be given; and from him who does not produce anything, even what he has will be taken away from him."

Generosity never diminishes the giver but makes him or her more blessed and truly rich. For you can never give what you never owned in the first place. And what you have never owned you cannot truly enjoy because they make you anxious, afraid and insecure that once they are used up, they can only be replenished with difficulty. It's a pity that there are people with so much yet act like dirt poor, while there are poor people with very little who behave like they are exceptionally rich. The real poverty that is appalling is not so much material poverty as the poverty of the heart.

31
JANUARY

Friday

Ps 51:3–4, 5–6a, 6bcd–7, 10–11
Be merciful, O Lord,
for we have sinned.

3RD WEEK IN ORDINARY TIME
St. John Bosco, priest
Psalter: Week 3 / (White)

1st Reading: 2 S 11:1–4a, 5–10a, 13–17*

One afternoon, David got up from his siesta and took a walk on the roof of the royal house. From the rooftop, he saw a woman bathing; and the woman was very beautiful. David sent to inquire about the woman, and was told, "She is Bathsheba, daughter of Eliam and wife of Uriah, the Hittite." So David sent messengers to have her brought to him; and he had intercourse with her just after she had purified herself after her monthly period. (…) As the woman saw she was with child, she sent word to David, "I am with child."

David then sent a message to Joab, "Send me Uriah the Hittite." So Joab sent Uriah to David. When Uriah came, David asked him about Joab, how the people were and how the war was proceeding. Then he told Uriah, "Go down to your house and wash your feet." (…) The next morning, David wrote Joab a letter to be taken by hand by Uriah, in which he said, "Place Uriah in the front row where the fighting is very fierce and then withdraw from him so that he may be struck down and die." When Joab was attacking the city, he assigned Uriah to a place which he knew was being defended by strong warriors. And the defenders attacked the men of Joab. Some of David's soldiers and officers were killed; Uriah the Hittite also died.

Gospel: Mk 4:26–34

Jesus also said, "In the kingdom of God it is like this: a man scatters seed upon the soil. Whether he is asleep or awake, be it day or night, the seed sprouts and grows; he knows not how. The soil produces of itself; first, the blade; then, the ear; then the full grain in the ear. And when it is ripe for harvesting, they take the sickle for the cutting: the time for the harvest has come."

Jesus also said, "What is the kingdom of God like? To what shall we compare it? It is like a mustard seed which, when sown, is the smallest of all the seeds scattered upon the soil. But once sown, it grows up and becomes the largest of the plants in the garden, and even grows branches so big, that the birds of the air can take shelter in its shade." Jesus used many such stories, in order to proclaim the word to them in a way that they would be able to understand. He would not teach them without parables; but privately, to his disciples, he explained everything.

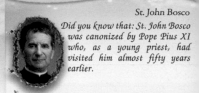

St. John Bosco
Did you know that: St. John Bosco was canonized by Pope Pius XI who, as a young priest, had visited him almost fifty years earlier.

Many things can't simply be explained easily. They defy the logical sequence of how things unfold; their processes do not follow the natural order; they cannot be quantified and therefore, they are confounding. It is no wonder Jesus used symbolic stories to illustrate what the Kingdom of God is. For these stories invite us to reflect, think further and churn them in our heads until its multitude of meanings emerge and bring us into greater insight and learning. For God's reign is not meant to be understood at once but to be discovered through time, slowly, painstakingly, with patience. It is after all worth the wait and the effort.

3RD WEEK IN ORDINARY TIME
Psalter: Week 3 / (Green / White)

Saturday

Ps 51:12–13, 14–15, 16–17
Create a clean heart in me,
O God.

01
FEBRUARY

1st Reading: 2 S 12:1–7a, 10-17*

So Yahweh sent the prophet Nathan to David. Nathan went to the king and said to him, "There were two men in a city: one was rich; the other, poor. The rich man had many sheep and cattle, but the poor man had only one little ewe lamb he had bought. He himself fed it and it grew up with him and his children. It shared his food, drank from his cup and slept on his lap. It was like a daughter to him. Now a traveler came to the rich man, but he would not take from his own flock or herd to prepare food for the traveler. Instead, he took the poor man's lamb and prepared that for his visitor." David was furious because of this man and told Nathan, "As Yahweh lives, the man who has done this deserves death! He must return the lamb fourfold for acting like this and showing no compassion."

Nathan said to David, "You are this man! It is Yahweh, God of Israel, who speaks: 'I anointed you king over Israel and saved you from Saul's hands; Now the sword will never be far from your family because you have despised me and taken the wife of Uriah the Hittite for yourself. (…) David said to Nathan, "I have sinned against Yahweh." Nathan answered him, "Yahweh has forgiven your sin; you shall not die. However, because you have dared to despise Yahweh by doing such a thing, the child that is born to you shall die." Then Nathan went to his home. (…)

Gospel: Mk 4:35–41

On that same day, when evening had come, Jesus said to them, "Let's go across to the other side of the lake." So they left the crowd, and took him along in the boat he had been sitting in, and other boats set out with him. Then a storm gathered and it began to blow a gale. The waves spilled over into the boat, so that it was soon filled with water. Jesus was in the stern, sleeping on a cushion.

They woke him up, and said, "Master, don't you care if we drown?" And rising up, Jesus rebuked the wind, and ordered the sea, "Quiet now! Be still!" The wind dropped, and there was a great calm. Then Jesus said to them, "Why are you so frightened? Do you still have no faith?"

But they were terrified, and they said to one another, "Who can this be? Even the wind and the sea obey him!"

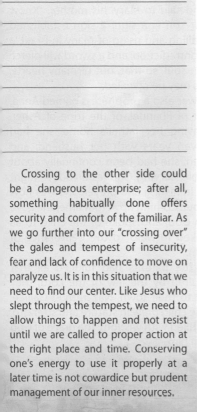

Crossing to the other side could be a dangerous enterprise; after all, something habitually done offers security and comfort of the familiar. As we go further into our "crossing over" the gales and tempest of insecurity, fear and lack of confidence to move on paralyze us. It is in this situation that we need to find our center. Like Jesus who slept through the tempest, we need to allow things to happen and not resist until we are called to proper action at the right place and time. Conserving one's energy to use it properly at a later time is not cowardice but prudent management of our inner resources.

02
FEBRUARY

Sunday

Ps 24:7, 8, 9, 10
Who is this king of glory?
It is the Lord!

1st Reading: Mal 3:1–4

Thus says the Lord God: Now I am sending my messenger ahead of me, to clear the way; then, suddenly, the Lord, for whom you long, will enter the Sanctuary. The envoy of the Covenant which you so greatly desire, already comes, says Yahweh of hosts. Who can bear the day of his coming and remain standing when he appears? For he will be like fire in the foundry and like the lye used for bleaching.

He will be as a refiner or a fuller. He will purify the sons of Levi and refine them, like gold and silver. So Yahweh will have priests who will present the offering as it should be. Then Yahweh will accept with pleasure the offering of Judah and Jerusalem, as in former days.

2nd Reading: Heb 2:14–18

And because all those children share one same nature of flesh and blood, Jesus, likewise, had to share this nature. This is why his death destroyed the one holding the power of death, that is the devil, and freed those who remained in bondage all their lifetime, because of the fear of death.

Jesus came, to take by the hand, not the angels but the human race. So, he had to be like his brothers and sisters, in every respect, in order to be the high priest, faithful to God and merciful to them, a priest, able to ask pardon, and atone for their sins. Having been tested through suffering, he is able to help those who are tested.

Gospel: Lk 2:22–40 (or Lk 2:22–32)

When the day came for the purification according to the law of Moses, they brought the baby up to Jerusalem, to present him to the Lord, as it is written in the law of the Lord: *Every firstborn male shall be consecrated to God.* And they offered a sacrifice, as ordered in the law of the Lord: *a pair of turtledoves or two young pigeons.*

There lived in Jerusalem, at this time, a very upright and devout man named Simeon; the Holy Spirit was in him. He looked forward to the time when the Lord would comfort Israel; and he had been assured, by the Holy Spirit, that he would not die before seeing the Messiah of the Lord. So, he was led into the temple by the Holy Spirit at the time the parents brought the child Jesus, to do for him according to the custom of the Law.

Simeon took the child in his arms, and blessed God, saying,

"Now, O Lord, you can dismiss your servant in peace,for you have fulfilled your word and my eyes have seen your salvation, which you display for all the people to see.

"Here is the light you will reveal to the nations, and the glory of your people Israel."

His father and mother wondered at what was said about the child. Simeon blessed them, and said to Mary, his mother, "Know this: your son is a sign; a sign established for the falling and rising of many in Israel, a sign of contradiction; and a sword will pierce your own soul, so that, out of many hearts, thoughts may be revealed."

There was also a prophetess named Anna, daughter of Phanuel, of the tribe of Asher. After leaving her father's home, she had been seven years with her husband; and since then, she had been continually about the temple, serving God, as a widow, night and day, in fasting and prayer. She was now eighty-four. Coming up at that time, she gave praise to God, and spoke of the child to all who looked forward to the deliverance of Jerusalem.

When the parents had fulfilled all that was required by the law of the Lord, they returned to their town, Nazareth in Galilee. There, the child grew in stature and strength, and was filled with wisdom: the grace of God was upon him.

Reading: A poor insignificant couple from a backwater town presents their child in the Temple with an offering signifying their simple status. They are just one among the many faithful who line up to fulfil their religious duties. Yet Simeon detected something special about the child. His spiritual sensibilities honed by countless hours of prayers and attentive listening to God led him to go to the Temple on the precise day the unknown couple from Nazareth would bring their child. Now he can rest in peace; he has seen his heart's desire.

Reflection: It is sometimes a source of amazement how some people have the knack to be at the right place at the right time. We call them lucky. Sometimes we suspect them to have advance secret knowledge of the things to come. Thus their choices hit jackpot prize anytime. In things spiritual however, all is fair and the field is levelled for everyone. Nobody has an edge over the other. After all, it is first a gift of God given freely to all. It is our capacity to respond to this gift that differentiates us from others. It is what differentiated Simeon from his contemporaries. He accepted God's gift and waited patiently for its coming. His beard had turned white but his hope in God's promise remained fresh as ever. And when the favourable time arrived Simeon was ready. He sang the song that was locked for a long time in his heart: a song that bared the richness of the life he dedicated to God in response to God's gift given a long time ago; a life that he gives back to God without regret.

Response: If we but only reflect, we will realize that all we have are gifts from the Lord. So when was the last time we gave thanks to this generous God of ours? Was our thank you as profound and soulful as Simeon's thanksgiving? If we but pause today and recall the many wonderful things God has done in our life, we might be capable of weaving a thanksgiving prayer coming straight from the heart.

03
FEBRUARY

Monday
Ps 3:2–3, 4–5, 6–7
Lord, rise up and save me.

4TH WEEK IN ORDINARY TIME
St. Blaise, bishop & martyr
St. Ansgar, bishop
Psalter: Week 4 / (Green / Red / White)

1st Reading: 2 S 15:13–14, 30; 16:5–13

Gospel: Mk 5:1–20

They arrived at the other side of the lake, in the region of the Gerasenes. No sooner did Jesus leave the boat than he was met by a man with evil spirits, who had come from the tombs. The man lived among the tombs, and no one could restrain him, even with a chain. He had often been bound with fetters and chains; but he would pull the chains apart and smash the fetters; and no one had the strength to control him. Night and day he stayed among the tombs on the hillsides, and was continually screaming, and beating himself with stones.

When he saw Jesus from afar, he ran and fell at his feet, and cried with a loud voice, "What do you want with me, Jesus, Son of the Most High God? For God's sake, I beg you, do not torment me!" He said this, because Jesus had commanded, "Evil spirit, come out of the man!" When Jesus asked the evil spirit, "What is your name?" it replied, "Legion is my name, for we are many." And it kept begging Jesus, not to send them out of that region.

Now a great herd of pigs was feeding on the hillside, and the evil spirits begged him, "Send us to the pigs, and let us go into them." So Jesus let them go. The evil spirits came out of the man and went into the pigs; and immediately, the herd rushed down the cliff; and all were drowned in the lake. The herdsmen fled, and reported this in the town and in the countryside. So all the people came to see what had happened.

They came to Jesus, and saw the man freed of the evil spirits, sitting there, clothed and in his right mind; the same man who had been possessed by the legion. They were afraid. And when those who had seen it, told what had happened to the man and to the pigs, the people begged Jesus to leave their neighborhood.

When Jesus was getting into the boat, the man, who had been possessed, begged to stay with him. Jesus would not let him, and said, "Go home to your people, and tell them how much the Lord has done for you, and how he has had mercy on you." So he went throughout the country of Decapolis, telling everyone how much Jesus had done for him; and all the people were astonished.

St. Blaise
Did you know that: The practice of the ceremony in which two crossed candles are held under people's throats during St. Blaise feast day became popular when he was revered in a cult as one of the "Fourteen Holy Helpers."

A journey to the other side could open new possibilities and challenges. Jesus was met by a demoniac who was violent and unrestrainable. He probably did not expect such a welcome committee. Nevertheless, He turned the surprise into another surprise of His own. He showed Himself as firmly in control of the demoniac without domination but by engaging the legion of demons inside the latter for a talk. This led to a resolution acceptable to all, the man possessed was freed, the demons were not tormented, but went ahead anyway to their destruction and the people who could not believe begged Him to leave. The irony in the story is that the demoniac was freed and sang the praises of Jesus while the people of the place continued to be "possessed" by their fears. Indeed truth is stranger than fiction.

4TH WEEK IN ORDINARY TIME
Psalter: Week 4 / (Green)

Tuesday

Ps 86:1–2, 3–4, 5–6
Listen, Lord, and answer me.

04
FEBRUARY

1st Reading: 2 S 18:9–10, 14b, 24–25a, 30 – 19:3

Gospel: Mk 5:21–43

Jesus then crossed to the other side of the lake; and while he was still on the shore, a large crowd gathered around him. Jairus, an official of the synagogue, came up and, seeing Jesus, threw himself at his feet; and begged him earnestly, "My little daughter is at the point of death. Come and lay your hands on her, so that she may get well and live."

Jesus went with him, and many people followed, pressing around him. Among the crowd was a woman who had suffered from bleeding for twelve years. She had suffered a lot at the hands of many doctors and had spent everything she had, but instead of getting better, she was worse. Because she had heard about Jesus, this woman came up behind him and touched his cloak, thinking, "If I just touch his clothing, I shall get well." Her flow of blood dried up at once, and she felt in her body that she was healed of her complaint. But Jesus was conscious that healing power had gone out from him, so he turned around in the crowd, and asked, "Who touched my clothes?" His disciples answered, "You see how the people are crowding around you. Why do you ask who touched you?" But he kept looking around to see who had done it. Then the woman, aware of what had happened, came forward, trembling and afraid. She knelt before him, and told him the whole truth.

Then Jesus said to her, "Daughter, your faith has saved you. Go in peace and be free of this illness."

While Jesus was still speaking, some people arrived from the official's house to inform him, "Your daughter is dead. Why trouble the Master any further?" But Jesus ignored what they said, and told the official, "Do not fear, just believe." And he allowed no one to follow him except Peter, James, and John, the brother of James.

When they arrived at the house, Jesus saw a great commotion, with people weeping and wailing loudly. Jesus entered, and said to them, "Why all this commotion and weeping? The child is not dead, but asleep."

They laughed at him. So Jesus sent them outside, and went with the child's father and mother and his companions into the room, where the child lay. Taking her by the hand, he said to her, "Talitha kumi!" which means, "Little girl, get up!"

The girl got up at once and began to walk around. (She was twelve years old.) The parents were amazed, greatly amazed. Jesus strictly ordered them not to let anyone know about it; and he told them to give her something to eat.

A woman suffering from bleeding and a girl of twelve were restored to health that day. Two marginalized sectors of society found completeness and healing. It is worth noting that the woman who was of right age willed herself to be healed by approaching Jesus and touching His cloak whereas the girl-child had to be helped by her father's intercession due to her minor age and helplessness. Two images of healing, one is actively willed while the other is dependent on others. Both approaches got what was wanted. So, the question is who are we when we have something to ask from God, an adult mature person who knows what to ask for, or a child who puts his or her trust in the hands of others?

05
FEBRUARY

Wednesday
Ps 32:1–2, 5, 6, 7
Lord, forgive the wrong
I have done.

4TH WEEK IN ORDINARY TIME
St. Agatha, virgin & martyr
Psalter: Week 4 / (Red)

1st Reading: 2 S 24:2, 9–17*

The following day, before David awoke, Yahweh's word had come to the prophet Gad, David's seer, "Go, and give David this message: I offer you three things and I will let one of them befall you according to your own choice." So Gad went to David and asked him, "Do you want three years of famine in your land? Or do you want to be pursued for three months by your foes while you flee from them? Or do you want three days' pestilence in your land? Now, think and decide what answer I shall give him who sent me."

David answered Gad, "I am greatly troubled. Let me fall into the hands of Yahweh whose mercy is abundant; but let me not fall into human hands."

So Yahweh sent a pestilence on Israel from morning until the appointed time, causing the death of seventy thousand men from Dan to Beersheba. When the angel stretched forth his hand toward Jerusalem to destroy it, Yahweh would punish no more and said to the angel who was causing destruction among the people, "It is enough, hold back your hand." The angel of Yahweh was already at the threshing floor of Araunah, the Jebusite.

When David saw the angel striking the people, he spoke to Yahweh and said, "I have sinned and acted wickedly, but these are only the sheep; what have they done? Let your hand strike me and my father's family."

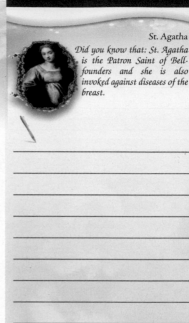

St. Agatha
Did you know that: St. Agatha is the Patron Saint of Bell-founders and she is also invoked against diseases of the breast.

Gospel: Mk 6:1–6

Jesus returned to his own country, and his disciples followed him. When the Sabbath came, he began to teach in the synagogue, and most of those who heard him were astonished. But they said, "How did this come to him? What kind of wisdom has been given to him, that he also performs such miracles? Who is he but the carpenter, the Son of Mary, and the brother of James and Joses and Judas and Simon? His sisters, too, are they not here among us?" So they took offense at him. And Jesus said to them, "Prophets are despised only in their own country, among their relatives, and in their own family." And he could work no miracles there, but only healed a few sick people, by laying his hands on them.

Jesus himself was astounded at their unbelief.

We always feel safe when we are in our own environment. After all, home is where the heart is and the heart resides in places where it is comfortable and secure. However, home or hometown could also be a place that constricts, that prevents us to be who we are if it runs contrary to preordained notions and the conventional wisdom of that place. Thus Jesus was boxed as the carpenter's son, the brother of so and so. This carries the tag of someone who should not be different from us. Thus his hometown missed what the other towns enjoyed when they accepted Jesus for who He was and not as interpreted by His town mates.

4TH WEEK IN ORDINARY TIME
St. Paul Miki & Companions, martyrs
Psalter: Week 4 / (Red)

Thursday
1 Chr 29:10, 11ab, 11d-12a, 12bcd
Lord, you are exalted over all.

06
FEBRUARY

St. Paul Miki

Did you know that: Regent Emperor Hideyoshi had the part of St. Paul Miki's & his companions' ears cut off and marched them through the various towns with blood streaming down their faces to warn others of the consequences of being a Christian.

1st Reading: 1 K 2:1–4, 10–12

When David was about to die, he gave his son Solomon this instruction, "I am about to go the way of all creatures. Be strong and show yourself a man. Keep the commandments of Yahweh your God and walk in his ways. Keep his statutes, his commands, his ordinances and declarations written in the law of Moses, that you may succeed in whatever you do and wherever you go. If you do so, Yahweh will fulfill the promise he made to me: 'If your sons take care to walk before me faithfully with their whole heart and their whole soul, you shall always have one of your descendants on the throne of Israel.'

Then David rested with his ancestors and was buried in the city of David. David reigned over Israel for forty years: seven years in Hebron and thirty-three years in Jerusalem. So Solomon sat on the throne of David his father and his reign was firmly established.

Gospel: Mk 6:7–13

Jesus called the Twelve to him, and began to send them out two by two, giving them authority over evil spirits. And he ordered them to take nothing for the journey, except a staff: no food, no bag, no money in their belts. They were to wear sandals and were not to take an extra tunic.

And he added, "In whatever house you are welcomed, stay there until you leave the place. If any place doesn't receive you, and the people refuse to listen to you, leave after shaking the dust off your feet. It will be a testimony against them."

So they set out to proclaim that this was the time to repent. They drove out many demons and healed many sick people by anointing them.

What we do on behalf of the People of God will always be God's mission not ours. And as a reminder, Jesus sent His disciples in pairs. No one will claim exclusive authorship for what he or she did on behalf of the Lord. They are not even to rely on their own strengths and endowments as signified by their not bringing of food, bag, money and extra tunics. We are but mere instruments of God in this mission. It is He who will initiate, support and bring the work to a happy conclusion in His own time. What does this truth imply? It is a more relaxed interpretation of our collaboration in God's mission; thus we can relax. The mission might not be accomplished in our lifetime but surely will happen since God is the author of it all.

07
FEBRUARY

Friday

Ps 18:31, 47 & 50, 51
Blessed be God my salvation!

4TH WEEK IN ORDINARY TIME
Psalter: Week 4 / (Green)

1st Reading: Sir 47:2–11

Gospel: Mk 6:14–29

King Herod also heard about Jesus, because his name had become well-known. Some people said, "John the Baptist has been raised from the dead, and that is why miraculous powers are at work in him." Others thought, "He is Elijah," and others, "He is a prophet like the prophets of times past." When Herod was told of this, he thought, "I had John beheaded; yet, he has risen from the dead!"

For this is what had happened: Herod had ordered John to be arrested; and had had him bound and put in prison because of Herodias, the wife of his brother Philip. Herod had married her; and John had told him, "It is not right for you to live with your brother's wife." So Herodias held a grudge against John and wanted to kill him; but she could not, because Herod respected John. He knew John to be an upright and holy man, and kept him safe. And he liked listening to him; although he became very disturbed whenever he heard him.

Herodias had her chance on Herod's birthday, when he gave a dinner for all the senior government officials, military chiefs, and the leaders of Galilee. On that occasion, the daughter of Herodias came in and danced; and she delighted Herod and his guests. The king said to the girl, "Ask me for anything you want and I will give it to you." And he went so far as to say with many oaths, "I will give you anything you ask, even half my kingdom." She went out and said to her mother, "What shall I ask for?" The mother replied, "The head of John the Baptist." The girl hurried to the king and made her request, "I want you to give me the head of John the Baptist, here and now, on a dish."

The king was very displeased, but he would not refuse in front of his guests because of his oaths. So he sent one of the bodyguards, with orders to bring John's head. He went and beheaded John in prison; then he brought the head on a dish and gave it to the girl. And the girl gave it to her mother. When John's disciples heard of this, they came and took his body and buried it.

Poor John: he was the victim of a woman's wrath. It's shocking what smouldering anger is capable of. It does not rest, is always on the lookout to get even, ever tenacious and creative in a vindictive way. Who would ever have thought that a birthday would be the occasion of John's demise? It's amazing how much energy we expend sometimes on useless feelings such as anger like Herodias, subservience like the daughter, and fear of shame like Herod. In the end, we are left with nothing but a head detached from its shoulder, thus a useless head. It is not only John but also these three who literally lost their heads that night.

4TH WEEK IN ORDINARY TIME
St. Jerome Emiliani, priest
St. Josephine Bakhita, virgin
Psalter: Week 4 / (Green / White)

Saturday
Ps 119:9, 10, 11, 12, 13, 14
Lord, teach me your statutes.

08
FEBRUARY

St. Josephine Bakhita

Did you know that: St. Josephine Bakhita was kidnapped into slavery, and since she was too frightened to remember her name, she was dubbed by her captors Bakhita, meaning, "lucky one."

How do we balance work and rest especially if we are on a roll, our work is thriving, and people can't get enough of us? We tend to continue enjoying the fruits of our success without regard to health and wellbeing. Yet Jesus advised His disciples to go to a remote place and recharge. They had to recover their energy and inner balance in order to be fruitful still. It is not only movement that brings success but sitting still and being quiet; getting in touch with our inner world is as equally important. Thus, equilibrium between action and non-action, between doing and being, between motion and stillness, between work and prayer: this is the tried and tested recipe for success.

1st Reading: 1 K 3:4–13

The king used to sacrifice at Gibeon, the great high place; on the altar there he had offered a thousand burnt offerings. It was in Gibeon, during the night, that Yahweh appeared to Solomon in a dream and said, "Ask what you want me to give you."

Solomon answered, "You have shown your servant David my father a great and steadfast love because he served you faithfully and was righteous and sincere towards you. You have given him proof of your steadfast love in making a son of his sit on his throne this day. And now, O Yahweh my God, you have made your servant king in place of David my father, although I am but a young boy who does not know how to undertake anything. Meantime, your servant is in the midst of your people whom you have chosen—a people so great that they can neither be numbered nor counted.

Give me, therefore, an understanding mind in governing your people that I may discern between good and evil. For who is able to govern this multitude of people of yours?"

Yahweh was pleased that Solomon had made this request. And he told him, "Because you have requested this rather than long life or wealth or even vengeance on your enemies; indeed, because you have asked for yourself understanding to discern what is right, I shall grant you your request. I now give you a wise and discerning mind such as no one has had before you nor anyone after you shall ever have. I will also give you what you have not asked for, both wealth and fame; and no king shall be your equal during your lifetime."

Gospel: Mk 6:30–34

The apostles returned and reported to Jesus all they had done and taught. Then he said to them, "Let us go off by ourselves into a remote place and have some rest." For there were so many people coming and going that the apostles had no time even to eat. And they went away in the boat to a secluded area by themselves.

But people saw them leaving, and many could guess where they were going. So, from all the towns, they hurried there on foot, arriving ahead of them.

As Jesus went ashore, he saw a large crowd, and he had compassion on them, for they were like sheep without a shepherd. And he began to teach them many things.

09
FEBRUARY

Sunday

Ps 112:4-5, 6-7, 8-9
The just man is a light in darkness
to the upright.

1st Reading: Is 58:7-10

Thus says the Lord: Fast by sharing
your food with the hungry,
bring to your house the homeless,
clothe the one you see naked
and do not turn away from your own kin.
Then will your light break forth as the dawn
and your healing come in a flash.
Your righteousness will be your vanguard,
the glory of Yahweh your rearguard.
Then you will call and Yahweh will answer,
you will cry and he will say, I am here.
If you remove from your midst the yoke,
the clenched fist and the wicked word,
if you share your food with the hungry
and give relief to the oppressed,
then your light will rise in the dark,
your night will be like noon.

2nd Reading: 1 Cor 2:1-5

When I came to reveal to you the
mystery of God's plan, I did not count
on eloquence or on a show of learning. I was
determined, not to know anything among
you, but Jesus, the Messiah, and a crucified
Messiah. I, myself, came weak, fearful and
trembling; my words and preaching were
not brilliant, or clever to win listeners. It was,
rather, a demonstration of spirit and power,
so that, your faith might be a matter, not of
human wisdom, but of God's power.

Gospel: Mt 5:13-16

Jesus said to his disciples, "You are the
salt of the earth. But if salt has lost its
saltiness, how can it be made salty again? It
has become useless. It can only be thrown
away and people will trample on it.

"You are the light of the world. A city
built on a mountain cannot be hidden. No
one lights a lamp and covers it; instead, it is
put on a lamp stand, where it gives light to
everyone in the house. In the same way, your
light must shine before others, so that they
may see the good you do, and praise your
Father in heaven."

Reading: Jesus, like all good teachers, taught His disciples not only to appeal to their rational and logical side but also to teach them metaphorically to stimulate the creative part of their thinking process. He used everyday mundane objects in life such as the salt that flavors food and light that drives the darkness away. Then, He drew connections between these earthly things to things that are spiritual. In this way, there would be no dichotomy between teaching and life, between physical realities and the spirit.

Reflection: Jesus was teaching his disciples by using metaphorical language. It forced them to think and apply the metaphors of salt and light into their own following of the Lord. The Teacher led them to reflect upon themselves and came up with their own answers. This method empowers the learners by not being passive but active participants in the learning process in the search for truth. The Jesus pedagogy is not one of spoon feeding. It invites the students to be active partners in the learning process.

Response: It's a good day to sit at the feet of the Master and allow His teaching to permeate my life's choices. Reading the bible today might be a good idea to refresh myself and drink deep from the wellspring of His Word.

10 FEBRUARY

Monday

Ps 132:6–7, 8–10
Lord, go up to the place
of your rest!

5TH WEEK IN ORDINARY TIME
St. Scholastica , virgin
Psalter: Week 1 / (White)

1st Reading: 1 K 8:1–7, 9–13

Then Solomon assembled before him in Jerusalem the elders of Israel and all the heads of the tribes, as well as the leaders of the ancestral houses of the Israelites, to bring up the Ark of the Covenant of Yahweh from the city of David, which is Zion.

All the Israelites assembled near king Solomon in the month of Ethanim, the seventh month. When all the elders of Israel arrived, the priests carried the Ark of Yahweh and brought it up together with the Tent of Meeting and all the holy vessels that were in the tent. After the priests and Levites had brought them up, king Solomon with the entire congregation of Israel that had assembled before him and were with him before the Ark, sacrificed so many sheep and oxen that they could neither be counted nor numbered. Then the priests laid the Ark of the Covenant of Yahweh in its place in the inner Sanctuary of the house—the Most Holy Place—underneath the wings of the cherubim. The cherubim had their wings spread out over the place of the ark, providing a covering above the Ark and its poles.

There was nothing in the Ark except the two tablets of stone which Moses placed there at Horeb, where Yahweh made a Covenant with the Israelites when they came out of the land of Egypt. And when the priests came out of the Holy Place, such a cloud filled Yahweh's house that the priests could not continue to minister. Indeed, the glory of Yahweh filled his house.

Then Solomon said, "Yahweh has said that he would dwell in thick darkness. So the house I have built you will be your house, a place for you to dwell in forever."

Gospel: Mk 6:53–56

Having crossed the lake, Jesus and his disciples came ashore at Gennesaret, where they tied up the boat. As soon as they landed, people recognized Jesus, and ran to spread the news throughout the countryside. Wherever he was, they brought to him the sick lying on their mats; and wherever he went, to villages, towns or farms, they laid the sick in the marketplace, and begged him to let them touch just the fringe of his cloak. And all who touched him were cured.

St. Scholastica

Did you know that: St. Scholastica was selected as the main motif for a high value commemorative coin: the Austria 50 Euro 'The Christian Religious Orders', issued on March 13, 2002. On the obverse (heads) side of the coin, Scholastica is depicted alongside Benedict.

Now Jesus has a following. His name precedes Him wherever He goes. The life of the simple carpenter's son is changed forever. Yet, did this newfound fame change His person? It seemed that Jesus remained steady throughout His rise from obscurity to fame, and from fame to notoriety. It didn't change His person a bit. It only showed the tremendous inner resources He had that kept His inner balance intact amidst the changes in His life. Life's surprises did not change Him. It is He who showed how we can handle our ever-changing life experience by holding on to what we have inside.

Tuesday

Ps 84:3, 4, 5 & 10, 11
How lovely is your dwelling place,
Lord, mighty God!

11
FEBRUARY

1st Reading: 1 K 8:22–23, 27–30

Solomon stood before the altar of Yahweh in the presence of all the assembly of Israel. He raised his hands towards heaven and said, "O Yahweh, God of Israel, there is no God like you either in heaven or on earth! You keep your Covenant and show loving-kindness to your servants who walk before you wholeheartedly. But will God really live among people on earth? If neither heavens nor the highest heavens can contain you, how much less can this house which I have built! Yet, listen to the prayer and supplication of your servant, O Yahweh my God; hearken to the cries and pleas which your servant directs to you this day. Watch over this house of which you have said, 'My Name shall rest there.' Hear the prayer of your servant in this place.

"Listen to the supplication of your servant and your people Israel when they pray in this direction; listen from your dwelling place in heaven and, on listening, forgive."

Gospel: Mk 7:1–13

One day, the Pharisees gathered around Jesus, and with them were some teachers of the law who had just come from Jerusalem. They noticed that some of his disciples were eating their meal with unclean hands, that is, without washing them. Now the Pharisees, and in fact all the Jews, never eat without washing their hands, for they follow the tradition received from their ancestors. Nor do they eat anything, when they come from the market, without first washing themselves. And there are many other traditions they observe; for example, the ritual washing of cups, pots and plates. So the Pharisees and the teachers of the law asked him, "Why do your disciples not follow the tradition of the elders, but eat with unclean hands?"

Jesus answered, "You shallow people! How well Isaiah prophesied of you when he wrote: *This people honors me with their lips, but their heart is far from me. The worship they offer me is worthless, for what they teach are only human rules.* You even put aside the commandment of God to hold fast to human tradition." And Jesus commented, "You have a fine way of disregarding the commandments of God in order to enforce your own traditions! For example, Moses said: *Do your duty to your father and your mother, and: Whoever curses his father or his mother is to be put to death.* But according to you, someone could say to his father or mother, 'I already declared *Corban* (which means "offered to God") what you could have expected from me.' In this case, you no longer require him to do anything for his father or mother; and so you nullify the word of God through the tradition you have handed on. And you do many other things like that."

When God and human pride collides in the hearts and minds of people, God usually takes a beating. Take, for example, the gospel today wherein God's commandments in time became supplanted by human rules. The people enforcing it will not hear of any contrary arguments even if in their hearts they know that it has merits. They feel personally for the status quo. It is not about what is right or wrong that is at stake. It is about personal pride. When this happens, sound reason takes a backseat. When criticized, resentment will set in, which in time, will turn to hatred. And so Jesus' fate is not something hidden. The day He took on the religious leaders and their hypocrisy was the day His death march began.

12
FEBRUARY

Wednesday
Ps 37:5-6, 30-31, 39-40
The mouth of the just
murmurs wisdom.

5TH WEEK IN ORDINARY TIME
Psalter: Week 1 / (Green)

1st Reading: 1 K 10:1-10

The queen of Sheba heard about Solomon's fame, and came to test him with difficult questions. She arrived in Jerusalem with a vast retinue and with camels loaded with spices and an abundance of gold and precious stones. When she came to Solomon, she told him all that she had on her mind and Solomon answered all her questions. There was nothing that the king could not explain to her. And when the queen of Sheba had seen all the wisdom of Solomon, the palace he had built, the food on his table, the residence of his officials, the attendance of his servants and their clothing, his cupbearers, and the burnt offerings which he offered at Yahweh's house, it left her breathless.

Then she said to the king, "All that I heard in my own land concerning you and your wisdom was true. But I did not believe the reports until I came and saw with my own eyes. And what did I see! I was told only half the story; for your wisdom and wealth surpass the report I heard.

Fortunate are your wives! Fortunate are your servants who are ever in your presence and hear your wisdom! Blessed be Yahweh your God, who has looked kindly on you and has put you on the throne of Israel! Because of Yahweh's eternal love for Israel, he has made you king so that you may dispense justice and righteousness."

Then she gave the king a hundred and twenty talents of gold, spices in abundance, and precious stones. Such an abundance of spices as those which the queen of Sheba gave to king Solomon was never again seen.

Gospel: Mark 7:14-23

Jesus then called the people to him again and said to them, "Listen to me, all of you, and try to understand. Nothing that enters a person from the outside can make that person unclean. It is what comes from within that makes a person unclean. Let everyone who has ears listen."

When Jesus got home and was away from the crowd, his disciples asked him about this saying, and he replied, "So even you are dull? Do you not see that whatever comes from outside cannot make a person unclean, since it enters not the heart but the stomach, and is finally passed out?"

Thus Jesus declared that all foods are clean.

And he went on, "What comes out of a person is what defiles him, for evil designs come out of the heart: theft, murder, adultery, jealousy, greed, maliciousness, deceit, indecency, slander, pride and folly. All these evil things come from within and make a person unclean."

Each culture has their taboos connected to food. This is a testament to, more than a critique of, the very important role food has in our daily lives. We recreate ourselves everyday by the nourishment we take in. That is why people are so concerned with what food they take in because it becomes part of them; it is absorbed by the body. But Jesus declared all food to be good. They are not the cause of our moral lapses and defects. When taken in moderation they contribute to our wellbeing. What prompts us to do evil is what is stored in the heart and not in the stomach. Thus we have to take extra care of the nourishments we give to our hearts as much as we are attentive to the food we take to feed our body.

Thursday

Ps 106:3–4, 35–36, 37 & 40
Remember us, O Lord,
as you favor your people.

13
FEBRUARY

1st Reading: 1 K 11:4–13

In Solomon's old age, his wives led him astray to serve other gods and, unlike his father David, his heart was no longer wholly given to Yahweh his God. For he served Astarte the goddess of the Sidonians, and Milcom, the idol of the Ammonites. He did what displeased Yahweh and, unlike his father David, was unfaithful to him. Solomon even built a high place for Chemosh, the idol of Moab, on the mountain east of Jerusalem and also for Molech, the idol of the Ammonites. He did the same for all his foreign wives who burned incense and sacrificed to their gods.

Yahweh became angry with Solomon because his heart had turned away from Yahweh, the God of Israel. Yahweh appeared to him twice and commanded him not to follow other gods. But he did not obey Yahweh's command. Therefore, Yahweh said to Solomon, "Since this has been your choice and you have kept neither my Covenant nor the statutes I commanded you, I will take the kingdom from you and give it to your servant. Nevertheless, I will not do this during your lifetime for the sake of your father David; I will take it from your son. But I will not take it all; I will reserve one tribe for your son for the sake of David my servant, and for the sake of Jerusalem, the city which I have chosen."

Gospel: Mk 7:24–30

When Jesus left that place, he went to the border of the Tyrian country. There, he entered a house, and did not want anyone to know he was there; but he could not remain hidden. A woman, whose small daughter had an evil spirit, heard of him, and came and fell at his feet. Now this woman was a pagan, a Syrophoenician by birth, and she begged him to drive the demon out of her daughter.

Jesus told her, "Let the children be fed first, for it is not right to take the children's bread and throw it to the puppies." But she replied, "Sir, even the puppies under the table eat the crumbs from the children's bread." Then Jesus said to her, "You may go your way; because of such a response, the demon has gone out of your daughter." And when the woman went home, she found her child lying in bed, and the demon gone.

The greater the need, the stronger should be our persistence. This was shown by the Syrophoenician woman who did not flinch at the implied rejection of her request by Jesus. What she begged was not for her, it was for her daughter; thus she could put her own pride at stake because it was her concern for others that made her determined. If it is for ourselves what we ask for, we are prone to sensitivity and personalize the negative response. But if it is for others, we tend to forget the self because we are focused on the other. Thus to love outside of ourselves make us stronger, more resilient, more firm in our resolve. We become better. Love allows us to surpass our narrow-mindedness and narcissism. Love amplifies our strength to the maximum.

14
FEBRUARY

𝔉riday
Ps 81:10–11ab, 12–13, 14–15
I am the Lord, your God;
hear my voice.

5TH WEEK IN ORDINARY TIME
St. Cyril, monk
St. Methodius, bishop
Psalter: Week 1 / (White)

1st Reading: 1 K 11:29–32; 12:19

Once, when Jeroboam went out of Jerusalem, the prophet Ahijah of Shiloh found him on the road. The two of them were alone in the open country when Ahijah, who had a new garment on, clutched and tore it into twelve pieces. He then said to Jeroboam, "Take ten pieces for yourself for this is the word of Yahweh, the God of Israel:' I am about to tear the kingdom from Solomon's hands to give you ten tribes. Only one tribe shall be left to him for the sake of my servant David and Jerusalem, the city which I have chosen out of all the tribes of Israel.

So Israel has been in rebellion against the house of David to the present time.

Gospel: Mk 7:31–37

Jesus set out: from the country of Tyre he passed through Sidon and, skirting the sea of Galilee, he came to the territory of Decapolis. There, a deaf man, who also had difficulty in speaking, was brought to him. They asked Jesus to lay his hand upon him.

Jesus took him apart from the crowd, put his fingers into the man's ears, and touched his tongue with spittle. Then, looking up to heaven, he said with a deep sigh, "Ephphata!" that is, "Be opened!" And immediately, his ears were opened, his tongue was loosened, and he began to speak clearly. Jesus ordered them not to tell anyone about it; but the more he insisted, the more they proclaimed it. The people were completely astonished and said, "He has done all things well; he makes the deaf hear and the dumb speak."

Sts. Methodius & Cyril
Did you know that: Sts. Methodius and Cyril are brothers who invented the Glagolitic and Cyrillic alphabets respectively.

Anything that is closed presents a wall, and an obstacle that impedes our capacity to move forward. It represents a hindrance. The deaf and speech-impaired man in our Gospel is tormented by a formidable barrier before he can enjoy a meaningful life. He has difficulty expressing his thoughts and feelings and his capacity to understand others is hindered by his inability to hear. Thus his ears and tongue must be loosened from the bond that ties them down. He must be liberated from his physical chains of disability. Jesus opened that which had been closed for some time. This is His specialty. Anything that has calcified, hardened or been barred for a long time does not have a chance to stop Him. Even the gates of death could not hold Him. "Ephpheta," "be opened" my heart and mind to the things of God. Stop feigning sleep.

Saturday

Ps 106:6–7ab, 19–20, 21–22
Remember us, O Lord,
as you favor your people.

15
FEBRUARY

1st Reading: 1 K 12:26–32; 13:33–34*

Jeroboam thought, "The kingdom could return to the house of David. Should this people go up to offer sacrifices in Yahweh's house in Jerusalem, their heart would turn again to their master, Rehoboam king of Judah. They would kill me and go back to him." And so the king sought advice and made two golden calves. Then he said to the people, "You have been going up to Jerusalem long enough. Here are your gods, O Israel, who brought you up out of the land of Egypt." He put one of these in Bethel, the other in Dan. And so Jeroboam made the people sin; the people went as far as Dan to accompany one of them. (...)

After this, however, Jeroboam did not abstain from doing evil. Instead he made priests for the high places from among the people. He consecrated anyone who wanted to be a priest for the high places. And this became the sin of the family of Jeroboam for which it was to be cut off and destroyed from the face of the earth.

Gospel: Mk 8:1–10

Jesus was in the midst of another large crowd, that obviously had nothing to eat. So he called his disciples and said to them, "I feel sorry for these people, because they have been with me for three days and now have nothing to eat. If I send them to their homes hungry, they will faint on the way; some of them have come a long way."

His disciples replied, "Where, in a deserted place like this, could we get enough bread to feed these people?" He asked them, "How many loaves have you?" And they answered, "Seven."

Then he ordered the crowd to sit down on the ground. Taking the seven loaves and giving thanks, he broke them, and handed them to his disciples to distribute. And they distributed them among the people. They also had some small fish. So Jesus said a blessing, and asked that these be shared as well.

The people ate and were satisfied, and they picked up the broken pieces left over, seven baskets full. Now those who had eaten were about four thousand in number. Jesus sent them away, and immediately got into the boat with his disciples, and went to the region of Dalmanutha.

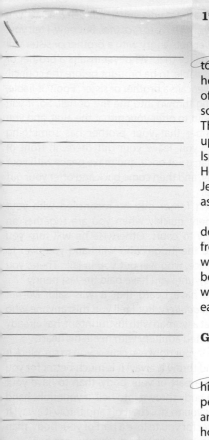

Jesus never dwells only on the problem at hand. He also looks for solutions or makes one. Thus the problem of food and distance from its source did not stop Him from addressing the present concern. He did not answer their problem with another problem. He asked the apostles for their resources first and from there crafted His response. He did not lament the fact that they had too little. What was there He multiplied. The people had their fill with much to spare. Jesus finds ways to address unexpected problems. He does great things because the word "impossible" is not part of His vocabulary.

16
FEBRUARY

Sunday

Ps 119:1-2, 4-5, 17-18, 33-34
Blessed are they who follow
the law of the Lord!

1st Reading: Sir 15:15–20*

*I*f you wish, you can keep the commandments and it is in your power to remain faithful. (...) Life and death are set before man: whichever a man prefers will be given him. How magnificent is the wisdom of the Lord! He is powerful and all-seeing. His eyes are on those who fear him. He knows all the works of man. He has commanded no one to be godless and has given no one permission to sin.

2nd Reading: 1 Cor 2:6–10

*B*rothers and sisters: In fact, we do speak of wisdom to the mature in faith, although it is not a wisdom of this world or of its rulers, who are doomed to perish. We teach the mystery, and secret plan, of divine wisdom, which God destined from the beginning, to bring us to glory.

No ruler of this world ever knew this; otherwise, they would not have crucified the Lord of glory. But as Scripture says: Eye has not seen, ear has not heard, nor has it dawned on the mind, what God has prepared for those who love him. God has revealed it to us, through his Spirit, because the Spirit probes everything, even the depth of God.

Gospel: Mt 5:17–37 (or Mt 5:20–22a, 27–28, 33–34a, 37)

*J*esus said to his disciples, "Do not think that I have come to annul the law and the prophets. I have not come to annul them, but to fulfi ll them. I tell you this: as long as heaven and earth last, not the smallest letter or dot in the law will change, until all is fulfilled.

"So then, whoever breaks the least important of these commandments, and teaches others to do the same, will be the least in the kingdom of heaven. On the other hand, whoever obeys them, and teaches others to do the same, will be great in the kingdom of heaven. I tell you, if your sense of right and wrong is not keener than that of the Lawyers and the Pharisees, you will not enter the kingdom of heaven.

"You have heard, that it was said to our people in the past: *Do not commit murder; anyone who murders will have to face trial.* But now, I tell you: whoever gets angry with a brother or sister will have to face trial. Whoever insults a brother or sister is liable, to be brought before the council. Whoever calls a brother or sister "Fool!" is liable, of being thrown into the fire of hell. So, if you are about to offer your gift at the altar, and you remember that your brother has something against you, leave your gift there, in front of the altar; go at once, and make peace with your brother, and then come back and offer your gift to God.

"Don't forget this: be reconciled with your opponent quickly when you are together on the way to court. Otherwise he will turn you over to the judge, who will hand you over to the police, who will put you in jail. There, you will stay, until you have paid the last penny.

"You have heard that it was said: *Do not commit adultery.* But I tell you this: anyone who looks at a woman with lustful intent, has already committed adultery with her in his heart.

"So, if your right eye causes you to sin, pluck it out and throw it away! It is much better for you to lose a part of your body, than to have your whole body thrown into hell. If your right hand causes you to sin, cut it off and throw it away! It is better for you to lose a part of your body, than to have your whole body thrown into hell.

"It was also said: *Anyone who divorces his wife, must give her a written notice of divorce.* But what I tell you is this: if a man divorces his wife, except in the case of unlawful union, he causes her to commit adultery. And the man who marries a divorced woman commits adultery.

"You have also heard that people were told in the past: *Do not break your oath; an oath sworn to the Lord must be kept.* But I tell you this: do not take oaths. Do not swear by the heavens, for they are God's throne; nor by the earth, because it is his foot stool; nor by Jerusalem, because it is the city of the great king. Do not even swear by your head, because you cannot make a single hair white or black. Let your 'Yes' mean 'Yes' and your 'No' mean 'No.' Anything else you say comes from the evil one."

Reading: Jesus reminded His disciples that He did not come to annul the Law and the Prophets but to fulfil them to the fullest through a proper and sound appreciation of their precepts. It is an evaluation that is both a source of freedom and joy if practiced in one's daily life. He cited some of these precepts and how they are to be interpreted so as to give flesh and bone to His teaching.

Reflection: Jesus may look very unconventional, unlike the teachers of that time. But looks are deceiving for He does not come to bring a new teaching and do away with the old. He came to fulfill them to the fullest. Thus he reminded His hearers that the Laws and the Prophets ought to be followed. The moral and ethical life must have a basis. It is not dependent on what feels good lest we fall into thinking that we are the measure of what is good and true and beautiful. It is always good to have a common reference point to evaluate our actions. Jesus is not someone who detests the old ways. He only presents them in a new way that makes them always relevant: the archaic that never goes out of style.

Response: Stop and ponder the "laws" for good living that we intentionally break because we think they are too insignificant to be bothered with: the white lies we make, the promises we do not keep and the countless other little law-breaking things we make. Today is a good day to make a resolution to be faithful in anything no matter how small and insignificant this may be.

17
FEBRUARY

Monday

Ps 119:67, 68, 71, 72, 75, 76
Be kind to me, Lord,
and I shall live.

6TH WEEK IN ORDINARY TIME
The Seven Holy Founders of the
Order of Servites
Psalter: Week 2 / (Green / White)

1st Reading: Jas 1:1-11

James, a servant of God, and of the Lord Jesus Christ, sends greetings to the twelve tribes scattered among the nations.

Consider yourselves fortunate, my brothers and sisters, when you meet with every kind of trial, for you know, that the testing of your faith makes you steadfast. Let your steadfastness become perfect, with deeds, that you, yourselves, may be perfect and blameless, without any defect.

If any of you is lacking in wisdom, ask God, who gives to all easily and unconditionally. But ask with faith, not doubting, for the one who doubts is like a wave driven and tossed on the sea by the wind. Such a person should not expect anything from the Lord, since the doubter has two minds and his conduct will always be insecure.

Let the believer who is poor, boast, in being uplifted, and let the rich one boast, in being humbled, because he will pass away like the flower of the field. The sun rises and its heat dries the grass; the flower withers and its beauty vanishes. So, too, will the rich person fade away, even in the midst of his pursuits.

Gospel: Mark 8:11-13

The Pharisees came and started to argue with Jesus. Hoping to embarrass him, they asked for some heavenly sign. Then his spirit was moved. He gave a deep sigh and said, "Why do the people of this present time ask for a sign? Truly, I say to you, no sign shall be given to this people." Then he left them, got into the boat again, and went to the other side of the lake.

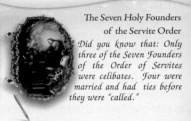

The Seven Holy Founders
of the Servite Order
Did you know that: Only three of the Seven Founders of the Order of Servites were celibates. Four were married and had ties before they were "called."

Signs are comforting. They assure us that we are on the right track or not and therefore we can easily adjust and reorient ourselves. Signs help us see well especially if we are in an unfamiliar and out-of-the-way place. But people who have trod familiar roads do not need signs anymore. They know the terrain as intimately as the palm of their hand. Their own experience is a better guide. Because of this the Pharisees who traversed the byways and hiways of holiness and faithfulness to God should have known better when Jesus came. They should have known that Jesus came from above. Yet they were obstinate and hard-headed. This exasperates the Lord. They do not need signs. What they need is a change of heart.

Tuesday

Ps 94:12-13a, 14-15, 18-19
Blessed the man you instruct,
O Lord.

18
FEBRUARY

1st Reading: Jas 1:12-18

Happy are those who patiently endure trials, because, afterward, they will receive the crown of life, which the Lord promised to those who love him. No one, when tempted, should say, "This temptation comes from God." God is never tempted, and he can never tempt anyone. Instead, each of us is lured, and enticed, by our own evil desire. Once this desire has conceived, it gives birth to sin, and sin, when fully grown, gives birth to death.

Do not be deceived, my beloved. Every good and perfect gift comes from above, from the Father of Light, in whom there is no change, or shadow of a change. By his own will, he gave us life, through the word of truth, that we might be a kind of offering to him, among his creatures.

Gospel: Mark 8:14-21

The disciples had forgotten to bring more bread, and had only one loaf with them in the boat. Then Jesus warned them, "Keep your eyes open, and beware of the yeast of the Pharisees and the yeast of Herod." And they said to one another, "He saw that we have no bread."

Aware of this, Jesus asked them, "Why are you talking about the loaves you are short of? Do you not see or understand? Are your minds closed? Have you eyes that don't see and ears that don't hear? And do you not remember when I broke the five loaves among five thousand? How many baskets full of leftovers did you collect?" They answered, "Twelve." "And having distributed seven loaves to the four thousand, how many wicker baskets of leftovers did you collect?" They answered, "Seven." Then Jesus said to them, "Do you still not understand?"

When minds and hearts are not in synch there is bound to be misunderstanding. We communicate at different levels; meanings and intentions are misinterpreted. This is the reason why the disciples could not understand the words of their Master. They are stuck in the ordinary and the mundane, while Jesus' discourse is of a higher plane, of the spiritual realm whose resonances in life is deeper than physical realities. The disciples have not yet attained the maturity of spirit to keep abreast with Jesus. They are indeed students at the feet of the Teacher. They will not understand for a long time. But they will get there someday.

19

FEBRUARY

Wednesday

Ps 15:2-3a, 3bc-4ab, 5
Who shall live on your holy
mountain, O Lord?

6TH WEEK IN ORDINARY TIME
Psalter: Week 2 / (Green)

1st Reading: Jas 1:19-27

My beloved, be quick to hear but slow to speak, and slow to anger, for human anger does not fulfill the justice of God. So get rid of any filth, and reject the prevailing evil, and welcome the word that has been planted in you, and has the power to save you.

Be doers of the word, and not just hearers, lest you deceive yourselves. The hearer, who does not become a doer, is like that one, who looked at himself in the mirror; he looked, and then promptly forgot what he was like. But those who fix their gaze on the perfect law of freedom, and hold onto it, not listening and then forgetting, but acting on it, will find blessing on their deeds.

Those who think they are religious, but do not restrain their tongue, deceive themselves, and their religion is in vain. In the sight of God, our Father, pure and blameless religion lies in helping the orphans, and widows in their need, and keeping oneself from the world's corruption.

Gospel: Mark 8:22-26

When Jesus and his disciples came to Bethsaida, Jesus was asked to touch a blind man who was brought to him. He took the blind man by the hand and led him outside the village. When he had put spittle on his eyes and laid his hands upon him, he asked, "Can you see anything?" The man, who was beginning to see, replied, "I see people! They look like trees, but they move around." Then Jesus laid his hands on his eyes again and the man could see perfectly. His sight was restored and he could see everything clearly.

Then Jesus sent him home, saying, "Do not return to the village."

Seeing clearly is a process. It does not come with having a functional pair of eyes but the capacity to discern the deeper reality of the object in sight. The blind man who had been in darkness for a long time could not clearly see people. They looked like trees. Thus Jesus had to lay His hands once again on his eyes before perfect sight is restored. For some people it takes a lifetime before they clearly can see things as they are. Their darkness is too thick that it takes a special intervention from God before they can see things in the light. Then, they realize they cannot go back to their former ways, like the blind who was enjoined not to go back to his village, to what was familiar and comfortable. Seeing opens a new horizon. A new road beckons. Once you see clearly you can never go back to your former life again.

Thursday

Ps 34: 2-3, 4-5, 6-7
The Lord hears
the cry of the poor.

20
FEBRUARY

1st Reading: Jas 2:1-9

My brothers and sisters, if you truly believe in our glorified Lord, Jesus Christ, you will not discriminate between persons. Suppose a person enters the synagogue where you are assembled, dressed magnificently and wearing a gold ring; at the same time, a poor person enters dressed in rags. If you focus your attention on the well dressed and say, "Come and sit in the best seat," while, to the poor one you say, "Stay standing, or else sit down at my feet," have you not, in fact, made a distinction between the two? Have you not judged, using a double standard?

Listen, my beloved brothers and sisters, did God not choose the poor of this world to receive the riches of faith, and to inherit the kingdom, which he has promised to those who love him? Yet, you despise them! Is it not the rich who are against you, and drag you to court? Do they not insult the holy name of Christ by which you are called?

If you keep the law of the kingdom, according to Scripture: Love your neighbor as yourself, you do well; but if you make distinctions between persons, you break the law, and are condemned by the same law.

Gospel: Mark 8:27-33

Jesus set out with his disciples for the villages around Caesarea Philippi; and on the way he asked them, "Who do people say I am?" And they told him, "Some say, you are John the Baptist; others say, you are Elijah or one of the prophets."

Then Jesus asked them, "But you, who do you say I am?" Peter answered, "You are the Messiah." And he ordered them not to tell anyone about him.

Jesus then began to teach them that the Son of Man had to suffer many things and be rejected by the elders, the chief priests and the teachers of the law. He would be killed, and after three days rise again. Jesus said all this quite openly, so that Peter took him aside and began to protest strongly. But Jesus, turning around, and looking at his disciples, rebuked Peter, saying, "Get behind me, Satan! You are thinking not as God does, but as people do."

Friendship allows us to know each other better. The longer time we spend with one another gives us the chance to map out contours of each other's person that are not accessible to mere acquaintants. This is the reason why we believe in the testimony of the apostles. It is they who have seen, heard and touched the Lord. Their knowledge of the Lord is the product of their time spent with Him. Thus they can declare with confidence that Jesus is the Messiah. But even then, they still had to grow in knowledge as to what kind of Messiah the Lord is. Peter on behalf of others could not accept a suffering vulnerable Messiah so off tangent to the triumphant Messiah that they hoped Him to be; hence the rebuke. It will take Peter and the other disciples a longer time before their knowledge of Jesus will be such that they too will embrace suffering and death, the way Jesus did, without hesitation.

21
FEBRUARY

Friday
Ps 112:1-2, 3-4, 5-6
Blessed the man who greatly
delights In the Lord's command.

6TH WEEK IN ORDINARY TIME
St. Peter Damian, bishop & doctor
Psalter: Wevek 2 / (Green / White)

1st Reading: Jas 2:14-24, 26

What good is it, my brothers and sisters, to profess faith, without showing works? Such faith has no power to save you. If a brother or sister is in need of clothes or food, and one of you says, "May things go well for you; be warm and satisfied," without attending to their material needs, what good is that? So, it is, for faith without deeds: it is totally dead.

Say to whoever challenges you, "You have faith and I have good deeds; show me your faith apart from actions and I, for my part, will show you my faith in the way I act." Do you believe there is one God? Well enough, but do not forget, that the demons, also, believe, and tremble with fear!

You foolish one, do you have to be convinced, that faith without deeds is useless? Think of our father Abraham. Was he not justified by the act of offering his son Isaac on the altar? So you see, his faith was active, along with his deeds, and became perfect by what he did. The word of Scripture was thus fulfilled, Abraham believed in God so he was considered a righteous person and he was called the friend of God.

So you see, a person is justified by works, and not by faith alone. So, just as the body is dead without its spirit, so faith, without deeds is also dead.

Gospel" Mark 8:34—9:1

Jesus called the people and his disciples, and said, "If you want to follow me, deny yourself; take up your cross and follow me. For if you choose to save your life, you will lose it; and if you lose your life for my sake, and for the sake of the Gospel, you will save it.

"What good is it, to gain the whole world, while destroying your soul? There is nothing more precious than your soul. I tell you, if anyone is ashamed of me and of my words, among this adulterous and sinful people, the Son of Man will also be ashamed of him, when he comes in the glory of his Father with the holy angels."

And he went on to say, "Truly I tell you, there are some here who will not die before they see the kingdom of God coming with power."

St. Peter Damian

Did you know that: St. Peter Damian became a saint without a formal canonization. His cult existed since his death at Faenza, at Fonte-Avellana, at Monte Cassino, and at Cluny.

Following someone means the willingness to be led and be taught. This entails self divestment. Someone full of himself or herself cannot listen to others. The harder the lessons are, the more effort one must exert to accept it. Learning is easy if we have confidence and trust in the teacher. After all, it is the person of the teacher that carries more weight in the teaching process. It is not his or her words alone nor his or her action apart. It is the totality of his or her person. It is for this reason why following of Jesus entails trust and confidence in Him. Following is easy if one believes. Faith matters. May we have it in abundance to follow the Lord even unto death.

Saturday

Ps 23:1-3a, 4, 5, 6
The Lord is my shepherd;
there is nothing I shall want.

22
FEBRUARY

1st Reading: 1 P 5:1–4

*B*eloved: I now address myself to those elders among you; I, too, am an elder, and a witness to the sufferings of Christ, hoping to share the glory that is to be revealed. Shepherd the flock which God has entrusted to you, guarding it, not out of obligation, but, willingly, for God's sake; not as one looking for a reward, but with a generous heart; do not lord it over, those in your care, rather be an example to your flock. Then, when the Chief Shepherd appears, you will be given a crown of unfading glory.

Gospel: Mt 16:13–19

*J*esus came to Caesarea Philippi. He asked his disciples, "Who do people say the Son of Man is?" They said, "For some of them, you are John the Baptist; for others Elijah, or Jeremiah, or one of the prophets."

Jesus asked them, "But you, who do you say I am?" Peter answered, "You are the Messiah, the Son of the living God." Jesus replied, "It is well for you, Simon Barjona, for it is not flesh or blood that has revealed this to you, but my Father in heaven.

"And now I say to you: You are Peter; and on this Rock I will build my Church; and never will the powers of death overcome it.

"I will give you the keys of the kingdom of heaven: whatever you bind on earth shall be bound in heaven; and whatever you unbind on earth shall be unbound in heaven."

What we confess stands on steady ground, on the rock of Peter's own solid faith in Jesus. This should give us assurances that what we have inherited from the apostles could withstand the scrutiny of time and people. However some of us still give in to doubt. Others disillusioned by the outside practice of the faith or of the people entrusted to safeguard it bail out and shop for other faith groups that might restore their sense of balance and peace. But aren't we convinced that what we have has been guaranteed by Jesus? After all we received the faith from the Apostles. It is they who have seen, heard and touched Him. Outside their testimony, all would be conjectures. May we remain in the solid ground of Peter's confession, ever vigilant to safeguard the faith but not too narrow-minded as to close ourselves from the wisdom of other faith traditions that might illumine our understanding of our own faith.

23
FEBRUARY

Sunday

Ps 103:1-2, 3-4, 8, 10, 12-13
The Lord is kind and merciful.

1ˢᵗ Reading: Lev 19:1–2, 17–18

*Y*ahweh spoke to Moses and said, "Speak to the entire assembly of the people of Israel and say to them: Be holy for I, Yahweh, your God, am holy.

"Do not hate your brother in your heart; rebuke your neighbor frankly so as not to share in his guilt. Do not seek revenge or nurture a grudge against one of your people, but love your neighbor as yourself; I am Yahweh."

2ⁿᵈ Reading: 1 Cor 3:16–23

*B*rothers and sisters: "Do you not know that you are God's temple, and that God's Spirit abides within you? If anyone destroys the temple of God, God will destroy him. God's temple is holy, and you are this temple.

Do not deceive yourselves. If anyone of you considers himself wise in the ways of the world, let him become a fool, so that he may become wise. For the wisdom of this world is foolishness in God's eyes. To this, Scripture says: *God catches the wise in their own wisdom.* It also says: *The Lord knows the reasoning of the wise, that it is useless.*

Because of this, let no one boast about human beings, for everything belongs to you; Paul, Apollos, Cephas—life, death, the present and the future. Everything is yours, and you, you belong to Christ, and Christ is of God.

Gospel: Mt 5:38–48

*J*esus said to his disciples: "You have heard, that it was said: *An eye for an eye and a tooth for a tooth.* But I tell you this: do not oppose evil with evil; if someone slaps you on your right cheek, turn and offer the other. If someone sues you in court for your shirt, give him your coat as well. If someone forces you to go one mile, go two miles with him. Give when asked, and do not turn your back on anyone who wants to borrow from you.

"You have heard, that it was said: *Love your neighbor and do not do good to your enemy.* But this I tell you: love your enemies; and pray for those who persecute you, so that you may be children of your Father in Heaven. For he makes his sunrise on both the wicked and the good; and he gives rain to both the just and the unjust.

"If you love those who love you, what is special about that? Do not even tax collectors do as much? And if you are friendly only to your friends, what is so exceptional about that? Do not even the pagans do as much? As for you, be perfect, as your heavenly Father is perfect."

Reading: Jesus quotes to His listener the sayings and maxims used to govern their response to certain situations. This is reflective of the mentalities and attitudes of people towards enemies and friends; that is, you exact a pound of flesh for a pound taken from you, and concern yourself only with people who love you. But Jesus pointed out their limitations and instead uses a higher standard for right conduct. His reference is His loving Father in heaven. Thus, over and above our common considerations, one must strive for the ideal and not for what is practical.

Reflection: Jesus did tell His disciples to follow the Law and the Prophets but they must exercise right judgment and not get stuck only with the letter of the Law but to look higher and see the spirit that permeates the Law, that is, love. This standard should also be used in everyday common sayings that are usually accepted without question because they seem to be practical and just, like exacting payment for debt obtained and loving only those who love you. But this kind of logic runs contrary to the logic of love. It is too easy and convenient. Love when it is genuine needs hard work. That's why the seat of love, the heart, is a muscle. It needs to be exercised to maintain its capacity to go beyond the easy and the practical. It has to be strong so as not to get tired loving even if it is uncomfortable to do so.

Response: When was the last time you allowed yourself to be "vulnerable" for the sake of love? It may seem foolish but people who love are not weak. In fact they are so strong that they can bear the burdens of true love. So, allow yourself to be weak for the sake of love today and feel strong in participating in God's awesome power of Love.

24
FEBRUARY

Monday
Ps 19:8,9,10, 15
The precepts of the Lord
give joy to the heart.

7TH WEEK IN ORDINARY TIME
Psalter: Week 3 / (Green)

1st Reading: Jas 3:13-18

*B*eloved: If you consider yourself wise and learned, show it by your good life, and let your actions, in all humility, be an example for others. But if your heart is full of bitter jealousy, and ambition, do not try to show off; that would be covering up the truth; this kind of wisdom does not come from above, but from the world, and it is earthly and devilish. Wherever there is jealousy and ambition, you will also find discord, and all that is evil. Instead, the wisdom that comes from above is pure and peace-loving. (…)

Gospel: Mark 9:14-29

*W*hen they came to the place where they had left the disciples, they saw many people around them and some teachers of the law arguing with them. When the people saw Jesus, they were astonished and ran to greet him.

He asked, "What are you arguing about with them?" A man answered him from the crowd, "Master, I brought my son to you, for he has a spirit, deaf and mute. Whenever the spirit seizes him, it throws him down and he foams at the mouth, grinds his teeth and becomes stiff all over. I asked your disciples to drive the spirit out, but they could not."

Jesus replied, "You faithless people! How long must I be with you? How long must I put up with you? Bring him to me." And they brought the boy to him.

As soon as the spirit saw Jesus, it shook and convulsed the boy, who fell on the ground and began rolling about, foaming at the mouth. Then Jesus asked the father, "How long has this been happening to him?" He replied, "From childhood. And it has often thrown him into the fire and into the water to destroy him. If you can do anything, have pity on us and help us."

Jesus said to him, "Why do you say, 'If you can?' All things are possible for one who believes." Immediately, the father of the boy cried out, "I do believe, but help the little faith I have."

Jesus saw that the crowd was increasing rapidly, so he ordered the evil spirit, "Dumb and deaf spirit, I command you: Leave the boy and never enter him again." The evil spirit shook and convulsed the boy and with a terrible shriek came out. The boy lay like a corpse and people said, "He is dead." But Jesus took him by the hand and raised him; and the boy stood up. After Jesus had gone indoors, his disciples asked him privately, "Why couldn't we drive out the spirit? And he answered, "Only prayer can drive out this kind, nothing else."

The disciples were asked to effect a particular healing. It was a boy oppressed by a dumb and deaf spirit. It was just one of those days when they were at a loss how to explain their impotence before something which they had lorded over before. It was just an ordinary case yet there they were embarrassed at their own inadequacy. It is in this context that arguments began. Expectations were not met, hope was dashed to the ground, the friendly atmosphere turned sour with disappointment. And then Jesus found them. He remedied the case by expelling the cause of the little boy's illness. And order was once again restored. That day, Jesus taught His disciples a valuable lesson that would stay with them forever. When faced with an enormous task beyond their skill, they should not resort to defensive behaviour but to prayer.

Tuesday

Ps 55:7-8-9-10a, 10b-11a, 23
Throw your cares on the Lord,
and he will support you.

25
FEBRUARY

1st Reading: Jas 4:1–10

Beloved: What causes these fights and quarrels among you? Is it not your cravings, that make war within your own selves? When you long for something you cannot have, you kill for it, and when you do not get what you desire, you squabble and fight. The fact is, you do not have what you want, because you do not pray for it. You pray for something, and you do not get it, because you pray with the wrong motive, of indulging your pleasures. You adulterers! Don't you know, that making friends with the world makes you enemies of God? Therefore, whoever chooses to be the world's friend becomes God's enemy.

Can you not see the point of the saying in Scripture: "The longing of the spirit, he sent to dwell in us, is a jealous longing?" But God has something better to give, and Scripture also says, *God opposes the proud but he gives his favor to the humble*. Give in, then, to God; resist the devil, and he will flee from you. Draw close to God and he will come close to you. Clean your hands, you sinners, and purify your hearts, you doubters. Recognize your distress, be miserable and weep. Turn your laughter into tears and your joy into sadness. Humble yourselves before the Lord and he will raise you up.

Gospel: Mk 9:30–37

Jesus and his disciples made their way through Galilee; but Jesus did not want people to know where he was because he was teaching his disciples. And he told them, "The Son of Man will be delivered into the hands of men. They will kill him, but three days after he has been killed, he will rise." The disciples, however, did not understand these words and they were afraid to ask him what he meant.

They came to Capernaum and, once inside the house, Jesus asked them, "What were you discussing on the way?" But they did not answer, because they had been arguing about who was the greatest.

Then he sat down, called the Twelve and said to them, "If someone wants to be first, let him be last of all and servant of all." Then he took a little child, placed him in their midst, and putting his arms around him he said to them, "Whoever welcomes a child such as this in my name, welcomes me; and whoever welcomes me, welcomes not me, but the One who sent me."

Jesus talks about suffering and death, the vulnerable lot of the Son of Man in human hands while His disciples argue who among them is the greatest. They are clearly coming from different planes. This must be one of the times when Jesus' patience was tested. After all the times the disciples spent with Him, they could still not get it. Yet Jesus continued hoping and believing in His unruly lot. He did not give up on them. It was because of this that they willingly laid down their lives for the One who patiently taught them what true greatness really meant. And His teaching had a lasting impact because He lived what He taught. He walked the talk. Hence His words and His actions affirming and confirming each other was a teaching style that transformed His apostles.

26
FEBRUARY

Wednesday

Ps 49:2–3, 6–7, 8–10, 11
Blessed are the poor in spirit;
the Kingdom of heaven is theirs!

7TH WEEK IN ORDINARY TIME
Psalter: Week 3 / (Green)

1st Reading: Jas 4:13–17

*B*eloved: Listen now, you who speak like this, "Today or tomorrow we will go off to this city and spend a year there; we will do business and make money." You have no idea what tomorrow will bring. What is your life? No more than a mist, which appears for a moment and then disappears. Instead of this, you should say, "God willing, we will live and do this or that." But no! You boast of your plans: this brazen pride is wicked. Anyone who knows what is good, and does not do it, sins.

Gospel: Mk 9:38–40

*J*ohn said to Jesus, "Master, we saw someone who drove out demons by calling upon your name, and we tried to forbid him, because he does not belong to our group." Jesus answered, "Do not forbid him, for no one who works a miracle in my name can soon after speak evil of me. For whoever is not against us is for us."

Owning exclusive rights of Jesus is bad business for Him who came that all might be saved. His love is without borders. Thus from the onset of His ministry, Jesus taught His disciples not to be jealous of others who were using His name casting out demons but did not belong to their group. These people could not malign the source of their own fruitfulness in their ministry. He is simply too big for all of us. The feeling of threat from others with the same activity as ours should not mobilize us towards defense and offense. Rather than concentrating on eliminating each other, our efforts should be directed to serving the community. If we ever have to compete with them, let us compete who among us could serve our brothers and sisters more. The only competition allowed among the followers of Jesus is the competition to service.

Thursday

27 FEBRUARY

Ps 49:14–15ab, 15cd–16, 17–18, 19–20

Blessed are the poor in spirit; the Kingdom of heaven is theirs!

1ˢᵗ Reading: Jas 5:1–6

So, now, for what concerns the rich, cry and weep, for the misfortunes that are coming upon you. Your riches are rotting, and your clothes, eaten up by the moths. Your silver and gold have rusted, and their rust grows into a witness against you. It will consume your flesh, like fire, for having piled up riches, in these, the last days.

You deceived the workers who harvested your fields, but, now, their wages cry out to the heavens. The reapers' complaints have reached the ears of the Lord of hosts. You lived in luxury and pleasure in this world, thus, fattening yourselves for the day of slaughter. You have easily condemned, and killed the innocent since they offered no resistance.

Gospel: Mk 9:41–50

Jesus said to his disciples, "If anyone gives you a drink of water because you belong to Christ and bear his name, truly, I say to you, he will not go without reward.

"If anyone should cause one of these little ones who believe in me to stumble and sin, it would be better for him to be thrown into the sea with a great millstone around his neck.

"If your hand makes you fall into sin, cut it off! It is better for you to enter life without a hand, than with two hands to go to hell, to the fire that never goes out. And if your foot makes you fall into sin, cut it off! It is better for you to enter life without a foot, than with both feet to be thrown into hell. And if your eye makes you fall into sin, tear it out! It is better for you to enter the kingdom of God with one eye, than, keeping both eyes, to be thrown into hell, where the worms that eat them never die, and the fire never goes out. The fire itself will preserve them.

"(…)Salt is a good thing; but if it loses Its saltiness, how can you make it salty again? Have salt in yourselves and be at peace with one another."

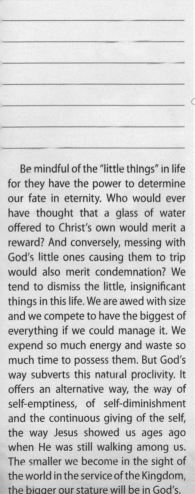

Be mindful of the "little things" in life for they have the power to determine our fate in eternity. Who would ever have thought that a glass of water offered to Christ's own would merit a reward? And conversely, messing with God's little ones causing them to trip would also merit condemnation? We tend to dismiss the little, insignificant things in this life. We are awed with size and we compete to have the biggest of everything if we could manage it. We expend so much energy and waste so much time to possess them. But God's way subverts this natural proclivity. It offers an alternative way, the way of self-emptiness, of self-diminishment and the continuous giving of the self, the way Jesus showed us ages ago when He was still walking among us. The smaller we become in the sight of the world in the service of the Kingdom, the bigger our stature will be in God's.

28
FEBRUARY

Friday

Ps 103:1-2, 3-4, 8-9, 11-12
The Lord is kind and merciful.

7TH WEEK IN ORDINARY TIME
Psalter: Week 3 / (Green)

1st Reading: Jas 5:9–12

Beloved, do not fight among yourselves and you will not be judged. See, the judge is already at the door. Take for yourselves, as an example of patience, the suffering of the prophets, who spoke in the Lord's name. See how those who were patient are called blessed. You have heard of the patience of Job and know how the Lord dealt with him in the end. *For the Lord is merciful and shows compassion.*

Above all, my beloved, do not swear, either by heaven or by earth, or make a habit of swearing. Let your yes be yes and your no be no, lest you become liable for judgment.

Gospel: Mk 10:1–12

Jesus went to the province of Judea, beyond the Jordan River. Once more, crowds gathered around him and, once more, he taught them, as he always did. Some (Pharisees came and) put him to the test with this question: "Is it right for a husband to divorce his wife?" He replied, "What law did Moses give you?" They answered, "Moses allowed us to write a certificate of dismissal in order to divorce."

Then Jesus said to them, "Moses wrote this law for you, because you have hearts of stone. But in the beginning of creation God made them male and female; and because of this, man has to leave father and mother and be joined to his wife; and the two shall become one body. So, they are no longer two, but one body. Therefore, let no one separate what God has joined."

When they were indoors at home, the disciples again asked him about this, and he told them, "Whoever divorces his wife and marries another, commits adultery against his wife; and the woman who divorces her husband and marries another, also commits adultery."

Our God is a mature God whose sense of responsibility to what He has promised is rock steady. It does not change with the passage of time. It's the reason why Jesus can in no way accept the dissolution of marriage that is founded on the love of God whose very nature is unchangeable, irrevocable and forever valid. God will never renege on His promise. That is why it is presupposed that those who undertake marriage are already of right age, capable of right judgment and responsible for the decision made. Marriage is not something to be taken lightly because it touches on a mystery bigger than us. We participate in the very essence of God. Thus if ever a marriage really breaks up, it is not God who is unfaithful one. It is us.

Saturday

Ps 141:1-2, 3 & 8
Let my prayer come like incense before you.

01
MARCH

1st Reading: Jas 5:13-20

Beloved: Are any among you, discouraged? They should pray. Are any of you happy? They should sing songs to God. If anyone is sick, let him call on the elders of the Church. They shall pray for him, anointing him with oil in the name of the Lord. The prayer said in faith will save the sick person; the Lord will raise him up and if he has committed any sins, he will be forgiven.

There will be healing, if you confess your sins to one another, and pray for each other. The prayer of the upright man has great power, provided he perseveres. Elijah was a human being, like ourselves, and when he prayed, earnestly, for it not to rain, no rain fell for three and a half years. Then he prayed again: the sky yielded rain and the earth produced its fruit.

Brothers, if any one of you strays far away from the truth, and another person brings him back to it, be sure of this: he who brings back a sinner from the wrong way, will save his soul from death and *win forgiveness for many sins*.

Gospel: Mk 10:13-16

People were bringing their little children to him to have him touch them; and the disciples rebuked them for this.

When Jesus noticed it, he was very angry and said, "Let the children come to me and don't stop them, for the kingdom of God belongs to such as these. Truly, I say to you, whoever does not receive the kingdom of God like a child will not enter it." Then he took the children in his arms and, laying his hands on them, blessed them.

Little things take time to grow but they are worth investing in. After all, from the little acorn comes an oak tree. But it takes patience and long vision to invest in that which takes years to grow. And this is where Jesus excels most, minding the little ones and making them grow towards their potential. He does not mind the discomfort of touching so many children and through them consequently, touching also their parents who feel good seeing their children thus blessed by someone they admire. It takes greatness to see potential where others like the disciples see only distractions. They could not see that in front of God they too were no more than mere children. They have a lot to learn. Jesus showed them another truth to be reflected upon: there is nothing so ordinary and too banal that God will not take time to mind them. All have worth in God's divine sight.

1st Reading: Is 49:14–15

Zion said: "Yahweh has forsaken me, my Lord has forgotten me." Can a woman forget the baby at her breast and have no compassion on the child of her womb? Yet though she forget, I will never forget you.

2nd Reading: 1 Cor 4:1–5

Brothers and sisters: Let everyone, then, see us as the servants of Christ, and stewards of the secret works of God. Being stewards, faithfulness shall be demanded of us; but I do not mind if you, or any human court, judges me. I do not even judge myself; my conscience, indeed, does not accuse me of anything, but that is not enough for me to be set right with God: the Lord is the one who judges me.

Therefore, do not judge before the time, until the coming of the Lord. He will bring to light whatever was hidden in darkness, and will disclose the secret intentions of the hearts. Then, each one will receive praise from God.

Gospel: Mt 6:24–34

" Jesus said to his disciples, "No one can serve two masters; for he will either hate one and love the other; or he will be loyal to the first and look down on the second. You cannot, at the same time, serve God and money.

Therefore, I tell you, not to be worried about food and drink for yourself, or about clothes for your body. Is not life more important than food; and is not the body more important than clothes? Look at the birds of the air; they do not sow, they do not harvest, and do not store food in barns; and yet, your heavenly Father feeds them. Are you not less worthy than they are?

"Can any of you add a day to your life by worrying about it? Why are you so worried about your clothes? Look at how the flowers in the fields grow. They do not toil or spin. But I tell you, that not even Solomon, in all his glory, was clothed like one of these. If God so clothes the grass in the field, which blooms today and is to be burned in an oven tomorrow, how much more will he clothe you? What little faith you have!

"Do not worry, and say: What are we going to eat? What are we going to drink? or: What shall we wear? The pagans busy themselves with such things; but your heavenly Father knows that you need them all. Set your heart, first, on the kingdom and righteousness of God; and all these things will also be given to you. Do not worry about tomorrow, for tomorrow will worry about itself. Each day has enough trouble of its own."

Reading: Jesus is teaching His disciples to commit themselves only to one Master so as not to experience the tension of being divided. This adherence to only one would enable them to harness their energies and creativity effectively.

Reflection: Faithfulness today is a very lonely word. In a world full of choices, we have opened ourselves to many possibilities and we experience the poverty of not being able to have it all. Thus sometimes, to free ourselves from the stricture of conventions and generally accepted rules of conduct and behavior we demolish customs and traditions. We do away with the meta narratives of our community and choose our individual feelings and situations instead as the yardstick of what is good and acceptable. But there are things bigger than us. They somehow influence our behavior and decisions in life simply because to do so would conserve values bigger than our own concerns. If we but step back for a while and shift our focus from ourselves to the wider community, we will see that the collective discernment of the past still retains a certain validity to the present. Perhaps what we should do is not to destroy them and start anew, but to creatively interpret them for the present age.

Response: This might be a good day for me to visit some of the values and codes of conduct that I inherited from my family and see whether they are life-affirming and conserve the well-being of the community or not. I will have to thank the Lord for giving me such help in navigating my way within a community.

03
MARCH

Monday
Ps 111:1–2, 5–6, 9 & 10c
The Lord will remember
his covenant for ever.

8TH WEEK IN ORDINARY TIME
St. Katharine Drexel, virgin
Psalter: Week 4 / (Green / White)

1st Reading: 1 P 1:3–9

Let us praise God, the Father of our Lord Jesus Christ, for his great mercy. In raising Jesus Christ from the dead, he has given us new life, and a living hope. The inheritance that does not corrupt, nor goes bad, nor passes away, was reserved for you, in heaven, since God's power shall keep you faithful, until salvation is revealed, in the last days.

There is cause for joy, then, even though you may, for a time, have to suffer many trials. Thus will your faith be tested, like gold in a furnace. Gold, however, passes away, but faith, worth so much more, will bring you, in the end, praise, glory and honor, when Jesus Christ appears.

You have not, yet, seen him, and, yet, you love him; even without seeing him, you believe in him, and experience a heavenly joy beyond all words, for you are reaching the goal of your faith: the salvation of your souls.

Gospel: Mk 10:17–27

Just as Jesus was setting out on his journey again, a man ran up, knelt before him and asked, "Good Master, what must I do to have eternal life?"

Jesus answered, "Why do you call me good? No one is good but God alone. You know the commandments: Do not kill; do not commit adultery; do not steal; do not bear false witness; do not cheat; honor your father and mother." The man replied, "I have obeyed all these commandments since my childhood."

Then Jesus looked steadily at him and loved him; and he said, "For you, one thing is lacking. Go, sell what you have, and give the money to the poor; and you will have riches in heaven. Then, come, and follow me." On hearing these words, his face fell and he went away sorrowful, for he was a man of great wealth.

Jesus looked around and said to his disciples, "How hard it is for those who have riches to enter the kingdom of God!" The disciples were shocked at these words, but Jesus insisted, "Children, how hard it is to enter the kingdom of God! It is easier for a camel to go through the eye of the needle than for one who is rich to enter the kingdom of God."

They were more astonished than ever and wondered, "Who, then, can be saved?" Jesus looked steadily at them and said, "For human beings it is impossible, but not for God; all things are possible with God."

St. Katharine Drexel

Did you know that: St. Katharine Drexel founded the Sisters of the Blessed Sacrament for the Black and the Native American peoples. She is the second only recognized American born saint in 2000.

We should never ask God what to do when we are not ready to risk it all. We might fulfill the minimal demands and feel good about it, considering that even these are difficult for many, but this does not impress God one bit. We might boast about this achievement but God wants something more. And when we dare ask Him what more we should do, we ran the risk of bursting our illusion of being good and of being just in front of God. He will demand all that we have. He will deliberately impoverish us. And once we are empty, He will lavish us with the richness of His grace. We will want for nothing for having God in us will suffice.

Tuesday

Ps 98:1, 2–3ab, 3cd–4
The Lord has made known his salvation.

04
MARCH

St. Casimir

Did you know that: St. Casimir is the Patron Saint of Lithuania and one of the chief patron saints of Russia.

_____
_____
_____
_____
_____
_____
_____
_____
_____
_____

This is a continuation of our reflection yesterday on letting go of everything for God. There is indeed an exchange for what we have given up for the Kingdom. But there is a catch, the economics of heaven is different from earthly commerce. It is not a one to one exchange of goods with equal value. The odds are stacked high on the part of God, He deliberately loses to us because some of the things exchanged are neither seen nor felt; we are not even aware of it sometimes but it is there. Only a heart that is sensitive to the workings of the divine can discern his or her blessedness. A material exchange for the things we have given up for the Lord is a poor exchange. A life lived meaningfully and fruitful is a good bargain that the Lord willingly exchanges for the pittance that we offer.

1st Reading: 1 P 1:10–16

Beloved: This was the salvation for which the prophets so eagerly looked when, in days past, they foretold the favor of God, with regard to you. But they could only investigate when the Spirit of Christ present within them, pointed out the time and the circumstances, of this—the sufferings of Christ, and the glories which would follow.

It was revealed to them, that they were working, not for themselves, but for you. Thus, in these days, after the Holy Spirit has been sent from heaven, the Gospel's preachers have taught you these mysteries, which even the angels long to see.

So, then, let your spirit be ready. Be alert, with confident trust, in the grace you will receive, when Jesus Christ appears. Like obedient children, do not return to your former life, given over to ignorance and passions. Imitate the one who called you. As he is holy, so you, too, be holy, in all your conduct, since Scripture says: *Be holy for I am holy.*

Gospel: Mk 10:28–31

Peter spoke up and said, "We have given up everything to follow you." Jesus answered, "Truly, there is no one who has left house, or brothers or sisters, or father or mother, or children, or lands, for my sake, and for the Gospel, who will not receive his reward. I say to you: even in the midst of persecution, he will receive a hundred times as many houses, brothers, sisters, mothers, children, and lands in the present time; and, in the world to come, eternal life. Do pay attention: many who now are the first will be last, and the last, first."

Lent

The Season of Lent starts on Ash Wednesday and ends on Holy Thursday before the Evening Mass of the Lord's Supper. From then on until Easter Sunday the Church celebrates the Easter Triduum of Christ's passion and death, burial, and resurrection.

Lent is characterized by penance for our past sins, works of mercy especially toward the poor, and personal preparation for the renewal of our baptismal promises on Easter Vigil. Thus Lent has two features: penitential and baptismal. Our tears of penance renew in our hearts and souls the water of baptism.

The ashes imposed on us on Ash Wednesday remind us that we are dust and to dust we shall return and that therefore the entire life of a Christian should be marked by works of self-denial and generosity. The traditional discipline of Lent consists of constant prayer and reading of God's word, fasting on Ash Wednesday and Good Friday, abstinence from meat on Fridays, and works of mercy especially to those who have less in life. What is important is that through prayer and good works we allow God's grace to bring about our interior conversion. The sacrament of penance should accompany our Lenten observance.

Holy Week is the high point of the Lenten season. It opens with the procession with blessed palms and the gospel reading of the passion and death of Our Savior. The triumphal entry into Jerusalem ended on Calvary, but we know that Good Friday led to Easter Sunday.

The biblical readings and prefaces extol the virtue of conversion of life, the need to fulfil our baptismal promises, joyful acceptance of daily trials for the love of God, and unselfish service to all who need our assistance.

05
MARCH

Wednesday

Ps 51:3–4, 5–6, 12–13, 14, 17
Be merciful, O Lord,
for we have sinned.

ASH WEDNESDAY
Psalter: Week 4 / (Violet)

1st Reading: Jl 2:12–18*

Yahweh says, "Yet even now, return to me with your whole heart; with fasting, weeping and mourning. Rend your heart, not your garment. Return to Yahweh, your God — gracious and compassionate."(…) Blow the trumpet in Zion, proclaim a sacred fast, call a solemn assembly.

Gather the people, sanctify the community, bring together the elders, even the children and infants at the breast. Let the bridegroom leave his bed, and the bride her room.

Between the vestibule and the altar, let the priests, Yahweh's ministers, weep and say: Spare your people, Yahweh. Do not humble them or make them an object of scorn among the nations. Why should it be said among the people: Where is their God? Yahweh has become jealous for his land; he has had pity on his people.

2nd Reading: 2 Cor 5:20—6:2

Gospel: Mt 6:1–6, 16–18

Jesus said to his disciples, "Be careful not to make a show of your good deeds before people. If you do so, you do not gain anything from your Father in heaven. When you give something to the poor, do not have it trumpeted before you, as do those who want to be noticed in the synagogues and in the streets, in order to be praised by people. I assure you, they have their reward.

"If you give something to the poor, do not let your left hand know what your right hand is doing, so that your gift remains really secret. Your Father, who sees what is kept secret, will reward you.

"When you pray, do not be like those who want to be noticed. They love to stand and pray in the synagogues or on street corners, in order to be seen by everyone. I assure you, they have their reward. When you pray, go into your room, close the door, and pray to your Father who is with you in secret; and your Father who sees what is kept secret will reward you.

"When you fast, do not put on a miserable face, as do the hypocrites. They put on a gloomy face, so that people can see they are fasting. I tell you this: they have been paid in full already. When you fast, wash your face and make yourself look cheerful, because you are not fasting for appearances or for people, but for your Father, who sees beyond appearances. And your Father who sees what is kept secret, will reward you."

Righteousness is not something for display. It is a way of life that is the product of consistency in words and actions. You do not ascribe it to yourself. It is others who begin to notice your spiritual growth and they affirm it by their testimony and belief in the righteousness that you displayed all along. Righteousness if flaunted loses its power to influence and transform others. It becomes a superficial and cheap effort to impress. This is why Jesus warned His disciples not to resort to this kind of gimmickry. Better strive for holiness in secret to avoid the distraction of having to deal with people's attention. Since a righteous life cannot be contained, when that comes, you are strong enough to realize that it is not you but the righteous God who took possession of you who attracted them.

THURSDAY AFTER ASH WEDNESDAY
Psalter: Week 4 / (Violet)

Thursday

Ps 1:1–2, 3, 4 & 6
Blessed are they who hope
in the Lord.

06
MARCH

1st Reading: Dt 30:15–20

Moses said to the people, "See, I set before you on this day life and good, evil and death. I command you to love Yahweh, your God and follow his ways. Observe his commandments, his norms and his laws, and you will live and increase, and Yahweh will give you his blessing in the land you are going to possess. But if your heart turns away and does not listen, if you are drawn away and bow before other gods to serve them, I declare on this day that you shall perish. You shall not last in the land you are going to occupy on the other side of the Jordan.

"Let the heavens and the earth listen, that they may be witnesses against you. I have set before you life and death, blessing and curse. Therefore, choose life that you and your descendants may live, loving Yahweh, listening to his voice, and being one with him. In this is life for you and length of days in the land which Yahweh swore to give to your ancestors, to Abraham, Isaac and Jacob."

Gospel: Lk 9:22–25

Jesus said to his disciples, "The Son of Man must suffer many things. He will be rejected by the elders and chief priests and teachers of the law, and be put to death. Then after three days he will be raised to life."

Jesus also said to all the people, "If you wish to be a follower of mine, deny yourself and take up your cross each day, and follow me! For if you choose to save your life, you will lose it; but if you lose your life for my sake, you will save it. What does it profit you to gain the whole world, if you destroy or damage yourself?"

Jesus never promised His disciples an easy life. As a matter of fact, early on, He already disclosed to them the kind of end He would have: an ignoble death but one that would lead to new life. However, His disciples could not grasp the significance of His last words on death and being raised to new life. The very idea of death troubled them. Thus the invitation of Jesus on denying the self and taking up the cross fell on deaf ears. It would take the very death and resurrection of Jesus to convince them to embrace this path. Even then, it would be a long time before some of them became fully convinced.

07
MARCH

Friday

Ps 51:3-4, 5-6ab, 18-19
A heart contrite and humbled,
O God, you will not spurn.

FRIDAY AFTER ASH WEDNESDAY
Psalter: Week 4 / (Violet)

1st Reading: Is 58:1-9a

Thus says the Lord God: Cry out aloud for all you are worth; raise your voice like a trumpet blast; tell my people of their offenses, Jacob's family of their sins.

Is it true that they seek me day after day, longing to know my ways, as a people that does what is right and has not forsaken the word of its God? They want to know the just laws and not to drift away from their God.

"Why are we fasting," they complain, "and you do not even see it? We are doing penance and you never notice it. "

Look, on your fast days you push your trade and you oppress your laborers.

Yes, you fast but end up quarreling, striking each other with wicked blows. Fasting as you do will not make your voice heard on high.

Is that the kind of fast that pleases me, just a day to humble oneself? Is fasting merely bowing down one's head, and making use of sackcloth and ashes? Would you call that fasting, a day acceptable to Yahweh?

See the fast that pleases me: breaking the fetters of injustice and unfastening the thongs of the yoke, setting the oppressed free and breaking every yoke.

Fast by sharing your food with the hungry, bring to your house the homeless, clothe the one you see naked and do not turn away from your own kin.

Then will your light break forth as the dawn and your healing come in a flash.

Your righteousness will be your vanguard, the glory of Yahweh your rearguard.

Then you will call and Yahweh will answer, you will cry and he will say, I am here.

Gospel: Mt 9:14-15

The disciples of John came to Jesus with the question, "How is it, that we and the Pharisees fast on many occasions, but not your disciples?"

Jesus answered them, "How can you expect wedding guests to mourn as long as the bridegroom is with them? The time will come, when the bridegroom will be taken away from them, and then, they will fast."

Joy is the by product of a life lived for Jesus. No wonder, many saints were known to be advocates or provocateurs of joy. The reason why the Son of Man came into the world is precisely to bring back to us this capacity to know joy that we lost when we deliberately turned our back on God's friendship. From that time on, we tried to win back God's favour through a life of penance, mortification and sacrifice. But Jesus came and befriended us again. We have joy back in our midst. There is no reason to be unhappy. That is why Jesus' disciples do not fast. That will come when Jesus will be separated from them.

Saturday

Ps 86:1-2, 3-4, 5-6
Teach me your way, O Lord,
that I may walk in your truth.

08

MARCH

1st Reading: Is 58:9b–14

Thus says the Lord: If you remove from your midst the yoke, the clenched fist and the wicked word, if you share your food with the hungry and give relief to the oppressed, then your light will rise in the dark, your night will be like noon. Yahweh will guide you always and give you relief in desert places. He will strengthen your bones; he will make you as a watered garden, like a spring of water whose waters never fail. Your ancient ruins will be rebuilt, the age-old foundations will be raised. You will be called the Breach-mender, and the Restorer of ruined houses. If you stop profaning the Sabbath and doing as you please on the holy day, if you call the Sabbath a day of delight and keep sacred Yahweh's holy day, if you honor it by not going your own way, not doing as you please and not speaking with malice, then you will find happiness in Yahweh, over the heights you will ride triumphantly, and feast joyfully on the inheritance of your father Jacob. The mouth of Yahweh has spoken.

Gospel: Lk 5:27–32

Jesus went out, and noticing a tax collector named Levi, sitting in the tax-office, he said to him, "Follow me!" So Levi, leaving everything, got up and followed Jesus.

Levi gave a great feast for Jesus, and many tax collectors came to his house, and took their places at the table with the other people. Then the Pharisees and their followers complained to Jesus' disciples, "How is it, that you eat and drink with tax collectors and sinners?" But Jesus spoke up, "Healthy people don't need a doctor, but sick people do. I have not come to call the just, but sinners, to a change of heart."

Not all those considered sinners are stubborn of heart. We might be surprised to learn that beneath the sinful exterior is someone sincerely looking for meaning in life. Levi is a such case. He was at his tax collector's table doing his "sinful" job during an ordinary day. Yet, someone extraordinary passed by and invited him to a life that he could not have conceived of before. He is given a chance; he will not allow it to pass. It's amazing sometimes how people condemn others without even bothering to give them a chance to reform. Or even if they were given the chance were not accorded the necessary companionship and support to help them overcome their sinful situation. Jesus did not only invite Levi, He also showed His confidence and support by attending Levi's feast and defending him in front of people who would not allow him to change. Levi found someone who would risk for him. For someone like him following Jesus would be a no brainer.

09
MARCH

Sunday

Ps 51:3-4, 5-6, 12-13, 17
Be merciful, O Lord,
for we have sinned.

1ˢᵗ Reading: Gen 2:7-9; 3:1-7

Then Yahweh God formed man, dust drawn from the clay, and breathed into his nostrils a breath of life and man became alive with breath. God planted a garden in Eden in the east and there he placed man whom he had created. Yahweh God caused to grow from the ground every kind of tree that is pleasing to see and good to eat, also the tree of Life in the middle of the garden and the tree of the Knowledge of Good and Evil.

Now the serpent was the most crafty of all the wild creatures that Yahweh God had made. He said to the woman, "Did God really say: You must not eat from any tree in the garden?" The woman said to the serpent, "We may eat the fruit of the trees in the garden, but of the fruit of the tree that is in the middle of the garden God said: You must not eat, and you must not touch it or you will die." The serpent said to the woman, "You will not die, but God knows that the day you eat it, your eyes will be opened and you will be like gods, knowing good and evil."

The woman saw that the fruit was good to eat, and pleasant to the eyes, and ideal for gaining knowledge. She took its fruit and ate it and gave some to her husband who was with her. He ate it. Then their eyes were opened and both of them knew they were naked. So they sewed leaves of a fig tree together and made themselves loincloths.

2ⁿᵈ Reading: Rom 5:12-19

Brothers and sisters: Sin entered the world through one man; and through sin, death; and later on, death spread to all humankind, because all sinned. As long as there was no law, they could not speak of disobedience, but sin was already in the world. This is why, from Adam to Moses, death reigned among them, although their sin was not disobedience, as in Adam's case—this was not the true Adam, but foretold the other, who was to come.

Such has been the fall, but God's gift goes far beyond. All died, because of the fault of one man, but how much more does the grace of God spread, when the gift he granted, reaches all, from this unique man, Jesus Christ. Again, there is no comparison between the gift, and the offense of one man. The disobedience that brought condemnation was of one sinner, whereas the grace of God brings forgiveness to a world of sinners. If death reigned through the disobedience of one and only one person, how much more, will there be a reign of life, for those who receive the grace, and the gift of true righteousness, through the one person, Jesus Christ.

Just as one transgression brought sentence of death to all, so, too, one man's good act has brought justification and light to all; and, as the disobedience of only one, made all sinners, so the obedience of one person, allowed all to be made just and holy.

Gospel: Mt 4:1-11

At that time, the Spirit led Jesus into the desert, that he might be put to the test by the devil. After Jesus fasted forty days and nights he was famished.

Then the tempter came to him and said, "If you are the Son of God, order these stones to turn into bread." But Jesus answered, "Scripture says: *One does not live on bread alone, but on every word that comes from the mouth of God.*"

Then the devil took Jesus to the Holy City, set him on the highest wall of the temple, and said to him, "If you are the Son of God, throw yourself down, for scripture says: *God has given orders to his angels concerning you. Their hands will hold you up, lest you hurt your foot against a stone.*" Jesus answered, "But scripture also says: *You shall not put the Lord your God to the test.*"

Then the devil took Jesus to a very high mountain, and showed him all the nations of the world in all their greatness and splendor. And he said, "All this I will give you, if you kneel down and worship me." Then Jesus answered, "Be off, Satan! Scripture says: *Worship the Lord your God and serve him alone!*"

Then the devil left him; and angels came to serve him.

Reading: Jesus went to the desert to fortify Himself for the work ahead after His baptism in the river Jordan. When He was physically weak, the devil made his pitch and tried to tempt him. It was Jesus' adherence to the Word of God that made Satan flee.

Reflection: Countless men and women have prepared themselves before embarking on a life-changing venture by confronting their very own selves. This usually means leaving the ordinary and familiar in their lives and spending some time in silence, mortification and prayer. It is a test of inner strength because what is buried deep in the heart and mind surfaces during this period of preparation. The temptation of Jesus is a classic temptation. It deals with the basic needs of everyone, from the will to survive, the need to be loved and be special and the will to power. Jesus with deft and aplomb navigated these mundane concerns by firmly focusing His mind on the Word of God. It was His moral compass and guide. It did not fail Him. For "heaven and earth may pass away, but the Word of God will not." We too shall overcome if we cling firmly to God's word.

Response: I am usually beset by countless challenges and temptations everyday. How do I fare? Am I like Jesus who stood firmly in God's unchanging world or do I give in to compromises, back deals or indifference? Perhaps today is a good day to stand my ground with the Word of God as my shield.

10
MARCH

Monday

Ps 19:8, 9, 10, 15
Your words, Lord,
are Spirit and life.

1ST WEEK OF LENT
Psalter: Week 1 / (Violet)

1st Reading: Lev 19:1–2, 11–18

Gospel: Mt 25:31–46

*J*esus said to his disciples, When the Son of Man comes in his glory with all his angels, he will sit on the throne of his glory. All the nations will be brought before him; and, as a shepherd separates the sheep from the goats, so will he do with them, placing the sheep on his right hand and the goats on his left. The king will say to those on his right, 'Come, blessed of my Father! Take possession of the kingdom prepared for you from the beginning of the world. For I was hungry, and you fed me. I was thirsty, and you gave me something to drink. I was a stranger, and you welcomed me into your home. I was naked, and you clothed me. I was sick, and you visited me. I was in prison, and you came to see me.'

"Then the righteous will ask him, 'Lord, when did we see you hungry, and give you food; thirsty, and give you something to drink; or a stranger, and welcome you; or naked, and clothe you? When did we see you sick, or in prison, and go to see you?'

"The king will answer, 'Truly I say to you: just as you did it for one of the least of these brothers or sisters of mine, you did it to me.'

"Then he will say to those on his left, 'Go, cursed people, out of my sight, into the eternal fire, which has been prepared for the devil and his angels! For I was hungry, and you did not give me anything to eat; I was thirsty, and you gave me nothing to drink; I was a stranger, and you did not welcome me into your house; I was naked, and you did not clothe me; I was sick, and in prison, and you did not visit me.'

"They, too, will ask, 'Lord, when did we see you hungry, thirsty, naked or a stranger, sick or in prison, and did not help you?' The king will answer them, 'Truly I say to you: just as you did not do it for one of the least of these, you did not do it for me.' And these will go into eternal punishment; but the just, to eternal life."

What we do here on earth echoes in eternity. This is why we have to be mindful of what we do here below. Sometimes it is not so much the big faults that will condemn us but the little transgressions that we tend to overlook. For the big sins are always before us; they don't allow us to be at peace. We might struggle for a time but inevitably we will give in to repentance and confess these big sins. Not so the smaller faults. They tend to be bypassed. Thus there will be a big surprise on judgment day when these little things will condemn us before the judge and ruler of the world. It pays to be mindful and aware of our actions now, especially our tendency to neglect the little ones of God. Little they may be here on earth but they sure have a big say in the judgment to come.

Tuesday

Ps 34:4–5, 6–7, 16–17, 18–19
From all their distress
God rescues the just.

11
MARCH

1st Reading: Is 55:10–11

Thus says Yahweh: As the rain and the snow come down from the heavens and do not return till they have watered the earth, making it yield seed for the sower and food for others to eat, so is my word that goes forth out of my mouth: it will not return to me idle, but it shall accomplish my will, the purpose for which it has been sent.

Gospel: Mt 6:7–15

Jesus said to his disciples, "When you pray, do not use a lot of words, as the pagans do; for they believe that, the more they say, the more chance they have of being heard. Do not be like them. Your Father knows what you need, even before you ask him.

"This, then, is how you should pray:
Our Father in heaven,
holy be your name,
your kingdom, come,
your will, be done
on earth, as in heaven.
Give us today, our daily bread.
Forgive us our debts,
as we forgive those who are in debt to us.
Do not bring us to the test,
but deliver us from the evil one.

"If you forgive others their wrongdoings, your Father in heaven will also forgive yours. If you do not forgive others, then your Father will not forgive you."

Prayer is something private and individual. We can never teach others how we pray for they might not have the necessary disposition that we have while praying. We can only encourage them and show them our own prayer life to stimulate their own desire to have intimacy with God. We may even share with them our prayers but they have to find on their own this sense of connection and deep relationship with the Father. That is why Jesus may have taught us the only prayer that directly came from Him, but we could never recreate His disposition and inner reality.

12
MARCH

Wednesday
Ps 51:3–4, 12–13, 18–19
A heart contrite and humbled,
O God, you will not spurn.

1ST WEEK OF LENT
Psalter: Week 1 / (Violet)

1st Reading: Jon 3:1–10

The word of Yahweh came to Jonah a second time: "Go to Nineveh, the great city, and announce to them the message I give you."

In obedience to the word of Yahweh, Jonah went to Nineveh. It was a very large city, and it took three days just to cross it. So Jonah walked a single day's journey and began proclaiming, "Forty days more and Nineveh will be destroyed."

The people of the city believed God. They declared a fast, and all of them, from the greatest to the least, put on sackcloth.

Upon hearing the news, the king of Nineveh got up from his throne, took off his royal robe, put on sackcloth and sat down in ashes. He issued a proclamation throughout Nineveh:

"By the decree of the king and his nobles, no people or beasts, herd or flock, will taste anything; neither will they eat nor drink. But let people and beasts be covered with sackcloth. Let everyone call aloud to God, turn from his evil ways and violence. Who knows? God may yet relent, turn from his fierce anger and spare us."

When God saw what they did and how they turned from their evil ways, he had compassion and did not carry out the destruction he had threatened upon them.

Gospel: Lk 11:29–32

As the crowd increased, Jesus spoke the following words: "People of the present time are troubled people. They ask for a sign, but no sign will be given to them except the sign of Jonah. As Jonah became a sign for the people of Nineveh, so will the Son of Man be a sign for this generation. The Queen of the South will rise up on Judgment Day with the people of these times and accuse them, for she came from the ends of the earth to hear the wisdom of Solomon; and here, there is greater than Solomon. The people of Nineveh will rise up on Judgment Day with the people of these times and accuse them, for Jonah's preaching made them turn from their sins, and here, there is greater than Jonah."

Jonah, the prophet of the Old Testament, was commissioned by God to preach repentance to the people of Nineveh and he tried to run away from his mandate. That was him exercising his own freedom. But God is also free to pursue His own plan and when these two freedoms collide, it is God's will that triumphs and Jonah found himself in the soil of Nineveh to do what God had ordered him. And the people repented. The judgment of God was averted. And here in our Gospel hundreds of years after is someone greater than Jonah. He too was commissioned by the Father to preach repentance first to His people Israel; unlike Jonah He obeyed. But He is not successful. His unconditional obedience did not guarantee that the mission would be a success. And so God can in His freedom pursue His plans, but humanity has to cooperate. If not, the plan of God will remain a plan until proper disposition makes it workable.

Thursday

Ps 138:1–2ab, 2cde–3, 7c–8
Lord, on the day I called for help,
you answered me.

13
MARCH

1st Reading: Est C:12, 14–16, 23–25

Seized with anguish in her fear of death, queen Esther likewise had recourse to the Lord. Then she prayed to the Lord God of Israel:

"My Lord, you who stand alone, come to my help; I am alone and have no help but you. Through my own choice I am endangering my life.

"As a child I was wont to hear from the people of the land of my forebears that you, O Lord, chose Israel from among all people, and our fathers from among their ancestors to be your lasting heritage; that you did for them, all that you have promised.

"Remember us, Lord; reveal yourself in the time of our calamity. Give me courage, King of gods and master of all power. Make my words persuasive when I face the lion; turn his heart against our enemy, that the latter and his like may be brought to their end.

"Save us by your hand; help me who am alone and have none but you, O Lord."

Gospel: Mt 7:7–12

Jesus said to his disciples, "Ask, and you will receive; seek, and you will find; knock, and the door will be opened. For everyone who asks, receives; whoever seeks, finds; and to him who knocks, the door will be opened. Would any of you give a stone to your son, when he asks for bread? Or give him a snake, when he asks for a fish? However bad you may be, you know how to give good things to your children. How much more, then, will your Father in heaven give good things to those who ask him!

"So, do to others whatever you would that others do to you: there, you have the law and the prophets."

The injunction of Jesus towards the end of the Gospel is a good guide for better living with others. We do to others what we want them to do to us. The measure is easy and right at hand. It is our very self. We need not imagine anything outside us. Yet we still fall into the trap of isolating the self from others. We tend to compete with them rather than make them our allies. If we but look at them as a reflection of who we are, we will realize that we have the same dreams and aspirations; deep down we want the same things. Thus the word of the Lord: "Do unto others whatever you would others do to you."

14
MARCH

Friday
Ps 130:1–2, 3–4, 5–7a, 7bc–8
If you, O Lord, mark iniquities,
who can stand?

1ST WEEK OF LENT
Psalter: Week 1 / (Violet)

1st Reading: Ezk 18:21–28

Thus says Yahweh, "If the sinner turns from his sin, observes my decrees and practices what is right and just, he will live; he will not die. None of the sins he committed will be charged against him; he will live, as a consequence of his righteous deeds. Do I want the death of the sinner?—word of Yahweh. Do I not, rather, want him to turn from his ways and live?

But if the righteous man turns away from what is good, and commits sins as the wicked do, will he live? His righteous deeds will no longer be credited to him; but he will die, because of his infidelity and his sins.

But you say: Yahweh's way is not just! Why, Israel! Is my position wrong? Is it not rather that yours is wrong? If the righteous man turns from his righteous deeds, and sins, then he dies, because of his sins. And if the wicked man does what is good and right, after turning from the sins he committed, he will save his life. He will live and not die, because he has opened his eyes; and turned from the sins he had committed.

Gospel: Mt 5:20–26

Jesus said to his disciples, "I tell you, if your sense of right and wrong is not keener than that of the Lawyers and the Pharisees, you will not enter the kingdom of heaven.

"You have heard, that it was said to our people in the past: *Do not commit murder; anyone who murders will have to face trial.* But now, I tell you: whoever gets angry with a brother or sister will have to face trial. Whoever insults a brother or sister is liable, to be brought before the council. Whoever calls a brother or sister "Fool!" is liable, of being thrown into the fire of hell. So, if you are about to offer your gift at the altar, and you remember that your brother has something against you, leave your gift there, in front of the altar; go at once, and make peace with your brother, and then come back and offer your gift to God.

"Don't forget this: be reconciled with your opponent quickly when you are together on the way to court. Otherwise he will turn you over to the judge, who will hand you over to the police, who will put you in jail. There, you will stay, until you have paid the last penny."

Anger as an emotion is something human and normal. Everybody feels this from time to time. Even Jesus displayed anger on several occasions. As a human emotion, it is something neutral. It is just the way it is. But what one does as a consequence of anger is where the judgment of good or bad enters. Jesus gets angry at the stubbornness of the people of His time. He tries to teach them the truth but they consistently reject Him. His anger comes from His sadness that salvation is at hand yet people do not avail of it. He never wished them ill. The same thing cannot be said for most of us. We have difficulty handling our anger. We also get angry most of the time for the wrong reason. That is why the Gospel counsels us to address our anger immediately before it gets the better of us. We should do it early or be sorry later on.

Saturday

Ps 119:1–2, 4–5, 7–8
Blessed are they who follow
the law of the Lord!

15
MARCH

1st Reading: Dt 26:16–19

*M*oses spoke to the people saying, "On this day, Yahweh, your God, commands you to fulfill these norms and these commandments. Obey them now and put them into practice with all your heart and with all your soul.

"Today Yahweh has declared to you that he will be your God, and so you shall follow his ways, observing his norms, his commandments and his laws, and listening to his voice.

"Today Yahweh has declared that you will be his very own people even as he had promised you, and you must obey all his commandments. He, for his part, will give you honor, renown and glory, and set you high above all the nations he has made, and you will become a nation consecrated to Yahweh, your God, as he has declared."

Gospel: Mt 5:43–48

*J*esus said to his disciples, "You have heard, that it was said: *Love your neighbor and do not do good to your enemy.* But this I tell you: love your enemies; and pray for those who persecute you, so that you may be children of your Father in Heaven. For he makes his sunrise on both the wicked and the good; and he gives rain to both the just and the unjust.

"If you love those who love you, what is special about that? Do not even tax collectors do as much? And if you are friendly only to your friends, what is so exceptional about that? Do not even the pagans do as much? As for you, be perfect, as your heavenly Father is perfect."

It takes real courage to love especially our enemies. We sometimes glorify those who are not averse to the use of force to protect their interest and sneer at those who continue to love even if the situation is hopeless. We see courage in the former and stupidity in the latter. But those who readily use force are not courageous; they simply are violent. They act according to the primitive instinct common to all humanity. It takes more effort to love especially those not worthy. It is more exhausting. It is because of this that those who know how to love are stronger. Their strength is not physical but something transcendental.

16
MARCH

Sunday

Ps 33:4–5, 18–19, 20, 22
Lord, let your mercy be on us,
as we place our trust in you.

1st Reading: Gen 12:1–4a

Yahweh said to Abram, "Leave your country, your family and your father's house, for the land I will show you. I will make you a great nation. I will bless you and make your name great, and you will be a blessing. I will bless those who bless you, and whoever curses you, I will curse, and in you all people of the earth will be blessed."

So Abram went as Yahweh had told him, and Lot went with him.

2nd Reading: 2 Tim 1:8b–10

Dear brothers and sisters, do your share in laboring for the Gospel, with the strength of God. He saved us and called us—a calling which proceeds from his holiness. This did not depend on our merits, but on his generosity and his own initiative. This calling, given to us from all time, in Christ Jesus has just been manifested with the glorious appearance of Christ Jesus, our Lord, who destroyed death, and brought life and immortality to light, in his Gospel.

Gospel: Mt 17:1–9

Jesus took with him Peter and James, and his brother John, and led them up a high mountain, where they were alone. Jesus' appearance was changed before them: his face shone like the sun, and his clothes became white as snow. Then suddenly, Moses and Elijah appeared to them, talking with Jesus.

Peter spoke up and said to Jesus, "Master, it is good for us to be here. If you wish, I will make three tents: one for you, one for Moses, and one for Elijah."

Peter was still speaking, when a bright cloud covered them with its shadow; and a voice from the cloud said, "This is my Son, the Beloved, my Chosen One. Listen to him."

On hearing the voice, the disciples fell to the ground, full of fear. But Jesus came, touched them, and said, "Stand up, do not be afraid!" When they raised their eyes, they no longer saw anyone except Jesus. And as they came down the mountain, Jesus commanded them not to tell anyone what they had seen, until the Son of Man be raised from the dead.

Reading: Jesus brought the three disciples closest to Him to the top of the mountain. There, his glory was revealed with the appearances of Moses, the Law receiver and Elijah, the greatest among the prophets of old. Then, God in His heaven once again confirmed the status of the Lord as the Beloved. Overwhelmed, the disciples wanted to stay longer but Jesus had to go down and continue His mission. Then He warned them not to disclose the messianic secret until the appointed time.

Reflection: One deeply exhilarating experience of a human person is to go up and to be elevated as it points directly to his or her first attempt to get up without help from others. Just look at the joy of a baby making tentative efforts to stand on his or her own. From the floor the baby finds himself or herself standing above it. This experience is later borrowed in symbolic language to mean a meeting of the divine. In the case of Jesus, it is to disclose His divine origin. It is not He but the Apostles who will encounter the divine in Him that they somehow overlooked when He was with them on the level and ordinary plane of life. It is sometimes a good idea to be detached from the ordinary and mundane concerns of life and climb our own mountain of prayer and good works to see the glory of God shining before us.

Response: It would be a good idea to go to a place that transports me to heights simply because it is charged with so much spiritual meaning to me. I might go to a shrine, a park or a garden that helps me focus my mind on God and allows me to see His beauty that is ever ancient yet ever new.

_____
_____
_____
_____
_____
_____
_____
_____
_____
_____
_____
_____

17
MARCH

Monday

Ps 79:8, 9, 11 and 13
Lord, do not deal with us
according to our sins.

2ND WEEK OF LENT
Psalter: Week 2 / (Violet)

1st Reading: Dn 9:4b–10

I prayed to Yahweh, my God, and made this confession: "Lord God, great and to be feared, you keep your Covenant and love for those who love you and observe your commandments. We have sinned; we have not been just; we have been rebels, and have turned away from your commandments and laws. We have not listened to your servants, the prophets, who spoke in your name to our kings, leaders, fathers and to all the people of the land.

"Lord, justice is yours; but ours is a face full of shame, as it is to this day— we, the people of Judah, the inhabitants of Jerusalem, the whole of Israel, near and far away, in all the lands where you have dispersed us because of the infidelity we have committed against you. Ours is the shame, O Lord, for we, our kings, princes and fathers, have sinned against you. We hope for pardon and mercy from the Lord, our God, because we have rebelled against him. We have not listened to the voice of Yahweh, our God, or followed the laws which he has given us through his servants, the prophets."

Gospel: Lk 6:36–38

J esus said to his disciples, "Be merciful, just as your Father is merciful.

"Don't be a judge of others and you will not be judged; do not condemn and you will not be condemned; forgive and you will be forgiven; give and it will be given to you, and you will receive in your sack good measure, pressed down, full and running over. For the measure you give will be the measure you receive back."

Again this is a rewording of Jesus' exhortation to do to others what you will have others do to you. It means that the measure we give to others will be the measure given to us. More importantly, this will be the measure used in heaven to evaluate our fittingness or the lack of it to enter the house of God. This is something easy to follow. We need not memorize a long list of do's and don'ts. We are the measure. The I for once is seen in a positive light.

Tuesday

Ps 50:8–9, 16bc–17, 21 and 23
To the upright, I will show the
saving power of God.

18
MARCH

1st Reading: Is 1:10, 16–20

*H*ear the warning of Yahweh, rulers of Sodom. Listen to the word of God, people of Gomorrah. Wash and make yourselves clean. Remove from my sight the evil of your deeds. Put an end to your wickedness and learn to do good. Seek justice and keep in line the abusers; give the fatherless their rights and defend the widow.

"Come," says Yahweh, "let us reason together. Though your sins be like scarlet, they will be white as snow; though they be as crimson red, they will be white as wool. If you will obey me, you will eat the goods of the earth; but if you resist and rebel, the sword will eat you instead." Truly Yahweh has spoken.

Gospel: Mt 23:1–12

*J*esus said to the crowds and to his disciples, "The teachers of the law and the Pharisees have sat down on the chair of Moses. So you shall do and observe all they say; but do not do as they do, for they do not do what they say. They tie up heavy burdens and load them on the shoulders of the people, but they do not even lift a finger to move them. They do everything in order to be seen by people: they wear very wide bands of the law around their foreheads, and robes with large tassels. They enjoy the first places at feasts and the best seats in the synagogues, and they like being greeted in the marketplace, and being called 'Master' by the people.

"But you, do not let yourselves be called Master, because you have only one Master, and all of you are brothers and sisters. Neither should you call anyone on earth Father, because you have only one Father, he who is in heaven. Nor should you be called Leader, because Christ is the only Leader for you. Let the greatest among you be the servant of all. For whoever makes himself great shall be humbled, and whoever humbles himself shall be made great."

What makes a teacher generally effective is not so much the good content of his or her teaching but the quality of his or her personhood. But taken to extreme, the teacher will invest so much in external appearances rather than on the knowledge he or she is supposed to pass. That is why Jesus told the crowds that in front of such teachers, better to focus on their words rather than on who they are because who they are internally and externally do not correspond to their teachings. In this case, their word has more weight than their being. They may not be exemplars of righteousness but they could still be the voice.

19
MARCH

Wednesday
Ps 89:2-3, 4-5, 27, 29
The son of David will live forever.

SOLEMNITY OF ST. JOSEPH,
HUSBAND OF MARY
Psalter: Proper / (White)

1ˢᵗ Reading: 2 S 7:4–5a, 12–14a, 16

2ⁿᵈ Reading: Rom 4:13, 16–18, 22

*B*rothers and sisters: If God promised Abraham, or rather his descendants, that the world would belong to him, this was not because of his obeying the law, but because he was just, and a friend of God, through faith.

For that reason, faith is the way, and all is given, by grace; and the promises of Abraham are fulfilled for all his descendants, not only for his children according to the law, but, also, for all the others, who have believed.

Abraham is the father of all of us, as it is written: *I will make you the father of many nations.* He is our father, in the eyes of Him, who gives life to the dead, and calls into existence, what does not yet exist, for this is the God in whom he believed.

Abraham believed, and hoped against all expectation, thus, becoming the father of many nations, as he had been told: *See how many will be your descendants.*

This was taken into account, for him to attain righteousness.

Gospel: Mt 1:16, 18–21, 24a

*J*acob was the father of Joseph, the husband of Mary, and from her came Jesus who is called the Christ —the Messiah.

This is how Jesus Christ was born: Mary his mother had been given to Joseph in marriage, but before they lived together, she was found to be pregnant through the Holy Spirit.

Then Joseph, her husband, made plans to divorce her in all secrecy. He was an upright man, and in no way did he want to disgrace her.

While he was pondering over this, an angel of the Lord appeared to him in a dream and said, "Joseph, descendant of David, do not be afraid to take Mary as your wife. She has conceived by the Holy Spirit, and now she will bear a son. You shall call him 'Jesus' for he will save his people from their sins."

When Joseph awoke, he did what the angel of the Lord had told him to do, and he took his wife to his home.

Joseph is the silent man of the Gospel. He never had a speaking part. Yet he played an important role in salvation history. He provided the proper lineage to Jesus as the Messiah from the roots of Jesse, a descendant from the house David. He was portrayed as "pondering over" his course of action when he found out that Mary was pregnant. He was a man prone to deep thoughts before making a decision. This is probably the reason why Joseph was chosen to carry a ministry that God had not asked any man before. He thought before he acted. Once he was sure of what to do, he set things in motion without looking back. God is in need of a man who once convinced will not go back from his words. Silent but reliable, Joseph became the Father of the Son of God here below.

Thursday

Ps 1:1–2, 3, 4 and 6
Blessed are they who hope
in the Lord.

20
MARCH

1st Reading: Jer 17:5–10

This is what Yahweh says, "Cursed is the man who trusts in human beings and depends on a mortal for his life, while his heart is drawn away from Yahweh!

"He is like a bunch of thistles in dry land, in parched desert places, in a salt land where no one lives and who never finds happiness.

"Blessed is the man who puts his trust in Yahweh and whose confidence is in him! He is like a tree planted by the water, sending out its roots towards the stream.

"He has no fear when the heat comes, his leaves are always green; the year of drought is no problem and he can always bear fruit.

"Most deceitful is the heart. What is there within man, who can understand him? I, Yahweh, search the heart and penetrate the mind. I reward each one according to his ways and the fruit of his deeds."

Gospel: Lk 16:19–31

Jesus said to the Pharisees, "Once there was a rich man who dressed in purple and fine linen and feasted every day. At his gate lay Lazarus, a poor man covered with sores, who longed to eat just the scraps falling from the rich man's table. Even dogs used to come and lick his sores. It happened that the poor man died, and angels carried him to take his place with Abraham. The rich man also died, and was buried. From the netherworld where he was in torment, the rich man looked up and saw Abraham afar off, and with him Lazarus at rest.

"He called out, 'Father Abraham, have pity on me, and send Lazarus, with the tip of his finger dipped in water, to cool my tongue, for I suffer so much in this fire!'

"Abraham replied, 'My son, remember that in your lifetime you were well-off, while the lot of Lazarus was misfortune. Now he is in comfort, and you are in agony. But that is not all. Between your place and ours a great chasm has been fixed, so that no one can cross over from here to you, or from your side to us.'

"The rich man implored once more, 'Then I beg you, Father Abraham, send Lazarus to my father's house, where my five brothers live. Let him warn them, so that they may not end up in this place of torment.' Abraham replied, 'They have Moses and the prophets. Let them listen to them.' But the rich man said, 'No, Father Abraham; but if someone from the dead goes to them, they will repent.'

"Abraham said, 'If they will not listen to Moses and the prophets, they will not be convinced, even if someone rises from the dead.'"

It is not only our deliberate acts of evil that will convict us someday but also what we have not done simply because we have not paid attention and were too immersed in our own affairs. It is thus that inattention could be deadly to our future fate. How many times do we fail to respond to the call to love not because we are heartless or evil but simply because we are not aware? Our focus is somewhere else. Our immediate environment is neglected. We are like a sprinkler that throws water afar yet the grasses around us wither and die because no water is given them. If we focus on where we are, there are many opportunities to love. Our salvation may not be that far. It may be just right beside us.

21
MARCH

Friday
Ps 105:16–17, 18–19, 20–21
Remember the marvels
the Lord has done.

2ND WEEK OF LENT
Psalter: Week 2 / (Violet)

1st Reading: Gen 37:3–4, 12–13a, 17b–28a*

Israel loved Joseph more than any of his other children, for he was the son of his old age and he had a coat with long sleeves made for him. His brothers who saw that their father loved him more than he loved them, hated him and could no longer speak to him in a friendly way. (...) They saw him in the distance and before he reached them, they plotted to kill him. They said to one another, "Here comes the specialist in dreams! Now's the time! Let's kill him and throw him into a well. We'll say a wild animal devoured him. Then we'll see what his dreams were all about!" But Reuben heard this and tried to save him from their hands saying, "Let us not kill him; shed no blood! Throw him in this well in the wilderness, but do him no violence." This he said to save him from them and take him back to his father. (…)

Gospel: Mt 21:33–43, 45–46

Jesus said to the chief priests and the elders of the people, "Listen to another example: There was a landowner who planted a vineyard. He put a fence around it, dug a hole for the wine press, built a watchtower, leased the vineyard to tenants, and then, went to a distant country. When harvest time came, the landowner sent his servants to the tenants to collect his share of the harvest. But the tenants seized his servants, beat one, killed another, and stoned a third. "Again, the owner sent more servants; but they were treated in the same way.

"Finally, he sent his son, thinking, 'They will respect my son.' But when the tenants saw the son, they thought, 'This is the one who is to inherit the vineyard. Let us kill him, and his inheritance will be ours.' So they seized him, threw him out of the vineyard and killed him.

"Now, what will the owner of the vineyard do with the tenants when he comes?" They said to him, "He will bring those evil men to an evil end, and lease the vineyard to others, who will pay him in due time."

And Jesus replied, "Have you never read what the Scriptures say? *The stone which the builders rejected has become the cornerstone. This was the Lord's doing, and we marvel at it.* Therefore I say to you: the kingdom of heaven will be taken from you, and given to a people who will produce its fruit." When the chief priests and the Pharisees heard these parables, they realized that Jesus was referring to them. They would have arrested him, but they were afraid of the crowd, who regarded him as a prophet.

The truth is sometimes stranger than fiction. Here is a group of people convinced of their faithfulness to God, acclaimed and esteemed as such but only to be told by Jesus of their real standing before the God whom they served. It was too painful to accept. Hence the tendency for violence to soothe the wounded ego and pride. Some people make a career out of their holiness and will defend it tooth and nail. They cannot see that holiness is a process and continues throughout. It does not stop at a certain point in time. Had the chief priests and the Pharisees taken the words of Jesus as a challenge rather than a condemnation, they would have changed and encountered real holiness. Instead what they had was an empty and hollow claim that they had to defend all their lives.

Saturday

Ps 103:1–2, 3–4, 9–10, 11–12
The Lord is kind and merciful.

22
MARCH

1st Reading: Mic 7:14–15, 18–20

Gospel: Lk 15:1–3, 11–32*

*T*ax collectors and sinners were seeking the company of Jesus, all of them eager to hear what he had to say. But the Pharisees frowned at this, muttering, "This man welcomes sinners and eats with them." So Jesus told them this parable: "There was a man with two sons. The younger said to his father, 'Give me my share of the estate.' So the father divided his property between them. Some days later, the younger son gathered all his belongings and started off for a distant land, where he squandered his wealth in loose living. Having spent everything, he was hard pressed when a severe famine broke out in that land. (...)

"Finally coming to his senses, he said, 'How many of my father's hired workers have food to spare, and here I am starving to death! I will get up and go back to my father, and say to him, Father, I have sinned against God, and before you. I no longer deserve to be called your son. Treat me then as one of your hired servants.' With that thought in mind, he set off for his father's house.

"He was still a long way off, when his father caught sight of him. His father was so deeply moved with compassion that he ran out to meet him, threw his arms around his neck and kissed him. The son said, 'Father, I have sinned against Heaven and before you. I no longer deserve to be called your son.'

"But the father turned to his servants: 'Quick!' he said. 'Bring out the finest robe and put it on him! Put a ring on his finger and sandals on his feet! Take the fattened calf and kill it! We shall celebrate and have a feast, for this son of mine was dead, and has come back to life; he was lost, and is found!' And the celebration began.

"Meanwhile, the elder son had been working in the fields. As he returned and approached the house, he heard the sound of music and dancing. He called one of the servants and asked what it was all about. The servant answered, 'Your brother has come home safe and sound, and your father is so happy about it that he has ordered this celebration, and killed the fattened calf.'

"The elder son became angry, and refused to go in. His father came out and pleaded with him. The son, very indignant, said, 'Look, I have slaved for you all these years. Never have I disobeyed your orders. Yet you have never given me even a young goat to celebrate with my friends. But when this son of yours returns, after squandering your property with loose women, you kill the fattened calf for him!'

"The father said, 'My son, you are always with me, and everything I have is yours. But this brother of yours was dead, and has come back to life; he was lost, and is found. And for that we had to rejoice and be glad.'"

The Parable of the Prodigal Son or of the Prodigal Father is a study in contrast about what love should and should not be. The Father loved His sons to the point of prodigality. This enabled him to endure the crass disrespect of the younger son and the cold resentful obedience of the elder son. The two sons love themselves so much. The younger went far away with his inheritance to live a life of license that he thought was freedom. Yet when he was down, he recalled his Father's love and this was his salvation. Not so with the elder son whose self love demanded that he be pampered by the father. The father's loving presence was not enough. He could not enjoy that which the younger son recalled from afar. Perhaps he also needed to be exiled to realize that which he had nearby but always had overlooked.

23
MARCH

Sunday

Ps 95:1–2, 6–7, 8–9
If today you hear his voice,
harden not your hearts.

1ˢᵗ Reading: Ex 17:3–7

*I*n those days, the people thirsted for water there and grumbled against Moses, "Why did you make us leave Egypt to have us die of thirst with our children and our cattle?"

So Moses cried to Yahweh, "What shall I do with the people? They are almost ready to stone me!" Yahweh said to Moses, "Go ahead of the people and take with you the elders of Israel. Take with you the staff with which you struck the Nile, and go. I will stand there before you on the rock at Horeb. You will strike the rock and water will flow from it and the people will drink." Moses did this in the presence of the elders of Israel.

The place was called Massah and Meribah because of the complaints of the Israelites, who tested Yahweh saying, "Is Yahweh with us or not?"

2ⁿᵈ Reading: Romans 5:1–2, 5–8

*B*rothers and sisters, by faith, we have received true righteousness, and we are at peace with God, through Jesus Christ, our Lord. Through him, we obtain this favor, in which we remain, and we even boast to expect the glory of God.

And hope does not disappoint us, because the Holy Spirit has been given to us, pouring into our hearts the love of God.

Consider, moreover, the time that Christ died for us: when we were still helpless and unable to do anything. Few would accept to die for an upright person; although, for a very good person, perhaps someone would dare to die. But see how God manifested his love for us: while we were still sinners, Christ died for us.

Gospel: Jn 4:5–15, 19b–26, 39a, 40-42 (or Jn: 4:5-42)

*J*esus came to a Samaritan town called Sychar, near the land that Jacob had given to his son Joseph. Jacob's well is there. Tired from his journey, Jesus sat down by the well; it was about noon. Now a Samaritan woman came to draw water, and Jesus said to her, "Give me a drink." His disciples had just gone into town to buy some food.

The Samaritan woman said to him, "How is it that you, a Jew, ask me, a Samaritan and a woman, for a drink?" (For Jews, in fact, have no dealings with Samaritans.) Jesus replied, "If you only knew the gift of God! If you knew who it is, who is asking you for a drink, you yourself would have asked me, and I would have given you living water."

The woman answered, "Sir, you have no bucket, and this well is deep; where is your living water? Are you greater than our ancestor Jacob, who gave us this well; he drank from it himself, together with his sons and his cattle?"

Jesus said to her, "Those who drink of this water will be thirsty again; but those, who drink of the water that I shall give, will never be thirsty; for the water, that I shall give, will become in them a spring of water, welling up to eternal life."

The woman said to him, "Give me this water, that I may never be thirsty, and never have to come here to draw water." Jesus said, "Go, call your husband, and come back here."

The woman then said to him, "I see you are a prophet; tell me this: Our ancestors came to this mountain to worship God; but you Jews, do you not claim that Jerusalem is the only place to worship God?"

Jesus said to her, "Believe me, woman, the hour is coming when you shall worship the Father, but that will not be on this mountain nor in Jerusalem. You worship what you do not know; we worship what we know, because salvation is from the Jews. But the hour is coming, and is even now here, when the true worshipers will worship the Father in Spirit and truth; for that is the kind of worshippers the Father wants. God is Spirit, and those who worship him must worship in Spirit, and truth."

The woman said to him, "I know that the Messiah (that is the Christ) is coming. When he comes, he will tell us everything." And Jesus said, "I who am talking to you, I am he."

In that town many Samaritans believed in him when they heard the woman who declared, "He told me everything I did." So, when they came to him, they asked him to stay with them, and Jesus stayed there two days. After that, many more believed because of his own words, and they said to the woman, "We no longer believe because of what you told us; we have heard for ourselves, and we know that this is the Savior of the world."

Reading: Jesus passed through a Samaritan town. The Samaritans are traditionally hostile to the Jews who look down on them as inferior since they do not go to worship God in the Temple of Jerusalem. In a well, traditionally associated with Jacob-Israel, Jesus encounters a Samaritan woman and asks for a drink of water. Prejudice and bias get in the way. But what started as a wary exchange between strangers turns into a relationship that is echoed for eternity. The woman believed and shared it to her fellow town folks. From her, a town's people became adherents of Jesus.

Reflection: Sometimes, God pretends to have a need of us in order to befriend us, just as Jesus relied on the Samaritan woman for His drink to quench His thirst. He could very well have gotten it Himself but He chose to appear to need her help to facilitate a connection that otherwise would have been difficult considering their difference in status. It was at first awkward though civil. The woman displayed proper courtesy albeit with a bit of apprehension. But the conversation with Jesus caught her unawares for it was actually she who was in need of quenching her deeper thirst, the thirst of the soul which was way beyond Jesus' physical thirst. And she believed. From a potential giver of plain water to a happy recipient of the "water of life," she shared her newfound wealth and remained one of the best of friends of Him who was formerly a stranger but now her Lord and Master.

Response: I have many "thirsts" in this life but do I take a moment to identify and sort them out? Perhaps some are not really "life-threatening." As a matter of fact I might be the better without it. But there are some that I have to attend to in order to grow in this life. It might be a good idea to seek and drink from the "water of life" today, and from there, try to quench the thirst of others in any way I can.

24
MARCH

Monday

Ps 42:2, 3; 43:3, 4
Athirst is my soul for the living God.
When shall I go and behold the face of God?

3RD WEEK OF LENT
Psalter: Week 3 / (Violet)

1st Reading: 2 K 5:1–15b*

*N*aaman was the army commander of the king of Aram. This man was highly regarded and enjoyed the king's favor, for Yahweh had helped him lead the army of the Arameans to victory. But this valiant man was sick with leprosy. One day some Aramean soldiers raided the land of Israel and took a young girl captive who became a servant to the wife of Naaman. She said to her mistress, "If my master would only present himself to the prophet in Samaria, he would surely cure him of his leprosy."

Naaman went to tell the king what the young Israelite maidservant had said. The king of Aram said to him, "Go to the prophet, and I shall also send a letter to the king of Israel." (...)

Elisha, the man of God, came to know that the king of Israel had torn his clothes, so he sent this message to him: "Why have you torn your clothes? Let the man come to me, that he may know that there is a prophet in Israel." So Naaman came with his horses and chariots, and stopped before the house of Elisha. Elisha then sent a messenger to tell him, "Go to the river Jordan and wash seven times, and your flesh shall be as it was before, and you shall be cleansed." (...)

So Naaman went down to the Jordan where he washed himself seven times as Elisha had ordered. His skin became soft like that of a child and he was cleansed. Then Naaman returned to the man of God with all his men. He entered and said to him, "Now I know that there is no other God anywhere in the world but in Israel. I ask you to accept these gifts from your servant."

Gospel: Lk 4:24–30

*J*esus said to the people in the synagogue at Nazareth, "No prophet is honored in his own country. Truly, I say to you, there were many widows in Israel in the days of Elijah, when the heavens withheld rain for three years and six months and a great famine came over the whole land. Yet, Elijah was not sent to any of them, but to a widow of Zarephath, in the country of Sidon. There were also many lepers in Israel in the time of Elisha, the prophet; and no one was healed except Naaman, the Syrian."

On hearing these words, the whole assembly became indignant. They rose up and brought him out of the town, to the edge of the hill on which Nazareth is built, intending to throw him down the cliff. But he passed through their midst and went his way.

Everybody wants to be recognized and loved. And having encountered that, we hold on to it and defend it. The Israelites glory in their being the chosen race, the people beloved by God. It is therefore a shock when Jesus pointed out from their history that there were instances when God preferred the pagans over them. They could not take this sitting down. And so the act of violence ensued. Jesus had to walk away from their pettiness and leave with his life intact. It is not Jesus whom the people should kill. It should have been their false sense of honor and pride.

SOLEMNITY OF THE ANNUNCIATION OF THE LORD
Psalter: Proper / (White)

Tuesday

Ps 40:7–8a, 8b–9, 10, 11
Here am I, Lord;
I come to do your will.

25
MARCH

1st Reading: Is 7:10–14; 8:10

Yahweh addressed Ahaz, "Ask for a sign from Yahweh your God, let it come either from the deepest depths or from the heights of heaven."

But Ahaz answered, "I will not ask, I will not put Yahweh to the test."

Then Isaiah said, "Now listen, descendants of David. Have you not been satisfied trying the patience of people, that you also try the patience of my God? Therefore the Lord himself will give you a sign: *The Virgin* is with child and bears a son and calls his name *Immanuel.*

Devise a plan and it will be thwarted, make a resolve and it will not stand, for God-is-with-us.

2nd Reading: Heb 10:4–10

Gospel: Lk 1:26–38

In the sixth month, the angel Gabriel was sent from God, to a town of Galilee called Nazareth. He was sent to a virgin, who was betrothed to a man named Joseph, of the family of David; and the virgin's name was Mary.

The angel came to her and said, "Rejoice, full of grace, the Lord is with you!" Mary was troubled at these words, wondering what this greeting could mean.

But the angel said, "Do not fear, Mary, for God has looked kindly on you. You shall conceive and bear a son; and you shall call him Jesus. He will be great, and shall rightly be called Son of the Most High. The Lord God will give him the kingdom of David, his ancestor; he will rule over the people of Jacob forever; and his reign shall have no end."

Then Mary said to the angel, "How can this be, since I am a virgin?" And the angel said to her, "The Holy Spirit will come upon you and the power of the Most High will overshadow you; therefore, the holy child to be born of you shall be called Son of God. Even your relative, Elizabeth, is expecting a son in her old age, although she was unable to have a child; and she is now in her sixth month. With God nothing is impossible."

Then Mary said, "I am the handmaid of the Lord, let it be done to me as you have said." And the angel left her.

Today we celebrate the Incarnation of the Son of God in the womb of the Virgin Mary. This happens just right after the spring equinox (March 20) begins. This is the time when night and day are more or less of equal length. The characteristic of this season lends a rich symbolism to the nature of the baby conceived. He is equally human (represented by the night) and divine (represented by the day). Perhaps it is the logic of the season that our forefathers in faith adopted to explain the mystery of Christ rather than the logic of a correct and precise date of Jesus' conception and birth. They used the language of the cosmos in order to convey the truth that is too big to be encapsulated in mere plain words.

26 MARCH

1st Reading: Dt 4:1, 5–9

Moses spoke to the people and said, "And now, Israel, listen to the norms and laws which I teach that you may put them into practice. And you will live and enter and take possession of the land which Yahweh, the God of your fathers, gives you.

"See, as Yahweh, my God, ordered me, I am teaching you the norms and the laws that you may put them into practice in the land you are going to enter and have as your own. If you observe and practice them, other peoples will regard you as wise and intelligent. When they come to know of all these laws, they will say, "There is no people as wise and as intelligent as this great nation." For in truth, is there a nation as great as ours, whose gods are as near to it as Yahweh, our God, is to us whenever we call upon him? And is there a nation as great as ours whose norms and laws are as just as this law which I give you today?

"But be careful and be on your guard. Do not forget these things which your own eyes have seen nor let them depart from your heart as long as you live. But on the contrary, teach them to your children and to your children's children."

Gospel: Mt 5:17–19

Jesus said to his disciples, "Do not think that I have come to annul the law and the prophets. I have not come to annul them, but to fulfill them. I tell you this: as long as heaven and earth last, not the smallest letter or dot in the law will change, until all is fulfilled.

"So then, whoever breaks the least important of these commandments, and teaches others to do the same, will be the least in the kingdom of heaven. On the other hand, whoever obeys them, and teaches others to do the same, will be great in the kingdom of heaven."

Jesus may come across as a maverick but He is not a nihilist of the Law and the Prophets. What He does is not to demolish them but to bring out their real essence. He is not therefore abolishing them. He is bringing them to their fullest sense. However people tend to stay on the literal surface meaning of the letter of the Law. They are too lazy to sink deep into its mystery in order to have a better appreciation of it. They would rather choose the easy way. It requires hard work to really enter into the essence of the Law. And so Jesus is not only in battle with the literalist unimaginative interpreters of the Law. He is also combating their laziness so that they can truly understand its meaning.

Thursday

Ps 95:1-2, 6-7, 8-9
If today you hear his voice,
harden not your hearts.

27
MARCH

1st Reading: Jer 7:23–28

Thus says Yahweh, "One thing I did command them: Listen to my voice and I will be your God and you will be my people. Walk in the way I command you and all will be well with you. But they did not listen and paid no attention. They followed the bad habits of their stubborn heart and turned away from me.

"From the time I brought their ancestors out of Egypt until this day I have continually sent them my servants, the prophets; but this stiff-necked people did not listen. They paid no attention and were worse than their ancestors.

"You may say all these things to them but they will not listen. You will call them but they will not answer. This is a nation that did not obey Yahweh and refused to be disciplined. Truth has perished and is no longer heard from their lips."

Gospel: Lk 11:14–23

One day, Jesus was driving out a demon, which was mute. When the demon had been driven out, the mute person could speak, and the people were amazed. Yet some of them said, "He drives out demons by the power of Beelzebul, the chief of the demons." Others wanted to put him to the test, by asking him for a heavenly sign.

But Jesus knew their thoughts, and said to them, "Every nation divided by civil war is on the road to ruin, and will fall. If Satan also is divided, his empire is coming to an end. How can you say that I drive out demons by calling upon Beelzebul? If I drive them out by Beelzebul, by whom do your sons drive out demons? They will be your judges, then.

"But if I drive out demons by the finger of God; would not this mean that the kingdom of God has come upon you? As long as a man, strong and well armed, guards his house, his goods are safe. But when a stronger man attacks and overcomes him, the challenger takes away all the weapons he relied on, and disposes of his spoils.

"Whoever is not with me is against me, and whoever does not gather with me, scatters."

Division is a characteristic of the devil's handiwork. He turns one against the other until unity is destroyed. Where discord is, there you will find him. But the same thing cannot be said among their ranks. They are united in their effort to sow disunity in the world. For divided they are easily vanquished. They gain strength in their numbers. And so Jesus points the contradiction in His accusers' words. If He is the devil's instrument, how could He work against the devil? What He does is not random healing of the possessed but a consistent ministry of driving out demons. If it was all for a show, it would have been limited to a few and its efficacy be but momentary. His enemies could not just admit that His works are good and therefore holy. They would rather ascribe it to the demon than to admit it. That is why Jesus is angry at them. Their stubbornness is consciously willed.

28
MARCH

Friday

Ps 81:6c–8a, 8bc–9, 10–11ab, 14 & 17
I am the Lord your God:
hear my voice.

3RD WEEK OF LENT
Psalter: Week 3 / (Violet)

1st Reading: Hos 14:2–10

Thus says the Lord: Return to your God, Yahweh, O Israel! Your sins have caused your downfall. Return to Yahweh with humble words. Say to him, "Oh, you who show compassion to the fatherless, forgive our debt, be appeased. Instead of bulls and sacrifices, accept the praise from our lips.

Assyria will not save us: no longer shall we look for horses, nor ever again shall we say 'Our gods' to the work of our hands."

I will heal their disloyalty and love them with all my heart, for my anger has turned from them.

I shall be like dew to Israel, like the lily will he blossom. Like a cedar, he will send down his roots; his young shoots will grow and spread.

His splendor will be like an olive tree, his fragrance, like a Lebanon cedar.

They will dwell in my shade again, they will flourish like the grain, they will blossom like a vine, and their fame will be like Lebanon wine.

What would Ephraim do with idols, when it is I who hear and make him prosper? I am like an evergreen cypress tree; all your fruitfulness comes from me.

Who is wise enough to grasp all this? Who is discerning and will understand? Straight are the ways of Yahweh: the just walk in them, but the sinners stumble.

Gospel: Mk 12:28–34

A teacher of the law had been listening to this discussion and admired how Jesus answered them. So he came up and asked him, "Which commandment is the first of all?"

Jesus answered, "The first is: *Hear, Israel! The Lord, our God, is One Lord; and you shall love the Lord, your God, with all your heart, with all your soul, with all your mind and with all your strength.* And after this comes a second commandment: *You shall love your neighbor as yourself.* There is no commandment greater than these two."

The teacher of the law said to him, "Well spoken, Master; you are right when you say that he is one, and there is no other besides him. To love him with all our heart, with all our understanding and with all our strength, and to love our neighbor as ourselves is more important than any burnt offering or sacrifice."

Jesus approved this answer and said, "You are not far from the kingdom of God." And after that, no one dared to ask him any more questions.

No one can do wrong with love. It is the foundation of all other laws. However, love could be used so many times even for the wrong reasons so much so that it loses its power to inspire and ignite the heart. It becomes only a word for the lips to pronounce but bereft of its majestic weight and stature. But despite the abuses love is subjected to it never goes out of style. After all, with proper discernment, in the many instances that love has been misused, people realize that it is the person not the love that broke someone's heart, wounded friendship and did ill to others. The meaning of love derived from God remains valid and true. It is for this reason that some teachers of the Law found friendship with Jesus. Many might have been His enemies from their ranks, but there were always some who were not far from the kingdom of God.

Saturday
Ps 51:3–4, 18–19, 20–21ab
*It is mercy I desire,
and not sacrifice.*

29
MARCH

1ˢᵗ Reading: Hos 6:1–6

Come, let us return to Yahweh. He who shattered us to pieces, will heal us as well; he has struck us down, but he will bind up our wounds.

Two days later he will bring us back to life; on the third day, he will raise us up, and we shall live in his presence.

Let us strive to know Yahweh. His coming is as certain as the dawn; his judgment will burst forth like the light; he will come to us as showers come, like spring rain that waters the earth.

O Ephraim, what shall I do with you? O Judah, how shall I deal with you? This love of yours is like morning mist, like morning dew that quickly disappears.

This is why I smote you through the prophets, and have slain you by the words of my mouth.

For it is love that I desire, not sacrifice; it is knowledge of God, not burnt offerings.

Gospel: Lk 18:9–14

Jesus told another parable to some people, fully convinced of their own righteousness, who looked down on others: "Two men went up to the temple to pray; one was a Pharisee, and the other a tax collector. The Pharisee stood by himself, and said, 'I thank you, God, that I am not like other people, grasping, crooked, adulterous, or even like this tax collector. I fast twice a week, and give a tenth of all my income to the temple.'

"In the meantime the tax collector, standing far off, would not even lift his eyes to heaven, but beat his breast, saying, 'O God, be merciful to me, a sinner.'

"I tell you, when this man went back to his house, he had been reconciled with God, but not the other. For whoever makes himself out to be great will be humbled, and whoever humbles himself will be raised up."

Beauty shines most when it is not conscious of itself. This is also true in holiness. If one is not conscious of one's virtue the more it will have the power to inspire others. For whatever is true and genuine does not need our help to promote it. It needs no justification or advertisement for it to be real. Being unselfconscious is therefore the ingredient that makes holiness holier. And perhaps this is where our battle lies with ourselves. For after having acquired the virtue, we must protect it from our tendency to seek praise and recognition. In the end, we should not only be afraid of the devil out there who might try to rob our holiness from us. We also have to watch ourselves.

30

MARCH

Sunday

Ps 23:1-3a, 3b-4, 5, 6
The Lord is my shepherd,
there is nothing I shall want.

1ˢᵗ Reading: 1 S 16:1b, 6–7, 10–13a

*Y*ahweh asked Samuel, "How long will you be grieving Saul whom I have rejected as king of Israel? Fill your horn with oil and be on your way to Jesse the Bethlehemite, for I have chosen my king from among his sons."

As they came, Samuel looked at Eliab the older and thought, "This must be Yahweh's anointed." But Yahweh told Samuel, "Do not judge by his looks or his stature for I have rejected him. Yahweh does not judge as man judges; humans see with the eyes; Yahweh sees the heart."

Jesse presented seven of his sons to Samuel who said, "Yahweh has chosen none of them. But are all your sons here?" Jesse replied, "There is still the youngest, tending the flock just now." Samuel said to him, "Send for him and bring him to me; we shall not sit down to eat until he arrives." So Jesse sent for his youngest son and brought him to Samuel. He was a handsome lad with a ruddy complexion and beautiful eyes. And Yahweh spoke, "Go, anoint him for he is the one." Samuel then took the horn of oil and anointed him in his brothers' presence. From that day onwards, Yahweh's spirit took hold of David.

2ⁿᵈ Reading: Eph 5:8–14

*B*rothers and sisters, you were once darkness, but, now, you are light, in the Lord. Behave as children of light; the fruits of light are kindness, justice and truth, in every form.

You, yourselves, search out what pleases the Lord, and take no part in works of darkness, that are of no benefit; expose them instead. Indeed, it is a shame even to speak of what those people do in secret, but as soon as it is exposed to the light, everything becomes clear; and what is unmasked, becomes clear through light. Therefore it is said: "Awake, you who sleep, arise from the dead, that the light of Christ may shine on you."

Gospel: Jn 9:1, 6–9, 13–17, 34–38

(or Jn 9:1-41)

*A*s Jesus walked along, he saw a man who had been blind from birth. He made paste with spittle and clay, and rubbed it on the eyes of the blind man. Then he said, "Go and wash in the Pool of Siloam." (This word means *sent*.) So the blind man went and washed and came back able to see. His neighbors, and all the people who used to see him begging, wondered. They said, "Isn't this the beggar who used to sit here?" Some said, "He's the one." Others said, "No, but he looks like him." But the man himself said, "I am he."

The people brought the man who had been blind to the Pharisees. Now it was a Sabbath day when Jesus made mud paste and opened his eyes. The Pharisees asked him again, "How did you recover your sight?" And he said, "He put paste on my eyes, and I washed, and now I see." Some of the Pharisees said, "That man is not from God, for he works on the Sabbath"; but others wondered, "How can a sinner perform such miraculous signs?" They were divided, and they questioned the blind man again, "What do you think of this man who opened your eyes?" And he answered, "He is a prophet!"

They answered him, "You were born a sinner and now you teach us!" And they expelled him. Jesus heard that they had expelled him. He found him and said, "Do you believe in the Son of Man?" He answered, "Who is he, that I may believe in him?" Jesus said, "You have seen him and he is speaking to you." He said, "Lord, I believe"; and he worshiped him.

Reading: Jesus healed a blind man on the Sabbath; this raised a veritable storm of indignation from the religious authorities who ruled that such act was not sanctioned by God. But people were divided: how could something that good come from someone evil? The blind was rebuked as a sinner when he dared declared his healer a prophet, for his blindness before was indicative of his sinfulness. Cast out from the Temple, he was found by Jesus and consequently, through an act of faith, he found his Saviour.

Reflection: Some people relish the fact that someone is inferior to them and feel bad if the status quo is changed. They take delight in the misery of others and enforce a code that legitimizes their pettiness. Such is the case of the people and the Pharisee of today's Gospel. They would not believe that the blind man who was a sinner in their midst could find healing and wholeness. That was too scandalous since he had to suffer more as punishment for sins committed in this life. So they maligned him and his healer and declared unholy the healing that had taken place on a holy day. The blind man who now could see should have been the sign that told them God is now walking in their land. Their deeds reveal that their spiritual blindness was far greater than the physical blindness of the man.

Response: When was the last time I rejoiced at the blessings of others? Perhaps I have to remind someone today how blessed he or she is and invite her or him to thanksgiving and praise to the God who is overly generous to us.

31
MARCH

Monday
Ps 30:2 & 4, 5–6, 11–12a & 13b
I will praise you, Lord,
for you have rescued me.

4TH WEEK OF LENT
Psalter: Week 4 / (Violet)

1st Reading: Is 65:17–21

Thus says Yahweh, "I now create new heavens and a new earth, and the former things will not be remembered, nor will they come to mind again. Be glad forever and rejoice in what I create; for I create Jerusalem to be a joy and its people to be a delight. I will rejoice over Jerusalem and take delight in my people. The sound of distress and the voice of weeping will not be heard in it any more. You will no longer know of dead children or of adults who do not live out a lifetime. One who reaches a hundred years will have died a mere youth, but one who fails to reach a hundred will be considered accursed. They will build houses and dwell in them; they will plant crops and eat their fruit."

Gospel: Jn 4:43–54

When the two days were over, Jesus left for Galilee. Jesus himself said that no prophet is recognized in his own country. Yet the Galileans welcomed him when he arrived, because of all the things which he had done in Jerusalem during the Festival, and which they had seen. For they, too, had gone to the feast.

Jesus went back to Cana of Galilee, where he had changed the water into wine. At Capernaum there was an official, whose son was ill, and when he heard that Jesus had come from Judea to Galilee, he went and asked him to come and heal his son, for he was at the point of death.

Jesus said, "Unless you see signs and wonders, you will not believe!" The official said, "Sir, come down before my child dies." And Jesus replied, "Go, your son lives!"

The man had faith in the word that Jesus spoke to him, and went his way. As he was approaching his house, his servants met him, and gave him the good news, "Your son has recovered!" So he asked them at what hour the child began to recover, and they said to him, "The fever left him yesterday, at about one o'clock in the afternoon." And the father realized that that was the time when Jesus had told him, "Your son lives!" And he became a believer, he and all his family.

Jesus performed this second miraculous sign when he returned from Judea to Galilee.

In contrast to Nazareth where Jesus could hardly work miracles because of their unbelief, Galilee is a place of fecundity for the Lord. This is where He first performed His miracle way before His time, the miracle of the wine in a wedding feast. Here in this Gospel, He will again perform another miraculous sign, that is, the healing of the official's son. Where there is faith in Him, Jesus' power manifests itself all the more. He need not pry open the minds and hearts of people. They are already predisposed. This tremendous saving in time and energy of Jesus is therefore channelled to more productive things. Possibilities multiply when there is cooperation.

Tuesday

Ps 46:2–3, 5–6, 8–9
The Lord of hosts is with us;
our stronghold is the God of Jacob.

01
APRIL

1ˢᵗ Reading: Ezk 47:1–9, 12

Gospel: Jn 5:1–16

There was a feast of the Jews, and Jesus went up to Jerusalem. Now, by the Sheep Gate in Jerusalem, there is a pool (called Bethzatha in Hebrew) surrounded by five galleries. In these galleries lay a multitude of sick people: blind, lame and paralyzed.

(All were waiting for the water to move, for at times an angel of the Lord would descend into the pool and stir up the water; and the first person to enter the pool, after this movement of the water, would be healed of whatever disease that he had.)

There was a man who had been sick for thirty-eight years. Jesus saw him, and because he knew how long this man had been lying there, he said to him, "Do you want to be healed?" And the sick man answered, "Sir, I have no one to put me into the pool when the water is disturbed; so while I am still on my way, another steps down before me."

Jesus then said to him, "Stand up, take your mat and walk!" And at once the man was healed, and he took up his mat and walked.

Now that day happened to be the Sabbath. So the Jews said to the man who had just been healed, "It is the Sabbath, and the law doesn't allow you to carry your mat." He answered them, "The one who healed me said to me, 'Take up your mat and walk!'" They asked him, "Who is the one who said to you: Take up your mat and walk?" But the sick man had no idea who it was who had cured him, for Jesus had slipped away among the crowd that filled the place.

Afterward Jesus met him in the temple court and told him, "Now you are well; don't sin again, lest something worse happen to you." And the man went back and told the Jews that it was Jesus who had healed him. So the Jews persecuted Jesus because he performed healings like that on the Sabbath.

Unhappy is a sick person with no one to attend to his or her needs. There is no one to ease the burden and the suffering such sickness brings. This is what happened to the man sick for thirty-eight years. As much as he desired healing in the miraculous pool of Bethzatha, nobody was there to help him. Each one was preoccupied with his or her own sickness. They could not spare any sympathy for him. Thus whenever the pool's water was disturbed, those wishing to be healed and their cohorts pushed and shoved one another in an effort to be the first to touch the waters. It was a hopeless situation indeed for that man. However, Jesus passed by and took pity on Him. Not even the prohibition to refrain from work on the Sabbath could deter Him to help the sick man. He had suffered enough because of his fate. He should not be deprived of healing even on a holy day. Only great persons can transcend the prohibition to love even though it is legitimated by human laws. They are extraordinary because they see beyond the ordinary that most of us see.

02
APRIL

Wednesday
Ps 145:8-9, 13cd-14, 17-18
The Lord is gracious and merciful.

4TH WEEK OF LENT
Psalter: Week 4 / (Violet)

1st Reading: Is 49:8-15

Gospel: Jn 5:17-30

Jesus replied the Jews, "My Father goes on working and so do I." And the Jews tried all the harder to kill him, for Jesus not only broke the *Sabbath* observance, but also made himself equal with God, calling God his own *Father.*"

Jesus said to them, "Truly, I assure you, the Son cannot do anything by himself, but only what he sees the Father do. And whatever he does, the Son also does. The Father loves the Son and shows him everything he does; and he will show him even greater things than these, so that you will be amazed.

"As the Father raises the dead and gives them life, so the Son gives life to whom he wills. In the same way, the Father judges no one, for he has entrusted all judgment to the Son, and he wants all to honor the Son, as they honor the Father. Whoever ignores the Son, ignores as well the Father who sent him.

"Truly, I say to you, anyone who hears my word and believes him who sent me, has eternal life; and there is no judgment for him, because he has passed from death to life.

"Truly, the hour is coming and has indeed come, when the dead will hear the voice of the Son of God and, on hearing it, will live. For the Father has life in himself, and he has given to the Son also to have life in himself. And he has empowered him as well to carry out Judgment, for he is Son of Man.

"Do not be surprised at this: the hour is coming when all those lying in tombs will hear my voice and come out; those who have done good shall rise to live, and those who have done evil will rise to be condemned.

"I can do nothing of myself. As I hear, so I judge, and my judgment is just, because I seek not my own will, but the will of him who sent me."

Little boys usually tend to imitate their fathers. Fathers, after all, are the most significant male figures they have in their young lives. The more the father is involved in the rearing of his son, the more will be his influence on the little boy's life. Jesus had a good recollection of His Father in heaven. His Father must have been very much a part of His life. No wonder He mirrors His Father even in His own actions. We need more positive role models of fatherhood in this world to help male children acquire values that will anchor them later in their lives.

Thursday

Ps 106:19–20, 21–22, 23
Remember us, O Lord,
as you favor your people.

03 APRIL

1st Reading: Ex 32:7–14

Gospel: Jn 5:31–47

*J*esus said to the Jews, "If I bore witness to myself, my testimony would be worthless. But Another One is bearing witness to me, and I know that his testimony is true when he bears witness to me. John also bore witness to the truth when you sent messengers to him, but I do not seek such human testimony; I recall this for you, so that you may be saved.

"John was a burning and shining lamp, and for a while you were willing to enjoy his light. But I have greater evidence than that of John—the works which the Father entrusted to me to carry out. The very works I do bear witness: the Father has sent me. Thus he who bears witness to me is the Father who sent me. You have never heard his voice and have never seen his likeness; therefore, as long as you do not believe his messenger, his word is not in you.

"You search in the Scriptures, thinking that in them you will find life; yet Scripture bears witness to me. But you refuse to come to me, that you may live. I am not seeking human praise; but I know that the love of God is not within you, for I have come in my Father's name and you do not accept me. If another comes in his own name, you will accept him. As long as you seek praise from one another, instead of seeking the glory which comes from the only God, how can you believe?

"Do not think that I shall accuse you to the Father. Moses himself, in whom you placed your hope, accuses you. If you believed Moses, you would believe me, for he wrote of me. But if you do not believe what he wrote, how will you believe what I say?"

Our faith in Jesus is guaranteed by a "cloud of witnesses" according to Hebrews 12:1. This, Jesus claimed as much. In today's Gospel He presented His own list of witnesses starting from His Father, as evidenced by the work He did in obedience to the Father, John the Baptist and the Scriptures. These are heavy weight witnesses. The catch is it takes time to appreciate the testimonies that they made. They have to be pondered upon, prayed upon and later be accepted in faith. The good place to start is the Scriptures. There we have the will of the Father regarding what the Messiah will do for His people and the testimonies of John. Perhaps it is high time that we get to re-acquaint ourselves with the Man behind the Book.

04
APRIL

Friday
Ps 34:17–18, 19–20, 21 & 23
The Lord is close to the brokenhearted.

4TH WEEK OF LENT
Psalter: Week 4 / (Violet)

1st Reading: Wis 2:1a, 12–22

Led by mistaken reasons they think, "Life is short and sad and there is no cure for death. It was never heard that anyone came back from the netherworld. Let us set a trap for the righteous, for he annoys us and opposes our way of life; he reproaches us for our breaches of the law and accuses us of being false to our upbringing. He claims knowledge of God and calls himself son of the Lord. He has become a reproach to our way of thinking; even to meet him is burdensome to us. He does not live like others and behaves strangely.

"According to him we have low standards, so he keeps aloof from us as if we were unclean. He emphasizes the happy end of the righteous and boasts of having God as father.

"Let us see the truth of what he says and find out what his end will be. If the righteous is a son of God, God will defend him and deliver him from his adversaries.

"Let us humble and torture him to prove his self-control and test his patience. When we have condemned him to a shameful death, we may test his words."

This is the way they reason, but they are mistaken, blinded by their malice. They do not know the mysteries of God nor do they hope for the reward of a holy life; they do not believe that the blameless will be recompensed.

Gospel: Jn 7:1–2, 10, 25–30

Jesus went around Galilee; he would not go about in Judea, because the Jews wanted to kill him. Now the Jewish feast of the Tents was at hand. But after his brothers had gone to the festival, he also went up, not publicly but in secret.

Some of the people of Jerusalem said, "Is this not the man they want to kill? And here he is speaking freely, and they don't say a word to him? Can it be, that the rulers know that this is really the Christ? Yet we know where this man comes from; but when the Christ appears, no one will know where he comes from." So Jesus announced in a loud voice in the temple court where he was teaching, "You say that you know me and know where I come from! I have not come of myself; I was sent by the One who is true, and you don't know him. I know him, for I come from him, and he sent me."

They would have arrested him, but no one laid hands on him be cause his time had not yet come.

Now, Jesus' movement gets harder and harder. Those opposed to Him are already pooling resources to constrict His activities. He has to skip some places and go in secret to destinations He wants to be. He needs to do His task of proclaiming the Good News no matter the consequences. Therefore, Jesus had to clarify to people doubting Him on the basis that the provenance of the Messiah is supposed to be unknown yet they know where He comes from. He has to tell them that He comes from the Father whom He alone knows very well. It was galling to those who believed that they are God's chosen people. So another reason is added why they have to silence Jesus. His truth is too brutal to their ears.

Saturday

Ps 7:2–3, 9bc–10, 11–12
O Lord, my God,
in you I take refuge.

05
APRIL

1st Reading: Jer 11:18–20

Yahweh made it known to me and so I know! And you let me see their scheming: "Take care, even your kinsfolk and your own family are false with you, and behind your back they freely criticize you. Do not trust them when they approach you in a friendly way."

But I was like a gentle lamb led to the slaughter. I did not know it was against me that they were plotting, "Let us feed him with trials and remove him from the land of the living and let his name never be mentioned again."

Yahweh, God of Hosts, you who judge with justice and know everyone's heart and intentions, let me see your vengeance on them, for to you I have entrusted my cause.

Gospel: Jn 7:40–53

Many who had been listening to these words began to say, "This is the Prophet." Others said, "This is the Christ." But some wondered, "Would the Christ come from Galilee? Doesn't Scripture say that the Christ is a descendant of David and from Bethlehem, the city of David?" The crowd was divided over him. Some wanted to arrest him, but no one laid hands on him.

The officers of the temple went back to the chief priests, who asked them, "Why didn't you bring him?" The officers answered, "No one ever spoke like this man." The Pharisees then said, "So you, too, have been led astray! Have any of the rulers or any of the Pharisees believed in him? Only these cursed people, who have no knowledge of the law!"

Yet one of them, Nicodemus, who had gone to Jesus earlier, spoke out, "Does our law condemn people without first hearing them and knowing the facts?" They replied, "Do you, too, come from Galilee? Look it up and see for yourself that no prophet is to come from Galilee."

And they all went home.

The people are now divided, for or against Jesus. They could not simply make up their mind how to understand Him. Is He a Prophet or the Christ? In addition, if He is the Christ, should it not be that His place of origin is supposed to be unknown? On the other hand, isn't it that the Messiah should come from the line of David and from Bethlehem? Questions upon questions arise regarding who Jesus is. And above this commotion lords over the haughty dismissal of the religious authorities of that time. Those who follow Jesus are ignorant of the Law. The situation is tense. It will be a matter of time before things will get out of hand.

06
APRIL

Sunday

Ps 130:1-2, 3-4, 5-6, 7-8
With the Lord there is mercy
and fullness of redemption.

1st Reading: Ezk 37:12–14

So prophesy! Say to them: This is what Yahweh says: I am going to open your tombs; I shall bring you out of your tombs, my people; and lead you back to the land of Israel. You will know that I am Yahweh, O my people! when I open your graves and bring you out of your graves; when I put my spirit in you, and you live. I shall settle you in your land; and you will know that I, Yahweh, have done what I said I would do."

2nd Reading: Rom 8:8–11

Brothers and sisters: Those walking according to the flesh cannot please God.

Yet your existence is not in the flesh, but in the spirit, because the Spirit of God is within you. If you did not have the Spirit of Christ, you would not belong to him. But Christ is within you; though the body is branded by death as a consequence of sin, the spirit is life and holiness. And if the Spirit of Him who raised Jesus from the dead is within you, He who raised Jesus Christ from among the dead will also give life to your mortal bodies. Yes, he will do it through his Spirit who dwells within you.

Gospel: Jn 11:3–7, 17, 20–27, 33–45 (or Jn 11:1-45)

Martha and Mary sent this message to Jesus, "Lord, the one you love is sick." On hearing this, Jesus said, "This illness will not end in death; rather it is for God's glory, and the Son of God will be glorified through it."

It is a fact that Jesus loved Martha and her sister and Lazarus; yet, after he heard of the illness of Lazarus, he stayed two days longer in the place where he was. Only then did he say to his disciples, "Let us go into Judea again."

When Jesus came, he found that Lazarus had been in the tomb for four days.

When Martha heard that Jesus was coming, she went to meet him, while Mary remained sitting in the house. Martha said to Jesus, "If you had been here, my brother would not have died. But I know that whatever you ask from God, God will give you." Jesus said, "Your brother will rise again."

Martha replied, "I know that he will rise in the resurrection, at the last day." But Jesus said to her, "I am the resurrection. Whoever believes in me, though he die, shall live. Whoever lives and believes in me will never die. Do you believe this?"

Martha then answered, "Yes, Lord, I have come to believe that you are the Christ, the Son of God, he who is coming into the world."

When Jesus saw her weeping, and the Jews also weeping, who had come with her, he was moved to the depths of his spirit and troubled. Then he asked, "Where have you laid him?" They answered, "Lord, come and see." Jesus wept. The Jews said, "See how he loved him!" But some of them said, "If he could open the eyes of the blind man, could he not have kept this man from dying?"

Jesus, again deeply moved, drew near to the tomb. It was a cave with a stone laid across the entrance. Jesus said, "Take the stone away." Martha said to him, "Lord, by now he will smell, for this is the fourth day." Jesus replied, "Have I not told you that, if you believe, you will see the glory of God?" So they removed the stone.

Jesus raised his eyes and said, "Father, I thank you, for you have heard me. I knew that you hear me always; but my prayer was for the sake of these people, that they may believe that you sent me." When Jesus had said this, he cried out in a loud voice, "Lazarus, come out!"

The dead man came out, his hands and feet bound with linen strips, and his face wrapped in a cloth. Jesus said to them, "Untie him, and let him go."

Many of the Jews who had come with Mary believed in Jesus when they saw what he did.

Reading: Martha sent news to Jesus that Lazarus His best friend was sick. He tarried two days more before going to see him and found him buried. This was the occasion where Jesus showed His being Lord of the living and the dead. The tragedy of Lazarus became a demonstration of Jesus' power over life and death.

open display of emotion affirms the full humanity of Jesus at its best. But He is not only human, He is also fully divine. He called out to Lazarus to leave the place of death and come back to the living. And thus the human plane of sadness and death was transformed into the divine plane of joy and life since Jesus was around.

Reflection: The death of a loved one could be a devastating experience. The sense of loss is simply hard to bear alone. But thanks to the community around who condole and mourn with those left behind for they facilitate the grieving and moving forward and provide the necessary support to ease the burden. Jesus Himself felt this sense of loss many times over. He even wept for some of them such as this death of Lazarus, His friend. This

Response: Knowing that death brings the pain of loss and separation, it might be a good idea to console those who grieve, not only those who have lost someone in this life but more so those who have experienced dying and death in forms other than physical death. Today let us affirm our belief in life and share that enthusiasm especially to those who experience its lack.

Happy are those who do not see but Believe

Monday

Ps 23:1–3a, 3b–4, 5, 6
Even though I walk in the dark valley
I fear no evil; for you are at my side.

5TH WEEK OF LENT
Psalter: Week 1 / (Violet)

1st Reading: Dn 13:1–9, 15–17, 19–30, 33–62* (or 13:14c–62)

There lived in Babylon a man named Joakim, who was married to a very beautiful, God-fearing woman, Susanna, Hilkiah's daughter, whose pious parents had trained her in the law of Moses. (…) After the people had left at noon, Susanna would go into her husband's garden for a walk. The two old men began to lust for her as they watched her enter the garden every day. (…) Susanna entered the garden, as usual, with only two maids. She decided to bathe, for it was a hot day. (…) She said to the maids, "Bring me oil and ointments, and shut the garden doors while I bathe." When the maids had left, the two elders hurried to her and said, "Look, the garden doors are shut and no one sees us. We desire to possess you. If you refuse to give in, we will testify that you sent your maids away, for there was a young man here with you. (…)

Susanna was condemend to death. She cried aloud, "Eternal God, nothing is hidden from you; you know all things before they come to be. You know that these men have testified falsely against me. Would you let me die, though I am not guilty of all their malicious charges?" The Lord heard her.(…) The whole assembly shouted and blessed God, for helping those who hope in him. They turned against the two elders who, through Daniel's efforts, had been convicted by their own mouths (…)

Gospel: Jn 8:1–11

Jesus went to the Mount of Olives. At daybreak Jesus appeared in the temple again. All the people came to him, and he sat down and began to teach them. Then the teachers of the law and the Pharisees brought in a woman who had been caught in the act of adultery. They made her stand in front of everyone. "Master," they said, "this woman has been caught in the act of adultery. Now the law of Moses orders that such women be stoned to death; but you, what do you say?" They said this to test Jesus, in order to have some charge against him. Jesus bent down and started writing on the ground with his finger. And as they continued to ask him, he straightened up and said to them, "Let anyone among you who has no sin be the first to throw a stone at her." And he bent down, again, writing on the ground. As a result of these words, they went away, one by one, starting with the elders, and Jesus was left alone, with the woman standing before him. Then Jesus stood up and said to her, "Woman, where are they? Has no one condemned you?" She replied, "No one." And Jesus said, "Neither do I condemn you; go away and don't sin again."

We are sometimes quick to condemn, driven by what we thought as righteous anger but in the end simply coming out of our pettiness. After all, we have in one way or another participated in sins we so strongly condemn in others. It is as if by projecting this sin as horrible and warranting punishment on others, we wash ourselves clean. But Jesus comes to uncover what is hidden in the deepest recesses of our hearts. The people who brought the adulterous woman for condemnation to Jesus were also fallible, weak sinners like her. They have to be reminded of this so that they would be merciful and understanding of others who have strayed and have given in to momentary weakness. That day, it was not only the sinful woman who was rescued but some of the people who recovered their humanity because of Jesus.

Tuesday

Ps 102:2-3, 16-18, 19-21
O Lord, hear my prayer,
and let my cry come to you.

08 APRIL

1st Reading: Num 21:4-9

From Mount Hor the Israelites set out by the Red Sea road to go around the land of Edom. The people were discouraged by the journey and began to complain against God and Moses, "Why have you brought us out of Egypt to die in the wilderness? There is neither bread nor water here and we are disgusted with this tasteless manna."

Yahweh then sent fiery serpents against them. They bit the people and many of the Israelites died. Then the people came to Moses and said, "We have sinned, speaking against Yahweh and against you. Plead with Yahweh to take the serpents away."

Moses pleaded for the people and Yahweh said to him, "Make a fiery serpent and set it on a standard; whoever has been bitten and then looks at it shall live."

So Moses made a bronze serpent and set it on a standard. Whenever a man was bitten, he looked towards the bronze serpent and he lived.

Gospel: Jn 8:21-30

Jesus said to the Pharisees, "I am going away, and though you look for me, you will die in your sin. Where I am going you cannot come." The Jews wondered, "Why does he say that we can't come where he is going? Will he kill himself?"

But Jesus said, "You are from below and I am from above; you are of this world and I am not of this world. That is why I told you that you will die in your sins. And you shall die in your sins, unless you believe that I am He."

They asked him, "Who are you?"; and Jesus said, "Just what I have told you from the beginning. I have much to say about you and much to condemn; but the One who sent me is truthful and everything I learned from him, I proclaim to the world."

They didn't understand that Jesus was speaking to them about the Father. So Jesus said, "When you have lifted up the Son of Man, then you will know that I am He and that I do nothing of myself, but I say just what the Father taught me. He who sent me is with me and has not left me alone; because I always do what pleases him."

As Jesus spoke like this, many believed in him.

Misunderstanding upon misunderstanding pile up between Jesus and the religious authorities of that time. The communication breakdown between them is such that it will inevitably lead to hostility and violence. But why can't they meet halfway? After all, both are concerned about the right way of following God. The differences they have are not that big as to represent an insurmountable obstacle to overcome. Then pride gets in the way. The Pharisees loathe to be told that their way of righteousness has erred and is now a stumbling block to the simple and poor people who do not have the luxury and privileges they enjoy. The affairs of the spirit have become inaccessible to most. Jesus whose heart is firmly set on the vast majority who are the little ones of the Gospel, placed Himself on collision course with these spiritual elites. Terrible consequences will arise from this choice.

09
APRIL

Wednesday
Dn 3:52, 53, 54, 55, 56
Glory and praise for ever!

5TH WEEK OF LENT
Psalter: Week 1 / (Violet)

1st Reading: Dn 3:14–20, 91–92, 95

Gospel: Jn 8:31–42

Jesus went on to say to the Jews who believed in him, "You will be my true disciples, if you keep my word. Then you will know the truth, and the truth will set you free." They answered him, "We are the descendants of Abraham and have never been slaves of anyone. What do you mean by saying: You will be free?"

Jesus answered them, "Truly, I say to you, whoever commits sin is a slave. But the slave doesn't stay in the house forever; the son stays forever. So, if the Son makes you free, you will be really free.

"I know that you are the descendants of Abraham; yet you want to kill me because my word finds no place in you. For my part, I speak of what I have seen in my Father's presence, but you do what you have learned from your father."

They answered him, "Our father is Abraham." Then Jesus said, "If you were Abraham's children, you would do as Abraham did. But now you want to kill me, the one who tells you the truth—the truth that I have learned from God. That is not what Abraham did; what you are doing are the works of your father."

The Jews said to him, "We are not illegitimate children; we have one Father, God." Jesus replied, "If God were your Father you would love me, for I came forth from God, and I am here. And I didn't come by my own decision, but it was he himself who sent me."

The conversation Jesus has with His new followers sought to clarify their questions and put to rest their doubts and suspicions. After all, a lifetime of tradition, customs and beliefs are being rewritten by Jesus' preaching. To say goodbye to those that had shaped their lives and faith is not an easy task. And so Jesus has to assure them of what they will get in return. They will get to know their real Father through Him. This will be a slow, frustrating sometimes hopeless endeavour. Some of His hearers were so set in their ways that no amount of persuasion could make them embrace the teachings of Jesus Christ. But Jesus will continue anyway. This is why He was sent by the Father: to preach the Good News in and out of season.

Thursday

Ps 105:4-5, 6-7, 8-9
The Lord remembers
his covenant for ever.

10
APRIL

1st Reading: Gen 17:3-9

Abram fell face down and God said to him, "This is my Covenant with you: you will be the father of a multitude of nations. No longer will you be called Abram, but Abraham, because I will make you the father of a multitude of nations. I will make you more and more famous; I will multiply your descendants; nations shall spring from you, kings shall be among your descendants. And I will establish a covenant, an everlasting Covenant between myself and you and your descendants after you; from now on I will be your God and the God of your descendants after you, for generations to come. I will give to you and your descendants after you the land you are living in, all the land of Canaan, as an everlasting possession and I will be the God of your race."

God said to Abraham, "For your part, you shall keep my covenant, you and your descendants after you, generation after generation."

Gospel: Jn 8:51-59

Jesus said to the Jews, "Truly, I say to you, if anyone keeps my word, he will never experience death." The Jews replied, "Now we know that you have a demon. Abraham died and the prophets as well, but you say, 'Whoever keeps my word will never experience death.' Who do you claim to be? Do you claim to be greater than our father Abraham, who died? And the prophets who also died?"

Then Jesus said, "If I were to praise myself, it would count for nothing. But he who gives glory to me is the Father, the very one you claim as your God, although you don't know him. I know him, and if I were to say that I don't know him, I would be a liar like you. But I know him and I keep his word. As for Abraham, your ancestor, he looked forward to the day when I would come; and he rejoiced when he saw it." The Jews then said to him, "You are not yet fifty years old and you have seen Abraham?" And Jesus said, "Truly, I say to you, before Abraham was, I am." They then picked up stones to throw at him, but Jesus hid himself and left the temple.

The conversion that Jesus worked hard for His hearers came to nothing. They were not ready to give up the familiar, comfortable and reassuring brand of faith that they have received. They would not embrace anything that unsettles them. And so the discussion and debate becomes heated. A harsh word here and some strong replies there led inevitably to animosity and discord. This culminated in the people picking up stones to throw at Jesus. There is now no use talking to one another for the lines have been drawn. From now on, Jesus will have to contend not only with their unbelief. He will also have to face their hatred.

11
APRIL

Friday

Ps 18:2–3a, 3bc–4, 5–6, 7
In my distress I called upon the
Lord, and he heard my voice.

5TH WEEK OF LENT
Psalter: Week 1 / (Violet)

1st Reading: Jer 20:10–13

I hear many people whispering, "Terror is all around!

Denounce him! Yes, denounce him!"

All my friends watch me to see if I will slip: "Perhaps he can be deceived," they say; "then we can get the better of him and have our revenge."

But Yahweh, a mighty warrior, is with me.

My persecutors will stumble and not prevail; that failure will be their shame and their disgrace will never be forgotten.

Yahweh, God of Hosts, you test the just and probe the heart and mind.

Let me see your revenge on them, for to you I have entrusted my cause.

Sing to Yahweh! Praise Yahweh and say: he has rescued the poor from the clutches of the wicked!

Gospel: Jn 10:31–42

The Jews then picked up stones to throw at him; so Jesus said, "I have openly done many good works among you, which the Father gave me to do. For which of these do you stone me?"

The Jews answered, "We are not stoning you for doing a good work, but for insulting God; you are only a man, and you make yourself God."

Then Jesus replied, "Is this not written in your law: I said, you are gods? So those who received this word of God were called gods, and the Scripture is always true. What then should be said of the one anointed, and sent into the world, by the Father? Am I insulting God when I say, 'I am the Son of God'?

"If I am not doing the works of my Father, do not believe me. But if I do them, even if you have no faith in me, believe because of the works I do; and know that the Father is in me, and I in the Father."

Again they tried to arrest him, but Jesus escaped from their hands. He went away again to the other side of the Jordan, to the place where John had baptized, and there he stayed.

Many people came to Jesus, and said, "John worked no miracles, but he spoke about you, and everything he said was true." And many in that place became believers.

As a continuation of the theme of conflict between Jesus and His hearers, this reading fits into the picture. Yesterday, the Gospel ends with the people wanting to stone Jesus who hid Himself and left the Temple. Now we still have the strands of people picking stones to throw at Jesus, but this time, Jesus faces them and asks the reason for their violent behaviour. As if Jesus does not give up easily on people. Even if the going gets rough and emotions get in the way, Jesus will not simply walk away. But then His audience have enough already. When He avoids their stones, they want to arrest Him. So Jesus has to leave. No matter how much He tries, there are some things that cannot be.

Saturday

Jer 31:10, 11–12abcd, 13
The Lord will guard us.
as a shepherd guards his flock.

12
APRIL

1st Reading: Ezk 37:21–28

Gospel: Jn 11:45–56

*M*any of the Jews who had come with Mary believed in Jesus when they saw what he did; but some went to the Pharisees and told them what Jesus had done. So the chief priests and the Pharisees called together the Council.

They said, "What are we to do? For this man keeps on performing many miraculous signs. If we let him go on like this, all the people will believe in him and, as a result of this, the Romans will come and destroy our Holy Place and our nation."

Then one of them, Caiaphas, who was High Priest that year, spoke up, "You know nothing at all! It is better to have one man die for the people than to let the whole nation be destroyed."

In saying this Caiaphas did not speak for himself, but being High Priest that year, he foretold like a prophet that Jesus would die for the nation, and not for the nation only, but also would die in order to gather into one the scattered children of God. So, from that day on, they were determined to kill him.

Because of this, Jesus no longer moved about freely among the Jews. He withdrew instead to the country near the wilderness, and stayed with his disciples in a town called Ephraim.

The Passover of the Jews was at hand, and people from everywhere were coming to Jerusalem to purify themselves before the Passover. They looked for Jesus and, as they stood in the temple, they talked with one another, "What do you think? Will he come to the festival?"

And now, the enmity between Jesus and some of the Jews, especially the religious and political leaders, has reached its climax. They cannot tolerate Him further. He has to go. And so a principle has been drawn to legitimize their act of violence towards one man. He must be sacrificed for the greater good. This thought must have comforted them somehow. They have cast their actions into something even patriotic, for the preservation of order and the survival of the nation. Funny how sometimes we too legitimize our patently bad actions by couching them with some good intent. We try to do mind games with our conscience. No matter what people do to justify themselves, sins committed will always be sins before us.

13
APRIL

Sunday

Ps 22:8-9, 17-18, 19-20, 23-24
My God, my God,
why have you abandoned me?

1st Reading: Is 50:4–7

2nd Reading: Phil 2:6–11

Gospel: Mt 27: 11-54 (or Mt 26:14—27:66)

Jesus stood before the governor. Pilate asked him, "Are you the king of the Jews?" Jesus answered, "You say so."

The chief priests and the elders of the people accused him, but he made no answer. Pilate said to him, "Do you hear all the charges they bring against you?" But he did not answer even one question, so that the governor wondered greatly. At Passover, it was customary for the governor to release any prisoner the people asked for. Now, there was a well-known prisoner called Barabbas. When the people had gathered, Pilate asked them, "Whom do you want me to set free: Barabbas, or Jesus called the Messiah?" for he knew that Jesus had been handed over to him out of envy.

While Pilate was sitting in court, his wife sent him this message, "Have nothing to do with that holy man. Because of him, I had a dream last night that disturbed me greatly." But the chief priests and the elders of the people stirred up the crowds, to ask for the release of Barabbas and the death of Jesus. When the governor asked them again, "Which of the two do you want me to set free?" they answered, "Barabbas!" Pilate said to them, "And what shall I do with Jesus called the Messiah?" All answered, "Crucify him!" Pilate asked, "Why? What evil has he done?" But they shouted louder, "Crucify him!"

Pilate saw that he was getting nowhere, and that there could be a riot. He asked for water, washed his hands before the people, and said, "I am innocent of this man's blood. Do what you want!" And all the people answered, "His blood be on us and on our children!" Then Pilate set Barabbas free, but had Jesus scourged, and handed over to be crucified. The Roman soldiers took Jesus into the palace of the governor and the whole troop gathered around him. They stripped him and dressed him in a purple cloak. Then, weaving a crown of thorns, they forced it onto his head, and placed a reed in his right hand. They knelt before Jesus and mocked him, saying, "Hail, king of the Jews!" They spat on him, took the reed from his hand and struck him on the head with it. When they had finished mocking him, they pulled off the purple cloak and dressed him in his own clothes, and led him out to be crucified. On the way they met a man from Cyrene called Simon, and forced him to carry the cross of Jesus. When they reached the place called Golgotha, which means the Skull, they offered him wine mixed with gall. He tasted it but would not drink it. There they crucified him, and divided his clothes among themselves, casting lots to decide what each one should take. Then they sat down to guard him. The statement of his offense was displayed above his head, and it read, "This is Jesus, the King of the Jews." They also crucified two thieves with him, one on his right hand and one on his left.

The people passing by shook their heads and insulted him, saying, "Aha! You, who destroy the temple and in three days rebuild it, save yourself—if you are God's Son—and come down from the cross!"

In the same way the chief priests, the elders and the teachers of the law mocked him. They said, "The man who saved others cannot save himself. Let the king of Israel come down from his cross and we will believe in him. He trusted in God; let God rescue him if God wants to, for he himself said, 'I am the Son of God.'" Even the thieves who were crucified with him insulted him.

From midday, darkness fell over all the land until mid-afternoon. At about three o'clock, Jesus cried out in a loud voice, "Eloi, Eloi, lamma sabbacthani?" which means: My God, my God, why have you forsaken me? As soon as they heard this, some of the bystanders said, "He is calling for Elijah." And one of them ran, took a sponge and soaked it in vinegar and, putting it on a reed, gave it to him to drink. Others said, "Leave him alone, let us see whether Elijah will come to save him."

Then Jesus cried out again in a loud voice and gave up his spirit. At that very moment, the curtain of the temple Sanctuary was torn in two from top to bottom, the earth quaked, rocks were split, tombs were opened, and many holy people who had died were raised to life. They came out of the tombs after the Resurrection of Jesus, entered the Holy City, and appeared to many.

The captain and the soldiers who were guarding Jesus, having seen the earthquake and everything else that had happened, were terribly afraid, and said, "Truly, this was God's Son."

Reading: Jesus was brought before the civil authority of Jerusalem, Pilate, governor of Jerusalem. Despite his effort to free Jesus whom he sees as clearly innocent of the charge, he finally relented due to the pressures exerted by the religious authorities, and had Jesus crucified. His death may have been that of a criminal but it revealed His true identity to the captain supervising His crucifixion.

Reflection: The Palm Sunday celebration is a liturgy of paradox and contrast. In the first part we celebrate the triumphant entry of Jesus to Jerusalem, while the Gospel reading in the second part talks about His passion and death. This probably reminds us of the paradoxical nature of our existence too. We are joyful as redeemed sons and daughters of God, but we experience the passion of our sinfulness which sometimes leads us to an experience of death and the loss of meaning of our existence. Today's celebration may well remind us that triumph and defeat, joy and sadness, life and death are two concepts that are inseparable. One has little or hollow meaning without the other serving as a contrasting principle. But Jesus Christ who bursts open everything that He touches has enriched our understanding of these dual concepts. He added a third: there is new life after death; not the same life that one had prior to dying but a renewed and transformed life afterwards.

Response: The passion of the Lord points to His passion for humanity. It might be a good day for us to reflect what we have done on behalf of humanity. There are various ways we can do to make the world a better place to live. Why don't we start by scaling down our wants. Let us make an inventory of what we truly need in order to live meaningfully and start giving to those with nothing, that which are excesses of our legitimate needs.

14
APRIL

Monday

Ps 27:1, 2, 3, 13–14
The Lord is my light
and my salvation.

MONDAY OF HOLY WEEK
Psalter: Week 2 / (Violet)

1st Reading: Is 42:1–7

*H*ere is my servant whom I uphold, my chosen one in whom I delight. I have put my spirit upon him, and he will bring justice to the nations.

He does not shout or raise his voice. Proclamations are not heard in the streets. A broken reed he will not crush, nor will he snuff out the light of the wavering wick.

He will make justice appear in truth. He will not waver or be broken until he has established justice on earth; the islands are waiting for his law.

Thus says God, Yahweh, who created the heavens and stretched them out, who spread the earth and all that comes from it, who gives life and breath to those who walk on it: I, Yahweh, have called you for the sake of justice; I will hold your hand to make you firm; I will make you as a Covenant to the people, and as a light to the nations, to open eyes that do not see, to free captives from prison, to bring out to light those who sit in darkness.

Gospel: Jn 12:1–11

*S*ix days before the Passover, Jesus came to Bethany, where he had raised Lazarus, the dead man, to life. Now they gave a dinner for him, and while Martha waited on them, Lazarus sat at the table with Jesus.

Then Mary took a pound of costly perfume, made from genuine spikenard, and anointed the feet of Jesus, wiping them with her hair. And the whole house was filled with the fragrance of the perfume.

Judas Iscariot—the disciple who was to betray Jesus—remarked, "This perfume could have been sold for three hundred silver coins, and the money given to the poor." Judas, indeed, had no concern for the poor; he was a thief, and as he held the common purse, he used to help himself to the funds.

But Jesus spoke up, "Leave her alone. Was she not keeping it for the day of my burial? (The poor you always have with you, but you will not always have me.)" Many Jews heard that Jesus was there and they came, not only because of Jesus, but also to see Lazarus whom he had raised from the dead. So the chief priests thought about killing Lazarus as well, for many of the Jews were drifting away because of him, and believing in Jesus.

The High Priest who articulated the dogma of one man sacrificed for the good of many now has to contend with another, Lazarus. For it was because of him that Jews now come in droves to Jesus, driven by curiosity or genuine desire to know the truth that the teachings of the religious leaders have obscured. The people now have sensed hope. Lazarus will be one of the collateral damages in their quest to silence Jesus and His teachings. But they could not do it by themselves. Someone from the party of Jesus must collaborate with them. And here in our Gospel, Judas Iscariot who betrayed Jesus was introduced with a motive to do so. He was weak in front of money. Not even the sweet perfume of Mary's loving service to Jesus would melt his heart already led astray by Mammon.

Tuesday

Ps 71:1-2, 3-4a,
5ab-6ab, 15 & 17
I will sing of your salvation.

15
APRIL

1st Reading: Is 49:1-6

Gospel: Jn 13:21-33, 36-38

Jesus was distressed in spirit, and said plainly, "Truly, one of you will betray me." The disciples then looked at one another, wondering whom he meant. One of the disciples, the one Jesus loved, was reclining near Jesus; so Simon Peter signalled him to ask Jesus whom he meant. And the disciple, who was reclining near Jesus, asked him, "Lord, who is it?" Jesus answered, "I shall dip a piece of bread in the dish, and he to whom I give it, is the one." So Jesus dipped the bread in the dish and gave it to Judas Iscariot, the son of Simon. As Judas took the piece of bread, Satan entered into him. Jesus then said to him, "What you are going to do, do quickly." None of the others, reclining at the table, understood why Jesus had said this to Judas. As Judas had the common purse, they may have thought that Jesus was telling him, "Buy what we need for the feast," or, "Give something to the poor." Judas left as soon as he had eaten the bread. It was night.

When Judas had gone out, Jesus said, "Now is the Son of Man glorified, and God is glorified in him. God will glorify him, and he will glorify him very soon. My children, I am with you for only a little while; you will look for me, but as I already told the Jews, now I tell you: where I am going you cannot come."

Simon Peter said to him, "Lord, where are you going?" Jesus answered, "Where I am going you cannot follow me now, but afterward you will." Peter said, "Lord, why can't I follow you now? I am ready to give my life for you." "To give your life for me?" Jesus asked Peter. "Truly I tell you, the cock will not crow, before you have denied me three times."

Yesterday's Gospel speaks of Judas Iscariot as being too concerned with money. He used to help himself from the common purse since it was entrusted to him. Now he will push his robbery further by planning to betray Jesus to the High Priest and his Council in exchange for a fee. We can only guess what happened to Judas along the way. He was called by Jesus to be His disciple and was treated as a friend and brother. Yet he strayed. Not even the love of his Master was enough to set his heart right. He chose the lesser portion, and with him, all those who choose money and its derivatives above righteousness. They place their confidence on things that they can never bring when they die to console them in the next life.

16
APRIL

Wednesday
Ps 69:8–10, 21–22, 31 & 33–34
Lord, in your great love,
answer me.

WEDNESDAY OF HOLY WEEK
Psalter: Week 2 / (Violet)

1st Reading: Is 50:4–9a

The Lord Yahweh has taught me so I speak as his disciple and I know how to sustain the weary. Morning after morning he wakes me up to hear, to listen like a disciple.

The Lord Yahweh has opened my ear.

I have not rebelled, nor have I withdrawn.

I offered my back to those who strike me, my cheeks to those who pulled my beard; neither did I shield my face from blows, spittle and disgrace.

I have not despaired, for the Lord Yahweh comes to my help. So, like a flint I set my face, knowing that I will not be disgraced.

He who avenges me is near. Who then will accuse me? Let us confront each other. Who is now my accuser? Let him approach. If the Lord Yahweh is my help, who will condemn me?

Gospel: Mt 26:14–25

One of the Twelve, who was called Judas Iscariot, went to the chief priests and said, "How much will you give me if I hand him over to you?" They promised to give me thirty pieces of silver; and from then on, he kept looking for the best way to hand Jesus over to them.

On the first day of the Festival of Unleavened Bread, the disciples came to Jesus and said to him, "Where do you want us to prepare the Passover meal for you?" Jesus answered, "Go into the city, to the house of a certain man, and tell him, 'The Master says: My hour is near, and I will celebrate the Passover with my disciples in your house.'"

The disciples did as Jesus had ordered, and prepared the Passover meal. When it was evening, Jesus sat at table with the Twelve. While they were eating, Jesus said, "Truly I say to you: one of you will betray me." They were deeply distressed, and they asked him, one after the other, "You do not mean me, do you, Lord?"

He answered, "The one who dips his bread with me will betray me. The Son of Man is going as the Scriptures say he will. But alas for that one who betrays the Son of Man: better for him not to have been born." Judas, the one who would betray him, also asked, "You do not mean me, Master, do you?" Jesus replied, "You have said it."

Matthew provides us with more details on the circumstances of Judas' betrayal of Jesus than John's Gospel yesterday. For instance he provides us with information on how much the agreed price was between him and the chief priests upon his handing over of Jesus to them. It was thirty pieces of silver which according to Exodus 21:32 was the ransom price of a servant. This is how much the chief priests looked at Jesus. Insulting as it might have been, Jesus in the real sense of the word is a servant. First, to the will of the Father and second, He came to serve and not to be served. Paradoxically, the betrayal of Judas and the pittance the chief priests were willing to pay for Jesus' arrest highlighted His mission as the Servant of God and humanity.

HOLY THURSDAY
Psalter: Proper / (White)

Thursday

Ps 116:12-13, 15-16bc, 17-18
Our blessing cup is a communion
with the Blood of Christ

17
APRIL

Chrism Mass:
1st **Reading: Is 61:1-3a, 6a, 8b-9**
Ps 89: 21-22, 25 & 27
For ever I will sing the goodness of the Lord.
2nd **Reading: Rev 1:5-8**
Gospel: Lk 14:16–21

Evening Mass of the Lord's Supper:
1st **Reading: Ex 12:1-8,11-14**
2nd **Reading: 1Cor 11:23-26**
Gospel: Jn 13:1-15

*I*t was before the feast of the Passover. Jesus realized that his hour had come to pass from this world to the Father; and as he had loved those who were his own in the world, he would love them with perfect love.

They were at supper, and the devil had already put into the mind of Judas, son of Simon Iscariot, to betray him. Jesus knew that the Father had entrusted all things to him, and as he had come from God, he was going to God. So he got up from the table, removed his garment, and taking a towel, wrapped it around his waist. Then he poured water into a basin, and began to wash the disciples' feet, and to wipe them with the towel he was wearing.

When he came to Simon Peter, Simon asked him, "Why, Lord, do you want to wash my feet?" Jesus said, "What I am doing you cannot understand now, but afterward you will understand it." Peter replied, "You shall never wash my feet!"

Jesus answered him, "If I do not wash you, you can have no part with me." Then Simon Peter said, "Lord, wash not only my feet, but also my hands and my head!"

Jesus replied, "Whoever has taken a bath does not need to wash (except the feet), for he is clean all over. You are clean, though not all of you." Jesus knew who was to betray him; because of this he said, "Not all of you are clean."

When Jesus had finished washing their feet, he put on his garment again, went back to the table, and said to them, "Do you understand what I have done to you? You call me Master and Lord, and you are right, for so I am. If I, then, your Lord and Master, have washed your feet, you also must wash one another's feet. I have given you an example, that as I have done, you also may do."

This is a moving scene between the Master and His disciples. On the eve of His Passion, Jesus shared a fellowship meal with His own. He also left them with a memory of humble service. The Teacher, for the last time, taught His followers by example. Washing the feet is a menial job reserved for servants. Yet, here is the person whom they all esteemed stooping low to wash their feet. This was too much for Peter. He dreamed of a glorious, triumphant future with his Master. Not a future of humble service and renunciation of the self. He tried to escape it but to no avail. From then on, Peter had to contend with the fact that his greatness would be measured in terms of how much he served and gave himself for others. The Last Supper would also be the last of his ambition to power according to the ways of the world.

18
APRIL

𝓕riday

Ps 31:2, 6, 12–13, 15–16, 17, 25
Father, into your hands
I commend my spirit.

**GOOD FRIDAY OF THE
LORD'S PASSION**
Psalter: Proper / (Red)

1ˢᵗ Reading: Is 52:13 – 53:12

2ⁿᵈ Reading: Heb 4:14–16; 5:7–9

*B*rothers and sisters: We have a great high priest, Jesus, the Son of God, who has entered heaven. Let us, then, hold fast to the faith we profess. Our high priest is not indifferent to our weaknesses, for he was tempted, in every way, just as we are, yet, without sinning. Let us, then, with confi dence, approach the throne of grace. We will obtain mercy and, through his favor, help in due time.

Christ, in the days of his mortal life, offered his sacrifi ce with tears and cries. He prayed to him, who could save him from death, and he was heard, because of his humble submission. Although he was Son, he learned, through suffering, what obedience was, and, once made perfect, he became the source of eternal salvation, for those who obey him.

Gospel: John 18:1 – 19:42*

*W*hen Jesus had finished speaking, he went with his disciples to the other side of the Kidron Valley. There was a garden there, which Jesus entered with his disciples.

Now Judas, who betrayed him, knew the place, since Jesus had often met there with his disciples. So Judas took soldiers and some servants from the chief priests and Pharisees, and they went to the garden with lanterns, torches and weapons.

Jesus knew all that was going to happen to him; he stepped forward and asked, "Who are you looking for?" They answered, "Jesus the Nazarene." Jesus said, "I am he." Judas, who betrayed him, stood there with them. When Jesus said, "I am he," they moved backwards and fell to the ground. He then asked a second time, "Who are you looking for?" and they answered, "Jesus the Nazarene." Jesus replied, "I told you that I am he. If you are looking for me, let these others go." So what Jesus had said came true: "I have not lost one of those you gave me."

Simon Peter had a sword; he drew it and struck Malchus, the High Priest's servant, cutting off his right ear. But Jesus said to Peter, "Put your sword into its sheath! Shall I not drink the cup which the Father has given me?" The guards and the soldiers, with their commander, seized Jesus and bound him; and they took him fi rst to Annas. Annas was the father-in-law of Caiaphas, who was the High Priest that year; and it was Caiaphas who had told the Jews, "It is better that one man should die for the people." (...)

The arrest, passion and crucifixion of Jesus are the culmination of the ongoing enmity between Him and some of the religious and political authorities of that time. This hostility will now involve many other people, some with unwilling participation while others would be adroitly manipulated by the chief priests who sense that they now have the upper hand. On one side is the powerful, elite class of the Jewish society of that time together with their minions. On the other side is the small circle of Jesus' companions, the three Marys, prominent among them, His Mother Mary, and the disciple whom He loved. The others scattered like dry leaves thrown in the wind. Their fear is stronger than their love for Jesus. But these four small, insignificant and weak followers stood with firm resolve to be with Jesus till the end. Theirs is the love that fears not even death. Their courage is a testament that no matter how hopeless the situation may be, a remnant will always remain faithful to God till the end.

THE VIGIL IN THE HOLY NIGHT OF EASTER
Psalter: Proper / (White)

Saturday
Ps 118: 1-2, 16-17, 22-23
Alleluia, alleluia, alleluia

19
APRIL

1st **Reading:** Gen 1—2:2 (or 1:1, 26-31a)
2nd **Reading:** Gen 22:1-18 (or 22:1-2, 9a,10-13, 15-18)
3rd **Reading:** Ex 14:15—15:1
4th **Reading:** Is 54:5-14
5th **Reading:** Is 55:1-11
6th **Reading:** Bar 3:9-15, 32—4:4
7th **Reading:** Ezk 36:16-17a, 18-28

Reading: Rom 6:3-11
Gospel: Matthew 28:1-10

After the Sabbath, at dawn on the first day of the week, Mary Magdalene and the other Mary went to visit the tomb. Suddenly there was a violent earthquake: an angel of the Lord descending from heaven, came to the stone, rolled it from the entrance of the tomb, and sat on it. His appearance was like lightning and his garment white as snow. When they saw the angel, the guards were struck with terror.

The angel said to the women, "Do not be afraid, for I know that you are looking for Jesus, who was crucified. He is not here, for he is risen as he said. Come, see the place where they laid him; then go at once and tell his disciples that he is risen from the dead, and is going before you to Galilee. You will see him there. This is my message for you."

In fear, yet with great joy, the women left the tomb and ran to tell the news to his disciples.

Suddenly, Jesus met them on the way and said, "Rejoice!" The women approached him, embraced his feet and worshiped him. But Jesus said to them, "Do not be afraid! Go and tell my brothers to set out for Galilee; there, they will see me."

This Saturday is traditionally called Black Saturday for black stands for mourning and for death. And tonight's celebration will celebrate the passage of the Christian community's journey from the darkness of sin, betrayal and death to the wonderful light of the resurrection, new hope and peace. Mary of Magdala and the other Mary will be the first among the followers of Jesus to see this light returning from darkness. They will carry this light to the other disciples whose feeble and fragile faith like a dying ember will receive a jolt of hope to resurrect anew their faith in their Master whom they abandoned because of fear. This time, the dark memory of their momentary cowardice will be swept away by this marvelous news. A new day will dawn. Easter will come to them early while the world is still wrapped in darkness.

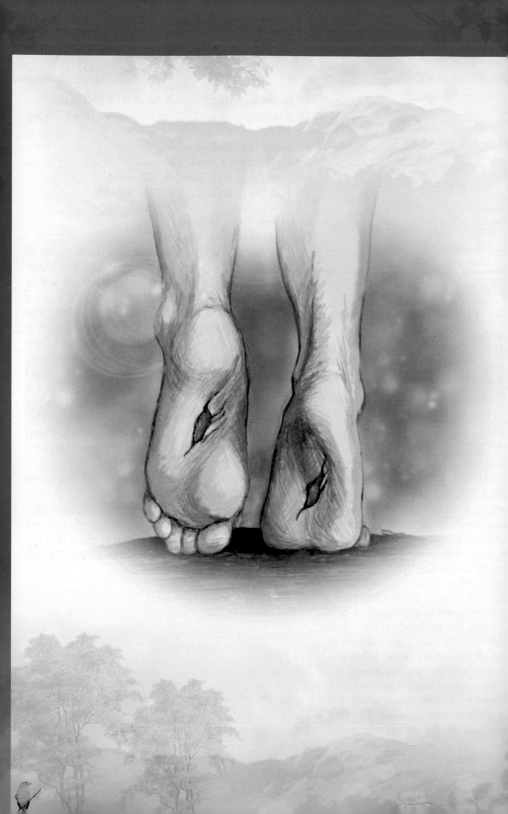

Easter

*T*he Evening Mass of the Lord's Supper on Holy Thursday ushers in the Easter Triduum of Christ's passion and death (Good Friday), burial (Holy Saturday), and resurrection (Easter Sunday). The Easter Triduum is the most solemn celebration in the liturgical year when we commemorate the paschal mystery of Christ in which we participate through baptism and Holy Eucharist. The renewal of baptismal promises on Easter Vigil and in all the Masses on Easter Sunday culminates our Lenten observance. The sprinkling with holy water and the lighted candles in our hands evoke the most significant moment in our lives: our baptism when God claimed us as his sons and daughters.

The joy of the resurrection of Our Lord flows over to the next fifty days of the Easter Season until Pentecost Sunday. The chanting of the Alleluia and the lighted paschal candle keep alive the solemn and memorable celebration of the Easter Vigil. The biblical readings and prefaces remind us that the risen Christ is always present among us and that we can recognize him in the proclaimed word and in the breaking of bread that is the Eucharist.

Two important feasts unfold the other aspects of Christ's resurrection: Ascension and Pentecost. After forty days Christ ascended into heaven bringing up with him the redeemed human race. In a world oppressed by misery the Ascension enlivens our hope that heaven is our final home.

Seated at the right hand of the Father, Jesus Christ sent down the Holy Spirit upon the Church on the day of Pentecost. On this day the Holy Spirit sent forth the Apostles into the whole world to preach the gospel and to baptize. Pentecost is the culmination of Christ's death and resurrection. He ascended into heaven in order to send the Holy Spirit that would continue among us the work of salvation that he had begun. We exist in the era of the Holy Spirit. In some way the sacrament of confirmation is like our own Pentecost; for it is through this sacrament that the Holy Spirit anoints us to go forth and proclaim around us in word and good example the gospel of Christ.

Sunday

Ps 118:1–2, 16–17, 22–23
This is the day the Lord has made;
let us rejoice and be glad.

1st Reading: Acts 10:34a, 37–43

Peter then spoke to the people, "Truly, I realize that God does not show partiality. No doubt you have heard of the event that occurred throughout the whole country of the Jews, beginning from Galilee, after the baptism John preached. You know how God anointed Jesus, the Nazorean with the Holy Spirit, and power. He went about doing good, and healing all who were under the devil's power, because God was with him; we are witnesses of all that he did throughout the country of the Jews, and in Jerusalem itself. Yet, they put him to death, by hanging him on a wooden cross.

But God raised him to life on the third day, and let him manifest himself, not to all the people, but to the witnesses that were chosen beforehand by God—to us, who ate and drank with him after his resurrection from death. And he commanded us to preach to the people, and to bear witness, that he is the one appointed by God, to judge the living and the dead. All the prophets say of him, that everyone who believes in him has forgiveness of sins, through his name."

2nd Reading: Col 3:1–4 (or 1 Cor 5:6b–8)

Brothers and sisters, if you are risen with Christ, seek the things that are above, where Christ is seated at the right hand of God. Set your mind on the things that are above, not on earthly things. For you have died and your life is now hidden with Christ in God. When Christ, who is your life, reveals himself, you also will be revealed with him in glory.

Gospel: Jn 20:1–9
or Lk 24: 13–35
(Evening Masses)

On the first day after the Sabbath, Mary of Magdala came to the tomb early in the morning while it was still dark, and she saw that the stone blocking the tomb had been moved away. She ran to Peter, and the other disciple whom Jesus loved, and she said to them, "They have taken the Lord out of the tomb and we don't know where they have laid him."

Peter then set out with the other disciple to go to the tomb. They ran together, but the other disciple outran Peter and reached the tomb first. He bent down and saw the linen cloths lying flat, but he did not enter.

Then Simon Peter came, following him, and entered the tomb; he, too, saw the linen cloths lying flat. The napkin, which had been around his head, was not lying flat like the other linen cloths, but lay rolled up in its place. Then the other disciple, who had reached the tomb first, also went in; he saw and believed. Scripture clearly said that Jesus must rise from the dead, but they had not yet understood that.

Reading: Under the cover of darkness, Mary of Magdala went to the tomb in order to embalm the body of the Lord but she saw the stone blocking the tomb moved away. Gripped by fear she reported the incident to the apostles, two of whom ran to find out. Peter, who entered first, saw only the empty tomb; the other disciple on the other hand believed.

Reflection: The two disciples almost always take the center stage of this drama of the empty tomb. While Mary of Magdala sometimes stays in the background, it is forgotten that it was she first who courageously went to the tomb in order to dignify the body of the Lord with the proper burial ritual. Probably it's because her silence and unassuming presence make us tend to gloss over her and focus on the more popular disciple whom Jesus loved and Peter who takes charge every time. Her name recall to the readers tends to be nil. But it was she who had the privilege of seeing the Risen Lord first. Her intuition led her to seek Him whom she loved in the confines of the tomb, a place for the dead, but found Him instead very much alive in the garden, the place of life and fecundity. Mary of Magdala is the apostle to the apostles. May she help us relish the joy of the Lord's resurrection that we celebrate today.

Response: In our faith community, we tend to acknowledge only those who are prominent in service or those whose help are widely seen and felt. But how about the "little ones" who labor in the background? Their contribution tends to be drowned by the help extended by the more flamboyant, popular members of our church. Today might be a good day to thank them for services rendered without calling attention to themselves.

_____

_____

_____

_____

_____

_____

_____

_____

_____

_____

_____

21
APRIL

Monday

Ps 16:1–2a & 5, 7–8, 9–10, 11
Keep me safe, O God,
you are my hope.

OCTAVE OF EASTER, MONDAY
Psalter: Proper / (White)

1st Reading: Acts 2:14, 22–33*

Then Peter stood up with the Eleven and, with a loud voice, addressed them, (…) Fellow Israelites, listen to what I am going to tell you about Jesus of Nazareth. God accredited him and through him did powerful deeds and wonders and signs in your midst, as you well know. You delivered him to sinners to be crucified and killed, and, in this way, the purpose of God, from all times, was fulfilled. But God raised him to life and released him from the pain of death; because it was impossible for him to be held in the power of death. David spoke of him when he said: I saw the Lord before me at all times; he is by my side, that I may not be shaken. Therefore, my heart was glad and my tongue rejoiced; my body, too, will live in hope. Because you will not forsake me in the abode of the dead, nor allow your Holy One to experience corruption. You have made known to me the paths of life, and your presence will fill me with joy. (…)

This Messiah is Jesus; and we are all witnesses that God raised him to life. He has been exalted at God's right side; and the Father has entrusted the Holy Spirit to him; this Spirit, he has just poured upon us, as you now see and hear.

Gospel: Mt 28:8–15

In fear, yet with great joy, the women left the tomb and ran to tell the news to his disciples. Suddenly, Jesus met them on the way and said, "Rejoice!" The women approached him, embraced his feet and worshiped him. But Jesus said to them, "Do not be afraid! Go and tell my brothers to set out for Galilee; there, they will see me."

As the women proceeded on their way, some of the guards went into the city, and reported to the chief priests all that had happened. The chief priests met with the elders, and decided to give the soldiers a large sum of money, with this order, "Say that his disciples came by night while you were asleep, and stole the body of Jesus. If Pilate comes to know of this, we will explain the situation and keep you out of trouble." The soldiers accepted the money and did as they were told. This story has circulated among the Jews until this day.

Two tales of the empty tomb circulated that day. The first tale told of the resurrection, the passage to death and new life while the second tale was of deception, of thievery, with the intent to mislead. Whatever the impact the two tales had during that time, we are aware that the significant tale was the first. It touched the small band of Jesus so much so that they made the necessary passage from cowardice to boldness, from being dispersed to becoming a group again, from despair to hope. And the resolve they had during the first Easter morn birthed a new movement that is alive until now. Mary of Magdala was the new "Gabriel" who brought tidings of great joy not only to the apostles but to those who would find renewed hope in the resurrection.

Tuesday

Ps 33:4–5, 18–19, 20 and 22
The earth is full
of the goodness of the Lord.

22

APRIL

1st Reading: Acts 2:36–41

*P*eter said to the people, "Let Israel, then, know for sure, that God has made Lord and Christ this Jesus, whom you crucified."

When they heard this, they were deeply troubled. And they asked Peter and the other apostles, "What shall we do, brothers?"

Peter answered: "Each of you must repent and be baptized in the name of Jesus Christ, so that your sins may be forgiven. Then, you will receive the gift of the Holy Spirit. For the promise of God was made to you and your children, and to all those from afar, whom our God may call."

With many other words Peter gave the message; and appealed to them, saying, "Save yourselves from this crooked generation." So, those who accepted his word were baptized; some three thousand persons were added to their number that day.

Gospel: Jn 20:11–18

*M*ary stood weeping outside the tomb; and as she wept, she bent down to look inside. She saw two angels in white, sitting where the body of Jesus had been, one at the head, and the other at the feet. They said, "Woman, why are you weeping?" She answered, "Because they have taken my Lord and I don't know where they have put him."

As she said this, she turned around and saw Jesus standing there, but she did not recognize him. Jesus said to her, "Woman, why are you weeping? Who are you looking for?" She thought it was the gardener and answered him, "Sir, if you have taken him away, tell me where you have put him, and I will go and take him away."

Jesus said to her, "Mary!" She turned, and said to him, "Rabboni!"—which means Master. Jesus said to her, "Do not touch me, because I have not yet ascended to the Father. But go to my brothers and say to them: I am ascending to my Father, who is your Father, to my God, who is your God."

So Mary of Magdala went and announced to the disciples, "I have seen the Lord, and this is what he said to me."

Not even the darkness of death and the apparent helplessness of Jesus during the crucifixion took away the love and esteem that Mary of Magdala had with Him. She still called Him her Lord and is now weeping over His missing body. Her grief made her a little bit inattentive to the one she spoke. She could not see her Lord with tears in her eyes. But she was called by her name and things changed. She knew at once. Her sorrow gave way to joy. How many times have we succumbed to despair at the utter helplessness of our situation. And how many times have we turned things around simply because God called us by our name? Like Mary of Magdala, we have been called a long long time ago. In our mother's womb God called us and mentioned us by name (Is. 49:1). If we go back from time to time to the experience of that first call, we will not cave in to any darkness that comes in our life.

23
APRIL

Wednesday
Ps 105:1–2, 3–4, 6–7, 8–9
Rejoice, O hearts
that seek the Lord.

OCTAVE OF EASTER, WEDNESDAY
Psalter: Proper / (White)

1st Reading: Acts 3:1–10
Gospel: Lk 24:13–35*

That same day, two followers of Jesus were going to Emmaus, a village seven miles from Jerusalem, and they were talking to each other about all the things that had happened. While they were talking and debating these things, Jesus himself approached and began to accompany them, but their eyes were not able to recognize him. He asked, "What is it you are talking about?" The two stood still, looking sad. Then the one named Cleophas answered, "Why, it seems you are the only traveler to Jerusalem who doesn't know what has happened there these past few days." And he asked, "What is it?" They replied, "It is about Jesus of Nazareth. He was a prophet, you know, mighty in word and deed before God and the people. But the chief priests and our rulers sentenced him to death. They handed him over to be crucified. We had hoped that he would redeem Israel.

It is now the third day since all this took place. It is also true that some women of our group have disturbed us. When they went to the tomb at dawn, they did not find his body; and they came and told us that they had had a vision of angels, who said that Jesus was alive. Some of our people went to the tomb and found everything just as the women had said, but they did not find a body in the tomb." He said to them, "How dull you are, how slow of understanding! Is the message of the prophets too difficult for you to understand? Is it not written that the Christ should suffer all this, and then enter his glory?" (…) As they drew near the village they were heading for, Jesus made as if to go farther. But they prevailed upon him, "Stay with us, for night comes quickly. The day is now almost over." So he went in to stay with them. When they were at table, he took the bread, said a blessing, broke it, and gave each a piece.

Then their eyes were opened, and they recognized him; but he vanished out of their sight. And they said to one another, "Were not our hearts burning within us when he was talking to us on the road and explaining the Scriptures?" They immediately set out and returned to Jerusalem. There, they found the Eleven and their companions gathered together. They were greeted by these words: "Yes, it is true, the Lord is risen! He has appeared to Simon!" Then the two told what had happened on the road to Emmaus, and how Jesus had made himself known, when he broke bread with them.

Emmaus is a journey of faith. Little did the two disciples know that they would be changed forever because of that walk. In their hour of uncertainty, a mysterious stranger appeared to help them navigate their confusion, their doubts and disbelief. It was the most fruitful walk they ever had. For, unknown to them, it was the risen Lord Himself walking with them, guiding them, teaching them to understand what had transpired in their lives. So their hearts were burning and their eyes were opened by His Word and the Breaking of the Bread. They started their walk unsure and afraid. They continue now with purpose and renewed hope because they have encountered the Lord on their way to Emmaus.

Thursday

Ps 8:2ab and 5, 6–7, 8–9
O Lord, our God, how wonderful
your name in all the earth!

24
APRIL

1st Reading: Acts 3:11–26
Gospel: Lk 24:35–48

The two disciples told what had happened on the road to Emmaus, and how Jesus had made himself known, when he broke bread with them.

While they were still talking about this, Jesus himself stood in their midst. (He said to them, "Peace to you.") In their panic and fright they thought they were seeing a ghost, but he said to them, "Why are you upset, and how does such an idea cross your minds? Look at my hands and feet, and see that it is I myself! Touch me, and see for yourselves, for a ghost has no flesh and bones as I have!" (As he said this, he showed his hands and feet.)

Their joy was so great that they still could not believe it, as they were astonished; so he said to them, "Have you anything to eat?" And they gave him a piece of broiled fi sh. He took it, and ate it before them.

Then Jesus said to them, "Remem ber the words I spoke to you when I was still with you: Everything written about me in the law of Moses, in the prophets and in the psalms must be fulfilled." Then he opened their minds to understand the Scriptures. And he said, "So it was written: the Messiah had to suffer, and on the third day rise from the dead. Then repentance and forgiveness in his name would be proclaimed to all nations, Chrisbeginning from Jerusalem. And you are witnesses of these things.

And so the two disciples now give testimony of their experience on the way to Emmaus. Their story is just one among the other stories that testify to the Lord's resurrection. But these will not just be stories; the Lord Himself appears in their midst with His gift of peace. His appearance settled the doubts of the many. They will not spend their time thinking "How could it be?" The time to move on begins. Jesus has to say His goodbye to His small band of faithful. They were a sorry lot but Jesus believed in them. They will now witness to Him whom they have seen, touched and heard.

25
APRIL

Friday

Ps 118:1–2 & 4, 22–24, 25–27a
The stone rejected by the builders
has become the cornerstone.

OCTAVE OF EASTER, FRIDAY
Psalter: Proper / (White)

1ˢᵗ Reading: Acts 4:1–12

Gospel: Jn 21:1–14

Jesus revealed himself to the disciples by the Lake of Tiberias. He appeared to them in this way: Simon Peter, Thomas who was called the Twin, Nathanael of Cana in Galilee, the sons of Zebedee and two other disciples were together; and Simon Peter said to them, "I'm going fishing." They replied, "We will come with you." And they went out and got into the boat, but that night they caught nothing.

When the sun came up, Jesus was standing on the shore, but the disciples did not know that it was Jesus. Jesus called out, "Friends, have you anything to eat?" They answered, "Nothing." Then he said to them, "Throw the net on the right side of the boat and you will find something." When they had lowered the net, they were not able to pull it in because of the great number of fish.

Then the disciple Jesus loved said to Peter, "It's the Lord!" At these words, "It's the Lord!" Simon Peter put on his clothes, for he was stripped for work, and jumped into the water. The other disciples came in the boat, dragging the net full of fish; they were not far from land, about a hundred meters.

When they landed, they saw a charcoal fire with fish on it, and some bread. Jesus said to them, "Bring some of the fish you've just caught." So Simon Peter climbed into the boat and pulled the net to shore. It was full of big fish— one hundred and fifty-three—but, in spite of this, the net was not torn.

Jesus said to them, "Come and have breakfast." And not one of the disciples dared to ask him, "Who are you?" for they knew it was the Lord. Jesus came and took the bread and gave it to them, and he did the same with the fish.

This was the third time that Jesus revealed himself to his disciples after rising from the dead.

The swirl of events that had marked their lives forever must have been too big for Peter to digest at once. Their Lord and Master had been killed. Peter disowned Him when He was most vulnerable. He may have a change of heart now but the rumor that He is alive is too much to accept. Peter needs to sort things out. He might not know how to manage the events unfolding but at least he knows how to fish very well. This is the trade where he is in control. So he thought. They labored all night but caught nothing. Peter must have been in the edge of despair when the Lord stepped in. He reintroduced Himself to His disciples by re-enacting the very first time He called them. That day was a fresh beginning for all of them. The darkness and the shame of the Holy Week are behind them. A new sun rises for the Son of God has finally risen from the dead.

Saturday

Ps 118:1 & 14–15ab, 16–18, 19–21
I will give thanks to you,
for you have answered me.

26
APRIL

1st Reading: Acts 4:13–21

They were astonished at the boldness of Peter and John, considering that they were uneducated and untrained men. They recognized, also, that they had been with Jesus, but, as the man who had been cured stood beside them, they could make no reply.

So they ordered them to leave the council room while they consulted with one another. They asked, "What shall we do with these men? Everyone who lives in Jerusalem knows, that a remarkable sign has been given through them, and we cannot deny it. But to stop this from spreading any further among the people, let us warn them never again to speak to anyone in the name of Jesus." So they called them back and charged them not to speak, or teach at all, in the name of Jesus.

But Peter and John answered them, "Judge for yourselves, whether it is right in God's eyes, for us to obey you, rather than God. We cannot stop speaking about what we have seen and heard." Then the council threatened them once more and let them go. They could find no way of punishing them because of the people, who glorified God for what had happened.

Gospel: Mk 16:9–15

After Jesus rose early on the first day of the week, he appeared first to Mary of Magdala, from whom he had driven out seven demons. She went and reported the news to his followers, who were now mourning and weeping. But when they heard that he lived, and had been seen by her, they would not believe it.

After this he showed himself in another form to two of them, as they were walking into the country. These men also went back and told the others, but they did not believe them. Later Jesus showed himself to the Eleven while they were at table. He reproached them for their unbelief, and hardness of heart, in refusing to believe those who had seen him after he had risen.

Then he told them, "Go out to the whole world and proclaim the Good News to all creation."

Why did Jesus first appear to Mary of Magdala? Was it intentional or was she just at the right place at the right time? Whatever it may be, this will be never taken from her. She was the first to see the risen Lord, and the privileged bearer of the good news to others. But her testimony was not enough to convince the others. A series of resurrection appearances will have to take place before the disciples will be convinced. Anything that big probably needs to be repeated before it can be understood.

27

APRIL

Sunday

Ps 118:2-4, 13-15, 22-24
Give thanks to the Lord
for he is good, his love is everlasting.

1st Reading: Acts 2:42–47

The whole community were faithful to the teaching of the apostles, the common life of sharing, the breaking of bread and the prayers.

A holy fear came upon all the people, for many wonders and miraculous signs were done by the apostles. Now, all the believers lived together, and shared all their belongings. They would sell their property, and all they had, and distribute the proceeds to others, according to their need. Each day, they met together, in the temple area; they broke bread in their homes; they shared their food, with great joy and simplicity of heart; they praised God and won the people's favor. And every day, the Lord added to their number, those who were being saved.

2nd Reading: 1 P 1:3–9

Let us praise God, the Father of our Lord Jesus Christ, for his great mercy. In raising Jesus Christ from the dead, he has given us new life, and a living hope. The inheritance that does not corrupt, nor goes bad, nor passes away, was reserved for you, in heaven, since God's power shall keep you faithful, until salvation is revealed, in the last days.

There is cause for joy, then, even though you may, for a time, have to suffer many trials. Thus will your faith be tested, like gold in a furnace. Gold, however, passes away, but faith, worth so much more, will bring you, in the end, praise, glory and honor, when Jesus Christ appears.

You have not, yet, seen him, and, yet, you love him; even without seeing him, you believe in him, and experience a heavenly joy beyond all words, for you are reaching the goal of your faith: the salvation of your souls.

Gospel: Jn 20:19–31

On the evening of that day, the first day after the Sabbath, the doors were locked where the disciples were, because of their fear of the Jews. But Jesus came, and stood among them, and said to them, "Peace be with you!" Then he showed them his hands and his side. The disciples, seeing the Lord, were full of joy.

Again Jesus said to them, "Peace be with you! As the Father has sent me, so I send you." After saying this, he breathed on them, and said to them, "Receive the Holy Spirit! Those whose sins you forgive, they are forgiven; those whose sins you retain, they are retained."

Thomas, the Twin, one of the Twelve, was not with them when Jesus came. The other disciples told him, "We have seen the Lord." But he replied, "Until I have seen in his hands the print of the nails, and put my finger in the mark of the nails and my hand in his side, I will not believe."

Eight days later, the disciples were again inside the house and Thomas was with them. Although the doors were locked, Jesus came and stood in their midst and said, "Peace be with you!" Then he said to Thomas, "Put your finger here, and see my hands; stretch out your hand, and put it into my side. Do not continue in your unbelief, but believe!"

Thomas said, "You are my Lord and my God." Jesus replied, "You believe because you see me, don't you? Happy are those who have not seen and yet have come to believe."

There were many other signs that Jesus gave in the presence of his disciples, but they are not recorded in this book. These are recorded, so that you may believe that Jesus is the Christ, the Son of God. Believe, and you will have life through his name!

Reading: Behind locked doors the Lord revealed Himself to the Apostles. He breathed on them the Holy Spirit and sent them for mission. Eight days later He appeared again this time with Thomas present who had doubted the first apparition. This time he believed and declared the post resurrection belief that the church holds until now.

Reflection: Now Jesus doesn't have to mask His divinity to His disciples. If before He tempered His display of power to them, now He lets go of this self-imposed limitation and allows His Godhead to shine through. Bursting the gates of death and emerging triumphant, no locked doors created by human hands, could deter the Risen Lord. Not even the doubts of some disciples, prominent among whom was Thomas, could stop the momentum of Easter. There are things to be done ahead. So the Lord commissioned His disciples to continue His work. There is a transfer of authorship of His mission to the disciples. Their time had come. The Master and Teacher had made a master and teacher to His once fumbling, weak and slow-in-understanding followers. He could now plan His return to the Father. The mission rests on capable hands.

Response: Have we ever thought of the purpose why we were born? Perhaps the reason why we are still restless today is because we have not yet done that for which we were born. It will not be easy. But today is a blessed day to reflect and see what God wants me to do. Spending a quiet time for this exercise might help us reorient our life to something meaningful and productive.

28
APRIL

Monday

Ps 2:1–3, 4–7a, 7b–9
Blessed are all who take refuge
in the Lord.

2ND WEEK OF EASTER
St. Peter Chanel, priest & martyr
St. Louis Grignion de Montfort, priest
Psalter: Week 2 / (White / Red)

1st Reading: Acts 4:23–31

As soon as Peter and John were set free, they went to their friends and reported what the chief priests and elders had said to them.

When they heard it, they raised their voices as one, and called upon God, "Sovereign Lord, maker of heaven and earth, of the sea and everything in them, you have put these words in the mouth of David, our father and your servant, through the Holy Spirit: *Why did the pagan nations rage and the people conspire in folly? The kings of the earth were aligned; and the princes gathered together against the Lord and against his Messiah.* For indeed, in this very city, Herod, with Pontius Pilate and the pagans, together, with the people of Israel, conspired against your holy servant, Jesus, whom you anointed. Thus, indeed, they brought about whatever your powerful will had decided, from all time, would happen. But now, Lord, see their threats against us; and enable your servants to speak your word with all boldness. Stretch out your hand, to heal, and to work signs and wonders, through the name of Jesus, your holy servant." When they had prayed, the place where they were gathered together shook; and they were all filled with the Holy Spirit and began to speak the word of God boldly.

Gospel: Jn 3:1–8

Among the Pharisees there was a ruler of the Jews named Nicodemus. He came to Jesus by night and said, "Rabbi, we know that you have come from God to teach us, for no one can perform miraculous signs like yours unless God is with him." Jesus replied, "Truly, I say to you, no one can see the kingdom of God unless he is born again from above." Nicodemus said, "How can there be rebirth for a grown man? Who could go back to his mother's womb and be born again?" Jesus replied, "Truly, I say to you: No one can enter the kingdom of God without being born of water and Spirit. What is born of the flesh is flesh, and what is born of the Spirit is spirit. Because of this, don't be surprised when I say, 'You must be born again from above.' The wind blows where it pleases and you hear its sound, but you don't know where it comes from or where it is going. It is like that with everyone who is born of the Spirit."

St. Peter Chanel
Did you know that: After St. Peter Chanel was martyred by a band of native warriors, clubbing the missionary to death and cutting up his body with hatchets, the whole island of Futuna was converted to Catholicism.

This will be the beginning of the Gospel trilogy that involves Nicodemus. He was an important member of the religious leaders but felt the need to talk with Jesus. Not yet strong to declare his belief in the Lord, he came under cover of darkness. His fear of being caught by his peers and his desire to know more about Jesus made him cautious. He had many questions. These had to be settled first before he made his judgment whether to be with or against Jesus. His questions were direct and earnest. Here is a man who genuinely hungered for the truth. Whether he would find it or not during the time of Jesus, still he was a man on the right track to find that which he had been looking for through the years.

Tuesday

Ps 93:1ab, 1cd–2, 5
The Lord is king;
he is robed in majesty.

29
APRIL

St. Catherine of Siena

Did you know that: St. Catherine of Siena, the only lay woman in the history of the Church to receive the title Doctor of the Church, suffered from anorexia nervosa.

_____

_____

_____

_____

_____

_____

_____

_____

_____

_____

_____

_____

_____

_____

_____

_____

This is the second part of the Gospel trilogy involving Nicodemus. Jesus continues to instruct him on the truth about Himself. At first, Nicodemus will have a hard time understanding him. All that Jesus says seem to be abstract and does not make sense. But Nicodemus, the seeker of truth perseveres. "How can this be?" was all he could say for the moment. Things are not yet clear. But little by little comprehension will set in. It may take a long time. For some it will even take a lifetime. Still, Nicodemus made the first step. This is after all the most crucial step when making the journey of faith.

1st Reading: Acts 4:32–37

The whole community of believers was one in heart and mind. No one claimed private ownership of any possession; but rather, they shared all things in common. With great power, the apostles bore witness to the resurrection of the Lord Jesus, for all of them were living in an exceptional time of grace.

There was no needy person among them, for those who owned land or houses, sold them and brought the proceeds of the sale. And they laid it at the feet of the apostles, who distributed it, according to each one's need. This is what a certain Joseph did. He was a Levite from Cyprus, whom the apostles called Barnabas, meaning: "The encouraging one." He sold a field which he owned and handed the money to the apostles.

Gospel: Jn 3:7b–15

Jesus said to Nicodemus, "Because of this, don't be surprised when I say, 'You must be born again from above.' The wind blows where it pleases and you hear its sound, but you don't know where it comes from or where it is going. It is like that with everyone who is born of the Spirit."

Nicodemus asked again, "How can this be?" And Jesus answered, "You are a teacher in Israel, and you don't know these things!

"Truly, I say to you, we speak of what we know and we witness to the things we have seen, but you don't accept our testimony. If you don't believe when I speak of earthly things, what then, when I speak to you of heavenly things? No one has ever gone up to heaven except the one who came from heaven, the Son of Man.

"As Moses lifted up the serpent in the desert, so must the Son of Man be lifted up, so that whoever believes in him may have eternal life."

30
APRIL

Wednesday

Ps 34:2–3, 4–5, 6–7, 8–9
The Lord hears the cry
of the poor.

2ND WEEK OF EASTER
St. Pius V, pope
Psalter: Week 2 / (White)

1st Reading: Acts 5:17–26

The High Priest and all his supporters, that is, the party of the Sadducees, became very jealous of the apostles; so they arrested them and had them thrown into the public jail. But an angel of the Lord opened the door of the prison during the night, brought them out, and said to them, "Go and stand in the temple court and tell the people the whole of this living message." Accordingly, they entered the temple at dawn and resumed their teaching.

When the High Priest and his supporters arrived, they called together the Sanhedrin, that is the full Council of the elders of Israel. They sent word to the jail to have the prisoners brought in. But when the temple guards arrived at the jail, they did not find them inside; so they returned with the news, "We found the prison securely locked, and the prison guards at their post outside the gate; but when we opened the gate, we found no one inside."

Upon hearing these words, the captain of the temple guard and the high priests were baffled, wondering where all of this would end. Just then, someone arrived with the report, "Look, those men whom you put in prison are standing in the temple, teaching the people." Then the captain went off with the guards and brought them back, but without any show of force, for fear of being stoned by the people.

Gospel: Jn 3:16–21

Jesus said to Nicodemus, "Yes, God so loved the world that he gave his only Son that whoever believes in him may not be lost, but may have eternal life. God did not send the Son into the world to condemn the world; instead, through him the world is to be saved. Whoever believes in him will not be condemned. He who does not believe is already condemned, because he has not believed in the name of the only Son of God.

"This is how Judgment is made: Light has come into the world, and people loved darkness rather than light, because their deeds were evil. For whoever does wrong hates the light, and doesn't come to the light, for fear that his deeds will be seen as evil. But whoever lives according to the truth comes into the light, so that it can be clearly seen that his works have been done in God.

St. Pius V
Did you know that: It was St. Pope Pius V who promulgated the Roman Catechism, the Roman Missal, and the Roman Breviary used until Vatican II.

The last part of the gospel trilogy involving Nicodemus leaves us a resounding note on love. The love of God to the world is confirmed by Jesus not only by His testimony but more so by His presence. He is the love incarnate of the Father to the world. And so Jesus' appearance to the world should not be feared. Only those who are incapable of love will abhor Him since He will be a sign and presence of what they have missed throughout their lives. The heart that has been long dead will find it difficult to live again in love. And so the blessing of God's love incarnate became for many a sign of their condemned lives. They will therefore exert all efforts to extinguish this reminder of what they have lost in life.

FEAST OF ST. JOSEPH, THE WORKER
Psalter: Proper / (White)

Thursday

Ps 90:2, 3–4, 12–13, 14 & 16
Lord, give success
to the work of our hands.

01
MAY

1st Reading: Gen 1:26–2:3 (or Col 3:14-15, 17, 23-24)

God said, "Let us make man in our image, to our likeness. Let them rule over the fish of the sea, over the birds of the air, over the cattle, over the wild animals, and over all creeping things that crawl along the ground." So God created man in his image; in the image of God he created him; male and female he created them. God blessed them and said to them, "Be fruitful and increase in number, fill the earth and subdue it, rule over the fish of the sea and the birds of the sky, over every living creature that moves on the ground."

God said, "I have given you every seed-bearing plant which is on the face of all the earth, and every tree that bears fruit with seed. It will be for your food. To every wild animal, to every bird of the sky, to everything that creeps along the ground, to everything that has the breath of life, I give every green plant for food." So it was. God saw all that he had made, and it was very good. There was evening and there was morning: the sixth day.

That was the way the sky and earth were created and all their vast array. By the seventh day the work God had done was completed, and he rested on the seventh day from all the work he had done. And God blessed the seventh day and made it holy, because on that day he rested from all the work he had done in his creation.

Gospel: Mt 13:54–58

Jesus went to his hometown and taught the people in their synagogue. They were amazed and said, "Where did he get this wisdom and these special powers? Isn't he the carpenter's son? Isn't Mary his mother and aren't James, Joseph, Simon and Judas his brothers? Aren't all his sisters living here? Where did he get all these things?" And so they took offense at him.

Jesus said to them, "The only place where prophets are not welcome is his hometown and in his own family." And he did not perform many miracles there because of their lack of faith.

We will always be tied to our roots. Those who know who we are have the tendency to evaluate our claim against our background; thus it could be of help or a burden to us. The town mates of Jesus knew His family so well. They could not get past their notion that He was just one of them, coming from an ordinary family that lived ordinary lives. He had no right to be above them. He had to go back to His station in life. This was the reason for the sad state of Jesus not being able to perform many miracles. He was up against the expectations of people who said He was not who He claimed to be. Their unbelief robbed Him of the full extent of His potency. Jesus could not insist if He was not given the chance..

02
MAY

Friday
Ps 27:1, 4, 13–14
One thing I seek: to dwell
in the house of the Lord.

2ND WEEK OF EASTER
St. Athanasius, bishop & doctor
Psalter: Week 2 / (White)

1st Reading: Acts 5:34–42
Gospel: Jn 6:1–15

Jesus went to the other side of the Sea of Galilee, near Tiberias, and large crowds followed him, because of the miraculous signs they saw, when he healed the sick. So he went up into the hills and sat down there with his disciples.

Now the Passover, the feast of the Jews, was at hand.

Then lifting up his eyes, Jesus saw the crowds that were coming to him, and said to Philip, "Where shall we buy bread so that these people may eat?" He said this to test Philip, for he himself knew what he was going to do. Philip answered him, "Two hundred silver coins would not buy enough bread for each of them to have a piece."

Then one of Jesus' disciples, Andrew, Simon Peter's brother, said, "There is a boy here who has five barley loaves and two fi sh; but what good are these for so many?"

Jesus said, "Make the people sit down." There was plenty of grass there, so the people, about five thousand men, sat down. Jesus then took the loaves, gave thanks, and distributed them to those who were seated. He did the same with the fish, and gave them as much as they wanted. And when they had eaten enough, he told his disciples, "Gather up the pieces left over, that nothing may be lost." So they gathered them up and filled twelve baskets with bread, that is, with pieces of the fi ve barley loaves left over by those who had eaten.

When the people saw the miracle which Jesus had performed, they said, "This is really the Prophet, the one who is to come into the world."

Jesus realized that they would come and take him by force to make him king; so he fled to the hills by himself.

St. Athanasius
Did you know that: St. Athanasius championed the statement of belief we now know as the Nicene Creed.

In every movement or organization, logistical problems do pop out from time to time. Sometimes they turn into a nightmare. Our gospel today presents such typical scenario. After a day's work Jesus went to the other side of Galilee but the people could not get enough of Him. They hungered for more so they followed Him to the other side. Then their hunger became physically real. It would be a problem how to feed them. Yet every problem presents an opportunity. In this case, it was the opportunity of sharing what one had no matter how small. The poor offering of the little boy became the avenue for the feeding of the multitude. For a miracle does not require much. It is the willingness to give the little that we have that unleashes the abundant blessings of God to us.

FEAST OF STS. PHILIP AND JAMES, APOSTLES
Psalter: Proper / (Red)

Saturday

Ps 19:2–3, 4–5
Their message goes out through all the earth.

03
MAY

1st Reading: 1 Cor 15:1–8

Let me remind you, brothers and sisters, of the Good News that I preached to you, and which you received, and on which, you stand firm. By that gospel, you are saved, provided that you hold to it, as I preached it. Otherwise, you will have believed in vain.

In the first place, I have passed on to you what I, myself, received: that Christ died for our sins, as Scripture says; that he was buried; that he was raised on the third day, according to the Scriptures; that he appeared to Cephas and then to the Twelve. Afterward, he appeared to more than five hundred brothers and sisters together; most of them are still alive, although some have already gone to rest. Then he appeared to James, and after that, to all the apostles. And last of all, he appeared to the most despicable of them, this is, to me.

Gospel: Jn 14:6–14

Jesus said, "I am the way, the truth and the life; no one comes to the Father but through me. If you know me, you will know the Father also; indeed you know him, and you have seen him."

Philip asked him, "Lord, show us the Father, and that is enough." Jesus said to him, "What! I have been with you so long and you still do not know me, Philip? Whoever sees me sees the Father; how can you say, 'Show us the Father'? Do you not believe that I am in the Father and the Father is in me?

"All that I say to you, I do not say of myself. The Father who dwells in me is doing his own work. Believe me when I say that I am in the Father and the Father is in me; at least believe it on the evidence of these works that I do.

"Truly, I say to you, the one who believes in me will do the same works that I do; and he will even do greater than these, for I am going to the Father. Everything you ask in my name, I will do, so that the Father may be glorified in the Son. Indeed, anything you ask, calling upon my name, I will do it."

Jesus never fails to mention His Father. In everything He does, He always links it with His Father. This probably made His disciples curious to get to know more about the Father that Jesus Christ was most proud of. And so Jesus revealed to them something even more startling. Not only was He intimately connected with His Father, He had and was the unique access to Him. He dwells in the Father and the Father dwells in Him. These are not mere words but Jesus puts forward His own works as evidence of His claim. James and John and the rest of the disciples could therefore be rest assured that the words of Jesus were true because they were confirmed by His actions.

04
MAY

Sunday

Ps 16:1-2, 5, 7-8, 9-10, 11
Lord, you will show us the path of life.

1st Reading: Acts 2:14, 22–33*

Then Peter stood up with the Eleven and, with a loud voice, addressed them, (…) "Fellow Israelites, listen to what I am going to tell you about Jesus of Nazareth. God accredited him and through him did powerful deeds and wonders and signs in your midst, as you well know. You delivered him to sinners to be crucified and killed, and, in this way, the purpose of God, from all times, was fulfilled. But God raised him to life and released him from the pain of death; because it was impossible for him to be held in the power of death. (…)

"Friends, I don't need to prove that the patriarch David died and was buried; his tomb is with us to this day. But he knew, that God had sworn to him, that one of his descendants would sit upon his throne and, as he was a prophet, he foresaw and spoke of the resurrection of the Messiah. So he said, that *he would not be left in the region of the dead, nor would his body experience corruption.*

"This Messiah is Jesus; and we are all witnesses that God raised him to life. He has been exalted at God's right side; and the Father has entrusted the Holy Spirit to him; this Spirit, he has just poured upon us, as you now see and hear."

2nd Reading: 1 P 1:17–21

Dear brothers and sisters, you call upon a Father who makes no distinction between persons, but judges, according to each one's deeds; take seriously, then, these years which you spend in a strange land. Remember that, you were freed from the useless way of life of your ancestors, not with gold and silver, but with the precious blood of the Lamb without a spot or blemish. God, who has known Christ before the world began, revealed him to you in the last days. Through him, you have faith in God, who raised him from the dead, and glorified him, in order that you might put all your faith and hope in God.

Gospel: Lk 24:13–35

That same day, two followers of Jesus were going to Emmaus, a village seven miles from Jerusalem, and they were talking to each other about all the things that had happened. While they were talking and debating these things, Jesus himself approached and began to accompany them, but their eyes were not able to recognize him.

He asked, "What is it you are talking about?" The two stood still, looking sad. Then the one named Cleophas answered, "Why, it seems you are the only traveler to Jerusalem who doesn't know what has happened there these past few days." And he asked, "What is it?"

They replied, "It is about Jesus of Nazareth. He was a prophet, you know, mighty in word and deed before God and the people. But the chief priests and our rulers sentenced him to death. They handed him over to be crucified. We had hoped that he would redeem Israel.

It is now the third day since all this took place. It is also true that some women of our group have disturbed us. When they went to the tomb at dawn, they did not find his body; and they came and told us that they had had a vision of angels, who said that Jesus was alive. Some of our people went to the tomb and found everything just as the women had said, but they did not find a body in the tomb."

He said to them, "How dull you are, how slow of understanding! Is the message of the prophets too difficult for you to understand? Is it not written that the Christ should suffer all this, and then enter his glory?" Then starting with Moses, and going through the prophets, he explained to them everything in the Scriptures concerning himself.

As they drew near the village they were heading for, Jesus made as if to go farther. But they prevailed upon him, "Stay with us, for night comes quickly. The day is now almost over." So he went in to stay with them. When they were at table, he took the bread, said a blessing, broke it, and gave each a piece.

Then their eyes were opened, and they recognized him; but he vanished out of their sight. And they said to one another, "Were not our hearts burning within us when he was talking to us on the road and explaining the Scriptures?"

They immediately set out and returned to Jerusalem. There, they found the Eleven and their companions gathered together. They were greeted by these words: "Yes, it is true, the Lord is risen! He has appeared to Simon!" Then the two told what had happened on the road to Emmaus, and how Jesus had made himself known, when he broke bread with them.

Reading: Two other disciples are on the road to Jerusalem passing by Emmaus. The word has spread that the Lord's body has not been found in the tomb. On their way they meet a stranger who explains to them the fate of the Messiah according to Scriptures. When they reach Emmaus, they invite the mysterious stranger to stay with them. He reenacts the scene of the Last Supper and at once they recognize Him to be their missing Lord. With haste they set out to Jerusalem at once and there affirm the good news that awaits them: the Lord is truly risen!

Reflection: There are many journeys we undertake in this lifetime. Some demand that we do it alone but if there is an opportunity, it is always good to have a companion nearby to share the adventure. But in reality, we are never alone in this life, Jesus always journeys with us in a guise. It is only a matter of discovering His hidden identity in the many people and events that come our way. Discovering His hidden presence demands awareness and attentiveness in the now. We do not allow the ghost of the past and the fears of the future to drown our sense of wonder at the present. With this, we will hopefully arrive at the heavenly Jerusalem to meet the Lord who is truly risen.

Response: There are people now who are in difficult journeys of their life. Some of them might be close to us. Why not walk with them for a while and lend a helping hand by way of presence. Let us also pause and pray for those whom we could not accompany and entrust them to the loving companionship of the Lord who comes and walks with us in disguise.

_____
_____
_____
_____
_____
_____
_____
_____

05
MAY

Monday
Ps 119:23–24, 26–27, 29–30
Blessed are they who follow
the law of the Lord!

3RD WEEK OF EASTER
Psalter: Week 3 / (White)

1st Reading: Acts 6:8–15

Stephen, full of grace and power, did great wonders and miraculous signs among the people. Some persons then came forward, who belonged to the so-called Synagogue of Freedmen, from Cyrene, Alexandria, Cilicia and Asia. They argued with Stephen. But they could not match the wisdom and the spirit with which he spoke. As they were unable to face the truth, they bribed some men to say, "We heard him speak against Moses and against God."

So they stirred up the people, the elders and the teachers of the law; they took him by surprise, seized him and brought him before the Council. Then they produced false witnesses, who said, "This man never stops speaking against our Holy Place and the law. We even heard him say that Jesus, the Nazorean, will destroy our Holy Place and change the customs which Moses handed down to us." And all who sat in the Council fixed their eyes on him; and his face appeared to them like the face of an angel.

Gospel: Jn 6:22–29

Next day, the people, who had stayed on the other side, realized that only one boat had been there, and that Jesus had not entered it with his disciples; but rather, the disciples had gone away alone. Other boats from Tiberias landed near the place where all these people had eaten the bread. When they saw that neither Jesus nor his disciples were there, they got into the boats and went to Capernaum looking for Jesus.

When they found him on the other side of the lake, they asked him, "Master, when did you come here?"

Jesus answered, "Truly, I say to you, you look for me, not because of the signs which you have seen, but because you ate bread and were satisfied. Work then, not for perishable food, but for the lasting food which gives eternal life. The Son of Man will give it to you, for he is the one on whom the Father has put his mark."

Then the Jews asked him, "What shall we do? What are the works that God wants us to do?" And Jesus answered them, "The work God wants is this: that you believe in the One whom God has sent."

More and more people are now looking for Jesus. The miraculous signs He did must have picked the curiosity of some while others genuinely believed. So it is a mixed lot that came looking for Jesus. Resources are now mobilized to get to know this new Teacher who is causing such a sensation never before known in the land of Israel. Bigger boats are now employed. People are willing to put their money on someone that will give them hope. But Jesus knew that most of them were looking for a quick fix to their problems. The bread that satisfied them worked only to address their physical needs. Jesus invited them to a better and lasting solution to their problems. They had to believe in Him as the One sent by the Father so that His word and work would shape them to a kind of life worthy of eternity.

Tuesday

Ps 31:3cd–4, 6 & 7b & 8a, 17 & 21ab
Into your hands, O Lord,
I commend my spirit.

06
MAY

1st Reading: Acts 7:51—8:1a

Stephen said to the people, "But you are a stubborn people. You hardened your hearts and closed your ears. You have always resisted the Holy Spirit, just as your fathers did. Was there a prophet whom your ancestors did not persecute? They killed those who announced the coming of the Just One, whom you have now betrayed and murdered; you, who, received the law through the angels but did not fulfill it."

When they heard this reproach, they were enraged; and they gnashed their teeth against Stephen. But he, full of the Holy Spirit, fixed his eyes on heaven and saw the glory of God, and Jesus at God's right hand; so he declared: "I see the heavens open, and the Son of Man at the right hand of God."

But they shouted and covered their ears with their hands, and rushed together upon him. They brought him out of the city and stoned him; and the witnesses laid down their cloaks at the feet of a young man named Saul. As they were stoning him, Stephen prayed saying: "Lord Jesus, receive my spirit." Then he knelt down and said in a loud voice: "Lord, do not hold this sin against them." And when he had said this, he died.

Saul was there, approving his murder. This was the beginning of a great persecution against the Church in Jerusalem. All, except the apostles, were scattered throughout the region of Judea and Samaria.

Gospel: Jn 6:30–35

The crowd said to Jesus, "Show us miraculous signs, that we may see and believe you. What sign do you perform? Our ancestors ate manna in the desert; as Scripture says: They were given bread from heaven to eat."

Jesus then said to them, "Truly, I say to you, it was not Moses who gave you the bread from heaven. My Father gives you the true bread from heaven. The bread God gives is the One who comes from heaven and gives life to the world." And they said to him, "Give us this bread always."

Jesus said to them, "I am the bread of life; whoever comes to me shall never be hungry, and whoever believes in me shall never be thirsty."

As Jesus attracted a large amount of attention, not all were sold out on His credentials. There had been too many charlatans who had walked their land. So their demands on Jesus to legitimize Himself before their eyes got bigger and bigger. For instance, now they demanded miraculous signs. The many wonders the Lord had made do not impress them at all. It had to be something on their own terms and done specifically for them. The miracle of the multiplication of the bread is something that they could dismiss with another miracle that happened in their history, the manna in the desert. But Jesus showed them the difference between the two. Whereas Moses was dependent on the power of God, Jesus was not. He was in complete possession of His own faculty to effect the miracle. And the true miracle was not the physical bread multiplied but He who is the true bread from heaven that came down to satisfy the deep seated hunger of humanity.

07
MAY

Wednesday

Ps 66:1–3a, 4–5, 6–7a
Let all the earth cry out to God
with joy.

3RD WEEK OF EASTER
Psalter: Week 3 / (White)

1st Reading: Acts 8:1b–8

This was the beginning of a great persecution against the Church in Jerusalem. All, except the apostles, were scattered throughout the region of Judea and Samaria. Devout men buried Stephen and mourned deeply for him. Saul, meanwhile, was trying to destroy the church. He entered house after house and dragged off men and women, and had them put in jail.

At the same time, those who were scattered went about, preaching the word. Philip went down to a town of Samaria and proclaimed the Christ there. All the people paid close attention to what Philip said as they listened to him, and saw the miraculous signs that he did. For, in cases of possession, the unclean spirits came out shrieking loudly. Many people, who were paralyzed or crippled, were healed. So there was great joy in that town.

Gospel: Jn 6:35–40

Jesus said to the crowd, "I am the bread of life; whoever comes to me shall never be hungry, and whoever believes in me shall never be thirsty. Nevertheless, as I said, you refuse to believe, even when you have seen. Yet all those whom the Father gives me will come to me, and whoever comes to me, I shall not turn away. For I have come from heaven, not to do my own will, but the will of the One who sent me.

"And the will of him who sent me is that I lose nothing of what he has given me, but instead that I raise it up on the last day. This is the will of the Father, that whoever sees the Son and believes in him shall live eternal life; and I will raise him up on the last day."

This is a continuation on Jesus' discussion on the theme of bread with His listeners. This will be a long discourse perhaps because bread as staple food has an important role to play in the life of people. It also figures prominently in the life of Israel, when they were saved by God from starvation in the desert, when bread that dropped from heaven sustained their journey. But the manna they received only sustained their physical life enabling them to survive. The bread that is Jesus is of better quality because it ensures eternal life. All they have to do is believe in Him to receive this bread. It will be a long and sometimes bitter conversation between Jesus and those among whom He worked so hard to convince.

Thursday

Ps 66:8–9, 16–17, 20
Let all the earth cry out to God
with joy.

08
MAY

1st Reading: Acts 8:26–40*

An angel of the Lord said to Philip, "Go south, toward the road that goes down from Jerusalem to Gaza, the desert road." So he set out and, it happened that, an Ethiopian was passing along that way. He was an official in charge of the treasury of the queen of the Ethiopians. He had come on pilgrimage to Jerusalem and was on his way home. He was sitting in his carriage and reading the prophet Isaiah.

The Spirit said to Philip, "Go and catch up with that carriage." So Philip ran up and heard the man reading the prophet Isaiah; and he asked, "Do you really understand what you are reading?" The Ethiopian replied, "How can I, unless someone explains it to me?" He then invited Philip to get in and sit beside him. This was the passage of Scripture he was reading: *He was led like a sheep to be slaughtered; like a lamb that is dumb before the shearer, he did not open his mouth. He was humbled and deprived of his rights. Who can speak of his descendants? For he was uprooted from the earth.*

The official asked Philip, "Tell me, please, does the prophet speak of himself or of someone else?" Then Philip began to tell him the Good News of Jesus, using this text of Scripture as his starting point. As they traveled down the road, they came to a place where there was some water. Then the Ethiopian official said, "Look, here is water; what is to keep me from being baptized?"

Then he ordered the carriage to stop. Both Philip and the Ethiopian went down into the water and Philip baptized him. When they came out of the water, the Spirit of the Lord took Philip away. The Ethiopian saw him no more, but he continued on his way full of joy. (…)

Gospel: Jn 6:44–51

Jesus said to the crowd, "No one can come to me unless he is drawn by the Father who sent me; and I will raise him up on the last day. It has been written in the Prophets: They shall all be taught by God. So whoever listens and learns from the Father comes to me.

"For no one has seen the Father except the One who comes from God; he has seen the Father. Truly, I say to you, whoever believes has eternal life.

"I am the bread of life. Though your ancestors ate the manna in the desert, they died. But here you have the bread from heaven, so that you may eat of it, and not die. I am the living bread from heaven; whoever eats of this bread will live forever. The bread I shall give is my flesh, and I will give it for the life of the world."

Now Jesus ramps up the rhetoric. He says that only those whom the Father draws to Him will come and follow Him. In short those who would reject Him had been rejected beforehand by the Father. This explains their inability to believe and accept His word. This must have soured the peoples' feelings toward Him. After all, the Jews had always prided themselves to be the chosen people, the apple of God's eye. Jesus even further rubbed salt to their wounded feelings when He declared that He is the true bread that came down from heaven that is far superior to the bread that their ancestors ate in the desert. That day, these words would cement enmity between Him and some of the Jews.

09
MAY

Friday

Ps 117:1bc, 2
Go out to all the world
and tell the Good News.

3RD WEEK OF EASTER
Psalter: Week 3 / (White)

1st Reading: Acts 9:1–20*

Saul considered nothing but violence and death for the disciples of the Lord (…)

As he traveled along and was approaching Damascus, a light from the sky suddenly flashed around him. He fell on the ground and heard a voice saying to him, "Saul, Saul! Why do you persecute me?" and he asked, "Who are you, Lord?" The voice replied, "I am Jesus, whom you persecute. Now get up, and go into the city; there, you will be told what you are to do."

The men who were travelling with him stood there speechless: they had heard the sound, but could see no one. Saul got up from the ground and, opening his eyes, he could not see. They took him by the hand and brought him to Damascus. He was blind; and he did not eat or drink for three days.

There was a disciple in Damascus named Ananias, to whom the Lord called in a vision, "Ananias!" He answered, "Here I am, Lord!" Then the Lord said to him, "Go, at once, to straight street and ask, at the house of Judas, for a man of Tarsus named Saul. (…)

So Ananias left and went to the house. He laid his hands upon Saul and said, "Saul, my brother, the Lord Jesus, who appeared to you on your way here, has sent me to you, so that you may receive your sight, and be filled with the holy Spirit." Immediately, something like scaes fell from his eyes and he could see; he got up and was baptized. Then he took food and was strengthened. (…)

Gospel: Jn 6:52–59

The Jews were arguing among themselves, "How can this man give us his flesh to eat?" So Jesus replied, "Truly, I say to you, if you do not eat the flesh of the Son of Man and drink his blood, you have no life in you. The one who eats my flesh and drinks my blood lives eternal life, and I will raise him up on the last day.

"My flesh is really food, and my blood is truly drink. Those who eat my flesh and drink my blood, live in me, and I in them. Just as the Father, who is life, sent me, and I have life from the Father, so whoever eats me will have life from me. This is the bread from heaven; not like that of your ancestors, who ate and later died. Those who eat this bread will live forever."

Jesus spoke in this way in Capernaum when he taught them in the synagogue.

Jesus' discourse on the living bread becomes muddled as debate upon debate pile up between Him and His listeners who refuse to understand and believe. His critics have to resort now to a literal interpretation, a tactic akin to bringing the discussion which employs symbolic and creative metaphors on the empirical and material level. They could therefore conclude falsity on a claim that could not be backed up by physical and tangible proofs. If this is the mindset of the other party, there could be no fruitful dialogue that would ensue. And so, Jesus must have appeared as strange and a little bit loose in the head that day for them. On the part of Jesus' party, they would appear as hard and obstinate of heart. No meaningful communication would follow afterwards; instead polemics would ensue throughout between them.

3RD WEEK OF EASTER
St. Damien de Veuster, priest
Psalter: Week 3 / (White)

Saturday

10
MAY

Ps 116:12–13, 14–15, 16–17
How shall I make a return to the Lord
for all the good he has done for me?

St. Damien de Veuster

Did you know that: St. Damien de Veuster is considered a "martyr of charity" and called "the Apostle of the Lepers."

_____
_____
_____
_____
_____
_____
_____
_____
_____
_____

Because of this, even some of the followers of Jesus would get confused. Caught between the emotionally charged conversations, some would loose their balance and perspectives. The teachings they heard from the Lord even in secret would not be enough to save their faith in their Teacher and Master. This led to an exodus of followers; their confusion and lack of understanding was greater than their faith in Him whom they followed for a time. Such sad partings happen even in the tightest group or organization. You retain some, you lose some. Jesus will experience being abandoned several times over by those whom He called friends. This training must have toughened Him to face the horrors of His Passion.

1st Reading: Acts 9:31–42*

There was a disciple in Joppa named Tabitha, which means Dorcas, or Gazelle. She was always doing good works and helping the poor. At that time, she fell sick and died. After having washed her body, they laid her in the upstairs room. As Lydda is near Joppa, the disciples, on hearing that Peter was there, sent two men to him with the request, "Please come to us without delay."

So Peter went with them. On his arrival they took him upstairs to the room. All the widows crowded around him in tears, showing him the clothes that Dorcas had made while she was with them. Peter made them all leave the room and then he knelt down and prayed. Turning to the dead body he said, "Tabitha, stand up." She opened her eyes, looked at Peter and sat up. Peter gave her his hand and helped her up. Then he called in the saints and widows and presented her to them alive. This became known throughout all of Joppa and many people believed in the Lord because of it.

So Peter went with them. On his arrival, they took him upstairs to the room. All the widows crowded around him in tears, showing him the clothes that Dorcas had made while she was with them. Peter made them all leave the room; and then, he knelt down and prayed. Turning to the dead body, he said, "Tabitha, stand up." She opened her eyes, looked at Peter and sat up. Peter gave her his hand and helped her up. Then he called in the saints and widows, and presented her to them alive. This became known throughout all of Joppa; and many people believed in the Lord because of it.

Gospel: Jn 6:60–69

Many of Jesus' followers said, "This language is very hard! Who can accept it?"

Jesus was aware that his disciples were murmuring about this, and so he said to them, "Does this offend you? Then how will you react when you see the Son of Man ascending to where he was before? It is the spirit that gives life, not the flesh. The words that I have spoken to you are spirit and they are life. But among you there are some who do not believe."

From the beginning, Jesus knew who would betray him. So he added, "As I have told you, no one can come to me unless it is granted by the Father."

After this, many disciples withdrew and no longer followed him. Jesus asked the Twelve, "Will you also go away?" Peter answered him, "Lord, to whom shall we go? You have the words of eternal life. We now believe and know that you are the Holy One of God."

11
MAY

Sunday

Ps 23:1-3a, 3b–4, 5, 6
The Lord is my shepherd;
there is nothing I shall want.

1st Reading: Acts 2:14a, 36–41

*T*hen Peter stood up with the Eleven and, with a loud voice, addressed them, "Let Israel then know for sure that God has made Lord and Christ this Jesus whom you crucified."

When they heard this, they were deeply troubled. And they asked Peter and the other apostles, "What shall we do, brothers?"

Peter answered: "Each of you must repent and be baptized in the name of Jesus Christ, so that your sins may be forgiven. Then you will receive the gift of the Holy Spirit. For the promise of God was made to you and your children, and to all those from afar whom our God may call."

With many other words Peter gave the message and appealed to them saying, "Save yourselves from this crooked generation." So those who accepted his word were baptized; some three thousand persons were added to their number that day.

2nd Reading: 1 P 2:20b–25

*B*eloved, if you endure punishment when you have done well, that is a grace before God.

This is your calling: remember Christ who suffered for you, leaving you an example so that you may follow in his way. *He did no wrong and there was no deceit in his mouth.* He did not return insult for insult and, when suffering, he did not curse but put himself in the hands of God who judges justly. He went to the cross burdened with our sins so that we might die to sin and live an upright life. *For by his wounds you have been healed.* You were like stray sheep, but you have come back to the Shepherd and Guardian of your souls.

Gospel: Jn 10:1–10

*J*esus said, "Truly, I say to you, anyone who does not enter the sheepfold by the gate, but climbs in some other way, is a thief and a robber. But the shepherd of the sheep enters by the gate. The keeper opens the gate to him and the sheep hear his voice; he calls each of his sheep by name and leads them out. When he has brought out all his own, he goes before them and the sheep follow him for they know his voice. A stranger they will not follow, rather they will run away from him because they don't recognize a stranger's voice."

Jesus used this comparison, but they did not understand what he was saying to them.

So Jesus said, "Truly, I say to you, I am the gate of the sheep. All who came were thieves and robbers, and the sheep did not hear them. I am the gate. Whoever enters through me will be saved; he will go in and out freely and find food.

"The thief comes to steal and kill and destroy, but I have come that they may have life, life in all its fullness."

Reading: Jesus used the imagery of the sheepfold in order to convey a lesson. He likens Himself to the sheepfold's gate through which anyone who enters will be saved.

Reflection: Heaven and salvation are concepts that defy our neat and orderly reasoning. They are too big a reality to be captured by mere words. Thus, images such as the sheepfold, with its sense of security, due to its sturdy walls and food in abundance inside, convey in a human way some understanding of such realities that cannot be contained by human concepts. This is where our capacity for symbolic thinking enters the picture. For only those who know the art of thinking beyond the literal and the rational sequential process can relish the truths that come from higher domains. And so Jesus as the shepherd and the gate of the sheepfold invites us to contemplate the mystery of His being. It is a task that demands time, perhaps an eternity for us to grasp a bit of who He really is.

Response: Many of us have a bias towards the left brain operation that deals with the linear, sequential and rational way of the thinking process. Our right brain which is the domain of creativity is hardly utilized. If the saying "two heads are better than one" is true, then it would be to our interest to develop the weak part of our brain operations. So why don't we make a conscious effort to develop the capacity for whole-brain thinking? There are many materials in the internet about this. Perhaps this is what we need to spice up our spiritual life by awaking our capacity for wonder and enchantment.

12
MAY

Monday

Ps 42:2–3; 43:3,4
Athirst is my soul
for the living God.

4TH WEEK OF EASTER
St. Nereus and St. Achilleus, martyrs
St. Pancras, martyr
Psalter: Week 4 / (White / Red)

1st Reading: Acts 11:1–18*

News came to the apostles and the brothers and sisters in Judea that even foreigners had received the word of God. So, when Peter went up to Jerusalem, these Jewish believers began to argue with him, "You went to the home of uncircumcised people and ate with them!"

So Peter began to give them the facts as they had happened, "I was at prayer in the city of Joppa when, in a trance, I saw a vision. Something like a large sheet came down from the sky and drew near to me, landing on the ground by its four corners. As I stared at it, I saw four-legged creatures of the earth, wild beasts and reptiles, and birds of the sky. Then I heard a voice saying to me: 'Get up, Peter, kill and eat!' I replied, 'Certainly not, Lord! No common or unclean creature has ever entered my mouth.' A second time the voice from the heavens spoke, 'What God has made clean, you must not call unclean.' This happened three times, and then it was all drawn up into the sky. At that moment, three men, who had been sent to me from Caesarea, arrived at the house where we were staying. The Spirit instructed me to go with them without hesitation (…)

When they heard this, they set their minds at rest and praised God saying, "Then God has granted life-giving repentance to the pagan nations as well."

Gospel: Jn 10:11–18

Jesus said, "I am the good shepherd. The good shepherd gives his life for the sheep. Not so the hired hand, or any other person who is not the shepherd, and to whom the sheep do not belong. They abandon the sheep as soon as they see the wolf coming; then the wolf snatches and scatters the sheep. This is because the hired hand works for pay and cares nothing for the sheep.

"I am the good shepherd. I know my own and my own know me, as the Father knows me and I know the Father. Because of this, I give my life for my sheep.

"I have other sheep which are not of this fold. These I have to lead as well, and they shall listen to my voice. Then there will be one flock, since there is one shepherd."

"The Father loves me, because I lay down my life in order to take it up again. No one takes it from me, but I lay it down freely. It is mine to lay down and to take up again: this mission I received from my Father."

St. Nereus and St. Achilleus

Did you know that: Sts. Nereus and Achilleus were Roman soldiers who persecuted Christians. They were converted and together with the niece of the emperor, they were martyred.

Jesus employs a beautiful imagery of attention and care to those He called His own. This is easily understood by His listeners since the image of a shepherd was part and parcel of their life. Jesus uses this as a teaching device that people can emotionally relate to because it is part of their experience. This makes the teaching stick better in the minds of those whom He taught. Thus, Jesus is a Teacher who has methods in teaching and communication skills. His added sets of competencies to His formidable person made Him an effective preacher of His time. He was as human as could be when teaching something about the divine.

Tuesday

Ps 87:1b–3, 4–5, 6–7
All you nations, praise the Lord.

13 MAY

1ˢᵗ Reading: Acts 11:19–26

Those who had been scattered, because of the persecution over Stephen, traveled as far as Phoenicia, Cyprus and Antioch, proclaiming the message, but only to the Jews. But there were some natives of Cyprus and Cyrene among them who, on coming into Antioch, spoke also to the Greeks, giving them the good news of the Lord Jesus. The hand of the Lord was with them so that a great number believed and turned to the Lord.

News of this reached the ears of the Church in Jerusalem, so they sent Barnabas to Antioch. When he arrived and saw the manifest signs of God's favor, he rejoiced and urged them all to remain firmly faithful to the Lord; for he, himself, was a good man, filled with the Holy Spirit and faith. Thus large crowds came to know the Lord.

Then Barnabas went off to Tarsus, to look for Saul; and when he found him, he brought him to Antioch. For a whole year, they had meetings with the Church and instructed many people. It was in Antioch that the disciples were first called Christians.

Gospel: Jn 10:22–30

The time came for the feast of the Dedication.

It was winter, and Jesus walked back and forth in the portico of Solomon. The Jews then gathered around him and said to him, "How long will you keep us in doubt? If you are the Messiah, tell us plainly." Jesus answered, "I have already told you, but you do not believe. The works I do in my Father's name proclaim who I am, but you don't believe because, as I said, you are not my sheep.

"My sheep hear my voice and I know them; they follow me and I give them eternal life. They shall never perish, and no one will ever steal them from me. What my Father has given me, is greater than all things else. To snatch it out of the Father's hand, no one is able! I and the Father are One."

In today's gospel, we continue the theme from yesterday of the sheep who knows his or her shepherd from yesterday. The people who hold on to their allegiance for or against Jesus are getting impatient. He has ruffled the feathers of the powerful elites; He must be the One longed for by Israel to come. Yet they had to be sure. And so they exerted pressure on Jesus to reveal who He really was. But Jesus would not appease their doubts and uncertainties. These fence-setters would not get assurances as to whom they could safely place their bets. The fact that they still do not get it despite the words and actions of Jesus means they are not His sheep. Their eyes are blind; their ears are deaf to the many signs and affirmations that the Lord did in their midst. These seal their fate as not Jesus' own.

14
MAY

Wednesday

Ps 113:1–2, 3–4, 5–6, 7–8
The Lord will give him a seat
with the leaders of his people.

**FEAST OF ST. MATTHIAS,
APOSTLE**
Psalter: Proper / (Red)

1st Reading: Acts 1:15–17, 20–26

*P*eter stood up in the midst of the community— about one hundred and twenty in all—and he said, "Brothers, it was necessary that the Scriptures referring to Judas be fulfilled. The Holy Spirit had spoken through David about the one who would lead the crowd coming to arrest Jesus. He was one of our number and had been called to share our common ministry. In the Book of Psalms it is written: *Let his house become deserted and may no one live in it*. But it is also written: *May another take his office*. Therefore, we must choose someone from among those who were with us during all the time that the Lord Jesus moved about with us, beginning with John's baptism until the day when Jesus was taken away from us. One of these has to become, with us, a witness to his resurrection." Then they proposed two: Joseph, called Barsabbas, also known as Justus, and Matthias. They prayed: "You know, Lord, what is in the hearts of all. Show us, therefore, which of the two you have chosen to replace Judas in this apostolic ministry which he deserted to go to the place he deserved."

Then they drew lots between the two and the choice fell on Matthias who was added to the eleven apostles.

Gospel: Jn 15:9–17

*J*esus said to his disciples, "As the Father has loved me, so I have loved you. Remain in my love! You will remain in my love if you keep my commandments, just as I have kept my Father's commandments and remain in his love.

"I have told you all this, that my own joy may be in you, and your joy may be complete. This is my commandment: Love one another as I have loved you! There is no greater love than this, to give one's life for one's friends; and you are my friends, if you do what I command you.

"I shall not call you servants any more, because servants do not know what their master is about. Instead, I have called you friends, since I have made known to you everything I learned from my Father.

"You did not choose me; it was I who chose you and sent you to go and bear fruit, fruit that will last. And everything you ask the Father in my name, he will give you.

"This is my command, that you love one another."

Keeping the commandments of the one who loves us should be a breeze. We are assured that whatever He wills for us is for our own good, no matter how much it will discomfort us, or go contrary to our own wishes and desires. We are at least assured that it comes from a heart whose only concern is our good. This is probably why Jesus calls us friends instead of servants. For a friend is never commanded to do things. Only servants are commanded to blind obedience. As friends we know where the command of Jesus comes from. It comes from a loving heart who desires our very own good more than we do. This is the motivation for our joy. That is why we can follow without regret.

Thursday

Ps 89:2–3, 21–22, 25 & 27
For ever, I will sing
the goodness of the Lord!

15
MAY

St. Isidore

Did you know that: St. Isidore the Farmer was canonized together with four great figures of the Catholic Reformation, i.e. St. Ignatius of Loyola, St. Teresa of Avila, St. Francis Xavier, and St. Philip Neri.

_____
_____
_____
_____
_____
_____
_____
_____
_____
_____
_____
_____
_____

Doing service to assure the comfort of others is not a menial task. It is a good task, something that each of us should think about. If we but from time to time think of doing something for the good of others, the world would be a better place than it is right now. Jesus showed us the impulse that must underlie our service to others. It should be grounded on a love that does not feel diminished by humility. For humility as a virtue, does not humiliate. Only false humility does that. Humble service, if taken to heart, assures our blessedness. For it is not something easy. Only those with great spiritual strength have the capacity to do and sustain such an act.

1st Reading: Acts 13:13–25

From Paphos, Paul and his companions set sail and came to Perga in Pamphylia. There, John left them and returned to Jerusalem, while they went on from Perga and came to Antioch in Pisidia. On the Sabbath day they entered the synagogue and sat down. After the reading of the law and the prophets, the officials of the synagogue sent this message to them, "Brothers, if you have any word of encouragement for the assembly, please speak up."

So Paul arose, motioned to them for silence and began, "Fellow Israelites and, also, all you who fear God, listen. The God of our people Israel chose our ancestors; and after he had made them increase during their stay in Egypt, he led them out by powerful deeds. For forty years he fed them in the desert; and after he had destroyed seven nations in the land of Canaan, he gave them their land as an inheritance. All this took four hundred and fifty years. After that, he gave them Judges, until Samuel the prophet. Then they asked for a king; and God gave them Saul, son of Kish, of the tribe of Benjamin; and he was king for forty years. After that time, God removed him and raised up David as king, to whom he bore witness saying: I have found David, the son of Jesse, a man after my own heart, who will do all I want him to do.

"It is from the descendants of David that God has now raised up the promised Savior of Israel, Jesus. Before he appeared, John proclaimed a baptism of repentance for all the people of Israel. As John was ending his life's work, he said: 'I am not what you think I am, for, after me, another one is coming, whose sandal I am not worthy to untie.'"

Gospel: Jn 13:16–20

Jesus said to his disciples, "Truly, I say to you, the servant is not greater than his master, nor is the messenger greater than he who sent him.Understand this, and blessed are you, if you put it into practice.

"I am not speaking of you all, because I know the ones I have chosen, and the Scripture has to be fulfilled which says: *The one who shares my table will rise up against me.* I tell you this now before it happens, so that when it does happen, you may know that I am He.

"Truly, I say to you, whoever welcomes the one I send, welcomes me; and whoever welcomes me, welcomes the One who sent me."

16
MAY

Friday
Ps 2:6–7, 8–9, 10–11ab
You are my Son;
this day I have begotten you!

4TH WEEK OF EASTER
Psalter: Week 4 / (White)

1st Reading: Acts 13:26–33

Paul said in the synagogue, "Brothers, children and descendants of Abraham, and you, also, who fear God, it is to you that this message of salvation has been sent. It is a fact, that the inhabitants of Jerusalem, and their leaders, did not recognize Jesus. Yet, in condemning him, they fulfilled the words of the prophets that are read every Sabbath, but not understood. Even though they found no charge against him that deserved death, they asked Pilate to have him executed. And after they had carried out all that had been writ-ten concerning him, they took him down from the cross and laid him in a tomb.

"But God raised him from the dead, and for many days thereafter, he showed himself, to those who had come up with him from Galilee to Jerusalem. They have now become his witnesses before the people. We, ourselves, announce to you this Good News: All that God promised our ancestors, he has fulfilled, for us, their descendants, by raising Jesus, according to what is written in the second psalm: *You are my Son, today I have begotten you.*"

Gospel: Jn 14:1–6

Jesus said to his disciples, "Do not be troubled! Trust in God and trust in me! In my Father's house there are many rooms; otherwise, I would not have told you that I go to prepare a place for you. After I have gone and prepared a place for you, I shall come again and take you to me, so that where I am, you also may be. Yet you know the way where I am going."

Thomas said to him, "Lord, we don't know where you are going; how can we know the way?" Jesus said, "I am the way, the truth and the life; no one comes to the Father but through me."

Saying goodbye is not always easy. That is why Jesus tells His disciples that His going away for a while will actually benefit them. He will prepare their rooms in His Father's house. Then He will return to take them with Him. This might blunt the pain of separation but it does not succeed in eliminating the sadness that His parting will cause. Thomas himself expressed the doubts of his peers, they might not be able to know the way to follow Jesus when He leaves. And so Jesus has to assure them of His abiding love for them. He Himself will ensure that they will get to the place where He is through Him. They might not be together in the near future, but their unity, forged in love, will cut across the separation of time and space so that they will always remain together in that love.

Saturday

Ps 98:1, 2-3ab, 3cd-4
All the ends of the earth have seen the saving power of God.

17
MAY

1st Reading: Acts 13:44–52

The following Sabbath almost the entire city gathered to listen to Paul, who spoke a fairly long time about the Lord. But the presence of such a crowd made the Jews jealous. So they began to oppose, with insults, whatever Paul said.

Then Paul and Barnabas spoke out firmly, saying, "It was necessary, that God's word be first proclaimed to you, but since you now reject it, and judge yourselves to be unworthy of eternal life, we turn to non-Jewish people. For thus we were commanded by the Lord: I have set you as a light to the pagan nations, so that you may bring my salvation to the ends of the earth."

Those who were not Jews rejoiced, when they heard this, and praised the message of the Lord; and all those, destined for everlasting life, believed in it. Thus the word spread, throughout the whole region.

Some of the Jews, however, incited God-fearing women of the upper class, and the leading men of the city, as well, and stirred up an intense persecution against Paul and Barnabas. Finally, they had them expelled from their region. The apostles shook the dust from their feet, in protest against this people, and went to Iconium, leaving; the disciples, filled with joy and the Holy Spirit.

Gospel: Jn 14:7–14

Jesus said to his disciples, "If you know me, you will know the Father also; indeed you know him, and you have seen him." Philip asked him, "Lord, show us the Father, and that is enough." Jesus said to him, "What! I have been with you so long and you still do not know me, Philip? Whoever sees me, sees the Father; how can you say, 'Show us the Father'? Do you not believe that I am in the Father and the Father is in me?

"All that I say to you, I do not say of myself. The Father who dwells in me is doing his own work. Believe me when I say that I am in the Father and the Father is in me; at least believe it on the evidence of these works that I do.

"Truly, I say to you, the one who believes in me will do the same works that I do; and he will even do greater than these, for I am going to the Father. Everything you ask in my name, I will do, so that the Father may be glorified in the Son. Indeed, anything you ask, calling upon my name, I will do it."

People will sometimes compliment a father how his son is his spitting image. And the father finds joy in the fact that he will be perpetuated through the son. But in the case of Jesus, it is He who claims that He is the mirror image of the Father. Those who see Him, see the Father as well. This filial pride gives us a glimpse of how intimate Jesus is with His Father. Within the divine conversation the Father must have constantly assured the Son of their similarity and likeness. And the Son seeing the fact itself as truth is confident enough to claim this with His disciples. We can only surmise how tenderness and intimacy is expressed within the Godhead, but one thing is clear at least. You are only happy to be the mirror of somebody else's features, gestures and habits if you truly love that person. It will not be a burden at all but an honor.

18
MAY

Sunday

Ps 33:1-2, 4-5, 18-19
Lord, let your mercy be on us,
as we place our trust in you.

1st Reading: Acts 6:1–7

*I*n those days, as the number of disciples grew, the so-called Hellenists complained against the so-called Hebrews, because their widows were being neglected in the daily distribution. So the Twelve summoned the whole body of disciples together, and said, "It is not right, that we should neglect the word of God to serve at tables. So, friends, choose from among yourselves seven respected men, full of Spirit and wisdom, that we may appoint them to this task. As for us, we shall give ourselves to prayer, and to the ministry of the word."

The whole community agreed; and they chose Stephen, a man full of faith and the Holy Spirit; Philip, Prochorus, Nicanor, Timon, Parmenus and Nicolaus of Antioch, who was a proselyte. They presented these men to the apostles, who, first prayed over them, and then, laid hands upon them.

The word of God continued to spread, and the number of the disciples in Jerusalem increased greatly; and even many priests accepted the faith.

2nd Reading: 1 P 2:4–9

*B*eloved, Jesus is the living stone rejected by people but chosen by God and precious to him. On drawing close to him, you also became living stones built into a spiritual temple, a holy community of priests offering spiritual sacrifices which please God through Jesus Christ. Scripture says: *See, I lay in Zion a chosen and precious cornerstone; whoever believes in him will not be disappointed.*

This means honor for you who believed, but for unbelievers also *the stone which the builders rejected has become the cornerstone* and it is *a stone to stumble over, a rock which lays people low*. They stumble over it in rejecting the Word, but the plan of God is fulfilled in this.

You are a *chosen race, a community of priest-kings, a consecrated nation, a people God has made his own to proclaim his wonders.* For he called you from your darkness to his own wonderful light.

Gospel: Jn 14:1–12

*J*esus said to his disciples, "Do not be troubled; trust in God and trust in me. In my Father's house there are many rooms. Otherwise I would not have told you that I go to prepare a place for you. After I have gone and prepared a place for you, I shall come again and take you to me, so that where I am, you also may be. Yet you know the way where I am going."

Thomas said to him, "Lord, we don't know where you are going; how can we know the way?" Jesus said, "I am the way, the truth and the life; no one comes to the Father but through me. If you know me, you will know the Father also; indeed you know him and you have seen him."

Philip asked him, "Lord, show us the Father and that is enough." Jesus said to him, "What! I have been with you so long and you still do not know me, Philip? Whoever sees me sees the Father; how can you say: 'Show us the Father'? Do you not believe that I am in the Father and the Father is in me?

"All that I say to you, I do not say of myself. The Father who dwells in me is doing his own work. Believe me when I say that I am in the Father and the Father is in me; at least believe it on the evidence of these works that I do.

"Truly, I say to you, the one who believes in me will do the same works that I do; and he will even do greater than these, for I am going to the Father."

Reading: Jesus calmed the fears of His apostles regarding their future. It is assured since they have a room prepared already for them in His Father's house. If they believe in Jesus, they will not get lost on their way to the Father nor will they feel a stranger before Him when the time comes. They who have seen, heard and touched the Lord have already seen, heard and touched the Father because of the deep intimacy of the Son to the Father.

optimism accusing us of clinging to an illusion or false hope, but what have they as an alternative? Their claim to an alternative meaningful life still demands an act of faith on those who follow it. And so between the two messiahs or multiple messiahs that present different visions of life, whom do we choose? May our faith be strong enough to believe that Jesus' vision for us is the best portion among the lot.

Reflection: Many of us cannot help worrying about the future. Time sometimes terrorizes us. But with Jesus, time ceases to intimidate because He promises a glorious future for those who believe. It is only a matter of attitude on our part whether we hold firmly to this promise or doubt it. In the end, it is we who are the author of the misery or the joy of our living. Some people might attack our Christian

Response: Making an act of faith in Jesus tends to be mechanical sometimes without our awareness or the full participation of our being. It would be good to pause today and make a sincere proclamation of our faith in Jesus, relishing every word, allowing it to penetrate our whole being so that we can stand for that act of faith no matter what the world will say for or against it.

19
MAY

Monday
Ps 115:1-2, 3-4, 15-16
Not to us, O Lord,
but to your name give the glory.

5TH WEEK OF EASTER
Psalter: Week 1 / (White)

1st Reading: Acts 14:5–18*

A move was made by pagans and Jews, together with their leaders, to harm the apostles and to stone them. But Paul and Barnabas learned of this and fled to the Lycaonian towns of Lystra and Derbe. (…) There was a crippled man in Lystra who had never been able to stand or walk. One day, as he was listening to the preaching, Paul looked intently at him and saw that he had the faith to be saved. So he said with a loud voice, "Stand upright on your feet." And the man leaped up and began walking. When the people saw what Paul had done, they cried out in the language of Lycaonia, "The gods have come to us in human likeness!" They named Barnabas Zeus, and Paul they called Hermes, since he was the chief speaker. (…) When Barnabas and Paul heard this, they tore their garments, to show their indignation, and rushed into the crowd, shouting, "Friends, why are you doing this? We are human beings, with the same weakness you have, and we are now telling you to turn away from these useless things, to the living God who made the heavens, the earth, the sea and all that is in them. In past generations, he allowed each nation to go its own way, though he never stopped making himself known; for he is continually doing good, giving you rain from heaven and fruitful seasons, providing you with food, and filling your hearts with gladness." Even these words could hardly keep the crowd from offering sacrifice to them.

Gospel: Jn 14:21–26

Jesus said to his disciples, "Whoever keeps my commandments is the one who loves me. If he loves me, he will also be loved by my Father; I too shall love him and show myself clearly to him."

Judas—not Judas Iscariot—asked Jesus, "Lord, how can it be that you will show yourself clearly to us and not to the world?" Jesus answered him, "If anyone loves me, he will keep my word and my Father will love him; and we will come to him and live with him. But if anyone does not love me, he will not keep my words; and these words that you hear are not mine, but the Father's who sent me.

"I told you all this while I am still with you. From now on the Helper, the Holy Spirit whom the Father will send in my name, will teach you all things, and remind you of all that I have told you."

The Helper, the Holy Spirit, is introduced in the gospel today. This is another assurance of Jesus that while He is gone, He will not leave His disciples orphaned. Someone from the Trinity will always be with them. Just as Jesus comes to do the will of the Father, so the Holy Spirit will teach and remind them of all that Jesus told them. In the end, we can see the teamwork and harmony within the Godhead. The Father puts His plan into operation, the Son and the Holy Spirit cooperate in perfect accord. No one makes an initiative by Himself. The Three Persons, within the Trinity, always act in perfect harmony. It is because of this that when someone acts in the name of any of the Persons in the Godhead but it contradicts the teaching of Jesus, that is a sure sign that he or she is an impostor. For the Son only says what His Father tells Him and the Spirit reminds us of all Jesus said and taught. The Trinity cannot contradict itself.

Tuesday

Ps 145:10–11, 12–13ab, 21
Your friends make known, O Lord,
the glorious splendor of your kingdom.

20
MAY

St. Bernardine of Siena

Did you know that: St. Bernardine of Siena was a great preacher and reformer who could project his voice so that he could be heard by up to 30 thousand people in the open air.

1st Reading: Acts 14:19–28

Some Jews arrived from Antioch and Iconium and turned the people against Paul and Barnabas. They stoned Paul and dragged him out of the town, leaving him for dead. But, when his disciples gathered around him, he stood up and returned to the town. And the next day, he left for Derbe with Barnabas.

After proclaiming the gospel in that town and making many disciples, they returned to Lystra and Iconium, and on to Antioch. They were strengthening the disciples, and encouraging them to remain firm in the faith; for they said, "We must go through many trials to enter the kingdom of God." In each church they appointed elders and, after praying and fasting, they commended them to the Lord, in whom they had placed their faith.

Then they traveled through Pisidia, and came to Pamphylia. They preached the word in Perga and went down to Attalia. From there, they sailed back to Antioch, where they had first been commended to God's grace, for the task they had now completed.

On their arrival, they gathered the Church together, and told them all that God had done through them, and how he had opened the door of faith to the non-Jews. They spent a fairly long time there with the disciples.

Gospel: Jn 14:27–31a

Jesus said to his disciples, "Peace be with you! My peace I give to you; not as the world gives peace do I give it to you. Do not be troubled! Do not be afraid! You heard me say, 'I am going away, but I am coming to you.' If you loved me, you would be glad that I go to the Father, for the Father is greater than I.

"I have told you this now before it takes place, so that when it does happen you may believe. There is very little left for me to tell you, for the prince of this world is at hand, although there is nothing in me that he can claim. But see, the world must know that I love the Father, and that I do what the Father has taught me to do. Come now, let us go."

From the 14th of May until now, it seems that the gospels are all about Jesus making preparations to leave behind those whom He calls friends. It is a long series of farewell. It seems that Jesus is taking too much time to say His goodbyes. For isn't it that the more intimate we are with one another, the harder the separation will be. Jesus experienced this very human feeling of attachment. But no matter how hard it is for Him, He remained focused on His task. The mission given Him by the Father must be done. If the price is the pain of separation from those He called His own, He is willing to pay the price. But meanwhile, He will try to comfort His friends. It is them and their good that will preoccupy Him throughout. He will always love them till the very end.

21
MAY

Wednesday
Ps 122:1-2, 3-4ab, 4cd-5
Let us go rejoicing
to the house of the Lord.

5TH WEEK OF EASTER
St. Christopher Magallanes, priest
and Companions, martyrs
Psalter: Week 1 / (White / Red)

1st Reading: Acts 15:1-6

Some persons, who had come from Judea to Antioch, were teaching the brothers in this way, "Unless you are circumcised, according to the law of Moses, you cannot be saved."

Because of this, there was trouble; and Paul and Barnabas had fierce arguments with them. For Paul told the people to remain as they were, when they became believers. Finally, those who had come from Jerusalem suggested that Paul and Barnabas and some others go up to Jerusalem, to discuss the matter with the apostles and elders.

They were sent on their way by the Church. As they passed through Phoenicia and Samaria they reported how the non-Jews had turned to God; and there was great joy among all the brothers and sisters.

On their arrival in Jerusalem, they were welcomed by the Church, the apostles and the elders, to whom they told all what God had done through them. Some believers, however, who belonged to the party of the Pharisees, stood up and said, that non-Jewish men must be circumcised and instructed to keep the law of Moses. So the apostles and elders met together to consider this matter.

Gospel: Jn 15:1-8

Jesus said to his disciples, "I am the true vine and my Father is the vine grower. If any of my branches doesn't bear fruit, he breaks it off; and he prunes every branch that does bear fruit, that it may bear even more fruit. You are already made clean by the word I have spoken to you. Live in me as I live in you. The branch cannot bear fruit by itself, but has to remain part of the vine; so neither can you, if you don't remain in me.

"I am the vine and you are the branches. As long as you remain in me and I in you, you bear much fruit; but apart from me you can do nothing. Whoever does not remain in me is thrown away, as they do with branches, and they wither. Then they are gathered and thrown into the fire and burned.

"If you remain in me and my words remain in you, you may ask whatever you want, and it will be given to you. My Father is glorified when you bear much fruit: it is then that you become my disciples."

St. Christopher Magallanes

Did you know that: St. Christopher Magallanes and his companions were falsely charged of promoting Cristero Rebellion which was a mass popular uprising and attempted counter-revolution against the anti-Catholicism of the ruling Mexican government. This resulted to years of persecution of Mexican Catholics and the Catholic Church in Mexico.

Intimacy with Jesus is the source of fruitfulness in our life and work. There is no other way, for to graft ourselves onto Jesus means that His tremendous power and creativity is there at our disposal. We will count not only on our own strengths and capacities; Jesus Himself will work with us. The vine, being Jesus, and we, as the branches are a beautiful image of how we are supposed to remain with one another. It also gives a beautiful example of how Jesus allows us authorship of good works in this world while He remains hidden in the center, supporting our initiatives and guiding our works toward completion. After all, vines tend to be covered by the luxuriant branches hiding it from view. May we always remain in Him who keeps us fruitful throughout.

Thursday

22 MAY

Ps 96:1–2a, 2b–3, 10
Proclaim God's marvelous deeds
to all the nations.

St. Rita of Cascia
Did you know that: St. Rita of Cascia, together with St. Jude, is also the Patron of Impossible Cases.

1st Reading: Acts 15:7–21

As the discussions became heated, Peter stood up and said to them, "Brothers, you know that from the beginning, God chose me among you, so that non-Jews could hear the Good News from me, and believe. God, who can read hearts, put himself on their side, by giving the Holy Spirit to them, just as he did to us. He made no distinction between us and them, and cleansed their hearts through faith. So, why do you want to put God to the test? Why do you lay on the disciples, a burden that neither our ancestors nor we, ourselves, were able to carry? We believe, indeed, that we are saved through the grace of the Lord Jesus, just as they are."

The whole assembly kept silent as they listened to Paul and Barnabas tell of all the miraculous signs and wonders that God had done, through them, among the non-Jews.

After they had finished, James spoke up, "Listen to me, brothers. Symeon has just explained how God first showed his care, by taking a people for himself from non-Jewish nations. And the words of the prophets agree with this, for Scripture says,

After this I will return and rebuild the booth of David which has fallen; I will rebuild its ruins and set it up again. Then, the rest of humanity will look for the Lord, and all the nations will be consecrated to my Name. So says the Lord, who does today what he decided from the beginning.

Because of this, I think that we should not make difficulties for those non-Jews who are turning to God. Let us just tell them, not to eat food that is unclean from having been offered to idols; to keep themselves from prohibited marriages; and not to eat the flesh of animals that have been strangled; or any blood. For, from the earliest times, Moses has been taught in every place, and every Sabbath his laws are recalled."

Gospel: Jn 15:9–11

Jesus said to his disciples, "As the Father has loved me, so I have loved you. Remain in my love! You will remain in my love if you keep my commandments, just as I have kept my Father's commandments and remain in his love.

"I have told you all this, that my own joy may be in you, and your joy may be complete."

Jesus never tires of telling His disciples how He loved them. Even unto the end, He affirms this love for each and every one of them. Perhaps, it's because love is such a complex reality that it has to be affirmed over and over again until it takes root in the consciousness of the beloved. We may sometimes feel that talking about love is cheap in this uncertain and unfaithful time we live. But still love can never be diminished by the infidelity of some. After all, its existence is possible only because there is a faithful God who loves us first; therefore we can also love. Jesus still believes in love that is articulated and acted upon. We must put our trust in Him who sustains all our love in this world and beyond.

23
MAY

Friday

Ps 57:8-9, 10 & 12
I will give you thanks
among the peoples, O Lord.

5TH WEEK OF EASTER
Psalter: Week 1 / (White)

1st Reading: Acts 15:22–31

The apostles and elders, together with the whole Church, decided to choose representatives from among them, to send to Antioch with Paul and Barnabas. These were Judas, known as Barsabbas, and Silas, both leading men among the brothers. They took with them the following letter:

"Greetings from the apostles and elders, your brothers, to the believers of non-Jewish birth in Antioch, Syria and Cilicia. We have heard, that some persons from among us have worried you with their discussions, and troubled your peace of mind. They were not appointed by us. But now, it has seemed right to us, in an assembly, to choose representatives, and to send them to you, along with our beloved Barnabas and Paul, who have dedicated their lives to the service of our Lord Jesus Christ. We send you, then, Judas and Silas, who, themselves, will give you these instructions by word of mouth.

We, with the Holy Spirit, have decided not to put any other burden on you except what is necessary: You are to abstain from blood; from the meat of strangled animals; and from prohibited marriages. If you keep yourselves from these, you will do well. Farewell."

After saying goodbye, the messengers went to Antioch, where they assembled the community and handed them the letter. When they read the news, all were delighted with the encouragement it gave them.

Gospel: Jn 15:12–17

Jesus said to his disciples, "This is my commandment: Love one another as I have loved you! There is no greater love than this, to give one's life for one's friends; and you are my friends, if you do what I command you.

"I shall not call you servants any more, because servants do not know what their master is about. Instead, I have called you friends, since I have made known to you everything I learned from my Father.

"You did not choose me; it was I who chose you and sent you to go and bear fruit, fruit that will last. And everything you ask the Father in my name, he will give you.

"This is my command, that you love one another."

And now, the rule to end all rules is given to the disciples. The commandment to love will be the supreme rule throughout their lives. After more than two thousand years, how has the community that Jesus started and still exists fare against this commandment to love? Have we understood what Jesus meant, or are we still grappling our way towards love that allows us to risk and even give our lives for our friends? The world has changed since then, but the rule remains valid even now. We need heroes of love who will show us how to do it. Is there anyone of us courageous enough to heed the commandment uttered a long time ago but still awaiting realization?

Saturday

Ps 100:1b–2, 3, 5
Let all the earth cry out to God
with joy.

24
MAY

_____
_____
_____
_____
_____
_____
_____
_____
_____
_____
_____
_____
_____
_____

1st Reading: Acts 16:1–10

Paul traveled on, to Derbeand then to Lystra. A disciple named Timothy lived there, whose mother was a believer of Jewish origin but whose father was a Greek. As the believers at Lystra and Iconium spoke well of him, Paul wanted Timothy to accompany him. So he took him and, because of the Jews of that place, who all knew that his father was a Greek, he circumcised him.

As they traveled from town to town, they delivered the decisions of the apostles and elders in Jerusalem, for the people to obey. Meanwhile, the churches grew stronger in faith, and increased in number, every day.

They traveled through Phrygia and Galatia, because they had been prevented by the Holy Spirit from preaching the message in the province of Asia. When they came to Mysia, they tried to go on to Bithynia, but the Spirit of Jesus did not allow them to do this. So, passing by Mysia, they went down to Troas.

There, one night, Paul had a vision. A Macedonian stood before him and begged him, "Come over to Macedonia and help us!" When he awoke, he told us of this vision; and we understood that the Lord was calling us, to give the Good News to the Macedonian people.

Gospel: Jn 15:18–21

Jesus said to his disciples, "If the world hates you, remember that the world hated me before you. This would not be so if you belonged to the world, because the world loves its own. But you are not of the world, since I have chosen you from the world; because of this the world hates you.

"Remember what I told you: the servant is not greater than his master; if they persecuted me, they will also persecute you. If they kept my word, they will keep yours as well. All this they will do to you on account of my name, because they do not know the One who sent me."

Outsiders will always feel this sense of alienation, of not being accepted in a group as long as he or she does not conform to the culture of the group in question. This is the feeling of Jesus relative to the world. He paid so much to be "in the group" by leaving behind His divine estate and pitch His tent among us. Still He was not accepted by the world. His message is too hard to bear. Thus if He, the Master and Teacher is an outsider, all those who follow Him will always feel this sense of not belonging to the world. This is probably one of the reasons why Jesus spent so much time preparing His disciples before He left. Hard times will be their lot ahead. Until the very end, Jesus never thought of Himself and His good. His thoughts remained throughout with those He loved as an example of a love that does not measure.

25
MAY

Sunday

Ps 66:1-3, 4-5, 6-7, 16, 20
Let all the earth cry out to God
with joy.

1st Reading: Acts 8:5–8, 14–17

Philip went down to a town of Samaria and proclaimed the Christ there. All the people paid close attention to what Philip said as they listened to him, and saw the miraculous signs that he did. For, in cases of possession, the unclean spirits came out shrieking loudly. Many people, who were paralyzed or crippled, were healed. So there was great joy in that town.

Now, when the apostles in Jerusalem heard that the Samaritans had accepted the word of God, they sent Peter and John to them. They went down and prayed for them, that they might receive the Holy Spirit; for he had not as yet come down upon any of them, since they had only been baptized in the name of the Lord Jesus. So Peter and John laid their hands on them and they received the Holy Spirit.

2nd Reading: 1 P 3:15–18

Beloved, bless the Lord Christ in your hearts. Always have an answer ready, when you are called upon, to account for your hope, but give it simply and with respect. Keep your conscience clear, so that those who slander you may be put to shame by your upright, Christian living. Better to suffer for doing good, if it is God's will, than for doing wrong.

Remember how Christ died, once, and for all, for our sins. He, the just one, died for the unjust, in order to lead us to God. In the body, he was put to death, in the spirit, he was raised to life.

Gospel: Jn 14:15–21

Jesus said to his disciples, "If you love me, you will keep my commandments; and I will ask the Father and he will give you another Helper to be with you forever, that Spirit of truth whom the world cannot receive because it neither sees him nor knows him. But you know him for he is with you and will be in you.

"I will not leave you orphans, I am coming to you. A little while and the world will see me no more, but you will see me because I live and you will also live. On that day you will know that I am in my Father and you in me, and I in you.

"Whoever keeps my commandments is the one who loves me. If he loves me, he will also be loved by my Father; I too shall love him and show myself clearly to him."

Reading: Jesus asks His followers to show their love for Him by keeping His commandments. He assures them of a helper, the Paraclete, so that they will not feel orphaned or abandoned. If they show their love for Jesus through obedience to His words, they will be loved by the Father and the Son, and the Spirit will dwell within them.

Reflection: The last words we speak to our love ones before departing are usually words of tenderness, counsels and assurances. In this regard Jesus is no different from us. His humanity fully shines despite His transformation in the Resurrection. He still remains the Son of God and the Son of Mary. What is surprising is the seeming reluctance of the Lord to part ways with His own friends. This human sentiment shining through His divinity assures us that from that time onwards, one of the Trinity can understand intimately how it is to be human. God has been inexorably linked to humanity. The world can rest in peace. There is someone like us and representing us in the Godhead.

Response: Jesus reminds us that our love for Him is shown in our obedience to His command. He has two which can be collapsed into one, that is, "love God and neighbor," or the double law of love. Have I really loved God and neighbor or do I prefer to love one over the other? It would be good to examine our following of the Lord today and evaluate it according to the standards of the command to love.

26
MAY

Monday

Ps 149:1b–2, 3–4, 5–6a & 9b
The Lord takes delight
in his people.

6TH WEEK OF EASTER
St. Philip Neri, priest
Psalter: Week 2 / (White)

1st Reading: Acts 16:11–15

We put out to sea from Troas and sailed straight across to Samothrace Island; and the next day, to Neapolis. From there, we went inland to Philippi, the leading city of the district of Macedonia, and a Roman colony. We spent some days in that city.

On the Sabbath, we went outside the city gate, to the bank of the river, where we thought the Jews would gather to pray. We sat down and began speaking to the women who were gathering there. One of them was a God-fearing woman, named Lydia, from the city of Thyatira, a dealer in purple cloth.

As she listened, the Lord opened her heart to respond to what Paul was saying. After she had been baptized, together with her household, she invited us to her house, "If you think I am faithful to the Lord, come and stay at my house." And she persuaded us to accept her invitation.

St. Philip Neri

Did you know that: St. Philip Neri is one of the saints who showed the humorous side of holiness in his life.

Gospel: Jn 15:26–16:4a

Jesus said to his disciples, "From the Father, I will send you the Spirit of truth. When this Helper has come from the Father, he will be my witness, and you, too, will be my witnesses, for you have been with me from the beginning.

"I tell you all this to keep you from stumbling and falling away. They will put you out of the synagogue. Still more, the hour is coming, when anyone who kills you will claim to be serving God; they will do this, because they have not known the Father or me. I tell you all these things now so that, when the time comes, you may remember that I told you about them."

Jesus now discloses the fate that awaits those who will persevere in following Him once He is gone. He never gives false hopes and promises to His own. He will strengthen and prepare them for the trials ahead but they will know what is in store for them if they remain faithful to His teachings. The only assurance He gives is that they will never be abandoned. The Holy Spirit will be with them as co-witnesses for Jesus in this world. Coming from others, these words meant to console would sound hollow and empty. But on the lips of Jesus, they have the backing and guarantee of His words and actions that have never been known to be false. His integrity guarantees that what He says is true. These words probably were the source of strength for those who remained faithful even at the foot of the cross. These will also give those who gave in to momentary fear and cowardice the courage to regroup, to believe once again and to continue the cause that Jesus had left in their hands.

Tuesday
27 MAY

Ps 138:1–2ab, 2cde–3, 7c–8
Your right hand saves me,
O Lord.

St. Augustine of Canterbury

Did you know that: St. Augustine of Canterbury was the pioneer in founding the dioceses of London and Rochester, and establishing a See, and building a cathedral and monastery at Canterbury.

_____
_____
_____
_____
_____
_____
_____
_____
_____
_____
_____
_____
_____
_____
_____
_____
_____

The time for mentoring is slowly coming to an end. It is not the glory of the Teacher if His pupils remain so. They too must become teachers themselves so that what they have learned from their Master will reach a wider audience. And so Jesus consoles His own with the assurance that the Spirit, the Helper will be sent to them to help them spread the truth of Jesus. They will lose the physical presence of the Lord, but the Spirit will abide forever in their hearts to make them feel that they are never abandoned by the Master who taught and prepared them to continue the mission once He is gone.

1ˢᵗ Reading: Acts 16:22–34

They set the crowd against them; and the officials tore the clothes off Paul and Silas and ordered them to be flogged. And after inflicting many blows on them, they threw them into prison, charging the jailer to guard them safely. Upon receiving these instructions, he threw them into the inner cell and fastened their feet in the stocks.

About midnight, Paul and Silas were praying and singing hymns to God, and the other prisoners were listening. Suddenly, a severe earthquake shook the place, rocking the prison to its foundations. Immediately, all the doors flew open and the chains of all the prisoners fell off. The jailer woke up to see the prison gates wide open. Thinking that the prisoners had escaped, he drew his sword to kill himself, but Paul shouted to him, "Do not harm yourself! We are all still here."

The jailer asked for a light, then rushed in, and fell at the feet of Paul and Silas. After he had secured the other prisoners, he led them out and asked, "Sirs, what must I do to be saved?" They answered, "Believe in the Lord Jesus Christ and you, and your household, will be saved." Then they spoke the word of God to him and to all his household.

Even at that hour of the night, the jailer took care of them and washed their wounds; and he, and his whole household, were baptized at once. He led them to his house, spread a meal before them and joyfully celebrated with his whole household his newfound faith in God.

Gospel: Jn 16:5–11

Jesus said to his disciples, "Now I am going to the One who sent me, and none of you asks me where I am going; instead you are overcome with grief, because of what I have said.

"Believe me, it is better for you that I go away, because as long as I do not go away, the Helper will not come to you. But if I go away, I will send him to you, and when he comes, he will vindicate the truth before a sinful world; and he will vindicate the paths of righteousness and justice.

"What is the world's sin, in regard to me? Disbelief. What is the path of righteousness? It is the path I walk, by which I go to the Father; and you shall see me no more. What is the path of justice? It is the path on which the prince of this world will always stand condemned."

28
MAY

Wednesday
Ps 148:1–2, 11–12, 13–14
Heaven and earth
are full of your glory.

6TH WEEK OF EASTER
Psalter: Week 2 / (White)

1st Reading: Acts 17:15, 22 – 18:1*

Paul stood up in the Areopagus hall and said, "Athenian citizens, I note that, in every way, you are very religious. As I walked around, looking at your shrines, I even discovered an altar with this inscription: To an unknown God. Now, what you worship as unknown, I intend to make known to you.

"God, who made the world and all that is in it, does not dwell in sanctuaries made by human hands, being as he is Lord of heaven and earth. Nor does his worship depend on anything made by human hands, as if he were in need. Rather, it is he who gives life and breath and everything else, to everyone. From one stock he created the whole human race, to live throughout all the earth, and he fixed the time and the boundaries of each nation. He wanted them to seek him by themselves, even if it was only by groping for him, that they succeed in finding him.

Yet, he is not far from any one of us. For, in him, we live and move, and have our being; as some of your poets have said: for we, too, are his offspring. If we are indeed God's offspring, we ought not to think of divinity as something like a statue of gold or silver, a product of human art and imagination." (…)

When they heard Paul speak of a resurrection from death, some made fun of him, while others said, "We must hear you on this topic some other time." At that point Paul left. But a few did join him, and believed. Among them were Dionysius, a member of the Areopagus court, a woman named Damaris, and some others.

After this, Paul left Athens and went to Corinth.

Gospel: Jn 16:12–15

Jesus said to his disciples, "I still have many things to tell you, but you cannot bear them now. When he, the Spirit of truth comes, he will guide you into the whole truth.

"For he will not speak of his own authority, but will speak what he hears, and he will tell you about the things which are to come. He will take what is mine and make it known to you; in doing this, he will glorify me. All that the Father has is mine; for this reason, I told you that the Spirit will take what is mine, and make it known to you."

Here Jesus affirms again His commitment not to leave His own orphaned and uncertain. He promises to send the Holy Spirit who will lead them into the whole truth. But the Holy Spirit will not reveal something new that Jesus has not told His disciples before. The Spirit will simply take what is Jesus' truth and give it to the disciples, deepen it and make it part of their consciousness so that they too will have the mind of Jesus. The Spirit therefore will guarantee that the disciples will never forget. Our memories will be safeguarded by the Spirit lest we misrepresent the truth of our Lord.

Thursday
Ps 98:1, 2–3ab, 3cd–4
The Lord has revealed to the nations his saving power.

29 MAY

1st Reading: Acts 18:1–8

Paul left Athens and went to Corinth. There, he found a Jew named Aquila, a native of Pontus, who had recently come from Italy with his wife Priscilla, following a decree of the Emperor Claudius, which ordered all Jews to leave Rome. Paul went to visit them, and then stayed and worked with them, because they shared the same trade of tent making. Every Sabbath, he held discussions in the synagogue, trying to convince both Jews and Greeks.

When Silas and Timothy came down from Macedonia, Paul was able to give himself wholly to preaching, and proving to the Jews that Jesus was the Messiah. One day, when they opposed him and insulted him, he shook the dust from his clothes in protest, saying, "Your blood be on your own heads! I am innocent. I am not to blame if, from now on, I go to the non-Jews."

So Paul left there and went to the house of a God-fearing man named Titus Justus, who lived next door to the synagogue. A leading man of the synagogue, Crispus, along with his whole household, believed in the Lord. On hearing Paul, many more Corinthians believed and were baptized.

Gospel: Jn 16:16–20

Jesus said to his disciples, "A little while, and you will see me no more; and then a little while, and you will see me."

Some of the disciples wondered, "What does he mean by, 'A little while, and you will not see me; and then a little while, and you will see me'? And why did he say, 'I go to the Father'?" And they said to one another, "What does he mean by 'a little while'? We don't understand."

Jesus knew that they wanted to question him; so he said to them, "You are puzzled because I told you that in a little while you will see me no more, and then a little while later you will see me.

"Truly, I say to you, you will weep and mourn while the world rejoices. You will be sorrowful, but your sorrow will turn to joy."

Sorrow and joy come together. They deepen the meaning of each other because of the contrast in experience they afford one another. And the going away of Jesus will give the disciples such contrast. When Jesus will be torn violently from them by death, their sorrow will plumb the depths of despair and hopelessness. Only their memory of His words and teachings and their faith in Him will support them in this time of trial. Only their love for Him will make them strong. But this faith and love will be vindicated when Jesus will rise triumphant from death and return to them. Their joy will know no bounds. Jesus is true to His words. Doubts will cease. The liberating feeling of having placed their faith in someone who is truthful and worthy of belief will comfort them throughout their lives.

30
MAY

Friday
Ps 47:2-3, 4-5, 6-7
God is king of all the earth.

16TH WEEK OF EASTER
Psalter: Week 2 / (White)

1st Reading: Acts 18:9–18

One night, in a vision, the Lord said to Paul, "Do not be afraid, but continue speaking and do not be silent, for many people in this city are mine. I am with you, so no one will harm you." So Paul stayed a year and a half in that place, teaching the word of God among them.

When Gallio was governor of Achaia, the Jews made a united attack on Paul and brought him before the court. And they accused him, "This man tries to persuade us to worship God in ways that are against the law."

Paul was about to speak in his own defense when Gallio said to the Jews, "If it were a matter of a misdeed or vicious crime, I would have to consider your complaint. But since this is a quarrel about teachings and divine names that are proper to your own law, see to it yourselves: I refuse to judge such matters." And he sent them out of the court.

Then the people seized Sosthenes, a leading man of the synagogue, and beat him in front of the tribunal; but Gallio paid no attention to it.

Paul stayed on with the disciples in Corinth for many days; he then left them and sailed off with Priscilla and Aquila for Syria. And as he was no longer under a vow he had taken, he shaved his head before sailing from Cenchreae.

Gospel: Jn 16:20–23

Jesus said to his disciples, "Truly, I say to you, you will weep and mourn while the world rejoices. You will be sorrowful, but your sorrow will turn to joy. A woman in childbirth is in distress because her time is at hand. But after the child is born, she no longer remembers her suffering because of her great joy: a human being is born into the world.

"You feel sorrowful now, but I will see you again, and your hearts will rejoice; and no one will take your joy from you. When that day comes you will not ask me anything. Truly, I say to you, whatever you ask the Father in my name, he will give you."

Joy that is borne out of sorrow is a transformed joy, not the exuberant, carefree happiness of spontaneous joy but a more sober, realistic and responsible joy. After all it is born of sacrifice and momentary pain. It knows how to relish the present because it faced squarely the sadness of the past. Jesus invites His disciples to such joy. He tries to console them from their mourning by pointing to a gloriously joyful future ahead. And once they have it, joy can never be taken away from them. The night of weeping will cease. If they have passed this path already, there is no other direction except to happiness that lasts forever with Jesus.

FEAST OF THE VISITATION OF THE BLESSED VIRGIN MARY
Psalter: Proper / (White)

Saturday

Is 12:2-3, 4bcd, 5-6
Among you is the great and Holy One of Israel.

31
MAY

_____
_____
_____
_____
_____
_____
_____
_____
_____
_____
_____
_____
_____
_____
_____
_____

1st Reading: Zep 3:14–18a

Cry out with joy, O daughter of Zion; rejoice, O people of Israel! Sing joyfully with all your heart, daughter of Jerusalem!

Yahweh has lifted your sentence and has driven your enemies away. Yahweh, the King of Israel is with you; do not fear any misfortune.

On that day, they will say to Jerusalem: Do not be afraid nor let your hands tremble, for Yahweh your God is within you, Yahweh, saving warrior. He will jump for joy on seeing you, for he has revived his love. For you he will cry out with joy, as you do in the days of the feast.

I will drive away the evil I warned you about, and you will no longer be shamed.

Gospel: Lk 1:39–56

Mary then set out for a town in the hill country of Judah. She entered the house of Zechariah and greeted Elizabeth. When Elizabeth heard Mary's greeting, the baby leapt in her womb. Elizabeth was filled with the Holy Spirit, and, giving a loud cry, said, "You are most blessed among women; and blessed is the fruit of your womb! How is it, that the mother of my Lord comes to me? The moment your greeting sounded in my ears, the baby within me suddenly leapt for joy. Blessed are you, who believed that the Lord's word would come true!"

And Mary said,

"My soul proclaims the greatness of the Lord,
my spirit exults in God, my savior!
He has looked upon his servant, in her lowliness, and people, forever, will call me blessed.
The Mighty One has done great things for me,
Holy is his Name!
From age to age, his mercy extends to those who live in his presence.
He has acted with power and done wonders, and scattered the proud with their plans.
He has put down the mighty from their thrones, and lifted up those who are downtrodden.
He has filled the hungry with good things, but has sent the rich away empty.
He held out his hand to Israel, his servant, for he remembered his mercy, even as he promised to our fathers, to Abraham and his descendants forever."

Mary remained with Elizabeth about three months, and then returned home.

Those who believe that the promise of the Lord will be done to them will always have reason to sing His praise. Their mouths will always acclaim His goodness. Everyday will be a blessing despite its own share of burden. Mary did not heed her own condition of pregnancy but went posthaste to help her cousin Elizabeth who bore a child in her old age. These two women had their share of hardships and challenges in life. But their faith in God and His promise remained unshaken. And so the trouble of their world is momentarily forgotten. In this snapshot of the event, they are only conscious of their blessings from God. Mary sang her song of thanksgiving. It is also the song of Elizabeth and all those who never stop believing in the kindness of God.

01
JUNE

Sunday

Ps 47:2–3, 6–7, 8–9
God mounts his throne to shouts of joy:
a blare of trumpets for the Lord.

1st Reading: Acts 1:1–11

In the first part of my work, Theophilus, I wrote of all that Jesus did and taught, from the beginning until the day when he ascended to heaven.

But first he had instructed, through the Holy Spirit, the apostles he had chosen. After his passion, he presented himself to them, giving many signs, that he was alive; over a period of forty days he appeared to them and taught them concerning the kingdom of God. Once, when he had been eating with them, he told them, "Do not leave Jerusalem but wait for the fulfillment of the Father's promise about which I have spoken to you: John baptized with water, but you will be baptized with the Holy Spirit within a few days."

When they had come together, they asked him, "Is it now that you will restore the kingdom of Israel?" And he answered, "It is not for you to know the time and the steps that the Father has fixed by his own authority. But you will receive power when the Holy Spirit comes upon you; and you will be my witnesses in Jerusalem, throughout Judea and Samaria, even to the ends of the earth."

After Jesus said this, he was taken up before their eyes and a cloud hid him from their sight. While they were still looking up to heaven, where he went, suddenly, two men dressed in white stood beside them and said, "Men of Galilee, why do you stand here looking up at the sky? This Jesus, who has been taken from you into heaven, will return in the same way as you have seen him go there."

2nd Reading: Eph 1:17–23

Brothers and sisters, may the God of Christ Jesus our Lord, the Father of glory, reveal himself to you, and give you a spirit of wisdom and revelation, that you may know him.

May he enlighten your inner vision, that you may appreciate the things we hope for, since we were called by God. May you know how great is the inheritance, the glory, God sets apart for his saints; may you understand, with what extraordinary power, he acts in favor of us who believe.

He revealed his almighty power in Christ when he raised him from the dead, and had him sit at his right hand in heaven, far above all rule, power, authority, dominion, or any other supernatural force that could be named, not only in this world, but in the world to come as well.

Thus has God put all things under the feet of Christ and set him above all things, as head of the church, which is his body, the fullness of him, who fills all in all.

Gospel: Mt 28:16–20

As for the eleven disciples, they went to Galilee, to the mountain where Jesus had told them to go. When they saw Jesus, they bowed before him, although some doubted.

"All authority has been given to me in heaven and on earth. Go, therefore, and make disciples of all nations. Baptize them in the Name of the Father and of the Son and of the Holy Spirit, and teach them to observe all that I have commanded you. I am with you always, even to the end of the world."

Reading: On a mountain in Galilee, Jesus now has to go to the Father. His disciples have gone there to worship Him and to listen to His last words. He gives them the mission to make disciples of all nations and baptize them according to the Trinitarian formula. He assures them of His continued presence in their ministry.

Reflection: Even during the last moments of Jesus with His disciples, some still hold doubts in their hearts. The resurrection is too big a mystery for them to grasp. However, it did not impede them to go to the mountain where Jesus is to ascend to His Father. Their doubt was not a hindrance to follow Him. Faith takes time to grow but if there is love, it will hold the line until belief sets in. Some of the disciples may not have entirely understood what was happening but in the end, they will prove themselves worthy of the Lord's confidence and esteem.

Response: There are people who struggle with their faith. Some have questions that if left unanswered would seriously harm their belief. A little time spent with the likes of them might ease their burden and turn their unbelief into solid faith. Likewise guiding the little ones to our faith might be a good start to help propagate our faith. A time spent with children and explaining to them in the simplest way the articles of our faith would aid them in their journey towards a mature faith in the future.

_____

_____

_____

_____

_____

_____

_____

_____

02
JUNE

Monday
Ps 68:2–3ab, 4–5acd, 6–7ab
Sing to God,
O kingdoms of the earth.

7TH WEEK OF EASTER
Sts. Marcellinus and Peter, martyrs
Psalter: Week 3 / (White / Red)

1st Reading: Acts 19:1–8

While Apollos was in Corinth, Paul traveled through the interior of the country and came to Ephesus. There, he found some disciples, whom he asked, "Did you receive the Holy Spirit when you became believers?" They answered, "We have not even heard that anyone may receive the Holy Spirit." Paul then asked, "What kind of baptism have you received?" And they answered, "The baptism of John."

Paul then explained, "John's baptism was for conversion, but he himself said they should believe in the one who was to come, and that one is Jesus." Upon hearing this, they were baptized in the name of the Lord Jesus. Then Paul laid his hands on them and the Holy Spirit came down upon them; and they began to speak in tongues and to prophesy. There were about twelve of them in all.

Paul went into the synagogue; and for three months he preached and discussed there boldly, trying to convince them about the kingdom of God.

Gospel: Jn 16:29–33

The disciples said to Jesus, "Now you are speaking plainly and not in veiled language! Now we see that you know all things, even before we question you. Because of this we believe that you came from God."

Jesus answered them, "You say that you believe? The hour is coming, indeed it has come, when you will be scattered, each one to his home, and you will leave me alone. Yet I am not alone, for the Father is with me.

"I have told you all this, so that in me you may have peace. You will have trouble in the world; but, courage! I have overcome the world."

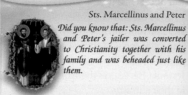

Sts. Marcellinus and Peter

Did you know that: Sts. Marcellinus and Peter's jailer was converted to Christianity together with his family and was beheaded just like them.

Veiled language is something irritating. It teases and taxes the brain, disclosing, while at the same time, hiding its real meaning. This is the reason why many do not have the patience to follow the teachings of the Lord. But now, He is commended for speaking plainly. They could understand Him; now they can believe. But then, the truths of heaven are never captured by plain human words. Jesus had to use symbolic language to convey a truth whose understanding would come at a later time. For that is the nature of the mystery greater than us. We have to spend time to grasp it but even then, we cannot fully comprehend the mystery. Our understanding will always increase as time goes by, but always will be short of the real meaning of the mystery. This is the motivation for our joy. That is why we can follow without regret.

Tuesday

Ps 68:10–11, 20–21
Sing to God,
O kingdoms of the earth.

03
JUNE

St. Charles Lwanga

Did you know that: St. Charles Lwanga was an Ugandan Catholic catechist martyred for his faith together with many Anglicans and Catholics during the reign of King Mwanga II.

_____

_____

_____

_____

_____

_____

_____

_____

_____

_____

_____

Prayers are nothing but conversations with God. The more spontaneous they are the more endearing and intimate. Just as the prayer of Jesus to His Father in this gospel is a free-flowing conversation that comes out from the heart, prayers are not supposed to be a struggle to put into words what we want to tell the Father. After all, He knows what we need before we even utter them. Some prayers are listened to and responded immediately. There are prayers that have to wait, while others are not responded to according to request. There are also favors that are withheld. Whatever the outcome of our prayers, they are always for our own good. What is most important is our growth in friendship and intimacy with our partner in this divine conversation and sustain such act.

1st Reading: Acts 20:17–27

From Miletus, Paul sent word to Ephesus, summoning the elders of the Church. When they came to him, he addressed them, "You know how I lived among you, from the first day I set foot in the province of Asia; how I served the Lord in humility, through the sorrows and trials that the Jews caused me. You know, that I never held back from doing anything that could be useful for you; I spoke publicly and in your homes; and I urged Jews, and non-Jews, alike, to turn to God and believe in our Lord Jesus.

"But now, I am going to Jerusalem, chained by the Spirit, without knowing what will happen to me there. Yet, in every city, the Holy Spirit warns me, that imprisonment and troubles await me. Indeed, I put no value on my life; if only I can finish my race; and complete the service to which I have been assigned by the Lord Jesus, to announce the good news of God's grace.

"I now feel sure, that none of you, among whom I have gone about proclaiming the kingdom of God, will ever see me again. Therefore, I declare to you, this day, that my conscience is clear with regard to all of you. For I have spared no effort in fully declaring to you God's will."

Gospel: Jn 17:1–11a

Jesus lifted up his eyes to heaven and said, "Father, the hour has come! Give glory to your Son, that the Son may give glory to you. You have given him power over all humanity, so that he may give eternal life to all those you entrusted to him. For this is eternal life: to *know* you, the only true God, and the One you sent, Jesus Christ.

"I have glorified you on earth and finished the work that you gave me to do. Now, Father, give me, in your presence, the same glory I had with you before the world began.

"I have made your name known to those you gave me from the world. They were yours, and you gave them to me, and they kept your word. And now they *know* that whatever you entrusted to me, is indeed from you. I have given them the teaching I received from you, and they accepted it, and know in truth that I came from you; and they believe that you sent me.

"I pray for them. I do not pray for the world, but for those who belong to you, and whom you have given to me. Indeed all I have is yours, and all you have is mine; and now they are my glory. I am no longer in the world, but they are in the world, and I come to you. Holy Father, keep those you have given me in your name, so that they may be one, as we also are."

04

JUNE

Wednesday

Ps 68:29–30, 33–35a, 35bc–36ab

Sing to God,
O kingdoms of the earth.

7TH WEEK OF EASTER
Psalter: Week 3 / (White)

1st Reading Act 20:28-38

Paul spoke to the presbyters of the Church of Ephesus, "Keep watch over yourselves, and over the whole flock the Holy Spirit has placed into your care. Shepherd the Church of the Lord that he has won, at the price of his own blood. I know that, after I leave, ruthless wolves will come among you and not spare the flock. And, from among you, some will arise, corrupting the truth, and inducing the disciples to follow them.

"Be on the watch, therefore, remembering that, for three years, night and day, I did not cease to warn everyone, even with tears. Now, I commend you to God, and to his grace-filled word, which is able to make you grow and gain the inheritance that you shall share with all the saints.

"I have not looked for anyone's silver, gold or clothing. You, yourselves, know, that these hands of mine have provided for both my needs and the needs of those who were with me. In every way, I have shown you that by working hard one must help the weak, remembering the words that the Lord Jesus himself said, 'Happiness lies more in giving than in receiving.'"

After this discourse, Paul knelt down with them and prayed. Then, they all began to weep and threw their arms around him and kissed him. They were deeply distressed because he had said that they would never see him again. And they went with him even to the ship.

Gospel: Jn 17:11b–19

Jesus prayed, saying, "Holy Father, keep those you have given me in your name, so that they may be one, as we also are. When I was with them, I kept them safe in your name; and not one was lost, except the one who was already lost, and in this, the Scripture was fulfilled. And now I come to you; in the world I speak these things, so that those whom you gave me, might have joy—all my joy within themselves.

"I have given them your word; and the world has hated them, because they are not of the world, just as I am not of the world, I do not ask you to remove them from the world, but to keep them from the evil one. They are not of the world, just as I am not of the world. Consecrate them in the truth. Your word is truth.

"I have sent them into the world as you sent me into the world; and for their sake, I go to the sacrifice by which I am consecrated, so that they too may be consecrated in truth."

Jesus never forgets His friends. Even on the verge of His glorification, when mundane concerns fade in the background, Jesus never forgets for a moment His own. He commends them to the Father for safe-keeping. Yet His love does not blind Him from what is to be done. The disciples must stay in the world to continue what He has started, to consecrate the world in the truth of the Father. His love does not spoil them. He only asks that they be kept from the evil one, that no matter how the latter persecutes and inflicts pain on them, they will remain steadfast and strong in the faith. May the prayer of Jesus remain valid for all times and in all places.

Thursday

05
JUNE

Ps 16:1–2a and 5, 7–8, 9–10, 11
Keep me safe, O God,
you are my hope.

St. Boniface

Did you know that: St. Boniface is known as the Apostle of Germany. He not only brought the Christian faith but also the Roman Christian civilization to this portion of Europe.

_____
_____
_____
_____
_____
_____
_____
_____
_____
_____
_____
_____
_____
_____

Jesus looks beyond those who believe in Him now as well as those who will believe in Him on the strength of the testimony of His present believers. He wishes to share with them what He has enjoyed with the Father. In this prayer, we catch a glimpse of the dynamics of God. The overflow of love within the Trinity is such that they need not hold on to it to be satisfied. They can share it freely since it comes from an inexhaustible supply within the Triune God. And so Jesus wishes to share the very life He has with the Father to His followers. They too will know someday the bliss within the Godhead.

1st Reading: Acts 22:30; 23:6–11

The next day, the commander wanted to know for certain, the charges the Jews were making against Paul. So, he released him from prison and called together the High Priest and the whole Council; and they brought Paul down and made him stand before them.

Paul knew, that part of the Council were Sadducees and others Pharisees; so he spoke out in the Council, "Brothers, I am a Pharisee, son of a Pharisee. It is for the hope in the resurrection of the dead that I am on trial here."

At these words, an argument broke out between the Pharisees and the Sadducees, and the whole assembly was divided. For the Sadducees claim that, there is neither resurrection, nor angels nor spirits; while the Pharisees acknowledge all these things.

Then, the shouting grew louder; and some teachers of the law of the Pharisee party protested, "We find nothing wrong with this man. Maybe a spirit or an angel has spoken to him."

With this, the argument became so violent that the commander feared that Paul would be torn to pieces by them. He, therefore, ordered the soldiers to go down and rescue him from their midst, and take him back to the fortress.

That night, the Lord stood by Paul and said, "Courage! As you have borne witness to me here, in Jerusalem, so must you do in Rome."

Gospel: Jn 17:20–26

Jesus prayed, saying, "I pray not only for these. but also for those who through their word will believe in me. May they all be one, as you Father are in me and I am in you. May they be one in us, so that the world may believe that you have sent me.

"I have given them the glory you have given me, that they may be one as we are one: I in them and you in me. Thus they shall reach perfection in unity; and the world shall *know* that you have sent me, and that I have loved them, just as you loved me.

"Father, since you have given them to me, I want them to be with me where I am, and see the glory you gave me, for you loved me before the foundation of the world.

"Righteous Father, the world has not known you, but I have known you, and these have *known* that you have sent me. As I revealed your name to them, so will I continue to reveal it, so that the love with which you loved me may be in them, and I also may be in them."

06
JUNE

Friday
Ps 103:1–2, 11–12, 19–20ab
The Lord has established
his throne in heaven.

7TH WEEK OF EASTER
St. Norbert, bishop
Psalter: Week 3 / (White)

1st Reading: Acts 25:13b–21

King Agrippa, and his sister Bernice, arrived in Caesarea to greet Festus. As they were to stay there several days, Festus told the king about Paul's case, and said to him,

"We have here, a man, whom Felix left as a prisoner. When I was in Jerusalem, the chief priests, and the elders of the Jews, accused him, and asked me to sentence him. I told them, that it is not the custom of the Romans to hand over a man, without giving him an opportunity to defend himself in front of his accusers. So they came, and I took my seat, without delay, on the tribunal, and sent for the man.

"When the accusers had the floor, they did not accuse him of any of the crimes that I was led to think he had committed; instead, they quarreled with him, about religion, and about a certain Jesus, who has died, but whom Paul asserted to be alive. I did not know what to do about this case, so I asked Paul if he wanted to go to Jerusalem, to be tried there. But Paul appealed, to be judged by the emperor. So I ordered, that he be kept in custody until I send him to Caesar."

Gospel: Jn 21:15–19

After they had finished breakfast, Jesus said to Simon Peter, "Simon, son of John, do you love me more than these do?" He answered, "Yes, Lord, you know that I love you." And Jesus said, "Feed my lambs."

A second time Jesus said to him, "Simon, son of John, do you love me?" And Peter answered, "Yes, Lord, you know that I love you." Jesus said to him, "Look after my sheep." And a third time he said to him, "Simon, son of John, do you love me?"

Peter was saddened because Jesus asked him a third time, "Do you love me?" and he said, "Lord, you know everything; you know that I love you." Jesus then said, "Feed my sheep! Truly, I say to you, when you were young, you put on your belt and walked where you liked. But when you grow old, you will stretch out your hands, and another will put a belt around you, and lead you where you do not wish to go."

Jesus said this to make known the kind of death by which Peter was to glorify God. And he added, "Follow me!"

St. Norbert
Did you know that: St. Norbert is the founder of the Order of Canons Regular of Prémontré, popularly known as White Canons.

Love grows in intensity as time goes by. It could also lose its force. Jesus however invites Peter into deeper intimacy with Him again by His triple interrogation of the love Peter has for Him. He gives Peter the chance to redeem himself from his triple denial of the Lord during His passion. This episode from the past will be buried this day if Peter will be up to the occasion. Each time the Lord asks Peter and he affirms his love, a corresponding responsibility is placed upon him. This will allow Peter to validate his declaration of love by his readiness to do what the Lord commands him to do. Blessed is that day when Peter was redeemed by love.

Saturday

Ps 11:4, 5 & 7
The just will gaze on your face,
O Lord.

07
JUNE

1st Reading: Acts 28:16–20, 30–31

Upon our arrival in Rome, the captain turned the prisoners over to the military governor, but permitted Paul to lodge in a private house, with the soldier who guarded him.

After three days, Paul called together the leaders of the Jews. When they had gathered, he said to them: "Brothers, though I have not done anything against our people, or against the traditions of our fathers, I was arrested in Jerusalem, and handed over to the Romans. They examined me, and wanted to set me free, for they saw nothing in my case that deserved death. But the Jews objected, so I was forced to appeal to Caesar without the least intention of bringing any case against my own people. Therefore, I have asked to see you, and speak with you, since it is because of the hope of Israel, that I bear these chains."

Paul stayed for two whole years in a house he himself rented without any hindrance all those who came to see him. He proclaimed the kingdom of God and taught the truth about Jesus Christ, the Lord, quite openly and without any hindrance.

Gospel: Jn 21:20–25

Peter looked back and saw that the disciple Jesus loved was following as well, the one who had reclined close to Jesus at the supper, and had asked him, "Lord, who is to betray you?" On seeing him, Peter asked Jesus, "Lord, what about him?" Jesus answered, "If I want him to remain until I come, is that any concern of yours? Follow me!"

Because of this, the rumor spread in the community that this disciple would not die. Yet Jesus did not say to Peter, "He will not die," but, "Suppose I want him to remain until I come back, what concern is that of yours?"

It is this disciple who testifies about the things and has written these things down, and we know that his testimony is true. But Jesus did many other things; if all were written down, I think the world itself could not contain the books that should be written.

The gospels are not autobiographies of the Lord. They are faith accounts of the people who knew Him because they had heard, touched and seen the Lord. For this reason, there are many things that the Lord did which are not recorded. The gospel today says as much. This gives us an orientation on how to profit from our reading of the gospels. They are meant to awaken faith in Jesus who is the man behind the book. They are not meant to give us information into the life history of the Lord.

08
JUNE

Sunday

Ps 104:1, 24, 29-30, 31, 34
Lord, send out your Spirit,
and renew the face of the earth.

1st Reading: Acts 2:1–11

When the day of Pentecost came, they were all together in one place. And suddenly, out of the sky, came a sound, like a strong rushing wind; and it filled the whole house where they were sitting. There appeared tongues, as if of fire, which parted and came to rest upon each one of them. All were filled with the Holy Spirit and began to speak other languages, as the Spirit enabled them to speak.

Staying in Jerusalem were religious Jews from every nation under heaven. When they heard this sound, a crowd gathered, all excited, because each heard them speaking in his own language. Full of amazement and wonder, they asked, "Are not all these who are speaking Galileans? How is it, that we hear them in our own native language? Here are Parthians, Medes and Elamites; and residents of Mesopotamia, Judea and Cappadocia; Pontus and Asia; Phrygia, Pamphylia, Egypt; and the parts of Libya belonging to Cyrene; and visitors from Rome; both Jews and foreigners who accept Jewish beliefs, Cretians and Arabians; and all of us hear them proclaiming in our own language what God, the Savior, does."

2nd Reading: 1 Cor 12:3b–7, 12–13

Brothers and sisters, I tell you that nobody inspired by the Spirit of God may say, "A curse on Jesus," as no one can say, "Jesus is the Lord," except by the Holy Spirit.

There is diversity of gifts, but the Spirit is the same. There is diversity of ministries, but the Lord is the same. There is diversity of works, but the same God works in all. The Spirit reveals his presence in each one with a gift that is also a service.

As the body is one, having many members, and all the members, while being many, form one body, so it is with Christ. All of us, whether Jews or Greeks, slaves or free, have been baptized in one Spirit, to form one body, and all of us have been given, to drink from the one Spirit.

Gospel: Jn 20:19–23

On the evening of that day, the first day after the Sabbath, the doors were locked where the disciples were, because of their fear of the Jews. But Jesus came, and stood among them, and said to them, "Peace be with you!" Then he showed them his hands and his side. The disciples, seeing the *Lord*, were full of joy.

Again Jesus said to them, "Peace be with you! As the Father has sent me, so I send you." After saying this, he breathed on them, and said to them, "Receive the Holy Spirit! Those whose sins you forgive, they are forgiven; those whose sins you retain, they are retained."

Reading: Fear tends to lock us into our own self. We lock out others afraid to venture into the wild threatening world outside. But Jesus is not one to be hindered by our own fears and insecurities. He tears them apart and offers us the possibility of engaging the world again. He brings His peace which casts aside the gloom of our defeat, our weaknesses and infidelities.

Reflection: The first gift of Jesus to His bewildered disciples when He appeared to them was "Peace." It was the peace that had seen violence and death and had overcome it. It was a peace that would never give in to doubt and despair anymore. It is the peace of those who have "walked the valleys of death" and lived. This is a very big gift that one can give to others. This is a product of a life that has known hardship and has overcome it. Very few possess this kind of treasure. When the going is rough, we tend to seek persons who could give us proper perspectives of what we are undergoing. Usually these are people who have undergone the same ordeal themselves and have survived. We draw strength from their wisdom and tranquillity. We believe their words because they embody those words themselves. And so Jesus' peace is a genuine peace. The disciples will be settled from that time on. The moment of fear has passed by.

Response: Today I would like to give peace and tranquillity to others by being peaceful myself. I will not try to struggle nor compete even with myself. I will just be contented with who I am and what I have today and share these with others.

09
JUNE

Monday

Ps 121:1bc–2, 3–4, 5–6, 7–8
Our help is from the Lord,
who made heaven and earth.

10TH WEEK IN ORDINARY TIME
St. Ephrem, deacon & martyr
Psalter: Week 2 / (Green / White)

1st Reading: 1 K 17:1–6

Elijah, the prophet from Tishbe in Gilead, said to Ahab, "As Yahweh, the God of Israel whom I serve lives, neither dew shall drop nor rain fall except at my command."

Then the word of Yahweh came to Elijah, "Leave this place and go eastward. Hide yourself by the brook Cherith, east of the Jordan. You shall drink from the brook and, for your food, I have commanded the ravens to feed you there." So Elijah obeyed the word of Yahweh and went to live by the brook Cherith, east of the Jordan. There the ravens brought him bread in the morning and meat in the evening; and he drank from the brook.

Gospel: Mt 5:1–12

When Jesus saw the crowds, he went up the mountain. He sat down and his disciples gathered around him. Then he spoke and began to teach them:

"Fortunate are those who are poor in spirit, for theirs is the kingdom of heaven.

"Fortunate are those who mourn; they shall be comforted.

"Fortunate are the gentle; they shall possess the land.

"Fortunate are those who hunger and thirst for justice, for they shall be satisfied.

"Fortunate are the merciful, for they shall find mercy.

"Fortunate are those with pure hearts, for they shall see God.

"Fortunate are those who work for peace; they shall be called children of God.

"Fortunate are those who are persecuted for the cause of righteousness, for theirs is the kingdom of heaven.

"Fortunate are you, when people insult you and persecute you and speak all kinds of evil against you because you are my followers. Be glad and joyful, for a great reward is kept for you in God. For that is how this people persecuted the prophets who lived before you.

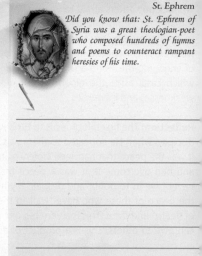

St. Ephrem

Did you know that: St. Ephrem of Syria was a great theologian-poet who composed hundreds of hymns and poems to counteract rampant heresies of his time.

The valuation of fortune and misfortune is usually dependent on what one holds dear and important. In a world steeped in materialistic orientation, outward appearances are esteemed rather than interiority. Jesus considers fortunate those whom the world normally abhors. It is because they have something that can never be taken away from them. It is embedded in their being. We have two choices before us: to be considered fortunate by the world or to be fortunate according to the standards of heaven. Whatever decisions we make will shape the orientation and direction of the life we will lead.

Tuesday

Ps 4:2-3, 4-5, 7b-8
Lord, let your face shine on us.

10
JUNE

1st Reading: 1 K 17:7-16

After a while, the brook dried up because no rain had fallen in the land. Then Yahweh spoke to Elijah, "Go to Zarephath of the Sidonites and stay there. I have given word to a widow there, to give you food." So Elijah went to Zarephath. On reaching the gate of the town, he saw a widow gathering sticks. He called to her and said, "Bring me a little water in a vessel that I may drink."

As she was going to bring it, he called after her and said, "Bring me also a piece of bread." But she answered, "As Yahweh your God lives, I have no bread left, but only a handful of flour in a jar and a little oil in a jug. I am just now gathering some sticks so that I may go in and prepare something for myself and my son to eat— and die."

Elijah then said to her, "Do not be afraid. Go, and do as you have said. But first make me a little cake of it and bring it to me. Then make some for yourself and your son. For this is the word of Yahweh, the God of Israel, 'The jar of meal shall not be emptied nor shall the jug of oil fail, until the day when Yahweh sends rain to the earth.'"

So she went and did as Elijah told her; and she had food for herself, Elijah and her son from that day on. The jar of flour was not emptied nor did the jug of oil fail, in accordance with what Yahweh had said through Elijah.

Gospel: Mt 5:13-16

Jesus said to his disciples, "You are the salt of the earth. But if salt has lost its saltiness, how can it be made salty again? It has become useless. It can only be thrown away and people will trample on it.

"You are the light of the world. A city built on a mountain cannot be hidden. No one lights a lamp and covers it; instead, it is put on a lamp stand, where it gives light to everyone in the house. In the same way, your light must shine before others, so that they may see the good you do, and praise your Father in heaven."

Once a precious commodity whose weight equaled the value of gold in equal quantity, salt flavors and preserves food. It cleans and is usually believed to cast away evil when flung in the air. Our being equated to salt shows the value and esteem that the Lord has for us. And like salt we are enjoined to spice up the world with holy lives, preserving the values of the Kingdom even if it goes out of fashion in this changing world, and contributing to transforming this sinful world into a civilization of love.

The second imagery that Jesus used for us is light. We are the light of the world darkened by sinful structures that block the light of God. But this light is not ours, it is the reflection of the light of Jesus in our life. The amount of light we can absorb from Him is dependent on our quality as instruments of His light

11
JUNE

Wednesday
Ps 98:1, 2–3ab, 3cd–4, 5–6
The Lord has revealed
to the nations his saving power.

10TH WEEK IN ORDINARY TIME
St. Barnabas, apostle
Psalter: Week 2 / (Red)

1st Reading: Acts 11:21b–26; 13:1–3

*T*he hand of the Lord was with them so that a great number believed and turned to the Lord.

News of this reached the ears of the Church in Jerusalem, so they sent Barnabas to Antioch. When he arrived and saw the manifest signs of God's favor, he rejoiced and urged them all to remain firmly faithful to the Lord; for he, himself, was a good man, filled with the Holy Spirit and faith. Thus large crowds came to know the Lord.

Then Barnabas went off to Tarsus, to look for Saul; and when he found him, he brought him to Antioch. For a whole year, they had meetings with the Church and instructed many people. It was in Antioch that the disciples were first called Christians.

There were at Antioch–in the Church which was there–prophets and teachers: Barnabas, Symeon known as Niger, Lucius of Cyrene, Manaen who had been brought up with Herod, and Saul. On one occasion, while they were celebrating the Lord and fasting, the Holy Spirit said to them, "Set apart for me Barnabas and Saul to do the work for which I have called them." So, after fasting and praying, they laid their hands on them and sent them off.

Gospel: Mt 10:7–13 (or Mt 5:17–19)

*J*esus said to his apostles, "Go, and proclaim this message: The kingdom of heaven is near. Heal the sick, bring the dead back to life, cleanse the lepers, and drive out demons. Freely have you received, freely give. Do not carry any gold or silver or money in your purses. Do not take a traveling bag, or an extra shirt, or sandals, or a walking stick: workers deserve to be compensated.

"When you come to a town or a village, look for a worthy person, and stay there until you leave.

"When you enter the house, wish it peace. If the people are worthy people, your peace will rest on them; if they are not worthy people, your blessing will come back to you."

Jesus never formed His disciples to stay with Him forever. For it is no merit to a teacher to have his students forever at his side. They have to expand their horizons by using whatever they have learned from their Master. They have to show that they have truly understood what the Teacher taught them. They have to be teachers themselves in their own right. But for now, the disciples are apprentices. They need to go back to their Teacher from time to time to share their experiences of successes and failures. They still need His guidance. In this gospel, the disciples are given a chance to participate in God's mission. They are now co-workers of Jesus in doing the will of the Father.

Thursday

Ps 65:10, 11, 12–13
It is right to praise you in Zion,
O God.

12
JUNE

1st Reading: 1 K 18:41–46

Elijah said to Ahab, "Go up, eat and drink, for the sound of rain is rushing in." So Ahab went up to eat and drink. Elijah, in the meantime, went to the top of Carmel, bowed to the ground and put his face between his knees. Then he said to his servant, "Go up and look in the direction of the sea." The man went up, looked, and said, "There is nothing." Then Elijah said, "Go again;" and seven times he went. At the seventh time, he perceived a little cloud, the size of a man's hand, rising out of the sea. Elijah told him, "Go, tell Ahab: Prepare your chariot and go down before the rain stops you." A little later the sky grew dark with clouds and wind, and a strong rain fell. Ahab was riding on his way to Jezreel. As for Elijah, the hand of Yahweh was on him, and tucking his cloak in his belt, he ran before Ahab to the entrance of Jezreel.

Gospel: Mt 5:20–26

Jesus said to his disciples, "I tell you, if your sense of right and wrong is not keener than that of the Lawyers and the Pharisees, you will not enter the kingdom of heaven.

"You have heard, that it was said to our people in the past: *Do not commit murder; anyone who murders will have to face trial*. But now, I tell you: whoever gets angry with a brother or sister will have to face trial. Whoever insults a brother or sister is liable, to be brought before the council. Whoever calls a brother or sister "Fool!" is liable, of being thrown into the fire of hell. So, if you are about to offer your gift at the altar, and you remember that your brother has something against you, leave your gift there, in front of the altar; go at once, and make peace with your brother, and then come back and offer your gift to God.

"Don't forget this: be reconciled with your opponent quickly when you are together on the way to court. Otherwise he will turn you over to the judge, who will hand you over to the police, who will put you in jail. There, you will stay, until you have paid the last penny."

Doing the minimum in our spiritual life is not enough. Jesus cautions His followers to be righteous in a much broader way than the teachers of the Law and the Pharisees. They have to act more than what the Law places at face value. For the spirit of the Law is usually not captured by plain words alone. The literal sense of the Law does not do justice to the scope and breadth that it covers. Jesus reminds them that murder is not just killing the physical life of persons; it also includes the act of insulting and humiliating people in public. The ensuing hostility between parties robs them of their abilities to enjoy life to the fullest. Only reconciliation will restore the equilibrium and bring them back towards normal life.

13
JUNE

Friday
Ps 27:7–8a, 8b–9abc, 13–14
I long to see your face, O Lord.

10TH WEEK IN ORDINARY TIME
St. Anthony of Padua, priest & doctor
Psalter: Week 2 / (White)

1st Reading: 1 K 19:9a, 11–16

On reaching the place, Elijah came to the cave and stayed in it. Then the word of Yahweh came to him, "What are you doing here, Elijah?"

Then Yahweh said, "Go up and stand on the mount, waiting for Yahweh." And Yahweh passed by.

There was first a windstorm, wild wind which rent the mountains and broke the rocks into pieces before Yahweh, but Yahweh was not in the wind. After the storm, an earthquake, but Yahweh was not in the earthquake; after the earthquake, a fire, but Yahweh was not in the fire; after the fire, the murmur of a gentle breeze. When Elijah perceived it, he covered his face with his cloak, went out and stood at the entrance of the cave.

Then he heard a voice addressing him again, "What are you doing here, Elijah?" He answered, "I am burning with jealous love for Yahweh, the God of Hosts, because the Israelites have forsaken your Covenant, thrown down your altars and slain your prophets with the sword. No one is left but myself, yet they still seek my life to take it away."

Yahweh said to him, "Take the road back through the desert and go to Damascus, for you must anoint Hazael as king of Syria. You shall also anoint Jehu, son of Nimshi, as king over Israel. And Elisha, son of Shaphat, from Abel Meholah, you shall anoint as prophet in your place."

St. Anthony of Padua
Did you know that: St. Anthony of Padua was canonized saint less than a year after his death.

Gospel: Mt 5:27–32

Jesus said to his disciples, "You have heard that it was said: *Do not commit adultery*. But I tell you this: anyone who looks at a woman with lustful intent, has already committed adultery with her in his heart.

"So, if your right eye causes you to sin, pluck it out and throw it away! It is much better for you to lose a part of your body, than to have your whole body thrown into hell. If your right hand causes you to sin, cut it off and throw it away! It is better for you to lose a part of your body, than to have your whole body thrown into hell.

"It was also said: *Anyone who divorces his wife, must give her a written notice of divorce*. But what I tell you is this: if a man divorces his wife, except in the case of unlawful union, he causes her to commit adultery. And the man who marries a divorced woman commits adultery."

Again Jesus talks of the spirit of the Law that must be taken into account in our spiritual and moral life. He wants His disciples to understand the Law beyond its surface meaning until they come to the very heart: that an offense occurs when one begins doing what is prohibited. Thus adultery begins with one's lustful look at a woman. Every time one entertains a temptation, one deliberately weakens the will to resist. Ultimately without self-discipline, the fall into sin follows. For sin has a long history. The completion of the act is merely the end of a long series of unhindered sinful acts.

Saturday

Ps 16:1b–2a & 5, 7–8, 9–10
You are my inheritance, O Lord.

14 JUNE

1st Reading: 1 K 19:19–21

*E*lijah left. He found Elisha, son of Shaphat, who was plowing with twelve yoke of oxen; he was following the twelfth. Elijah passed by him and cast his cloak over him. Elisha left the oxen, ran after Elijah and said, "Let me say goodbye to my father and mother; then I will follow you." Elijah said to him, "Return if you want, don't worry about what I did." However, Elisha turned back, took the yoke of oxen and slew them. He roasted their meat on the pieces of the yoke and gave it to his people who ate of it. After this, he followed Elijah and began ministering to him.

Gospel: Mt 5:33–37

*J*esus said to his disciples, "You have also heard that people were told in the past: *Do not break your oath; an oath sworn to the Lord must be kept.* But I tell you this: do not take oaths. Do not swear by the heavens, for they are God's throne; nor by the earth, because it is his foot stool; nor by Jerusalem, because it is the city of the great king. Do not even swear by your head, because you cannot make a single hair white or black. Let your 'Yes' mean 'Yes' and your 'No' mean 'No.' Anything else you say comes from the evil one."

Promises are made not to be broken but to be fulfilled. They are the present articulation of what we intend to do in the future. A promise usually gives additional backing to one's words. They are resorted to when the other party has doubts and fears that need to be assuaged. But one need not make any promises if one's intention is clear from the very beginning. Sincerity doesn't need the backing of a sworn oath. The words spoken plainly and clearly are enough to guarantee your position. Today Jesus encourages us to make our word our bond.

15
JUNE

Sunday

Dn 3:52, 53, 54, 55 — Glory and praise for ever!

1st Reading: Ex 34:4b-6, 8-9

Moses went up Mount Sinai in the early morning, as Yahweh has commanded. And Yahweh came down in a cloud and stood there with him, and Moses called on the name of Yahweh. Then Yahweh passed in front of him and cried out, "Yahweh, Yahweh is a God full of pity and mercy, slow to anger and abounding in truth and loving kindness."

Moses hastened to bow down to the ground and worshiped. He then said, "If you really look kindly on me, my Lord, please come and walk in our midst and even though we are a stiff-necked people, pardon our wickedness and our sin and make us yours."

2nd Reading: 2 Cor 13:11-13

Brothers and sisters, be happy, strive to be perfect, have courage, be of one mind and live in peace. And the God of love and peace will be with you. Greet one another with a holy kiss. All the saints greet you.

The grace of Christ Jesus the Lord, the love of God and the fellowship of the Holy Spirit be with you all.

Gospel: Jn 3:16-18

Yes, God so loved the world that he gave his only Son that whoever believes in him may not be lost, but may have eternal life. God did not send the Son into the world to condemn the world; instead, through him the world is to be saved. Whoever believes in him will not be condemned. He who does not believe is already condemned, because he has not believed in the name of the only Son of God.

Reading: Jesus now discloses to Nicodemus the truth about His personhood. He shared His privileged status as the Son sent by the Father to save the world. It is belief in the Son that will lead to salvation.

Reflection: Love is the very essence of our Trinitarian God, for it is, after all, the overflowing, abundant love of the Father that made Him begot His only Son who came from His very own substance. He could have chosen to be alone for all eternity, complete and whole unto Himself but His love so overflows that He decided to have a community of Persons within the Godhead, the Father and the Son, and the Holy Spirit who is the love of the Father to the Son, and the Son who receives this love and returns it to the Father. Thus this "community of love" presides over the whole creation in love. It follows therefore that the way to our divinization is no other than the path of love.

Response: Have I told the people close to me lately that I love them? It may sound corny and so banal, what with the many "I love yous" spoken insincerely. But I will not mind this negative thought today. I will reach out to those who matter to me and I will tell them straight faced that I love them.

16
JUNE

Monday

Ps 5:2–3ab, 4b–6a, 6b–7
Lord, listen to my groaning.

11TH WEEK IN ORDINARY TIME
Psalter: Week 3 / (Green)

1st Reading: 1 K 21:1–16*

*N*aboth, a man from Jezreel, owned a vineyard just beside the palace of Ahab, king of Samaria. Ahab asked Naboth, "Give me your vineyard which is near my house that I may use it for a vegetable garden. I will give you a better vineyard in exchange. Or, if you prefer, I will pay you its price."

But Naboth said to Ahab, "Yahweh forbid that I should give you the inheritance of my fathers."

So Ahab went home angry and sad because of what Naboth had told him, that he would not give him the inheritance of his fathers. So he lay down on his bed with his face turned toward the wall and refused to eat.

His wife Jezebel came to him and said, "Why are you so angry that you refuse to eat?" He answered, "I spoke to Naboth the Jezreelite and asked him to sell me his vineyard or to exchange it for another one in exchange; but he answered: I will not give you my vineyard."

His wife Jezebel said to him, "Are you not king of Israel? Get up and eat and be joyful, for I will give you the vineyard of Naboth of Jezreel."

So Jezebel wrote letters using Ahab's name and sealed them with his seal, and sent the letters to the elders and important persons living near Naboth. This is what she wrote in the letters: "Declare a fast and put Naboth on trial. Get two scoundrels to accuse him in this way: 'You have cursed God and the king.' Then take him out and stone him to death."

The people, the elders and the important persons who lived in his city did as Jezebel had instructed them in the letters she sent to them. They declared a fast and put Naboth on trial. The two worthless fellows came in and sat facing him, accusing Naboth before the people, "Naboth cursed God and the king!" So the people took him outside the city and stoned him to death. They then sent word to Jezebel that Naboth had been stoned and was dead. (...)

As soon as Ahab heard that Naboth was dead, he went down to the vineyard of Naboth and took possession of it.

Gospel: Mt 5:38–42

*J*esus said to his disciples, "You have heard, that it was said: *An eye for an eye and a tooth for a tooth*. But I tell you this: do not oppose evil with evil; if someone slaps you on your right cheek, turn and offer the other. If someone sues you in court for your shirt, give him your coat as well. If someone forces you to go one mile, go two miles with him. Give when asked, and do not turn your back on anyone who wants to borrow from you."

If we react to a situation it is usually by instinct. We need not think what we have to do. We give back what we receive automatically. And so Jesus cautions us today to do away with reaction. It does not change but abets the already negative environment. We are called to transform the negative into positive. We need to transform the bad to the good. Doing so means we have to start with ourselves. This calls for a sacrifice of the ego.

Tuesday

Ps 51:3–4, 5–6ab, 11 & 16
Be merciful, O Lord,
for we have sinned.

17
JUNE

1st Reading: 1 K 21:17–29

Yahweh spoke to Elijah of Tishbe, "Go down to meet Ahab, king of Israel, in Samaria. He is taking possession of the vineyard of Naboth. Say to him: 'Have you killed and have taken possession at the same time?' Then give him this word of mine: 'Dogs shall lick your blood in the very place where the dogs licked the blood of Naboth.'"

Ahab then said to Elijah, "Who, better than my enemy, could find me here and now!" Elijah answered, "I have come to you because you have done what Yahweh abhors. This is Yahweh's word: 'I will bring disgrace on you. I will sweep you away and cut off every male of your family, from the lowliest to the greatest. Your family will disappear like the families of Jeroboam and Baasa, because you have offended me and have dragged Israel into sin.' There is another word of Yahweh to Jezebel: 'The dogs shall devour Jezebel within the territory of Jezreel.' If anyone of Ahab's line dies in the city, he shall be devoured by dogs; if in the green country, the birds of the air shall feed on him."

There was no one like Ahab, urged by his wife Jezebel, in doing what Yahweh abhorred. He did horrible things and ran after unclean idols just as the Amorites had done, from whom Yahweh had taken the land to give it to Israel.

On hearing these words, Ahab tore his clothes and put on sackcloth. He fasted as he lay in sackcloth and moved around despondently. Then Yahweh said to Elijah the Tishbite, "Have you seen how Ahab has humbled himself? Because of this I will not bring about the disaster during his reign; during his son's reign disgrace will fall on his family."

Gospel: Mt 5:43–48

Jesus said to his disciples, "You have heard, that it was said: *Love your neighbor and do not do good to your enemy.* But this I tell you: love your enemies; and pray for those who persecute you, so that you may be children of your Father in Heaven. For he makes his sunrise on both the wicked and the good; and he gives rain to both the just and the unjust.

"If you love those who love you, what is special about that? Do not even tax collectors do as much? And if you are friendly only to your friends, what is so exceptional about that? Do not even the pagans do as much? As for you, be perfect, as your heavenly Father is perfect."

Love is easier when the objects of love are people close to you. It does not even require an effort. Love flows automatically to those who makes us feel good. But love is greater when directed to those who will harm us. It requires tremendous strength on our part. The needed strength sometimes goes beyond human capacities. It has to tap into the divine. Jesus encourages love of enemies for this forces us to connect with the Father always. Since we need His strength we have to be in continuous intimacy with Him. Loving one's enemies guarantees our friendship with God.

Wednesday

Ps 31:20, 21, 24
Let your hearts take comfort,
all who hope in the Lord.

11TH WEEK IN ORDINARY TIME
Psalter: Week 3 / (Green)

1st Reading: 2 K 2:1, 6–14*

Yahweh took Elijah up to heaven in a whirlwind. It happened this way: (…) When Elijah and Elisha stood by the Jordan Elijah took his mantle, rolled it, and struck the water with it. The water parted to both sides and they crossed over on dry ground.

As they were talking on the way, a chariot of fire with horses of fire stood between them, and Elijah was taken up to heaven in a whirlwind. Elisha saw him and cried out, "Father, my father, chariots of Israel and its horsemen!"

When Elisha lost sight of him, he took hold of his own clothes and tore them. He then picked up the mantle which had fallen from Elijah and returned to the banks of the Jordan. He took the cloak that had fallen off Elijah, hit the water with it, and asked, "Where is the Yahweh, the God of Elijah?" When he hit the water again, it divided and Elisha crossed over.

Gospel: Mt 6:1–6, 16–18

Jesus said to his disciples "Be careful not to make a show of your good deeds before people. If you do so, you do not gain anything from your Father in heaven. When you give something to the poor, do not have it trumpeted be fore you, as do those who want to be noticed in the synagogues and in the streets, in order to be praised by people. I assure you, they have their reward.

"If you give something to the poor, do not let your left hand know what your right hand is doing, so that your gift remains really secret. Your Father, who sees what is kept secret, will reward you.

"When you pray, do not be like those who want to be noticed. They love to stand and pray in the synagogues or on street corners, in order to be seen by everyone. I assure you, they have their reward. When you pray, go into your room, close the door, and pray to your Father who is with you in secret; and your Father who sees what is kept secret will reward you.

"When you fast, do not put on a miserable face, as do the hypocrites. They put on a gloomy face, so that people can see they are fasting. I tell you this: they have been paid in full already. When you fast, wash your face and make yourself look cheerful, because you are not fasting for appearances or for people, but for your Father, who sees beyond appearances. And your Father, who sees what is kept secret, will reward you."

Genuine goodness need not trumpet itself. The very act of doing good is its own reward. It is most happy when it realizes itself. For a good deed that wants to be rewarded by recognition does not spring from a good heart but a heart in need. It is as poor as the recipients of the deed it has done, probably much poorer. It is therefore not a virtue but a way to fill up one's inner poverty. Jesus knows this very well. So today he invites us to do good according to the style of the Father and His own: one that is unobtrusive and sincere.

11TH WEEK IN ORDINARY TIME
St. Romuald, abbot
Psalter: Week 3 / (Green / White)

Thursday
Ps 97:1–2, 3–4, 5–6, 7
Rejoice in the Lord, you just!

19
JUNE

St. Romuald

Did you know that: St. Romuald was the founder of several monasteries and hermitages; among those are Fonte Avellana and Camaldoli.

_____
_____
_____
_____
_____
_____
_____
_____
_____
_____
_____
_____
_____

Our way of praying to the Father varies from one person to another. It depends on our person and our degree of intimacy with the Father. But the common thing we do is to start with words. We string words together to communicate with the Father. This at least could be shared. What cannot be transferred is the disposition behind the utterances of the same words. In today's Gospel, Jesus taught His disciples the words He used to talk to His Father. It is the first step to initiate His friends in an intimate relationship with the Father. He can show them by example how a life lived in proximity to the Father is. But it would be the personal effort of the disciples to awaken their love for the Father while praying.

1st Reading: Sir 48:1–14

Then came the prophet Elijah, like a fire, his words a burning torch.

He brought a famine on the people and in his zealous love had them reduced in number.

Speaking in the name of the Lord he closed the heavens, and on three occasions called down fire.

How marvelous you were, Elijah, in your wondrous deeds! Who could ever boast of being your equal? By the word of the Most High you brought a dead man back to life; you brought kings to destruction and thrust famous men from their beds.

You heard a rebuke at Sinai and sentences of punishment at Horeb; you anointed kings to be avengers and prophets to succeed you.

You were taken up by a whirlwind of flames in a chariot drawn by fiery horses.

It was written that you should be the one to calm God's anger in the future, before it broke out in fury, to turn the hearts of fathers to their sons and to restore the tribes of Jacob.

Happy are those who will see you and those who die in love, for we too shall live.

Such was Elijah, taken up in a whirlwind, and Elisha was filled with his spirit.

During his life no leader could shake him, no one dominated him. Nothing was too difficult for him and even in death his body prophesied. In life he worked wonders, in death his deeds were amazing.

Gospel: Mt 6:7–15

Jesus said to his disciples "When you pray, do not use a lot of words, as the pagans do; for they believe that, the more they say, the more chance they have of being heard. Do not be like them. Your Father knows what you need, even be fore you ask him.

"This, then, is how you should pray: Our Father in heaven, holy be your name, your kingdom, come, your will, be done on earth, as in heaven.

'Give us today, our daily bread.

'Forgive us our debts, as we forgive those who are in debt to us.

'Do not bring us to the test, but deliver us from the evil one.'

"If you forgive others their wrong doings, your Father in heaven will also forgive yours. If you do not forgive others, then your Father will not forgive you."

20

JUNE

𝔉riday
Ps 132:11, 12, 13–14, 17–18
The Lord has chosen Zion
for his dwelling.

11TH WEEK IN ORDINARY TIME
Psalter: Week 3 / (Green)

1st Reading: 2 K 11:1-4, 9-18, 20*

In the seventh year, Jehoiada the chief priest, summoned the officers of the royal guard and of the Carites to the house of Yahweh. After concluding a pact with them under oath, he showed them the king's son.

The commanders of the guards did what Jehoiada the priest had told them to do; and they showed up with all their men, those who were to go off duty on the Sabbath as well as those who were to come on duty on that day. Jehoiada entrusted to the officers the spears and shields of king David which were in the house of Yahweh. And then the guards stood from the southern corner of the house to the north, surrounding the altar and the house of Yahweh. Then Jehoiada, the priest, brought out the king's son, crowned him and put the bracelets on him, then proclaimed and consecrated him king. All clapped their hands, shouting and crying out, "Long live the king!"

When Athaliah heard the noise of the people, she approached the crowd surrounding the house of Yahweh. (…) Jehoiada the priest commanded the officers, "Surround her and bring her out to the courtyard, and kill anyone who tries to defend her." He gave this order, because he thought, "She should not die in the house of Yahweh." They brought her out, and when they reached the palace of the king, by the horses' entrance, there, they killed her.

Jehoiada made a Covenant between Yahweh and the king and the people so they would be the people of Yahweh. All the citizens went to the temple of Baal and destroyed it. They broke the altars and the images into pieces, and killed Mattan, the priest of Baal, before his altar. Then Jehoiada, the priest, posted guards over the house of Yahweh. All the citizens were happy and the city was at peace. Now regarding Athaliah, she had died by the sword in the king's palace.

Gospel: Mt 6:19-23

Jesus said to his disciples, "Do not store up treasures for yourself here, on earth, where moth and rust destroy it; and where thieves can steal it. Store up treasures for yourself with God, where no moth or rust can destroy it, nor thief come and steal it. For where your treasures is, there, also, will your heart be.

"The lamp of the body is the eye; if your eyes are sound, your whole body will be full of light. If your eyes are diseased, your whole body will be full of darkness. If, then, the light in you is darkness, how great is that darkness!"

We call the things we have accumulated here on earth as possessions, for rightly they are. We are the ones who possess them not the other way around. It is us who have control over them. Sadly what happens is sometimes we are the ones possessed by our possessions. They enslave us to the point that we become too preoccupied with them. We lose sight of the fact that they are temporary and passing. We will not have them forever. They will all be left behind when we die. And so they are meant to be enjoyed and shared. They are good servants who use them to do good here on earth. They can guarantee our life beyond if used wisely and prudently. But once they gain ascendance over us, they turn us into very bad masters. They become tyrants that will drive us literally and figuratively to hell.

Saturday

21
JUNE

Ps 89:4–5, 29–30, 31–32, 33–34
Forever I will maintain my love
for my servant.

St. Aloysius Gonzaga

Did you know that: St. Aloysius Gonzaga's name was changed to Robert before his death, in honor of his confessor, St. Robert Bellarmine.

1st Reading: 2 Chr 24:17–25*

The Judaeans abandoned the house of Yahweh, the God of their ancestors, and worshiped the Asherah poles and idols. Because of this sinful activity, God was angry with Judah and Jerusalem. He sent them prophets to bring them back to Yahweh, but when the prophets spoke, they would not listen. The spirit of God took control of Zechariah, son of Jehoiada the priest. He stood up before the people and said, "God says this: Why are you disobeying the commandments of Yahweh? You cannot prosper. You have abandoned Yahweh and he will abandon you." They then plotted against him and, by order of the king, stoned him in the court of Yahweh's house. King Joash forgot the kindness of Jehoiada, the father of Zechariah, and killed Jehoiada's son who cried out as he died, "Let Yahweh see and do justice!" (…) When a year had gone by, the Aramaean army made war on Joash. They reached Judah and Jerusalem, and killed all the officials among the people, sending back to the king of Damascus all that they had plundered from them. Though the Aramaean army was small, Yahweh delivered into its power an army of great size for they had abandoned him, the Code of their ancestors. (…)

Gospel: Mt 6:24–34

Jesus said to his disciples, "No one can serve two masters; for he will either hate one and love the other; or he will be loyal to the first and look down on the second. You cannot, at the same time, serve God and money. Therefore, I tell you, not to be worried about food and drink for yourself, or about clothes for your body. Is not life more important than food; and is not the body more important than clothes? Look at the birds of the air; they do not sow, they do not harvest, and do not store food in barns; and yet, your heavenly Father feeds them. Are you not less worthy than they are?

"Can any of you add a day to your life by worrying about it? Why are you so worried about your clothes? Look at how the flowers in the fields grow. They do not toil or spin. But I tell you, that not even Solomon, in all his glory, was clothed like one of these. If God so clothes the grass in the field, which blooms today and is to be burned in an oven tomorrow, how much more will he clothe you? What little faith you have!

"Do not worry, and say: What are we going to eat? What are we going to drink? or: What shall we wear? The pagans busy themselves with such things; but your heavenly Father knows that you need them all. Set your heart, first, on the kingdom and righteousness of God; and all these things will also be given to you. Do not worry about tomorrow, for tomorrow will worry about itself. Each day has enough trouble of its own."

Serving two masters at the same time is a bad decision. It divides our energy, creativity and efficacy. We will fail both in the end or we will be forced to choose one over the other. And so instead of wasting our time and effort it is better to choose just one master whom we can serve well. Jesus presents a Master who is worth our while. He presents His Father Who takes care of His own very well. In the end one will not even know who serves whom. It is an investment of a lifetime that is forever open to anyone who cares.

1st Reading: Dt 8:2–3,14b–16a

*M*oses said to the people, "Remember how Yahweh, your God, brought you through the desert for forty years. He humbled you, to test you and know what was in your heart, whether you would keep his commandments or not. He made you experience want, he made you experience hunger, but he gave you manna to eat which neither you nor your fathers had known, to show you that one does not live on bread alone, but also by everything that comes from the mouth of God.

"Then do not let your heart become proud and do not forget Yahweh, your God, who brought you out of the land of Egypt, the house of slavery. It is he who has led you across this great and terrible desert, full of fiery serpents and scorpions, an arid land where there is no water. But for you he made water gush forth from the hardest rock. And he fed you in the desert with manna which your fathers did not know."

2nd Reading: 1 Cor 10:16–17

*B*rothers and sisters, "The cup of blessing that we bless, is it not a communion with the blood of Christ? And the bread that we break, is it not a communion with the body of Christ? The bread is one, and so we, though many, form one body, sharing the one bread."

Gospel: Jn 6:51–58

*J*esus said to the crowd, "I am the living *bread from heaven*; whoever eats of this bread will live forever. The bread I shall give is my flesh, and I will give it for the life of the world."

The Jews were arguing among themselves, "How can this man give us his flesh to eat?" So Jesus replied, "Truly, I say to you, if you do not eat the flesh of the Son of Man and drink his blood, you have no life in you. The one who eats my flesh and drinks my blood lives eternal life, and I will raise him up on the last day.

"My flesh is really food, and my blood is truly drink. Those who eat my flesh and drink my blood, live in me, and I in them. Just as the Father, who is life, sent me, and I have life from the Father, so whoever eats me will have life from me. This is the *bread from heaven*; not like that of your ancestors, who ate and later died. Those who eat this bread will live forever."

If God so clothes the grass
in the fi eld, which blooms today and
is to be burned in an oven tomorrow,
how much more will he clothe you?

Reading: Jesus had been giving them the living bread discourse which the Jews repeatedly misunderstood. Jesus is once again speaking in veiled languages whose real meaning is known only to those whom Jesus wishes to disclose the meaning.

Reflection: The Lord's bread of life discourse is one of the contentious arguments He has with the Jews who insist on a literalist's approach to the words of Jesus. If this is the case, the claims of Jesus are hard to believe. The eating of His flesh and the drinking of His blood to have life would be an absurd and macabre assertion. However, Jesus speaks on a different plane. He points to the manna that temporarily saved wandering Israel in the desert when they were hungry as a bread of temporary relief. It rained from heaven. He who came from heaven descended as the bread that will usher eternal life. To understand Him means to draw from various sources of knowledge such as history, customs and traditions. This is the main conflict He has with the Jews. They use elementary brain process of literal thinking while Jesus employs multiple brain operations of the creative and symbolic thinking. These two brain operations are hard pressed to meet. This inevitably led to open conflict and hostility.

Response: Bread is a nourishing food. It is actually delightful to eat if we know where to source it. Today, I will try to share good bread with those close to me. I will make an effort to bake or buy one to be enjoyed with friends. And perhaps, I will make a pitch of inviting them to a mass some time where we can enjoy the bread of life, Jesus Himself, during communion time.

_____
_____
_____
_____
_____
_____
_____
_____
_____
_____

23
JUNE

Monday
Ps 60:3, 4–5, 12–13
Help us with your right hand,
O Lord, and answer us.

12TH WEEK IN ORDINARY TIME
Psalter: Week 4 / (Green)

1st Reading: 2 K 17:5–8, 13–15a, 18

The army of the king of Asshur subjected the whole of Israel, coming to Samaria and laying siege to it for three years. In the ninth year of the reign of Hoshea, the king of Assyria captured Samaria, exiled the Israelites to Asshur and made them settle in Halah, at the banks of Habor, the river of Gozan, as well as in the cities of the Medes.

This happened because the children of Israel had sinned against Yahweh, their God, who had brought them out of the land of Egypt, where they were subject to Pharaoh. But they had turned back to other gods. They followed the customs of the nations which Yahweh had driven out before them. Yahweh warned Israel and Judah through the mouth of every prophet and seer, saying: "Turn from your evil ways and keep my commandments and precepts according to the laws which I commanded your fathers and which I have sent to you by my servants, the prophets."

But they did not listen and refused, as did their fathers, who did not believe in Yahweh, their God. They despised his statutes and the Covenant he had made with their fathers, and the warnings he had given them. They went after worthless idols and they themselves became worthless, following the nations which surrounded them, in spite of what Yahweh had said, "Do not do as they do."

So Yahweh became indignant with Israel and cast them far away from his presence, leaving only the tribe of Judah.

Gospel: Mt 7:1–5

Jesus said to his disciples, "Do not judge; and you will not be judged. In the same way you judge others, you will be judged; and the measure you use for others will be used for you. Why do you look at the speck in your brother's eye, and not see the plank in your own eye? How can you say to your brother, 'Come, let me take the speck from your eye,' as long as that plank is in your own? Hypocrite, remove the plank out of your own eye; then, you will see clearly, to remove the speck out of your brother's eye."

The best teachers and guides are those with experience. It is something that can never be taught. It can only be acquired in time. So Jesus cautions us against playing teacher and guide before our time comes. We might worsen our brother's or our sister's condition by our naive advice. This is true especially in the area of spirituality. It takes years to have some understanding on how the Spirit works. Usually we find out through our own spiritual journey. The learning and insights do help a lot to equip us to help others navigate our own spiritual journeys. But until then, when we have not yet settled our own, we remain students like the rest at the feet of the Master. We do not play judge, teacher nor guide but are co-journeyers with others.

SOLEMNITY OF THE NATIVITY OF ST. JOHN THE BAPTIST
Psalter: Proper / (White)

Tuesday

Ps 139:1-3, 13-14, 14-15
I praise you for I am wonderfully made.

24
JUNE

1st Reading: Is 49:1–6

Listen to me, O islands, pay attention, people from distant lands. Yahweh called me from my mother's womb; he pronounced my name before I was born. He made my mouth like a sharpened sword.

He hid me in the shadow of his hand. He made me into a polished arrow set apart in his quiver. He said to me, "You are Israel, my servant, through you I will be known."

"I have labored in vain," I thought, "and spent my strength for nothing." Yet what is due me was in the hand of Yahweh, and my reward was with my God. I am important in the sight of Yahweh, and my God is my strength.

And now Yahweh has spoken, he who formed me in the womb to be his servant, to bring Jacob back to him, to gather Israel to him. He said: "It is not enough that you be my servant, to restore the tribes of Jacob, to bring back the remnant of Israel. I will make you the light of the nations, that my salvation will reach to the ends of the earth."

2nd Reading: Acts 13:22–26

Gospel: Lk 1:57–66, 80

When the time came for Elizabeth, she gave birth to a son. Her neighbors and relatives heard that the merciful Lord had done a wonderful thing for her, and they rejoiced with her.

When, on the eighth day, they came to attend the circumcision of the child, they wanted to name him Zechariah after his father. But his mother said, "Not so; he shall be called John." They said to her, "But no one in your family has that name!" and they made signs to his father for the name he wanted to give him. Zechariah asked for a writing tablet, and wrote on it, "His name is John;" and they were very surprised. Immediately, Zechariah could speak again, and his first words were in praise of God.

A holy fear came on all in the neighborhood, and throughout the hill country of Judea the people talked about these events. All who heard of it, pondered in their minds, and wondered, "What will this child be?" For they understood that the hand of the Lord was with him.

As the child grew up, he was seen to be strong in the Spirit; and he lived in the desert, until the day when he appeared openly in Israel.

We recall today the birth of a miracle child. His birth has been a product of conspiracy from heaven. It was so humanly impossible that not even his own father believed at first. But here today we celebrate his birth. God is generous to his parents for his coming took away their shame. His mother, who was thought barren, had now produced a child. Not just any ordinary child but someone whom no one born of a woman could surpass in greatness. He deserved his name. For through him, God has been generous also to the rest of humanity. John's birth assured us that the Messiah is coming hot on his heels. John, who is God's generosity to the world, is a sign that God has irrevocably committed Himself to humanity.

25
JUNE

Wednesday
Ps 119:33, 34, 35, 36, 37, 40
Teach me the way of your decrees,
O Lord.

12TH WEEK IN ORDINARY TIME
Psalter: Week 4 / (Green)

1st Reading: 2 K 22:8–13; 23:1–3

Hilkiah, the high priest, said to Shaphan, the secretary, "I have found the Book of the Law in the house of Yahweh." And he entrusted the Book to Shaphan who read it. Then Shaphan went to the king and said, "We have gathered the money in the house, and this has been turned over to the caretakers of the house to make the repairs."

And Shaphan added, "The priest Hilkiah has turned over a book to me." And Shaphan read the book to the king. When the king heard the contents of the book, he tore his clothes and commanded Hilkiah, Ahikam, Achbor, the secretary Shaphan, and Asaiah, his minister, to do the following, "Go and consult Yahweh about the threats in this book which you have found. Consult him for me, for the people and for the whole of Judah, since our fathers did not listen to what this book says nor to its ordinances. This is why the anger of Yahweh is ready to burn against us."

The king summoned to his side all the leaders of Judah and Jerusalem. Then he went up to the house of Yahweh, followed by all the people of Judah and Jerusalem. The priests with the prophets and all the people went with him, from the youngest to the oldest. When all were gathered, he read to them the Book of the Law found in the house of Yahweh.

The king stood by the pillar; he made a Covenant in the presence of Yahweh, promising to follow him, to keep his commandments and laws, and to respect his ordinances. He promised to keep this Covenant according to what was written in the book with all his heart and with all his soul. And all the people promised with him.

Gospel: Mt 7:15–20

Jesus said to his disciples, "Beware of false prophets: they come to you in sheep's clothing; but inside, they are voracious wolves. You will recognize them by their fruits. Do you ever pick grapes from thorn bushes; or figs, from thistles?

"A good tree always produces good fruit. A rotten tree produces bad ruit. A good tree cannot produce bad fruit; and a rotten tree cannot bear good fruit. Any tree that does not bear good fruit is cut down and thrown into the fire. So then, you will know them by their fruit."

External appearances are important in this physical world of ours. No wonder many of us preoccupy ourselves with our external looks! A veritable industry has been formed out of this need to look good. It is an industry that thrives well even in economic crises. But there are things that cosmetics cannot provide. It can never be faked for too long. That is what Jesus is warning His disciples. Outside appearances are easily manipulated. One is hard pressed to judge which one is real or fake. So He points out a new criterion for discerning what is true and what is not: to look at the good done by a person manifested consistently in time because it springs from the quality of the heart that comes from within.

Thursday

Ps 79:1b–2, 3–5, 8, 9
For the glory of your name,
O Lord, deliver us.

26
JUNE

1st Reading: 2 K 24:8–17*

At that time, the officials of Nebuchadnezzar, king of Babylon, came to attack Jerusalem, surrounding the city. Nebuchadnezzar came while the city was being besieged by his men.

Jehoiachin, king of Judah, surrendered, together with his mother, his servants, his leaders and the palace officials. It was the eighth year of the reign of Nebuchadnezzar. Nebuchadnezzar captured them and he took away the treasures of the house of Yahweh and of the king's house. He also destroyed all the objects of gold which Solomon, king of Israel, had made for the Sanctuary of Yahweh. So the word Yahweh had spoken, was fulfilled.

Nebuchadnezzar carried off into exile all the leaders and prominent men, the blacksmiths and locksmiths, all the men of valor fit for war. A total of ten thousand were exiled to Babylon. Only the poorest sector of the population was left. Nebuchadnezzar also carried away Jehoiachin, with his mother, his wives, the ministers of the palace, and the prominent men of the land.

So all the prominent people, numbering seven thousand, the blacksmiths, numbering a thousand, and all the men fit for war were deported to Babylon by the king of Babylon.

He made Mattaniah, Jehoiachin's uncle, king of Jerusalem, in place of Jehoiachin. And he changed his name to Zedekiah.

Gospel: Mt 7:21–29

Jesus said to his disciples, "Not everyone who says to me, 'Lord! Lord!' will enter the kingdom of heaven, but the one who does the will of my heavenly Father. Many will say to me on that day, 'Lord, Lord, did we not speak in your name? Did we not cast out devils and perform many miracles in your name?' Then I will tell them openly, 'I have never known you; away from me, you evil people!'

"Therefore, anyone who hears these words of mine, and acts according to them, is like a wise man, who built his house on rock. The rain poured down, the rivers flooded, and the wind blew and struck that house. But it did not collapse, because it was built on rock. But anyone who hears these words of mine, and does not act accordingly, is like a fool who built his house on sand. The rain poured, the rivers flooded, and the wind blew and struck that house; it collapsed, and what a terrible collapse that was!"

When Jesus had finished this dis course, the crowds were struck by the way he taught, because he taught with authority, unlike their teachers of the law.

Paying lip service alone to our faith is cheap. It will not buy us passage towards the kingdom. Jesus said as much in this gospel. We have to hear and believe, and in believing proclaim what we believe and in proclaiming we walk the talk. These three are inter-related. Not one can live apart from the other. For in hearing the word of Jesus, we make a conscious decision to believe. We may not fully grasp the extent of the mystery of faith but at least we have an understanding that hopefully will grow with time. And it is our belief that prompts our speech and action. Our words explain why we are doing things; and our actions confirm the validity of our words. In doing so, we build a good foundation for our future: a future shared with Him in whom our faith rests!

27
JUNE

Friday

Ps 103:1–2, 3–4, 6–7, 8, 10
The Lord's kindness is everlasting
to those who fear him.

**SOLEMNITY OF THE
MOST SACRED HEART OF JESUS**
Psalter: Proper / (White)

1st Reading: Dt 7:6–11

Moses said to the people, "You are a people consecrated to Yahweh, your God. Yahweh has chosen you from among all the peoples on the face of the earth, that you may be his own people. Yahweh has bound himself to you and has chosen you, not because you are the most numerous among all the peoples (on the contrary, you are the least). Rather, he has chosen you because of his love for you and to fulfill the oath he made to your fathers. Therefore, with a firm hand Yahweh brought you out from slavery in Egypt, from the power of Pharaoh.

"So know that Yahweh, your God, is the true and faithful God. He keeps his covenant, and his love reaches to the thousandth generation for those who love him and fulfill his commandments, but he punishes in their own persons those who hate him and he repays them without delay.

"So keep the commandments, the norms and the laws that today I command you to practice.

2nd Reading: 1 Jn 4:7–16

Gospel: Mt 11:25–30

On that occasion, Jesus said, "Father, Lord of heaven and earth, I praise you; because you have hidden these things from the wise and learned, and revealed them to simple people. Yes, Father, this was your gracious will.

"Everything has been entrusted to me by my Father. No one knows the Son except the Father; and no one knows the Father except the Son, and those to whom the Son chooses to reveal him.

"Come to me, all you who are weary and burdened, and I will give you rest. Take my yoke upon you and learn from me, for I am gentle and humble of heart; and you will find rest. For my yoke is easy; and my burden is light."

There is a divine bias for the simple people. God seems to reserve the best things to those who are not great in this world. Does this mean that God is also prone for our human tendencies to have preference on one over the other? But if we think about it, all of us are in a way little and small in the eyes of God. There is nothing that we can boast of in front of Him to make our statures bigger than what it may seem. In the end, His bias is for all of us. It is our fault that we think highly of ourselves or allow the world to delude us that we are a cut above the rest. It is us who leave behind our lowly stature in exchange for the puny honor of this world. It is us who choose the lowly part and not God.

IMMACULATE HEART OF THE BLESSED VIRGIN MARY

Psalter: Week 4 / (White)

Saturday

1 Sam 2:1, 4–5, 6–7, 8abcd
My heart exults in the Lord,
my Savior.

28

JUNE

1st Reading: Is 61:9–11

Their descendants shall be known among the nations and their offspring among the people. All who see them will acknowledge that they are a race Yahweh has blessed.

I rejoice greatly in Yahweh, my soul exults for joy in my God, for he has clothed me in the garments of his salvation, he has covered me with the robe of his righteousness, like a bridegroom wearing a garland, like a bride adorned with jewels.

For as the earth brings forth its growth, and as a garden makes seeds spring up, so will the Lord Yahweh make justice and praise spring up in the sight of all nations.

Gospel: Lk 2:41–51

Every year, the parents of Jesus went to Jerusalem for the Feast of the Passover, as was customary. And when Jesus was twelve years old, he went up with them, according to the custom of this feast. After the festival was over, they returned, but the boy Jesus remained in Jerusalem; and his parents did not know it.

They assumed that he was in their group of travelers, and, after walking the whole day, they looked for him among their relatives and friends. As they did not find him, they went back to Jerusalem, searching for him; and, on the third day, they found him in the temple, sitting among the teachers, listening to them and asking questions. And all the people were amazed at his understanding and his answers.

His parents were very surprised when they saw him; and his mother said to him, "Son, why have you done this to us? Your father and I were very worried while searching for you." Then he said to them, "Why were you looking for me? Did you not know that I must be in my Father's house?" But they did not understand this answer.

Jesus went down with them, returning to Nazareth, and he continued to be obedient to them. As for his mother, she kept all these things in her heart.

The heart of Mary is the most famous organ of her body. It has even surpassed in popularity the womb that bore the Savior in this world. After all, it is her heart that was tasked the most by her ministry of becoming the mother of the Son of God. From the Annunciation to the birth and Presentation of the Lord in the Temple, down to the Lord's public ministry and His Passion, Death and Resurrection, Mary's heart constantly pondered on the gradual unfolding of her Son's being. She may not have fully understood at that time, but the memory of her Son kept in her heart made her steadfast in her belief in her Son and Lord. This is why Mary's heart is Immaculate and pure. It endured so much for her Son because it was where she kept all her memory of Him.

29
JUNE

Sunday

Ps 34:2–3, 4–5, 6–7, 8–9
The angel of the Lord will rescue
those who fear him.

1st Reading: Acts 12:1–11

About that time king Herod decided to persecute some members of the Church. He had James, the brother of John, killed with the sword, and when he saw how it pleased the Jews, he proceeded to arrest Peter also.

This happened during the festival of the Unleavened Bread. Herod had him seized and thrown into prison with four squads, each of four soldiers, to guard him. He wanted to bring him to trial before the people after the Passover feast, but while Peter was kept in prison, the whole Church prayed earnestly for him.

On the very night before Herod was to bring him to trial, Peter was sleeping between two soldiers, bound by a double chain, while guards kept watch at the gate of the prison.

Suddenly, an angel of the Lord stood there and a light shone in the prison cell. The angel tapped Peter on the side and woke him saying, "Get up quickly!" At once, the chains fell from Peter's wrists. The angel said, "Put on your belt and your sandals." Peter did so; and the angel added, "Now, put on your cloak and follow me."

Peter followed him out; yet he did not realize that what was happening with the angel was real; he thought he was seeing a vision. They passed the first guard, and then the second, and they came to the iron door leading out to the city, which opened by itself for them. They went out and made their way down a narrow alley, when suddenly the angel left him.

Then Peter recovered his senses and said, "Now I know that the Lord has sent his angel and has rescued me from Herod's clutches and from all that the Jews had in store for me."

2nd Reading: 2 Tim 4:6–8, 17–18

As for me, I am already poured out as a libation, and the moment of my departure has come. I have fought the good fight, I have finished the race, I have kept the faith. Now, there is laid up for me the crown of righteousness, with which the Lord, the just judge, will reward me, on that day, and not only me, but all those who have longed for his glorious coming.

But the Lord was at my side, giving me strength to proclaim the word fully, and let all the pagans hear it. So I was rescued from the lion's mouth. The Lord will save me from all evil, bringing me to his heavenly kingdom. Glory to him for ever and ever. Amen!

Gospel: Mt 16:13–19

Jesus came to Caesarea Philippi. He asked his disciples, "Who do people say the Son of Man is?" They said, "For some of them, you are John the Baptist; for others Elijah, or Jeremiah, or one of the prophets."

Jesus asked them, "But you, who do you say I am?" Peter answered, "You are the Messiah, the Son of the living God." Jesus replied, "It is well for you, Simon Barjona, for it is not flesh or blood that has revealed this to you, but my Father in heaven.

"And now I say to you: You are Peter; and on this Rock I will build my Church; and never will the powers of death overcome it.

"I will give you the keys of the kingdom of heaven: whatever you bind on earth shall be bound in heaven; and whatever you unbind on earth shall be unbound in heaven."

Reading: After a successful public ministry, Jesus now asks His disciples who He is according to people's perception. They in turn report to Him the various opinions people have about Him ranging from the mighty prophets of old till John who recently caused quite a stir in the land of Israel. Then Jesus asked His disciples who they thought He was. Peter answered on behalf of the group the profession of faith in the personhood of Jesus that we still profess. It is through Peter's confession that the Church of Jesus will be built securely here on earth.

Reflection: Friendship matters a lot in knowing a person better. Friends have special access to secrets usually not known by the public. This is the advantage of the disciples. Their intimacy with Jesus led them to understand the mystery of His being more than if they were mere acquaintances only. That is why Peter, on behalf of his group, could confidently proclaim the faith we now have in Jesus. This does not come from mere repetition of claimed assertions or by rote memory. This is a product of a relationship that provides venues to get to know each other better.

Response: Have I disclosed who I really am to my friends? Or am I holding back some things about me that I am afraid to share with them. Perhaps today is a good day to answer the repeated questions of a friend or friends concerning myself. Giving them access to who I really am would be a good gift to them today.

30
JUNE

Monday

Ps 50:16bc–17, 18–19, 20–21, 22–23
Remember this,
you who never think of God.

13TH WEEK IN ORDINARY TIME
The First Martyrs of Holy Roman Church
Psalter: Week 1 / (Green / Red)

1st Reading: Am 2:6–10, 13–16

Yahweh says this, "Because Israel has sinned, not once but three times; and even more, I will not relent. They sell the just for money and the needy for a pair of sandals; they tread on the head of the poor and trample them upon the dust of the earth, while they silence the right of the afflicted; a man and his father go to the same woman to profane my holy name; they stretch out upon garments taken in pledge, beside every altar; they take the wine of those they swindle and are drunk in the house of their God.

It was I who destroyed the Amorites before them, whose height was like the height of the cedar; a people as sturdy as an oak. I destroyed their fruit above and their roots below.

It was I who brought you up from the land of Egypt and led you forty years in the wilderness to take possession of the land of the Amorites.

Behold, I will crush you to the ground, as a cart does when it is full of sheaves. The swift shall be unable to flee and the strong man shall lose his strength. The warrior shall not save himself nor the bowman stand his ground. The swift of foot shall not escape nor the horseman save himself. Even the most stout-hearted among the warriors shall flee away naked on that day," says Yahweh.

Gospel: Mt 8:18–22

When Jesus saw the crowd pressing around him, he gave orders to cross to the other side of the lake. A teacher of the law approached him; and said, "Master, I will follow you wherever you go." Jesus said to him, "Foxes have holes and birds have nests, but the Son of Man has nowhere to lay his head." Another disciple said to him, "Lord, let me go and bury my father first." But Jesus said to him, "Follow me, and let the dead bury their dead."

Another disciple said to him, "Lord, let me go and bury my father first." But Jesus said to him, "Follow me, and let the dead bury their dead."

Following the Lord is a serious decision. One has to be ready before signifying such intent. For the Lord does not accept half-hearted responses. It is either all or nothing. This is with regard to those who want to follow them by their own will. There are others whom the Lord sought out Himself. They may not be that ready but it is the Lord who asks them to follow Him. It is He who will supply what they lack. All they have to do is cooperate with God and He will take care of the rest.

13TH WEEK IN ORDINARY TIME
Bl. Junipero Serra, priest
Psalter: Week 1 / (Green / White)

Tuesday

Ps 5:4b–6a, 6b–7, 8
Lead me into your justice,
Lord.

01
JULY

Bl. Junipero Serra
Did you know that: Blessed Junipero Serra's name was taken from St. Francis of Assisi's childlike companion Brother Juniper.

1st Reading: Am 3:1–8; 4:11–12

Hear this word which Yahweh speaks against you, people of Israel, against the whole family which he brought up from the land of Egypt.

"Only you have I known of all the families of the earth; therefore I will call you to account for all your wrongdoings."

Do two walk together unless they have agreed?

Does a lion roar in the forest when it has no prey? Does a young lion growl in its den unless it has seized something?

Does a bird get caught in a snare if the snare has not been baited? Does a tiger spring up from the ground unless it has caught something?

If a trumpet sounds in a city, will the people not be frightened?

If disaster strikes a city, has not Yahweh caused it? Yet Yahweh does nothing without revealing his plan to his servants, the prophets. If the lion roars, who will not be afraid? If Yahweh speaks, who will not prophesy?

"I overthrew you, a divine punishment, as happened to Sodom and Gomorrah; you were like a brand snatched from the blaze, yet you never returned to me," says Yahweh.

"Therefore, I will deal with you in my own way, Israel, and since I will do this to you, prepare, Israel, to meet your God!"

Gospel: Mt 8:23–27

Jesus got into the boat and his disciples followed him. Without warning, a fierce storm burst upon the lake, with waves sweeping the boat. But Jesus was asleep.

The disciples woke him up and cried, "Lord save us! We are lost!" But Jesus answered, "Why are you so afraid, you of little faith?" Then he stood up and rebuked the wind and sea; and it became completely calm.

The disciples were astonished. They said, "What kind of man is he? Even the winds and the sea obey him."

There are people so centered that they can wade through storms and turbulence without being ruffled. Jesus slept through the storm while His disciples struggled mightily against it. In the end they had to call on the Lord for help. He got up, rebuked the elements, and peace and calm was restored. His inner calmness and peace irradiates outside Him and affects a change in the environment around Him.

02
JULY

Wednesday

Ps 50:7, 8–9, 10–11, 12–13, 16bc–17
To the upright I will show
the saving power of God.

13TH WEEK IN ORDINARY TIME
Psalter: Week 1 / (Green)

1st Reading: Am 5:14–15, 21–24

*S*eek good and shun evil, that you may live. Then Yahweh, the God of hosts, as you have claimed, will be with you.

Hate wickedness and love virtue, and let justice prevail in the courts; perhaps Yahweh, the God of hosts, will take pity on the remnant of Joseph.

I hate, I reject your feasts, I take no pleasure when you assemble to offer me your burnt offerings. Your cereal offerings, I will not accept! Your offerings of fattened beasts, I will not look upon!

Away with the noise of your chanting, away with your strumming on harps. But let justice run its course like water, and righteousness be like an everflowing river.

Gospel: Mt 8:28–34

*W*hen Jesus reached Gadara, on the other side, he was met by two men, possessed by devils, who came out from the tombs. They were so fierce that no one dared to pass that way. They cried out, "Son of God, leave us alone! Have you come here to torment us before the time?"

Some distance away there was a large herd of pigs feeding. So the demons begged him, "If you drive us out, send us into that herd of pigs." Jesus ordered them, "Go!" So the demons left the men and went into the pigs. The whole herd rushed down the cliff into the lake and was drowned.

The men in charge of the pigs ran off to the town, where they told the whole story; and also what had happened to the men possessed with the demons. The whole town went out to meet Jesus; and when they saw him, they begged him to leave their region.

When things are not in their proper places, there is chaos. The demons have no claim to the two persons they possess. That is why they are fierce. They have to fight tooth and nail over that which they had taken illegally and by force. But they meet the Lord who puts right the things out of their places. In a desperate last pleading since the Lord is stronger than them, they ask to be sent into a herd of pigs. These are unclean animals according to the Jewish law. When possessed, the pigs in turn rush to the sea which is the mythical abode of Leviathan, the ancient monster that represents loss of order. And thus everything is once again in their rightful place. The two demoniacs are back to sanity and the evil ones to their home. Order is restored except for the townspeople who are comfortable where they are.

FEAST OF ST. THOMAS, APOSTLE
Psalter: Proper / (Red)

Thursday

Ps 117:1bc, 2
Go out to all the world and tell
the Good News.

03
JULY

1st Reading: Eph 2:19–22

Brothers and sisters, now, you are no longer strangers or guests, but fellow citizens of the holy people: you are of the household of God. You are the house, whose foundations are the apostles and prophets, and whose cornerstone is Christ Jesus. In him, the whole structure is joined together, and rises, to be a holy temple, in the Lord. In him, you, too, are being built, to become the spiritual Sanctuary of God.

Gospel: Jn 20:24–29

Thomas, the Twin, one of the Twelve, was not with them when Jesus came. The other disciples told him, "We have seen the Lord." But he replied, "Until I have seen in his hands the print of the nails, and put my finger in the mark of the nails and my hand in his side, I will not believe."

Eight days later, the disciples were again inside the house and Thomas was with them. Although the doors were locked, Jesus came and stood in their midst and said, "Peace be with you!" Then he said to Thomas, "Put your finger here, and see my hands; stretch out your hand, and put it into my side. Do not continue in your unbelief, but believe!"

Thomas said, "You are my Lord and my God." Jesus replied, "You believe because you see me, don't you? Happy are those who have not seen and yet have come to believe."

Today we celebrate the feast of Thomas commonly called the "Doubter." Thanks to him, healthy skepticism becomes part of our spiritual quest for truth. What is remarkable with Thomas is the fact that when he was confronted by the Risen Lord, he let go of his doubts and believed. He was humble enough to accept that he erred. Intellectual honesty demands that we question with the right intention and believe when confronted with the right reason. Doubting is not an ideology to be defended but an instrument to get into the truth with conviction.

04
JULY

Friday
Ps 119:2, 10, 20, 30, 40, 131
One does not live by bread alone, but by every
word that comes from the mouth of God.

13TH WEEK IN ORDINARY TIME
St. Elizabeth of Portugal
married woman, queen
Psalter: Week 1 / (Green / White

1st Reading: Am 8:4–6, 9–12

*H*ear this, you, who trample on the needy, to do away with the weak of the land. You who say, "When will the new moon or the Sabbath feast be over that we may open the store and sell our grain? Let us lower the measure and raise the price; let us cheat and tamper with the scales, and even sell the refuse with the whole grain. We will buy up the poor for money and the needy for a pair of sandals."

Yahweh says, "On that day, I will make the sun go down at noon; and darken the earth in broad daylight.

I will turn your festivals into mourning and all your singing into wailing. Everyone will mourn, covered with sackcloth; and every head will be shaved. I will make them mourn, as for an only son, and bring their day to a bitter end."

Yahweh says, "Days are coming when I will send famine upon the land; not hunger for bread or thirst for water, but for hearing the word of Yahweh.

"Men will stagger from sea to sea, wander to and fro, from north to east, searching for the word of Yahweh; but they will not find it."

Gospel: Mt 9:9–13

*A*s Jesus moved on from there, he saw a man named Matthew, at his seat in the customhouse; and he said to him, "Follow me!" And Matthew got up and followed him. Now it happened, while Jesus was at table in Matthew's house, many tax collectors and sinners joined Jesus and his disciples. When the Pharisees saw this, they said to his disciples, "Why is it, that your master eats with sinners and tax collectors?"

When Jesus heard this, he said, "Healthy people do not need a doctor, but sick people do. Go, and find out what this means: What I want is mercy, not sacrifice. I did not come to call the righteous, but sinners."

St. Elizabeth of Portugal
Did you know that: St. Elizabeth of Portugal, wife of the king of Portugal, was a great-niece of St. Elizabeth of Hungary, daughter of the king of Hungary.

For Matthew it was just an ordinary day as he dispensed with his work. Little did he know that his life would take a turn that day when Jesus passed by him. He was invited and he responded. He did not think twice. Perhaps he had been mulling things over for a time. Perhaps he was in search of something he could not find in his ordinary life. How many times it seemed that we could change a person's life simply by inviting him out of the life he lived but missed it because we never took the chance. Jesus took His chances with Matthew and succeeded. Another life was changed for the better simply because someone cared.

13TH WEEK IN ORDINARY TIME
St. Anthony Zaccaria, priest
Psalter: Week 1 / (Green / White)

Saturday

Ps 85:9ab and 10, 11–12, 13–14
The Lord speaks of peace
to his people.

05
JULY

St. Anthony Zaccaria

Did you know that: St. Anthony Zaccaria, founder of the Clerics of St. Paul, is one of the many saints with incorruptible body.

1st Reading: Am 9:11–15

"On that day, I shall restore the fallen hut of David and wall up its breaches, and raise its ruined walls; and so build it as in days of old.

"They shall conquer the remnant of Edom, and the neighboring nations, upon which my name has been called." Thus says Yahweh, the one who will do this.

Yahweh says also, "The days are coming when the plowman will overtake the reaper and the treader of grapes overtake the sower. The mountains shall drip sweet wine and all the hills shall melt.

"I shall bring back the exiles of my people Israel; they will rebuild the desolate cities and dwell in them. They will plant vineyards and drink their wine; they will have orchards and eat their fruit. I shall plant them in their own country and they shall never again be rooted up from the land which I have given them," says Yahweh your God.

Gospel: Mt 9:14–17

The disciples of John came to him with the question, "How is it, that we and the Pharisees fast on many occasions, but not your disciples?"

Jesus answered them, "How can you expect wedding guests to mourn as long as the bridegroom is with them? The time will come, when the bridegroom will be taken away from them, and then, they will fast.

"No one patches an old coat with a piece of unshrunken cloth, for the patch will shrink and tear an even bigger hole in the coat. In the same way, you don't put new wine into old wine skins. If you do, the wine skins will burst and the wine will be spilt. No, you put new wine into fresh skins; then both are preserved."

We tend to find contrast in what we do with what others do and insist that ours is the better way to do things. Perhaps it's the reason why the disciples of John had to confront Jesus with the strange way His disciples behaved which was different from theirs and that of the Pharisees. And so Jesus had to tell them of something that they lacked which made them cling to the old methods. It had to do with perspectives. They had not yet discovered the perspectives of the bridegroom that Israel had waited for too long. As long as they did not recognize that God had finally visited them through Jesus, they would continue their mournful fasting throughout their lives.

06
JULY

Sunday

Ps 145:1-2, 8-9, 10-11, 13-14
I will praise your name forever,
my King and my God.

1st Reading: Zec 9:9–10

Thus says the Lord: Rejoice greatly, daughter of Zion!

Shout for joy, daughter of Jerusalem!

For your king is coming, just and victorious, humble and riding on a donkey, on a colt, the foal of a donkey.

No more chariots in Ephraim, no more horses in Jerusalem, for he will do away with them.

The warrior's bow shall be broken when he dictates peace to the nations.

He will reign from sea to sea, and from the River to the ends of the earth.

2nd Reading: Rom 8:9, 11–13

Brothers and sisters, your existence is not in the flesh, but in the spirit, because the Spirit of God is within you. If you did not have the Spirit of Christ, you would not belong to him. And, if the Spirit of him, who raised Jesus from the dead, is within you, he, who raised Jesus Christ from among the dead, will also give life to your mortal bodies. Yes, he will do it, through his Spirit, who dwells within you.

Then, brothers, let us leave the flesh and no longer live according to it. If not, we will die. Rather, walking in the spirit, let us put to death the body's deeds, so that we may live.

Gospel: Mt 11:25–30

On that occasion, Jesus said, "Father, Lord of heaven and earth, I praise you; because you have hidden these things from the wise and learned, and revealed them to simple people. Yes, Father, this was your gracious will.

"Everything has been entrusted to me by my Father. No one knows the Son except the Father; and no one knows the Father except the Son, and those to whom the Son chooses to reveal him.

"Come to me, all you who are weary and burdened, and I will give you rest. Take my yoke upon you and learn from me, for I am gentle and humble of heart; and you will find rest. For my yoke is easy; and my burden is light."

Reading: Jesus speaks of three things in this reading. First, He thanks the Father for having preference in revealing the things of heaven to simple people. Second, He also affirms His uniqueness as the only way to access the Father. Lastly, He invites all who work and carry heavy burdens to carry His yoke so that they may be refreshed..

Reflection: Our generation seems to be an anxious and overworked lot. We seldom take time to really care for ourselves. Our capacity to recreate is even impaired. Gorging on food, binging on drinks, staying out late at night is equated with fun and entertainment. But are they? In the end, they only wreak havoc on our physical and mental wellness. It even impairs our spiritual state by robbing us of the time to really listen to our inner self. It is in this busy, chaotic lifestyle that Jesus steps in and presents HImself as an alternative to the many things we do to lighten ourselves. We might have to invest to get to know Him better and we come out the better.

Response: To have your burden taken off your back is a refreshing experience. How many times have others helped me with my burdens? Do I help also in return? Today, I will consciously try to ease the burden of others by way of companionship, by listening to them with compassion, or by just assuring them of my prayers. May I lighten their burden by the conscious act I do for them.

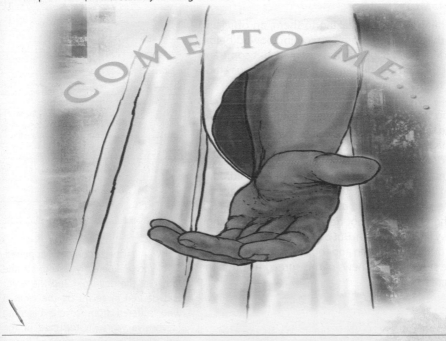

07
JULY

Monday
Ps 145:2–3, 4–5, 6–7, 8–9
The Lord is gracious and merciful.

14TH **WEEK IN ORDINARY TIME**
Psalter: Week 2 / (Green)

1st Reading: Hos 2:16, 17c–18, 21–22

Thus says Yahweh: So I am going to allure her, lead her once more into the desert, where I can speak to her tenderly.

Then I will give back her vineyards, make the Valley of Achor a door of hope.

There, she will answer me, as in her youth, as when she came out of the land of Egypt.

On that day, Yahweh says, you will call me my husband, and never again: my Baal.

You will be my spouse forever, betrothed in justice and integrity; we will be united in love and tenderness.

I will espouse you in faithfulness; and you will come to know Yahweh.

Gospel: Mt 9:18–26

While Jesus was speaking to them, an official of the synagogue came up to him, bowed before him and said, "My daughter has just died, but come and place your hands on her, and she will live." Jesus stood up and followed him with his disciples.

Then a woman, who had suffered from a severe bleeding for twelve years, came up from behind and touched the edge of his cloak; for she thought, "If I only touch his cloak, I will be healed." Jesus turned, saw her and said, "Courage, my daughter, your faith has saved you." And from that moment, the woman was cured.

When Jesus arrived at the official's house and saw the flute players and the excited crowd, he said, "Get out of here! The girl is not dead. She is only sleeping!" And they laughed at him. But once the crowd had been turned out, Jesus went in and took the girl by the hand, and she stood up. The news of this spread through the whole area.

Two miracles in one day happened. One was deliberately asked by the father of the dead girl and the other was desired in secret by the woman who suffered from severe bleeding for twelve years. In the case of the girl, it was Jesus who touched her to wholeness and life while the woman had to touch Jesus' cloak from behind to be healed. The former was willed by Jesus; the woman was restored to health because of her faith. Perhaps these two images of healing will help us understand better how miracles work in our life.

Tuesday

Ps 115:3–4, 5-6, 7ab–8, 9–10
The house of Israel trusts
in the Lord.

08
JULY

1st Reading: Hos 8:4–7, 11–13

Thus says Yahweh: Without my approval they set up kings and without my blessing appointed leaders. With their silver and gold they fashioned idols to their own ruin. To me, Samaria, your calf is loathsome; and my anger blazes against you. How long will you remain defiled? The calf is yours, Israel, a craftsman has made it; it is not God and will be broken into pieces. As they sow the wind, they will reap the whirlwind. Stalk without flower, it will never yield flower, or if they do, foreigners will devour it.

Ephraim built many altars; but his altars made him more guilty. I wrote out for him the numerous precepts of my law; but they look on them as coming from foreigners. They offer sacrifices to me because they are those who eat the meat; but Yahweh does not accept their sacrifices, for he is mindful of their sin and remembers their wickedness. They will return to Egypt.

Gospel: Mt 9:32–38

As they were going away, some people brought to Jesus a man who was dumb, because he was possessed by a demon. When the demon was driven out, the dumb man began to speak. The crowds were astonished and said, "Nothing like this has ever been seen in Israel." But the Pharisees said, "He drives away demons with the help of the prince of demons."

Jesus went around all the towns and villages, teaching in their synagogues and proclaiming the good news of the kingdom; and he cured every sickness and disease. When he saw the crowds, he was moved with pity; for they were harassed and help-less, like sheep without a shepherd. Then he said to his disciples, "The harvest is abundant, but the workers are only few. Ask the master of the harvest to send workers to gather his harvest."

No matter how much Jesus tried, He could only reach a few. There were simply too many people who needed help. But instead of giving in to helplessness and despair, He looked forward to a time when there would be many "harvesters" working alongside Him. Oftentimes we think of fellow workers of the Lord as a special elite group of people that would be difficult to follow. We tend to forget that in our own state of life, we could extend help by being conscious of our faith and allowing it to shape our choices and decisions. Our example, in word and deed of a lived faith, is enough to do our share in advancing the work of God.

09
JULY

Wednesday

Ps 105:2–3, 4–5, 6–7

Seek always the face of the Lord.

14TH WEEK IN ORDINARY TIME

St. Augustine Zhao Rong, priest
& Companions, martyrs

Psalter: Week 2 / (Green / Red)

1st Reading: Hos 10:1–3, 7–8, 12

Israel was a spreading vine, rich in fruit. The more his fruit increased, the more altars he built; the more his land prospered, the more he adorned his sacred stones.

Their heart is divided! They shall pay for it. Their altars will be thrown down and their sacred stones broken to pieces.

Now they say, "We have no king (because we have no fear of God) and what good would a king do us?"

As for the king of Samaria, he has been carried off like foam on water.

The idolatrous high places—the sin of Israel—will be destroyed. Thorn and thistle will creep over the altars. Then they will say to the mountains: "Cover us," and to the hills: "Fall on us."

Plow new ground, sow for yourselves justice and reap the harvest of kindness. It is the time to go seeking Yahweh until he comes to rain salvation on you.

Gospel: Mt 10:1–7

Jesus called his Twelve disciples to him, and gave them authority over unclean spirits, to drive them out, and to heal every disease and sickness.

These are the names of the Twelve apostles: first Simon, called Peter, and his brother Andrew; James, the son of Zebedee, and his brother John; Philip and Bartholomew; Thomas and Matthew, the tax collector; James, the son of Alphaeus, and Thaddaeus; Simon, the Canaanite, and Judas Iscariot, the man who would betray him. Jesus sent these twelve mission, with the instructions: "Do not visit pagan territory and do not enter a Samaritan town. Go, instead, to the lost sheep of the people of Israel.

"Go, and proclaim this message: The kingdom of heaven is near."

St. Augustine Zhao Rong

Did you know that: St. Augustine Zhao Rong and Companions was canonized on October 1, 2000, which coincided the Anniversary of the Triumph of the Communist Revolution in 1948.

And so Jesus has to extend His reach by turning His disciples into fellow harvesters for God's vineyard. He has to trust that they would be equal to the task. However, the authority He gives them is a measured authority. They have to undergo training before full responsibility will be handed over to them. Thus begins the story of the twelve. They will be mentored by Jesus according to the ways of the Kingdom. He also gives them a smaller geographical area that they can comfortably cover. They will go only to the lost sheep of the people of Israel. This would do for the moment. Their time to take over would come eventually.

Thursday

Ps 80:2ac and 3b, 15–16
Let us see your face, Lord,
and we shall be saved..

10
JULY

1st Reading: Hos 11:1–4, 8e–9

Thus says Yahweh: I loved Israel when he was a child; out of Egypt I called my son. But the more I have called, the further have they gone from me—sacrificing to the Baals, burning incense to the idols.

Yet, it was I who taught Ephraim to walk, taking them by the arms; yet, little did they realize that it was I who cared for them. I led them with cords of human kindness, with leading strings of love, and I became for them as one who eases the yoke upon their neck and stoops down to feed them.

How can I give you up, Ephraim? Can I abandon you like Admah or make you like Zeboiim? My heart is troubled within me and I am moved with compassion. I will not give vent to my great anger; I will not return to destroy Ephraim, for I am God and not human. I am the Holy One in your midst; and I do not want to come to you in anger.

Gospel: Mt 10:7–15

Jesus said to his apostles, "Go, and proclaim this message: The kingdom of heaven is near. Heal the sick, bring the dead back to life, cleanse the lepers, and drive out demons. Freely have you received, freely give. Do not carry any gold or silver or money in your purses. Do not take a traveling bag, or an extra shirt, or sandals, or a walking stick: workers deserve to be compensated.

"When you come to a town or a village, look for a worthy person, and stay there until you leave.

"When you enter the house, wish it peace. If the people are worthy people, your peace will rest on them; if they are not worthy people, your blessing will come back to you.

"And if you are not welcomed, and your words are not listened to, leave that house or that town, and shake the dust off your feet. I assure you, it will go easier for the people of Sodom and Gomorrah on the day of judgment, than it will for the people of that town."

The mission has been spelled out. Now is the time to execute it. However Jesus gives them certain provisions for their journey. They will go only with their clothes on and stay in one house while they minister to a town. There are also prohibitions: absolutely no extra baggage nor walking stick nor any money while on the road. They will have to depend on the generosity of God who is the author and sustainer of the works they do.

11
JULY

Friday
Ps 51:3–4, 8–9, 12–13, 14 and 17
My mouth will declare your praise.

14ᵀᴴ WEEK IN ORDINARY TIME
St. Benedict, abbot
Psalter: Week 2 / (White)

1ˢᵗ Reading: Hos 14:2–10

Thus says Yahweh: Return to your God, Yahweh, O Israel!

Your sins have caused your downfall. Return to Yahweh with humble words. Say to him, "Oh, you who show compassion to the fatherless, forgive our debt, be appeased.

Instead of bulls and sacrifices, accept the praise from our lips. Assyria will not save us: no longer shall we look for horses, nor ever again shall we say 'Our gods' to the work of our hands."

I will heal their disloyalty and love them with all my heart, for my anger has turned from them.

I shall be like dew to Israel, like the lily will he blossom.

Like a cedar, he will send down his roots; his young shoots will grow and spread.

His splendor will be like an olive tree, his fragrance, like a Lebanon cedar.

They will dwell in my shade again, they will flourish like the grain, they will blossom like a vine, and their fame will be like Lebanon wine.

What would Ephraim do with idols, when it is I who hear and make him prosper? I am like an evergreen cypress tree; all your fruitfulness comes from me.

Who is wise enough to grasp all this? Who is discerning and will understand?

Straight are the ways of Yahweh: the just walk in them, but the sinners stumble.

Gospel: Mt 10:16–23

Jesus said to his apostles, "Look, I send you out like sheep among wolves. You must be as clever as snakes and as innocent as doves. Be on your guard with people, for they will hand you over to their courts, and they will flog you in their synagogues. You will be brought to trial before rulers and kings because of me, so that you may witness to them and the pagans.

"But when you are arrested, do not worry about what you are to say, or how you are to say it; when the hour comes, you will be given what you are to say. For it will not be you who speak, but the Spirit of your Father, speaking through you.

"Brother will hand over his brother to death, and a father his child; children will turn against their parents and have them put to death. Everyone will hate you because of me, but whoever stands firm to the end will be saved.

"When they persecute you in one town, flee to the next. I tell you the truth, you will not have passed through all the towns of Israel before the Son of Man comes."

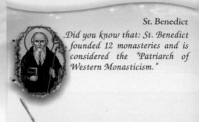

St. Benedict
Did you know that: St. Benedict founded 12 monasteries and is considered the "Patriarch of Western Monasticism."

Even if God is the sender of missionaries, still it pays for them to exercise prudence and human sensibilities. They will work amidst various contending forces. They must be able to navigate themselves as much as possible without compromising the mission. However, when push comes to shove, they have to remain firm and unwavering. Help will be given when it is needed, but not in the way the world thinks it should be. God works in ways that the world sometimes does not comprehend. Whatever it may be, we are assured that the better part has been chosen by God Himself.

14TH WEEK IN ORDINARY TIME
Psalter: Week 2 / (Green / White)

Saturday

Ps 93:1ab, 1cd-2, 5
The Lord is king;
he is robed in majesty.

12
JULY

1st Reading: Is 6:1–8

In the year that King Uzziah died I saw the Lord seated on a throne, high and exalted; the train of his robe filled the Temple. Above him were seraphs, each with six wings: two to cover the face, two to cover the feet, and two to fly with.

They were calling to one another: "Holy, holy, holy is Yahweh Sabaoth. All the earth is filled with his glory!" At the sound of their voices the foundations of the threshold shook and the temple was filled with smoke. I said, "Poor me! I am doomed! For I am a man of unclean lips living among a people of unclean lips, and yet I have seen the King, Yahweh Sabaoth."

Then one of the seraphs flew to me; in his hands was a live coal which he had taken with tongs from the altar. He touched my mouth with it and said,"

See, this has touched your lips; your guilt is taken away and your sin is forgiven."

Then I heard the voice of the Lord, "Whom shall I send? And who will go for us?" I answered, "Here I am. Send me!"

Gospel: Mt 10:24–33

Jesus said to his apostles, "A student is not above his teacher, nor a slave above his master. A student should be content to become like his teacher, and the slave like his master. If the head of the household has been called Beelzebul, how much more, those of his household! So, do not be afraid of them!

"There is nothing covered that will not be uncovered. There is nothing hidden that will not be made known. What I am telling you in the dark, you must speak in the light. What you hear in private, proclaim from the housetops.

"Do not be afraid of those who kill the body, but have no power to kill the soul. Rather, be afraid of him who can destroy both body and soul in hell. For a few cents you can buy two sparrows. Yet not one sparrow falls to the ground without your Father knowing. As for you, every hair of your head has been counted. Do not be afraid: you are worth more than many sparrows!

"Whoever acknowledges me before others, I will acknowledge before my Father in heaven. Whoever rejects me before others, I will reject before my Father in heaven."

Continuing the theme of mission, Jesus seemed to give His disciples a foretaste of what's in store for them. Since they cannot be greater than Him, their Teacher and Guide, what He has undergone, they too will undergo. It may be daunting for some who at once will think of the calumnies and persecutions the Lord had to deal with in His lifetime. Of course the cross looms large and foreboding in the horizon. That's why it is not good to follow the Lord half-heartedly. We cannot choose our paths; to give up halfway would be a waste of time and energy expended during the first half of the journey. Fear is to be acknowledged but it should be set aside. We follow Him till the end.

13
JULY

Sunday

Ps 65:10, 11, 12–13, 14
The seed that falls on good ground
will yield a fruitful harvest.

1st Reading: Is 55:10–11

Thus says Yahweh: As the rain and the snow come down from the heavens and do not return till they have watered the earth, making it yield seed for the sower and food for others to eat, so is my word that goes forth out of my mouth: it will not return to me idle, but it shall accomplish my will, the purpose for which it has been sent.

2nd Reading: Rom 8:18–23

Brothers and sisters: I consider, that the suffering of our present life cannot be compared with the glory that will be revealed, and given to us. All creation is eagerly expecting the birth, in glory, of the children of God. For, if now, the created world was unable to attain its purpose, this did not come from itself, but from the one who subjected it. But it is not without hope; for even the created world, will be freed from this fate of death, and share the freedom and glory of the children of God.

We know, that the whole creation groans and suffers the pangs of birth. Not creation alone, but even ourselves; although the Spirit was given to us, as a foretaste of what we are to receive, we groan in our innermost being, eagerly awaiting the day, when God will give us full rights, and rescue our bodies as well.

Gospel: Mt 13:1–23 (or Mt 13:1-9)

That same day, Jesus left the house and sat down by the lakeside. Many people gathered around him. So he got into a boat, and sat down, while the crowds stood on the shore; and he spoke to them in parables about many things.

Jesus said, "The sower went out to sow; and, as he sowed, some seeds fell along the path; and the birds came and ate them up. Other seeds fell on rocky ground, where there was little soil, and the seeds sprouted quickly, because the soil was not deep. But as soon as the sun rose, the plants were scorched; and they withered, because they had no roots. Again, other seeds fell among thistles; and the thistles grew and choked the plants. Still, other seeds fell on good soil and produced a crop: some a hundredfold, others sixty, and others thirty. If you have ears, then hear!"

Then his disciples came to him and said, "Why do you speak to them in parables?"

Jesus answered, "To you it has been given to know the secrets of the kingdom of heaven, but not to these people. For the one who has will be given more; and he will have in abundance. But the one who does not have will be deprived of even what he has. That is why I speak to them in parables; because they look and do not see; they hear; but they do not listen or understand.

"In them, the words of the prophet Isaiah are fulfilled: *However much you hear, you do not understand; however much you see, you do not perceive.*

"For the heart of this people has grown dull. Their ears hardly hear and their eyes dare not see. If they were to see with their eyes, hear with their ears and understand with their heart, they would turn back, and I would heal them.

"But blessed are your eyes, because they see; and your ears, because they hear.

"For I tell you, many prophets and righteous people have longed to see the things you see, but they did not see them; and to hear the things you hear, but they did not hear them.

"Now listen to the parable of the sower.

"When a person hears the message of the kingdom, but does not take it seriously, the devil comes and snatches away what was sown in his heart. This is the seed that fell along the footpath.

"The seed that fell on rocky ground stands for the one who hears the word, and accepts it at once with joy. But such a person has no roots, and endures only for a while. No sooner is he harassed or persecuted because of the word, than he gives up.

"The seed that fell among the thistles is the one who hears the word; but then, the worries of this life and the love of money choke the word; and it does not bear fruit.

"As for the seed that fell on good soil, it is the one who hears the word and understands it; this seed bears fruit and produces a hundred, or sixty, or thirty times more."

Reading: Jesus taught by using the everyday experiences of common people. In this case, He used the experience of a farmer. The parable of the sower and the seeds mirrors how people respond to the word.

Reflection: Words have innate potentialities. Once they are spoken they get a life of their own. They can change lives. They can influence our decisions. That's why we seek men and women of wisdom to listen to their words when we are at a loss. Their counsel can lead us back to our inner balance. They can help guide us back to the path we have lost. But reception is also important in hearing words. For if one is not properly disposed to it, these words loose their power. They become sterile unable to bear fruit. Jesus knows this truth very well, hence the parable of the seeds that fell on different types of ground. The story is a miniature of who we are in front of His word.

Response: Have I been profiting from the words of others lately? More importantly, do I have the proper disposition to listen to the words of others? Today, I will try to consciously listen to others and have a genuine interest in what they have to say.

14
JULY

Monday
Ps 50:8–9, 16bc–17, 21 & 23
To the upright I will show
the saving power of God.

15TH WEEK IN ORDINARY TIME
St. Kateri Tekakwitha, virgin
Psalter: Week 3 / (Green / White)

1st Reading: Is 1:10–17

"Hear the warning of Yahweh, rulers of Sodom. Listen to the word of God, people of Gomorrah."

"What do I care," says Yahweh" for your endless sacrifices? I am fed up with your burnt offerings, and the fat of your bulls. The blood of fatlings, and lambs and he-goats I abhor, when you come before me and trample on my courts.

"Who asked you to visit me? I am fed up with your oblations. I grow sick with your incense. Your New Moons, Sabbaths and meetings, evil with holy assemblies, I can no longer bear.

"I hate your New Moons and appointed feasts. They burden me. When you stretch out your hands I will close my eyes; the more you pray, the more I refuse to listen, for your hands are bloody.

"Wash and make yourselves clean.

"Remove from my sight the evil of your deeds. Put an end to your wickedness and learn to do good. Seek justice and keep in line the abusers; give the fatherless their rights and defend the widow."

Gospel: Mt 10:34 – 11:1

Jesus said to his apostles, "Do not think that I have come to establish peace on earth. I have not come to bring peace, but a sword. For I have come to set a man against his father, and a daughter against her mother, a daughter-in-law against her mother-in-law. Each one will have as enemies, those of one's own family.

"Whoever loves father or mother more than me, is not worthy of me. And whoever loves son or daughter more than me, is not worthy of me. And whoever does not take up his cross and follow me, is not worthy of me. Whoever finds his life will lose it; but whoever loses his life, for my sake, will find it.

"Whoever welcomes you, welcomes me; and whoever welcomes me, welcomes him who sent me. The one who welcomes a prophet, as a prophet, will receive the reward of a prophet; the one who welcomes a just man, because he is a just man, will receive the reward of a just man. And if anyone gives even a cup of cold water to one of these little ones, because he is my disciple, I assure you, he will not go unrewarded."

When Jesus had finished giving his twelve disciples these instructions, he went on from there, to teach and to proclaim his message in their towns.

St. Kateri Tekakwitha

Did you know that: St. Kateri Tekakwitha, the first native American to be canonized, was the daughter of a pagan Mohawk chief.

More things are piled up on the shoulders of those who choose to follow Jesus. It is as if pressures are calibrated to keep pace with our growing strengths. There seems to be no end in sight to all possible discomfort and pain one must be willing to take in order to be a disciple of Jesus. These probably are told in advance so that there will be no blaming afterwards when the going gets rough on the road to discipleship. Jesus wants His disciples to be wide-eyes with what they are signing into. He does not promise a life on a bed of roses. What He promises is a victorious glorious life in the end. He or she who desires that life must be ready to pay for what will happen in between.

15TH WEEK IN ORDINARY TIME
St. Bonaventure, bishop & doctor
Psalter: Week 3 / (White)

Tuesday

15
JULY

Ps 48:2–3a, 3b–4, 5–6, 7–8
God upholds his city for ever.

St. Bonaventure

Did you know that: St. Bonaventure is often referred to as the "second founder" of the Franciscan Order.

1st Reading: Is 7:1–9

When Ahaz son of Jotham, the son of Uzziah, was king of Judah, king Rezin of Aram and Pekah son of Remaliah, king of Israel, laid siege to Jerusalem but they were unable to capture it.

When the news reached the house of David, "Aram's troops are encamped in Ephraim," the heart of the king and the hearts of the people trembled as the trees of the forest tremble before the wind.

Yahweh then said to Isaiah: "Go with your son *A-remnant-will-return*, and meet Ahaz at the end of the aqueduct of the Upper Pool, on the road to the Washer man's Field.

"Say to him, stay calm and fear not; do not lose courage before these two stumps of smoldering firebrands—the fierce anger of Rezin the Aramean and the blazing fury of the son of Remaliah. You know that Aram, Ephraim and Remaliah's son have plotted against Judah, saying: Let us invade and scare it, let us seize it and put the son of Tabeel king over it. But the Lord Yahweh says:

"It shall not be so; it shall not come to pass.

"For Damascus is only the head of Aram and Rezin the lord of Damascus.

"Samaria is only the head of Ephraim and Remaliah's son is only the lord of Samaria.

"Within fifty-six years, Ephraim will be shattered and will no longer be a people.

"But if you do not stand firm in faith, you, too, will not stand at all."

Gospel: Mt 11:20–24

Jesus began to denounce the cities in which he had performed most of his miracles, because the people there did not change their ways. "Alas for you Chorazin and Bethsaida! If the miracles worked in you had taken place in Tyre and Sidon, the people there would have repented long ago in sackcloth and ashes. But I assure you, for Tyre and Sidon; It will be more bearable for Tyre and Sidon on the day of judgment than for you. And you, Capernaum, will you be lifted up to heaven? You will be thrown down to the place of the dead! For if the miracles which were performed in you had been performed in Sodom, it would still be there today! But I tell you, it will be more bearable for Sodom on the day of judgment than for you."

Denounce is a strong negative word. For Jesus to denounce the cities, mentioned in this Gospel, must mean that He was fed up with their blindness and hard-headedness. But what made them so stubborn amidst the many signs and wonders that the Lord did in their midst? One can only guess, but it is sad to see the opportunity given them pass by. It was all a waste not only on their part but on the part of Jesus too who gave time and effort for their sake.

16
JULY

Wednesday
Ps 94:5-6, 7-8, 9-10, 14-15
The Lord will not abandon
his people.

15TH WEEK IN ORDINARY TIME
Our Lady of Mount Carmel
Psalter: Week 3 / (Green / White)

1st Reading: Is 10:5-7, 13b-16

*T*hus says Yahweh: Woe to Assyria, the rod of my anger, the staff of my fury!

Against a godless nation I send him, against a people who provoke my wrath I dispatch him, to plunder and pillage, to tread them down like mud in the streets.

But the mind of his king is far from this, his heart harbors other thoughts; what he wants is to destroy, to make an end of all nations.

For the king says:

"By my own strength I have done this and by my own wisdom, for I am clever.

"I have moved the frontiers of people, I have plundered treasures, I have brought inhabitants down to the dust, I have toppled kings from their thrones.

"As one reaches into a nest, so my hands have reached into nations' wealth.

"As one gathers deserted eggs, so have I gathered the riches of the earth.

"No one flapped a wing or opened its mouth to chirp a protest."

Does the ax claim more credit than the man who wields it?

Does the saw magnify itself more than the one who uses it?

This would be like a rod wielding the man who lifts it up; will those not made of wood, be controlled by the cudgel?

This is why Yahweh Sabaoth, is ready to send a wasting sickness upon the king's sturdy warriors.

Beneath his plenty, a flame will burn like a consuming fire.

Gospel: Mt 11:25-27

*O*n that occasion, Jesus said, "Father, Lord of heaven and earth, I praise you; because you have hidden these things from the wise and learned, and revealed them to simple people. Yes, Father, this was your gracious will.

"Everything has been entrusted to me by my Father. No one knows the Son except the Father; and no one knows the Father except the Son, and those to whom the Son chooses to reveal him."

Knowing somebody well presupposes deep intimacy. Jesus glories in His deep relationship with the Father and readily boasts about it. What more, He shares this bond with those who will follow Him, holding nothing back for Himself. It is a sharing that springs from someone who could not wait to share the delight He has with His Father whose heart is firmly set for the simple lowly people of this world. It would be wonderful to access this Father from Jesus Himself.

Thursday

17 JULY

Ps 102:13–14ab & 15, 16–18, 19–21
From heaven the Lord looks down
on the earth.

1st Reading: Is 26:7–9, 12, 16–19

Let the righteous walk in righteousness. You make smooth the path of the just, and we only seek the way of your laws, O Yahweh.

Your name and your memory are the desire of our hearts. My soul yearns for you in the night; for you my spirit keeps vigil.

When your judgments come to earth, the world's inhabitants learn to be upright.

Yahweh, please give us peace; for all that we accomplish is your work. For they sought you in distress, they cried out to you in the time of their punishment.

As a woman in travail moans and writhes in pain, so are we now in your presence.

We conceived, we had labor pains, but we gave birth to the wind. We have not brought salvation to the land; the inhabitants of a new world have not been born.

Your dead will live! Their corpses will rise! Awake and sing, you who lie in the dust!

Let your dew fall, O Lord, like a dew of light, and the earth will throw out her dead.

Gospel: Mt 11:28–30

Jesus said, "Come to me, all you who are weary and burdened, and I will give you rest. Take my yoke upon you and learn from me, for I am gentle and humble of heart; and you will find rest. For my yoke is easy; and my burden is light."

Carrying things tends to weary us in the long run. That's why it is wise to unload some of these burdens from time to time, to give ourselves breathing space and recover our strengths. People tend to hold on to their burden especially the psycho-emotional ones. They occupy precious space in the heart and grow heavier through the years. But the yoke of Jesus is light for one burdened only by the demands of love. Since love is a power that can do all things, bear all things and suffer all things, it can lighten even the heaviest of load. Love makes everything good and light.

18 JULY

Friday

Is 38:10, 11, 12abcd, 16
You saved my life, O Lord;
I shall not die.

15TH WEEK IN ORDINARY TIME
St. Camillus de Lellis, priest
Psalter: Week 3 / (Green / White)

1st Reading: Is 38:1-6, 21-22, 7-8

In those days Hezekiah fell mortally ill and the prophet Isaiah, son of Amoz, went to him with a message from Yahweh, "Put your house in order for you shall die; you shall not live."

Hezekiah turned his face to the wall and prayed to Yahweh, "Ah Yahweh! Remember how I have walked before you in truth and wholeheartedly, and done what is good in your sight." And Hezekiah wept bitterly.

Then the word of Yahweh came to Isaiah, "Go and tell Hezekiah what Yahweh, the God of his father David, says: I have heard your prayer and I have seen your tears. See! I am adding fifteen years to your life and I will save you and this city from the power of the king of Assyria. I will defend it for my sake and for the sake of David my servant.

Isaiah then said, "Bring a fig cake to rub on the ulcer and let Hezekiah be cured!"

Hezekiah asked, "What is the sign that I shall go up to the house of Yahweh?" Isaiah answered, "This shall be for you a sign from Yahweh, that he will do what he has promised. See! I shall make the shadow descending on the stairway of Ahaz go back ten steps." So the sunlight went back the ten steps it had covered on the stairway.

Gospel: Mt 12:1-8

It happened that, Jesus was walking through the wheat fields on a Sabbath. His disciples were hungry; and they began to pick some heads of wheat, to crush and to eat the grain. When the Pharisees noticed this, they said to Jesus, "Look at your disciples! They are doing what is prohibited on the Sabbath!"

Jesus answered, "Have you not read what David did, when he and his men were hungry? He went into the House of God, and they ate the bread offered to God, though neither he nor his men had the right to eat it, but only the priests. And have you not read in the law, how, on the Sabbath, the priests in the temple desecrate the Sabbath, yet they are not guilty?

"I tell you, there is greater than the temple here. If you really knew the meaning of the words: *It is mercy I want, not sacrifice,* you would not have condemned the innocent.

"Besides, the Son of Man is Lord of the Sabbath."

St. Camillus de Lellis

Did you know that: St. Camillus de Lellis founded the Order of St. Camillus variously known as Agonizants, Camillians, Clerks Regular Ministers of the Infirm, Fathers of a Good Death, and Order of the Servants of the Sick,

Doing acts of mercy trumps sacrifice especially on the personal level and directed to oneself anytime. For the former benefits the others while the latter is more of the self. The benefits one gains from doing personal sacrifices are annulled when one begins to take a "holier than thou stance" relative to others who cannot and would not engage in such practices. Perhaps it is not really the act itself that Jesus condemns. After all, any self development activity helps improve who we are and has a social effect. It is the attitude that might arise from it that is undesirable; that is, an elitist appreciation of oneself while scorning others.

15TH WEEK IN ORDINARY TIME
Psalter: Week 3 / (Green / White)

Saturday
Ps 10:1-2, 3-4, 7-8, 14
Do not forget the poor, O Lord!

19
JULY

1st Reading: Mic 2:1–5

Woe to those who plot wickedness and plan evil even on their beds! When morning comes they do it, as soon as it is within their reach.

If they covet fields, they seize them. Do they like houses? They take them. They seize the owner and his household; both, the man and his property.

This is why Yahweh speaks, "I am plotting evil against this whole brood, from which your necks cannot escape. No more shall you walk with head held high, for it will be an evil time."

On that day, they will sing a taunting song against you; and a bitter lamentation will be heard, "We have been stripped of our property in our homeland. Who will free us from the wicked who allots our fields."

Truly, no one will be found in the assembly of Yahweh to keep a field for you.

Gospel: Mt 12:14–21

The Pharisees went out, and made plans to get rid of Jesus. As Jesus was aware of their plans, he left that place. Many people followed him, and he cured all who were sick. But he gave them strict orders not to make him known.

In this way, Isaiah's prophecy was fulfilled:

Here is my servant, whom I have chosen; the one I love, and with whom I am pleased. I will put my spirit upon him; and he will announce my judgment to the nations.

He will not argue or shout, nor will his voice be heard in the streets. The bruised reed he will not crush, nor snuff out the smoldering wick until he brings justice to victory, and in him, all the nations will put their hope.

Jesus deemed it wise to walk away from a conflict. He is not known to have been a coward but it is He Himself who had counseled His disciples to be cunning as snakes and meek as doves. Nothing could be gained from a head-on collision with the religious authorities. The mission is still too young to be orphaned of its initiator. And so Jesus searches for a friendly place and cures those in search for wholeness and meaningful lives. The fighting will be left for another day. Meanwhile, a lot of work still needs to be done.

1st Reading: Wis 12:13,16–19

There is no other god besides you, one who cares for everyone, who could ask you to justify your judgments;

Your strength is the source of your justice and because you are the Lord of all, you can be merciful to everyone.

To those who doubt your sovereign power you show your strength and you confound the insolence of those who ignore it. But you, the Lord of strength, judge with prudence and govern us with great patience, because you are able to do anything at the time you want.

In this way you have taught your people that a righteous person must love his human fellows; you have also given your people cause for hope by prompting them to repent of their sin.

2nd Reading: Rom 8:26–27

Brothers and sisters, we are weak but the Spirit comes to help us. How to ask? And what shall we ask for? We do not know, but the spirit intercedes for us without words, as if with groans. And He who sees inner secrets knows the desires of the Spirit, for he asks for the hoy ones what is pleasing to God.

Gospel: Mt 13:24-43 (or Mt 13:24-30)

Jesus told the people another parable, "The kingdom of heaven can be compared to a man, who sowed good seed in his field. While everyone was asleep, his enemy came, and sowed weeds among the wheat, and went away.

"When the plants sprouted and produced grain, the weeds also appeared. Then, the servants of the owner came, and said to him, 'Sir, was it not good seed that you sowed in your field? Where did the weeds come from?' He answered them, 'This is the work of an enemy.' They asked him, 'Do you want us to go and pull up the weeds?' He told them, 'No, when you pull up the weeds, you might uproot the wheat with them. Let them grow together, until harvest; and, at harvest time, I will say to the workers: Pull up the weeds first, tie them in bundles and burn them; then gather the wheat into my barn.'"

Jesus offered them another parable: "The kingdom of heaven is like a mustard seed that a man took and sowed in his field.

"It is smaller than all other seeds, but once it is fully grown, it is bigger than any garden plant; like a tree, the birds come and rest in its branches."

He told them another parable, "The kingdom of heaven is like the yeast that a woman took, and hid in three measures of flour, until the whole mass of dough began to rise."

Jesus taught all these things to the crowds by means of parables; he did not say anything to them without using a parable. This fulfilled what was spoken by the Prophet: *I will speak in parables. I will proclaim things kept secret since the beginning of the world.*

Then he sent the crowds away and went into the house. And his disciples came to him, saying, "Explain to us the parable of the weeds in the field." Jesus answered them, "The one who sows the good seed is the Son of Man. The field is the world; the good seed are the people of the kingdom; the weeds are those who follow the evil one. The enemy who sows the weeds is the devil; the harvest is the end of time, and the workers are the angels.

"Just as the weeds are pulled up and burned in the fire, so will it be at the end of time. The Son of Man will send his angels, and they will weed out of his kingdom all that is scandalous and all who do evil. And these will be thrown into the blazing furnace, where there will be weeping and gnashing of teeth. Then the just will shine, like the sun, in the kingdom of their Father. If you have ears, then hear."

Reading: Again Jesus uses imagery taken from agriculture to teach about the Kingdom of Heaven. He prefers to use the symbol of the sower and the seed to convey His teachings. However, since He uses parables to do so, the meaning of His words is not easily accessible. Sometimes, He has to explain them to His disciples in private so that they may understand.

Reflection: The good and the bad, the sacred and the profane tend to live side by side. It is as if they could not exist without the other. The more renowned the place as a center of holiness, the more commercialism and consumerism is attracted around it giving rise to many commercial pursuits in support of the holy activities going on. It is thus with a certain dose of realism that Jesus told the parable of the good sower whose work is sabotaged by the enemy who sowed weeds among the wheat. It happens in the real world that we live in. It is present in the hearts of each and every one of us. In this regard Jesus counsels patience and allows the process of the wheat and the weeds to finish. It is only during harvest time that the two could be safely separated. We too should have the patience to live in a world of contrasts. Meanwhile let us strive to make our wheat outgrow our weeds within.

Response: How do I behave amidst the differences that I have with others? Do I fit in or do I insist on doing things my own way by removing their uniqueness and individuality and insisting that they be a clone of me? Today, I will try to integrate myself amidst the diversity that I find in my environment. I will allow them to grow with me and let time teach us to pull the weeds of differences that hinder our friendship instead.

21 JULY

Monday

Ps 50:5–6, 8–9, 16bc–17, 21 & 23
To the upright I will show
the saving power of God.

16TH WEEK IN ORDINARY TIME
St. Lawrence of Brindisi, priest & doctor
Psalter: Week 4 / (Green / White)

1st Reading: Mic 6:1–4, 6–8

Listen to what Yahweh said to me, "Stand up, let the mountains hear your claim, and the hills listen to your plea."

Hear, O mountains, Yahweh's complaint! Foundations of the earth, pay attention! For Yahweh has a case against his people, and will argue it with Israel.

"O my people, what have I done to you? In what way have I been a burden to you? Answer me.

"I brought you out of Egypt; I rescued you from the land of bondage; I sent Moses, Aaron and Miriam to lead you.

"What shall I bring when I come to Yahweh and bow down before God the most high? Shall I come with burnt offerings, with sacrifices of yearling calves? Will Yahweh be pleased with thousands of rams, with an overabundance of oil libations? Should I offer my firstborn for my sins, the fruit of my body for my wrongdoing?

"You have been told, O man, what is good and what Yahweh requires of you: to do justice, to love mercy, and to walk humbly with your God."

Gospel: Mt 12:38–42

Some teachers of the law and some Pharisees spoke up, "Teacher, we want to see a sign from you." Jesus answered them, "An evil and unfaithful people want a sign; but no sign will be given, them except the sign of the prophet Jonah. In the same way, as Jonah spent three days and three nights in the belly of the whale, so will the Son of Man spend three days and three nights in the heart of the earth.

"At the judgment, the people of Nineveh will rise with this generation, and condemn it; because they reformed their lives at the preaching of Jonah, and here, there is greater than Jonah. At the judgment, the Queen of the South will stand up and condemn you. She came from the ends of the earth to hear the wisdom of Solomon; and here, there is greater than Solomon. "

St. Lawrence of Brindisi
Did you know that: St. Lawrence of Brindisi died on his birthday in Lisbon after finishing his mission as the Viceroy of Naples.

Signs are confirmatory by nature. We ask them from time to time to assure ourselves that we are on the right track. Some teachers of the Law and Pharisees asked the Lord for a sign. Perhaps they want to rest their doubts and be sure of their decisions before committing themselves to the Lord. Perhaps they just want to trap Him and disregard any signs He may make since their minds were set on a negative course of action. Whatever their frame of mind, Jesus was vexed with them. He had been performing countless signs of miracles and wonders in front of them for a period of time already. If it did not convince them, one more would not make a dent on their unbelief.

16TH WEEK IN ORDINARY TIME
St. Mary Magdalene
Psalter: Week 4 / (White)

Tuesday

22
JULY

Ps 63:2, 3–4, 5–6, 8–9
My soul is thirsting for you,
O Lord my God.

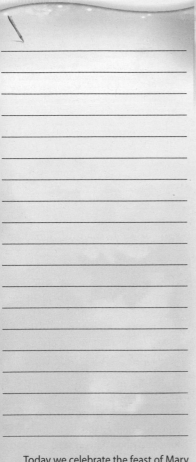

1st Reading: Song 3:1–4b (or 2 Cor 5:14–17)

The Bride says: On my bed at night I looked for the one I love, I sought him without finding him; I called him and he did not answer.

I will rise and go about the city, through the streets and the squares; I will seek the love of my heart...

I sought him without finding him; the watchmen came upon me, those who patrol the city." Have you seen the love of my heart?"

As soon as I left them, I found the love of my heart. I held him and would not let him go till I had brought him to my mother's house to the room of her who conceived me.

Gospel: Jn 20:1–2, 11–18

On the first day after the Sabbath, Mary of Magdala came to the tomb early in the morning while it was still dark, and she saw that the stone blocking the tomb had been moved away. She ran to Peter, and the other disciple whom Jesus loved, and she said to them, "They have taken the Lord out of the tomb and we don't know where they have laid him."

Mary stood weeping outside the tomb; and as she wept, she bent down to look inside. She saw two angels in white, sitting where the body of Jesus had been, one at the head, and the other at the feet. They said, "Woman, why are you weeping?" She answered, "Because they have taken my Lord and I don't know where they have put him."

As she said this, she turned around and saw Jesus standing there, but she did not recognize him. Jesus said to her, "Woman, why are you weeping? Who are you looking for?" She thought it was the gardener and answered him, "Sir, if you have taken him away, tell me where you have put him, and I will go and take him away."

Jesus said to her, "Mary!" She turned, and said to him, "Rabboni!"—which means Master. Jesus said to her, "Do not touch me, because I have not yet ascended to the Father. But go to my brothers and say to them: I am ascending to my Father, who is your Father, to my God, who is your God."

So Mary of Magdala went and announced to the disciples, "I have seen the Lord, and this is what he said to me."

Today we celebrate the feast of Mary of Magdala, the woman who earned a distinction of being one of the followers of Jesus who did not abandon Him even at the lowest moment of her Lord's life. Little is known about her and the persistent caricature of her as a sinful woman is altogether false. But she figured prominently in the resurrection event. She was the first to see the Risen Lord and announce the good news to the still hesitant, fearful disciples. Henceforth she will be called "apostle to the apostles"–an honor she earned through her constant unwavering adherence to Jesus even in moments when hope was nowhere in sight.

23
JULY

Wednesday
Ps 71:1-2, 3-4a, 5-6ab, 15 & 17
I will sing of your salvation.

16TH WEEK IN ORDINARY TIME
St. Bridget of Sweden, religious
Psalter: Week 4 / (Green / White)

1st Reading: Jer 1:1, 4–10

These are the words of Jeremiah, son of Hilkiah, one of the priests at Anathoth in the territory of Benjamin.

A word of Yahweh came to me, "Even before I formed you in the womb I have known you; even before you were born I had set you apart, and appointed you a prophet to the nations!"

I said, "Ah, Lord Yahweh! I do not know how to speak; I am still young!"

But Yahweh replied, "Do not say; 'I am still young', for now you will go, whatever be the mission I am entrusting to you, and you will speak of whatever I command you to say. Do not be afraid of them, for I will be with you to protect you—it is Yahweh who speaks!"

Then Yahweh stretched out his hand and touched my mouth and said to me," Now I have put my words in your mouth. See! Today I give you authority over nations and over kingdoms to uproot and to pull down, to destroy and to overthrow, to build and to plant."

Gospel: Mt 13:1–9

That same day, Jesus left the house and sat down by the lakeside. Many people gathered around him. So he got into a boat, and sat down, while the crowds stood on the shore; and he spoke to them in parables about many things.

Jesus said, "The sower went out to sow; and, as he sowed, some seeds fell along the path; and the birds came and ate them up. Other seeds fell on rocky ground, where there was little soil, and the seeds sprouted quickly, because the soil was not deep. But as soon as the sun rose, the plants were scorched; and they withered, because they had no roots. Again, other seeds fell among thistles; and the thistles grew and choked the plants. Still, other seeds fell on good soil and produced a crop: some a hundredfold, others sixty, and others thirty. If you have ears, then hear!"

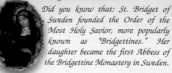

St. Bridget of Sweden

Did you know that: St. Bridget of Sweden founded the Order of the Most Holy Savior, more popularly known as "Bridgettines." Her daughter became the first Abbess of the Bridgettine Monastery in Sweden.

Farmers are generally good at their trade. They understand the factors that allow for a good harvest such as good seed, good soil and the likes. But no matter how careful they are, still things happen that negate a good harvest. Some seeds will fall on undesirable grounds, for once thrown, the seeds have a trajectory of their own. It is like the mission that God entrusted to each and every one of us. The recipients are not carefully scrutinized whether they are fertile soils from which the Word of God might grow a plentiful harvest or not. The seeds of the Good News are sown with a prayer that they would yield bountiful results. The different types of persons should not daunt us in the task. We sow and God takes care of the rest.

16TH WEEK IN ORDINARY TIME
St. Sharbel Makhluf, priest
Psalter: Week 4 / (Green / White)

Thursday
Ps 36:6–7ab, 8–9, 10–11
With you is the fountain of life, O Lord.

24
JULY

St. Sharbel Makhluf
Did you know that: St. Sharbel Makhluf was a Maronite Catholic, not a Roman Catholic. In his authority as universal head of the Catholic Church in all its parts, Pope Paul had the saint canonized and presided over it at St. Peter's Basilica.

_____
_____
_____
_____
_____
_____
_____
_____
_____
_____
_____
_____
_____

The Kingdom of God is revealed in parables. It is not accessible to eyes and ears that cannot leave behind the usual and literal. It is a language that is finer than our coarse, obvious and ordinary human discourse. That is why faith is a condition to savor its wealth of meanings. Faith opens our eyes to the wonders of God's love revealed to us in symbolic discourse. What was once arcane and incomprehensible becomes accessible to our human understanding. Perhaps it cannot be helped. The Kingdom is a divine reality that human words heave and groan to contain its meaning.

1st Reading: Jer 2:1–3, 7–8, 12–13

A word of Yahweh came to me, "Go and shout this in the hearing of Jerusalem. This is Yahweh's word:

I remember your kindness as a youth, the love of your bridal days, when you followed me in the wilderness, through a land not sown.

Israel was holy to Yahweh, the first fruits of his harvest. All who ate of it had to pay and misfortune fell on them— it is Yahweh who speaks.

I brought you to a fertile land to eat of the choicest fruit. As soon as you came you defiled my land and dishonored my heritage!

The priests did not ask, 'Where is Yahweh?' The masters of my teaching did not know me; the pastors of my people betrayed me; the prophets followed worthless idols and spoke in the name of Baal.

Be aghast at that, O heavens! Shudder, be utterly appalled—it is Yahweh who speaks—for my people have done two evils: they have forsaken me, the fountain of living water, to dig for themselves leaking cisterns that hold no water!

Gospel: Mt 13:10–17

Jesus' disciples came to him and said, "Why do you speak to them in parables?"

Jesus answered, "To you it has been given to know the secrets of the kingdom of heaven, but not to these people. For the one who has will be given more; and he will have in abundance. But the one who does not have will be deprived of even what he has. That is why I speak to them in parables; because they look and do not see; they hear; but they do not listen or understand.

"In them, the words of the prophet Isaiah are fulfilled: *However much you hear, you do not understand; however much you see, you do not perceive.*

"*For the heart of this people has grown dull. Their ears hardly hear and their eyes dare not see. If they were to see with their eyes, hear with their ears and understand with their heart, they would turn back, and I would heal them.* But blessed are your eyes, because they see; and your ears, because they hear.

"For I tell you, many prophets and righteous people have longed to see the things you see, but they did not see them; and to hear the things you hear, but they did not hear them."

25

JULY

Friday

Ps 126:1bc–2ab, 2cd–3, 4–5, 6
Those who sow in tears,
shall reap with shouts of joy.

FEAST OF ST. JAMES, APOSTLE
Psalter: Proper / (Red)

1st Reading: 2 Cor 4:7–15

Brothers and sisters, we carry this treasure in vessels of clay, so that this all surpassing power may not be seen as ours, but as God's. Trials of every sort come to us, but we are not discouraged. We are left without answer, but do not despair; persecuted but not abandoned, knocked down but not crushed. At any moment, we carry, in our person, the death of Jesus, so, that, the life of Jesus may also be manifested in us. For we, the living, are given up continually to death, for the sake of Jesus, so, that, the life of Jesus may appear in our mortal existence. And as death is at work in us, life comes to you.

We have received the same spirit of faith referred to in Scripture, that says: *I believed and so I spoke.* We also believe, and so we speak. We know that he, who raised the Lord Jesus, will also raise us, with Jesus, and bring us, with you, into his presence. Finally, everything is for your good, so that grace will come more abundantly upon you, and great will be the thanksgiving for the glory of God.

Gospel: Mt 20:20–28

The mother of James and John came to Jesus with her sons, and she knelt down, to ask a favor. Jesus said to her, "What do you want?" And she answered, "Here, you have my two sons. Grant, that they may sit, one at your right hand and one at your left, in your kingdom."

Jesus said to the brothers, "You do not know what you are asking. Can you drink the cup that I am about to drink?" They answered, "We can." Jesus replied, "You will indeed drink my cup; but to sit at my right or at my left is not for me to grant. That will be for those, for whom my Father has prepared it."

The other ten heard all this, and were angry with the two brothers. Then Jesus called them to him and said, "You know, that the rulers of nations behave like tyrants, and the powerful oppress them. It shall not be so among you: whoever wants to be great in your community, let him minister to the community. And if you want to be the first of all, make yourself the servant of all. Be like the Son of Man, who came not to be served, but to serve, and to give his life to redeem many."

Great powers entail great responsibilities. That's why one has to be ready to wield power responsibly. James and John desire power with Jesus. It is a legitimate desire. Jesus Himself did not rebuke them. However there are conditions in obtaining such power. Although the brothers believed that they could fulfill the requirements, still Jesus told them that it was not He but the Father who appointed. They just had to be ready. The ten got angry at such audacity but it is more because the brothers acted faster than them. They too had the same desire. Jesus is not yet finished with them. He will have a long way to go in purifying the intentions of His disciples.

Saturday

Ps 84: 3, 4, 5-6a & 8a, 11
How lovely is your dwelling place,
Lord, mighty God!

26
JULY

1st Reading: Jer 7: 1-11

These words were spoken by Yahweh, to Jeremiah, "Stand at the gate of Yahweh's house and proclaim this in a loud voice: Listen to what Yahweh says, all you people of Judah (who enter these gates to worship Yahweh). Yahweh the God of Israel says this:

"Amend your ways and your deeds and I will stay with you in this place. Rely not on empty words such as: 'Look, temple of Yahweh! Temple of Yahweh! This is the temple of Yahweh!'

"It is far better for you to amend your ways and act justly with all. Do not abuse the stranger, orphan or widow or shed innocent blood in this place or follow false gods to your own ruin. Then I will stay with you in this place, in the land I gave to your ancestors in times past and forever.

"But you trust in deceptive and useless words. 9 You steal, kill, take the wife of your neighbor; you swear falsely, worship Baal and follow foreign gods who are not yours. Then, after doing all these horrible things, you come and stand before me in this temple that bears my name and say, 'Now we are safe.'

"Is this house on which rests my name a den of thieves? I have seen this myself—it is Yahweh who speaks."

Gospel: Mt 13:24–30
(or from Lectionary of Saints)

Jesus told the people another parable, "The kingdom of heaven can be compared to a man, who sowed good seed in his field. While everyone was asleep, his enemy came, and sowed weeds among the wheat, and went away.

"When the plants sprouted and produced grain, the weeds also appeared. Then, the servants of the owner came, and said to him, 'Sir, was it not good seed that you sowed in your field? Where did the weeds come from?'

"He answered them, 'This is the work of an enemy.' They asked him, 'Do you want us to go and pull up the weeds?' He told them, 'No, when you pull up the weeds, you might uproot the wheat with them. Let them grow together, until harvest; and, at harvest time, I will say to the workers: Pull up the weeds first, tie them in bundles and burn them; then gather the wheat into my barn.'"

The sacred and profane, light and shadow, the good and the bad, these will forever exist as twins to one another. They are only significant when the other is present for they can be only understood in contrast to the other. This may be the reason why the owner of the field is not annoyed at all that weeds grow along with the wheat. He did not plant the former but he was not naïve enough to believe that they would not make an appearance. So he allowed them to grow together. There's no use weeding out the bad seeds. They are so alike and intertwined that one could not help destroy the other in the process of uprooting the weeds. And so God allows good and evil to thrive together. The harvest will determine who will go to the fire and who will go to the barn. God's patience allows us the time to change our ways. May we make use of such time to come out the better.

27
JULY

Sunday Ps 119:57, 72, 76–77, 127–128, 129–130
Lord, I love your commands.

1st Reading: 1 K 3:5, 7–12

It was in Gibeon, during the night, that Yahweh appeared to Solomon in a dream and said, "Ask what you want me to give you."

Solomon answered, "O Yahweh my God, you have made your servant king in place of David my father, although I am but a young boy who does not know how to undertake anything. Meantime, your servant is in the midst of your people whom you have chosen—a people so great that they can neither be numbered nor counted.

"Give me, therefore, an understanding mind in governing your people that I may discern between good and evil. For who is able to govern this multitude of people of yours?"

Yahweh was pleased that Solomon had made this request. And he told him, "Because you have requested this rather than long life or wealth or even vengeance on your enemies; indeed, because you have asked for yourself understanding to discern what is right, I shall grant you your request. I now give you a wise and discerning mind such as no one has had before you nor anyone after you shall ever have."

2nd Reading: Rom 8:28–30

Brothers and sisters, "We know that in everything, God works for the good of those who love him, whom he has called, according to his plan. Those whom he knew beforehand, he has also predestined, to be like his Son, similar to him, so, that, he may be the Firstborn among many brothers and sisters. And so, those whom God predestined, he called; and those whom he called, he makes righteous; and to those whom he makes righteous, he will give his glory."

Gospel: Mt 13:44–52 (or Mt 13:44-46)

Jesus said to his disciples, "The kingdom of heaven is like a treasure, hidden in a field. The one who finds it, buries it again; and so happy is he, that he goes and sells everything he has, in order to buy that field.

"Again, the kingdom of heaven is like a trader, who is looking for fine pearls. Once he has found a pearl of exceptional quality, he goes away, sells everything he has and buys it.

"Again, the kingdom of heaven is like a big fishing net, let down into the sea, in which every kind of fish has been caught. When the net is full, it is dragged ashore. Then they sit down and gather the good fish into buckets, but throw the bad away. That is how it will be at the end of time; the angels will go out to separate the wicked from the just, and to throw the wicked into the blazing furnace, where they will weep and gnash their teeth."

Jesus asked, "Have you understood all these things?" "Yes," they answered. So he said to them, "Therefore, every teacher of the law, who becomes a disciple of the kingdom of heaven, is like a householder, who can produce from his store things both new and old."

Reading: Continuing the theme of how the Kingdom of Heaven can be explained in terms of human concepts, Jesus now uses the imagery from the world of treasure hunters, traders and fishermen. Nothing is so banal and plain that it cannot disclose some truths regarding the Kingdom. The disciples who are already honed in the teaching style of Jesus now understand the point of the parable.

God. This time around we not only need scholars to theologize about our faith but more so, creative thinkers who will find ways and means to transmit the faith that touches not only the head but also the heart. Jesus has shown us the way. We need to recover this tradition to educate this world that has turned deaf ears to our concepts and principles because they have lost the power to stir the souls of people.

Reflection: In coaching others toward a meaningful life, we have to be creative just as Jesus was creative in stirring the hearts and minds of His listeners. He provided them with an emotional memory of His teachings. This lasts more than the beautiful concepts and ideas that we forward them. If we but just look around, the whole creation speaks of God. It is only a matter of sitting down and taking time to see in what manner we can use them to advance the project of

Response: I have been relying big time on my left brain operations of sequential logical thinking. I hardly have time to develop my right brain of the affective creative thinking. Today, I will start developing the right hemisphere of my brain by downloading from the internet references that will enhance my creative bents. There are also books that will guide me. I will invest in one to give me the skills to relish the symbolic, allegorical meanings in the bible.

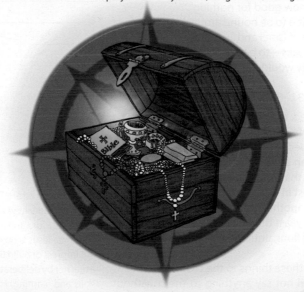

28
JULY

Monday

Dt 32:18–19, 20–21
You have forgotten God
who gave you birth.

17TH WEEK IN ORDINARY TIME
Psalter: Week 1 / (Green)

1st Reading: Jer 13:1–11

This is what Yahweh said to me: "Go! Buy yourself a linen belt and put it around your waist; do not put it in water." So I bought the belt as Yahweh ordered and put it around my waist.

The word of Yahweh came to me a second time, "Take the belt you bought, the one you put around your waist, and go to the torrent Perah; hide it there in a hole in the rock." I went and hid it as Yahweh instructed me.

After many days Yahweh said to me, "Go to the torrent Perah and get the belt I ordered you to hide there." I went to the torrent and dug up the belt but it was ruined and good for nothing; and Yahweh said to me, "In this way I will destroy the pride and great glory of Judah, this wicked people who refuse to heed what I say, this stubborn people who go after other gods to serve and worship them. And they shall become like this belt which is now good for nothing.

"For just as a belt is to be bound around a man's waist so was the people of Israel and Judah bound to me—it is Yahweh who speaks—to be my people, my glory and my honor; but they would not listen."

Gospel: Mt 13:31–35

Jesus offered the crowd another parable: "The kingdom of heaven is like a mustard seed that a man took and sowed in his field.

"It is smaller than all other seeds, but once it is fully grown, it is bigger than any garden plant; like a tree, the birds come and rest in its branches."

He told them another parable, "The kingdom of heaven is like the yeast that a woman took, and hid in three measures of flour, until the whole mass of dough began to rise."

Jesus taught all these things to the crowds by means of parables; he did not say anything to them without using a parable. This fulfilled what was spoken by the Prophet: I will speak in parables. I will proclaim things kept secret since the beginning of the world.

Teaching is an art. Those who are truly teachers know how to simplify complex concepts for the benefit of their students. Jesus is no exception. He does not impress or build up His reputation as a teacher by deliberately showing off His skills and learning. His main concern is for His audience to understand Him. And so, examples and analogies are drawn from everyday life. One has to exercise only his or her faculty of imagination to understand what is being revealed. But for those who overly intellectualize God and His works, all of Jesus' teachings will be incomprehensible. For God truly reveals what was hidden from ages to the simple and ordinary people.

Tuesday

Ps 79:8, 9, 11 & 13
For the glory of your name,
O Lord, deliver us.

29
JULY

St. Martha

Did you know that: The festival of Moors in the town of Villajoyosa, Spain is celebrated in honor of St. Martha.

_____
_____
_____
_____
_____
_____
_____
_____
_____
_____
_____
_____
_____
_____
_____

Despite being near to the Lord, the disciples have a long way to go before they can truly understand the teachings of Jesus. Their one great advantage from the rest is the ease of access to the Teacher. They can directly ask Him for clarification and get instant answers. This is a privilege not enjoyed by all. This reminds us that being close and intimate with Jesus has its own perks. One need not fall in line to get an answer for our doubts and uncertainties in life. The good news is, everyone can have this privilege. Jesus is no ordinary teacher hampered by our ordinary human conditions. He can attend to us simultaneously without breaking sweat. But we have to be His friends. Our chance to be one starts now.

1st Reading: Jer 14:17–22

This you will say to them: Let my eyes shed tears night and day without ceasing! For with a great wound has the virgin daughter of my people been wounded, a most grievous wound.

If I go into the country, I see those slain by the sword. If I enter the city I see the ravages of famine. For the prophet and the priest did not understand what was happening in the land.

Have you then rejected Judah forever? Do you abhor Zion? Why have you wounded us and left us with no hope of recovery?

We hoped for salvation but received nothing good; we waited for healing, but terror came!

Yahweh, we know our wickedness and that of our ancestors, and the times we have sinned against you.

For your name's sake do not despise us; do not dishonor the throne of your glory. Remember us. Do not break your Covenant with us!

Among the worthless idols of the nations, are there any who can bring rain, or make the skies send showers?

Only in you, Yahweh our God, do we hope, for it is you who do all this.

Gospel: Mt 13:36–43

Jesus sent the crowds away and went into the house. And his disciples came to him, saying, "Explain to us the parable of the weeds in the field." Jesus answered them, "The one who sows the good seed is the Son of Man. The field is the world; the good seed are the people of the kingdom; the weeds are those who follow the evil one. The enemy who sows the weeds is the devil; the harvest is the end of time, and the workers are the angels.

"Just as the weeds are pulled up and burned in the fire, so will it be at the end of time. The Son of Man will send his angels, and they will weed out of his kingdom all that is scandalous and all who do evil. And these will be thrown into the blazing furnace, where there will be weeping and gnashing of teeth. Then the just will shine, like the sun, in the kingdom of their Father. If you have ears, then hear. "

30
JULY

Wednesday

Ps 59:2–3, 4, 10–11, 17, 18
God is my refuge
on the day of distress.

1st Reading: Jer 15:10, 16–21

Woe is me, Mother, why did you bring me to the light?

A man of dissension throughout the land!

I owe them nothing, neither do they owe me, yet they all curse me!

I devoured your words when they came. They were my happiness and I felt full of joy when you made your name rest on me.

I never associate with worldly people, amusing myself with scoffers! When your hand was upon me I stood apart and you filled me with your anger.

Why is there no end to my sorrow or healing for my wound? Why do you deceive me, and why does my spring suddenly dry up?

Then Yahweh spoke to me, "If you return I will take you back and you will serve me again. Draw the gold from the dross and you will be as my own mouth. You must draw them to you and not go over to them. I will make you a fortress and a wall of bronze facing them; if they fight against you they will not overcome you; I am with you to free you and save you. I will redeem you from the wicked and free you from the hands of tyrants."

Gospel: Mt 13:44–46

Jesus said to his disciples, "The kingdom of heaven is like a treasure, hidden in a field. The one who finds it, buries it again; and so happy is he, that he goes and sells everything he has, in order to buy that field.

"Again, the kingdom of heaven is like a trader, who is looking for fine pearls. Once he has found a pearl of exceptional quality, he goes away, sells everything he has and buys it."

St. Peter Chrysologus
Did you know that: St. Peter Chrysologus was dubbed "Chrysologus", meaning "golden-worded", because of his exceptional oratorical eloquence.

We are ready to give up anything to have that which we truly desire. Jesus proposes to redirect our desire to what is essential, that is, the Kingdom of God. Having that, all things will be added to us in measure that is full, well pressed and shaken. For what we desire dictates our decisions and actions in life. And so to choose what is the most important for us is crucial. Again, today Jesus tells us to choose the Kingdom. Shall we give His proposal a chance, or shall we go our own merry way choosing what we think is best for ourselves?

Thursday

Ps 146:1b–2, 3–4, 5–6ab
Blessed is he whose help
is the God of Jacob.

31 JULY

St. Ignatius of Loyola
Did you know that: The book St.
Ignatius of Loyola read during
his recuperation and eventually
led to his "conversion" was
entitled "The Golden Legend"
by James of Voragine.

1st Reading: Jer 18:1–6

This is the word of Yahweh that came to Jeremiah: "Go down to the potter's house and there you will hear what I have to say."

So I went to the potter's house and found him working at the wheel. But the pot he was working on was spoiled in his hands, so he reworked it all over again into another pot that suits his desire.

Meanwhile Yahweh sent me his word, "People of Israel, can I not do with you what this potter does? As clay in the potter's hand so are you in my hands."

Gospel: Mt 13:47–53

Jesus said to his disciples, "The kingdom of heaven is like a big fishing net, let down into the sea, in which every kind of fish has been caught. When the net is full, it is dragged ashore. Then they sit down and gather the good fish into buckets, but throw the bad away. That is how it will be at the end of time; the angels will go out to separate the wicked from the just, and to throw the wicked into the blazing furnace, where they will weep and gnash their teeth."

Jesus asked, "Have you understood all these things?" "Yes," they answered. So he said to them, "Therefore, every teacher of the law, who becomes a disciple of the kingdom of heaven, is like a householder, who can produce from his store things both new and old."

When Jesus had finished these parables, he left that place.

The big fishing net as an image of the Kingdom is a beautiful image. It makes us imagine all sorts of people being dragged into it and given a chance. For the Kingdom is not discriminating. Experience has shown that people thought of as unfit have proven themselves worthy of the gift. A case example is Ignatius of Loyola whose feast we celebrate today. At first glance, he seemed to be a bad recruit: a noble man with a penchant for war. But history showed us otherwise. He turned out to be a good catch. And so the fishing net of the Kingdom is still being cast out to catch more people. May the likes of Ignatius be caught so that the Kingdom will expand in breadth and number.

01
AUGUST

Friday
Ps 69:5, 8–10, 14
Lord, in your great love,
answer me.

17TH WEEK IN ORDINARY TIME
St. Alphonsus Liguori, bishop & doctor
Psalter: Week 1 / (White)

1st Reading: Jer 26:1–9

At the beginning of the reign of Judah's king Jehoiakim son of Josiah, the word of Yahweh came to Jeremiah: Yahweh says this, "Stand in the courtyard of Yahweh's house and say to all who come from the towns of Judah to worship in Yahweh's house—all that I command you to say; do not omit anything! Perhaps they will listen to you. Perhaps each one will turn from his wicked ways. Then I will change my mind and forget the destruction that I have planned to inflict on them because of their wicked deeds.

Tell them: This is what Yahweh says:

"You have not obeyed me and you have failed to walk according to my law which I have set before you. You have not heeded my servants, the prophets, whom I have persistently sent to you. If you stubbornly close your ears to them, I will treat this house of mine as I treated the Sanctuary of Shiloh and let all the nations see that Jerusalem is a cursed city."

The priests, the prophets and all the people heard what Jeremiah said in Yahweh's house. When Jeremiah finished saying all that Yahweh had commanded, he was besieged by the priests and prophets saying, "You are bound to die! How dare you speak in Yahweh's Name telling us that this house will be treated like Shiloh and this city is to become a deserted ruin." And all the people gathered around Jeremiah in the house of Yahweh.

Gospel: Mt 13:54–58

Jesus went to his hometown and taught the people in their synagogue. They were amazed and said, "Where did he get this wisdom and these special powers? Isn't he the carpenter's son? Isn't Mary his mother and aren't James, Joseph, Simon and Judas his brothers? Aren't all his sisters living here? Where did he get all these things?" And so they took offense at him.

Jesus said to them, "The only place where prophets are not welcome is his hometown and in his own family." And he did not perform many miracles there because of their lack of faith.

St. Alphonsus Liguori
Did you know that: In 1732, St. Alphonsus Liguori founded the Congregation of the Holy Redeemer, an Order dedicated to preaching to the rural poor, popularly known as "Redemptorists."

Familiarity with someone sometimes robs us of the power to see beyond what we think we know. We get stuck with an image of that person that we do not allow to grow, develop and transform. Sometimes, this holding on to that familiar image is tinged with nostalgia and good memories. It represents a simple and uncomplicated knowledge of someone familiar. However, people change. They are full of surprises. This is the case of Jesus when He returns to His home town.

17TH WEEK IN ORDINARY TIME
St. Eusebius of Vercelli, bishop
St. Peter Julian Eymard, priest
Psalter: Week 1 / (Green / White)

Saturday

Ps 69:15–16, 30–31, 33–34
Lord, in your great love,
answer me.

02
AUGUST

St. Peter Julian Eymard
Did you know that: A reliquary containing the right arm humerus bone of St. Peter Julian Eymard is found in the Saint Jean Baptiste Catholic Church in New York City.

1st Reading: Jer 26:11–16, 24

The priests and the prophets said to the leaders of the people: "This man must die for he has spoken against the city as you have heard with your own ears!"

Jeremiah replied, "I have been sent by Yahweh to prophesy against this house and this city all that you have heard. Hence, reform your ways and your deeds and obey Yahweh your God that he may change his mind and not bring upon you the destruction he had intended.

"As for me I am in your hands; do with me whatever you consider just and right. But know that I am innocent; and if you take my life you commit a crime that is a curse on yourselves, on the city and the people. In truth it was Yahweh who sent me to say all that I said in your hearing."

Then the leaders, backed by the people, said to the priests and the prophets, "This man does not deserve death; he spoke to us in the Name of Yahweh."

As for Jeremiah he was befriended by Ahikam, son of Shaphan, and was not handed over to those who wanted him put to death.

Gospel: Mt 14:1–12

At that time, the reports about Jesus reached king Herod, and he said to his servants, "This man is John the Baptist. John has risen from the dead, and that is why miraculous powers are at work in John."

Herod had, in fact, ordered that John be arrested, bound in chains and put in prison, because of Herodias, the wife of his brother Philip. For John had said to Herod, "It is not right for you to have her as your wife." Herod wanted to kill him but he did not dare, because he feared the people, who regarded John as a prophet.

On Herod's birthday the daughter of Herodias danced among the guests; she so delighted Herod that he promised under oath to give her anything she asked for. The girl, following the advice of her mother, said, "Give me the head of John the Baptist, here, on a dish."

The king was very displeased, but because he had made his promise under oath, in the presence of his guests, he ordered it to be given to her. So he had John beheaded in prison, and his head brought on a dish and given to the girl. The girl then took it to her mother.

Then John's disciples came, took his body and buried it. Then they went and told Jesus.

There are things that will not rest easily. They come back to haunt and torment us. This is especially true if we have done something unjust and we know it. Our mind goes back from time to time to the injustice we have committed. That is why Herod sees John everywhere. Now that the news about Jesus reaches his ear, he immediately thinks of it as John resurrected. For it is said that there is no respite for the unjust. Their sins will always be before them. That is why blessed are the lowly and meek of heart. Theirs is a life free from the guilt of those who wield power unjustly.

03
AUGUST

Sunday

Ps 145:8–9, 15–16, 17–18
The hand of the Lord feeds us;
he answers all our needs.

1st Reading: Is 55:1–3

Thus says Yahweh: Come here, all you who are thirsty, come to the water! All who have no money, come!

Yes, without money and at no cost, buy and drink wine and milk.

Why spend money on what is not food and labor for what does not satisfy? Listen to me, and you will eat well; you will enjoy the richest of fare.

Incline your ear and come to me; listen, that your soul may live. I will make with you an everlasting Covenant, I will fulfill in you my promises to David.

2nd Reading: Rom 8:35, 37–39

Brothers and sisters: Who shall separate us from the love of Christ? Will it be trials, or anguish, persecution or hunger, lack of clothing, or dangers or sword?

No, in all of this, we are more than conquerors, thanks to him, who has loved us. I am certain, that neither death nor life, neither angels nor spiritual powers, neither the present nor the future, nor cosmic powers, were they from heaven, or from the deep world below, nor any creature whatsoever, will separate us from the love of God, which we have, in Jesus Christ, our Lord.

Gospel: Mt 14:13–21

When Jesus heard of the death of John the Baptist, he set out by boat for a secluded place, to be alone. But the people heard of it, and they followed him on foot from their towns. When Jesus went ashore, he saw the crowd gathered there, and He had compassion on them. And he healed their sick.

Late in the afternoon, his disciples came to him and said, "We are in a lonely place and it is now late. You should send these people away, so that they can go to the villages and buy something for themselves to eat."

But Jesus replied, "They do not need to go away; you give them something to eat." They answered, "We have nothing here but five loaves and two fishes." Jesus said to them, "Bring them here to me."

Then he made everyone sit down on the grass. He took the five loaves and the two fishes, raised his eyes to heaven, pronounced the blessing, broke the loaves, and handed them to the disciples to distribute to the people. And they all ate, and everyone had enough; then the disciples gathered up the leftovers, filling twelve baskets. About five thousand men had eaten there, besides women and children.

Reading: Hearing John's demise, Jesus sets out to a lonely place. He was easily traced by the people who had come on foot. This aroused the compassion of Jesus who healed some of their sick. It was late in the afternoon when the disciples advised Jesus to send the people away so they could buy food for themselves. He in turn proposed that they be fed by the disciples and worked a miracle on the little food that they had. On that day, a multitude was fed by the miracle of the loaves and the fish.

Reflection: Setbacks early in His ministry could have deterred men and women of lesser stature. John had been beheaded. Jesus was served a warning not to collide head on with the powers that be. But Jesus knew His mission and goal. Problems and obstacles are part and parcel of the task ahead. He would not retreat. He would only regroup His resources by withdrawing for a while since His time had not yet come. Yet even in His strategic retreat, logistical nightmare followed Him. The people who came on foot seeking Him had nothing to eat. Even His disciples were at a loss how to remedy the situation. It is in this difficult situation that great leaders show why they are leaders. They turn problems into opportunities. They make something big out of the little resources that they have. In the hands of Jesus the two fish and five loaves fed a multitude. It is a prelude for the things to come. This man has what it takes to confront the mighty and the powerful of the land.

Response: Feeding others with physical food can be a satisfying experience. It gives us a chance to do something that addresses one of the basic needs of a person. When was the last time I whipped up a meal for others? Today I might bring some snacks or viands that I could share with others.

04
AUGUST

Monday
Ps 119:9, 43, 79, 80, 95, 102
Lord, teach me your statutes.

18TH WEEK IN ORDINARY TIME
St. John Vianney, priest
Psalter: Week 2 / (White)

1st Reading: Jer 28:1–17

Gospel: Mt 14:22–36

*I*mmediately, Jesus obliged his disciples to get into the boat and go ahead of him to the other side, while he sent the crowd away.

And having sent the people away, he went up the mountain by himself, to pray. At nightfall, he was there alone. Meanwhile, the boat was very far from land, dangerously rocked by the waves, for the wind was against it.

At daybreak, Jesus came to them, walking on the sea. When they saw him walking on the sea, they were terrified, thinking that it was a ghost. And they cried out in fear. But at once, Jesus said to them, "Courage! Don't be afraid. It's me!" Peter answered, "Lord, if it is you, command me to come to you on the water."

Jesus said to him, "Come!" And Peter got out of the boat, and walked on the water to go to Jesus. But seeing the strong wind, he was afraid, and began to sink; and he cried out, "Lord, save me!" Jesus immediately stretched out his hand and took hold of him, saying, "Man of little faith, why did you doubt?"

As they got into the boat, the wind dropped. Then those in the boat bowed down before Jesus, saying, "Truly, you are the Son of God!"

They came ashore at Gennesaret. The local people recognized Jesus and spread the news throughout the region. So they brought to him all the sick people, begging him to let them touch just the hem of his cloak. All who touched it became perfectly well.

St. John Vianney
Did you know that: St. John Vianney, patron saint of parish priests and popularly known as the "Cure of Ars," yearned for the contemplative life of a monk, and four times he ran away from Ars.

Jesus prayed and calmly walked above the turbulent lake, whereas His disciples who went ahead had to contend with the furious winds and waves that were set against them. Perhaps prayer has the capacity to still our inner world so much so that the chaos of the world outside does not unsettle us. This sets us apart from those who are easily affected and become fearful when the going gets tough. When we take time to pray before facing the world, its challenges and obstacles cannot daunt us. Peter learned the hard way when he requested to meet the Lord halfway and his courage faltered. The waves would have swallowed him up had Jesus not extended his hands. He was not prayerful enough to navigate the turbulent waters of life on his own. He would have to pray as Jesus prayed to overcome.

18TH WEEK IN ORDINARY TIME
The Dedication of the Basilica
of Saint Mary Major
Psalter: Week 2 / (Green / White)

Tuesday

Ps 102:16–18, 19–21, 29 & 22–23
The Lord will build up Zion again,
and appear in all his glory.

05
AUGUST

1st Reading: Jer 30:1–2, 12–15, 18–22

This is another word that came to Jeremiah from Yahweh:

Yahweh, God of Israel says, "Write in a book all that I have communicated to you. Your wound is incurable, your injury is grievous. There is no one to plead your cause. There is a remedy for an ulcer but no healing for you! All your lovers have forgotten you; they care nothing for you. For I struck you as an enemy does, with a cruel punishment, because of your great guilt and the wickedness of your sin. Why cry out now that you are hurt? Is there no cure for your pain? Because of your great crime and grievous sin I have done this to you.

"I will restore my people into Jacob's tents and have pity on his dwellings. The city will be rebuilt over its ruins and the palace restored on its proper place. From them will come songs of praise and the sound of merrymaking.

"I will multiply them and they shall not be few. I will bestow honor on them and they shall not be despised. Their children will be as before and their community will be established before me. I will ask their oppressors to account.

"Their leader will be one of themselves, their ruler shall emerge from their midst. I will bring him close to me for who would dare to approach me? You shall be my people and I shall be your God."

Gospel: Mt 15:1–2, 10–14 (or Mt 14:22-36)

Some Pharisees, and teachers of the law, who had come from Jerusalem, gathered around Jesus. And they said to him, "Why don't your disciples follow the tradition of the elders? For they, they don't wash their hands before eating."

Jesus then called the people to him, and said to them, "Listen and understand: What enters into the mouth does not make a person unclean. What defiles a person is what comes out of his mouth."

After a while the disciples gathered around Jesus and said, "Do you know that the Pharisees were offended by what you said?" Jesus answered, "Every plant which my heavenly Father has not planted shall be uprooted. Pay no attention to them! They are blind, leading the blind. When a blind person leads another, the two will fall into a pit."

Today we celebrate the feast of the dedication of the Basilica of St. Mary Major, the first basilica ever dedicated to the Blessed Virgin Mary in the whole Christendom. This was done right after the Council of Ephesus that proclaimed Mary as the Mother of God. This basilica in turn had nurtured countless souls and directed them to the Son of Mary, her savior and God. Mary had been praised as the Star of the Sea in reference to her as the guide to the safe harbor of faith as we navigate the sea of life. We the modern disciples of the Lord can pass through the turbulence of life with calmness and without fear if we set our eyes firmly on Mary as our example and guide.

06
AUGUST

Wednesday

Ps 97:1–2, 5–6, 9
The Lord is king, the most high
over all the earth.

**FEAST OF THE
TRANSFIGURATION OF THE LORD**
Psalter: Proper / (White)

1st Reading: Dn 7:9–10, 13–14

I looked and saw the following:

Some thrones were set in place and One of Great Age took his seat. His robe was white, as snow, his hair, white as washed wool. His throne was flames of fire with wheels of blazing fire. A river of fire sprang forth and flowed before him. Thousands upon thousands served him and a countless multitude stood before him. Those in the tribunal took their seats and opened the book.

I continued watching the nocturnal vision:

One like a son of man came on the clouds of heaven. He faced the One of Great Age and was brought into his presence. Dominion, honor and kingship were given him, and all the peoples and nations of every language served him. His dominion is eternal and shall never pass away; his kingdom will never be destroyed.

2nd Reading: 2 P 1:16–19

Gospel: Mt 17:1–9

S ix days later, Jesus took with him Peter and James, and his brother John, and led them up a high mountain, where they were alone. Jesus' appearance was changed before them: his face shone like the sun, and his clothes became white as snow. Then suddenly, Moses and Elijah appeared to them, talking with Jesus.

Peter spoke up and said to Jesus, "Master, it is good for us to be here. If you wish, I will make three tents: one for you, one for Moses, and one for Elijah."

Peter was still speaking, when a bright cloud covered them with its shadow; and a voice from the cloud said, "This is my Son, the Beloved, my Chosen One. Listen to him."

On hearing the voice, the disciples fell to the ground, full of fear. But Jesus came, touched them, and said, "Stand up, do not be afraid!" When they raised their eyes, they no longer saw anyone except Jesus. And as they came down the mountain, Jesus commanded them not to tell anyone what they had seen, until the Son of Man be raised from the dead.

The Transfiguration of the Lord is another moment of revelation about what His true nature really is. This is witnessed only by His closest disciples, Peter, James and John. As to why Jesus did not allow the other disciples to glimpse His hidden glory as God, we can only surmise. Perhaps it is because He doesn't want to leak out prematurely His real identity. He needs only witnesses who according to the Jewish tradition have the strength especially if the attestation is by three. And so these chosen ones saw what others would have to wait for: the beatific vision of God. We can therefore excuse the incoherent stammering of the three after being dazzled by God's glory. In front of such divine manifestation, the mind is swept away, overwhelmed; the mouth cannot describe what has been seen.

18TH WEEK IN ORDINARY TIME
St. Sixtus II, pope
and Companions, martyrs
St. Cajetan, priest
Psalter: Week 2 / (Green / Red / White)

Thursday
Ps 51:12–13, 14–15, 18–19
Create a clean heart in me,
O God.

07
AUGUST

St. Cajetan
Did you know that: St. Cajetan established a montes pietatis (pawnshop) for the poor where they could borrow money with low interest.

1st Reading: Jer 31:31–34

The time is coming—it is Yahweh who speaks—when I will forge a new Covenant with the people of Israel and the people of Judah. It will not be like the one I made with their ancestors when I took them by the hand and led them out of Egypt. For they broke my Covenant although I was their Master, Yahweh declares.

This is the Covenant I shall make with Israel after that time: I will put my law within them and write it on their hearts; I will be their God and they will be my people.

And they will not have to teach each other, neighbor or brother, saying: 'Know Yahweh,' because they will all know me, from the greatest to the lowliest, for I will forgive their wrongdoing and no longer remember their sin.

Gospel: Mt 16:13–23

Jesus came to Caesarea Philippi. He asked his disciples, "Who do people say the Son of Man is?" They said, "For some of them, you are John the Baptist; for others Elijah, or Jeremiah, or one of the prophets."

Jesus asked them, "But you, who do you say I am?" Peter answered, "You are the Messiah, the Son of the living God." Jesus replied, "It is well for you, Simon Barjona, for it is not flesh or blood that has revealed this to you, but my Father in heaven.

"And now I say to you: You are Peter; and on this Rock I will build my Church; and never will the powers of death overcome it.

"I will give you the keys of the kingdom of heaven: whatever you bind on earth shall be bound in heaven; and whatever you unbind on earth shall be unbound in heaven."

Then he ordered his disciples not to tell anyone that he was the Christ.

From that day, Jesus began to make it clear to his disciples that he must go to Jerusalem; that he would suffer many things from the Jewish authorities, the chief priests and the teachers of the law; and that he would be killed and be raised on the third day. Then Peter took him aside and began to reproach him, "Never, Lord! No, this must never happen to you!" But he turned and said to Peter, "Get behind me, Satan! You are an obstacle in my path. You are thinking not as God does, but as people do."

Peter is a good representative of each and every one of us. He could be capable of deep penetrating insights that truly mark him as first among equal disciples, but he could also be dense and narrow minded sometimes which made Jesus praise him and, in the next breath, scold and reprimand him. Yet in all these, Peter never gave up his love for his Lord and Master. His heart was in the right place even though he was burdened by his own failings and weaknesses. And so Jesus never gave up on Peter whom He knew so well. Peter will later prove that he was worthy of such confidence when he sealed his love for the Lord with his life.

08
AUGUST

Friday

Dt 32:35cd–36ab, 39abcd, 41
It is I who deal death
and give life.

18TH WEEK IN ORDINARY TIME
St. Dominic, priest
Psalter: Week 2 / (White)

1st Reading: Nah 2:1, 3; 3:1–3, 6–7

See, there on the mountains, the feet of one who brings good news, one who proclaims peace.

Judah, celebrate your feasts and carry out your vows. For the wicked have been destroyed, they will not attack you anymore.

Yahweh will now restore Jacob's magnificence, like Israel' splendor. For they had been plundered, laid waste as a ravaged vineyard.

Woe to the bloody city, city of lies and booty, O city of unending plunder!

But what! Crack of whips, rumble of wheels and clatter of hoofs!

See the frenzied chargers, the flashing swords and glittering spears, the heaps of the wounded, the dead and dying–we trip over corpses!

I will pelt you with filth, I will treat you with contempt and make of you a shameful show, so that all who look on you will turn their backs in disgust and say: Nineveh—a city of lust—is in ruins. Who will mourn for her? Where can we find one to comfort her?

Gospel: Mt 16:24–28

Jesus said to his disciples, "If you want to follow me, deny yourself. Take up your cross and follow me. For whoever chooses to save his life will lose it, but the one who loses his life, for my sake, will find it. What will one gain by winning the whole world, if he destroys his soul? Or what can a person give, in exchange for his life?

"Know, that the Son of Man will come, in the glory of his Father with the holy angels, and he will reward each one according to his deeds. Truly, I tell you, there are some standing here who will not taste death, before they see the Son of Man coming in his kingdom."

St. Dominic

Did you know that: St. Dominic, the great founder of one of the Mendicant Orders—the Dominicans, was born twelve years before the other great founder of the Mendicant Order, St. Francis of Assisi.

Following is synonymous to risking. We give our all for a chance to follow someone faithfully and to the finish. That is why it is good business to know and be sure of who we follow. Our investment is such that giving up halfway because of disillusionment and falling out of faith would spell costly consequences. Jesus is making a pitch to us today to follow Him. He is candid about the fate of His disciples and does not water down what will happen as a consequence of such following. It is up to us whether we will cast our lot with Him or find others to follow. May we choose well and stand by our decision till the end.

Saturday
Ps 9:8–9, 10–11, 12–13
You forsake not those who seek you, O Lord.

09
AUGUST

St. Teresa Benedicta of the Cross
Did you know that: St. Teresa Benedicta of the Cross was a pupil of Edmund Husserl the founder of the 20th century philosophical school of phenomenology.

1st Reading: Hb 1:12 – 2:4

But you, are you not Yahweh from past ages? You, my holy God, you cannot die. You have set these people to serve your justice and you have made them firm as a rock, to fulfill your punishment.

Yahweh, your eyes are too pure to tolerate wickedness and you cannot look on oppression. Why, then, do you look on treacherous people and watch in silence while the evildoer swallows up one better than himself?

You treat human beings like the fish in the sea, like reptiles who are nobody's concern. This nation catches all on its hook, pulls them out with its net and piles them up in its dragnet. Pleased and delighted at their catch, they offer sacrifices to their net and burn incense to their dragnets, since these supplied them with fish in plenty and provided them with food in abundance. Will they continue, then, to constantly empty their nets, slaughtering nations without mercy?

I will stand in my watchtower and take up position on my battlements; I will see what he replies, if there is an answer to my question.

Then Yahweh answered me and said, "Write down the vision, inscribe it on tablets so it can be easily read, since this is a vision for an appointed time; it will not fail but will be fulfilled in due time. If it delays, wait for it, for it will come, and will not be deferred. Look: I don't look with favor on the one who gives way; the upright, on the other hand, will live by his faithfulness."

Gospel: Mt 17:14–20

A man approached Jesus, knelt before him and said, "Sir, have pity on my son who is an epileptic and is in a wretched state. He has often fallen into the fire and at other times into the water. I brought him to your disciples but they could not heal him."

Jesus replied, "O you people, faithless and misled! How long must I be with you? How long must I put up with you? Bring him here to me." And Jesus commanded the evil spirit to leave the boy, and the boy was immediately healed.

Later, the disciples approached Jesus and asked him privately, "Why couldn't we drive out the spirit?" Jesus said to them, "Because you have little faith. I say to you: if only you had faith the size of a mustard seed, you could tell that mountain to move from here to there, and the mountain would obey. Nothing would be impossible for you."

The size of our faith dictates the size of things we can do. Big faith means big enterprise, little faith means little results. The case of the epileptic child demonstrates the feeble faith the disciples still had. Their insecurities and doubts still get in the way. It is good though that they start with whatever little that they have and come out with the faith that could move mountains later on. And the Lord is there patiently guiding and mentoring them exercising patience and understanding. This tells us not to be afraid when we start with something small on our journey of faith. This is enough to start us towards a faith like that of the apostles.

10
AUGUST

Sunday

Ps 85: 9, 10, 11–12, 13–14
Lord, let us see your kindness,
and grant us your salvation.

1st Reading: 1 K 19:9a, 11–13a

On reaching the place, Elijah came to the cave and stayed in it. Then the word of Yahweh came to him, "What are you doing here, Elijah?" Then Yahweh said, "Go up and stand on the mount, waiting for Yahweh." And Yahweh passed by.

There was first a windstorm, wild wind which rent the mountains and broke the rocks into pieces before Yahweh, but Yahweh was not in the wind. After the storm, an earthquake, but Yahweh was not in the earthquake; after the earthquake, a fire, but Yahweh was not in the fire; after the fire, the murmur of a gentle breeze. When Elijah perceived it, he covered his face with his cloak, went out and stood at the entrance of the cave.

2nd Reading: Rom 9:1–5

Brothers and sisters: I tell you, sincerely, in Christ, and my conscience assures me in the Holy Spirit, that I am not lying: I have great sadness and constant anguish for the Jews. I would even desire, that, I myself, suffer the curse of being cut off from Christ, instead of my brethren: I mean, my own people, my kin. They are Israelites, whom God adopted, and on them, rests his glory. Theirs, are the Covenants, the law, the worship and the promises of God. They are descendants of the patriarchs, and from their race, Christ was born, he, who, as God, is above all distinctions. Blessed be He forever and ever: Amen!

Gospel: Mt 14:22–33

Immediately, Jesus obliged his disciples to get into the boat and go ahead of him to the other side, while he sent the crowd away.

And having sent the people away, he went up the mountain by himself, to pray. At nightfall, he was there alone. Meanwhile, the boat was very far from land, dangerously rocked by the waves, for the wind was against it.

At daybreak, Jesus came to them, walking on the sea. When they saw him walking on the sea, they were terrified, thinking that it was a ghost. And they cried out in fear. But at once, Jesus said to them, "Courage! Don't be afraid. It's me!" Peter answered, "Lord, if it is you, command me to come to you on the water."

Jesus said to him, "Come!" And Peter got out of the boat, and walked on the water to go to Jesus. But seeing the strong wind, he was afraid, and began to sink; and he cried out, "Lord, save me!" Jesus immediately stretched out his hand and took hold of him, saying, "Man of little faith, why did you doubt?"

As they got into the boat, the wind dropped. Then those in the boat bowed down before Jesus, saying, "Truly, you are the Son of God!"

Reading: After feeding the multitude, Jesus sent them away and obliged His disciples to go ahead while He remained to pray. The boat with the disciples had a rough ride. At daybreak Jesus went to them walking on the water which aroused their fear. Assured that it was their Lord, Peter begged that he be commanded to walk on the waters toward his Master. He sank because of his little faith and was rescued by the Lord. This incident on the lake made the disciples believe that Jesus is really the Son of God.

Reflection: In the Jewish tradition, darkness combined with strong wind and water signify chaos. It points to the early times before creation came to be. This reading presents to us a re-creation scene with Jesus as the main protagonist and the disciples being the re-created persons of the new dispensation in Christ. In this Gospel, the lordship of Jesus over chaos is solid and firm. There is no doubt that He is more than just human for being able to do this. Peter sank when he walked amidst the turbulence and was saved by the Lord who stretched His hands to take him out of the water. From incredulity and doubt, Peter was renewed into a firm believer of the Lord. This re-creative powers of the Lord on Peter spilled over to the other disciples who acknowledged Him as the true Son of God.

Response: There have been countless moments when I doubted. How many times must have I sunk in the waters of despair brought about by my unbelief? Today is a good day to make a confession of faith regarding who Jesus is for me. I will take some time and proclaim with my whole being that Jesus is my Lord and Savior.

11

AUGUST

Ps 148:1–2, 11–12, 13, 14
Heaven and earth
are filled with your glory.

19TH WEEK IN ORDINARY TIME
St. Clare, virgin
Psalter: Week 3 / (White)

1st Reading: Ezk 1:2–5, 24–28c

On the fifth of the month (it was the fifth year of the exile of king Jehoiachin) the word of Yahweh came to Ezekiel, son of Buzi, the priest, in the land of the Chaldeans by the banks of the Kebar. There the hand of Yahweh was upon me.

I looked: a windstorm came from the north bringing a great cloud. A fiery light inside it lit up all around it, while at the center there was something like a glowing metal.

In the center were what appeared to be four creatures with the same form; I heard the noise of their wings when they moved, similar to the roar of many waters, similar to the voice of the Most High, the noise of a multitude or of a camp. When they were not moving they lowered their wings.

I heard a noise above the platform over their heads. Above it was a throne resembling a sapphire; and high on this throne was a figure similar to that of a man. Then I saw a light as of glowing bronze, as if fire enveloped him from his waist upwards. And from his waist downwards it was as if fire gave radiance around him.

The surrounding light was like a rainbow in the clouds after a day of rain. This vision was the likeness of Yahweh's glory. On seeing it I fell on my face; and then I heard a voice speaking.

St. Clare
Did you know that: St. Clare of Assisi was the first woman founder of an Order to write her own Rule.

Gospel: Mt 17:22–27

While Jesus was in Galilee with the Twelve, he said to them, "The Son of Man will be delivered into the hands of men, and they will kill him. But he will rise on the third day." The Twelve were deeply grieved.

When they returned to Capernaum, the temple tax collectors came to Peter and asked him, "Does your master pay the temple tax?" He answered, "Yes."

Peter then entered the house; and immediately, Jesus asked him, "What do you think, Simon? Who pay taxes or tribute to the kings of the earth: their sons or strangers and aliens?" Peter replied, "Strangers and aliens." And Jesus told him, "The sons, then, are tax-free. But, so as not to offend these people, go to the sea, throw in a hook, and open the mouth of the first fish you catch. You will find a coin in it. Take the coin and give it to them for you and for me."

Jesus subjects Himself to human laws and obligations as a clear manifestation of how He fully embraced His humanity, God though He may be. This is part and parcel of His incarnation. He doesn't want to get exemptions and privileges simply because His Father is the governor of the whole universe. He took His place in the community of men and women without complaint. Contrast this with those who have entitlement mentalities that seek to bend the rules to suit their needs! We will profit well when we learn from the humility of Jesus and do what we are supposed to do for the good of the society in which we live.

19TH WEEK IN ORDINARY TIME
St. Jane Frances de Chantal, religious
Psalter: Week 3 / (Green / White)

Tuesday

Ps 119:14, 24, 72, 103, 111, 131
**How sweet to my taste
is your promise!**

12
AUGUST

St. Jane Frances de Chantal

Did you know that: St. Jane Frances de Chantal, founder of the Visitation nuns, was a mother of six children.

1st Reading: Ezk 2:8 – 3:4

Yahweh said to me, "Listen then, son of man, to what I say, and don't be a rebel among rebels. Open your mouth and take in what I'm about to say." I looked and saw a hand stretched out in front of me holding a scroll. He unrolled it before me; on both sides were written lamentations, groaning and woes. He said to me, "Son of man, eat what is given to you. Eat this scroll and then go; speak to the people of Israel." I opened my mouth and he made me eat the scroll; and then he said to me, "Eat and fill yourself with this scroll that I'm giving you." I ate it; and it tasted as sweet as honey.

He said, "Son of man, go to the Israelites; speak to them with my words."

Gospel: Mt 18:1–5, 10, 12–14

At that time, the disciples came to Jesus and asked him, "Who is the greatest in the kingdom of heaven?"

Then Jesus called a little child, set the child in the midst of the disciples, and said, "I assure you, that, unless you change, and become like little children, you cannot enter the kingdom of heaven. Whoever becomes humble, like this child, is the greatest in the kingdom of heaven, and whoever receives such a child, in my name, receives me.

"See that you do not despise any of these little ones; for I tell you, their angels in heaven continually see the face of my heavenly Father.

"What do you think of this? If someone has a hundred sheep and one of them strays, won't he leave the ninety-nine on the hillside, and go to look for the stray one? And I tell you, when he finally finds it, he is more pleased about it, than about the ninety-nine that did not go astray. It is the same with your Father in heaven. Your Father in heaven doesn't want even one of these little ones to perish."

Being conscious of one's greatness signifies an insecure hold onto imagined greatness. If one has to defend it to each and everyone constantly, then one's hold over it is tenuous and weak. There will be always someone much stronger who will come along and claim the title. That is why Jesus points out to the child as an exemplar of what greatness means. This is especially true in the case of the kingdom of heaven. The child accepts without counting what is given him or her. In heaven one does not contrast one's gifts with others to find out who has more and who has less. Each will have the friendship of God in equal measure.

13
AUGUST

Wednesday
Ps 113:1–2, 3–4, 5–6
The glory of the Lord is higher
than the skies.

19TH WEEK IN ORDINARY TIME
St. Pontian, pope & martyr
St. Hippolytus, priest & martyr
Psalter: Week 3 / (Green / Red)

1st Reading: Ezk 9:1–7; 10:18–22*

*Y*ahweh shouted loudly in my ears saying, "The punishment of the city is near; see, each one of these has in his hand his instrument of destruction." And six men came from the direction of the upper gate, which faces north, each one with his instrument of destruction. With them was a man clothed in linen, with writing materials at his side. They came; and stopped near the altar of bronze.

Then the glory of the God of Israel rose from the cherubim, where it rested; and went to the threshold of the house. yahweh called to the man clothed in linen; who had the material for writing at his side; and he said to him, "Pass through the center of the city, through Jerusalem, and trace a cross on the forehead of the men who sigh and groan, because of all the abominations committed in it."

I heard him say to the others, "Now you may pass through the city, after him, and strike. Your eyes shall not look with pity; show no mercy! Do away with them all— old men, young men, virgins, children and women—but do not touch anyone marked with a cross."

And, as they were told to begin with the Sanctuary, they struck the elders who were in front of the temple. Yahweh said to them, "Let the courts be filled with the slain and the temple be defiled with their blood: Go out!"

They went and slew the people in the city. (...)

Gospel: Mt 18:15–20

*J*esus said to his disciples, "If your brother has sinned against you, go and point out the fault to him, when the two of you are alone; and if he listens to you, you have won back your brother. If he doesn't listen to you, take with you one or two others, so that the case may be decided by the evidence of two or three witnesses. And if he refuses to listen to them, tell it to the assembled Church. But if he does not listen to the Church, then regard him as a pagan, or a tax collector.

"I say to you: whatever you bind on earth, heaven will keep bound; and whatever you unbind on earth, heaven will keep unbound.

"In like manner, I say to you, if, on earth, two of you agree in asking for anything, it will be granted to you by my heavenly Father; for where two or three are gathered in my name, I am there, among them."

St. Hippolytus
Did you know that: St. Pontian was the first pope who abdicated from his office to make way for his successor.

Breaking bonds is such a serious affair that Jesus made it deliberately difficult to do so. One has to undergo all the processes enumerated before one can legitimately break one's relationship with those one may have once called brothers or sisters. These show that Jesus puts premium on the preservation of the bond, of reconciliation and forgiveness. Only those who are deliberately set to break the relationship would have the stamina and the will to do so.

Thursday

Ps 78:56-57, 58-59, 61-62
Do not forget
the works of the Lord!

14
AUGUST

St. Maximilian Kolbe

Did you know that: St. Maximilian Kolbe, after undergoing starvation for two weeks, died with lethal injection of carbolic acid.

1st Reading: Ezk 12:1–12

Gospel: Mt 18:21 – 19:1

Peter asked Jesus, "Lord, how many times must I forgive the offenses of my brother or sister? Seven times?" Jesus answered, "No, not seven times, but seventy-seven times.

"This story throws light on the kingdom of Heaven: A king decided to settle accounts with his servants. Among the first of them was one who owed him ten thousand pieces of gold. As the man could not repay the debt, the king commanded that he be sold as a slave with his wife, his children and all his goods, as repayment.

"The servant threw himself at the feet of the king and said, 'Give me time, and I will pay you back everything.' The king took pity on him, and not only set him free, but even canceled his debt.

"When this servant left the king's presence, he met one of his fellow servants, who owed him a hundred pieces of silver. He grabbed him by the throat and almost choked him, shouting, 'Pay me what you owe!' His fellow servant threw himself at his feet and begged him, 'Give me time, and I will pay everything.' But the other did not agree, and sent him to prison until he had paid all his debt.

"Now the servants of the king saw what had happened. They were extremely upset, and so they went and reported everything to their lord. Then the lord summoned his servant and said, 'Wicked servant, I forgave you all that you owed me when you begged me to do so. Weren't you bound to have pity on your fellow servant, as I had pity on you?' The lord was now angry. He handed the wicked servant over to be punished, until he had paid the whole debt."

Jesus added, "So will my heavenly Father do with you, unless you sincerely forgive your brothers and sisters."

When Jesus had finished these sayings, he left Galilee and arrived at the border of Judea, on the other side of the Jordan River.

One of the most difficult things to do is to forgive. If the hurt is too deep, it takes a herculean effort before one can truly forgive and forget. And only a few are capable of this. The vast majority of us need time before we could truly heal into wholeness and move on without rancour and ill will to those who have offended us. That is why it is not easy to be the Lord's disciple. The demand is such that we have to truly believe in order to overcome. We have to acknowledge first our own sinfulness and believe that we have been forgiven of our entire debts. That's the only time we can forgive wholeheartedly. For what we don't have, we cannot give. To claim that we have been forgiven gives us the power to forgive others as well.

Friday

Ps 45:10, 11, 12, 16
The queen stands at your right
hand, arrayed in gold.

**SOLEMNITY OF THE
ASSUMPTION OF THE
BLESSED VIRGIN MARY**
Psalter: Proper / (White)

1st Reading: Rev 11:19a; 12:1–6a, 10ab
2nd Reading: 1 Cor 15:20–27

But no, Christ has been raised from the dead, and he comes before all those who have fallen asleep. A human being brought death; a human being also brings resurrection of the dead. For, as in Adam all die, so, in Christ, all will be made alive. However, each one in his own time: first Christ, then Christ's people, when he comes.

Then, the end will come, when Christ delivers the kingdom to God the Father, after having destroyed every rule, authority and power. for he must reign and put all enemies under his feet. the last enemy to be destroyed will be death. As scripture says: God has subjected everything under his feet. When we say that everything is put under his feet, we exclude, of course, the Father, who subjects everything to him.

Gospel: Lk 1:39–56

Mary then set out for a town in the hill country of Judah. She entered the house of Zechariah and greeted Elizabeth. When Elizabeth heard Mary's greeting, the baby leapt in her womb. Elizabeth was filled with the Holy Spirit, and, giving a loud cry, said, "You are most blessed among women; and blessed is the fruit of your womb! How is it, that the mother of my Lord comes to me? The moment your greeting sounded in my ears, the baby within me suddenly leapt for joy. Blessed are you, who believed that the Lord's word would come true!"

And Mary said, "My soul proclaims the greatness of the Lord, my spirit exults in God, my savior! He has looked upon his servant, in her lowliness, and people, forever, will call me blessed. The Mighty One has done great things for me, Holy is his Name! From age to age, his mercy extends to those who live in his presence. He has acted with power and done wonders, and scattered the proud with their plans. He has put down the mighty from their thrones, and lifted up those who are downtrodden. He has filled the hungry with good things, but has sent the rich away empty. He held out his hand to Israel, his servant, for he remembered his mercy, even as he promised to our fathers, to Abraham and his descendants forever."

Mary remained with Elizabeth about three months, and then returned home.

Today we celebrate the Assumption of the Blessed Virgin Mary with both body and soul into heaven. It is not only her feast but the feast of the whole humanity as well for whom the best representative is she. Her fate reveals that which await each and every one of us who are Christ's followers in the last days. She enjoyed it ahead of us being the most blessed among women who accepted the ministry of being the human mother of the Son of God. Today we join our voices with hers in a hymn of praise to God who made all these things possible because of His abiding love for humanity.

19TH WEEK IN ORDINARY TIME
St. Stephen of Hungary
Psalter: Week 3 / (Green / White)

Saturday

Ps 51:12–13, 14–15, 18–19
Create a clean heart in me,
O God.

16
AUGUST

St. Stephen of Hungary

Did you know that: St. Stephen of Hungary, who was canonized by Pope Gregory VII with his son St. Emeric, became the first canonized confessor king, a new category of saint. He is venerated as the patron saint of Hungary, kings, children who are dying, masons, stonecutters, and bricklayers.

1st Reading: Ezk 18:1–10, 13b, 30–32

The word of Yahweh came to me in these terms, "Why are you applying this proverb to the land of Israel: 'The parents have eaten sour grapes and the children's teeth are set on edge?" As I live, word of Yahweh, this proverb will no longer be quoted in Israel. All life is in my hands, the life of the parent and the life of the child are mine. The lives of both are in my hands; so, the one who sins will die.

Imagine a man who is righteous and practices what is just and right. He does not eat at the mountain shrines, or look towards the filthy idols of Israel, does not defile his neighbor's wife, or have intercourse with a woman during her period; he molests no one, pays what he owes, does not steal, gives food to the hungry and clothes to the naked, demands no interest on a loan and doesn't lend for interest, refrains from injustice, practices true justice, man to man, follows my decrees and obeys my laws in acting loyally. Because such a man is truly righteous, he will live, word of Yahweh.

But perhaps this man has a son, who steals and sheds blood, committing crimes which his father never did. Will such a man live? No, he will not! Because he has committed all these abominations he will die: his guilt will fall upon him. That is why I will judge you, Israel, each one according to his ways, word of Yahweh. Come back, turn away from your offenses, that you may not deserve punishment. Free yourselves from all the offenses you have committed and get a new heart and a new spirit. Why should you die, Israel?

I do not want the death of anyone, word of Yahweh, but that you be converted and live!"

Gospel: Mt 19:13–15

Little children were brought to Jesus, that he might lay his hands on them and pray for them. But the disciples scolded those who brought them. Jesus then said, "Let the children be! Don't hinder them from coming to me; for the kingdom of heaven belongs to those who are humble, like these children." Jesus laid his hands on them and went away.

Jesus never placed a barrier between Him and others. What's the use of His coming down on earth to be intimately close to us if in the end, obstacles are placed to make Him inaccessible? That is why He reprimanded His apostles who put a cordon around Him when children were brought that He might bless them. Perhaps they thought He needed space to rest. They must have thought of His comforts. But then He belongs to all and no one who desires to be close to Him will be denied.

1st Reading: Is 56:1, 6–7

This is what Yahweh says: Maintain what is and do what is just, for my salvation is close at hand, my justice is soon to come.

Yahweh says to the foreigners who join him, serving him and loving his name, keeping his Sabbath unprofaned and remaining faithful to his Covenant:

I will bring them to my holy mountain and give them joy in my house of prayer. I will accept on my altar their burnt offerings and sacrifices, for my house will be called a house of prayer for all the nations.

2nd Reading: Rom 11:13–15, 29–32

Brothers and sisters, listen to me, you who are not Jews: I am spending myself, as an apostle to the pagan nations, but I hope my ministry will be successful enough to awaken the jealousy of those of my race, and, finally, to save some of them. If the world made peace with God, when they remained apart, what will it be, when they are welcomed? Nothing less than, a passing from death to life; because the call of God, and his gifts, cannot be nullified.

Through the disobedience of the Jews, the mercy of God came to you who did not obey God. They, in turn, will receive mercy, in due time, after this disobedience, that brought God's mercy to you. So, God has submitted all to disobedience, in order to show his mercy to all.

Gospel: Mt 15:21–28

Leaving that place, Jesus withdrew to the region of Tyre and Sidon. A Canaanite woman from the area, came and cried out, "Lord, Son of David, have pity on me! My daughter is tormented by a demon." But Jesus did not answer her, not even a word. So his disciples approached him and said, "Send her away! See how she is shouting after us."

Then Jesus said to her, "I was sent only to the lost sheep of the nation of Israel."

But the woman was already kneeling before Jesus, and said, "Sir, help me!" Jesus answered, "It is not right to take the bread from the children and throw it to puppies." The woman replied, "That is true, sir, but even puppies eat the crumbs which fall from their master's table." Then Jesus said, "Woman, how great is your faith! Let it be as you wish." And her daughter was healed at that moment.

Reading: Jesus met a Canaanite woman who, desperate for a cure for her daughter, sought the Lord. Despite Jesus' initial rebuff she persisted, even taking the implied insult on her being not of the tribe of Israel. Because of her persistence and faith, her daughter got healed.

Reflection: A person of lesser stuff would have just walked away when Jesus began to speak of His exclusive ministry for the lost sheep of Israel. The Canaanite woman and her daughter did not belong to the race of Abraham. She neither had the right to ask nor impose healing for her daughter on Him. But she had something that made her hold her ground. It was desperation over a loved one's hopeless condition. This enabled her to forget about herself and allowed all her strength to work for the cure of her beloved daughter. Her selflessness made her a strong woman. She was able to do what she did because she loved her daughter that much. And so Jesus was won over. He granted the request of the mother who had suffered for love.

Response: The Canaanite woman facilitated the healing of her daughter by her persistence. Have I helped others towards the point of persistence? Or do I help only at my own convenience? Today I will try to identify those whom I would like to help even at the expense of my own comfort and pride.

18
AUGUST

Monday

Dt 32:18–19, 20, 21
You have forgotten God
who gave you birth.

20TH WEEK IN ORDINARY TIME
Psalter: Week 4 / (Green)

1st Reading: Ezk 24:15–23

The word of Yahweh came to me in these terms, "Son of man, I am about to suddenly take from you the delight of your eyes, but you are not to lament or weep or let your tears flow. Groan in silence and do not mourn for the dead; wear your turban, put on your sandals, do not cover your beard or eat the customary food of mourners."

I spoke to the people in the morning and my wife died that evening. The next morning I did as I had been commanded. Then the people said to me: "Explain to us the meaning of your actions." I said to them, "The word of Yahweh came to me in these terms: 'Say to Israel: I am about to profane my Sanctuary, your pride, the delight of your eyes for which you long. The sons and daughters you left behind will also fall by the sword, but you will do as I have done: you will not cover your beard or eat the customary food of mourners; you will keep your turbans on your heads and sandals on your feet. You will not lament or weep. Instead, because of your sin, you will waste away and groan among yourselves.'

Gospel: Mt 19:16–22

A young man approached Jesus and asked, "Master, what good work must I do to receive eternal life?" Jesus answered, "Why do you ask me about what is good? One, only, is good. If you want to enter eternal life, keep the commandments." The young man said, "Which commandments?" Jesus replied, *"Do not kill; do not commit adultery; do not steal; do not bear false witness; honor your father and mother. And love your neighbor as yourself."*

The young man said to him, "I have kept all these commandments. What do I still lack?" Jesus answered, "If you wish to be perfect, go, sell all that you possess, and give the money to the poor; and you will have treasure in heaven. Then come back and follow me."

On hearing this, the young man went away sad, for he was a man of great wealth.

Keeping the commandments is easy for some. They go through life, conscious of the dos and don'ts of their faith, and follow it conscientiously. With this they will be okay. It is only when they ask what more they can do to demonstrate their faith that problems may arise. For the bar of holiness is set high. Jesus, who left everything behind in obedience to God's will, is the standard. We are therefore forewarned never to ask God a question if we are not yet ready for the possible answer. Discipleship grows in strength in time. We must not force it to blossom prematurely.

Tuesday

Dt 32:26–27ab, 27cd–28, 30, 35cd–36ab
It is I who deal death and give life.

19 AUGUST

St. John Eudes

Did you know that: St. John Eudes wrote the first book ever written on the devotion to the Sacred Heart entitled, "Le Cœur Admirable de la Très Sainte Mère de Dieu".

_____

_____

_____

_____

_____

_____

_____

_____

_____

_____

_____

_____

1st Reading: Ezk 28:1–10

The word of Yahweh came to me in these terms, "Son of man, say to the prince of Tyre: You are very proud and self-satisfied: 'I am a god, I sit like a god in the heart of the sea.' Yet you are man and not a god; would you hold yourself as wise as God?

"You consider yourself wiser than Daniel; no secret is hidden from you. Your wisdom and know-how have earned you a fortune, gold and silver flowed to your treasury. Clever in trade, you became wealthy and, as your fortune increased, your heart became prouder.

"But now, Yahweh has spoken to you, to the one who is like God: I am bringing foreigners against you, the most feared of all the nations. Their sword will challenge your wisdom and debase your refined culture. They will bring you down to the pit and you will die in the depths of the sea. Will you be able to say 'I am a god' when your murderers are killing you? You are a man and not a god.

"You will die the death of the uncircumcised and perish at the hands of aliens, for I have spoken—word of Yahweh."

Gospel: Mt 19:23–30

Jesus said to his disciples, "Truly I say to you: it will be hard for one who is rich to enter the kingdom of heaven. Yes, believe me: it is easier for a camel to go through the eye of the needle than for the one who is rich to enter the kingdom of heaven."

On hearing this, the disciples were astonished and said, "Who, then, can be saved?" Jesus looked at them and answered, "For human beings it is impossible, but for God all things are possible."

Then Peter spoke up and said, "You see, we have given up everything to follow you. What, then, will there be for us?"

Jesus answered, "You, who have followed me, listen to my words: on the Day of Renewal, when the Son of Man sits on his throne in glory, you, also, will sit, on twelve thrones, to judge the twelve tribes of Israel. As for those who have left houses, brothers, sisters, father, mother, children or property for my Name's sake, they will receive a hundredfold, and be given eternal life. Many who are now first, will be last, and many who are now last, will be first."

Why is it so dangerous to be rich? Because you are against spiritual wisdom that says it is difficult for the rich to enter the Kingdom of God. The Gospel today tells as much. The consolation is that it does not express outrightly that the rich are excluded *de facto* from God's kingdom. It only talks about the hardship riches entail in entering God's kingdom. It is because of this that the rich of this world have to work overtime to be assured of salvation. And for those who feel exempted because of the lack of material wealth, they have to seriously see whether they have other forms of "riches" that might be a hindrance to the kingdom. In the end, it calls all of us to make a serious inventory of the "riches" we hold dear that might seal our fate in the final days to come.

20
AUGUST

Wednesday
Ps 23:1–3a, 3b–4, 5, 6
The Lord is my shepherd;
there is nothing I shall want.

20TH WEEK IN ORDINARY TIME
St. Bernard, abbot & doctor
Psalter: Week 4 / (White)

1st Reading: Ezk 34:1–11

Gospel: Mt 20:1–16

Jesus said to his disciples, "This story throws light on the kingdom of heaven: A landowner went out early in the morning, to hire workers for his vineyard. He agreed to pay each worker the usual daily wage, and sent them to his vineyard.

"He went out again, at about nine in the morning, and, seeing others idle in the town square, he said to them, 'You also, go to my vineyard, and I will pay you what is just.' So they went.

"The owner went out at midday, and, again, at three in the afternoon, and he made the same offer. Again he went out, at the last working hour—the eleventh— and he saw others standing around. So he said to them, 'Why do you stand idle the whole day?' They answered, 'Because no one has hired us.' The master said, 'Go, and work in my vineyard.'

"When evening came, the owner of the vineyard said to his manager, 'Call the workers and pay them their wage, beginning with the last and ending with the first.' Those who had gone to work at the eleventh hour came up, and were each given a silver coin. When it was the turn of the first, they thought they would receive more. But they, too, received one silver coin. On receiving it, they began to grumble against the landowner.

"They said, 'These last, hardly worked an hour; yet, you have treated them the same as us, who have endured the heavy work of the day and the heat.' The owner said to one of them, 'Friend, I have not been unjust to you. Did we not agree on one silver coin per day? So, take what is yours and go. I want to give to the last the same as I give to you. Don't I have the right to do as I please with what is mine? Why are you envious when I am kind?

"So will it be: the last will be first, the first will be last."

St. Bernard

Did you know that: St. Bernard of Clairvaux was the first Cistercian monk to be placed in the calendar of saints.

The parable seems to tell us that it is not our effort that will bring us to heaven but the generosity of Him who dwells in the heavenly kingdom. For no matter how much we try, we will only be worth "a day's wage." But even though we try later like the workers who were hired late, still we will get a day's worth wage if the owner wills it. And no one can question His action. He is the manager of His possessions and He will dispose of them according to His will. And so rather than fret whether we have received more than those who were late, let us just do what we can do for God. Let us rejoice that He is generous because all of us in the end do not deserve what we will receive.

Thursday

Ps 51:12–13, 14–15, 18–19
I will pour clean water on you
and wash away all your sins.

21
AUGUST

St. Piux X

Did you know that: St. Pope Pius X took his name in memory of Pius V, who had excommunicated Queen Elizabeth I, to signal that he intended to carry on their fight "against sects and rampant errors."

1st Reading: Ezk 36:23–28

Thus says Yahweh: I will make known the holiness of my great name, profaned among the nations because of you; and they will know that I am Yahweh, when I show them my holiness among you.

For I will gather you from all the nations and bring you back to your own land. Then I shall pour pure water over you and you shall be made clean—cleansed from the defilement of all your idols. I shall give you a new heart and put a new spirit within you. I shall remove your heart of stone and give you a heart of flesh. I shall put my spirit within you and move you to follow my decrees and keep my laws. You will live in the land I gave your ancestors; you shall be my people and I will be your God.

Gospel: Mt 22:1–14

Jesus continued speaking to them in parables: "This story throws light on the kingdom of heaven: A king gave a wedding banquet for his son. He sent his servants to call the invited guests to the banquet, but the guests refused to come.

"Again, he sent other servants, instructing them to say to the invited guests, 'I have prepared a banquet, slaughtered my fattened calves and other animals, and now, everything is ready. Come to the wedding!' But they paid no attention and went away, some to their farms, and some to their work. Others seized the servants of the king, insulted them and killed them.

"The king was furious. He sent his troops to destroy those murderers and burn their city. Then he said to his servants, 'The wedding banquet is prepared, but the invited guests were not worthy. Go instead to the main streets, and invite everyone you find to the wedding feast.'

"The servants went out into the streets and gathered all they found, good and bad alike, so that the hall was filled with guests.

The king came in to see the wedding guests, and he noticed a man not wearing a wedding garment. So he said to him, 'Friend, how did you get in without the wedding clothes?' But the man remained silent. So the king said to his servants, 'Bind his hands and feet and throw him into the outer darkness, where there is weeping and gnashing of teeth.'

"For many are called, but few are chosen."

The love of God is freely given but one should have the proper disposition to receive and enjoy it. This is where our efforts enter. To be partners with God we have to dispose ourselves to receive and nurture His gifts. These are the stuff from which we build our future with Him. Hence we have to prepare ourselves so as to benefit most from the free gratuitous love of God or we will spend eternity gnashing our teeth at the opportunity that passed us by simply because we were not ready when it knocked.

22
AUGUST

Friday
Ps 107:2–3, 4–5, 6–7, 8-9
Give thanks to the Lord;
his love is everlasting.

20TH WEEK IN ORDINARY TIME
The Queenship of the
Blessed Virgin Mary
Psalter: Week 4 / (White)

1st Reading: Ezk 37:1–14*

The hand of Yahweh was upon me. He brought me out and led me in spirit to the middle of the valley, which was full of bones. He made me walk to and fro among them; and I could see there was a great number of them on the ground, all along the valley; and that they were very dry.

Yahweh said to me, "Son of man, can these bones live again?" I said, "Lord Yahweh, only you know that." He then said, "Speak on my behalf concerning these bones; say to them:

Dry bones, hear the word of Yahweh! Yahweh says: I am going to put spirit in you and make you live. I shall put sinews on you and make flesh grow on you; I shall cover you with skin and give you my spirit, that you may live. And you will know that I am Yahweh."

I prophesied as I had been commanded; and then, there was a noise and commotion; the bones joined together. (…) But there was no spirit in them.

So Yahweh said to me, "Speak on my behalf and call on the spirit, son of man! (…) I prophesied as he had commanded me and breath entered them; they came alive, standing on their feet—a great, immense army!

He then said to me, "Son of man, these bones are all Israel. They keep saying: 'Our bones are dry, hope has gone, it is the end of us.' So prophesy! Say to them: This is what Yahweh says: I am going to open your tombs; I shall bring you out of your tombs, my people; and lead you back to the land of Israel. You will know that I am Yahweh, O my people! when I open your graves and bring you out of your graves; when I put my spirit in you, and you live. I shall settle you in your land; and you will know that I, Yahweh, have done what I said I would do."

Gospel: Mt 22:34-40

When the Pharisees heard how Jesus had silenced the Sadducees, they assembled together. One of them, a lawyer, questioned him to test him, "Teacher, which commandment of the law is the greatest?"

Jesus answered, *"You shall love the Lord your God with all your heart, with all your soul, and with all your mind.* This is the first and the most important of the commandments. The second is like it: *You shall love your neighbor as yourself.* The whole Law and the Prophets are founded on these two commandments."

We despair to think that we have to perform many things to qualify being good when all we have to do is one thing, that is, to love. But upon knowing this, we are again confronted with another difficulty, how to love? For the word love had been used and misused for a long time already. The word itself is sometimes suspect especially in this complicated world. So the challenge for us is to go back to the pristine meaning of love, that is, to go back again to the very Being of love, God. St. John in his gospel defines God as Love. And so God is the reference on how to love. And the more we contemplate God, the more we will know how to love.

20TH WEEK IN ORDINARY TIME
St. Rose of Lima, virgin
Psalter: Week 4 / (Green / White)

Saturday

Ps 85:9ab & 10, 11–12, 13–14
The glory of the Lord
will dwell in our land.

23
AUGUST

St. Rose of Lima

Did you know that: St. Rose of Lima became known as Rosa when an Indian maid declared her to be as beautiful as a rose. She is the Patron of Peru, of all Latin America, of the Indies and of the Philippines.

1st Reading: Ezk 43:1–7ab

The angel took me to the gate, facing east. Then I saw the glory of the God of Israel approaching from the east, with a sound like the sound of the ocean; and the earth shone with his glory. This vision was like the one I had seen when he came for the destruction of the city, and like the one I had seen on the bank of the river Chebar. Then I threw myself to the ground.

The glory of Yahweh arrived at the temple by the east gate. The spirit lifted me up and brought me into the inner court: the glory of Yahweh was filling the house. And I heard someone speaking to me from the temple while the man stood beside me. The voice said, "Son of man, you have seen the place of my throne, where I will place the soles of my feet, and live among the Israelites forever; and the people of Israel, they and their kings, will no longer defile my Holy Name with their prostitutions and the kings.

Gospel: Mt 23:1–12

Jesus said to the crowds and to his disciples. "The teachers of the law and the Pharisees have sat down on the chair of Moses. So you shall do and observe all they say; but do not do as they do, for they do not do what they say. They tie up heavy burdens and load them on the shoulders of the people, but they do not even lift a finger to move them. They do everything in order to be seen by people: they wear very wide bands of the law around their foreheads, and robes with large tassels. They enjoy the first places at feasts and the best seats in the synagogues, and they like being greeted in the marketplace, and being called 'Master' by the people.

"But you, do not let yourselves be called Master, because you have only one Master, and all of you are brothers and sisters. Neither should you call anyone on earth Father, because you have only one Father, he who is in heaven. Nor should you be called Leader, because Christ is the only Leader for you. Let the greatest among you be the servant of all. For whoever makes himself great shall be humbled, and whoever humbles himself shall be made great."

Being teachers in the service of God does not qualify us immediately as God's chosen ones. What we teach and what we do must form a uniform whole or else there will be a split between what we say and what we do. This is pointed by Jesus Himself with regard to the teachers of the Law and the Pharisees. What they have been teaching all along has not directed their lives and actions. Their words are therefore empty and hollow, not backed up by their examples. What they taught still remain valid. It can never be annulled by bad examples. The message remains true even if the medium is inadequate to convey its full meaning.

24
AUGUST

Sunday

Ps 138:1-2, 2-3, 6, 8
Lord, your love is eternal;
do not forsake the work of your hands.

1st Reading: Is 22:19-23

Thus says the Lord Yahweh Sabaoth: You will be deposed, strongman. I will hurl you down from where you are.

On that day I will summon my servant Eliakim, son of Hilkiah.

I will clothe him with your robe, I will strengthen him with your girdle, I will give him your authority, and he will be a father to the inhabitants of Jerusalem and to the people of Judah.

Upon his shoulder I will place the key of the house of David: what he opens, no one shall shut; what he shuts, no one shall open.

I will fasten him like a peg in a sure spot, and he will be a seat of honor in the house of his father.

2nd Reading: Rom 11:33-36

How deep are the riches, the wisdom and knowledge of God! His decisions cannot be explained, nor his ways understood! *Who has ever known God's thoughts? Who has ever been his adviser? Who has given him something first, so that God had to repay him?* For everything comes from him, has been made by him and has to return to him. To him be the glory for ever! Amen.

Gospel: Mt 16:13-20

Jesus came to Caesarea Philippi. He asked his disciples, "Who do people say the Son of Man is?" They said, "For some of them, you are John the Baptist; for others Elijah, or Jeremiah, or one of the prophets."

Jesus asked them, "But you, who do you say I am?" Peter answered, "You are the Messiah, the Son of the living God." Jesus replied, "It is well for you, Simon Barjona, for it is not flesh or blood that has revealed this to you, but my Father in heaven.

"And now I say to you: You are Peter; and on this Rock I will build my Church; and never will the powers of death overcome it.

"I will give you the keys of the kingdom of heaven: whatever you bind on earth shall be bound in heaven; and whatever you unbind on earth shall be unbound in heaven."

Then he ordered his disciples not to tell anyone that he was the Christ.

Reading: Amidst the backdrop of Caesarea Philippi, Jesus forced the issue of how He is perceived by the people. His disciples came up with various responses, all pointing out to His being an important personality akin to the mighty prophets of old or even of John the Baptist who stood against the authorities at that time and got beheaded. Then He asked his disciples point blank as to whom they thought He was. Peter, on behalf of the group, proclaimed Him Messiah and Son of God. Because of this, the Church of Christ will be founded on the solid declaration of faith by Peter.

Reflection: There is a time in our life when we have to lay down our all, when we have to risk everything because we are truly convinced and we do believe. This is what had happened to Peter when he was finally asked by Jesus who he thought Jesus was. Peter had been a follower for some time. He had been part of the most beautiful memories of Jesus. And now he had to give account of his own impression of his Teacher. Peter never hesitated. He proclaimed the faith that would be taken over by the church literally founded over his place of burial. Peter risked his all. He gained big time for that risk by being the rock on which the church of Jesus would be built.

Response: Am I proud of my faith or do I take it casually to the point that I don't make a stand when my faith is attacked. Today I will proudly wear my being a Christian and will help promote a better understanding of what I believe in my social network, in my workplace, in my community and in any place I can advance a correct appreciation of my belief.

25
AUGUST

Monday
Ps 96:1–2a, 2b–3, 4–5
Proclaim God's marvelous deeds
to all the nations.

21ST WEEK IN ORDINARY TIME
St. Louis
St. Joseph Calasanz, priest
Psalter: Week 1 / (Green / White)

1st Reading: 2 Thes 1:1–5, 11–12

From Paul, Sylvanus and Timothy, to the church of the Thessalonians, which is in God, our Father, and in Christ Jesus, the Lord.

May grace and peace be yours, from God, the Father, and Christ Jesus, the Lord.

Brothers and sisters, we should give thanks to God, at all times, for you. It is fitting to do so, for your faith is growing, and your love for one another, increasing. We take pride in you, among the churches of God, because of your endurance, and your faith in the midst of persecution and sufferings. In this, the just judgment of God may be seen; for you must show yourselves worthy of the kingdom of God, for which you are now suffering.

This is why we constantly pray for you; may our God make you worthy of his calling. May he, by his power, fulfill your good purposes, and your work, prompted by faith. In that way, the name of Jesus, our Lord, will be glorified through you, and you, through him, according to the loving plan of God and of Christ Jesus, the Lord.

Gospel: Mt 23:13–22

Jesus said to the crowds, "But woe to you, teachers of the law and Pharisees, you hypocrites! You shut the door to the kingdom of heaven in people's faces. You, yourselves, do not enter it, nor do you allow others to do so.

"Woe to you, scribes and Pharisees, you hypocrites! You devour widows' property; and as a show, you pray long prayers! Therefore, you shall receive greater condemnation. Woe to you, teachers of the law and Pharisees, you hypocrites! You travel by sea and land to make a single convert; yet, once he is converted, you make him twice as fit for hell as yourselves!

"Woe to you, blind guides! You say: To swear by the temple is not binding; but, to swear by the gold of the temple is binding. Foolish men! Blind men! Which is of more worth: the gold in the temple, or the temple which makes the gold a sacred treasure? You say: To swear by the altar is not binding, but to swear by the offering on the altar is binding. How blind you are! Which is of more value: the offering on the altar, or the altar which makes the offering sacred? Whoever swears by the altar, is swearing by the altar and by everything on it. Whoever swears by the temple, is swearing by the temple, and by God, who dwells in the temple. Whoever swears by heaven, is swearing by the throne of God, and by him, who is seated on it."

St. Joseph Calasanz
Did you know that: St. Joseph Calasanz, founder of the first free public school in modern Europe and the religious Order of the Pious Schools, more popularly known as Piarists, was a friend and supporter of Galileo Galilei.

The Lord's polemics with the teachers of the Law and the Pharisees increase in force as time passes by. It is their hard headedness that He is most angry about. If they only open their eyes a little bit and exercise self-examination, they will discover how much they have strayed from the path of righteousness. But they are not willing to change. They legitimize their crooked ways by deft manipulation of the Law. It is no longer a guide to righteous living but an instrument to preserve their status quo. Jesus will have none of this travesty. He will continue to criticize and confront this hypocrisy that has burdened God's people for so long.

Tuesday

26 AUGUST

Ps 96:10, 11–12, 13
The Lord comes
to judge the earth.

1st Reading: 2 Thes 2:1–3a, 14–17

Brothers and sisters, let us speak about the coming of Christ Jesus, our Lord, and our gathering to meet him. Do not be easily unsettled. Do not be alarmed by what a prophet says, or by any report, or by some letter said to be ours, saying, the day of the Lord is at hand.

Do not let yourselves be deceived, in any way. Apostasy must come first, when the man of sin will appear, to this end he called you, through the Gospel we preach, for he willed you, to share the glory of Christ Jesus, our Lord.

Because of that, brothers and sisters, stand firm and hold to the traditions that we taught you, by word or by letter. May Christ Jesus, our Lord, who has loved us, may God our Father, who, in his mercy, gives us everlasting comfort and true hope, strengthen you. May he encourage your hearts and make you steadfast in every good work and word.

Gospel: Mt 23:23–26

Jesus said, "Woe to you, teachers of the Law and Pharisees, you hypocrites! You do not forget the mint, anise and cumin seeds when you demand the tenth of everything; but then, you forget what is most fundamental in the law: justice, mercy and faith! You should have done these things without neglecting the others. Blind guides! You strain out a mosquito, but swallow a camel.

"Woe to you, teachers of the law and Pharisees, you hypocrites! You fill the plate and the cup, with theft and violence, and then pronounce a blessing over them. Blind Pharisee! Purify the inside first, then the outside, too, will be purified."

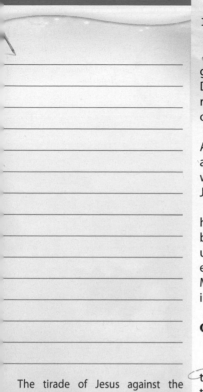

The tirade of Jesus against the teachers of the Law and the Pharisees continues. There seems to be no let up on the part of the Lord on His denunciation of their ways. But are they really that bad to warrant the divine anger? It seems that not all are hard-hearted and close-minded as we think they are. Some showed exceptional sensitivity and openness to Jesus' teachings. Just recall Nicodemus, Joseph of Arimathea and the synagogue official who asked healing for his daughter. It is not therefore their persons that Jesus condemns but their institutions that have calcified through time and have no energy to renew itself. The only way to awaken them from their torpor is through strong criticism. Jesus took upon Himself this thankless task to put religious institutions back on track. He would not be repaid with gratitude but with the cross.

27
AUGUST

Wednesday

Ps 128:1–2, 4–5
Blessed are those who
fear the Lord.

21ST WEEK IN ORDINARY TIME
St. Monica
Psalter: Week 1 / (White)

1st Reading: 2 Thes 3:6–10, 16–18

Brothers and sisters: We command you, beloved, to stay away from believers who are living in idleness, contrary to the traditions we passed on to you. You know, how you ought to follow our example: we worked while we were with you. Day and night, we labored and toiled so as not to be a burden to any of you. We had the right to act otherwise, but we wanted to give you an example.

Besides, while we were with you, we said clearly: If anyone is not willing to work, neither should that one eat.

May the Lord of peace give you his peace at all times and in every way. May the Lord be with you all.

I, Paul, write this greeting with my own hand. This is my signature in all my letters. This is how I write.

May the grace of Christ Jesus our Lord be with you.

Gospel: Mt 23:27–32

Jesus said, "Woe to you, teachers of the law and Pharisees, you hypocrites! You are like whitewashed tombs, beautiful in appearance; but, inside, there are only dead bones and uncleanness. In the same way, you appear religious to others, but you are full of hypocrisy and wickedness within.

"Woe to you, teachers of the law and Pharisees, you hypocrites! You build tombs for the prophets, and decorate the monuments of the righteous. You say: Had we lived in the time of our ancestors, we would not have joined them in shedding the blood of the prophets. So, you, yourselves, confess to be the descendants of those who murdered the prophets. And now, finish off what your ancestors began!"

St. Monica

Did you know that: Santa Monica, California was named after St. Monica, the mother of St. Augustine.

Time will later show that the institutions that Jesus hoped to reform to bring back righteousness to God's people would fight back and engineer His demise. They had enough of this upstart who dared try to criticize an institution that had been Israel's conscience and guide for a long time. Their pride had been wounded. The wall of hate was constructed. No amount of Jesus' admonition and appeal would ever move their hearts and minds to change. They would finish off as Jesus dared them to do, what their ancestors had began. They would silence this voice that had caused them inconvenience and harm.

Thursday

28 AUGUST

Ps 145:2–3, 4–5, 6–7
I will praise your name
for ever, Lord.

St. Augustine
Did you know that: St. Augustine is dubbed as the "Doctor of Grace".

1st Reading: 1 Cor 1:1–9

From Paul, called to be an apostle of Christ Jesus, by the will of God, and from Sosthenes, our brother, to God's Church which is in Corinth; to you, whom God has sanctified in Christ Jesus, and called, to be holy, together, with those, who, everywhere, call upon the name of our Lord Christ Jesus, their Lord and ours. Receive grace, and peace from God, our Father, and Christ Jesus, our Lord.

I give thanks, constantly, to my God, for you, and for the grace of God given to you, in Christ Jesus. For you have been fully enriched, in him, with words, as well as with knowledge, even as the testimony concerning Christ was confirmed in you. You do not lack any spiritual gift and only await the glorious coming of Christ Jesus, our Lord. He will keep you steadfast to the end, and you will be without reproach, on the day of the coming of our Lord Jesus. The faithful God will not fail you, after calling you to this fellowship with his Son, Christ Jesus, our Lord.

Gospel: Mt 24:42–51

Jesus said to his disciples, "Stay awake then, for you do not know on what day your Lord will come. Obviously, if the owner of the house knew at what time the thief was coming, he would certainly stay up and not allow his house to be broken into. So be alert, for the Son of Man will come at the hour you least expect.

"Imagine a faithful and prudent servant, whom his master has put in charge of his household, to give them food at the proper time. Fortunate, indeed, is that servant, whom his master will find at work when he comes. Truly I say to you, his lord will entrust him with everything he has.

"Not so with the bad servant, who thinks, 'My master is delayed.' And he begins to ill-treat his fellow servants, while eating and drinking with drunkards. But his master will come on the day he does not know, and at the hour he least expects. He will punish that servant severely; and place with him with the hypocrites. There will be weeping and gnashing of teeth."

Being watchful and being awake: these are beautiful imagery of what a disciple must be. It is not easy to be so. These demand preparation and a will to do so. There is always a tendency to relax and let go of the discipline when the Master is not around. Space and distance tend to bring out what has been buried in the hearts of all. Blessed then are those who remain constantly alert and on the watch. Their reliability amidst the Master's absence will earn them a place in His house.

29
AUGUST

Friday

Ps 71:1–2, 3–4a,
5–6ab, 15ab & 17
I will sing your salvation.

THE PASSION OF
ST. JOHN THE BAPTIST
Psalter: Proper / (Red)

1st Reading: Jer 1:17–19

The word of Yahweh came to me, "But you, get ready for action; stand up and say to them all that I command you. Be not scared of them or I will scare you in their presence! See, I will make you a fortified city, a pillar of iron with walls of bronze, against all the nations, against the kings and princes of Judah, against the priests and the people of the land.

"They will fight against you but shall not overcome you, for I am with you to rescue you—it is Yahweh who speaks."

Gospel: Mk 6:17–29

For this is what had happened: Herod had ordered John to be arrested; and had had him bound and put in prison because of Herodias, the wife of his brother Philip. Herod had married her; and John had told him, "It is not right for you to live with your brother's wife." So Herodias held a grudge against John and wanted to kill him; but she could not, because Herod respected John. He knew John to be an upright and holy man, and kept him safe. And he liked listening to him; although he became very disturbed whenever he heard him.

Herodias had her chance on Herod's birthday, when he gave a dinner for all the senior government officials, military chiefs, and the leaders of Galilee. On that occasion, the daughter of Herodias came in and danced; and she delighted Herod and his guests. The king said to the girl, "Ask me for anything you want and I will give it to you." And he went so far as to say with many oaths, "I will give you anything you ask, even half my kingdom." She went out and said to her mother, "What shall I ask for?" The mother replied, "The head of John the Baptist." The girl hurried to the king and made her request, "I want you to give me the head of John the Baptist, here and now, on a dish."

The king was very displeased, but he would not refuse in front of his guests because of his oaths. So he sent one of the bodyguards, with orders to bring John's head. He went and beheaded John in prison; then he brought the head on a dish and gave it to the girl. And the girl gave it to her mother. When John's disciples heard of this, they came and took his body and buried it.

John got into trouble when he pointed out the obvious that nobody wants . to talk about. Herod's union with Herodias, his brother's wife, is unlawful. But it is not Herod that he has to worry about the most. Herod still has respect for his person who has no qualms confronting the former of his transgression. It is Herodias who is implacable and unforgiving. And so a chance was grabbed without second thoughts and that is how the life of John, whom no man born of a woman could ever surpass, ended. He offered his life in service of the truth.

Saturday

Ps 33:12–13, 18–19, 20–21
Blessed the people the Lord has
chosen to be his own.

30
AUGUST

1st Reading: 1 Cor 1:26–31

Gospel: Mt 25:14–30

Jesus said to his disciples, "Imagine someone who, before going abroad, summoned his servants to entrust his property to them. He gave five talents of silver to one servant, two talents to another servant, and one talent to a third, to each, according to his ability; and he went away. He who received five talents went at once to do business with the talents, and gained another five. The one who received two talents did the same, and gained another two. But the one who received one talent dug a hole in the ground, and hid his master's money.

"After a long time, the master of those servants returned and asked for a reckoning. The one who had received five talents came with another five talents, saying, 'Lord, you entrusted me with five talents, but see, I have gained five more.' The master answered, 'Well done, good and faithful servant, since you have been faithful in a few things, I will entrust you in charge of many things. Come and share the joy of your master.'

" Then the one who had received two talents came and said, 'Lord, you entrusted me with two talents; with them I have gained two more.' The master said, 'Well done, good and faithful servant, since you have been faithful in little things, I will entrust you in charge of many things. Come and share the joy of your master.'

"Finally, the one who had received one talent came and said, 'Master, I know that you are a hard man. You reap what you have not sown, and gather what you have not scattered. I was afraid, so I hid your money in the ground. Here, take what is yours!' But his master replied, 'Wicked and worthless servant, you know that I reap where I have not sown, and gather where I have not scattered. You should have deposited my money in the bank, and given it back to me with interest on my return.

"Therefore, take the talent from him, and give it to the one who has ten. For to all those who have, more will be given, and they will have an abundance; but from those who are unproductive, even what they have will be taken from them. As for that useless servant, throw him out into outer darkness, where there will be weeping and gnashing of teeth."

God is a lousy finance manager. Perhaps, it is because He has so much good things spilling over out of His plenitude. He invests indiscriminately in His servants in varying measures. He does not discriminate, all are given a share. The only good thing we can say about Him as an investor is that He has the sense of whom to give more and whom to give less. This sense will be proven right for the one who was given a bigger share gives back double of the capital. While the one who received the least just gave it back, for he buried it out of fear. And so what little he has was taken away and given to him who had performed well. For God invests to lose. He gives it all to those who receives it and makes that investment grow.

31
AUGUST

Sunday

Ps 63:2, 3–4, 5–6, 8–9
My soul is thirsting for you,
O Lord my God.

1st Reading: Jer 20:7–9

*Y*ahweh, you have seduced me and I let myself be seduced.

You have taken me by force and prevailed.

I have become a laughingstock all day long; they all make fun of me, for every time I speak

I have to shout, "Violence! Devastation!" Yahweh's word has brought me insult and derision all day long.

So I decided to forget about him and speak no more in his name.

But his word in my heart becomes like a fire burning deep within my bones.

I try so hard to hold it in, but I cannot do it.

2nd Reading: Rom 12:1–2

I beg you, dearly beloved, by the mercy of God, to give yourselves, as a living and holy sacrifice, pleasing to God; that is the kind of worship for you, as sensible people. Don't let yourselves be shaped by the world where you live, but, rather, be transformed, through the renewal of your mind. You must discern the will of God: what is good, what pleases, what is perfect.

Gospel: Mt 16:21–27

*F*rom that day, Jesus began to make it clear to his disciples that he must go to Jerusalem; that he would suffer many things from the Jewish authorities, the chief priests and the teachers of the law; and that he would be killed and be raised on the third day.

Then Peter took him aside and began to reproach him, "Never, Lord! No, this must never happen to you!" But he turned and said to Peter, "Get behind me, Satan! You are an obstacle in my path. You are thinking not as God does, but as people do."

Then Peter took him aside and began to reproach him, "Never, Lord! No, this must never happen to you!" But he turned and said to Peter, "Get behind me, Satan! You are an obstacle in my path. You are thinking not as God does, but as people do."

Then Jesus said to his disciples, "If you want to follow me, deny yourself. Take up your cross and follow me. For whoever chooses to save his life will lose it, but the one who loses his life, for my sake, will find it. What will one gain by winning the whole world, if he destroys his soul? Or what can a person give, in exchange for his life?

"Know, that the Son of Man will come, in the glory of his Father with the holy angels, and he will reward each one according to his deeds."

Reading: After Peter's profession of faith, Jesus disclosed the fate that awaited Him, that of the cross, death and resurrection. Peter remonstrated with the Lord who in turn rebuked him. Then He taught them that following Him meant following even unto death.

Reflection: It is easier to follow those who are successful and famous. Everybody loves a winner. But to follow someone in good times and bad requires deep conviction. You have to be convinced of the justness of your cause. The disciples were not exempt from our human tendencies. They were on a roll when Jesus was popular and successful in His public ministry. But being the realist, He disclosed to them the kind of fate that inevitably awaited Him. He would have to drink the cup of suffering and death before His glorious resurrection. Even this momentary setback is bitter in the mouth of the disciples. Peter objected. This should not mar the triumph that they have right now. This is where the greatness of Jesus shines through. He does not promise His followers a rose-colored life but greatness that comes out from the willingness to suffer. Henceforth all who will follow Him will have no illusion on the kind of fate that awaits them. They will either follow Him or not, with eyes wide open.

Response: Am I a follower of the Lord only in good times and do I tend to fall behind when the going gets rough? Today I make an inventory of my brand of following the Lord and identify the times I broke lose when it was tough not to do so. I will make a sincere act of contrition for my failings and will resolve to start afresh with my discipleship to Christ.

01
SEPTEMBER

Monday
Ps 119:97, 98, 99, 100, 101, 102
Lord, I love your commands.

22ND WEEK IN ORDINARY TIME
Psalter: Week 2 / (Green)

1st Reading: 1 Cor 2:1–5

Brothers and sisters: When I came to reveal to you the mystery of God's plan, I did not count on eloquence or on a show of learning. I was determined, not to know anything among you, but Jesus, the Messiah, and a crucified Messiah. I, myself, came; weak, fearful and trembling; my words, and preaching, were not brilliant, or clever to win listeners. It was, rather, a demonstration of spirit and power, so, that, your faith might be a matter, not of human wisdom, but of God's power.

Gospel: Lk 4:16–30

When Jesus came to Nazareth, where he had been brought up, he entered the synagogue on the Sabbath, as he usually did. He stood up to read, and they handed him the book of the prophet Isaiah.

Jesus then unrolled the scroll and found the place where it is written: *"The Spirit of the Lord is upon me. He has anointed me, to bring good news to the poor; to proclaim liberty to captives; and new sight to the blind; to free the oppressed; and to announce the Lord's year of mercy."*

Jesus then rolled up the scroll, gave it to the attendant and sat down; and the eyes of all in the synagogue were fixed on him. Then he said to them, "Today, these prophetic words come true, even as you listen."

All agreed with him, and were lost in wonder, while he spoke of the grace of God. Nevertheless they asked, "Who is this but Joseph's Son?" So he said, "Doubtless you will quote me the saying: Doctor, heal yourself! Do here, in your town, what they say you did in Capernaum."

Jesus added, "No prophet is honored in his own country. Truly, I say to you, there were many widows in Israel in the days of Elijah, when the heavens withheld rain for three years and six months and a great famine came over the whole land. Yet, Elijah was not sent to any of them, but to a widow of Zarephath, in the country of Sidon. There were also many lepers in Israel in the time of Elisha, the prophet; and no one was healed except Naaman, the Syrian."

On hearing these words, the whole assembly became indignant. They rose up and brought him out of the town, to the edge of the hill on which Nazareth is built, intending to throw him down the cliff. But he passed through their midst and went his way.

Goodwill is usually maintained if we but stick to less contentious topics in our speech and speak of motherhood statements with which everyone agrees. However, once we point out people's failures and defects, a conflict situation arises. Goodwill is lost. Hostility replaces the once friendly atmosphere. Jesus was acceptable to His townsfolk until such time that He waded into the controversy of His person. The people who knew Him were awed by His speech yet they could not do away with their doubts about Him since they knew His origin. So, Jesus, pointing the reason for the lack of miracles in His town, earned their ire. Love and respect were lost. Jesus would never make significant inroads in His town for the rest of His life.

Tuesday

Ps 145:8–9, 10–11, 12–13ab, 13cd–14
The Lord is just in all his ways.

02
SEPTEMBER

1st Reading: 1 Cor 2:10b–16

*B*rothers and sisters: God has revealed it to us, through his Spirit, because the Spirit probes everything, even the depth of God.

Who, but his own spirit, knows the secrets of a person? Similarly, no one, but the Spirit of God, knows the secrets of God. We have not received the spirit of the world, but the Spirit who comes from God and, through him, we understand what God, in his goodness, has given us.

So we speak of this, not in terms inspired by human wisdom, but in a language taught by the Spirit, explaining a spiritual wisdom to spiritual persons. The one who remains on the psychological level does not understand the things of the Spirit. They are foolishness for him; and he does not understand, because they require a spiritual experience. On the other hand, the spiritual person judges everything, but no one judges him. Who has known the mind of God so as to teach him? But we have the mind of Christ.

Gospel: Lk 4:31–37

*J*esus went down to Capernaum, a town of Galilee, and began teaching the people at the Sabbath meetings. They were astonished at the way he taught them, for his word was spoken with authority.

In the synagogue, there was a man possessed by an evil spirit, who shouted in a loud voice, "What do you want with us, Jesus of Nazareth? Have you come to destroy us? I recognize you: you are the Holy One of God." Then Jesus said to him sharply, "Be silent and leave this man!" The evil spirit then threw the man down in front of them, and came out of him without doing him harm.

Amazement seized all these people, and they said to one another, "What does this mean? He commands the evil spirits with authority and power. He orders, and you see how they come out!" And news about Jesus spread throughout the surrounding area.

They say that if you want to get to know yourself better, ask your enemies for they will tell you in detail all your failures and shortcomings. On the part of Jesus, the evil spirits disclosed His identity as the Holy One of God. That is the most embarrassing thing they could say about Him. And coming from the mouth of enemies, this testimony should weigh far more important than those coming from Jesus' friends. The evil spirits will never voluntarily disclose the grandeur of Jesus' being had they had other bad things to say about Him.

03
SEPTEMBER

Wednesday

Ps 33:12–13, 14–15, 20–21
Blessed the people
the Lord has chosen to be his own.

22ND WEEK IN ORDINARY TIME
St. Gregory the Great, pope & doctor
Psalter: Week 2 / (White)

1st Reading: 1 Cor 3:1–9

Brothers and sisters: I could not, friends, speak to you as spiritual persons but as fleshly people, for you are still infants in Christ. I gave you milk, and not solid food, for you were not ready for it, and, up to now, you cannot receive it, for you are still of the flesh. As long as there is jealousy and strife, what can I say, but that you are at the level of the flesh, and behave like ordinary people.

While one says: "I follow Paul," and the other: "I follow Apollos," what are you, but people still at a human level? For what is Apollos? What is Paul?

They are ministers; and through them, you believed, as it was given by the Lord, to each of them. I planted, Apollos watered the plant, but God made it grow. So neither the one who plants nor the one who waters is anything, but God, who makes the plant grow.

The one who plants and the one who waters work to the same end, and the Lord will pay each, according to their work. We are fellow workers with God, but you are God's field and building.

Gospel: Lk 4:38–44

Leaving the synagogue, Jesus went to the house of Simon. His mother-in-law was suffering from high fever, and they asked him to do something for her. Bending over her, he rebuked the fever, and it left her. Immediately, she got up and waited on them.

At sunset, people suffering from many kinds of sickness were brought to Jesus. Laying his hands on each one, he healed them. Demons were driven out, howling as they departed from their victims, "You are the Son of God!" He rebuked them and would not allow them to speak, for they knew he was the Messiah.

Jesus left at daybreak and looked for a solitary place. People went out in search of him, and finding him, they tried to dissuade him from leaving. But he said, "I have to go to other towns, to announce the good news of the kingdom of God. That is what I was sent to do." And Jesus continued to preach in the synagogues of Galilee.

St. Gregory the Great

.Did you know that: As a monk, St. Gregory the Great composed some prayers in what is known as Gregorian Sacramentary and oversaw the musical development that is still called Gregorian Chant.

Jesus leaves the synagogue and immediately radiates healing and wholeness wherever He goes. Having been recharged in the holy place He now has the energy to do His ministry. Perhaps this passage tells us that Jesus is most effective when He starts His day with a prayer. After a long day's work, He still has space for a solitary moment with His Father. He does not consider it a loss of time for rest. It amplifies the benefits He gets from a night of sleep. This constancy in prayer will be one of the cherished memories of His disciples about Him. They must have rightly intuited that the source of Jesus' fecundity in mission is His time spent in communion with God His Father.

Thursday

Ps 24:1bc–2, 3–4ab, 5–6
To the Lord belongs the earth
and all that fills it.

04
SEPTEMBER

1st Reading: 1 Cor 3:18–23

Brothers and sisters: Do not deceive yourselves. If anyone of you considers himself wise in the ways of the world, let him become a fool, so that he may become wise. For the wisdom of this world is foolishness in God's eyes. To this, Scripture says: *God catches the wise in their own wisdom.* It also says: *The Lord knows the reasoning of the wise, that it is useless.*

Because of this, let no one boast about human beings, for everything belongs to you; Paul, Apollos, Cephas— life, death, the present and the future. Everything is yours, and you, you belong to Christ, and Christ is of God.

Gospel: Lk 5:1–11

One day, as Jesus stood by the Lake of Gennesaret, with a crowd gathered around him listening to the word of God, he caught sight of two boats, left at the water's edge by fishermen, now washing their nets. He got into one of the boats, the one belonging to Simon, and asked him to pull out a little from the shore. There he sat, and continued to teach the crowd. When he had finished speaking, he said to Simon, "Put out into deep water and lower your nets for a catch." Simon replied, "Master, we worked hard all night and caught nothing. But if you say so, I will lower the nets." This they did, and caught such a large number of fish that their nets began to break. They signaled their partners in the other boat to come and help them. They came, and they filled both boats almost to the point of sinking.

Upon seeing this, Simon Peter fell at Jesus' knees, saying, "Leave me, Lord, for I am a sinful man!" For he and his companions were amazed at the catch they had made, and so were Simon's partners, James and John, Zebedee's sons.

Jesus said to Simon, "Do not be afraid. You will catch people from now on." So they brought their boats to land and followed him, leaving everything.

This Gospel provides us information on the unique approach Jesus used to "catch" Simon Peter and James and John, Zebedee's sons. He was doing His normal rounds of preaching and it so happened by the lake of Gennesaret. Jesus espied these fishermen who were deeply concerned with their losses for that day rather than listening to His words. To catch their attention, he engaged the services of one of them, Simon Peter, and asked him to pull out a little from the shore. There He continued His preaching and when He finished, He told Simon to put into the deep. Little did Simon know that on that day, it was not only him and his companions who caught so much fish. Jesus also would make a good haul of three disciples who would later form the inner circle of the group.

05
SEPTEMBER

Friday

Ps 37:3–4, 5–6, 27–28, 39–40
The salvation of the just
comes from the Lord.

22ND WEEK IN ORDINARY TIME
Psalter: Week 2 / (Green)

1st Reading: 1 Cor 4:1–5

Brothers and sisters: Let everyone, then, see us as the servants of Christ, and stewards of the secret works of God. Being stewards, faithfulness shall be demanded of us; but I do not mind if you, or any human court, judges me. I do not even judge myself; my conscience, indeed, does not accuse me of anything, but that is not enough for me to be set right with God: the Lord is the one who judges me.

Therefore, do not judge before the time, until the coming of the Lord. He will bring to light whatever was hidden in darkness, and will disclose the secret intentions of the hearts. Then, each one will receive praise from God.

Gospel: Lk 5:33–39

Some people asked Jesus, "The disciples of John fast often and say long prayers, and so do the disciples of the Pharisees. Why is it, that your disciples eat and drink?" Then Jesus said to them, "You can't make wedding guests fast while the bridegroom is with them. But later, the bridegroom will be taken from them; and they will fast in those days."

Jesus also told them this parable: "No one tears a piece from a new coat to put it on an old one; otherwise the new coat will be torn, and the piece taken from the new coat will not match the old coat. No one puts new wine into old wine skins; otherwise the new wine will burst the skins and be spilled, and the skins will be destroyed as well. But new wine must be put into fresh skins. Yet, no one who has tasted old wine is eager to drink new wine, but says, 'The old is good.'"

Some people are afraid to try something new. They are most comfortable with the usual and the tested. That is why the scribes and Pharisees are uncomfortable with the way Jesus' disciples behave. They are out of line from the usual and so they complained to Jesus. But Jesus gave them a framework to understand where His disciples came from. They discovered the liberating joy of being in the groom's presence. This wonderful time will not be taken away from them. They will do their fasting and prayer when the bridegroom leaves. But meanwhile, they will rejoice. This joy could have been had by the scribes and Pharisees had they but accepted Jesus. They however did not. They preferred the gloom of their customs and traditions rather than the Good News brought by Jesus.

22ND WEEK IN ORDINARY TIME
Psalter: Week 2 / (Green / White)

Saturday

Ps 145:17-18, 19-20, 21
The Lord is near to all
who call upon him.

06
SEPTEMBER

1st Reading: 1 Cor 4:6b–15

Brothers and sisters: Learn by this example, not to believe yourselves superior by siding with one against the other. How, then, are you more than the others? What have you that you have not received? And if you received it, why are you proud, as if you did not receive it?

So, then, you are already rich and satisfied, and feel like kings, without us! I wish you really were kings, so that we might enjoy the kingship with you! It seems to me, that God has placed us, the apostles, in the last place, as if condemned to death, and as spectacles for the whole world, for the angels as well as for mortals.

We are fools for Christ, while you show forth the wisdom of Christ. We are weak, you are strong. You are honored, while we are despised. Until now we hunger and thirst, we are poorly clothed and badly treated, while moving from place to place. We labor, working with our hands. People insult us and we bless them, they persecute us and we endure everything; they speak evil against us, and ours are works of peace. We have become like the scum of the earth, like the garbage of humankind until now.

I do not write this to shame you, but to warn you, as very dear children. Because, even though you may have ten thousand guardians in the Christian life, you have only one father; and it was I who gave you life in Christ through the Gospel.

Gospel: Lk 6:1–5

One Sabbath Jesus was going through a field of grain, and his disciples began to pick heads of grain, crushing them in their hands for food. Some of the Pharisees asked them, "Why do you do what is forbidden on the Sabbath?" Then Jesus spoke up and asked them, "Have you never read what David did when he and his men were hungry? He entered the house of God, took and ate the bread of the offering, and even gave some to his men, though only priests are allowed to eat that bread." And Jesus added, "The Son of Man is Lord and rules over the Sabbath."

Jesus' movement is now gaining recognition. He is placed under surveillance by the spiritual guardians of the nation. It is no wonder therefore that they keep on complaining to Jesus about how unorthodox and out of line His disciples were. They make it their business to know what is going on in this new group. Instead of getting annoyed, Jesus capitalized on their criticisms by opening their eyes to a perspective that they neglected simply because they had been steeped in the legalistic framework of their faith. These precedents were made by heroes of the nation in breaking certain rules because they put premium on the good of their men rather than man-made laws and conventions. He is now inviting them to refocus their vision. He is inviting them to partake of the freedom of the sons and daughters of God.

07
SEPTEMBER

Sunday

Ps 95:1–2, 6–7, 8–9
If today you hear his voice,
harden not your hearts.

1st Reading: Ezk 33:7–9

The word of Yahweh came to me in these terms, "For your part, son of man, I have set you as a watchman for Israel; and when you hear my word, you must give them my warning. When I say to the wicked: 'Wicked man, you shall die for sure,' if you do not warn the wicked man to turn from his ways, he will die because of his sin; but I will also call you to account for his blood. If you warn the wicked man to turn from his ways and he does not do so, he will die for his sin; but you, yourself, will be saved."

2nd Reading: Rom 13:8–10

Brothers and sisters: Do not be in debt to anyone. Let this be the only debt of one to another: Love. The one who loves his or her neighbor fulfills the law. For the commandments: Do not commit adultery, do not kill, do not covet, and whatever else, are summarized in this one: You will love your neighbor as yourself. Love cannot do the neighbor any harm; so love fulfills the whole law.

Gospel: Mt 18:15–20

Jesus said to his disciples, "If your brother has sinned against you, go and point out the fault to him, when the two of you are alone; and if he listens to you, you have won back your brother. If he doesn't listen to you, take with you one or two others, so that the case may be decided by the evidence of two or three witnesses. And if he refuses to listen to them, tell it to the assembled Church. But if he does not listen to the Church, then regard him as a pagan, or a tax collector.

"I say to you: whatever you bind on earth, heaven will keep bound; and whatever you unbind on earth, heaven will keep unbound.

"In like manner, I say to you, if, on earth, two of you agree in asking for anything, it will be granted to you by my heavenly Father; for where two or three are gathered in my name, I am there, among them."

Reading: Jesus teaches the communitarian dimension of sin and forgiveness. It is only when available remedies of dialogue, having witnesses and involving the community fail to settle the dispute between parties that one could legitimately cut ties with the other. The community's decision will be upheld in heaven. Likewise, when the community gathers to ask and pray, the Father will grant their request and Jesus will be in their midst praying with them.

Reflection: The wellbeing and harmony of the community is threatened when two or more members are not at peace with one another. It is because of its repercussion to the community that every conflict is a communitarian responsibility. First, on effort to reconcile is done on the level of the conflicting parties; then, with their close friends and acquaintances up to the assembly, when the first two efforts on mediation fail. It is thus not a simple matter when we do something wrong even on the personal level. There will always be a social dimension to our every act. With this in mind, it is imperative to develop a clear social conscience that takes the common good as a factor in every act we do. The world would be a better place if we care enough for the good of others as we care for our own good.

Response: I usually have occasions of misunderstanding with others. Sometimes I become passionate with the differences that we have. But today is a day of healing and reconciliation. I will forgive those who hurt me and I will ask forgiveness from those whom I have hurt today.

08
SEPTEMBER

Monday
Ps 13:6ab, 6c
With delight I rejoice in the Lord.

FEAST OF THE NATIVITY OF THE BLESSED VIRGIN MARY
Psalter: Proper / (White)

1st Reading: Mic 5:1–4a (or Rom 8:28–30)
Gospel: Mt 1:1–16, 18–23

This is the account of the genealogy of Jesus Christ, son of David, son of Abraham.

Abraham was the father of Isaac, Isaac the father of Jacob, Jacob the father of Judah and his brothers. Judah was the father of Perez and Zerah (their mother was Tamar), Perez was the father of Hezron, and Hezron of Aram. Aram was the father of Aminadab, Aminadab of Nahshon, Nahshon of Salmon.

Salmon was the father of Boaz. His mother was Rahab. Boaz was the father of Obed. His mother was Ruth. Obed was the father of Jesse.

Jesse was the father of David, the king. David was the father of Solomon. His mother had been Uriah's wife.

Solomon was the father of Rehoboam. Then came the kings: Abijah, Asaph, Jehoshaphat, Joram, Uzziah, Jotham, Ahaz, Hezekiah, Manasseh, Amon, Josiah.

Josiah was the father of Jechoniah and his brothers at the time of the deportation to Babylon.

After the deportation to Babylon, Jechoniah was the father of Salathiel and Salathiel of Zerubbabel.

Zerubbabel was the father of Abiud, Abiud of Eliakim, and Eliakim of Azor. Azor was the father of Zadok, Zadok the father of Akim, and Akim the father of Eliud. Eliud was the father of Eleazar, Eleazar of Matthan, and Matthan of Jacob.

Jacob was the father of Joseph, the husband of Mary, and from her came Jesus who is called the Christ —the Messiah.

This is how Jesus Christ was born: Mary his mother had been given to Joseph in marriage, but before they lived together, she was found to be pregnant through the Holy Spirit.

Then Joseph, her husband, made plans to divorce her in all secrecy. He was an upright man, and in no way did he want to disgrace her.

While he was pondering over this, an angel of the Lord appeared to him in a dream and said, "Joseph, descendant of David, do not be afraid to take Mary as your wife. She has conceived by the Holy Spirit, and now she will bear a son. You shall call him 'Jesus' for he will save his people from their sins."

All this happened in order to fulfill what the Lord had said through the prophet: *The virgin will conceive and bear a son, and he will be called Emmanuel*, which means: God-with-us.

Today, we celebrate the nativity of Mary. But the Gospel reading instead recalls the genealogy and the birth of our Lord. This is not accidental but intentional. The liturgy reminds us that the Blessed Virgin is intimately linked to her Son. All the privileges and graces she received are because she is the mother of our Lord. So we celebrate the birth of Mary by recalling her Son. She is blessed among women not by her own merit but because of the merits her Son gained for her. This also tells us that from birth, she had been marked by the divine for this singular honor. She was born to be the vessel of the Son of God who will also be called the Son of Mary, her very own Son.

23RD WEEK IN ORDINARY TIME
St. Peter Claver, priest
Psalter: Week 3 / (White)

Tuesday

Ps 149:1b–2, 3–4, 5–6a & 9b
The Lord takes delight
in his people.

09
SEPTEMBER

St. Peter Claver

Did you know that: St. Peter Claver was a brilliant Jesuit who called himself Aethiporum servus meaning "slave of Ethiops." He was afflicted with Parkinson's disease, which eventually caused his decline and death.

1st Reading: 1 Cor 6:1–11

Brothers and sisters: When you have a complaint against a brother, how dare you bring it before pagan judges, instead of bringing it before God's people? Do you not know, that you shall one day judge the world? And if you are to judge the world, are you incapable of judging such simple problems?

Do you not know, that we will even judge the angels? And could you not decide everyday affairs? But when you have ordinary cases to be judged, you bring them before those who are of no account in the Church! Shame on you! Is there not even one among you wise enough to be the arbiter among believers?

But no. One of you brings a suit against another one, and files that suit before unbelievers. It is already a failure that you have suits against each other. Why do you not rather suffer wrong and receive some damage? But no. You wrong and injure others, and those are your brothers and sisters. Do you not know that the wicked will not inherit the kingdom of God?

Make no mistake about it: those who lead sexually immoral lives, or worship idols, or who are adulterers, perverts, sodomites, or thieves, exploiters, drunkards, slanderers or embezzlers will not inherit the kingdom of heaven. Some of you were like that, but you have been cleansed, and consecrated to God and have been set right with God, by the name of the Lord Jesus, and the Spirit of our God.

Gospel: Lk 6:12–19

Jesus went out into the hills to pray, spending the whole night in prayer with God. When day came, he called his disciples to him, and chose Twelve of them, whom he called 'apostles': Simon, whom he named Peter, and his brother Andrew; James and John; Philip and Bartholomew; Matthew and Thomas; James son of Alpheus and Simon called the Zealot; Judas son of James, and Judas Iscariot, who would be the traitor.

Coming down the hill with them, Jesus stood in an open plain. Many of his disciples were there, and a large crowd of people, who had come from all parts of Judea and Jerusalem, and from the coastal cities of Tyre and Sidon. They gathered to hear him and to be healed of their diseases. And people troubled by unclean spirits were cured. The entire crowd tried to touch him, because of the power that went out from him and healed them all.

The weight of decision rests heavily upon the shoulders of Jesus. He has to select His inner circle from among the disciples. The apostles will be His closest collaborators among all others who follow Him. And so Jesus has to pray. For every momentous decisions He takes in His life is always preceded by deep communion with His Father. This intimacy He has with His Father even before the beginning of time will not be broken even by His incarnation. This habit will remain with Him throughout. In here, we get one secret of Jesus' fecundity. He never does things by Himself. The other Persons in the Trinity are always with Him.

10
SEPTEMBER

Wednesday

Ps 45:11–12, 14–15, 16–17
Listen to me, daughter;
see and bend your ear.

23RD WEEK IN ORDINARY TIME
Psalter: Week 3 / (Green)

1st Reading: 1 Cor 7:25–31

Brothers and sisters: With regard to those who remain virgins, I have no special commandment from the Lord, but I give some advice, hoping that I am worthy of trust by the mercy of the Lord. I think this is good in these hard times in which we live. It is good for someone to remain as he is. If you are married, do not try to divorce your wife; if you are not married, do not marry. He who marries does not sin, nor does the young girl sin who marries. Yet they will face disturbing experiences, and I would like to spare you.

I say this, brothers and sisters: time is running out, and those who are married must live as if not married; those who weep as if not weeping; those who are happy as if they were not happy; those buying something as if they had not bought it, and those enjoying the present life as if they were not enjoying it. For the order of this world is vanishing.

Gospel: Lk 6:20-26

Looking at his disciples, Jesus said, "Fortunate are you who are poor, for the kingdom of God is yours.

"Fortunate are you, who are hungry now, for you will be filled.

"Fortunate are you, who weep now, for you will laugh.

"Fortunate are you, when people hate you, when they reject you and insult you and number you among criminals, because of the Son of Man. Rejoice in that day, and leap for joy, for a great reward is kept for you in heaven. Remember, that is how the ancestors of the people treated the prophets.

"But alas for you, who have wealth, for you have been comforted now.

"Alas for you, who are full, for you will go hungry.

"Alas for you, who laugh now, for you will mourn and weep.

"Alas for you, when people speak well of you, for that is how the ancestors of the people treated the false prophets."

How can people who are at the losing end like the poor, the hungry, the weeping and the likes be ever fortunate in this world? Isn't it that they represent a sorry lot? That would probably be true if we set our sight only in the here and now, and in this world. But if we expand our horizon and include eternity, the words of Jesus make sense. They are true especially if we suffer all these because we follow Him faithfully. It is faith that makes us believe that a glorious future awaits those who suffer on behalf of the Lord. How to explain it might be a problem, limited as we are; but countless men and women have risked and found the word of the Lord to be true. And so we are not treading on new ground; a cloud of witnesses have been ahead of us. May their examples and their ultimate triumph inspire us to go on despite hardships and tribulations.

Thursday

Ps 139:1b–3, 13–14ab, 23–24
Guide me, Lord,
along the everlasting way.

11
SEPTEMBER

1st Reading: 1 Cor 8:1b–7, 11–13*

Brothers and sisters: "(…) Can we, then, eat meat from offerings to the idols? We know that an idol is without existence and that there is no God but one. People speak indeed of other gods in heaven and on earth and, in this sense, there are many gods and lords. Yet for us, there is but one God, the Father, from whom everything comes, and to whom we go. And there is one Lord, Christ Jesus, through whom everything exists, and through him, we exist. Not everyone, however, has that knowledge. For some persons, who, until recently, took the idols seriously, that food remains linked to the idol, and eating of it stains their conscience, which is unformed.

Then, with your knowledge, you would have caused your weak brother or sister to perish, the one for whom Christ died. When you disturb the weak conscience of your brother or sister, and sin against them, you sin against Christ himself. Therefore, if any food will bring my brother to sin, I shall never eat this food, lest my brother or sister fall.

Gospel: Lk 6:27–38

Jesus said to his disciples, "But I say to you who hear me: Love your enemies, do good to those who hate you. Bless those who curse you, and pray for those who treat you badly. To the one who strikes you on the cheek, turn the other cheek; from the one who takes your coat, do not keep back your shirt. Give to the one who asks, and if anyone has taken something from you, do not demand it back.

"Do to others as you would have others do to you. If you love only those who love you, what kind of grace is yours? Even sinners love those who love them. If you do favors to those who are good to you, what kind of grace is yours? Even sinners do the same. If you lend only when you expect to receive, what kind of grace is yours? For sinners also lend to sinners, expecting to receive something in return.

"But love your enemies and do good to them, and lend when there is nothing to expect in return. Then will your reward be great, and you will be sons and daughters of the Most High. For he is kind toward the ungrateful and the wicked. Be merciful, just as your Father is merciful.

"Don't be a judge of others and you will not be judged; do not condemn and you will not be condemned; forgive and you will be forgiven; give and it will be given to you, and you will receive in your sack good measure, pressed down, full and running over. For the measure you give will be the measure you receive back."

Love is okay as long as it is with those who love you in return. There is reciprocity and you only respond to what you have received. But to love enemies? Not to return hate with hate? This is something that will tax human capacities. And this is the invitation of Jesus in our Gospel today. To subject ourselves to the stress of love so that we will tax our resources and be moved to beg from someone whose strength to love beyond human measure is inexhaustible… God Himself. This invitation to selfless love is an invitation as well to intimacy with someone whose very self definition is love.

12
SEPTEMBER

Friday
Ps 84:3, 4, 5–6, 12
How lovely is your dwelling place,
Lord, mighty God!

23RD WEEK IN ORDINARY TIME
The Most Holy Name of Mary
Psalter: Week 3 / (Green / White)

1st Reading: 1 Cor 9:16–19, 22b–27

Brothers and sisters: Because I cannot boast of announcing the Gospel: I am bound to do it. Woe to me, if I do not preach the Gospel! If I preached voluntarily, I could expect my reward, but I have been trusted with this office, against my will. How can I, then, deserve a reward? In announcing the Gospel, I will do it freely, without making use of the rights given to me by the Gospel.

So, feeling free with everybody, I have become everybody's slave, in order to gain a greater number. To the weak, I made myself weak, to win the weak. So, I made myself all things to all people, in order to save, by all possible means, some of them. This, I do, for the Gospel, so that I, too, have a share of it.

Have you not learned anything from the stadium? Many run, but only one gets the prize. Run, therefore, intending to win it, as athletes, who impose upon themselves a rigorous discipline. Yet, for them the wreath is of laurels which wither, while for us, it does not wither.

So, then, I run, knowing where I go. I box, but not aimlessly in the air. I punish my body and control it, lest, after preaching to others, I myself should be rejected.

Gospel: Lk 6:39–42

Jesus offered this example, "Can a blind person lead another blind person? Surely both will fall into a ditch. A disciple is not above the master; but when fully trained, he will be like the master. So why do you pay attention to the speck in your brother's eye, while you have a log in your eye, and are not conscious of it? How can you say to your neighbor, 'Friend, let me take this speck out of your eye,' when you can't remove the log in your own? You hypocrite! First remove the log from your own eye, and then you will see clearly enough to remove the speck from your neighbor's eye."

To lead others demands that we ourselves have acquired a level of self-mastery above those whom we guide. This means that we have undergone certain formation or life experiences that have led to wisdom. Without these, we will be merely blind guides groping with those we lead in darkness. Perhaps in this Gospel, Jesus tells us the great necessity of being formed by Him our Teacher and Guide, that we learn His ways and transmit it to others by word and example. Otherwise we will depend on our own resources which are limited. This will hinder our effectivity. Today, let us genuinely submit to the school of Jesus so that we will learn from the best.

Saturday

Ps 116:12–13, 17–18
To you, Lord,
I will offer a sacrifice of praise.

13
SEPTEMBER

St. John Chrysostom

Did you know that: St. John Chrysostom was called "golden tongue" (chrysostomos) and is the Patron of Orators and Preachers.

_____
_____
_____
_____
_____
_____
_____
_____
_____
_____
_____
_____
_____

There is a saying that thought generates speech, and speech generates action. If this is true, then He who informs your thoughts will also influence your words and actions. Jesus points out that what is inside is manifested by how we speak and act externally. That is one motivation enough to select only what is good to store in our heart and mind. This is a strong invitation to us listeners to hear His words and to let it be the motivation of our speech and action. In doing so, we are building a strong foundation for our future like a house built on solid ground. We will have the mind and heart of Jesus. He will recognize us when He comes again in His glory.

1st Reading: 1 Cor 10:14–22

Therefore, dear friends, shun the cult of idols. I address you as intelligent persons; judge what I say. The cup of blessing that we bless, is it not a communion with the blood of Christ? And the bread that we break, is it not a communion with the body of Christ? The bread is one, and so we, though many, form one body, sharing the one bread.

Consider the Israelites. For them, to eat of the victim is to come into communion with its altar. What does all that mean? That the meat is really consecrated to the idol, or that the idol is a being. However, when the pagans offer a sacrifice, the sacrifice goes to the demons, not to God. I do not want you to come into fellowship with demons. You cannot drink, at the same time, from the cup of the Lord and from the cup of demons. You cannot share in the table of the Lord and in the table of the demons. Do we want, perhaps, to provoke the jealousy of the Lord? Could we be stronger than he?

Gospel: Lk 6:43–49

Jesus said to his disciples, "No healthy tree bears bad fruit, no poor tree bears good fruit. And each tree is known by the fruit it bears: you don't gather figs from thorns, or grapes from brambles. Similarly, the good person draws good things from the good stored in his heart, and an evil person draws evil things from the evil stored in his heart. For the mouth speaks from the fullness of the heart.

"Why do you call me, 'Lord! Lord!' and do not do what I say? I will show you what the one is like, who comes to me, and listens to my words, and acts accordingly. That person is like the builder who dug deep, and laid the foundations of his house on rock. The river overflowed, and the stream dashed against the house, but could not carry it off because the house had been well built.

"But the one who listens and does not act, is like a man who built his house on the ground without a foundation. The flood burst against it, and the house fell at once: and what a terrible disaster that was!"

14

SEPTEMBER

Ps 78:1bc-2, 34-35, 36-37, 38
Do not forget the works of the Lord!

1st Reading: Num 21:4b–9

The people were discouraged by the journey and began to complain against God and Moses, "Why have you brought us out of Egypt to die in the wilderness? There is neither bread nor water here and we are disgusted with this tasteless manna."

Yahweh then sent fiery serpents against them. They bit the people and many of the Israelites died. Then the people came to Moses and said, "We have sinned, speaking against Yahweh and against you. Plead with Yahweh to take the serpents away."

Moses pleaded for the people and Yahweh said to him, "Make a fiery serpent and set it on a standard; whoever has been bitten and then looks at it shall live."

So Moses made a bronze serpent and set it on a standard. Whenever a man was bitten, he looked towards the bronze serpent and he lived.

2nd Reading: Phil 2:6–11

Brothers and sisters: Though Christ Jesus was in the form of God, he did not regard equality with God as something to be grasped, but emptied himself, taking on the nature of a servant, made in human likeness, and, in his appearance, found, as a man.

He humbled himself by being obedient to death, death on the cross. That is why God exalted him and gave him the name which outshines all names, so, that, at the name of Jesus all knees should bend in heaven, on earth and among the dead, and all tongues proclaim, that Christ Jesus is the Lord, to the glory of God the Father.

Gospel: Jn 3:13–17

Jesus said to Nicodemus, "No one has ever gone up to heaven except the one who came from heaven, the Son of Man. As Moses lifted up the serpent in the desert, so must the Son of Man be lifted up, so that whoever believes in him may have eternal life.

"Yes, God so loved the world that he gave his only Son that whoever believes in him may not be lost, but may have eternal life. God did not send the Son into the world to condemn the world; instead, through him the world is to be saved."

Reading: In this reading, Nicodemus heard the secret testimony of Jesus regarding His person, His work and His fate. These sayings were not accessible to many.

Reflection: Some teachings are confined only to a few and done in secret. There is a very old tradition to this practice. For such knowledge is not meant to be shared to all at once. This is too big and dangerous if placed in the hands of those not ready. The recipients have to be formed and prepared before such knowledge can be transferred to them. Nicodemus probably made the cut of those few who were capable of receiving the secret teachings of the Lord. He dares even to come to Jesus in the dead of the night to know the truth. He is a man in search for knowledge and he found a ready Teacher in Jesus. It must have been a relief to both men who talked while the rest of the world slept. The search is over for Nicodemus. He has stumbled upon the Truth who is Jesus. And the Teacher can now impart the knowledge that He has been holding on for a long time.

Response: I tend to gloss over the hard truths of my faith simply because I don't have the patience to follow and understand the arguments and reasoning behind those faith statements. I would rather stay in my affective-driven response to my faith. But I have to have an understanding of what I believe. Today, I will try to start revisiting my catechisms by buying myself a book that expounds on the tenets of my faith.

15
SEPTEMBER

Monday
Ps 40:7–8a, 8b–9, 10, 17
Proclaim the death of the Lord
until he comes again.

24TH WEEK IN ORDINARY TIME
Our Lady of Sorrows
Psalter: Week 4 / (White)

1st Reading: 1 Cor 11:17–26, 33

Brothers and sisters: To continue with my advice, I cannot praise you, for your gatherings are not for the better but for the worse.

First, as I have heard, when you gather together, there are divisions among you and I partly believe it.

There may have to be different groups among you, so that it becomes clear who among you are genuine.

Your gatherings are no longer the Supper of the Lord, for each one eats at once, his own food, and, while one is hungry, the other is getting drunk. Do you not have houses in which to eat and drink? Or perhaps you despise the Church of God and desire to humiliate those who have nothing? What shall I say? Shall I praise you? For this I cannot praise you.

This is the tradition of the Lord that I received, and, that, in my turn, I have handed on to you; the Lord Jesus, on the night that he was delivered up, took bread and, after giving thanks, broke it, saying, "This is my body which is broken for you; do this in memory of me." In the same manner, taking the cup after the supper, he said, "This cup is the new Covenant, in my blood. Whenever you drink it, do it in memory of me." So, then, whenever you eat of this bread and drink from this cup, you are proclaiming the death of the Lord, until he comes.

So then, brothers, when you gather for a meal, wait for one another.

Gospel: Luke 7:1-10

When Jesus had finished teaching the people, he went to Capernaum. A Roman military officer lived there, whose servant was very sick and near to death, a man very dear to him. So when he heard about Jesus, he sent some elders of the Jews to persuade him to come and save his servant's life. The elders came to Jesus and begged him earnestly, saying, "He deserves this of you, for he loves our people and even built a synagogue for us."

Jesus went with them. He was not far from the house, when the Roman officer sent friends to give this message, "Sir, do not trouble yourself, for I am not worthy to welcome you under my roof. You see, I didn't approach you myself. Just give the order, and my servant will be healed. For I myself, a junior officer, give orders to my soldiers, and I say to this one, 'Go!' and he goes; and to the other, 'Come!' and he comes; and to my servant, 'Do this!' and he does it."

On hearing these words, Jesus was filled with admiration. He turned and said to the people with him, "I say to you, not even in Israel have I found such great faith." The people, sent by the captain, went back to his house; there they found that the servant was well.

The captain in today's Gospel displayed the right sensitivity and courtesy to the Jewish culture. He may have been a high ranking official in the Roman army, yet he did not impose his office when he asked for healing for his servant. He sent his Jewish friends to beg the Lord to do this. He knew that the Jews would not want to have any commerce with pagans, let alone enter their houses. Thus to save the Lord from this seeming indignity he only asked that Jesus order healing for his servant and he would believe. This acceptance of Jewish customs and his faith in the word of Jesus gave him the healing he so desired. His humility made his house happy and blessed that day.

24TH WEEK IN ORDINARY TIME
St. Cornelius, pope & martyr
St. Cyprian, bishop & martyr
Psalter: Week 4 / (Red)

Tuesday

Ps 100:1b–2, 3, 4, 5
We are his people;
the sheep of his flock.

16
SEPTEMBER

St. Cornelius

Did you know that: St. Cornelius' name means "battle horn" and he is represented in icons either holding some form of cow's horn or with a cow nearby.

_____
_____
_____
_____
_____
_____
_____
_____
_____
_____
_____
_____
_____
_____

Fetish is synonymous to inclination, fixation or engrossment. With this in mind, if Jesus has a fetish, it would be the urge to help the poor and the marginalized, the little ones of society. In all the four Gospels, Jesus could not help but extend His aid to those who were most in need. He did not know the poor widow of Naim. But what He knew was that, having been deprived of the only man she had, her son, she would be vulnerable throughout her life. Moved with pity and without being asked, Jesus raised the young man back to life. During that time, two lives were preserved, that of the son and that of his mother. Jesus' sensitivity brought back possibilities to them both and a new beginning filled with hope.

1st Reading: 1 Cor 12:12–14, 27–31a

Brothers and sisters: As the body is one, having many members, and all the members, while being many, form one body, so it is with Christ. All of us, whether Jews or Greeks, slaves or free, have been baptized in one Spirit, to form one body, and all of us have been given, to drink from the one Spirit.

The body has not just one member, but many.

Now, you are the body of Christ, and each of you, individually, is a member of it. So God has appointed us in the Church. First apostles, second prophets, third teachers. Then come miracles, then the gift of healing, material help, administration in the Church and the gift of tongues.

Are all apostles? Are all prophets? Are all teachers? Can all perform miracles, or cure the sick, or speak in tongues, or explain what was said in tongues? Be that as it may, set your hearts on the most precious gifts.

Gospel: Lk 7:11–17

Jesus went to a town called Naim. He was accompanied by his disciples and a great number of people. As he reached the gate of the town, a dead man was being carried out. He was the only son of his mother, and she was a widow; there followed a large crowd of townspeople.

On seeing her, the Lord had pity on her and said, "Don't cry." Then he came up and touched the stretcher, and the men who carried it stopped. Jesus then said, "Young man, I say to you, wake up!" And the dead man sat up and began to speak, and Jesus gave him to his mother. A holy fear came over them all, and they praised God saying, "A great prophet has appeared among us. God has visited his people." This news spread throughout Judea and the surrounding places.

17
SEPTEMBER

Wednesday

Ps 33:2–3, 4–5, 12 & 22
Blessed the people the Lord has chosen to be his own.

24TH WEEK IN ORDINARY TIME
St. Robert Bellarmine, bishop & doctor
Psalter: Week 4 / (Green / White)

1st Reading: 1 Cor 12:31 – 13:13

Brothers and sisters: Be that as it may, set your hearts on the most precious gifts, and I will show you a much better way.

If I could speak all the human and angelic tongues, but had no love, I would only be sounding brass or a clanging cymbal. If I had the gift of prophecy, knowing secret things, with all kinds of knowledge, and had faith great enough to remove mountains, but had no love, I would be nothing. If I gave everything I had to the poor, and even give up my body to be burned, if I am without love, it would be of no value to me.

Love is patient, kind, without envy. It is not boastful or arrogant. It is not ill-mannered, nor does it seek its own interest. Love overcomes anger and forgets offenses. It does not take delight in wrong, but rejoices in truth. Love excuses everything, believes all things, hopes all things, endures all things.

Love will never end. Prophecies may cease, tongues be silent and knowledge disappear. For knowledge grasps something of the truth and prophecy as well. And when what is perfect comes, everything imperfect will pass away. When I was a child, I thought and reasoned like a child, but when I grew up, I gave up childish ways. Likewise, at present, we see dimly, as in a mirror, but, then, it shall be face to face. Now, we know, in part, but then I will know as I am known. Now, we have faith, hope and love, these three, but the greatest of these is love.

Gospel: Lk 7:31–35

Jesus said to the crowds, "What comparison can I use for the people? What are they like? They are like children sitting in the marketplace, about whom their companions complain, 'We piped you a tune and you wouldn't dance; we sang funeral songs and you wouldn't cry.

"Remember John: he didn't eat bread or drink wine, and you said, 'He has an evil spirit.' Next, came the Son of Man, eating and drinking; and you say, 'Look, a glutton for food and wine, a friend of tax collectors and sinners.' But the children of Wisdom always recognize her work."

St. Robert Bellarmine

Did you know that: St. Robert Bellarmine is the Patron Saint of Catechists.

Jesus knows how to be witty when He replies to His accuser. He does this while having a good laugh out of it from time to time. So it is not all the time heavy and emotionally laden conversations between Him and His detractors. Jesus could be playful sometimes. This reminds us that once in a while. humor has the capacity to lighten a heavy discussion When positions have hardened and reason is not listened to anymore, a nice touch of irony might elicit some laughter to drain away the tensions and bring the opposing camp back again to the discussion with a clearer mind. It does not always pay to be serious all the time. Jesus showed us that even He had use for something laughable sometimes.

Thursday

Ps 118:1b-2, 16ab-17, 28
Give thanks to the Lord,
for he is good.

18 SEPTEMBER

1st Reading: 1 Cor 15:1–11

Gospel: Lk 7:36–50

One of the Pharisees asked Jesus to share his meal, so he went to the Pharisee's home, and as usual reclined at the table to eat. And it happened that, a woman of this town, who was known as a sinner, heard that he was in the Pharisee's house. She brought an alabaster jar of perfume, and stood behind him, at his feet, weeping. She wet his feet with tears; she dried them with her hair; she kissed his feet and poured the perfume on them.

The Pharisee who had invited Jesus was watching, and thought, "If this man were a prophet, he would know what sort of person is touching him; isn't this woman a sinner?"

Then Jesus spoke to the Pharisee and said, "Simon, I have something to ask you." He answered, "Speak, master." And Jesus said, "Two people were in debt to the same creditor. One owed him five hundred silver coins, and the other fifty. As they were unable to pay him back, he graciously canceled the debts of both. Now, which of them will love him more?"

Simon answered, "The one, I suppose, who was forgiven more." And Jesus said, "You are right." And turning toward the woman, he said to Simon, "Do you see this woman? You gave me no water for my feet when I entered your house; but she has washed my feet with her tears and dried them with her hair. You didn't welcome me with a kiss; but she has not stopped kissing my feet since she came in. You provided no oil for my head; but she has poured perfume on my feet. This is why, I tell you, her sins, her many sins, are forgiven, because of her great love. But the one who is forgiven little, has little love."

Then Jesus said to the woman, "Your sins are forgiven." The others reclining with him at the table began to wonder, "Now this man claims to forgive sins!" But Jesus again spoke to the woman, "Your faith has saved you; go in peace!"

In today's Gospel we heard two contrasting receptions of the Lord: that of Simon the Pharisee and that of the sinful woman. It is true that Simon invited the Lord for supper but He did not extend the usual niceties and courtesies that accompany such invitation. He only provided food but nothing beyond that. After all, he belonged to a powerful group of religious authorities, the Pharisees. Jesus should be grateful that he extended the honor of invitation to Him. On the other hand is a sinful woman who had no pretense to earthly greatness. She was only conscious of her littleness before the Lord. Thus she gave the best that she had, the costly bottle of perfume and her tears to welcome and honor the Lord. Between the two, where do we find ourselves? Are we made haughty by our achievements in this world that we are at the point of disrespect when we deal with Jesus? Or are we like the sinful woman who begs the Lord for mercy and offers Him the best that we have, meager as it is, in front of Him.

19
SEPTEMBER

Friday
Ps 17:1bcd, 6–7, 8b & 15
Lord, when your glory appears,
my joy will be full.

24TH WEEK IN ORDINARY TIME
St. Januarius, bishop & martyr
Psalter: Week 4 / (Green / Red)

1st Reading: 1 Cor 15:12–20

Brothers and sisters: Well, then, if Christ is preached as risen from the dead, how can some of you say, that there is no resurrection of the dead? If there is no resurrection of the dead, then Christ has not been raised. And if Christ has not been raised, our preaching is empty, and our belief comes to nothing. And we become false witnesses of God, attesting that he raised Christ, whereas he could not raise him, if indeed, the dead are not raised. If the dead are not raised, neither has Christ been raised. And if Christ has not been raised, your faith gives you nothing, and you are still in sin. Also, those who fall asleep, in Christ, are lost. If it is only for this life, that we hope in Christ, we are the most unfortunate of all people.

But no, Christ has been raised from the dead, and he comes before all those who have fallen asleep.

Gospel: Lk 8:1–3

Jesus walked through towns and countryside, preaching and giving the good news of the kingdom of God. The Twelve followed him, and also some women, who had been healed of evil spirits and diseases: Mary called Magdalene, who had been freed of seven demons; Joanna, wife of Chuza, Herod's steward; Suzanna; and others, who provided for them out of their own funds.

St. Januarius
Did you know that: St. Januarius is popular because of the miraculous liquefaction of his blood, which occurs every year in Naples.

Jesus as a holy man is unique in many ways among the other holy men of His time. For one, He does not shun the company and help of women. They are a welcome group in His band. Our Gospel today tells us that such a group of women followed the Lord. They also contributed in the movement of Jesus by way of monetary support. These were active women followers. Their secondary status against the males in the Jewish society of that time did not hinder them from their active roles. And this happened because they followed an enlightened and evolved Master. Jesus valued the women in His group and respected their contribution. We too should have a positive appreciation of women by virtue of our following the Lord.

24TH WEEK IN ORDINARY TIME

St. Andrew Kim Tae-gon, priest & martyr
St. Paul Chong Ha-sang, martyr
and Companions, martyrs
Psalter: Week 4 / (Red)

Saturday

Ps 56:10c–12, 13–14
I will walk in the presence of God,
in the light of the living.

20
SEPTEMBER

St. Andrew Kim Taegon

Did you know that: St. Andrew Kim Tae-yon was the first Korean born Catholic priest and was canonized during Pope John Paul II's visit to Korea together with Paul Chong Ha-sang, a lay apostle.

_____
_____
_____
_____
_____
_____
_____
_____
_____
_____
_____
_____
_____

Jesus never turned down requests that explained further His teachings. As a matter of fact He delighted in being questioned especially if those who did so genuinely sought enlightenment. And so He explained His parable of the seeds that fell on different grounds which seemed to be ordinary and mundane to the casual observer. Yet the deeper significance of the parable has a realism that could help His hearers respond accordingly to His teachings. Jesus is a very good Teacher. All we have to do is ask Him and allow Him to teach us the way. But is He the Teacher that we will follow or do we allow the "false teachers" of this world to dictate to us what to do?

1st Reading: 1 Cor 15:35–37, 42–49 *

Brothers and sisters: Some of you will ask: How will the dead be raised? With what kind of body will they come?

You fools! What you sow cannot sprout unless it dies. And what you sow is not the body of the future plant, but a bare grain of wheat or any other seed,(…)

It is the same with the resurrection of the dead. The body is sown in decomposition; it will be raised never more to die. It is sown in humiliation, and it will be raised for glory. It is buried in weakness, but the resurrection shall be with power. When buried, it is a natural body, but it will be raised as a spiritual body. For there shall be a spiritual body, as there is, at present, a living body. Scripture says that Adam, the first man, became a living being; but the last Adam has become a life-giving spirit. (…)

Gospel: Lk 8:4–15

As a great crowd gathered, and people came to him from every town, Jesus began teaching them with a story: "The sower went out to sow the seed. And as he sowed, some of the seed fell along the way, was trodden on, and the birds of the sky ate it up. Some seed fell on rocky ground; and no sooner had it come up than it withered, because it had no water. Some seed fell among thorns; the thorns grew up with the seed and choked it. But some seed fell on good soil and grew, producing fruit, a hundred times as much!" And Jesus cried out, "Listen then, if you have ears to hear!"

The disciples asked him, "What does this story mean?" And Jesus answered, "To you it has been given to know the mystery of the kingdom of God. But to others it is given in the form of stories, or parables, so that, seeing, they may not perceive; and hearing, they may not understand.

"Now, this is the point of the parable:

"The seed is the word of God. Those along the wayside are people who hear it; but immediately, the devil comes and takes the word from their minds, for he doesn't want them to believe and be saved. Those on the rocky ground are people who receive the word with joy; but they have no root; they believe for a while, and give way in time of trial. Among the thorns are people who hear the word, but, as they go their way, they are choked by worries, riches, and the pleasures of life; they bring no fruit to maturity. The good soil, instead, are people who receive the word, and keep it, in a gentle and generous mind, and, persevering patiently, they bear fruit."

21
SEPTEMBER
Sunday

Ps 145:2–3, 8–9, 17–18
The Lord is near to all
who call upon him.

1st Reading: Is 55:6–9

Seek Yahweh while he may be found; call to him while he is near.

Let the wicked abandon his way, let him forsake his thoughts, let him turn to Yahweh for he will have mercy, for our God is generous in forgiving.

For my thoughts are not your thoughts, my ways are not your ways, says Yahweh.

For as the heavens are above the earth, so are my ways higher than your ways, and my thoughts above your thoughts.

2nd Reading: Phil 1:20c–24, 27a

Brothers and sisters: Christ will be exalted through my person, whether I live or die. For to me, living is for Christ, and dying is even better. But if I am to go on living, I shall be able to enjoy fruitful labor. Which shall I choose? So I feel torn between the two. I desire greatly to leave this life and to be with Christ, which will be better by far, but it is necessary for you that I remain in this life.

Try, then, to adjust your lives according to the Gospel of Christ.

Gospel: Mt 20:1–16

Jesus told his disciples this parable, "This story throws light on the kingdom of heaven: A landowner went out early in the morning, to hire workers for his vineyard. He agreed to pay each worker the usual daily wage, and sent them to his vineyard.

"He went out again, at about nine in the morning, and, seeing others idle in the town square, he said to them, 'You also, go to my vineyard, and I will pay you what is just.' So they went.

"The owner went out at midday, and, again, at three in the afternoon, and he made the same offer. Again he went out, at the last working hour—the eleventh—and he saw others standing around. So he said to them, 'Why do you stand idle the whole day?' They answered, 'Because no one has hired us.' The master said, 'Go, and work in my vineyard.'

"When evening came, the owner of the vineyard said to his manager, 'Call the workers and pay them their wage, beginning with the last and ending with the first.' Those who had gone to work at the eleventh hour came up, and were each given a silver coin. When it was the turn of the first, they thought they would receive more. But they, too, received one silver coin. On receiving it, they began to grumble against the landowner.

"They said, 'These last, hardly worked an hour; yet, you have treated them the same as us, who have endured the heavy work of the day and the heat.' The owner said to one of them, 'Friend, I have not been unjust to you. Did we not agree on one silver coin per day? So, take what is yours and go. I want to give to the last the same as I give to you. Don't I have the right to do as I please with what is mine? Why are you envious when I am kind?'

"So will it be: the last will be first, the first will be last."

Reading: Again, Jesus uses the imagery of the landowner of a vineyard who came out to look for workers to his vineyard at different times of the day. When the time for paying wages came, the last to work received the same full day's pay as those who came the earliest. The latter murmured complaints but they were reminded of the original agreement that the landowner had with them. How he uses his money is entirely up to his own discretion.

Reflection: The values of the Kingdom are way beyond our understanding and ken. Whereas we always put monetary or its equivalent value to the things that we do, heaven is happy to multiply the greatest good and joy without considering the cost and amount. This is the reason why the landowner, who is the image of God, paid all workers, regardless of the time spent in working, the same amount. He was happy to share his resources equally to all without regard to their outputs. This does not sit well with those who worked ahead. They felt cheated because they expended more energy, spent more time and experienced more discomfort than the others. They demand a just compensation to their efforts. But come to think of it, when we are in God's house everything will be shared equally. No one will have more than the others because there will be no basis for comparison. This will simply fade away. What will remain is the abundant love of God that can never be exhausted. There will always be something more left behind for others once we get our share.

Response: Have I begrudged another's generosity especially if I am not the recipient? Rather than griping about it, I should commend and reinforce it so that generosity will grow in strength especially in the community that I live.

22
SEPTEMBER

Monday

Ps 15:2–3a, 3bc–4ab, 5
The just one shall live on your
holy mountain, O Lord.

25TH WEEK IN ORDINARY TIME
Psalter: Week 1 / (Green)

1st Reading: Pro 3:27–34

*D*o not hold back from those who ask your help, when it is in your power to do it. Do not say to your neighbor, "Go away! Come another time; tomorrow I will give it to you!" when you can help him now.

Do not plot evil against your neighbor who lives trustingly beside you, nor fight a man without cause when he has done you no wrong. Do not envy the man of violence or follow his example.

For Yahweh hates the wicked but guides the honest. He curses the house of the evildoer but blesses the home of the upright. If there are mockers, he mocks them in turn but he shows his favor to the humble.

Gospel: Lk 8:16–18

*J*esus said to the crowd, "No one, after lighting a lamp, covers it with a bowl or puts it under the bed; rather, he puts it on a lamp stand, so that people coming in may see the light. In the same way, there is nothing hidden that shall not be uncovered; nothing kept secret, that shall not be known clearly. Now, pay attention and listen well, for whoever produces, will be given more; but from those who do not produce, even what they seem to have will be taken away from them."

The purpose of the lamp is to shed light. That is what it is made for. The same thing is true for the word of Jesus. It is spoken for a purpose; that is, those who will hear it may be able to produce fruits to build God's kingdom. It is thus in the interest of the hearers to listen very well to this fertile word of Jesus. For the quality of its produce depends on how one listens well. If it is received and kept in one's heart and mind like Mary did, the word of Jesus will be the motivation of one's speech and action. People who have dedicated their lives in following God's word have never regretted. The saints and their testimonies showed us how fruitful they were and contented about it because they clung to Jesus' word. We too will experience their bliss if we harden not our hearts when we hear His word.

Tuesday

Ps 119:1, 27, 30, 34, 35, 44
Guide me, Lord, in the way
of your commands.

23
SEPTEMBER

St. Pius of Pietrelcina
Did you know that: St. Padre Pio, the first stigmatized priest in the history of the Church, was born Francesco Forgione and was given the name "Pius" (in Italian "Pio") when he joined the Capuchins.

_____
_____
_____
_____
_____
_____
_____
_____
_____
_____
_____
_____
_____
_____

Jesus' fame had already spread and many were following His every word. Not even His family could get close to Him now. They had to wait and send an emissary to tell Him that they were around. And something wonderful happened that day. That simple family who waited to see their Jesus was complemented by Him in a way that also disclosed their greatness. They had already heard the word of God and had done it in their lives. This is the reason why they stayed behind when Jesus made the rounds of Israel. They did not have to follow Him in His itinerant preaching. They were already doing what Jesus continues to exhort His hearers to do.

1st Reading: Pro 21:1–6, 10–13

*I*n the hands of Yahweh, the heart of the king is like running water; he directs it wherever he wishes.

To the eyes of man all his ways are honest but it is Yahweh who weighs the heart.

To do what is upright and just pleases Yahweh more than sacrifice.

Haughty looks, proud heart, the light of the wicked is sin.

The plans of a hardworking man result in earnings; poverty is for those who act too hastily.

To make a fortune by means of deceit is like running after the wind; the end is death.

The soul of the wicked desires nothing but evil; not even his friend is treated with compassion.

When the mocker is punished the ignorant man grows wise; when the wise man is instructed he grows in knowledge.

The Just One watches the house of the evildoer and hurls the wicked into misfortune. He who is deaf to the poor man's cry will not be heard when he himself calls out.

Gospel: Lk 8:19–21

*T*he mother and relatives of Jesus came to him; but they could not get to him because of the crowd. Someone told him, "Your mother and your brothers are standing outside and wish to meet you." Then Jesus answered, "My mother and my brothers are those who hear the word of God and do it."

24
SEPTEMBER

Wednesday

Ps 119:29, 72, 89, 101, 104, 163
Your word, O Lord,
is a lamp for my feet.

25TH WEEK IN ORDINARY TIME
Psalter: Week 1 / (Green)

1st Reading: Pro 30:5–9

*E*very word of God is true, he is a shield in whom man can find refuge. Add nothing to his words lest he rebuke you and take you for a liar.

O God, two things I beg of you, do not deny me them before I die. Keep lying and falsehood far away from me, give me neither poverty nor riches. Give me just as much food as I need lest, satisfied, I deny you and say, "Who is Yahweh?" Or else, out of necessity, I steal and profane the name of my God.

Gospel: Lk 9:1–6

*J*esus called his Twelve disciples and gave them power and authority to drive out all evil spirits and to heal diseases. And he sent them to proclaim the kingdom of God and to heal the sick. He instructed them, "Don't take anything for the journey, neither staff, nor bag, nor bread, nor money; and don't even take a spare tunic. Whatever house you enter, remain there until you leave that place. And wherever they don't welcome you, leave the town and shake the dust from your feet: it will be as a testimony against them."

So they set out, and went through the villages, proclaiming the good news and healing people everywhere.

Jesus' style of leadership is handing over power to those who follow Him and giving them an opportunity to produce something for themselves. He provides an avenue where His disciples can do something concrete and something that they can be proud of. He does not feel diminished simply because His followers exercise control and leadership over that which they do. Strange but very few have the capacity to let go of the remote control and allow others to select the show. The majority have this growing need for control just to show who is the leader or the boss. Jesus empowers. He shows genuine delight at the achievements of those He sent. If we could be a little bit more like Him, many people would be happy to do something for the benefit of others.

25TH WEEK IN ORDINARY TIME
Psalter: Week 1 / (Green)

Thursday

Ps 90:3-4, 5-6, 12-13, 14 & 17bc
In every age, O Lord,
you have been our refuge.

25
SEPTEMBER

1st Reading: Ecl 1:2-11

All is meaningless–says the Teacher–meaningless, meaningless! What profit is there for a man in all his work for which he toils under the sun?

A generation goes, a generation comes and the earth remains forever. The sun rises, the sun sets, hastening towards the place where it again rises. Blowing to the south, turning to the north, the wind goes round and round and after all its rounds it has to blow again.

All rivers go to the sea but the sea is not full; to the place where the rivers come from, there they return again.

All words become weary and speech comes to an end, but the eye has never seen enough nor the ear heard too much.

What has happened before will happen again; what has been done before will be done again: there is nothing new under the sun.

If they say to you, "See, it's new!" know that it has already been centuries earlier.

There is no remembrance of ancient people, and those to come will not be remembered by those who follow them.

Gospel: Lk 9:7-9

King Herod heard of all this, and did not know what to think, for people said, "This is John, raised from the dead." Others believed that Elijah, or one of the ancient prophets, had come back to life. As for Herod, he said, "I had John beheaded. Who is this man, about whom I hear such wonders?" And he was anxious to see him.

There are things we have done that do not simply die. They continue to haunt us. The more unjust it has been, the scarier is its ghost that visits us. This is what King Herod felt. He knew that he had John beheaded because of an impulsive promise. Now, another man, who does what John did before, comes to town. He makes Herod remember the man he put to death. That is why Herod has to see him. He will always feel uneasy unless he puts the ghost of John to rest. But even if he sees Jesus, he will never find peace. Like Herod, we will never find peace from our ghosts if we do not repent.

26
SEPTEMBER

Friday
Ps 144:1b & 2abc, 3–4
Blessed be the Lord, my Rock!

25TH WEEK IN ORDINARY TIME
Sts. Cosmas & Damian, martyrs
Psalter: Week 1 / (Green / Red)

1st Reading: Ecl 3:1–11

There is a given time for everything and a time for every happening under heaven:

A time for giving birth, a time for dying; a time for planting, a time for uprooting.

A time for killing, a time for healing; a time for knocking down, a time for building.

A time for tears, a time for laughter; a time for mourning, a time for dancing.

A time for throwing stones, a time for gathering stones; a time for embracing, a time to refrain from embracing.

A time for searching, a time for losing; a time for keeping, a time for throwing away.

A time for tearing, a time for sewing; a time to be silent and a time to speak.

A time for loving, a time for hating; a time for war, a time for peace.

What profit is there for a man from all his toils?

Finally I considered the task God gave to the humans. He made everything fitting in its time, but he also set eternity in their hearts, although they are not able to embrace the work of God from the beginning to the end.

Gospel: Lk 9:18–22

One day, when Jesus was praying alone, not far from his disciples, he asked them, "What do people say about me?" And they answered, "Some say, that you are John the Baptist; others say, that you are Elijah; and still others, that you are one of the prophets of old, risen from the dead." Again Jesus asked them, "But who do you say that I am?" Peter answered, "The Messiah of God." Then Jesus spoke to them, giving them strict orders not to tell this to anyone.

And he added, "The Son of Man must suffer many things. He will be rejected by the elders and chief priests and teachers of the law, and be put to death. Then after three days he will be raised to life."

Sts. Cosmas & Damian
Did you know that: Sts. Cosmas and Damian, twin brothers martyred during the persecution under Diocletian, are the patron of doctors, nurses, and pharmacists.

The longer we spend time with one another, the deeper is our knowledge of each other. It is no wonder that the disciples, with Peter as their mouthpiece were able to pierce the veil that hid the deepest identity of Jesus. While others could only think of Him as a prophet, the disciples knew Him to be the Messiah of God. Yet even this confession did not guarantee their complete and steadfast faith in Jesus. They scattered like leaves when their Lord and Master was being tried, sentenced and put to death. This shows us that faith proclamation needs time to be truly rooted in our hearts and minds. The disciples themselves took time before they fully embraced what they had proclaimed that day.

Saturday

Ps 90:3–4, 5–6, 12–13, 14 &17
In every age, O Lord,
you have been our refuge.

27
SEPTEMBER

St.Vincent de Paul

Did you know that: St. Vincent de Paul, the founder of the Congregation of the Mission, more popularly known as Vincentians or Lazarists, is dubbed as the "Great Apostle of Charity."

Jesus had hinted at His fate to His disciples more often. But they didn't want to face the fact. They were afraid of its implications. They would rather enjoy the moment of triumph that Jesus had with His following added every day. Yet Jesus would not allow them to sidestep the issue. They had to follow Him with eyes wide open not deluding themselves of a false glorious future. This also goes for each and every one of us. Following Jesus does not guarantee an easy and smooth life. On the contrary we will find it hard to be disciples of the Lord in this present age. And He wants to tell us at once so that we will know what we are signing up for when we make Him the Lord and Master of our life. Knowing that, do we have the courage to go on?

1st Reading: Ecl 11:9 – 12:8

Rejoice, young man, in your youth and direct well your heart when you are young; follow your desires and achieve your ambitions but recall that God will take account of all you do.

Drive sorrow from your heart and pain from your flesh, for youth and dark hair will not last. Be mindful of your Creator when you are young, before the time of sorrow comes when you have to say, "This gives me no pleasure," and before the sun, moon and stars withdraw their light, before the clouds gather again after the rain.

On the day when the guardians of the house tremble, when sturdy men are bowed and those at the mill stop working because they are too few, when it grows dim for those looking through the windows, and the doors are shut and the noise of the mill grows faint, the sparrow stops chirping and the birdsong is silenced, when one fears the slopes and to walk is frightening; yet the almond tree blossoms, the grasshopper is fat and the caper berry bears fruit that serves no purpose, because man goes forward to his eternal home and mourners gather in the street, even before the silver chain is snapped or the golden globe is shattered, before the pitcher is broken at the fountain or the wheel at the mill, before the dust returns to the earth from which it came and the spirit returns to God who gave it.

Meaningless! meaningless! the Teacher says; all is meaningless!

Gospel: Lk 9:43b–45

While all were amazed at everything Jesus did, he said to his disciples, "Listen, and remember what I tell you now: The Son of Man will be betrayed into the hands of men." But the disciples didn't understand this saying; something prevented them from grasping what he meant, and they were afraid to ask him about it.

1st Reading: Ezk 18:25–28

Thus says Yahweh: But you say: Yahweh's way is not just! Why, Israel! Is my position wrong? Is it not rather that yours is wrong? If the righteous man turns from his righteous deeds, and sins, then he dies, because of his sins. And if the wicked man does what is good and right, after turning from the sins he committed, he will save his life. He will live and not die, because he has opened his eyes; and turned from the sins he had committed.

2nd Reading: Phil 2:1–11

Brothers and sisters: If I may advise you, in the name of Christ, and if you can hear it, as the voice of love; if we share the same Spirit, and are capable of mercy and compassion, then I beg of you, make me very happy: have one love, one spirit, one feeling, do nothing through rivalry or vain conceit. On the contrary, let each of you gently consider the others, as more important than yourselves. Do not seek your own interest, but, rather, that of others. Your attitude should be the same as Jesus Christ had:

Though he was in the form of God, he did not regard equality with God as something to be grasped, but emptied himself, taking on the nature of a servant, made in human likeness, and, in his appearance, found, as a man, He humbled himself by being obedient, to death, death on the cross.

That is why God exalted him and gave him the name which outshines all names, so, that, at the name of Jesus all knees should bend in heaven, on earth and among the dead, and all tongues proclaim, that Christ Jesus is the Lord, to the glory of God the Father.

Gospel: Mt 21:28–32

Jesus went on to say, "What do you think of this? A man had two sons. He went to the first and said to him, 'Son, go and work today in my vineyard.' And the son answered, 'I don't want to.' But later he thought better of it and went. Then the father went to his other son and said the same thing to him. This son replied, 'I will go, sir,' but he did not go.

"Which of the two did what the father wanted?" They answered, "The first." And Jesus said to them, "Truly, I say to you: the publicans and the prostitutes are ahead of you on the way to the kingdom of heaven. For John came, to show you the way of goodness, and you did not believe him; but the publicans and the prostitutes did. You were witnesses of this, but you neither repented nor believed him."

Reading: Jesus tells the story of the two sons who were requested by their father to go to his vineyard to work. The first said flatly that he will not obey his father but thought the better of it afterwards and went anyway. The second promised to obey the father's request but failed to do so. His hearers commended the eldest son who in turn was a mirror of the publicans and the prostitutes who initially violated God's command but turned a new leaf and repented when they heard the preaching of John. On the other hand, the chief priests and the elders did not effectively take the role of the youngest son.

Reflection: An open rebellion that leads to repentance and consequent obedience is better than a passive obedience that later leads to a secret rebellion. That is why we are better off with people who are loud and transparent with their intentions than those whose mind we cannot read. We know at least what to expect from the former and will be genuinely surprised if they have a change of heart. On the other hand we will have a hard time reconciling the good attitude the former has shown us while secretly harboring seditious thoughts. The known sinners in Jesus' time were like that. They made no secrets of their opposition to God by the lives they led, yet at a point in time, they changed course and mended their ways. It was a shock to note that those who were so sure of receiving the kingdom were instead disinherited of their claimed birthright because their disobedience was not forthright.

Response: I may be both the elder and the younger son in my response to obedience but they are not ideal examples. I should mean what I say and say what I mean clearly and without pretence. Today I take my word seriously. My word is my bond.

29
SEPTEMBER

Monday

Ps 138:1–2ab, 2cde–3, 4–5
In the sight of the angels
I will sing your praises, Lord.

FEAST OF STS. MICHAEL, GABRIEL
AND RAPHAEL, ARCHANGELS
Psalter: Proper / (White)

1st Reading: Rev 12:7–12ab (Dn 7:9–10, 13–14)

War broke out in heaven, with Michael and his angels battling with the dragon. The dragon fought back with his angels, but they were defeated, and lost their place in heaven. The great dragon, the ancient serpent, known as the devil, or Satan, seducer of the whole world, was thrown out. He was hurled down to earth, together with his angels.

Then, I heard a loud voice from heaven:

"Now has salvation come, with the power and the kingdom of our God, and the rule of his anointed.

"For our brothers' accuser has been cast out, who accused them night and day, before God.

"They conquered him, by the blood of the Lamb, and by the word of their testimony, for they gave up their lives, going to death.

"Rejoice, therefore, O you heavens, and you who dwell in them; but woe to you, earth and sea, for the devil has come to you, in anger, knowing that he has but a little time."

Gospel: Jn 1:47–51

When Jesus saw Nathanael coming, he said of him, "Here comes an Israelite, a true one; there is nothing false in him." Nathanael asked him, "How do you know me?" And Jesus said to him, "Before Philip called you, you were under the fig tree, and I saw you."

Nathanael answered, "Master, you are the Son of God! You are the king of Israel!" But Jesus replied, "You believe because I said, 'I saw you under the fig tree.' But you will see greater things than that.

"Truly, I say to you, you will see the heavens opened, and the angels of God ascending and descending upon the Son of Man."

Nathanael's true self and his hidden thoughts were laid bare by Jesus. Because of these, he promptly proclaimed the divinity of the Lord. Isn't it that in our lives, we also feel the Lord unmasking us for who we are; He lays bare our soul. There is nothing that we can hide from Him. Sometimes, like Nathanael, we acknowledge His majesty. Some other times, because of shame or because of false pride, we turn away and leave Him. Jesus has no intention of embarrassing us when He looks into our inmost self. He loves us for who we are. Our pretensions will not add or subtract from that love. May we aspire to be like Nathanael where nothing is false within him. That is why it was easy for him to proclaim the Lordship of Jesus.

Tuesday

Ps 88:2–3, 4–5, 6, 7–8
Let my prayer come before you, Lord.

30
SEPTEMBER

St. Jerome

Did you know that: St. Jerome, translator of the Bible into its official version known as the Latin Vulgate, was born Eusebius Hieronymus Sophronius.

_____
_____
_____
_____
_____
_____
_____
_____
_____
_____
_____
_____

There is now a sense of urgency in the movements of Jesus. His time is drawing near. There is so much to be done yet. Time is of the essence. It is in this moment of preparation when things sometimes don't get on in the way we want it. Jesus wants to be near Jerusalem so He sent His people to prepare lodging for Him nearby, in a Samaritan town. But people would not welcome Him. They did this to all Jews who wanted to go to Jerusalem during the Feast. Jesus was not singled out. He was just one among the many casualties of the enmity between the Jews and the Samaritans. If Jesus was made of lesser stuff He would have given in to the tempting course of action proposed by the impulsive James and John. How about us in similar situations? Do our emotions get the better of us?

1st Reading: Job 3:1–3, 11–17, 20–23

At length it was Job who spoke, cursing the day of his birth. This is what he said: Cursed be the day I was born, and the night which whispered:
A boy has been conceived.
Why didn't I die at birth, or come from the womb without breath?
Why the knees that received me, why the breasts that suckled me?
For then I should have lain down asleep and been at rest with kings and rulers of the earth who built for themselves lonely tombs; or with princes who had gold to spare and houses stuffed with silver.
Why was I not stillborn, like others who did not see the light of morn?
There, the trouble of the wicked ceases, there, the weary find repose.
Why is light given to the miserable, and life to the embittered?
To those who long for death more than for hidden treasure?
They rejoice at the sight of their end, they are happy upon reaching the grave.
Why give light to a man whose path has vanished, whose ways God blocks at every side?

Gospel: Lk 9:51–56

As the time drew near when Jesus would be taken up to heaven, he made up his mind to go to Jerusalem. He sent ahead of him some messengers, who entered a Samaritan village to prepare a lodging for him. But the people would not receive him, because he was on his way to Jerusalem. Seeing this, James and John, his disciples, said, "Lord, do you want us to call down fire from heaven to reduce them to ashes?" Jesus turned and rebuked them, and they went on to another village.

01
OCTOBER

Wednesday
Ps 88:10bc–11, 12–13, 14–15
Let my prayer come
before you, Lord.

26TH WEEK IN ORDINARY TIME
St. Thérèse of the Child Jesus,
virgin & doctor
Psalter: Week 2 / (White)

1st Reading: Job 9:1–12, 14–16

Then Job answered:
Very well I know that it is so.
But how can a mortal be just before God?
If one were to contend with him, not once in a thousand times would he answer.
His power is vast, his wisdom profound.
Who has resisted him and come out unharmed?
He moves mountains before they are aware; he overturns them in his rage.
He makes the earth tremble
and its pillars quake.
He commands the sun, and it does not shine;
he seals off the light of the stars.
He alone stretches out the skies and treads on the waves of the seas.
He made the Bear and Orion, the Pleiades and every constellation.
His wonders are past all reckoning, his miracles beyond all counting.
He passes by, but I do not see him; he moves on, but I do not notice him.
If he snatches away, who can stop him?
Who can say to him, "What are you doing?"
How then can I answer him and find words to argue with him?
If he does not answer when I am right, shall I plead with my judge for mercy?
Even if I appealed and he answered, I do not believe that he would have heard.

Gospel: Lk 9:57–62

As Jesus and his disciples went on their way, a man said to him, "I will follow you wherever you go." Jesus said to him, "Foxes have holes and the birds of the air have nests; but the Son of Man has nowhere to lay his head."

To another, Jesus said, "Follow me!" But he answered, "Let me go back now, for, first, I want to bury my father." And Jesus said to him, "Let the dead bury their dead; as for you, leave them, and proclaim the kingdom of God."

Another said to him, "I will follow you, Lord, but first let me say goodbye to my family." And Jesus said to him, "Whoever has put his hand to the plow, and looks back, is not fit for the kingdom of God."

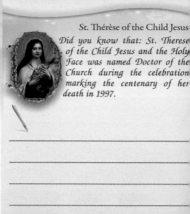

St. Thérèse of the Child Jesus
Did you know that: St. Thérèse of the Child Jesus and the Holy Face was named Doctor of the Church during the celebration marking the centenary of her death in 1997.

The invitation to be part of the team of Jesus continues until now. Many are called but only few respond willingly. It seems that we have a hundred and one reasons to postpone our response to God's call yet it only takes a hint from the worldly call before we go scurrying in its direction. It is therefore not a surprise to see many of those who hunger to know about God being unministered, neglected and abandoned. We are too preoccupied with worldly affairs that the work of the Lord takes a backseat in our priorities. Yet the Lord does not give up. The call is still on. Will you have your reasons too or will you stop hardening your heart to God's invitation?

Thursday

02
OCTOBER

Ps 27:7–8a, 8b–9abc, 13–14
I believe that I shall see the good things of the Lord in the land of the living.

1st Reading: Job 19:21–27

Have pity my friends, have pity,
for God's hand has struck me!
Why do you hound me as God does?
Will you never have enough of my flesh?'
Oh, that my words were written,
or recorded on bronze
with an iron tool, a chisel
or engraved forever on rock!
For I know that my Redeemer lives,
and he, the last, will take his stand on earth.
I will be there behind my skin,
and in my flesh I shall see God.
With my own eyes I shall see him—
I and not another. How my heart yearns!

Gospel: Luke 10:1–12

The Lord appointed seventy-two other disciples, and sent them, two by two, ahead of him, to every town and place, where he himself was to go. And he said to them, "The harvest is plentiful, but the workers are few. So you must ask the Lord of the harvest to send workers to his harvest. Courage! I am sending you like lambs among wolves. Set off without purse or bag or sandals; and do not stop at the homes of those you know.

"Whatever house you enter, first bless them, saying, 'Peace to this house!' If a friend of peace lives there, the peace shall rest upon that person. But if not, the blessing will return to you. Stay in that house, eating and drinking at their table, for the worker deserves to be paid. Do not move from house to house.

"When they welcome you to any town, eat what they offer you. Heal the sick who are there, and say to them: 'The kingdom of God has drawn near to you.'

"But in any town where you are not welcome, go to the marketplace and proclaim: 'Even the dust of your town that clings to our feet, we wipe off and leave with you. But know for a certainty that the kingdom of God has drawn near to you.' I tell you, that on the Day of Judgment it will be better for Sodom than for this town."

There is always a place for anyone who wants to work on God's project. After all, Jesus has designed it in such a way that He will not do all but leave space for others to own and continue the task that He has done. And He does train His disciples to the job. Earlier on, He gives them a chance for hands-on work. They must have the feel of the terrain so that when the time comes, they may be able to assume leadership without much difficulty. Meanwhile, they have to be mentored. And so we His modern followers are not called to do something unprepared. The capacities are already there; all Jesus does is to draw them out and to hone them. Every calling is therefore an opportunity for improvement.

03
OCTOBER

Friday

Ps 139:1-3, 7-8, 9-10, 13-14ab
Guide me, Lord, along the
everlasting way.

1st Reading: Job 38:1, 12–21; 40:3–5

Then Yahweh answered Job out of the storm:
Have you ever commanded the morning,
or shown the dawn its place,
that it might grasp the earth by its edges
and shake the wicked out of it,
when it takes a clay color
and changes its tint like a garment;
when the wicked are denied their own light,
and their proud arm is shattered?
Have you journeyed to where the sea begins
or walked in its deepest recesses?
Have the gates of death been shown to you?
Have you seen the gates of Shadow?
Have you an idea of the breadth of the earth?
Tell me, if you know all this.
Where is the way to the home of light,
and where does darkness dwell?
Can you take them to their own regions,
and set them on their homeward paths?
You know, for you were born before them,
and great is the number of your years!
Job said:
How can I reply, unworthy as I am!
All I can do is put my hand over my mouth.
I have spoken once, now I will not answer;
oh, yes, twice, but I will do no further.

Gospel: Lk 10:13–16

Jesus said, "Alas for you, Chorazin! Alas for you, Bethsaida! So many miracles have been worked in you! If the same miracles had been performed in Tyre and Sidon, they would already be sitting in ashes and wearing the sackcloth of repentance. Surely for Tyre and Sidon it will be better on the Day of Judgment than for you. And what of you, city of Capernaum? Will you be lifted up to heaven? You will be thrown down to the place of the dead.

"Whoever listens to you listens to me, and whoever rejects you rejects me; and he who rejects me, rejects the one who sent me."

No matter how much we try, there are things that will not go according to our wishes. Even Jesus has to contend with the fact that some places He so wished to save will go down on judgment day. For that is the risk of loving. We allow ourselves to be vulnerable. We run the risk of being hurt. Jesus experienced this whole range of emotions while still on earth. He lamented Chorazin and Bethsaida. The city of Capernaum too He foresaw as lost. Yet this did not stop Him from trying. As a matter of fact He tried till the very end. Giving up simply because it is hopeless is not Jesus' style. He showed us that love is tenacious and hopeful to the very end.

Saturday

Ps 119:66, 71, 75, 91, 125, 130
Lord, let your face shine
on me.

04
OCTOBER

St. Francis of Assisi

Did you know that: St. Francis of Assisi created the first nativity scene, which became widely popular up until now.

_____
_____
_____
_____
_____
_____
_____
_____
_____
_____
_____

1st Reading: Job 42:1-3, 5-6, 12-17

This was the answer Job gave to Yahweh:
I know that you are all powerful; no plan of yours can be thwarted. I spoke of things I did not understand, too wonderful for me to know. My ears had heard of you, but now my eyes have seen you. Therefore I retract all I have said, and in dust and ashes I repent.

Yahweh blessed Job's latter days much more than his earlier ones. He came to own fourteen thousand sheep, six thousand camels, a thousand yoke of oxen, and a thousand she-donkeys. He was also blessed with seven sons and three daughters. The first daughter he named Dove, the second Cinnamon, and the third Bottle of Perfume. Nowhere in the land was there found any woman who could compare in beauty with Job's daughters. Their father granted them an inheritance along with their brothers.

Job lived a hundred and forty years; he saw his children and their children to the fourth generation. He died old and full of years.

Gospel: Lk 10:17-24

The seventy-two disciples returned full of joy. They said, "Lord, even the demons obeyed us when we called on your name." Then Jesus replied, "I saw Satan fall like lightning from heaven. You see, I have given you authority to trample on snakes and scorpions and to overcome all the power of the Enemy, so that nothing will harm you. Nevertheless, don't rejoice because the evil spirits submit to you; rejoice, rather, that your names are written in heaven."

At that time, Jesus was filled with the joy of the Holy Spirit, and said, "I praise you, Father, Lord of heaven and earth, for you have hidden these things from the wise and learned, and made them known to little ones. Yes, Father, such has been your gracious will. I have been given all things by my Father, so that no one knows the Son except the Father, and no one knows the Father except the Son, and he to whom the Son chooses to reveal him."

Then Jesus turned to his disciples and said to them privately, "Fortunate are you to see what you see, for I tell you, that many prophets and kings would have liked to see what you see, but did not see it; and to hear what you hear, but did not hear it."

There is infectious joy in the air. The disciples rejoiced at their first successful ministry. Their Master partook in their joy, celebrating their little triumph. He gave His disciples the chance to revel in the good they had done because it would help them face the obstacles and hardships they would meet in the future. But Jesus directs their attention to what they should truly celebrate. It is not their success but the fact that they are now part of God's team. Their names are now in heaven. Successful or not later on, they should take comfort in the fact that God made them as their own. In our life, the source of our true joy should not be our work and its favorable result alone. Rather we should rejoice that God selected us to be His co-workers in the unfolding of His plan for the world.

05
OCTOBER

Sunday

Ps 80:9, 12, 13–14, 15–16, 19–20
The vineyard of the Lord
is the house of Israel.

1st Reading: Is 5:1–7

Let me sing for my beloved my love-
song about his vineyard.
My beloved had a vineyard on a fertile
hillside.
He dug it up, cleared the stones,
and planted the choicest vines.
He built there a watchtower
and hewed out a wine press as well.
Then he looked
for a crop of good grapes,
but it yielded only wild grapes.
Now, inhabitants of Jerusalem and people
of Judah,
judge between me and my vineyard.
What more was there to do
that I have not done for my vineyard?
Good grapes was the yield I expected.
Why did it yield only sour grapes?
Now I will let you know
what I am going to do
with my vineyard:
I will remove its hedge
and it will be burned;
I will break down its wall
and it will be trampled on.
I will make it a wasteland,
I will neither prune nor hoe it,
and briers and thorns will grow there.
I command the clouds, as well,
not to send rain on it.
The vineyard of Yahweh Sabaoth
is the people of Israel;
and the people of Judah
are his pleasant vine.
He looked for justice,
but found bloodshed;
He looked for righteousness
but heard cries of distress.

2nd Reading: Phil 4:6–9

Brothers and sisters: Do not be
anxious about anything. In
everything, resort to prayer and supplication,
together, with thanksgiving, and bring your
requests before God. Then, the peace of
God, which surpasses all understanding, will
keep your hearts and minds in Christ Jesus.

Finally, brothers and sisters, fill your minds
with whatever is truthful, holy, just, pure,
lovely and noble. Be mindful of whatever
deserves praise and admiration. Put into
practice what you have learned from me,
what I passed on to you, what you heard
from me or saw me doing, and the God of
peace will be with you.

Gospel: Mt 21:33–43

Jesus said to the chief priests and
elders, "Listen to another example:
There was a landowner who planted a
vineyard. He put a fence around it, dug a
hole for the wine press, built a watchtower,
leased the vineyard to tenants, and then,
went to a distant country. When harvest time
came, the landowner sent his servants to the
tenants to collect his share of the harvest.
But the tenants seized his servants, beat one,
killed another, and stoned a third.

"Again, the owner sent more servants; but
they were treated in the same way.

"Finally, he sent his son, thinking, 'They will
respect my son.' But when the tenants saw
the son, they thought, 'This is the one who is
to inherit the vineyard. Let us kill him, and his
inheritance will be ours.' So they seized him,
threw him out of the vineyard and killed him.

"Now, what will the owner of the vineyard
do with the tenants when he comes?" They
said to him, "He will bring those evil men
to an evil end, and lease the vineyard to
others, who will pay him in due time." And
Jesus replied, "Have you never read what the
Scriptures say? *The stone which the builders
rejected has become the cornerstone. This was
the Lord's doing, and we marvel at it.* Therefore
I say to you: the kingdom of heaven will be
taken from you, and given to a people who
will produce its fruit."

Reading: Again Jesus conveys His teaching by way of a parable which in this case is the Parable of the owner and his tenants. The unacceptable behavior of the tenants and their violence against the son of the owner mirrors the stature of the chief priests and the elders in front of God. They indicted themselves by their own judgment on what to do with the wicked tenants.

Reflection: Jesus has an ongoing conversation with the chief priests and elders in view of having a common agreement with the teachings of Jesus. However, the rift and the divide get wider and bigger. No matter how much Jesus tried, the religious leaders were set in their ways and convinced of their own righteousness. Thus they missed the time of their visitation. There is nothing as unfortunate as a closed mind and a hard head. Throw in pride and you have a deadly combination.

Response: How have I been behaving lately with regard to the things that I have? Do I have an owner's mentality or that of a steward? Today I am reminded by the Gospel that all I have comes from the Lord and I have to administer them wisely and should respond to this generous God with my own acts of generosity to others. I should care more for what I have and share these resources to others to the best that I can.

06
OCTOBER

Monday
Ps 111:1b–2, 7–8, 9 and 10c
The Lord will remember
his covenant for ever.

27TH WEEK IN ORDINARY TIME
St. Bruno, priest
Bl. Marie Rose Durocher, virgin
Psalter: Week 3 / (Green / White)

1st Reading: Gal 1:6–12*

Brothers and sisters: I am surprised at how quickly you have abandoned God, who called you, according to the grace of Christ, and have gone to another Gospel. Indeed, there is no other Gospel, but some people, who are sowing confusion among you, want to turn the Gospel of Christ upside down. (…) As I have said, I now say again: if anyone preaches the Gospel in a way other than you received it, fire that one! Are we to please humans or obey God? Do you think that I try to please people? If I were still trying to please people, I would not be a servant of Christ.

Let me remind you, brothers and sisters, that the Gospel we preached to you is not a human message, nor did I receive it from anyone, I was not taught of it; but it came to me, as a revelation from Christ Jesus.

Gospel: Lk 10:25–37

A teacher of the law came and began putting Jesus to the test. And he said, "Master, what shall I do to receive eternal life?" Jesus replied, "What is written in the law? How do you understand it?" The man answered, "It is written: *You shall love the Lord your God with all your heart, with all your soul, with all your strength and with all your mind. And you shall love your neighbor as yourself.*" Jesus replied, "What a good answer! Do this and you shall live." The man wanted to justify his question, so he asked, "Who is my neighbor?"

Jesus then said, "There was a man going down from Jerusalem to Jericho, and he fell into the hands of robbers. They stripped him, beat him and went off, leaving him half-dead.

"It happened that a priest was going along that road and saw the man, but passed by on the other side. Likewise a Levite saw the man, and passed by on the other side. But a Samaritan also was going that way; and when he came upon the man, he was moved with compassion. He went over to him, and cleaned his wounds with oil and wine, and wrapped them in bandages. Then he put him on his own mount, and brought him to an inn, where he took care of him.

"The next day, he had to set off; but he gave two silver coins to the innkeeper, and said, 'Take care of him, and whatever you spend on him, I will repay when I return.'"

Jesus then asked, "Which of these three, do you think, made himself neighbor to the man who fell into the hands of robbers?" The teacher of the law answered, "The one who had mercy on him." And Jesus said, "Then go and do the same."

St. Bruno
Did you know that: St. Bruno, the founder of the Carthusians, was not formally canonized but Pope Leo X granted the Carthusians permission to celebrate his feast.

It is easier to memorize the laws and precepts that would lead to a good life. If you possess a better than average intelligence, committing them to memory would be a breeze. But their actual application to life is something else. It is not only the brain that is involved here. The heart and soul must follow what has been recognized by the head. They too must give their own inputs to make the concepts operational. This is the area which we find most difficult. Concepts are easy to wrestle with; how to act on them is not. And so we are like the young man of the Gospel asking the Lord to show us the way. Jesus was not called Teacher for nothing. He teaches us the correct application of the things we learned from Him.

Tuesday

07

OCTOBER

Ps 139:1b–3, 13–14ab, 14c–15
Guide me, Lord,
along the everlasting way.

_____
_____
_____
_____
_____
_____
_____
_____
_____
_____
_____
_____
_____
_____

1st Reading: Gal 1:13–24

Brothers and sisters: You have heard of my previous activity in the Jewish community; I furiously persecuted the Church of God and tried to destroy it. For I was more devoted to the Jewish religion than many fellow Jews of my age, and I defended the traditions of my ancestors more fanatically.

But one day, God called me, out of his great love, he, who had chosen me from my mother's womb; and he was pleased to reveal, in me, his Son, that I might make him known among the pagan nations. Then, I did not seek human advice nor did I go up to Jerusalem, to those who were apostles before me. I immediately went to Arabia, and from there, I returned, again, to Damascus. Later, after three years, I went up to Jerusalem to meet Cephas, and I stayed with him for fifteen days. But I did not see any other apostle except James, the Lord's brother. On writing this to you, I affirm before God that I am not lying.

After that, I went to Syria and Cilicia. The churches of Christ in Judea did not know me personally; they had only heard of me: "He, who once persecuted us, is now preaching the faith he tried to uproot." And they praised God because of me.

Gospel: Lk 10:38–42

As Jesus and his disciples were on their way, he entered a village, and a woman called Martha welcomed him to her house. She had a sister named Mary, who sat down at the Lord's feet to listen to his words. Martha, meanwhile, was busy with all the serving, and finally she said, "Lord, don't you care that my sister has left me to do all the work? Tell her to help me!"

But the Lord answered, "Martha, Martha, you worry and are troubled about many things, whereas only one thing is needed. Mary has chosen the better part, and it will not be taken away from her."

Sitting at the feet of the Lord or serving Him by serving others: these are the two sides of following of the Lord. Both are equally important. But in the order of doing, listening to the voice of the Master and strengthening our relationship with Him takes precedence. Our doing should be grounded on our attentive listening to God and any apostolate that we undertake should spring from our prayer. Without this sitting at the master's feet, all our actions would be bereft of guidance and direction coming from the Lord. Putting into effect His will is already hard. Putting into operation our will would be harder. This is the reason why Mary had chosen the better portion. It was the better part to start working for God's project.

08
OCTOBER

Wednesday
Ps 117:1bc, 2
Go out to all the world,
and tell the Good News.

27TH WEEK IN ORDINARY TIME
Psalter: Week 3 / (Green)

1st Reading: Gal 2:1–2, 7–14

Brothers and sisters: After fourteen years, I, again, went up to Jerusalem with Barnabas, and Titus came with us. Following a revelation, I went, to lay before them the Gospel that I am preaching to the pagans. I had a private meeting with the leaders—lest I should be working, or have worked, in a wrong way. They recognized that I have been entrusted to give the Good News to the pagan nations, just as Peter has been entrusted to give it to the Jews. In the same way that God made Peter the apostle of the Jews, he made me the apostle of the pagans.

James, Cephas and John acknowledged the graces God gave me. Those men, who were regarded as the pillars of the Church, stretched out their hand to me and Barnabas, as a sign of fellowship; we would go to the pagans, and they, to the Jews. We should only keep in mind, the poor among them. I have taken care to do this.

When, later, Cephas came to Antioch, I confronted him, since he deserved to be blamed. Before some of James' people arrived, he used to eat with non-Jewish people. But when they arrived, he withdrew, and did not mingle anymore with them, for fear of the Jewish group. The rest of the Jews followed him in this pretense, and even Barnabas was part of this insincerity. When I saw that they were not acting in line with the truth of the Gospel, I said to Cephas publicly: If you, who are Jewish, agreed to live like the non-Jews, setting aside the Jewish customs, why do you, now, compel the non-Jews to live like Jews?

Gospel: Lk 11:1–4

One day, Jesus was praying in a certain place; and when he had finished, one of his disciples said to him, "Lord, teach us to pray, as John also taught his disciples." And Jesus said to them, "When you pray, say this:

Father, may your name be held holy,
may your kingdom come;
give us, each day, the kind of bread we need,
and forgive us our sins; for we also forgive
all who do us wrong;
and do not bring us to the test."

We have fond memories of those we love. These memories mark our understanding and appreciation of their person. The disciples' memory of Jesus is marked by His deep and profound prayer life. So much so that they were inspired to emulate His example. They asked Him to teach them how to pray. Because of this, the only prayer that Jesus taught them and us is the one recorded in the Gospel. The Our Father is simply strings of words that convey our sentiments to the Father. By itself it could not bring us to holiness. It is what happens inside, the inner transformation that matters. Jesus can only teach us the words He used while praying. It is our own personal labor to put substance to these borrowed words in our life.

27TH WEEK IN ORDINARY TIME
St. Denis, bishop & martyr
and Companions, martyrs
St. John Leonardi, priest
Psalter: Week 3 / (Green / Red / White)

Thursday

Ps 1:69–70, 71–72, 73–75
Blessed be the Lord, the God of
Israel; he has come to his people.

09 OCTOBER

St. Denis

*Did you know that: St. Denis
is one of the cephalophoric
saints which means he is
usually depicted as a saint who
carries his head that signifies
he was martyred by beheading.*

Persistence is the greater part of asking. This is proven in the Gospel by the insistent friend to the point of being a nuisance. The problem is, sometimes when we ask something from the Lord we are sensitive and easily slighted. A small delay, some inconveniences, that come with the asking and silence from God are interpreted as rejection and we easily give up, sore at the Lord who does not accede to our wishes. But beggars can't be choosers. They cannot dictate the terms in this particular transaction. They can only wait. So while waiting, we have to keep up the effort. God surrenders willingly to those who are persistent.

1st Reading: Gal 3:1–5

*H*ow foolish you are, Galatians! How could they bewitch you after Jesus Christ has been presented to you as crucified? I shall ask you only this: Did you receive the Spirit by the practice of the law, or by believing the message? How can you be such fools: you begin with the Spirit and end up with the flesh!

So, you have experienced all this in vain! Would that, it were not so! Did God give you the Spirit, and work miracles among you because of your observance of the law, or because you believed in his message?

Gospel: Lk 11:5–13

*J*esus said to his disciples, "Suppose one of you has a friend, and goes to his house in the middle of the night and says, 'Friend, lend me three loaves, for a friend of mine who is traveling has just arrived, and I have nothing to offer him.' Maybe your friend will answer from inside, 'Don't bother me now; the door is locked, and my children and I are in bed, so I can't get up and give you anything.' But I tell you, even though he will not get up and attend to you because you are a friend, yet he will get up because you are a bother to him, and he will give you all you need.

"And so I say to you, 'Ask, and it will be given to you; seek, and you will find; knock, and it will be opened to you. For the one who asks receives, and the one who searches finds, and to him who knocks the door will be opened.

"If your child asks for a fish, will you give him a snake instead? And if your child asks for an egg, will you give him a scorpion? If you sinful people know how to give good gifts to your children, how much more will your heavenly Father give the Holy Spirit to those who ask him."

10
OCTOBER

Friday
Ps 111:1b–2, 3–4, 5–6
The Lord will remember
his covenant for ever.

27TH WEEK IN ORDINARY TIME
Psalter: Week 3 / (Green)

1st Reading: Gal 3:7–14*

*B*rothers and sisters: (…) The Scriptures foresaw that, by the way of faith, God would give true righteousness to the non-Jewish nations. For God's promise to Abraham was this: *In you shall all the nations be blessed.* So, now, those who take the way of faith receive the same blessing as Abraham, who believed; but those who rely on the practice of the law are under a curse, for it is written: *Cursed is everyone who does not always fulfill everything written in the law.* (…)

Now Christ rescued us from the curse of the law, by becoming cursed himself, for our sake, as it is written: *there is a curse on everyone who is hanged on a tree.* So the blessing granted to Abraham, reached the pagan nations in, and, with Christ, and we received the promised Spirit, through faith.

Gospel: Lk 11:15–26

*Y*et some of the crowd said, "He drives out demons by the power of Beelzebul, the chief of the demons." Others wanted to put him to the test, by asking him for a heavenly sign.

But Jesus knew their thoughts, and said to them, "Every nation divided by civil war is on the road to ruin, and will fall. If Satan also is divided, his empire is coming to an end. How can you say that I drive out demons by calling upon Beelzebul? If I drive them out by Beelzebul, by whom do your sons drive out demons? They will be your judges, then.

"But if I drive out demons by the finger of God; would not this mean that the kingdom of God has come upon you? As long as a man, strong and well armed, guards his house, his goods are safe. But when a stronger man attacks and overcomes him, the challenger takes away all the weapons he relied on, and disposes of his spoils.

"Whoever is not with me is against me, and whoever does not gather with me, scatters.

"When the evil spirit goes out of a person, it wanders through dry lands, looking for a resting place; and finding none, it says, 'I will return to my house from which I came.' When it comes, it finds the house swept and everything in order. Then it goes to fetch seven other spirits, even worse than itself. They move in and settle there, so that the last state of that person is worse than the first."

Those who will not believe will always find a reason to reinforce their unbelief. They might go through the motions of searching for the truth but since their heart is set, no amount of proof will sway them. In today's Gospel, people accused Jesus of driving demons by the power of the prince of demons, Beelzebul. Others wanted that He justify Himself by way of heavenly signs. There was not much that could be done here since they had already judged Him. So Jesus did not indulge their pettiness. Rather he strove to reason with them to demonstrate that His healing could not possibly come from the evil one. After all, the healings He did were miraculous signs that unfolded before their very eyes yet they refused to believe. One more would not make a difference.

Saturday

Ps 105:2–3, 4–5, 6–7
The Lord remembers
his covenant for ever.

11
OCTOBER

1st Reading: Gal 3:22–29

*B*rothers and sisters: But the Scriptures have declared, that we are all prisoners of sin. So, the only way to receive God's promise is to believe in Jesus Christ.

Before the time of faith had come, the law confined us, and kept us in custody, until the time in which faith would show up. The law, then, was serving as a slave, to look after us until Christ came, so that we might be justified by faith. With the coming of faith, we are no longer submitted to this guidance.

Now, in Christ Jesus, all of you are sons and daughters of God, through faith. All of you, who were given to Christ through Baptism, have put on Christ. Here, there is no longer any difference between Jew or Greek, or between slave or freed, or between man and woman: but all of you are one, in Christ Jesus. And because you belong to Christ, you are of Abraham's race and you are to inherit God's promise.

Gospel: Lk 11:27–28

*A*s Jesus was speaking, a woman spoke from the crowd and said to him, "Blessed is the one who gave you birth and nursed you!" Jesus replied, "Truly blessed are those who hear the word of God, and keep it as well."

At first glance, Jesus seemed to deflect the praise given to His mother and re-channel it instead to those who hear God's word and keep it. But a deeper reading of His words will tell us that He is elevating the virtues of Mary, not because she was His biological mother but because she accepted the Word of God without hesitation and allowed herself to be God's vessel in the incarnation of His Son. It is true that Mary's blessedness will always be connected to Jesus. That is why the woman in the crowd praised her because she had an extraordinary Son. But the Son would not have been Man if not for Mary's docility to God's word. That is why the Son praised his mother because of her extraordinary reception of, and obedience to, the word of God.

12
OCTOBER

Sunday

Ps 23:1–3a, 3b–4, 5, 6
I shall live in the house of the Lord
all the days of my life.

1st Reading: Is 25:6–10a

On this mountain Yahweh Sabaoth will prepare for all peoples a feast of rich food and choice wines, meat full of marrow, fine wine strained.

On this mountain he will destroy the pall cast over all peoples, this very shroud spread over all nations, and death will be no more. The Lord Yahweh will wipe away the tears from all cheeks and eyes; he will take away the humiliation of his people all over the world: for Yahweh has spoken.

On that day you will say: This is our God. We have waited for him to save us, let us be glad and rejoice in his salvation. For on this mountain the hand of Yahweh rests.

2nd Reading: Phil 4:12–14,19–20

Brothers and sisters: I know what it is to be in want and what it is to have plenty. I am trained for both: to be hungry or satisfied, to have much or little. I can do all things in him who strengthens me. However, you did right in sharing my trials.

God, himself, will provide you with everything you need, according to his riches, and show you his generosity in Christ Jesus. Glory to God, our Father, for ever and ever: Amen.

Gospel: Mt 22:1–14 (or Mt 22:1-10)

Jesus continued speaking to the chief priests and elders in parables:

"This story throws light on the kingdom of heaven: A king gave a wedding banquet for his son. He sent his servants to call the invited guests to the banquet, but the guests refused to come.

"Again, he sent other servants, instructing them to say to the invited guests, 'I have prepared a banquet, slaughtered my fattened calves and other animals, and now, everything is ready. Come to the wedding!' But they paid no attention and went away, some to their farms, and some to their work. Others seized the servants of the king, insulted them and killed them.

"The king was furious. He sent his troops to destroy those murderers and burn their city. Then he said to his servants, 'The wedding banquet is prepared, but the invited guests were not worthy. Go instead to the main streets, and invite everyone you find to the wedding feast.'

"The servants went out into the streets and gathered all they found, good and bad alike, so that the hall was filled with guests.

"The king came in to see the wedding guests, and he noticed a man not wearing a wedding garment. So he said to him, 'Friend, how did you get in without the wedding clothes?' But the man remained silent. So the king said to his servants, 'Bind his hands and feet and throw him into the outer darkness, where there is weeping and gnashing of teeth.'

"For many are called, but few are chosen."

Reading: Today's Gospel speaks of a wedding banquet prepared by the king for his son's wedding. The invited guests did not come preferring to attend instead their own affairs. Some even did violence to the servants sent by the king and killed them. In anger, the king retaliated and having annihilated the ungrateful invited guests, he sent his servants once again to invite anyone who cared to come. But one had to be in festal garments when entering or risk the chance of being thrown out of the banquet hall.

Reflection: Familiarity sometimes makes us take for granted things that might have been otherwise hard to come by in a different setting. To be considered friend of the king and be one of his honored guests is a chance that ordinary mortals spend a lifetime just to be one. Yet since these friends have been so familiar with the regal presence, they are not as awed as common people are. Hence, they snub and were even irritated with such invitation. The same thing happens sometimes in the spiritual life. Those who are deemed "close" to or familiar with God are the ones who are not that awed with the holy life. Their sensibilities have been deadened by constant exposure to it that they have no qualms trampling upon it. It is not the result of their friendship with God. It is because pride has set in their hearts such privilege that they now have a bloated understanding of themselves.

Response: There are moments when I take God for granted, confident in the fact that He and I are friends. This should not go on. I must value my friendship with God. Today might be a good day to say a prayer of thanks to this God who befriended me and do something to someone today as an act of gratitude to this loving friend of mine.

13
OCTOBER

Monday

Ps 113:1b–2, 3–4, 5a & 6–7
Blessed be the name of the Lord
forever.

28TH WEEK IN ORDINARY TIME
Psalter: Week 4 / (Green)

1st Reading: Gal 4:22–24, 26–27, 31–5:1

*B*rothers and sisters: It says, that Abraham had two sons, one by a slave woman, the other by the free woman, his wife. The son of the slave woman was born in the ordinary way; but the son of the free woman was born in fulfillment of God's promise.

Here we have an allegory and the figures of two Covenants. The first is the one from Mount Sinai, represented through Hagar: her children have slavery for their lot.

But the Jerusalem above, who is our mother, is free. And Scripture says of her: *Rejoice, barren woman without children, break forth in shouts of joy, you who do not know the pains of childbirth, for many shall be the children of the forsaken mother, more than of the married woman.*

Brethren, we are not children of the slave woman, but of the free woman.

Christ freed us, to make us really free. So remain firm, and do not submit, again, to the yoke of slavery.

Gospel: Lk 11:29–32

*A*s the crowd increased, Jesus spoke the following words: "People of the present time are troubled people. They ask for a sign, but no sign will be given to them except the sign of Jonah. As Jonah became a sign for the people of Nineveh, so will the Son of Man be a sign for this generation. The Queen of the South will rise up on Judgment Day with the people of these times and accuse them, for she came from the ends of the earth to hear the wisdom of Solomon; and here, there is greater than Solomon. The people of Nineveh will rise up on Judgment Day with the people of these times and accuse them, for Jonah's preaching made them turn from their sins, and here, there is greater than Jonah."

Evil people are those who have been repeatedly shown signs in words and deeds that the time of salvation is near yet do not believe. Jesus tried hard to make them understand yet their hearts and minds were already hardened. They were not open to Jesus' teachings even if it was backed up by miraculous signs and wonders. Jesus was at the point of giving up. Yet He still reserved a last sign, that of His resurrection from the dead after three days, just as Jonah spent three days in the belly of the whale. What a great loss for the people of Jesus' time who did not open themselves to the teachings of Jesus! They lost eternity because of their persistent unbelief. People who are closed miss out on a lot of good things. May we of the present age not miss salvation by loosening our hearts and minds to God's word.

Tuesday

Ps 119:41, 43, 44, 45, 47, 48
Let your mercy come to me,
O Lord.

14
OCTOBER

St. Callistus I

Did you know that: St. Pope Callistus I biography, the main source of information about him, was written by his contemporary and enemy, St. Hippolytus.

1st Reading: Gal 5:1–6

Brothers and sisters: Christ freed us, to make us really free. So remain firm, and do not submit, again, to the yoke of slavery. I, Paul, say this to you: if you receive circumcision, Christ can no longer help you. Once more, I say, to whoever receives circumcision: you are now bound to keep the whole law. All you, who pretend to become righteous through the observance of the law, have separated yourselves from Christ, and have fallen away from grace.

As for us, through the Spirit and faith, we eagerly wait for the hope of righteousness. In Christ Jesus, it is irrelevant, whether we be circumcised or not; what matters is, faith, working through love.

Gospel: Lk 11:37–41

As Jesus was speaking, a Pharisee asked him to have a meal with him. So he went and sat at table. The Pharisee then wondered why Jesus did not first wash his hands before dinner. But the Lord said to him, "So then, you Pharisees, you clean the outside of the cup and the dish, but inside yourselves you are full of greed and evil. Fools! He who made the outside, also made the inside. But according to you, by the mere giving of alms everything is made clean."

Rituals make life easy by facilitating our movement from one area of our life to the next. For the Jews, eating meals has a sacral dimension; to enter into this sacred act and space, one must wash hands as a ritual cleansing of oneself coming from the profane world with its profane activities. Yet Jesus does not have the patience for such ceremonies that are only for outward appearances. He is more preoccupied with the interior cleanliness of the person. Outward rituals can be dispensed. They are not obligatory. But to be good interiorly is a must.

15
OCTOBER

Wednesday

Ps 1:1–2, 3, 4 & 6
Those who follow you, Lord,
will have the light of life.

28TH WEEK IN ORDINARY TIME
St. Teresa of Avila, virgin & doctor
Psalter: Week 4 / (White)

1st Reading: Gal 5:18–25

Brothers and sisters: When you are led by the Spirit you are not under the law.

You know what comes from the flesh: fornication, impurity and shamelessness, idol worship and sorcery, hatred, jealousy and violence, anger, ambition, division, factions, and envy, drunkenness, orgies and the like. I again say to you what I have already said: those who do these things shall not inherit the kingdom of God.

But the fruit of the Spirit is charity, joy and peace, patience, understanding of others, kindness and fidelity, gentleness and self-control. For such things there is no law or punishment. Those who belong to Christ have crucified the flesh with its vices and desires.

If we live by the Spirit, let us live in a spiritual way.

Gospel: Lk 11:42–46

The Lord said, "A curse is on you, Pharisees! To the temple you give a tenth of all, including mint and rue and other herbs, but you neglect justice and the love of God. These ought to be practiced, without neglecting the other obligations. A curse is on you, Pharisees, for you love the best seats in the synagogues and to be greeted in the marketplace. A curse is on you, for you are like tombstones of the dead which can hardly be seen; people don't notice them, and make themselves unclean by stepping on them."

Then a teacher of the law spoke up and said, "Master, when you speak like this, you insult us, too." And Jesus answered, "A curse is on you also, teachers of the law. For you prepare unbearable burdens and load them on the people, while you yourselves do not move a finger to help them."

St. Teresa of Avila
Did you know that: St. Teresa of Avila was the first woman to be honored as Doctor of the Church together with St. Catherine of Siena.

Cursing seems to be a heavy thing to do to others. We instinctively feel that people who curse go overboard. Yet here we are with Jesus cursing the Pharisees and the teachers of the Law. The air is thick with emotions. Jesus openly ridicules the religious leaders of His time. At first glance, it seemed that Jesus was too harsh with these two groups. Yet a closer reading reveals where His stance came from. It was because the Pharisees and the teachers of the Law had calcified in their belief that they were the keepers of righteousness. They have to be shaken from their false sense of the self so that they would see their folly. This is called tough love. It is not something easy. We would rather preserve peace by sweeping the hurtful truth and go on as if everything is normal. But Jesus would not. He could not bear the Pharisees and the teachers of the Law to remain where they were. If He was to be the bad guy, so be it. This is the price one pays sometimes if one loves passionately.

28TH WEEK IN ORDINARY TIME
St. Hedwig, religious
St. Margaret Mary Alacoque, virgin
Psalter: Week 4 / (Green / White)

Thursday

Ps 98:1, 2–3ab, 3cd–4, 5–6
The Lord has made known
his salvation.

16
OCTOBER

St. Margaret Mary Alacoque

Did you know that: St. Margaret Mary Alacoque is one of the three saints dubbed as "Saints of the Sacred Heart" because she was instrumental in the spread of the devotion to the Sacred Heart of Jesus.

1st Reading: Eph 1:1–10

Paul, an apostle of Christ Jesus, by the will of God, to the saints in Ephesus, to you, who share Christian faith: receive grace and peace from God, our Father, and from Jesus, the Lord. Blessed be God, the Father of Christ Jesus our Lord, who, in Christ, has blessed us from heaven, with every spiritual blessing. God chose us, in Christ, before the creation of the world, to be holy, and without sin in his presence. From eternity he destined us, in love, to be his adopted sons and daughters, through Christ Jesus, thus fulfilling his free and generous will. This goal suited him: that his loving-kindness, which he granted us in his beloved might finally receive all glory and praise. For, in Christ, we obtain freedom, sealed by his blood, and have the forgiveness of sins. In this, appears the greatness of his grace, which he lavished on us. In all wisdom and understanding, God has made known to us his mysterious design, in accordance with his loving-kindness, in Christ. In him, and under him, God wanted to unite, when the fullness of time had come, everything in heaven and on earth.

Gospel: Lk 11:47–54

The Lord said, "A curse is on you, for you build monuments to the prophets your ancestors killed. So you approve and agree with what your ancestors did. Is it not so? They got rid of the prophets, and you build monuments to them!

"For that reason the wisdom of God also said: I will send prophets and apostles and these people will kill and persecute some of them. But the present generation will have to answer for the blood of all the prophets that has been shed since the foundation of the world, from the blood of Abel to the blood of Zechariah, who was murdered between the altar and the Sanctuary. Yes, I tell you, the people of this time will have to answer for them all.

"A curse is on you, teachers of the law, for you have taken the key of knowledge. You yourselves have not entered, and you prevented others from entering."

As Jesus left that place, the teachers of the law and the Pharisees began to harass him, asking him endless questions, setting traps to catch him in something he might say.

The tirade of Jesus against the Pharisees and the teachers of the Law continues. He will not allow them to forget their historical errors. The truth may be hurtful but it has to be confronted. Any peace that is borne of compromise and not based on a genuine searching of the heart is bound to fail in the long run. An acknowledgement of the wrongs done and a genuine repentance and the seeking of forgiveness must be in place for peace to flourish. But the two groups have hardened their stance. It is not anymore the truth that matters but their pride wounded by Jesus' bold words. They now commence to find ways and means to silence truth. In the end, the truth will always find itself lonely.

17

OCTOBER

Friday

Ps 33:1–2, 4–5, 12–13
Blessed the people the Lord
has chosen to be his own.

28TH WEEK IN ORDINARY TIME
St. Ignatius of Antioch, bishop & martyr
Psalter: Week 4 / (Red)

1ˢᵗ Reading: Eph 1:11–14

*B*rothers and sisters: By a decree of him, who disposes all things, according to his own plan and decision, we, the Jews, have been chosen and called, and we were awaiting the Messiah, for the praise of his glory.

You, on hearing the word of truth, the Gospel that saves you, have believed in him.

And, as promised, you were sealed with the Holy Spirit, the first pledge of what we shall receive, on the way to our deliverance, as a people of God, for the praise of his glory.

Gospel: Lk 12:1–7

*M*eanwhile, such a numerous crowd had gathered that they crushed one another. Then Jesus spoke to his disciples in this way, "Beware of the yeast of the Pharisees, which is hypocrisy. Nothing is covered that will not be uncovered; or hidden, that will not be made known. Whatever you have said in darkness will be heard in daylight, and what you have whispered in hidden places, will be proclaimed from housetops.

"I tell you, my friends, do not fear those who put to death the body and, after that, can do no more. But I will tell you whom to fear: Fear the one who, after killing you, is able to throw you into hell. This one you must fear. Don't you buy five sparrows for two pennies? Yet not one of them has been forgotten by God. Even the hairs of your head have been numbered. Don't be afraid! Are you less worthy in the eyes of God than many sparrows?"

St. Ignatius of Antioch
Did you know that: St. Ignatius of Antioch is the bishop who first used the term "catholic" to describe the whole Church.

His clash with the Pharisees and the teachers of the Law left Jesus with no choice but to warn His disciples against being contaminated by the religious hypocrisy of these religious teachers. They may be able to cover it for a while and fool others by their display of piety, but a day will come when they will be unmasked for who they really are. In our life, we sometimes feel that we could cover up our acts, especially those that reveal our weaknesses. Yet time and time again we are shown that no secret remains as such permanently. But we never learn. The words of wisdom that Jesus imparted to His disciples during His time remain valid until today. Shall we therefore clean up our acts so that there will be no secrets to hide,? Or like the Pharisees will we continue conducting our lives as if it is business as usual?

Ps 145:10–11, 12–13, 17–18
Your friends make known,
O Lord, the glorious splendor
of your Kingdom.

1st Reading: 2 Tim 4:10–17b

Beloved: You must know, that Demas has deserted me, for the love of this world: he returned to Thessalonica. Crescens has gone to Galatia and Titus to Dalmatia. Only Luke remains with me. Get Mark and bring him with you, for he is a useful helper in my work. I sent Tychicus to Ephesus.

Bring with you the cloak I left at Troas, in Carpos' house, and also the scrolls, especially the parchments. Alexander, the metalworker, has caused me great harm. The Lord will repay him for what he has done. Distrust him, for he has been very much opposed to our preaching.

At my first hearing in court, no one supported me; all deserted me. May the Lord not hold it against them. But the Lord was at my side, giving me strength, to proclaim the word fully, and let all the pagans hear it. So I was rescued from the lion's mouth.

Gospel: Lk 10:1–9

After this, the Lord appointed seventy-two other disciples, and sent them, two by two, ahead of him, to every town and place, where he himself was to go. And he said to them, "The harvest is plentiful, but the workers are few. So you must ask the Lord of the harvest to send workers to his harvest. Courage! I am sending you like lambs among wolves. Set off without purse or bag or sandals; and do not stop at the homes of those you know.

"Whatever house you enter, first bless them, saying, 'Peace to this house!' If a friend of peace lives there, the peace shall rest upon that person. But if not, the blessing will return to you. Stay in that house, eating and drinking at their table, for the worker deserves to be paid. Do not move from house to house.

"When they welcome you to any town, eat what they offer you. Heal the sick who are there, and say to them: 'The kingdom of God has drawn near to you.'"

On-the-Job training is now part and parcel of the program before one is given a certificate of competency in his or her chosen field. It gives you a foretaste of the task you will handle in the future and the experience to handle most of the challenges that may crop up the job. Jesus did exactly that for His disciples. He sent them to have a feel of their future work ahead. And so meanwhile, since they were newcomers to the trade, sets of guidelines were given them. These would help them navigate the intricacies of doing God's work among people. Jesus' willingness to give them this chance showed how He trusted His group. This will probably play a great factor why most of them stayed even when He went up to heaven. He valued their persons and their contributions. In Jesus' team, they had the space to grow and contribute their talents and capacities to make the mission successful.

1st Reading: Is 45:1, 4–6

Thus says Yahweh to his anointed, to Cyrus:
"I have taken you by the right hand
to subdue nations before you
and strip kings of their armor,
to open the gateways before you
so that they will be closed no more.
"For the sake of Jacob my servant,
of Israel my chosen one,
I have called you by your name
and given you your mission
although you do not know me.
"I am Yahweh, and there is no other;
there is no God besides me.
I armed you when you did not know me,
so that, from the rising
to the setting of the sun,
all may know
that there is no one besides me;
I am Yahweh, and there is no other."

2nd Reading: 1 Thes 1:1–5b

From Paul, Sylvanus and Timothy, to the church of Thessalonica, which is in God, the Father, and in Christ Jesus, the Lord. May the peace and grace of God be with you.

We give thanks to God, at all times, for you, and remember you in our prayers. We constantly recall, before God, our Father, the work of your faith, the labors of your love, and your endurance, in waiting for Christ Jesus our Lord.

We remember, brothers and sisters, the circumstances of your being called. The Gospel we brought you was such, not only in words. Miracles, the Holy Spirit, and plenty of everything, were given to you.

Gospel: Mt 22:15–21

The Pharisees went away, considering how they could trap Jesus by his own words. They sent to him their disciples, along with members of Herod's party, saying, "Master, we know that you are an honest man, and truly teach God's way. You are not influenced by others, nor are you afraid of anyone. So tell us what you think: is it against the law to pay taxes to Caesar or not?"

But Jesus understood their evil intentions, and said to them, "Hypocrites, why are you trying to trap me? Show me the coin with which you pay taxes."

They showed him a silver coin, and Jesus said to them, "Whose head is this, and whose name?" They answered, "Caesar's." Then Jesus replied, "So give to Caesar what is Caesar's, and give to God what is God's."

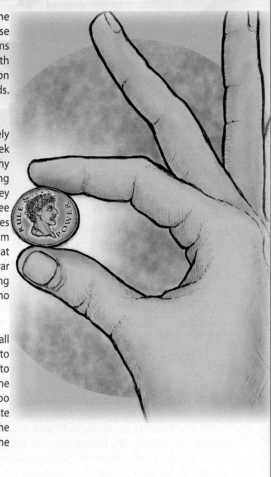

Reading: The hostility between Jesus and the religious authorities built up day by day. Because of this, the Pharisees plotted with the Herodians on how to trap Jesus. They tried to trip Him with a question that will either implicate Jesus on religious grounds or if not, on political grounds. Jesus sidestepped the trap with a clever reply.

Reflection: There are questions that genuinely seek the truth while there are questions that seek the downfall of the enemy. This is the reason why you have to be always on your toes when dealing with such people. You will never know when they will spring the trap. But Jesus is not the type to flee from such occasions. He knows where He comes from and the clarity of His purpose makes Him ready for such eventualities. It's because of this that the religious leaders could not beat Him in the war of words. A coalition of the aggrieved is beginning to form. Life will always be hard for those who stand for the truth.

Response: Am I honest in paying my taxes and all dues that I owe to others for services rendered to me? Jesus does not stop the payment of taxes to the government of His time because it ensures the environment where income could be made. I too should render a just account of all my legitimate income. I will be doing my share in ensuring the government's capacity to deliver services to the people.

20
OCTOBER

Monday

Ps 100:1b–2, 3, 4ab, 4c–5
The Lord made us,
we belong to him.

29TH WEEK IN ORDINARY TIME
St. Paul of the Cross, priest
Psalter: Week 1 / (Green / White)

1st Reading: Eph 2:1–10

Brothers and sisters: You were dead, through the faults and sins. Once, you lived through them, according to this world, and followed the Sovereign Ruler who reigns between heaven and earth, and who goes on working, in those who resist the faith. All of us belonged to them, at one time, and we followed human greed; we obeyed the urges of our human nature and consented to its desires. By ourselves, we went straight to the judgment, like the rest of humankind.

But God, who is rich in mercy, revealed his immense love. As we were dead through our sins, he gave us life, with Christ. By grace, you have been saved! And he raised us to life, with Christ, giving us a place with him in heaven.

In showing us such kindness, in Christ Jesus, God willed to reveal, and unfold in the coming ages, the extraordinary riches of his grace. By the grace of God, you have been saved, through faith. This has not come from you: it is God's gift. This was not the result of your works, so you are not to feel proud. What we are, is God's work. He has created us, in Christ Jesus, for the good works he has prepared, that we should devote ourselves to them.

Gospel: Lk 12:13–21

Someone in the crowd spoke to Jesus, "Master, tell my brother to share with me the family inheritance." He replied, "My friend, who has appointed me as your judge or your attorney?" Then Jesus said to the people, "Be on your guard and avoid every kind of greed, for even though you have many possessions, it is not that which gives you life."

And Jesus continued, "There was a rich man, and his land had produced a good harvest. He thought, 'What shall I do, for I am short of room to store my harvest? Alright, I know what I shall do: I will pull down my barns and I will build bigger ones, to store all this grain, which is my wealth.

"Then I will say to myself: My friend, you have a lot of good things put by for many years. Rest, eat, drink and enjoy yourself.' But God said to him, 'You fool! This very night your life will be taken from you. Tell me, who shall get all you have put aside?' This is the lot of the one who stores up riches for himself and is not wealthy in the eyes of God."

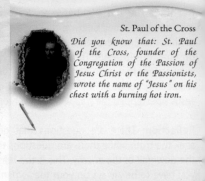

St. Paul of the Cross
Did you know that: St. Paul of the Cross, founder of the Congregation of the Passion of Jesus Christ or the Passionists, wrote the name of "Jesus" on his chest with a burning hot iron.

Family problems do happen especially if it involves inheritance. If the parents have not made a clear provision as to the division of the properties involved, misunderstanding and conflict may arise. And so one person among the crowd sought the help of Jesus to get what he thought was his legitimate share of the inheritance. He was probably banking on the moral authority that Jesus has acquired on the course of His ministry. But Jesus will not be simply dragged to an internal conflict between family members. Rather, He pointed to the root cause of the problem which is greed. Things would not have reached this point between the brothers had fairness governed their lives. And so Jesus told them what should be their true preoccupation first. They must grow rich before God by doing good. If such is the case, no problem of this sort will crop up. The heart will automatically do what is just and fair.

Tuesday

Ps 85:9ab–10, 11–12, 13–14
The Lord speaks of peace
to his people.

21
OCTOBER

1st Reading: Eph 2:12–22

Brothers and sisters: At that time, you were without Christ, you did not belong to the community of Israel; the Covenants of God, and his promises, were not for you; you had no hope, and were without God in this world. But now, in Christ Jesus, and by his blood, you, who were once far off, have come near.

For Christ is our peace; he, who has made the two people, one; destroying, in his own flesh, the wall—the hatred—which separated us. He abolished the law, with its commands and precepts. He made peace, in uniting the two people, in him; creating, out of the two, one New Man. He destroyed hatred and reconciled us both to God, through the cross, making the two, one body.

He came to proclaim peace; peace to you who were far off, peace to the Jews who were near. Through him, we—the two people—approach the Father, in one Spirit.

Now, you are no longer strangers or guests, but fellow citizens of the holy people: you are of the household of God. You are the house, whose foundations are the apostles and prophets, and whose cornerstone is Christ Jesus. In him, the whole structure is joined together, and rises, to be a holy temple, in the Lord. In him, you, too, are being built, to become the spiritual Sanctuary of God.

Gospel: Lk 12:35–38

Jesus said to his disciples, "Be ready, dressed for service, and keep your lamps lit, like people waiting for their master to return from the wedding. As soon as he comes and knocks, they will open the door to him. Happy are those servants whom the master finds wide-awake when he comes. Truly, I tell you, he will put on an apron, and have them sit at table, and he will wait on them. Happy are those servants, if he finds them awake when he comes at midnight or daybreak!"

During the early Christian community, people had this sense of alertness with regard to the second coming of Jesus. They lived in an apocalyptic time. That is why what they did and said was geared towards preparation for the coming of the Lord. But this sense has left us now. After more than two thousand years of waiting, we have lost this urgency and spiritual preparedness when the Master comes. Today, the Gospel reminds us that whether the Master's coming is near or not, we still have to be ready. This readiness should not be borne out of fear but of genuine love for the Master. Fear only makes us anxious and afraid, while love bestows the quality of joy in what we do because we have been always prepared. May we be prompt and proud when the Lord calls on us on the Last Day.

22
OCTOBER

Wednesday
29TH WEEK IN ORDINARY TIME
Psalter: Week 1 / (Green)

Is 12:2–3, 4bcd, 5–6
You will draw water joyfully
from the springs of salvation.

1st Reading: Eph 3:2–12*

You may have heard of the graces God bestowed on me, for your sake. By a revelation, he gave me the knowledge of his mysterious design, as I have explained in a few words. On reading them, you will have some idea of how I understand the mystery of Christ. This mystery was not made known to past generations, but only now, through revelations, given to holy apostles and prophets, by the Spirit. (…) This is the Good News, of which I have become minister, by a gift of God; a grace he gave me, when his power worked in me. This grace, was given to me, the least, among all the holy ones: to announce to the pagan nations, the immeasurable riches of Christ, and to make clear to all, how the mystery, hidden from the beginning, in God, the Creator of all things, is to be fulfilled. (…)

Gospel: Lk 12:39–48

Jesus said to his disciples, "Pay attention to this: If the master of the house had known at what time the thief would come, he would not have let his house be broken into. You also must be ready, for the Son of Man will come at an hour you do not expect."

Peter said, "Lord, did you tell this parable only for us, or for everyone?" And the Lord replied, "Imagine, then, the wise and faithful steward, whom the master sets over his other servants, to give them wheat at the proper time. Fortunate is this servant if his master, on coming home, finds him doing his work. Truly, I say to you, the master will put him in charge of all his property.

"But it may be that the steward thinks, 'My Lord delays in coming,' and he begins to abuse the male servants and the servant girls, eating and drinking and getting drunk. Then the master will come on a day he does not expect, and at an hour he doesn't know. He will cut him off, and send him to the same fate as the unfaithful.

"The servant who knew his master's will, but did not prepare and do what his master wanted, will be soundly beaten; but the one who does unconsciously what deserves punishment, shall receive fewer blows. Much will be required of the one who has been given much, and more will be asked of the one who has been entrusted with more."

It seems that our Gospels nowadays take an apocalyptic turn. No wonder since we are nearing the end of our liturgical calendar when we will celebrate the Christ the King Sunday. It is also the image of the things to come when this age will close and end. It will see the triumph of Jesus as King of heaven and earth. Meanwhile, we are led to think about our state of preparations for the great day. The Gospel also reminds us that we have been told ahead about this coming future. We have no cause to delay. A wise servant must handle his time as if it's the time when the Lord will come again in glory. He is burdened by this advanced knowledge. If he who already knows, yet does not do something to make himself ready, he will be punished more than those who are ignorant. For knowledge is both a blessing and a responsibility. How one uses it will spell the difference between salvation and damnation.

Thursday

Ps 33:1–2, 4–5, 11–12, 18–19
*The earth is full
of the goodness of the Lord.*

23
OCTOBER

St. John of Capistrano

Did you know that: St. John of Capistrano, dubbed as "the Soldier Priest", was married before he joined the Franciscans. He obtained a dispensation from the Pope first.

1st Reading: Eph 3:14–21

Brothers and sisters: And, now, I kneel in the presence of the Father, from whom, every family in heaven and on earth has received its name.

May he strengthen in you, the inner self, through his Spirit, according to the riches of his glory; may Christ dwell in your hearts, through faith; may you be rooted and founded in love.

All of this, so that you may understand, with all the holy ones, the width, the length, the height and the depth—in a word, that you may know the love of Christ, that surpasses all knowledge, that you may be filled, and reach the fullness of God. Glory to God, who shows his power in us, and can do much more than we could ask or imagine; glory to him, in the Church, and in Christ Jesus, through all generations, for ever and ever. Amen.

Gospel: Lk 12:49–53

Jesus said to his disciples, "I have come to bring fire upon the earth, and how I wish it were already kindled! But I have a baptism to undergo, and what anguish I feel until it is finished!

"Do you think that I have come to bring peace on earth? No, I tell you, but rather division. From now on, in one house five will be divided: three against two, and two against three. They will be divided, father against son and son against father; mother against daughter and daughter against mother; mother-in-law against her daughter-in-law, and daughter-in-law against her mother-in-law."

Now the words of Jesus take an ominous turn. What we thought as feel good teachings have now given way to the harsh realities that await those who cling to Jesus. Their lives will not be easy. They will make hard choices because they insist on following Jesus. This reminds us that our discipleship does not come cheap. Sometimes, we have to give up what we most hold dear, our loved ones. Perhaps this is the reason why many are called but few are chosen. We have no courage to pay the price when it is called for. If until now our lives have been beds of roses and no cross has ever rocked our world, then we should question ourselves. The pain of the cross is the clearest sign of our discipleship. Without that we have nothing to boast. May we stand firm in our following of the Lord even when it costs us dearly.

24
OCTOBER

$\mathcal{F}$riday
Ps 24:1–2, 3–4ab, 5–6
Lord, this is the people that longs to see your face.

29TH WEEK IN ORDINARY TIME
St. Anthony Mary Claret, bishop
Psalter: Week 1 / (Green / White)

1st Reading: Eph 4:1–6

$\mathcal{B}$rothers and sisters: Therefore, I, the prisoner of Christ, invite you, to live the vocation you have received. Be humble, kind, patient, and bear with one another in love. Make every effort to keep, among you, the unity of spirit, through bonds of peace. Let there be one body, and one Spirit, just as one hope is the goal of your calling by God.

One Lord, one faith, one baptism; one God, the Father of all, who is above all, and works through all, and is in all.

Gospel: Lk 12:54–59

$\mathcal{J}$esus said to the crowds, "When you see a cloud rising in the west, you say at once, 'A shower is coming'; and so it happens. And when the wind blows from the south, you say, 'It will be hot'; and so it is. You superficial people! You understand the signs of the earth and the sky, but you don't understand the present times. And why do you not judge for yourselves what is fit? When you go with your accuser before the court, try to settle the case on the way, lest he drag you before the judge, and the judge deliver you to the jailer, and the jailer throw you into prison. I tell you, you will not get out until you have paid the very last penny."

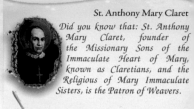

St. Anthony Mary Claret

Did you know that: St. Anthony Mary Claret, founder of the Missionary Sons of the Immaculate Heart of Mary, known as Claretians, and the Religious of Mary Immaculate Sisters, is the Patron of Weavers.

Today we celebrate a great saint, Anthony Mary Claret. Well, all saints are great by virtue of their holiness. Claret is just one among the many who witnessed to the transforming power of the Gospel when taken to heart in one's own life. But he can serve as a model on how we can be attentive to the signs of the times and act accordingly. He was not contented with doing the usual. He saw the great need of the church of his time and responded by his example of a holy life, his writings and sermons, his pastoral sensitivity as a bishop and finally his being a founder of a congregation whose sons would be (and are) at the forefront of combat between good and evil. Written by his own hands his life story can teach us a lot on how to be attentive to God's signs and act accordingly. We are not groping in the dark because others have gone ahead of us and have faced these problems squarely. The saints of God are our friends and guides.

Saturday

25 OCTOBER

Ps 122:1–2, 3–4ab, 4cd–5
Let us go rejoicing to the house
of the Lord.

1st Reading: Eph 4:7–16

Brothers and sisters: But to each of us, divine grace is given, according to the measure of Christ's gift. Therefore, it is said: *When he ascended to the heights, he brought captives and gave his gifts to people.*

He ascended, what does it mean, but, that he had also descended to the lower parts of the world? He, himself, who went down, then ascended far above all the heavens, to fill all things. As for his gifts, to some, he gave to be apostles; to others, prophets, or even evangelists; or pastors and teachers. So, he prepared those who belong to him, for the ministry, in order to build up the Body of Christ, until we are all united, in the same faith and knowledge of the Son of God. Thus, we shall become the perfect Man, upon reaching maturity, and sharing the fullness of Christ.

Then, no longer shall we be like children, tossed about by any wave, or wind of doctrine; and deceived by the cunning of people, who drag them along into error. Rather, speaking the truth, in love, we shall grow in every way, toward him, who is the head, Christ. From him, comes the growth of the whole body, to which a network of joints gives order and cohesion, taking into account, and making use of, the function of each one. So, the body builds itself, in love.

Gospel: Lk 13:1–9

One day, some people told Jesus what had occurred in the temple: Pilate had had Galileans killed, and their blood mingled with the blood of their sacrifices. Jesus asked them, "Do you think that these Galileans were worse sinners than all other Galileans, because they suffered this? No, I tell you. But unless you change your ways, you will all perish, as they did.

"And those eighteen persons in Siloah, who were crushed when the tower fell, do you think they were more guilty than all the others in Jerusalem? I tell you: no. But unless you change your ways, you will all perish, as they did."

And Jesus continued, "A man had a fig tree growing in his vineyard, and he came looking for fruit on it, but found none. Then he said to the gardener, 'Look here, for three years now I have been looking for figs on this tree, and I have found none. Cut it down, why should it continue to deplete the soil?' The gardener replied, 'Leave it one more year, so that I may dig around it and add some fertilizer; perhaps it will bear fruit from now on. But if it doesn't, you can cut it down.'"

Bad things happen to people not necessarily because they have done badly themselves. It is not a just dessert for some wrongs they did in the past. More often than not, they are just casualties of the evil done by others. They are the countless, nameless collateral damages of the bad deeds of some. In this case, we cannot blame God for the intentional evil done by our fellow human beings. We might accuse Him of not lifting a finger to stop them but who can dictate on God? He has His freedom to act or not and we cannot infringe on this radical freedom which He Himself allows us to have. We can only start with ourselves and make a thorough review whether we have used this freedom for the good or have ourselves contributed to the spiral of evil that happens in this world? Let the fruit of goodness blossom in our lives and perhaps, we will make our world a less evil place to live in.

1st Reading: Ex 22:20–26

Thus says Yahweh: You shall not wrong or oppress a stranger, for you were strangers in the land of Egypt. You shall not harm the widow or the orphan. If you do harm them and they cry out to me, I will hear them and my anger will blaze and I will kill you with the sword, and your own wives will be widows and your own children orphans.

If you lend money to any of my people who are poor, do not act like a moneylender and do not charge him interest.

If ever you take a person's cloak as a pledge, you must give it back to him by sunset, for it is all the covering he has for his body. In what else will he sleep? And when he cries to me I will hear him, for I am full of pity.

2nd Reading: 1 Thes 1:5c–10

Brothers and sisters: You, also, know how we dealt with you, for your sake. In return, you became followers of us, and of the Lord, when, on receiving the word, you experienced the joy of the Holy Spirit, in the midst of great opposition. And you became a model for the faithful of Macedonia and Achaia, since, from you, the word of the Lord spread to Macedonia and Achaia, and still farther. The faith you have in God has become news in so many places, that we need say no more about it. Others tell, of how you welcomed us, and turned from idols, to the Lord. For you serve the living and true God, and you wait for his Son, from heaven, whom he raised from the dead, Jesus, who frees us from impending trial.

Gospel: Mt 22:34–40

When the Pharisees heard how Jesus had silenced the Sadducees, they came together. One of them, a teacher of the Law, tried to test him with this question, "Teacher, which is the most important commandment in the Law?"

Jesus answered, "You shall love the Lord, your God, with all your heart, with all your soul and with all your mind. This is the first and the most important of the commandments. But after this there is another one very similar to it: You shall love your neighbor as yourself. The whole Law and the Prophets are founded on these two commandments."

Reading: The religious authorities in Jesus' time took turns trying to test and trap Jesus so as to dispose of Him. This time, they ask Him a religious question regarding the Law that has political implications which they might use against Him. But Jesus answered them with a principle that is equally valid be it in the religious or civil sphere. The Law of Love is the foundation of divine and human laws.

Reflection: Questions are meant to clarify and enhance one's understanding of the truth. But in the hands of enemies, it becomes a deadly weapon that can unmake the target of such malicious question. The religious authorities took turns in trapping Jesus with questions that may appear innocent but are deadly traps. It is a difficult time for the Lord and for His disciples. But the best defense against such line of questioning is no other than the truth itself. And Jesus sticks to the truth no matter what. It may offend the religious and civil authorities but the truth can withstand any form of scrutiny. The more the opponents of Jesus waylay Him with traps, the more He unmasks their hypocrisy by the truth that He brings. No wonder they had to kill Him. In this world, the truth will always and forever be lonely.

Response: Do I have the courage to stand up for the truth? How many times have I chosen to be silent rather than stand up for what is right when it will inconvenience me? A cowardly or an indifferent life is hardly a life worth living. Today I decide to make a stand for the truth and will act on it accordingly.

_____

_____

_____

_____

_____

_____

_____

27
OCTOBER

Monday
Ps 1:1–2, 3, 4 & 6
Behave like God
as his very dear children.

30TH WEEK IN ORDINARY TIME
Psalter: Week 2 / (Green)

1st Reading: Eph 4:32 – 5:8

Brothers and sisters: Be good and understanding, forgiving one another, as God forgave you, in Christ.

As most beloved children of God, strive to imitate him. Follow the way of love, the example of Christ, who loved you. He gave himself up for us, and became the offering and sacrificial victim, whose fragrance rises to God. And, since you are holy, there must not be among you, even a hint of sexual immorality, or greed, or any kind of impurity: these should not be named among you. So, too, for scandalous words, nonsense and foolishness, which are not fitting; instead, offer thanksgiving to God.

Know this: no depraved, impure, or covetous person, who serves the god 'Money,' shall have part in the kingdom of Christ and of God. Let no one deceive you with empty arguments, for these are the sins which God is about to condemn in people, who do not obey. Do not associate with such people. You were once darkness, but, now, you are light, in the Lord. Behave as children of light.

Gospel: Lk 13:10–17

Jesus was teaching in a synagogue on the Sabbath, and a crippled woman was there. An evil spirit had kept her bent for eighteen years, so that she could not straighten up at all. On seeing her, Jesus called her and said, "Woman, you are freed from your infirmity." Then he laid his hands upon her, and immediately she was made straight and praised God.

But the ruler of the synagogue was indignant, because Jesus had performed this healing on the Sabbath day, and he said to the people, "There are six days in which to work. Come on those days to be healed, and not on the Sabbath!"

But the Lord replied, "You hypocrites! Everyone of you unties his ox or his donkey on the Sabbath, and leads it out of the barn to give it water. And here you have a daughter of Abraham, whom Satan had bound for eighteen years. Should she not be freed from her bonds on the Sabbath?"

When Jesus said this, all his opponents felt ashamed. But the people rejoiced at the many wonderful things that happened because of him.

During the many times Jesus ruffled the feathers of the religious authorities, it was always about His healing of the sick during Sabbath, supposed to be a holy day where goodness is the supreme rule. Yet the religious customs and traditions nurtured by the spiritual elite rendered the day sterile and mournful. Even the basic impulse of human compassion was stifled in favor of the observance of the man-made laws and regulations. This kind of religious despotism did not sit well with Jesus. It is true that religion in one of its root meanings *"religare"* means to "bind." But it is a binding to a yoke that is easy and light. It is a bind that frees and not oppresses. And so Jesus let loose the liberating power of the Sabbath, that is, to give the woman the rest she craved from the oppression of her sickness of eighteen years. That day was truly Sabbath for her. She gained rest by the love of Jesus that does not rest in doing good.

FEAST OF STS. SIMON & JUDE, APOSTLES

Psalter: Proper / (Red)

Tuesday

Ps 19:2-3, 4-5
Their message goes out through all the earth.

28

OCTOBER

1st Reading: Eph 2:19-22

Brothers and sisters: Now, you are no longer strangers or guests, but fellow citizens of the holy people: you are of the household of God. You are the house, whose foundations are the apostles and prophets, and whose cornerstone is Christ Jesus. In him, the whole structure is joined together, and rises, to be a holy temple, in the Lord. In him, you, too, are being built, to become the spiritual Sanctuary of God.

Gospel: Lk 6:12-16

Jesus went out into the hills to pray, spending the whole night in prayer with God. When day came, he called his disciples to him, and chose Twelve of them, whom he called 'apostles': Simon, whom he named Peter, and his brother Andrew; James and John; Philip and Bartholomew; Matthew and Thomas; James son of Alpheus and Simon called the Zealot; Judas son of James, and Judas Iscariot, who would be the traitor.

There are major decisions in our lives that are sometimes heavy for us to bear alone. And so we resort to prayer, communing with God hoping that He will be with us when we finally make our choice. In the case of Jesus, this is not something added as an afterthought. Prayer always preceded His major decisions in life. In today's Gospel, Jesus is about to choose from among His disciples those who will be His closest collaborators. He needs to talk with His Father. This is clearly a big decision to make. But even with prayer, Jesus still made a mistake in the person of Judas Iscariot. This reminds us that things do not always go our way even if we have prayed over it. They have a purpose that we don't know. Surprises in life occur and we have to be ready. May our faith be big enough to accept when things go contrary to what we desire.

29
OCTOBER

Wednesday
Ps 145:10–11, 12–13ab, 13cd–14
The Lord is faithful
in all his words.

30TH WEEK IN ORDINARY TIME
Psalter: Week 2 / (Green)

1st Reading: Eph 6:1–9

Children, obey your parents, for, this is right: Honor your father and your mother. And this is the first commandment that has a promise: that you may be happy and enjoy long life in the land. And you, fathers, do not make rebels of your children, but educate them, by correction and instruction, which the Lord may inspire. Servants, obey your masters of this world with fear and respect, with simplicity of heart, as if obeying Christ. Do not serve, only when you are watched, or in order to please others, but become servants of Christ, who do God's will, with all your heart. Work willingly, for the Lord, and not for humans, mindful that the good each one has done, whether servant or free, will be rewarded by the Lord. And you, masters, deal with your servants in the same way, and do not threaten them, since you know that they, and you, have the same Lord, who is in heaven, and he treats all fairly.

Gospel: Lk 13:22–30

Jesus went through towns and villages teaching, and making his way to Jerusalem. Someone asked him, "Lord, is it true that few people will be saved?"

And Jesus answered, "Do your best to enter by the narrow door; for many, I tell you, will try to enter and will not be able. When once the master of the house has gone inside and locked the door, you will stand outside. Then you will knock at the door, calling, 'Lord, open to us!' But he will say to you, 'I do not know where you come from.'

"Then you will say, 'We ate and drank with you, and you taught in our streets!' But he will reply, 'I don't know where you come from. Away from me, all you workers of evil.'

"You will weep and grind your teeth, when you see Abraham, Isaac, and Jacob and all the prophets in the kingdom of God, and you yourselves left outside. Others will sit at table in the kingdom of God, people coming from east and west, from north and south. Some who are among the last, will be first; and some who are among the first, will be last!"

There is a time in our life when we preoccupy ourselves with eternity. This is true especially for those who feel their mortality slowly creeping in. They will therefore try to prepare provisions for their journey in the afterlife. This kind of preparation is consciously willed. Also, it is vulnerable to the surprise of sudden death where preparations made might not be enough to merit heaven. Thus Jesus' injunction to enter the narrow road is a better alternative. It's "very narrowness" will force us to think what are the truly essentials worth keeping so we may fit in its narrow frame and pass through. We need not prepare for heaven. The very choice we make of entering through the narrow gate will make us worthy of it.

Thursday

Ps 144:1b, 2, 9–10
Blessed be the Lord, my Rock!

30
OCTOBER

1st Reading: Eph 6:10–20

Brothers and sisters: Finally, be strong in the Lord, with his energy and strength. Put on the whole armor of God, to be able to resist the cunning of the devil. Our battle is not against human forces, but against the rulers and authorities and their dark powers, that govern this world. We are struggling against the spirits and supernatural forces of evil.

Therefore, put on the whole armor of God, that, in the evil day, you may resist, and stand your ground, making use of all your weapons. Take truth as your belt, justice as your breastplate, and zeal as your shoes, to propagate the Gospel of peace. Always hold in your hand, the shield of faith, to repel the flaming arrows of the devil. Finally, use the helmet of salvation, and the sword of the Spirit, that is, the word of God.

Pray, at all times, as the Spirit inspires you. Keep watch, together with sustained prayer and supplication for all the holy ones. Pray, also, for me, so that when I speak, I may be given words, to proclaim bravely, the mystery of the Gospel. Even when in chains, I am an ambassador of God; may he give me the strength to speak as I should.

Gospel: Lk 13:31–35

At that time some Pharisees came to Jesus and gave him this warning, "Leave this place and go on your way, for Herod wants to kill you." Jesus said to them, "Go and give that fox my answer: 'I drive out demons, and I heal today and tomorrow, and on the third day I finish my course!' Nevertheless, I must go on my way today, and tomorrow, and for a little longer; for it would not be fitting for a prophet to be killed outside Jerusalem.

"O Jerusalem, Jerusalem, you slay the prophets and stone those who are sent to you! How often have I tried to bring together your children, as a bird gathers her young under her wings. But you refused! From now on, *you will be left, with your temple.* And you will no longer see me until the time when you will say, *Blessed is he who comes in the name of the Lord!*"

At this point in time, the religious leaders who are out to destroy Jesus play the political card. They could not best Jesus on religious ground. He is always one step wiser than them, demolishing their arguments with aplomb. And so they have to drag their hostility towards the political front. After all, Jesus has no connections with anyone in power. He will surely be cowed and intimidated by their political clout. This was their mistake. Jesus did not come to please anyone except His Father, the ruler and governor of the universe. A mere Herod, king of Israel could not instill fear on Him. And so He dared to call Herod names that would surely fan his anger. He will not back out from this confrontation. Jesus shows courage that is not one of reckless abandon. He places His feet where His mouth is.

Friday

Ps 111:1–2, 3–4, 5–6
How great are the works
of the Lord!

30TH WEEK IN ORDINARY TIME
Psalter: Week 2 / (Green)

1st Reading: Phil 1:1–11

From Paul and Timothy, servants of Christ Jesus, to the saints in Philippi, with their bishops and deacons; to you all in Christ Jesus: May grace and peace be yours from God, our Father, and Christ Jesus the Lord.

I give thanks to my God, each time I remember you, and when I pray for you, I pray with joy. I cannot forget all you shared with me in the service of the Gospel, from the first day, until now. Since God began such a good work, in you, I am certain, that he will complete it in the day of Christ Jesus.

This is my hope for you, for I carry you all, in my heart: whether I am in prison, or defending and confirming the Gospel, you are with me and share the same grace.

God knows, that I love you dearly, with the love of Christ Jesus, and in my prayers, I ask that your love may lead you, each day, to a deeper knowledge and clearer discernment, that you may have good criteria for everything. So you may be pure of heart, and come, blameless, to the day of Christ, filled with the fruit of holiness, that comes through Christ Jesus, for the glory and praise of God.

Gospel: Lk 14:1–6

One Sabbath Jesus had gone to eat a meal in the house of a leading Pharisee, and he was carefully watched. In front of him was a man suffering from dropsy; so Jesus asked the teachers of the law and the Pharisees, "Is it lawful to heal on the Sabbath, or not?" But no one answered. Jesus then took the man, healed him, and sent him away. And he said to them, "If your lamb or your ox falls into a well on a Sabbath day, who among you doesn't hurry to pull it out?" And they could not answer.

We feel uneasy when we are watched. Our movements become stilted and our words guarded. We are not free. Jesus feels the same way too, probably right here in this Gospel. Yet He did not allow this feeling to overpower His love for those who are needy. He would not be constrained by others' careful watching. He will do what is the right thing to do even if others do not approve. And so, Jesus has to disappoint again His self-appointed guardians. He tried to expand their horizons by freeing them from the confines of their legalistic frame of mind. He has better luck with the man afflicted by dropsy. The teachers of the Law and the Pharisees are cases very hard to cure.

SOLEMNITY OF ALL SAINTS (ALL SAINTS' DAY)

Psalter: Proper / (White)

Saturday

Ps 24:1–2, 3–4, 5–6
Lord, this is the people
that longs to see your face.

01 NOVEMBER

1st Reading: Rev 7:2–4, 9–14*

I saw another angel, ascending from the sunrise, carrying the seal of the living God, and he cried out with a loud voice, to the four angels empowered to harm the earth and the sea, "Do not harm the earth or the sea or the trees, until we have sealed the servants of our God upon their foreheads." (…)

After this, I saw a great crowd, impossible to count, from every nation, race, people and tongue, standing before the throne, and the Lamb, clothed in white, with palm branches in their hands, and they cried out with a loud voice, "Who saves, but our God, who sits on the throne, and the Lamb?" (…) At that moment, one of the elders spoke up, and said to me, "Who are these people clothed in white, and where did they come from?" I answered, "Sir, it is you who know this." The elder replied, "They, are those who have come out of the great persecution; they have washed, and made their clothes white, in the blood of the Lamb.

2nd Reading: 1 Jn 3:1–3

Gospel: Mt 5:1–12a

When Jesus saw the crowds, he went up the mountain. He sat down and his disciples gathered around him. Then he spoke and began to teach them:

"Fortunate are those who are poor in spirit, for theirs is the kingdom of heaven. Fortunate are those who mourn; they shall be comforted. Fortunate are the gentle; they shall possess the land. Fortunate are those who hunger and thirst for justice, for they shall be satisfied.

"Fortunate are the merciful, for they shall find mercy. Fortunate are those with pure hearts, for they shall see God. Fortunate are those who work for peace; they shall be called children of God. Fortunate are those who are persecuted for the cause of righteousness, for theirs is the kingdom of heaven.

"Fortunate are you, when people insult you and persecute you and speak all kinds of evil against you because you are my followers. Be glad and joyful, for a great reward is kept for you in God."

Indeed fortunate are those who cling to God despite hardships and difficulties in this world. Their reward is assured in heaven. That is why we celebrate today the feast of all saints. These are the countless people who silently observed God's word in their lives and died in the odor of sanctity unknown to the world. They didn't need such recognition anyway. They have the better prize... heaven. In a world bent on trivializing the afterlife and robbing us of our hope of a better future, today's celebration reminds us that no matter how much heaven is being denied, we believe that there are people who have gone there. They may be nameless but we celebrate their good fate here on earth. And so candles and flowers have the right to take center stage today. We celebrate that which we hope we ourselves will achieve someday.

02
NOVEMBER

Sunday

Ps 23:1–3, 3–4, 5, 6
The Lord is my shepherd,
there is nothing I shall want.

1st Reading: Wis 3:1–9

The souls of the just are in the hands of God and no torment shall touch them. In the eyes of the unwise they appear to be dead. Their going is held as a disaster; it seems that they lose everything by departing from us, but they are in peace.

Though seemingly they have been punished, immortality was the soul of their hope. After slight affliction will come great blessings, for God has tried them and found them worthy to be with him; after testing them as gold in the furnace, he has accepted them as a holocaust.

At the time of his coming they will shine like sparks that run in the stubble. They will govern nations and rule over peoples, and the Lord will be their king forever.

Those who trust in him will penetrate the truth, those who are faithful will live with him in love, for his grace and mercy are for his chosen ones.

2nd Reading: Rom 6:3–9

Brothers and sisters: Don't you know, that in baptism, which unites us to Christ, we are all baptized and plunged into his death? By this baptism in his death, we were buried with Christ and, as Christ was raised from among the dead by the glory of the Father, we begin walking in a new life. If we have been joined to him by dying a death like his, so shall we be, by a resurrection like his.

We know, that our old self was crucified with Christ, so as to destroy what of us was sin, so that, we may no longer serve sin—if we are dead, we are no longer in debt to sin. But, if we have died with Christ, we believe we will also live with him. We know, that Christ, once risen from the dead, will not die again, and death has no more dominion over him.

Gospel: Mt 25:31–46

Jesus said to his disciples, "When the Son of Man comes in his glory with all his angels, he will sit on the throne of his glory. All the nations will be brought before him; and, as a shepherd separates the sheep from the goats, so will he do with them, placing the sheep on his right hand and the goats on his left.

"The king will say to those on his right, 'Come, blessed of my Father! Take possession of the kingdom prepared for you from the beginning of the world. For I was hungry, and you fed me. I was thirsty, and you gave me something to drink. I was a stranger, and you welcomed me into your home. I was naked, and you clothed me. I was sick, and you visited me. I was in prison, and you came to see me.'

"Then the righteous will ask him, 'Lord, when did we see you hungry, and give you food; thirsty, and give you something to drink; or a stranger, and welcome you; or naked, and clothe you? When did we see you sick, or in prison, and go to see you?' The king will answer, 'Truly I say to you: just as you did it for one of the least of these brothers or sisters of mine, you did it to me.'

"Then he will say to those on his left, 'Go, cursed people, out of my sight, into the eternal fire, which has been prepared for the devil and his angels! For I was hungry, and you did not give me anything to eat; I was thirsty, and you gave me nothing to drink; I was a stranger, and you did not welcome me into your house; I was naked, and you did not clothe me; I was sick, and in prison, and you did not visit me.'

"They, too, will ask, 'Lord, when did we see you hungry, thirsty, naked or a stranger, sick or in prison, and did not help you?' The king will answer them, 'Truly I say to you: just as you did not do it for one of the least of these, you did not do it for me.' And these will go into eternal punishment; but the just, to eternal life."

Reading: Jesus speaks of His glorious coming in the end times. The nations will be judged accordingly and the people will be separated according to their deeds. There will be reward for those who do good while punishment awaits the wicked. The things people do on behalf of the little ones of this earth, will have a great repercussion on judgement day.

Reflection: The small stuff may seem insignificant but in the long run they do matter because they tend to accumulate in time without our knowledge. Our awareness is focused on the big stuff. They are easily seen and could hardly be missed. Transposing this to the moral life, it's the big sin that we are so concerned about and gets attended to first. We are so bothered by it, probably because of its size; whereas we tend to sweep aside our small mistakes, small lapses in charity, our inattention to the needs of others. Our Gospel today reminds us that we cannot take the small things for granted. They can make or break our fate in the future.

Response: We may pass them by unaware of their hopeful stare that we might extend charity to their plight. We may have given our share of help without being mindful about it. Why not get to know these "little ones", the recipients of our help and make them feel that you see them as human persons. This will surely lighten their otherwise bleak and heavy day.

03
NOVEMBER

Monday

Ps 131:1bcde, 2, 3
In you, O Lord,
I have found my peace.

31ST WEEK IN ORDINARY TIME
St. Martin de Porres, religious
Psalter: Week 3 / (Green / White)

1st Reading: Phil 2:1–4

Brothers and sisters: If I may advise you, in the name of Christ, and if you can hear it, as the voice of love; if we share the same Spirit, and are capable of mercy and compassion, then I beg of you, make me very happy: have one love, one spirit, one feeling, do nothing through rivalry or vain conceit. On the contrary, let each of you gently consider the others, as more important than yourselves. Do not seek your own interest, but, rather, that of others.

Gospel: Lk 14:12–14

Jesus addressed the man who had invited him, and said, "When you give a lunch or a dinner, don't invite your friends, or your brothers and relatives, or your wealthy neighbors. For surely they will also invite you in return, and you will be repaid. When you give a feast, invite instead the poor, the crippled, the lame and the blind. Fortunate are you then, because they cannot repay you. You will be repaid at the resurrection of the upright."

St. Martin de Porres

Did you know that: St. Martin de Porres wanted badly to become a missionary but never left his hometown. Yet, even during his lifetime, many claimed to have seen him elsewhere as far as Africa, China, Peru, etc.

It is customary to show politeness to the host who invites us to their house. We refrain from giving suggestions until we have established a level of comfort that allows such privilege. We usually compliment their hospitality and honor it with an invitation to our house in return. But Jesus brings this dynamics onto a higher level. He not only says what he wants to say but suggests that the return invitation must be shunned in favor of a future payment for the upright of heart. In the Gospel, Jesus is not being cunning or stingy. He is not thinking of the cost when He will return the invitation of His host. Rather He is thinking of the blessings his host will receive if he gets to know the secret of generosity that does not seek to be repaid. If the host will understand it in human terms, he will be angry and feel insulted. But if he discerns the implication of Jesus' word, the chance for immortality will be opened wide for him on that day.

31ST WEEK IN ORDINARY TIME
St. Charles Borromeo, bishop
Psalter: Week 3 / (White)

Tuesday

04
NOVEMBER

Ps 22:26b–27, 28–30ab, 30e, 31–32
I will praise you, Lord,
in the assembly of your people.

St. Charles Borromeo

Did you know that: St. Charles Borromeo was the nephew of Pope Pius IV and the one of the only two cardinal-nephews to have been canonized.

_____
_____
_____
_____
_____
_____
_____
_____
_____
_____
_____

Jesus is in a meal setting; the atmosphere is convivial. Everyone is in a good frame of mind after a good meal and the exchange is lighthearted. It is in this context that one of the guests exclaimed about the bliss enjoyed by those who will be eating in the banquet of God. He has a basis. Probably everyone was happy around the table that day sharing the meal with Jesus. Then the harsh truth of the banquet in the Kingdom of God is revealed. It is intended for those invited but they will pass on the chance because they are too busy with their own concerns. Thus others will have a chance and they will respond to the invitation with the openness of those grateful for the opportunity given. And so silence will follow when understanding dawns on those around Jesus. For Jesus' company is fun only to those who are open to His word.

1st Reading: Phil 2:5–11

Brothers and sisters: Your attitude should be the same as Jesus Christ had: Though he was in the form of God, he did not regard equality with God as something to be grasped, but emptied himself, taking on the nature of a servant, made in human likeness, and, in his appearance, found, as a man, He humbled himself by being obedient, to death, death on the cross.

That is why God exalted him and gave him the Name which outshines all names, so, that, at the Name of Jesus all knees should bend in heaven, on earth and among the dead, and all tongues proclaim, that Christ Jesus is the Lord, to the glory of God the Father.

Gospel: Lk 14:15–24

One of those at the table said to Jesus, "Happy are those who eat at the banquet in the kingdom of God!"

Jesus replied, "A man once gave a feast and invited many guests. When it was time for the feast, he sent his servant to tell those he had invited to come, for everything was ready. But all alike began to make excuses. The first said, 'Please excuse me. I must go and see the piece of land I have just bought.' Another said: 'I am sorry, but I am on my way to try out the five yoke of oxen I have just bought.' Still another said, 'How can I come, when I've just got married?

"The servant returned alone, and reported this to his master. Upon hearing his account, the master of the house flew into a rage, and ordered his servant, 'Go out quickly, into the streets and alleys of the town, and bring in the poor, the crippled, the blind and the lame.'

"The servant reported after a while, 'Sir, your orders have been carried out, but there is still room.' The master said, 'Go out to the highways and country lanes, and force people to come in, to ensure that my house is full. I tell you, none of those invited will have a morsel of my feast.'"

05
NOVEMBER

Wednesday
Ps 27:1, 4, 13–14
The Lord is my light
and my salvation.

31ST WEEK IN ORDINARY TIME
Psalter: Week 3 / (Green)

1st Reading: Phil 2:12–18

Therefore, my dearest friends, as you always obeyed me while I was with you, even more, now, that I am far from you, continue working out your salvation "with fear and trembling." It is God who makes you, not only wish but also, carry out what pleases him. Do everything without grumbling, so, that, without fault or blame, you will be children of God, without reproach, among a crooked and perverse generation. You are a light among them, like stars in the universe, holding to the word of life. I shall feel proud of you, on the day of Christ, on seeing that my effort and labor have not been in vain. And if I am being poured out, as a libation over the sacrifice, and the offering of your faith, I rejoice and continue to share your joy; and, you, likewise should rejoice and share my joy.

Gospel: Lk 14:25–33

One day, when large crowds were walking along with Jesus, he turned and said to them, "If you come to me, unwilling to sacrifice your love for your father and mother, your spouse and children, your brothers and sisters, and indeed yourself, you cannot be my disciple. Whoever does not follow me, carrying his own cross, cannot be my disciple.

"Do you build a house without first sitting down to count the cost, to see whether you have enough to complete it? Otherwise, if you, have laid the foundation and are not able to finish it, everyone will make fun of you: 'This fellow began to build and was not able to finish.

"And when a king wages war against another king, does he go to fight without first sitting down to consider whether his ten thousand can stand against the twenty thousand of his opponent? And if not, while the other is still a long way off, he sends messengers for peace talks. In the same way, none of you may become my disciple, if he doesn't give up everything he has."

Following the Lord may seem romantic as an ideal but it involves real cost. You have to be ready to give up everything for Him. And so He counsels His would-be followers to sit down first and determine whether they can pay the price of discipleship without flinching. One has to be ready to give all or not bother at all. For to follow the Lord half-heartedly will only waste the efforts made thus far. It is here therefore that the injunction to love the Lord with all our heart, with all our mind and with all our being (Deut. 6,5) becomes clear. If we do this, the crosses that come our way will have its proper place. Even our sacrifices will have meaning. We will not be daunted. We will understand it as part of discipleship.

Thursday

Ps 105:2–3, 4–5, 6–7
Let hearts rejoice
who search for the Lord.

06
NOVEMBER

1st Reading: Phil 3:3–8a

Brothers and sisters: We are the true circumcised people, since we serve according to the Spirit of God, and our confidence is in Christ Jesus, rather than in our merits.

I, myself, do not lack those human qualities in which people have confidence. If some of them seem to be accredited with such qualities, how much more am I! I was circumcised when eight days old. I was born of the race of Israel, of the tribe of Benjamin; I am a Hebrew, born of Hebrews. With regard to the law, I am a Pharisee, and such was my zeal for the law that I persecuted the Church. As for being righteous according to the law, I was blameless.

But once I found Christ, all those things that I might have considered as profit, I reckoned as loss. Still more, everything seems to me, as nothing, compared with the knowledge of Christ Jesus, my Lord.

Gospel: Lk 15:1–10

Meanwhile tax collectors and sinners were seeking the company of Jesus, all of them eager to hear what he had to say. But the Pharisees and the teachers of the law frowned at this, muttering, "This man welcomes sinners and eats with them." So Jesus told them this parable:

"Who among you, having a hundred sheep and losing one of them, will not leave the ninety-nine in the wilderness, and seek the lost one till he finds it? And finding it, will he not joyfully carry it home on his shoulders? Then he will call his friends and neighbors together, and say, 'Celebrate with me, for I have found my lost sheep!' I tell you, in the same way, there will be more rejoicing in heaven over one repentant sinner, than over ninety-nine decent people, who do not need to repent.

"What woman, if she has ten silver coins and loses one, will not light a lamp, and sweep the house in a thorough search, till she finds the lost coin? And finding it, she will call her friends and neighbors, and say, 'Celebrate with me, for I have found the silver coin I lost!' I tell you, in the same way, there is rejoicing among the angels of God over one repentant sinner."

Those viewed as conventional sinners are not all bad. Some have had the misfortune to belong to such company but they too had the desire for redemption. That is why tax collectors and sinners were seeking Jesus. They had found somebody who did not condemn them outrightly but listened, comforted and led them towards genuine repentance. There was someone who was willing to give them a second chance. This tenderness displayed by Jesus towards sinners ought to remind us that love is the best incentive for those who go astray to return to the fold of God. It is mercy that they want and not harsh condemnation.

07
NOVEMBER

Friday
Ps 122:1–2, 3–4ab, 4cd–5
Let us go rejoicing
to the house of the Lord.

31ST WEEK IN ORDINARY TIME
Psalter: Week 3 / (Green)

1st Reading: Phil 3:17 – 4:1

Unite in imitating me, brothers and sisters, and look at those who walk in our way of life. For many live as enemies of the cross of Christ. I have said it to you many times, and now I repeat it with tears: they are heading for ruin; their belly is their god, and they feel proud of what should be their shame. They only think of earthly things. For us, our citizenship is in heaven, from where we await the coming of our Savior, Jesus Christ, the Lord. He will transfigure our lowly body, making it like his own body, radiant in glory, through the power which is his, to submit everything to himself.

Therefore, my brothers and sisters, whom I love and long for, you, my glory and crown, be steadfast in the Lord.

Gospel: Lk 16:1–8

Jesus told his disciples, "There was a rich man, whose steward was reported to him because of fraudulent service. He summoned the steward and asked him, 'What is this I hear about you? I want you to render an account of your service, for it is about to be terminated.

"The steward thought to himself, 'What am I to do now? My master will surely dismiss me. I am not strong enough to do hard work, and I am ashamed to beg. I know what I will do: I must make sure that when I am dismissed, there will be people who will welcome me into their homes.

"So he called his master's debtors, one by one. He asked the first debtor, 'How much do you owe my master?' The reply was, 'A hundred jars of oil.' The steward said, 'Here is your bill. Sit down quickly and write fifty.' To the second debtor he put the same question, 'How much do you owe?' The answer was, 'A hundred measures of wheat.' Then the steward said, 'Take your bill and write eighty.'

"The master commended the dishonest steward for his astuteness: for the people of this world are more astute, in dealing with their own kind, than are the people of light."

The gospel is cast in the negative. And if one is not discerning, he or she might think that astuteness in the service of deceit is being commended here. On the contrary, what is being presented is the technology of making friends as beneficial and may come in handy when one is in dire need. Thus we are being educated into the ways of surviving for the world to come by doing good to others, making friends and being generous. Although our salvation is a personal quest, still a crowd behind our back would be a great help. These are the people whom we come in contact with along the way and have experienced our kindness and generosity. For even though our salvation is primarily our own concern, it takes a village for one to be saved.

Saturday

Ps 112:1b–2, 5–6, 8a & 9
Blessed the man
who fears the Lord.

08
NOVEMBER

1st Reading: Phil 4:10–19

Brothers and sisters: I rejoice in the Lord because of your concern for me. You were indeed concerned for me before, but you had no opportunity to show it. I do not say this because of being in want; I have learned to manage with what I have. I know what it is to be in want and what it is to have plenty. I am trained for both: to be hungry or satisfied, to have much or little. I can do all things in him who strengthens me.

However, you did right in sharing my trials. You Philippians, remember that, in the beginning, when we first preached the Gospel, after I left Macedonia, you, alone, opened for me a debit and credit account, and when I was in Thessalonica, twice you sent me what I needed.

It is not your gift that I value, but rather, the interest increasing in your own account. Now, I have enough, and more than enough, with everything Epaphroditus brought me, on your behalf, and which I received as "fragrant offerings pleasing to God." God, himself, will provide you with everything you need, according to his riches, and show you his generosity in Christ Jesus.

Gospel: Lk 16:9–15

Jesus said to his disciples, "And so I tell you: use filthy money to make friends for yourselves, so that, when it fails, these people may welcome you into the eternal homes.

"Whoever can be trusted in little things can also be trusted in great ones; whoever is dishonest in slight matters will also be dishonest in greater ones. So if you have been dishonest in handling filthy money, who would entrust you with true wealth? And if you have been dishonest with things that are not really yours, who will give you that wealth which is truly your own?

"No servant can serve two masters. Either he does not like the one and is fond of the other, or he regards one highly and the other with contempt. You cannot give yourself both to God and to Money."

"The Pharisees, who loved money, heard all this and sneered at Jesus. He said to them, "You do your best to be considered righteous by people. But God knows the heart, and what is highly esteemed by human beings is loathed by God."

There is nothing here on earth that cannot be used for eternal life. Consider filthy money in our gospel today. Jesus counsels His hearers to use them to make friends. It may be dirty just as a broom is dirty, but it can sweep clean the way to eternal life. Thus money if used wisely for goodness can be an avenue for salvation. Perhaps Jesus pointed out the positive use of money because this is the easiest commodity that we can give to others. Sometimes we cannot part with our time nor can we share our talents to others because of so many engagements in life. But our money is not hampered by these considerations. It is the easiest to give in our attempts of charity. If we can only master the art of using money for our eternal benefits, we can be sure of a room in God's mansion.

09
NOVEMBER

Sunday

Ps 46:3, 4, 5–6, 8, 11
The waters of the river gladden the city of God, the holy dwelling of the Most High.

1st Reading: Ezk 47:1–2, 8–9, 12

The man brought me back to the entrance of the temple and I saw water coming out from the threshold of the temple and flowing eastward. The temple faced the east and the water flowed from the south side of the temple, from the south side of the altar. He then brought me out through the north gate and led me around the outside, to the outer gate facing the east; and there I saw the stream coming from the south side.

He said to me, "This water goes to the east, down to the Arabah, and when it flows into the sea of foul-smelling water, the water will become wholesome. Wherever the river flows, swarms of creatures will live in it; fish will be plentiful; and the seawater will become fresh. Wherever it flows, life will abound.

Near the river on both banks, there will be all kinds of fruit trees, with foliage that will not wither; and fruit that will never fail; each month they will bear a fresh crop, because the water comes from the temple. The fruit will be good to eat and the leaves will be used for healing.

2nd Reading: 1 Cor 3:9c–11, 16–17

Brothers and sisters: You are God's field and building.

I, as a good architect, according to the capacity given to me, I laid the foundation, and another is to build upon it. Each one must be careful how to build upon it. No one can lay a foundation other than the one which is already laid, which is Jesus Christ.

Do you not know that you are God's temple, and that God's Spirit abides within you? If anyone destroys the temple of God, God will destroy him. God's temple is holy, and you are this temple.

Gospel: Jn 2:13–22

As the Passover of the Jews was at hand, Jesus went up to Jerusalem. In the temple court he found merchants selling oxen, sheep and doves, and money-changers seated at their tables. Making a whip of cords, he drove them all out of the temple court, together with the oxen and sheep. He knocked over the tables of the money-changers, scattering the coins, and ordered the people selling doves, "Take all this away, and stop making a marketplace of my Father's house!"

His disciples recalled the words of Scripture: *Zeal for your house devours me like fire.*

The Jews then questioned Jesus, "Where are the miraculous signs which give you the right to do this?" And Jesus said, "Destroy this temple and in three days I will raise it up." The Jews then replied, "The building of this temple has already taken forty-six years, and will you raise it up in three days?"

Actually, Jesus was referring to the temple of his body. Only when he had risen from the dead did his disciples remember these words; then they believed both the Scripture and the words Jesus had spoken.

Reading: Jesus in this passage did a symbolic cleansing of the Temple from all commercial traffic. The Jews questioned His authority to do so and Jesus' reply was enigmatic. His words gained meaning only in the minds of the disciples after His death and resurrection.

Reflection: It's amazing how our inner self sometimes takes the form of the market. There is so much commercial traffic going on inside us. Even our relationship with God is not spared from these economic transactions. We give God our praise and reverence in exchange for His grace and blessing. Otherwise we withhold our favors if we think we do not get a good bargain. And here comes Jesus who cleans and drives all that defiles our inner sanctuary. It is supposed to be a holy place for it is there that we meet God. Yet it has become a marketplace.

Response: Today I make a list of all my commercial transactions with the Lord; how I try to pay or bribe Him to extend to me particular helps I badly need. And after having written them down, I will demolish them one by one and start afresh with my approach to God.

10
NOVEMBER

Monday
Ps 24:1b–2, 3–4ab, 5–6
Lord, this is the people
that longs to see your face.

32ND **WEEK IN ORDINARY TIME**
St. Leo the Great, pope & doctor
Psalter: Week 4 / (White)

1st Reading: Tit 1:1–9

From Paul, servant of God, apostle of Christ Jesus, at the service of God's chosen people, so that they may believe, and reach the knowledge of truth and godliness.

The eternal life we are waiting for was promised from the very beginning, by God, who never lies, and as the appointed time had come, he made it known, through the message entrusted to me by a command of God, our Savior.

Greetings to you, Titus, my true son in the faith we share. May grace and peace be with you from God the Father and Christ Jesus our Lord.

I left you in Crete because I wanted you to put right, what was defective, and appoint elders in every town, following my instructions. They must be blameless, married only once, whose children are believers, and not open to the charge of being immoral and rebellious. Since the overseer (or bishop) is the steward of God's House, he must be beyond reproach: not proud, hot-headed, over-fond of wine, quarrelsome, or greedy for gain.

On the contrary, he must be hospitable, a lover of what is good, wise, upright, devout and self-controlled. He must hold to the message of faith, just as it was taught, so that, in his turn, he may teach sound doctrine, and refute those who oppose it.

St. Leo the Great

Did you know that: St. Leo the Great is the first pope to be called the "Great" and famously known for persuading Attila the Hun not to invade Italy.

Gospel: Lk 17:1–6

Jesus said to his disciples, "Scandals will necessarily come and cause people to fall; but woe to the one who brings them about. It would be better for him to be thrown into the sea with a millstone around his neck. Truly, this would be better for that person, than to cause one of these little ones to fall.

"Listen carefully: if your brother offends you, tell him, and if he is sorry, forgive him. And if he offends you seven times in one day, but seven times he says to you, 'I'm sorry,' forgive him."

The apostles said to the Lord, "Increase our faith." And the Lord said, "If you have faith, even the size of a mustard seed, you may say to this tree, 'Be uprooted, and plant yourself in the sea!' and it will obey you."

Jesus is a tough act to follow. That is why the disciples ask for an increase in faith for, by their own strengths, they could never fulfill what following the Lord demands. They must not scandalize those who are still weak in the faith and be merciful to erring brothers and sisters. This demands a lot of spiritual strength. We do not always have control of ourselves and the disposition to do good. Our weaknesses sometimes get in the way. And so, the apostles were wise to ask the Lord the one thing that would carry them through. It is only through faith that we can safely navigate the waters of discipleship.

Tuesday

Ps 37:3–4, 8 & 23, 27 & 29
The salvation of the just comes from the Lord.

11
NOVEMBER

St. Martin of Tours

Did you know that: Martin Luther, an important figure of the Protestant Reformation, was named after St. Martin of Tours because he was baptized on the saint's feast day.

1st Reading: Tit 2:1–8, 11–14

Beloved: Let your words strengthen sound doctrine. Tell the older men to be sober, serious, wise, sound in faith, love and perseverance.

The older women, in like manner, must behave as befits holy women, not given to gossiping or drinking wine, but as good counselors, able to teach younger women to love their husbands and children, to be judicious and chaste, to take care of their households, to be kind, and submissive to their husbands, lest our faith be attacked.

Encourage the young men, to be self-controlled. Set them an example by your own way of doing. Let your teaching be earnest and sincere, and your preaching, beyond reproach. Then, your opponents will feel ashamed and will have nothing to criticize.

For the grace of God has appeared, bringing salvation to all, teaching us to reject an irreligious way of life, and worldly greed, and to live in this world, as responsible persons, upright and serving God, while we await our blessed hope—the glorious manifestation of our great God and Savior Christ Jesus. He gave himself for us, to redeem us from every evil, and to purify a people he wanted to be his own, and dedicated to what is good.

Gospel: Lk 17:7–10

Jesus said to the apostles, "Who among you would say to your servant, coming in from the fields after plowing or tending sheep, 'Go ahead and have your dinner'? No, you tell him, 'Prepare my dinner. Put on your apron, and wait on me while I eat and drink. You can eat and drink afterward.' Do you thank this servant for doing what you told him to do? I don't think so. And therefore, when you have done all that you have been told to do, you should say, 'We are no more than servants; we have only done our duty.'"

The world today is mired in an economic transaction mentality. Nothing is done for free. Everything has a corresponding pay whether pecuniary or other forms of payment such as praise, acknowledgement and the likes. This mindset has also crept into the church. Volunteerism and working without reward is slowly dying. That is why the gospel today is a timely reminder of what we ought to be. We are mere servants and we do not expect any rewards for the things we have done. This servanthood mentality also reminds us that we cannot demand from God when we do God's work. There is nothing to boast, for we are only doing what is expected of us. God owes us no debt. It is us however who will owe God if we do not do what we are expected to do as His servants.

12
NOVEMBER

Wednesday

Ps 23:1b–3a, 3bc–4, 5, 6
The Lord is my shepherd;
there is nothing I shall want.

32ND WEEK IN ORDINARY TIME
St. Josaphat, bishop & martyr
Psalter: Week 4 / (Red)

1st Reading: Tit 3:1–7

*B*eloved: Remind the believers, to be submissive to rulers and authorities, to be obedient, and to be ready for every good work. Tell them to insult no one; they must not be quarrelsome, but gentle and understanding with everyone.

We ourselves were once foolish, disobedient and misled. We were slaves of our desires, seeking pleasures of every kind. We lived in malice and envy, hateful, and hating each other. But God, our Savior, revealed his eminent goodness and love for humankind, and saved us, not because of good deeds we may have done, but for the sake of his own mercy, to the water of rebirth and renewal, by the Holy Spirit poured over us through Christ Jesus our Savior, so that, having been justified by his grace, we should become heirs, in hope of eternal life.

Gospel: Lk 17:11–19

*O*n the way to Jerusalem, Jesus passed through Samaria and Galilee, and as he entered a village, ten lepers came to meet him. Keeping their distance, they called to him, "Jesus, Master, have pity on us!" Jesus said to them, "Go, and show yourselves to the priests." Then, as they went on their way, they found they were cured. One of them, as soon as he saw that he was cleansed, turned back, praising God in a loud voice; and throwing himself on his face before Jesus, he gave him thanks. This man was a Samaritan.

Then Jesus asked him, "Were not all ten healed? Where are the other nine? Did none of them decide to return and give praise to God, but this foreigner?" And Jesus said to him, "Stand up and go your way; your faith has saved you."

St. Josaphat

Did you know that: St. Josaphat is the first saint of the Eastern Church to be formally canonized by Rome.

We think of healing in terms of being free from its physical manifestation. We breathe a sigh of relief. Our worries and distress are turned into joy. Yet physical healing is just the first stage of wholeness. The second stage is gratitude and acknowledgment of the Healer who makes us whole. Thus in our gospel today, the only one who was truly healed was the Samaritan leper who returned to thank the Lord. In the process he was not only healed from his physical malady, his spiritual bondage was also lifted through the forgiveness of his sins. The nine others who were healed may have returned to their homes happy, but only one went home joyful.

32ND WEEK IN ORDINARY TIME
St. Frances Xavier Cabrini, virgin
Psalter: Week 4 / (White)

Thursday

Ps 146:7, 8–9a, 9bc–10
Blessed is he whose help
is the God of Jacob.

13
NOVEMBER

St. Frances Xavier Cabrini

Did you know that: St. Frances Xavier Cabrini, an Italian citizen by birth, became the first American citizen canonized.

_____
_____
_____
_____
_____
_____
_____
_____
_____
_____
_____
_____
_____

Our generation loves to quantify things. We are trained to trust only those that can be observed and are accessible to our five senses. Those that are not are relegated to the sides. But this is not a new phenomenon. Even at the time of Jesus, the religious authorities who were supposed to be masters of the "hidden, imperceptible" things were demanding from Jesus the exact time when the Kingdom of God would come. They were so preoccupied with the date, they missed the signs. The greatest of signs that the Kingdom of God is now slowly configured was right in front of them yet they missed it. It is sad that sometimes the very thing we are looking for is the one thing we can't see.

1st Reading: Phlm 7–20

Beloved: I had great satisfaction and comfort on hearing of your charity, because the hearts of the saints have been cheered by you, brother.

Because of this, although in Christ I have the freedom to command what you should do, yet I prefer to request you, in love. The one talking is Paul, the old man, now prisoner for Christ. And my request is on behalf of Onesimus, whose father I have become while I was in prison.

This Onesimus has not been helpful to you, but now he will be helpful, both to you and to me. In returning him to you, I am sending you my own heart. I would have liked to keep him at my side, to serve me, on your behalf, while I am in prison for the Gospel, but I did not want to do anything without your agreement, nor impose a good deed upon you without your free consent.

Perhaps Onesimus has been parted from you for a while so that you may have him back forever, no longer as a slave, but better than a slave. For he is a very dear brother to me, and he will be even dearer to you. And so, because of our friendship, receive him, as if he were I myself. And if he has caused any harm, or owes you anything, charge it to me. I, Paul, write this and sign it with my own hand: I will pay it… without further mention of your debt to me, which is you yourself. So, my brother, please do me this favor, for the Lord's sake. Give me this comfort in Christ.

Gospel: Lk 17:20–25

The Pharisees asked Jesus when the kingdom of God was to come. He answered, "The kingdom of God is not like something you can observe, and say of it, 'Look, here it is!' or 'See, there it is!' for the kingdom of God is within you."

And Jesus said to his disciples, "The time is at hand, when you will long to see one of the glorious days of the Son of Man, but you will not see it. Then people will tell you, 'Look there! Look here!' Do not go with them, do not follow them. As lightning flashes from one end of the sky to the other, so will it be with the Son of Man; but first he must suffer many things, and be rejected by this generation."

14
NOVEMBER

Friday
Ps 119:1, 2, 10, 11, 17, 18
Blessed are they who follow
the law of the Lord!

32ND WEEK IN ORDINARY TIME
Psalter: Week 4 / (Green)

1st Reading: 2 Jn 4–9

I rejoiced greatly on meeting some of your children, who live in accordance with the truth, according to the command we have received from the Father. And now, I ask you, Lady—I write to you, not a new commandment, but that which we had, from the beginning—I ask you: let us love one another.

This is love: to walk according to his commandments. And this is the commandment: that you walk in love, as you have learned from the beginning.

Many deceivers have gone out into the world, people who do not acknowledge that Jesus is the Christ, who came in the flesh. They are impostors and antichrists. Take care of yourselves, that you do not lose the fruit of your labors, but receive a perfect reward. Everyone who goes beyond, and does not remain within the teaching of Christ, does not have God. The one who remains in the teaching, has both the Father and the Son.

Gospel: Lk 17:26–37

Jesus said to his disciples, "As it was in the days of Noah, so will it be on the day the Son of Man comes. In those days people ate and drank and got married; but on the day Noah entered the ark, the flood came and destroyed them all. So it was in the days of Lot: people ate and drank, and bought and sold, and planted and built; but on the day Lot left Sodom, God made fire and sulfur rain down from heaven, which destroyed them all. So will it be on the day the Son of Man is revealed.

"On that day, if you are on the rooftop, don't go down into the house to get your belongings; and if you happen to be in the fields, do not turn back. Remember Lot's wife! Whoever tries to save his life will lose it, but whoever gives his life will be born again.

"I tell you, though two men are sharing the same bed, it might happen that one will be taken, and the other left; though two women are grinding meal together, one might be taken and the other left."

"Then they asked Jesus, "Where will this take place, Lord?" And he answered, "Where the body is, there too will the vultures gather."

Our readings now take an ominous turn. It speaks of the end time and how it will come and catch everyone by surprise. This is not unusual for we are nearing the feast of Christ the King wherein the end time signifies the Kingship of Jesus over all realms of the universe. So the readings remind us to be ever vigilant. This is not to say that we wait with tense expectation. We do what we normally do, and if normal for you means doing God's will, then there is nothing to fear. It is only those who are not prepared who must be concerned.

32ND WEEK IN ORDINARY TIME
St. Albert the Great, bishop & doctor
Psalter: Week 4 / (Green / White)

Saturday

Ps 112:1–2, 3–4, 5–6
Blessed the man
who fears the Lord.

15
NOVEMBER

St. Albert the Great

Did you know that: St. Albert the Great translated, annotated, and publicized the work of Aristotle with the help of his student, St. Thomas Aquinas.

_____
_____
_____
_____
_____
_____
_____
_____
_____
_____
_____
_____

1ˢᵗ Reading: 3 Jn 5–8

*B*eloved, you do well to care for the brothers and sisters as you do. I mean, those coming from other places. They spoke of your charity before the assembled Church. It will be well, to provide them with what they need, to continue their journey, as if you did it for God. In reality, they have set out on the road, for his name without accepting anything from the pagans. We should receive such persons, making ourselves their cooperators in the work of the truth.

Gospel: Lk 18:1–8

*J*esus told his disciples a parable, to show them that they should pray continually, and not lose heart. He said, "In a certain town there was a judge, who neither feared God nor people. In the same town there was a widow, who kept coming to him, saying, 'Defend my rights against my adversary!' For a time he refused, but finally he thought, 'Even though I neither fear God nor care about people, this widow bothers me so much, I will see that she gets justice; then she will stop coming and wearing me out.'"

And Jesus said, "Listen to what the evil judge says. Will God not do justice for his chosen ones, who cry to him day and night, even if he delays in answering them? I tell you, he will speedily do them justice. But, when the Son of Man comes, will he find faith on earth?"

There are things in life that need persistence before they are attained. This is no truer as in the spiritual realm. We have to show tenacity and will as we plead God for graces we need. Our perseverance attests to our conviction that what we pray for is important to us. The time we spend praying for that particular intention also allows us to see the bigger picture: are we asking what is really appropriate for us or do we have to modify our request for that which we truly need. Time therefore has a way of purifying our prayer intentions. This goes to say that the length of time we spend in prayer is not wasted time. It allows us to school ourselves to ask what is appropriate next time.

1st Reading: Pro 31:10–13, 19–20, 30–31

The woman of character, where is she to be found? She is more precious than any jewel. Her husband has complete confidence in her; she will be of great benefit to him.

She brings him only good and not evil, all the days of her life. She has obtained wool and flax, and works them with skillful hands. She puts her hand to the distaff and her fingers hold the spindle. She reaches out her hand to the helpless and gives to the poor. Charm is deceptive and beauty useless; the woman who is wise is the one to praise.

May she enjoy the fruits of her labor and may all praise her for her works.

2nd Reading: 1 Thes 5:1–6

You do not need anyone to write to you about the delay, and the appointed time for these events. You know, that the day of the Lord will come like a thief in the night. When people feel secure, and at peace, the disaster will suddenly come upon them, as the birth pangs of a woman in labor, and they will not escape.

But you, beloved, are not in darkness; so that day will not surprise you like a thief. All of you are citizens of the light and the day; we do not belong to night and darkness. Let us not, therefore, sleep as others do, but remain alert and sober.

Gospel: Mt 25:14–30

Jesus told his disciples this parable, "Imagine someone who, before going abroad, summoned his servants to entrust his property to them. He gave five talents of silver to one servant, two talents to another servant, and one talent to a third, to each, according to his ability; and he went away. He who received five talents went at once to do business with the talents, and gained another five. The one who received two talents did the same, and gained another two. But the one who received one talent dug a hole in the ground, and hid his master's money.

"After a long time, the master of those servants returned and asked for a reckoning. The one who had received five talents came with another five talents, saying, 'Lord, you entrusted me with five talents, but see, I have gained five more.' The master answered, 'Well done, good and faithful servant, since you have been faithful in a few things, I will entrust you in charge of many things. Come and share the joy of your master.'

"Then the one who had received two talents came and said, 'Lord, you entrusted me with two talents; with them I have gained two more.' The master said, 'Well done, good and faithful servant, since you have been faithful in little things, I will entrust you in charge of many things. Come and share the joy of your master.'

"Finally, the one who had received one talent came and said, 'Master, I know that you are a hard man. You reap what you have not sown, and gather what you have not scattered. I was afraid, so I hid your money in the ground. Here, take what is yours!' But his master replied, 'Wicked and worthless servant, you know that I reap where I have not sown, and gather where I have not scattered. You should have deposited my money in the bank, and given it back to me with interest on my return.

"Therefore, take the talent from him, and give it to the one who has ten. For to all those who have, more will be given, and they will have an abundance; but from those who are unproductive, even what they have will be taken from them. As for that useless servant, throw him out into outer darkness, where there will be weeping and gnashing of teeth.'"

Reading: Jesus tells the Parable of the Talents to His listeners. It is about a master who entrusted varying amounts to his servants. Those with five and two talents doubled the amount on his return while the one entrusted with only one talent hid it in the ground for fear. The parable concludes with the two performing servants being given more while the unproductive servant ended up with nothing at all.

Reflection: Fear is the number one enemy of fruitfulness. This is shown in the parable of the gospel today. The one who received one talent from the Master focused so much on his fear that he overlooked the fact that the Master trusted him with just the right amount fitted for his talents and capacities. He was not able to gain momentum from this implied trust. He was blinded by his fear. Because of this, he condemned himself forever to an ordinary and uneventful life. He wanted to play safe. Nobody who doesn't risk will ever amount to something in this lifetime.

Response: What talents do I possess that still stand idle? Today is a good day to make an inventory of my strengths and make a plan how to harness and develop them effectively for the benefit of the greater community.

17
NOVEMBER

Monday
Ps 1:1–2, 3, 4 & 6
Those who are victorious
I will feed from the tree of life.

33RD WEEK IN ORDINARY TIME
St. Elizabeth of Hungary, religious
Psalter: Week 1 / (White)

1st Reading: Rev 1:1–4; 2:1–5

The Revelation of Jesus Christ. God gave it to him, to let his servants know what is soon to take place. He sent his angel to make it known to his servant, John, who reports everything he saw, for this is the word of God, and the declaration of Jesus Christ. Happy is the one who reads aloud these prophetic words, and happy those who hear them, and treasure everything written here, for the time is near.

From John, to the seven churches of Asia: receive grace and peace from him who is, who was, and who is to come, and from the seven spirits of God, which are before his throne. Write this, to the angel of the church in Ephesus, "Thus says the one who holds the seven stars in his right hand, and who walks among the seven golden lamp stands: I know your works, your difficulties and your patient suffering. I know, you cannot tolerate evildoers, but have tested those who call themselves apostles, and have proved them to be liars. You have persevered, and have suffered for my name without losing heart.

Nevertheless, I have this complaint against you: you have lost your first love. Remember from where you have fallen, and repent, and do what you used to do before. If not, I will come to you, and remove your lamp stand from its place; this, I will do, unless you repent.

Gospel: Lk 18:35–43

When Jesus drew near to Jericho, a blind man was sitting by the road, begging. As he heard the crowd passing by, he inquired what was happening, and they told him that Jesus of Nazareth was going by. Then he cried out, "Jesus, Son of David, have mercy on me!" The people in front of him scolded him. "Be quiet!" they said, but he cried out all the more, "Jesus, Son of David, have mercy on me!"

Jesus stopped, and ordered the blind man to be brought to him; and when he came near, Jesus asked him, "What do you want me to do for you?" And the man said, "Lord, that I may see!" Jesus said, "Receive your sight, your faith has saved you." At once the blind man was able to see, and he followed Jesus, giving praise to God. And all the people who were there also praised God.

St. Elizabeth of Hungary
.Did you know that: St. Elizabeth of Hungary was among the first members of the Franciscan Third Order which was newly founded during her time. She was also the first member to be declared a saint.

There are subtle barriers towards wholeness and healing. This is demonstrated in today's gospel wherein the blind man desiring to see, called on Jesus but was silenced by the people around him. It is rude and disrespectful to call on the Teacher in such a loud voice. Besides, what does He have to do with a blind man? So this sense of decorum which at first glance seemed appropriate is actually now a structure that hinders a blind man towards wholeness. But Jesus is famous for breaking conventions. He is not jealous with His dignity as to allow a loud pleading to deter Him from doing good. And so, the seemingly crass and rude blind man got his sight back simply because he did not allow human conventions to get in the way of his healing.

Tuesday

Ps 15:2–3a, 3bc–4ab, 5
I will seat the victor beside me on my throne.

18
NOVEMBER

St. Rose Philippine Duchesne

Did you know that: The Native Americans named St. Rose Philippine Duchesne "Quahkahkanumad" which stood for "Woman Who Prays Always."

1st Reading: Rev 3:1–6, 14–22*

Write this, to the angel of the church in Sardis, "(…) I know your worth: you think you live, but you are dead. Wake up, and strengthen that which is not already dead. For I have found your works to be imperfect in the sight of my God. Remember what you were taught; keep it, and change your ways. If you do not repent, I will come upon you, like a thief, at an hour you least expect.

Yet, there are some left in Sardis who have not soiled their robes; these will come with me, dressed in white, since they deserve it. The victor will be dressed in white, and I will never erase his name from the book of life(…)

Write this, to the angel of the church in Laodicea,

"(…) I know your works: you are neither cold nor hot. Would, that, you were cold or hot! You are lukewarm, neither hot nor cold; so I will spit you out of my mouth. You think you are rich, and have piled up so much, that you need nothing, but you do not realize, that you are wretched, and to be pitied; poor, blind and naked. (…)

"Look, I stand at the door and knock. If you hear my call, and open the door, I will come in to you, and have supper with you, and you, with me. I will let the victor sit with me, on my throne, just as I was victorious, and took my place with my Father, on his throne. (…)"

Gospel: Lk 19:1–10

Jesus entered Jericho and was passing through it. A man named Zaccheus lived there. He was a tax collector and a wealthy man. He wanted to see what Jesus was like, but he was a short man and could not see him because of the crowd. So he ran ahead and climbed up a sycamore tree. From there he would be able to see Jesus, who was going to pass that way. When Jesus came to the place, he looked up and said to him, "Zaccheus, come down quickly, for I must stay at your house today." So Zaccheus climbed down and received him joyfully. All the people who saw it began to grumble, and said, "He has gone as a guest to the house of a sinner." But Zaccheus spoke to Jesus, "Half of what I own, Lord, I will give to the poor, and if I have cheated anyone, I will pay him back four times as much." Looking at him Jesus said, "Salvation has come to this house today, for he is also a true son of Abraham. The Son of Man has come to seek and to save the lost."

We also feel like Zaccheus from time to time. We so badly want to see the Lord but the crowd of life's pressures and challenges prevents us from seeing Him. Our work, problem and other concerns form a barrier that hides Jesus from us. What shall we do with this obstacle? Let us imitate Zaccheus who climbed the sycamore tree. We too must climb our own tree of prayer and good works. And there from the vantage point of our spirituality, we will see that Jesus is in the midst of all our troubles and problems. He has never left our side. We can go on with our life secure that we are never alone even if we don't see Him from time to time.

19
NOVEMBER

Wednesday
Ps 150:1b–2, 3–4, 5–6
Holy, holy, holy Lord, mighty God!

33RD WEEK IN ORDINARY TIME
Psalter: Week 1 / (Green)

1st Reading: Rev 4:1–11

Gospel: Lk 19:11–28

Jesus was now near Jerusalem, and the people with him thought that God's reign was about to appear. So as they were listening to him, Jesus went on to tell them a parable. He said, "A man of noble birth went to a distant country in order to be crowned king, after which he planned to return home. Before he left, he summoned ten of his servants and gave them ten pounds of silver. He said, 'Put this money to work until I get back.' But his compatriots, who disliked him, sent a delegation after him with this message, 'We do not want this man to be our king.'

"He returned, however, appointed as king. At once he sent for the servants, to whom he had given the money, to find out what profit each had made. The first came in, and reported, 'Sir, your pound of silver has earned ten more pounds of silver.'

"The master replied, 'Well done, my good servant! Since you have proved yourself faithful in a small matter, I can trust you to take charge of ten cities.' The second reported, 'Sir, your pound of silver earned five more pounds of silver.' The master replied, 'And you, take charge of five cities!'

"The third came in, and said, 'Sir, here is your money, which I hid for safekeeping. I was afraid of you, for you are an exacting person: you take up what you did not lay down, and you reap what you did not sow.'

"The master replied, 'You worthless servant, I will judge you by your own words! So you knew I was an exacting person, taking up what I did not lay down, and reaping what I did not sow? Why, then, did you not put my money on loan, so that, when I got back, I could have collected it with interest?'

"Then the master said to those standing by, 'Take from him that pound, and give it to the one with ten pounds.' But they objected, 'Sir, he already has ten pounds!'

"The master replied, 'I tell you, everyone who has will be given more; but from those who have nothing, even what they have will be taken away. As for my enemies who did not want me to be their king, bring them in, and execute them right here in front me!'"

So Jesus spoke, and then he passed on ahead of them, on his way to Jerusalem.

Each of us has our own gifts and capacities. These endowments are part of our patrimony given by God. Although these gifts come in varying degrees still it is not whether we have more or less that matters but whether we have used these talents and abilities to the best it could be. There is no point in comparison. Others may look at it in terms of the monetary and status value such talents could bring. This is a very elementary assessment of God's gifts the the self-fulfilment and the knowledge that we have attained the best that we could ever be is the true measurement of having utilized God's gift wisely. Getting envious of another's achievement is a disservice to our loving and giving God. Not using it and keeping it for oneself likewise is another one.

Thursday

Ps 149:1b–2, 3–4, 5–6a & 9b
The Lamb has made us a kingdom
of priests to serve our God.

20
NOVEMBER

1st Reading: Rev 5:1–10

I, John, saw in the right hand of him who was seated on the throne, a scroll, written on both sides, sealed with seven seals. A mighty angel exclaimed, in a loud voice, "Who is worthy to open this and break the seals?"

But no one in heaven or on earth, or in the netherworld, was found able to open the book and read it. I wept much, when I saw that no one was found worthy to open the book and read it. Then, one of the elders said to me, "Do not weep. Look, the lion of the tribe of Judah, the shoot of David, has conquered; he will open the book of the seven seals."

And I saw next to the throne, with its four living creatures, and the twenty-four elders, a Lamb, standing, although it had been slain. I saw him with seven horns and seven eyes, which are the seven spirits of God, sent out to all the earth.

The Lamb moved forward, and took the book from the right hand of him who was seated on the throne. When he took it, the four living creatures and the twenty-four elders bowed before the Lamb. They all held in their hands, harps, and golden cups full of incense, which are the prayers of the holy ones.

This is the new song they sang: *You are worthy to take the book and open its seals, for you were slain, and by your blood, you purchased, for God, people, of every race, language and nation; and you made them a kingdom, and priests for our God, and they shall reign over the land.*

Gospel: Lk 19:41–44

*W*hen Jesus had come in sight of the city, he wept over it, and said, "If only today you knew the ways of peace! But now they are hidden from your eyes. Yet days will come upon you, when your enemies will surround you with barricades, and shut you in, and press on you from every side. And they will dash you to the ground and your children with you, and not leave stone upon stone within you, for you did not recognize the time and the visitation of your God."

When things go well with us and we are on a roll, we sometimes develop insensitivity to the promptings of God. We so believe in our wealth, health and the likes, especially when we are at the peak of our powers that we do not recognize the time and the visitation of our God. This is what happened to Jerusalem, the city of God. She was prosperous, thriving and secure even though she was under Roman rule. She also reveled in her special status as God's beloved, the seat of religious authority in all of Israel. And so her joy would turn into sorrow. This is the lot of those who have forgotten to tune themselves into their protector and guide - for those who are disconnected from their past will never have a glorious future.

21
NOVEMBER

Friday
Ps 119:14, 24, 72, 103, 111, 131
How sweet to my taste
is your promise!

33RD WEEK IN ORDINARY TIME
The Presentation of the Blessed Virgin Mary
Psalter: Week 1 / (White)

1st Reading: Rev 10:8–11

I, John, had heard a voice from heaven, spoke again, saying to me, "Go near the angel who stands on the sea and on the land, and take the small book open in his hand." So, I approached the angel and asked him for the small book; he said to me, "Take it and eat; although it be sweet as honey in your mouth, it will be bitter to your stomach."

I took the small book from the hand of the angel, and ate it. It was sweet as honey in my mouth, but when I had eaten it, it turned bitter in my stomach. Then, I was told, "You must, again, proclaim God's words, about many peoples, nations, tongues and kings."

Gospel: Lk 19:45–48

Jesus entered the temple area and began to drive out the merchants. And he said to them, "God says in the Scriptures, *My house shall be a house of prayer, but you have turned it into a den of robbers!*"

Jesus was teaching every day in the temple. The chief priests and teachers of the law wanted to kill him, and the elders of the Jews as well, but they were unable to do anything, for all the people were listening to him and hanging on his words.

The house of God ought to be a house of encounter with Him; yet, sad to say, we have the uncanny ability to transform it into something else for the sake of practicality or expediency. Because it's the only place big enough to accommodate our social gatherings, so it becomes a social hall from time to time. Or because it needs to be maintained we lease out some of its space for additional income. What was once a rare practice becomes permanent through time. The business built around it in time becomes immovable even though they are not really needed now since the parish has improved its sourcing of funds. The zeal of Jesus to preserve the house of God as a house of prayer and holiness ought to mobilize us to be ever vigilant that this be maintained as such. Sacred spaces should be free from mundane concerns.

33RD WEEK IN ORDINARY TIME
St. Cecilia, virgin & martyr
Psalter: Week 1 / (Red)

Saturday
Ps 144:1, 2, 9–10
Blessed be the Lord, my Rock!

22
NOVEMBER

St. Cecilia
Did you know that: St. Cecilia is the Patron of Musicians and is often depicted in art with a musical instrument in her hand.

_____
_____
_____
_____
_____
_____
_____
_____
_____
_____
_____

Our capacity to think is something wonderful. It enables us to solve questions even in the abstract realm. However, thinking like all other human faculties is not immune to contamination. It can be distorted by pride, self-interest, envy and the likes. The Sadducees are a religious people who believe that there is no resurrection. They have this hypothetical question that they tested on Jesus that showed the absurdity of such belief. The problem is, they saw it from a wrong angle. They thought that our human realities remain after the resurrection. So Jesus had to teach them the proper perspective. They acknowledged His superior wisdom but did they change their belief? What do you think?

1st Reading: Rev 11:4–12

These are *the two olive trees, and the two lamps, which are before the Lord of the earth.* If anyone intends to harm them, fire will come out of their mouths, to devour their enemies: this is how whoever intends to harm them will perish. (…)

But when my witnesses have fulfilled their mission, the beast that comes up from the abyss, will make war upon them, and will conquer and kill them. Their dead bodies will lie in the square of the great city, which the believers figuratively call Sodom, or Egypt, where their Lord was crucified. (…)

But after those three and a half days, a spirit of life, coming from God, entered them. They, then, stood up, and those who looked at them were seized with great fear. A loud voice from heaven called them, "Come up here." So they went up to heaven, in the midst of the clouds, in the sight of their enemies.

Gospel: Lk 20:27–40

Some Sadducees arrived. These people claim that there is no resurrection, and they asked Jesus this question, "Master, in the law Moses told us, 'If anyone dies leaving a wife but no children, his brother must take the wife, and any child born to them will be regarded as the child of the deceased.' Now, there were seven brothers: the first married, but died without children. The second married the woman, but also died childless. And then the third married her, and in this same way all seven died, leaving no children. Last of all the woman died. On the day of the resurrection, to which of them will the woman be a wife? For all seven had her as a wife."

And Jesus replied, "Taking a husband or a wife is proper to people of this world, but for those who are considered worthy of the world to come, and of resurrection from the dead, there is no more marriage. Besides, they cannot die, for they are like the angels. They are sons and daughters of God, because they are born of the resurrection.

"Yes, the dead will be raised, as Moses revealed at the burning bush, when he called the Lord *the God of Abraham and the God of Isaac and the God of Jacob.* For God is God of the living, and not of the dead, for to him everyone is alive."

Some teachers of the law then agreed with Jesus, "Master, you have spoken well." They didn't dare ask him anything else.

23
NOVEMBER

Sunday

Ps 23:1–2, 2–3, 5, 6
The Lord is my shepherd;
there is nothing I shall want.

1st Reading: Ezk 34:11–12, 15–17

Indeed Yahweh says this: I, myself, will care for my sheep and watch over them. As the shepherd looks after his flock when he finds them scattered, so will I watch over my sheep; and gather them from all the places where they were scattered in a time of cloud and fog. I, myself, will tend my sheep and let them rest, word of Yahweh. I will search for the lost and lead back the strays. I will bind up the injured and strengthen the weak; but the fat and strong will be eliminated. I will shepherd my flock with justice.

As for you, my flock—says Yahweh—I will distinguish between one sheep and another, and set apart rams and goats.

2nd Reading: 1 Cor 15:20–26, 28

Brothers and sisters: Christ has been raised from the dead, and he comes before all those who have fallen asleep. A human being brought death; a human being also brings resurrection of the dead. For, as in Adam all die, so, in Christ, all will be made alive. However, each one in his own time: first Christ, then Christ's people, when he comes.

Then, the end will come, when Christ delivers the kingdom to God the Father, after having destroyed every rule, authority and power. For he must reign and *put all enemies under his feet*. The last enemy to be destroyed will be death. When the Father has subjected everything to him, the Son will place himself under the One who subjected everything to him. From then on, God will be all in all.

Gospel: Mt 25:31–46

Jesus said to his disciples, "When the Son of Man comes in his glory with all his angels, he will sit on the throne of his glory. All the nations will be brought before him; and, as a shepherd separates the sheep from the goats, so will he do with them, placing the sheep on his right hand and the goats on his left.

"The king will say to those on his right, 'Come, blessed of my Father! Take possession of the kingdom prepared for you from the beginning of the world. For I was hungry, and you fed me. I was thirsty, and you gave me something to drink. I was a stranger, and you welcomed me into your home. I was naked, and you clothed me. I was sick, and you visited me. I was in prison, and you came to see me.'

"Then the righteous will ask him, 'Lord, when did we see you hungry, and give you food; thirsty, and give you something to drink; or a stranger, and welcome you; or naked, and clothe you? When did we see you sick, or in prison, and go to see you?' The king will answer, 'Truly I say to you: just as you did it for one of the least of these brothers or sisters of mine, you did it to me.'

"Then he will say to those on his left, 'Go, cursed people, out of my sight, into the eternal fire, which has been prepared for the devil and his angels! For I was hungry, and you did not give me anything to eat; I was thirsty, and you gave me nothing to drink; I was a stranger, and you did not welcome me into your house; I was naked, and you did not clothe me; I was sick, and in prison, and you did not visit me.'

"They, too, will ask, 'Lord, when did we see you hungry, thirsty, naked or a stranger, sick or in prison, and did not help you?' The king will answer them, 'Truly I say to you: just as you did not do it for one of the least of these, you did not do it for me.'

"And these will go into eternal punishment; but the just, to eternal life."

Reading: The Gospel speaks of the second coming of Jesus as a glorious and majestic King of heaven and earth. He will come to judge the nations and separate those who will enter the kingdom and those who will go to eternal punishment. The deeds that will determine reward and punishment are those done to the little ones of the earth. Jesus identifies Himself with them and if we attend to or ignore their needs, we also do the same to Jesus.

Reflection: Many charlatans throughout the ages have proclaimed the end of the world. Even in our lifetime alone, too many claims of the end time have been made. Yet the world still revolves around its orbit. Perhaps toying with other people's fears is the easiest way to access their allegiance. Besides, so many people don't want to make the necessary preparation to welcome the end time with confidence. This make them easy targets to those who preach fire and brimstone to increase their following. The gospel speaks of charity as a sure protection to what will come in the end. Yet how many heed this counsel?

Response: Have I been mindful of the poor lately? Do they figure in my plans this coming Christmas? Perhaps it is good to include them in my gift list and really think of something that will be meaningful and useful for them during the holiday season.

24
NOVEMBER

Monday

Ps 24:1bc–2, 3–4ab, 5–6
Lord, this is the people
that longs to see your face.

34TH WEEK IN ORDINARY TIME
St. Andrew Dung-Lac, priest & martyr
and Companions, martyrs
Psalter: Week 2 / (Red)

1st Reading: Rev 14:1–3, 4b–5

I, John, was given another vision: The Lamb was standing on Mount Zion, surrounded by one hundred and forty-four thousand people, who had his name, and his Father's name, written on their foreheads. A sound reverberated in heaven, like the sound of the roaring of waves, or deafening thunder; it was like a chorus of singers, accompanied by their harps.

They sing a new song before the throne, in the presence of the four living creatures and the elders, a song, which no one can learn, except the hundred and forty-four thousand, who have been taken from the earth. These are given, to follow the Lamb wherever he goes. They are the first taken from humankind, who are already of God and the Lamb. No deceit has been found in them; they are faultless.

Gospel: Lk 21:1–4

Jesus looked up and saw rich people putting their gifts into the treasury of the temple. He also saw a poor widow, who dropped in two small coins. And he said, "Truly, I tell you, this poor widow put in more than all of them. For all of them gave an offering from their plenty; but she, out of her poverty, gave all she had to live on."

St. Andrew Dung-Lac

Did you know that: Among St. Andrew Dung-Lac's group, 96 were Vietnamese, 11 were Spaniards, and 10 were French. They died at different times but were canonized together by Pope John Paul II.

Gifts are not measured in terms of quantity but in the quality of the giving. That is why the widow's offering bested the offerings of the rich not because it was bigger but because it came from a heart big enough to give all that it had without reserve. Seeing the quantity of the gift does not require much from us. But sensing the quality of the gift requires special sensitivity. Jesus is attentive to small details and we too would profit much if we are aware of these little things that make ordinary offerings such as two small coins special. Our life will be very much enriched.

34TH WEEK IN ORDINARY TIME
St. Catherine of Alexandria, virgin & martyr
Psalter: Week 2 / (Green / Red)

Tuesday

Ps 96:10, 11–12, 13
The Lord comes to judge
the earth.

25
NOVEMBER

St.. Catherine of Alexandria

Did you know that: St. Catherine of Alexandria was one of the voices who counseled St. Joan of Arc.

1st Reading: Rev 14:14–19

I, John, had this vision. I saw a white cloud, and the one sitting on it, like a *son of man*, wearing a golden crown on his head and a sharp sickle in his hand. An angel came out of the Sanctuary, calling loudly, to the one sitting on the cloud, "Put in your sickle and reap, for harvest time has come, and the harvest of the earth is ripe." He, who was sitting on the cloud, swung his sickle at the earth and reaped the harvest.

Then, another angel, who also had a sharp sickle, came out of the heavenly Sanctuary. Still, another angel, the one who has charge of the altar fire, emerged, and shouted to the first, who held the sharp sickle, "Swing your sharp sickle, and reap the bunches of the vine of the earth, for they are fully ripe." So, the angel swung his sickle and gathered in the vintage, throwing all the grapes into the great wine press of the anger of God.

Gospel: Lk 21:5–11

While some people were talking about the temple, remarking that it was adorned with fine stonework and rich gifts, Jesus said to them, "The days will come when there shall not be left one stone upon another of all that you now admire; all will be torn down." And they asked him, "Master, when will this be, and what will be the sign that this is about to take place?"

Jesus said, "Take care not to be deceived, for many will come in my name, saying, 'I am he; the time is near at hand!' Do not follow them. When you hear of wars and troubled times, don't be frightened; for all these things must happen first, even though the end is not so soon."

And Jesus said, "Nations will fight each other and kingdom will oppose kingdom. There will be great earthquakes, famines and plagues; in many places strange and terrifying signs from heaven will be seen."

Human achievements today are things to behold. They are even mind-boggling sometimes. It seems that there is no limit to what the human mind can do. Even the creativity of the past left behind monuments that still excites our wonder to this very day. But the truth is, no human made monuments will ever endure. The day will come when nothing will be left of what we have once admired. And so our gospel today reminds us not to put our complete trust in the things of the world. They come and go. Only one endures, that is, the Word of God. So as we labor to refine our human capacities, so much more should we labor to refine our spiritual achievements. These are the things that will endure forever.

1st Reading: Rev 15:1–4

I, John, saw another great and marvelous sign in the heavens: seven angels brought seven plagues, which are the last, for with these, the wrath of God will end. There was a sea of crystal, mingled with fire, and the conquerors of the beast, of its name and the mark of its name stood by it.

They had been given the celestial harps, and they sang the song of Moses, the servant of God, and the song of the Lamb: *Great and marvelous are your works, O Lord, God and Master of the universe. Justice and truth guide your steps, O King of the nations. Lord, who will not give honor and glory to your name? For you alone are holy. All the nations will come and bow before you, for they have now seen your judgments.*

Gospel: Lk 21:12–19

*J*esus said to the crowd, "Before all these things happen, people will lay their hands on you and persecute you; you will be delivered to the synagogues and put in prison, and for my sake you will be brought before kings and governors. This will be your opportunity to bear witness.

"So keep this in mind: do not worry in advance about what to say, for I will give you words and wisdom that none of your opponents will be able to withstand or contradict.

"You will be betrayed even by parents and brothers, by relatives and friends, and some of you will be put to death. But even though, because of my name, you will be hated by everyone, not a hair of your head will perish. By your patient endurance you will save your souls."

Discipleship has its cost. It is not merely a romantic feeling that we follow the one true Son of God but we will have damages to pay in this world. This at least was disclosed by Jesus to His disciples. He did not give them a false picture as to what they were entering into. He was honest to tell them that trials would be part and parcel of their lives. The only thing He promised was His never-failing help. Amidst all of these trials, He would be there. And so a potential disciple can weigh things out before deciding to follow. Jesus recruits without duplicity. Thus one can never blame the Lord for the cost of following Him has been laid down beforehand. We follow an honest and truthful Master. We ought to be one also.

Thursday

Ps 100:1b–2, 3, 4, 5
Blessed are they who are called
to the wedding feast of the Lamb.

27
NOVEMBER

1st Reading: Rev 18:1–2, 21–23; 19:1–3, 9a*

I, John, saw another angel, coming down from heaven. So great was his authority, that the whole earth was lit up with his glory. (…) A powerful angel picked up a boulder, the size of a large millstone, and threw it into the sea, saying:" With such violence will Babylon, the great city, be thrown down, never again to be seen. (…)

Never again, will the light of a lamp shine in you. The voice of bridegroom and bride will never, again, be heard in you. Because your traders were the world's great, and you led the nations astray by your magic spell. After this, I heard what sounded like the loud singing of a great assembly in heaven: *Alleluia! Salvation, glory and might belong to our God, for his judgments are true and just. He has condemned the great harlot who corrupted the world with her adultery. He has avenged his servants' blood, shed by her hand, in harlotry. Once more, they sang: Alleluia! The smoke from her goes up, for ever and ever! (…)*

Gospel: Lk 21:20–28

*J*esus said to his disciples, "When you see Jerusalem surrounded by armies, then know that the time has come when it will be reduced to a wasteland. If you are in Judea, flee to the mountains! If you are in Jerusalem, leave! If you are outside the city, don't enter it!

"For these will be the days of its punishment, and all that was announced in the Scriptures will be fulfilled. How hard will it be for pregnant women, and for mothers with babies at the breast! For a great calamity will come upon the land, and wrath upon this people. They will be put to death by the sword, or taken as slaves to other nations; and the pagans will trample upon Jerusalem, until the time of the pagans is fulfilled.

"Then there will be signs in sun and moon and stars, and on the earth anguish of nations, perplexed when they hear the roaring of the sea and its waves. People will faint with fear at the mere thought of what is to come upon the world, for the forces of the universe will be shaken. Then, at that time, they will see the Son of Man coming in a cloud with power and great glory.

"So, when you see things begin to happen, stand erect and lift up your heads, for your deliverance is drawing near."

We tend to look at the end time literature with fear. After all, it speaks of violence and cataclysm too terrifying to contemplate. And so we have two tendencies towards these writings. We fear them so much that we create a spirituality based on fear that God is not a loving God but a harsh and cold judge. On the other hand, we might dismiss them as mere literary style of writing and the language employed is symbolic and therefore not literal. And so we go our merry way. Whatever one's stance before the apocalyptic readings, we still have to look at our own preparedness to meet the Lord on the last day. It is not what will happen, for the end of time is a given, but how ready we are when the time comes that matters. We should not therefore preoccupy ourselves with the date and the exact occurrence of the apocalypse; rather, we should get ourselves ready when the time comes.

28
NOVEMBER

Friday
Ps 84:3, 4, 5–6a & 8a
Here God lives among his people.

34TH WEEK IN ORDINARY TIME
Psalter: Week 2 / (Green)

1st Reading: Rev 20:1-4, 11 – 21:2

I, John, saw an angel came down from heaven, holding in his hand the key to the Abyss, and a huge chain. He seized the monster, the ancient serpent, namely Satan or the devil, and chained him for a thousand years. He threw him into the abyss, and closed its gate with the key, then secured it with locks, that he might not deceive the nations in the future, until the thousand years have passed. Then, he will be released for a little while.

There were thrones, and seated on them were those with the power to judge. I, then, saw the spirits of those who had been beheaded, for having held the teachings of Jesus, and on account of the word of God. I saw all those, who had refused to worship the beast, or its image, or receive its mark on the forehead, or on the hand. They returned to life, and reigned with the Messiah for a thousand years. This is the first resurrection.

After that, I saw a great and splendid throne, and the one seated upon it. At once, heaven and earth disappeared, leaving no trace. I saw the dead, both great and small, standing before the throne, while books were opened. Another book, the book of life, was also opened. Then, the dead were judged, according to the records of these books, that is, each one according to his works.

The sea gave up the dead it had kept, as did death and the netherworld, so that all might be judged, according to their works. Then, death and the netherworld were thrown into the lake of fire. This lake of fire is the second death. All who were not recorded in the book of life were thrown into the lake of fire.

Then, I saw a new heaven and a new earth. The first heaven and the first earth had passed away, and no longer was there any sea. I saw the new Jerusalem, the holy city, coming down from God, out of heaven, adorned as a bride prepared for her husband.

Gospel: Lk 21:29-33

Jesus told his disciples this comparison, "Look at the fig tree and all the trees. As soon as their buds sprout, you know that summer is already near. In the same way, as soon as you see these things happening, you know that the kingdom of God is near. Truly, I tell you, this generation will not pass away, until all this has happened: heaven and earth will pass away, but my words will not pass away."

For those who have the sensitivity of spirit, nothing in the spiritual realm will ever catch them unawares. Even Jesus Himself tells us that signs will be there before the end will come. It is only a matter of reading and interpreting the signs correctly for one to prepare and not be surprised. It is the element of discernment that brings into the equation the importance of community. Alone, one could probably perceive the signs and thus respond accordingly. But if one discerns with the community, there is a greater chance that the result will be better, more attuned and refined by the collective discernment of the community. Many prophets of doom have predicted the end time but they have failed miserably. They did not submit their discernment to the greater community of believers. Jesus did not disclose the secret of reading signs to an individual apostle or to a select few. He told them all so that the discernment of the time would now rest in the hands of the community and not for a privileged few.

34TH WEEK IN ORDINARY TIME
Psalter: Week 2 / (Green/ White)

Saturday

29
NOVEMBER

Ps 95:1–2, 3–5, 6–7ab
Maranatha! Come, Lord Jesus!

1st Reading: Rev 22:1–7

John said: An angel showed me the river of life, clear as crystal, gushing from the throne of God, and of the Lamb. In the middle of the city, on both sides of the river, are the trees of life, producing fruit twelve times, once each month, the leaves of which are for healing the nations.

No longer will there be a curse; the throne of God and of the Lamb will be in the city, and God's servants will live in his presence. They will see his face, and his name will be on their foreheads. There will be no more night. They will not need the light of lamp, or sun, for God, himself, will be their light, and they will reign forever.

Then, the angel said to me, "These words are sure and true; the Lord God, who inspires the prophets, has sent his angel, to show his servants what must happen soon."

"I am coming soon! Happy are those who keep the prophetic words of this book."

Gospel: Lk 21:34–36

Jesus said to his disciples, "Be on your guard: don't immerse yourselves in a life of pleasure, drunkenness and worldly cares, lest that day catch you unaware, like a trap! For, like a snare, will that day come upon all the inhabitants of the earth. But watch at all times and pray, that you may be able to escape all that is going to happen, and to stand before the Son of Man."

Being on guard seems to evoke in some an image of tense vigilance that is tiresome. A more relaxed understanding of being on guard is being present to the moment, being mindful of what is happening in the now. It is not a tense expectation that something bad might happen during the watch. It is rather the openness to be surprised at any moment. It is like the wife who expects a husband's return after a long separation. She fusses over her welcome preparations, but all her being is attuned to the coming of her beloved. She does her work but every moment is a possible moment for the joy of reunion. If we reframe our understanding of how to be on guard while waiting for the end time, we will have a relaxed and enjoyable time of waiting.

30 NOVEMBER

Sunday

Ps 80:2-3, 15-16, 18-19
Lord, make us turn to you;
let us see your face and we shall be saved.

1st Reading: Is 63:16b-17; 64:2-7

You, O Yahweh, are our Father, from the beginning, you are our redeemer: this is your name. Why have you made us stray from your ways? Why have you let our heart become hard so that we do not fear you? Return for the sake of your servants, the tribes of your inheritance.

Let them witness your stunning deeds. No one has ever heard or perceived, no eye has ever seen a God besides you who works for those who trust in him.

You have confounded those who acted righteously and who joyfully kept your ways in mind. But you are angry with our sins, yet conceal them and we shall be saved.

All of us have become like the unclean; all our good deeds are like polluted garments; we have all withered like leaves, blown away by our iniquities. There is no one who calls upon your name, no one who rouses himself to lay hold of you. For you have hidden your face, you have given us up to the power of our evil acts. And yet, Yahweh, you are our Father; we are the clay and you are our potter; we are the work of your hand.

2nd Reading: 1 Cor 1:3-9

Brothers and sisters: Receive grace, and peace from God, our Father, and Christ Jesus, our Lord.

I give thanks, constantly, to my God, for you, and for the grace of God given to you, in Christ Jesus. For you have been fully enriched, in him, with words, as well as with knowledge, even as the testimony concerning Christ was confirmed in you. You do not lack any spiritual gift and only await the glorious coming of Christ Jesus, our Lord. He will keep you steadfast to the end, and you will be without reproach, on the day of the coming of our Lord Jesus. The faithful God will not fail you, after calling you to this fellowship with his Son, Christ Jesus, our Lord.

Gospel: Mk 13:33-37

Jesus said to his disciples, "Be alert and watch, for you don't know when the time will come. When a man goes abroad and leaves his home, he puts his servants in charge, giving to each one some responsibility; and he orders the doorkeeper to stay awake. So stay awake, for you don't know when the Lord of the house will come, in the evening or at midnight, when the cock crows or before dawn. If he comes suddenly, do not let him catch you asleep.

"And what I say to you, I say to all: Stay awake!"

Reading: The gospel speaks of being alert and watchful akin to servants charged by the master going abroad to do their responsibility, and like the doorkeeper to be vigilant lest he catches them slacking in their responsibilities or asleep when he returns. This vigilance is counseled to all who are waiting for the coming of the Lord.

Reflection: Vigilance makes us ready for anything. We will not be caught surprised and unaware. This is the admonition of the Lord to all His followers. In this world there are many temptations to slacken or even relax our principles drawn from the gospel. So many philosophies of life compete with the teachings of the Lord. They are seductive, very tempting and pleasing to our senses. It is only with the greatest vigilance that we can tear ourselves away sometimes from their hypnotic spell. We have to keep our gaze firmly on the Lord who will come. Meanwhile, we prepare. May the Lord see us awake when He comes again in His glory.

Response: Have I been vigilant in my work? Am I mindful and aware of what I do? This can be seen in the quality of my work output. Perhaps today, I will try to be more aware and mindful with what I do, and put heart and soul into it, no matter how small my work seem. Those who will benefit will find it delightful.

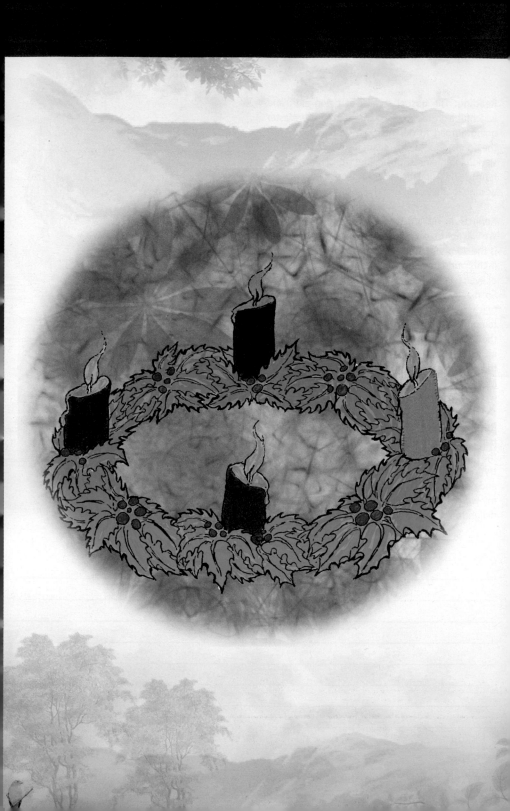

Advent

*T*he liturgical or Church year begins on the first Sunday of Advent. The season of Advent has four weeks. During this time the Christian people recall in joyful expectation the two comings of Jesus Christ into the world.

The first of these comings happened when he became incarnate in the womb of the Blessed Virgin Mary and was born on Christmas day. The second coming will take place on the Last Day when he will come in glory to judge the living and the dead.

The biblical readings and the prefaces of the Mass initially commemorate the second coming of Christ and then gradually shift the focus on his first coming by recalling the roles played by John the Baptist, his precursor, and the Blessed Virgin Mary, his mother.

From December 16, Filipino Catholics intensify their preparation for the birth of Our Lord by the special practice of Simbang Gabi whereby they relive the time when the Mary, Mother of God, awaited the birth of her Son.

Advent is not as strongly penitential in character as Lent. However, the proximity of Christmas joy should not eliminate the penitential spirit of Advent. Amidst our busy preparation for Christmas we should find time to pause and interiorize the meaning of Advent through prayer, self-denial, and works of generosity especially toward the poor.

01
DECEMBER

Monday

Ps 122:1–2, 3–4b, 4cd–5, 6–7, 8–9
Let us go rejoicing to the house
of the Lord.

1ST WEEK OF ADVENT
Psalter: Week 1 / (Violet)

1st Reading: Is 2:1–5

The vision of Isaiah, son of Amoz, concerning Judah and Jerusalem. In the last days, the mountain of Yahweh's house shall be set over the highest mountains and shall tower over the hills.

All the nations shall stream to it, saying, "Come, let us go to the mountain of Yahweh, to the house of the God of Jacob, that he may teach us his ways and we may walk in his paths. For the teaching comes from Zion, and from Jerusalem the word of Yahweh.

He will rule over the nations and settle disputes for many people. They will beat their swords into plowshares and their spears into pruning hooks. Nation will not raise sword against nation; they will train for war no more.

O nation of Jacob, come, let us walk in the light of Yahweh!"

Gospel: Mt 8:5–11

When Jesus entered Capernaum, an army captain approached him, to ask his help, "Sir, my servant lies sick at home. He is paralyzed and suffers terribly." Jesus said to him, "I will come and heal him."

The captain answered, "I am not worthy to have you under my roof. Just give an order and my boy will be healed. For I myself, a junior officer, give orders to my soldiers. And if I say to one, 'Go!' he goes; and if I say to another, 'Come!' he comes; and if I say to my servant, 'Do this!' he does it."

When Jesus heard this, he was astonished; and said to those who were following him, "I tell you, I have not found such faith in Israel. I say to you, many will come from east and west and sit down with Abraham, Isaac and Jacob at the feast in the kingdom of heaven."

The concept of command must be coupled with responsibility in order to temper the sense of power with personal integrity. The army captain in our reading showed why he was the one in command. He did not only wield the power of his office but showed that his people's welfare meant a lot to him. Thus he humbled himself in front of the Lord not to seek a personal favor but for his servant. In a human way he mirrored God's lordship over us. We are not mere subordinates but we have value and worth before Him. Thus the Son did not hesitate to "empty Himself" and take the form of a slave in order to effect our healing. In the first week of Advent, may we be guided by the army captain in our quest to prepare a fitting reception for the Lord when He comes in glory.

Tuesday

Ps 72:1-2, 7-8, 12-13, 17
Justice shall flourish in his time,
and fullness of peace forever.

02

DECEMBER

1st Reading: Is 11:1–10

From the stump of Jesse a shoot will come forth; from his roots a branch will grow and bear fruit.

The spirit of the Lord will rest upon him—a spirit of wisdom and understanding, a spirit of counsel and power, a spirit of knowledge and fear of Yahweh.

Not by appearances will he judge, nor by what is said must he decide, but with justice he will judge the poor and with righteousness decide for the meek.

Like a rod, his word will strike the oppressor, and the breath of his lips slay the wicked.

Justice will be the girdle of his waist, truth the girdle of his loins.

The wolf will dwell with the lamb, the leopard will rest beside the kid, the calf and the lion cub will feed together and a little child will lead them.

Befriending each other, the cow and the bear will see their young ones lie down together.

Like cattle, the lion will eat hay.

By the cobra's den the infant will play.

The child will put his hand into the viper's lair.

No one will harm or destroy over my holy mountain, for as water fills the sea the earth will be filled with the knowledge of Yahweh.

On that day the "Root of Jesse" will be raised as a signal for the nations. The people will come in search of him, thus making his dwelling place glorious.

Gospel: Lk 10:21–24

Jesus was filled with the joy of the Holy Spirit, and said, "I praise you, Father, Lord of heaven and earth, for you have hidden these things from the wise and learned, and made them known to little ones. Yes, Father, such has been your gracious will. I have been given all things by my Father, so that no one knows the Son except the Father, and no one knows the Father except the Son, and he to whom the Son chooses to reveal him."

Then Jesus turned to his disciples and said to them privately, "Fortunate are you to see what you see, for I tell you, that many prophets and kings would have liked to see what you see, but did not see it; and to hear what you hear, but did not hear it."

Spontaneous joy is a beauty to behold. It moves us to thanksgiving to the Ultimate Source of our joy, God Himself. Jesus' joy is not for Himself. It is for the little ones to whom the Father has revealed the things kept from the wise and the learned. It is for His disciples who have seen and heard what the great kings and prophets of old had yearned for but were not able to. In short, the locus of Jesus' joy is not the self but the others. This invites us to take genuine joy at the blessings others receive. It is to rejoice with them for their blessing is a testimony that God still walks in our land. To be genuinely happy for the good fortune of others is to show our contentment with our own blessings received from the same God.

03
DECEMBER

Wednesday

Ps 23:1–3a, 3b–4, 5, 6
I shall live in the house of the Lord
all the days of my life.

1ST WEEK OF ADVENT
St. Francis Xavier, priest
Psalter: Week 1 / (White)

1st Reading: Is 25:6–10a

On this mountain Yahweh Sabaoth will prepare for all peoples a feast of rich food and choice wines, meat full of marrow, fine wine strained.

On this mountain he will destroy the pall cast over all peoples, this very shroud spread over all nations, and death will be no more. The Lord Yahweh will wipe away the tears from all cheeks and eyes; he will take away the humiliation of his people all over the world: for Yahweh has spoken.

On that day you will say: This is our God. We have waited for him to save us, let us be glad and rejoice in his salvation. For on this mountain the hand of Yahweh rests.

Gospel: Mt 15:29–37

Jesus went to the shore of Lake Galilee, and then went up into the hills, where he sat down. Great crowds came to him, bringing the dumb, the blind, the lame, the crippled, and many with other infirmities. People carried them to the feet of Jesus, and he healed them. All were astonished when they saw the dumb speaking, the lame walking, the crippled healed, and the blind able to see; and they glorified the God of Israel.

Jesus called his disciples and said to them, "I am filled with compassion for these people; they have already followed me for three days and now have nothing to eat. I do not want to send them away fasting, or they may faint on the way." His disciples said to him, "And where shall we find enough bread in this wilderness to feed such a crowd?" Jesus said to them, "How many loaves do you have?" They answered, "Seven, and a few small fish."

Jesus ordered the people to sit on the ground. Then, he took the seven loaves and the small fish, and gave thanks to God. He broke them and gave them to his disciples, who distributed them to the people.

They all ate and were satisfied, and the leftover pieces filled seven wicker baskets.

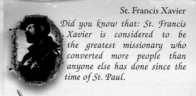

St. Francis Xavier

Did you know that: St. Francis Xavier is considered to be the greatest missionary who converted more people than anyone else has done since the time of St. Paul.

This is a beautiful episode of healing and feeding. Jesus was not only concerned with their physical infirmities and hunger, He also dealt with their spiritual maladies and want. Thus He is not a social worker dealing with earthly problems, nor a spiritual leader concerned only with the spiritual being of those around Him but the Lord and Savior who comes to bring wholeness and completeness to persons. The disciples didn't know this yet. They are still at a loss with regard to their Master's mission. Thus they continuously misunderstand Him. It is only through the Lord's patient mentoring that the disciples will understand that what Jesus does here on earth anticipates the things that will come in the future.

Thursday

Ps 118:1 & 8–9, 19–21, 25–27a
Blessed is he who comes
in the name of the Lord.

04
DECEMBER

St. John Damascene

Did you know that: St. John Damascene is regarded as Doctor of the Church and often referred to as "Doctor of Assumption" because of his writings on the Assumption of Mary.

_____
_____
_____
_____
_____
_____
_____
_____
_____
_____
_____
_____
_____
_____

1st Reading: Is 26:1–6

On that day this song will be sung in the land of Judah:

We have a strong city, he himself has set up walls and fortifications to protect us.

Open the gates!

Let the righteous nation enter, she who is firm in faithfulness.

You keep in perfect peace the one of steadfast mind, the one who trusts in you.

Trust in Yahweh forever, for Yahweh is an everlasting Rock.

He brought down those who dwell on high, he laid low the lofty city, he razed it to the ground, leveled it to the dust,

Now it is trampled the poor and the lowly tread upon it.

Gospel: Mt 7:21, 24–27

Jesus said to his disciples, "Not everyone who says to me, 'Lord! Lord!' will enter the kingdom of heaven, but the one who does the will of my heavenly Father.

"Therefore, anyone who hears these words of mine, and acts according to them, is like a wise man, who built his house on rock. The rain poured down, the rivers flooded, and the wind blew and struck that house. But it did not collapse, because it was built on rock. But anyone who hears these words of mine, and does not act accordingly, is like a fool who built his house on sand. The rain poured, the rivers flooded, and the wind blew and struck that house; it collapsed, and what a terrible collapse that was!"

It is not what we profess but what we do based on what we believe that matters. For words bereft of action are empty words, like sterile seeds that can never germinate and bear fruit. But even though action speaks louder than words, it will still be open to misinterpretation if we do not explain our actions through the spoken words. It is because of this that both have a role to play in having a clear solid faith. But a faith-based action is not easy. It is painstaking labor like putting up the house together brick by brick. It gains solidity only as we do the will of the Father one at a time. Storms will come but every time we hold on, we gain strength in doing what is right until it becomes part of our being.

05
DECEMBER

Friday

Ps 27:1, 4, 13–14
The Lord is my light
and my salvation.

1ST WEEK OF ADVENT
Psalter: Week 1 / (Violet)

1st Reading: Is 29:17–24

In a very short time, Lebanon will become a fruitful field and the fruitful field will be as a forest.

On that day the deaf will hear the words of the book, and out of the dark and obscurity the eyes of the blind will see.

The meek will find joy and the poor among men will rejoice in the Holy One of Israel.

For the tyrant will be no more and the scoffers gone forever, and all who plan to do evil will be cut down—those who by a word make you guilty, those who for a bribe can lay a snare and send home the just empty-handed.

Therefore Yahweh, Abraham's redeemer, speaks concerning the people of Jacob:

No longer will Jacob be ashamed; no longer will his face grow pale.

When he sees the work of my hands, his children again in his midst, they will sanctify my name, they will sanctify the Holy One of Jacob, and stand in awe of the God of Israel.

Those who err in spirit will understand; those who murmur will learn.

Gospel: Mt 9:27–31

As Jesus moved on from Capernaum, two blind men followed him, shouting, "Son of David, help us!" When he was about to enter the house, the blind men caught up with him; and Jesus said to them, "Do you believe that I am able to do what you want?" They answered, "Yes, sir!"

Then Jesus touched their eyes and said, "As you have believed, so let it be." And their eyes were opened. Then Jesus gave them a stern warning, "Be careful that no one knows about this." But as soon as they went away, they spread the news about him through the whole area.

There are prayers that need effort on our part before they can be fulfilled. Just like the two blind men who had to run after Jesus groping their way towards Him, shouting His name until they finally reached Him just before He entered the house. Even then, they had to demonstrate their faith to Him before healing could take place. This reminds us that prayer is a spiritual demonstration of the strength of our faith. The stronger we are, the bigger our capacity to wait and believe that everything will fall into place in God's own time. And so, as much as we are preoccupied with building up physical strength, the more investment in time and effort we must do developing those spiritual muscles that keep us going even though it is hard to play catch up with God.

1ST WEEK OF ADVENT
St. Nicholas, bishop
Psalter: Week 1 / (Violet / White)

Saturday

06
DECEMBER

Ps 147:1–2, 3–4, 5–6
Blessed are all who wait
for the Lord

St. Nicholas

Did you know that: St. Nicholas, often associated with Santa Claus, is considered by some modern scholars as the Christianized version of Poseidon for he is a favorite among Italian and Greek sailors and fisherfolks.

_____
_____
_____
_____
_____
_____
_____
_____
_____
_____
_____
_____
_____
_____

Projects succeed when there is focus and depth. This is the lesson we can glean from the Gospel today. Jesus saw the overwhelming need of the people. He knew He could not do it alone. He therefore empowered His disciples to replicate what He had been doing and entrusted them with responsibilities that would amplify His reach to people in need. But He cautioned them to limit themselves first to the lost sheep of Israel. They had to focus on what was possible to do. This ensures that little by little, the Kingdom of God expands day by day, slowly but surely.

1st Reading: Is 30:19–21, 23–26

O people of Zion, who dwell in Jerusalem, you will weep no more. When you cry, he will listen; when he hears, he will answer. When the Lord has given you the bread of anguish and the water of distress, he, your teacher will hide no longer. Your own eyes will see him, and your ear will listen to his words behind you: "This is the way, walk in it."

He will then give rain for the seed you sow and make the harvest abundant from the crops you grow. On that day your cattle will graze in wide pastures. Your beasts of burden will eat silage tossed to them with pitchfork and shovel.

For on the day of the great slaughter, when fortresses fall, streams of water will flow on every mountain and lofty hill.

The light of the moon will be as the light of the sun, and the light of the sun seven times greater, like the light of seven days, when Yahweh binds up the wounds of his people and heals the bruises inflicted by his blows.

Gospel: Mt 9:35—10:1, 5a, 6–8

Jesus went around all the towns and villages, teaching in their synagogues and proclaiming the good news of the kingdom; and he cured every sickness and disease. When he saw the crowds, he was moved with pity; for they were harassed and helpless, like sheep without a shepherd. Then he said to his disciples, "The harvest is abundant, but the workers are only few. Ask the master of the harvest to send workers to gather his harvest."

Jesus called his Twelve disciples to him, and gave them authority over unclean spirits, to drive them out and to heal every disease and sickness.

Jesus sent these Twelve on mission, with the instructions: "Go to the lost sheep of the people of Israel.

"Go, and proclaim this message: The kingdom of heaven is near. Heal the sick, bring the dead back to life, cleanse the lepers, and drive out demons. Freely have you received, freely give."

Sunday

Ps 85:9-10, 11-12, 13-14
Lord, let us see your kindness,
and grant us your salvation.

1st Reading: Is 40:1-5, 9-11

*B*e comforted, my people, be strengthened, says your God.

Speak to the heart of Jerusalem, proclaim to her that her time of bondage is at an end, that her guilt has been paid for, that from the hand of Yahweh she has received double punishment for all her iniquity.

A voice cries, "In the wilderness prepare the way for Yahweh. Make straight in the desert a highway for our God. Every valley will be raised up; every mountain and hill will be laid low. The stumbling blocks shall become level and the rugged places smooth. The glory of Yahweh will be revealed, and all mortals together will see it; for the mouth of Yahweh has spoken."

Go up onto the high mountain, messenger of good news to Zion, lift up your voice with strength, fear not to cry aloud when you tell Jerusalem and announce to the cities of Judah: Here is your God!

Here comes Yahweh Sabaoth with might; his strong arm rules for him; his reward is with him, and here before him is his booty.

Like a shepherd he tends his flock: he gathers the lambs in his arms, he carries them in his bosom, gently leading those that are with young.

2nd Reading: 2 P 3:8-14

*D*o not forget, beloved, that with the Lord, one day is like a thousand years, and a thousand years is like one day. The Lord does not delay in fulfilling his promise, though some speak of delay; rather, he gives you time, because he does not want anyone to perish, but that all may come to conversion. The Day of the Lord is to come like a thief. Then, the heavens will dissolve with a great noise; the elements will melt away by fire, and the earth, with all that is on it, will be burned up.

Since all things are to vanish, how holy and religious your way of life must be, as you wait for the day of God, and long for its coming, when the heavens will dissolve in fire, and the elements melt away in the heat. We wait for a *new heaven and a new earth*, in which justice reigns, according to God's promise.

Therefore, beloved, as you wait in expectation of this, strive, that God may find you rooted in peace, without blemish or fault.

Gospel: Mk 1:1-8

*T*his is the beginning of the Good News of Jesus Christ, the Son of God. It is written in the book of Isaiah, the prophet, *"I am sending my messenger ahead of you, to prepare your way. Let the people hear the voice calling in the desert: Prepare the way of the Lord, level his paths."*

So John began to baptize in the desert; he preached a baptism of repentance, for the forgiveness of sins. All Judea and all the people from the city of Jerusalem went out to John to confess their sins, and to be baptized by him in the river Jordan.

John was clothed in camel's hair and wore a leather belt around his waist. His food was locusts and honey. He preached to the people, saying, "After me comes one who is more powerful than I am; I have baptized you with water, but he will baptize you in the Holy Spirit."

Reading: The Gospel today is the introduction of the Gospel of Mark. It speaks of John who started his ministry in order to prepare the way for Someone who would come after him.

Reflection: It's not easy to play second fiddle especially if you too have your own set of followers and have been in the trade for some time. But that is precisely what John did. From the very beginning he knew his place and acted responsibly. No temptation for self-promotion or seeking out his own personal glory deterred him from his task. He was a man comfortable with himself. He did not need external signs of his stature. Even his lifestyle pointed to a conscious decision he made for himself. Clothed only in camel's hair with the barest of sustenance to support him, his greatness lay within. Playing second did not diminish who he was. He was God's servant and would remain as one no matter what.

Response: Advent is about disposing of our extras that we might have room for the Child to be born on Christmas. Let John be our guide today for simple living. Why don't we dispose all our accumulated things that we don't need anyway and give it to those who might have better use for it. Maybe, it is a good idea to start with our closet.

08
DECEMBER

Monday

Ps 98:1, 2–3, 3–4
Sing to the Lord a new song,
for he has done marvelous deeds.

SOLEMNITY OF THE
IMMACULATE CONCEPTION
OF THE BLESSED VIRGIN MARY
Psalter: Proper / (White)

1st Reading: Gen 3:9–15, 20

*Y*ahweh God called the man saying to him, "Where are you?" He said, "I heard your voice in the garden and I was afraid because I was naked, so I hid." God said, "Who told you that you were naked? Have you eaten of the tree I ordered you not to eat?" The man answered, "The woman you put with me gave me fruit from the tree and I ate it." God said to the woman, "What have you done?" The woman said, "The serpent deceived me and I ate."

Yahweh God said to the serpent, "Since you have done that, be cursed among all the cattle and wild beasts! You will crawl on your belly and eat dust all the days of your life. I will make you enemies, you and the woman, your offspring and her offspring. He will crush your head and you will strike his heel."

The man called his wife by the name of Eve, because she was the mother of all the living.

2nd Reading: Eph 1:3–6, 11–12

Gospel: Lk 1:26–38

*I*n the sixth month, the angel Gabriel was sent from God, to a town of Galilee called Nazareth. He was sent to a virgin, who was betrothed to a man named Joseph, of the family of David; and the virgin's name was Mary.

The angel came to her and said, "Rejoice, full of grace, the Lord is with you!" Mary was troubled at these words, wondering what this greeting could mean.

But the angel said, "Do not fear, Mary, for God has looked kindly on you. You shall conceive and bear a son; and you shall call him Jesus. He will be great, and shall rightly be called Son of the Most High. The Lord God will give him the kingdom of David, his ancestor; he will rule over the people of Jacob forever; and his reign shall have no end."

Then Mary said to the angel, "How can this be, since I am a virgin?" And the angel said to her, "The Holy Spirit will come upon you and the power of the Most High will overshadow you; therefore, the holy child to be born of you shall be called Son of God. Even your relative, Elizabeth, is expecting a son in her old age, although she was unable to have a child; and she is now in her sixth month. With God nothing is impossible."

Then Mary said, "I am the handmaid of the Lord, let it be done to me as you have said." And the angel left her.

Mary had a reason to rejoice on that blessed day when the angel Gabriel first brought the news to her. She was entrusted with a ministry that God had never asked before from any of the great personalities in the Old Testament. The divine confidence rests on the fragile shoulder of a girl-child of perhaps fourteen or fifteen years of age. Many speak about the obedience and docility of the Blessed Virgin. But few ever talk about her courage. To be chosen as the Mother of the Son of the Most High is a tall order. Yet, this simple maiden did not hesitate and carried the ministry with quiet courage and dignity. No wonder she was blessed among women. She was blessed with uncommon valor not found in anyone who preceded her.

Tuesday

Ps 96:1–2, 3, 10ac, 11–12, 13
The Lord our God comes
with power.

09
DECEMBER

St. Juan Diego

Did you know that: St. Juan Diego saw a Marian apparition in 1531 popularly known as Our Lady of Guadalupe which had a significant impact on the spread of the Catholic faith within Mexico. He was the first indigenous American saint canonized in 2002.

What makes God great is that even little ones have value. He will not allow one less from His flock when it gets lost even though He still has the numerical number to ignore the loss. Nothing is too trivial or too insignificant for a passionately loving God revealed by Jesus. This attachment is perhaps the motive why God deigned His Son to become one of His created beings. He wants to personally know His creatures in the most intimate way that He could. He allowed one of the Trinity to become like His creatures.

1st Reading: Is 40:1–11

Be comforted, my people, be strengthened, says your God. Speak to the heart of Jerusalem, proclaim to her that her time of bondage is at an end, that her guilt has been paid for, that from the hand of Yahweh she has received double punishment for all her iniquity.

A voice cries, "In the wilderness prepare the way for Yahweh. Make straight in the desert a highway for our God. Every valley will be raised up; every mountain and hill will be laid low. The stumbling blocks shall become level and the rugged places smooth. The glory of Yahweh will be revealed, and all mortals together will see it; for the mouth of Yahweh has spoken."

A voice says, "Cry." and I say, "What shall I cry?" "All flesh is grass, and all its beauty as the flower of the field. The grass withers, the flower wilts, when the breath of Yahweh blows upon it. The grass withers, the flower fades,' but the word of our God will forever stand. "Go up onto the high mountain, messenger of good news to Zion, lift up your voice with strength, fear not to cry aloud when you tell Jerusalem and announce to the cities of Judah:

Here is your God! Here comes Yahweh Sabaoth with might; his strong arm rules for him; his reward is with him, and here before him is his booty.

Like a shepherd he tends his flock: he gathers the lambs in his arms, he carries them in his bosom, gently leading those that are with young.

Gospel: Mt 18:12–14

Jesus said to his disciples, "What do you think of this? If someone has a hundred sheep and one of them strays, won't he leave the ninety-nine on the hillside, and go to look for the stray one? And I tell you, when he finally finds it, he is more pleased about it, than about the ninety-nine that did not go astray. It is the same with your Father in heaven. Your Father in heaven doesn't want even one of these little ones to perish."

10
DECEMBER

Wednesday

Ps 103:1–2, 3–4, 8 & 10
O bless the Lord, my soul!

2ND WEEK OF ADVENT
Psalter: Week 2 / (Violet)

1st Reading: Is 40:25–31

To whom, then, will you liken me or make me equal? says the Holy One.

Lift up your eyes and see: who has created all this?

He has ordered them as a starry host and called them each by name.

So mighty is his power, so great his strength, that not one of them is missing.

How can you say, O Jacob, how can you complain, O Israel, that your destiny is hidden from me, that your rights are ignored by Yahweh?

Have you not known, have you not heard that Yahweh is an everlasting God, the Creator of the ends of the earth?

He does not grow tired or weary, his knowledge is without limit.

He gives strength to the enfeebled, he gives vigor to the wearied.

Youth may grow tired and faint, young men will stumble and fall, but those who hope in Yahweh will renew their strength.

They will soar as with eagle's wings; they will run and not grow weary; they will walk and never tire.

Gospel: Mt 11:28–30

Jesus said to the crowds, "Come to me, all you who are weary and burdened, and I will give you rest. Take my yoke upon you and learn from me, for I am gentle and humble of heart; and you will find rest. For my yoke is easy; and my burden is light."

Burden is a matter of perspective. What is considered a burden by some is nothing to others. That is why Jesus' yoke is nothing to complain about because it is borne from the perspective of love. With love, sacrifices are counted as nothing. One is not focused on the pain but on the joy that one will harvest once the difficulties have been surmounted. Thus love sees not only the now but the future that will dawn. The yoke of love may be full of sacrifices but it is never considered heavy.

2ND WEEK OF ADVENT
St. Damasus I, pope
Psalter: Week 2 / (Violet / White)

Thursday
Ps 145:1 & 9, 10–11, 12–13ab
The Lord is gracious and merciful;
slow to anger, and of great kindness.

11
DECEMBER

St. Damasus

Did you know that: St. Pope Damasus I was a 60-year old deacon when he was elected Pope.

_____

_____

_____

_____

_____

_____

_____

_____

_____

_____

_____

_____

Jesus Himself now proclaims directly who will be one of our guides in navigating our way towards Christmas. It is John the Baptist, greatest among the sons of women but humble enough to accept that even he is unfit to untie the sandal straps of the Chosen One of God. It is John's humility which is his greatest virtue. Perhaps the Lord invites us to cultivate humility in this season of Advent for us to be numbered among the lowly shepherds who, on the first Christmas night, saw the baby Jesus ahead of the wise men from the east, and the rest of those who came.

1st Reading: Is 41:13–20

For I, Yahweh, your God, take hold of your right hand and say to you: "Fear not, I am your assistance."

Fear not, Jacob, poor worm, and you, people of Israel, so frail.

I am your redeemer, says Yahweh, the Holy One of Israel, your helper.

I will make you a thresher, new and with sharp double teeth: you will thresh hills and mountains, crushing them and reducing them to chaff.

You will winnow them, the wind will carry them off and the storm will scatter them. But you will rejoice in Yahweh and glory in the Holy One of Israel.

The poor and the afflicted seek water, and find none.

Their tongues are parched with thirst.

But I, Yahweh, will hear them; I, the God of Israel, will not forsake them.

I will open up streams over the barren heights and let the rivers flow through all the valleys;

I will turn the desert into lakes and brooks and the thirsty earth into a land of springs.

I will plant in the wilderness the cedar, the acacia, the myrtle and the olive; I will plant in the wasteland fir, cypress and pine— that all may see and know, consider and understand, that the hand of Yahweh has done this, that the Holy One of Israel has created it.

Gospel: Mt 11:11–15

Jesus said to the crowds, "I tell you this: no one greater than John the Baptist has arisen from among the sons of women; and yet, the least in the kingdom of heaven is greater than he. From the days of John the Baptist until now, the kingdom of heaven is something to be conquered; and violent men seize it.

"Up to the time of John, there was only prophesy: all the prophets and the law. And if you believe me, John is indeed that Elijah, whose coming was predicted. Let anyone with ears listen!"

12
DECEMBER

Friday

Jdt 13:18bcde, 19
You are the highest honor
of our race.

2ND WEEK OF ADVENT
Our Lady of Guadalupe
Psalter: Week 2 / (White)

1st Reading: Zec 2:14–17

"Sing and rejoice, O daughter of Zion, for I am about to come, I shall dwell among you," says Yahweh.

"On that day, many nations will join Yahweh and be my people, but my dwelling is among you. The people of Judah will be for Yahweh as his portion in his holy land. He will choose Jerusalem again.

"Keep still in Yahweh's presence, for he comes, having risen from his holy dwelling."

Gospel: Lk 1:39–47

Mary then set out for a town in the hill country of Judah. She entered the house of Zechariah and greeted Elizabeth. When Elizabeth heard Mary's greeting, the baby leapt in her womb. Elizabeth was filled with the Holy Spirit, and, giving a loud cry, said, "You are most blessed among women; and blessed is the fruit of your womb! How is it, that the mother of my Lord comes to me? The moment your greeting sounded in my ears, the baby within me suddenly leapt for joy. Blessed are you, who believed that the Lord's word would come true!"

And Mary said, "My soul proclaims the greatness of the Lord, my spirit exults in God, my savior!"

Wherever the Virgin Mary visits, joy spontaneously arises. She brings the joy of one who is pregnant with the divine and thus does not keep it to herself but generously brings it to others. Today we celebrate the feast of the Virgin of Guadalupe. Mary visited a lowly mestizo named Juan Diego and brought him the joy that would significantly alter the landscape of Catholicism in Mexico. Because of her, the Mexicans "leapt" for joy in receiving Jesus as their Lord and Savior. That visit transformed the whole nation.

2ND WEEK OF ADVENT
St. Lucy, virgin & martyr
Psalter: Week 2 / (Red)

Saturday

Ps 80:2ac & 3b, 15–16, 18–19
Lord, make us turn to you; let us see
your face and we shall be saved.

13
DECEMBER

St. Lucy

Did you know that: St. Lucy is the Patron Saint of the blind because according to legend it was plucked out by her torturers as part of the torture. However, in the end, God restored her eyes.

1st Reading: Sir 48:1–4, 9–11

Then came the prophet Elijah, like a fire, his words a burning torch.

He brought a famine on the people and in his zealous love had them reduced in number.

Speaking in the name of the Lord he closed the heavens, and on three occasions called down fire.

How marvelous you were, Elijah, in your wondrous deeds! Who could ever boast of being your equal?

You were taken up by a whirlwind of flames in a chariot drawn by fiery horses. It was written that you should be the one to calm God's anger in the future, before it broke out in fury, to turn the hearts of fathers to their sons and to restore the tribes of Jacob.

Happy are those who will see you and those who die in love, for we too shall live.

Gospel: Mt 17:9a, 10–13

As they came down the mountain, Jesus commanded them not to tell anyone what they had seen, until the Son of Man be raised from the dead.

The disciples asked him, "Why do the teachers of the law say that Elijah must come first?" Jesus answered, "So it is: first comes Elijah; and he will restore all things. But I tell you, Elijah has already come; and they did not recognize him; and they treated him as they pleased. And they will also make the Son of Man suffer."

Then the disciples understood that Jesus was referring to John the Baptist.

John the Baptist occupies a privileged place in the Lord's life story. After all, his birth was the herald that God once again walks among His people. When he grew up, he prepared the way of his Lord. That is why he was likened to the mighty prophet of old, Elijah. The latter had to contend with the priests of Baal in order to bring back wayward Israel to the worship of the one true God. John has to contend with God's own priests in order to bring back Israel's attention to what is important: it is mercy and not temple sacrifices that God wants.

14

DECEMBER

Sunday Lk 1:46–48, 49–50, 53–54
My soul rejoices in my God.

1st Reading: Is 61:1–2a, 10–11

The spirit of the Lord Yahweh is upon me, because Yahweh has anointed me to bring good news to the poor.

He has sent me to bind up broken hearts, to proclaim liberty to the captives, freedom to those languishing in prison; to announce the year of Yahweh's favor and the day of vengeance of our God. I rejoice greatly in Yahweh, my soul exults for joy in my God, for he has clothed me in the garments of his salvation, he has covered me with the robe of his righteousness, like a bridegroom wearing a garland, like a bride adorned with jewels.

For as the earth brings forth its growth, and as a garden makes seeds spring up, so will the Lord Yahweh make justice and praise spring up in the sight of all nations.

2nd Reading: 1 Thes 5:16–24

Brothers and sisters: Rejoice always, pray without ceasing and give thanks to God at every moment. This is the will of God, your vocation as Christians.

Do not quench the Spirit, do not despise the prophets' warnings. Put everything to the test and hold fast to what is good. Avoid evil, wherever it may be.

May the God of peace make you holy and bring you to perfection. May you be completely blameless, in spirit, soul and body, till the coming of Christ Jesus, our Lord; he who called you is faithful and will do it.

Gospel: Jn 1:6–8, 19–28

A man came, sent by God; his name was John.

He came to bear witness, as a witness to introduce the Light, so that all might believe through him.

He was not the Light, but a witness to introduce the Light.

This was the testimony of John, when the Jews sent priests and Levites to ask him, "Who are you?" John recognized the truth, and did not deny it. He said, "I am not the Messiah."

And they asked him, "Then who are you? Elijah?" He answered, "I am not." They said, "Are you the Prophet?" And he answered, "No." Then they said to him, "Tell us who you are, so that we can give some answer to those who sent us. How do you see yourself?" And John said, quoting the prophet Isaiah, "I am the _voice of one crying out in the wilderness: Make straight the way of the Lord!_"

Those who had been sent were Pharisees; and they put a further question to John, "Then why are you baptizing, if you are not the Messiah, or Elijah, or the Prophet?" John answered, "I baptize you with water, but among you stands one whom you do not know; although he comes after me, I am not worthy to untie the strap of his sandal."

This happened in Bethabara beyond the Jordan, where John was baptizing.

Reading: Again the Gospel speaks of John, clearly stating that he is not the promised Messiah but someone who prepares His way. The Pharisees try to ascertain his identity and once again John points to his role as the precursor of the One sent by God.

Reflection: John's character is an enigma. The miracle son of Zechariah and Elizabeth, he took away the shame of his parents when he was born. Now as a grown up, he faces the "shame" of having to insist on his secondary status to the one whose sandal strap he is not worthy to untie. Clearly he could have gotten more stature than what he had if he played along with the expectations of people. He was a child conceived in miracle; now he is spreading the miracle of humility to all who meet him. He doesn't have to be somebody other than himself.

Response: To be humble is a lifelong struggle. It needs a conscious decision on our part since it contradicts our human need to be recognized. Perhaps today is a good start to embark on our journey towards humility. Why not write down the many moments you think you have not handled well the praise and humiliation that have come your way. Find out the root cause or causes. It will give us a guide on how to be more humble next year.

_____

_____

_____

_____

_____

_____

_____

_____

_____

_____

15 DECEMBER

Monday

Ps 25:4–5ab, 6 & 7bc, 8–9
Teach me your ways, O Lord.

3RD WEEK OF ADVENT
Psalter: Week 3 / (Violet)

1st Reading: Num 24:2–7, 15–17a

He looked up and saw Israel camping, tribe by tribe; and the spirit of God came upon him and he uttered his song:

"Word of Balaam, son of Beor, the seer, the one who hears the words of God, and beholds the vision of the Almighty, in ecstasy, with eyes unveiled.

How goodly are your tents, Jacob, your encampments, Israel! Like valleys stretching far, like gardens beside a stream, like aloes planted by Yahweh, like cedars beside the waters.

His buckets are overflowing and his seeds are always watered. His king becomes stronger than Agag, and his kingdom grows.

Then Balaam pronounced his oracle: "Word of Balaam, son of Beor, the seer, the one who hears the words of God, who has knowledge from the Most High, and sees the vision of the Almighty, in ecstasy, with eyes unveiled. I see a figure, but not really. I behold him but not near. A star shall come forth from Jacob, he rises with a staff in his hand.

Gospel: Mt 21:23–27

Jesus had entered the temple and was teaching, when the chief priests, the teachers of the law and the Jewish authorities came to him, and asked, "What authority have you to act like this? Who gave you authority to do all this?"

Jesus answered them, "I will also ask you one question. If you answer me, then I will also tell you by what authority I do these things." Where did John's baptism come from? From heaven or from people?"

They discussed this among themselves, saying, "If we say, 'From heaven,' he will say, 'Then why did you not believe him?' And if we say, 'The baptism of John was merely something human', we've got to beware of the people, for all consider John to be a prophet." So they answered Jesus, "We do not know."

And Jesus said to them, "Neither will I tell you by what authority I do these things."

Those who will never believe will always have a reason to discredit you. That is why it is useless to argue with them. You will waste time and effort with those whose ways are set. It is like hitting your head against a brick wall. The religious and political leaders of Jesus' time had joined forces to make life difficult for Jesus. They questioned the ground of His action, that is, by whose authority He did all those things. Jesus refused to be dragged into their semantics. He cleverly sidestepped their trap by asking them a question Himself. He would not waste time arguing and justifying Himself to them. His works can stand the scrutiny of time.

Tuesday

Ps 34:2–3, 6–7, 17–18, 19 & 23
The Lord hears the cry of the poor

16
DECEMBER

1ˢᵗ Reading: Zep 3:1–2, 9–13

Thus says Yahweh: Woe to the rebellious, the defiled, the city that oppresses! She did not pay attention to the call nor accept the correction; she did not trust Yahweh; nor did she approach her God.

At that time, I will give truthful lips to the pagan nations, that all of them may call on the name of Yahweh, and serve him with the same zeal. From beyond the rivers of Ethiopia they will bring offerings to me.

On that day, you will no longer be ashamed of all your deeds, when you were unfaithful to me; I will have removed from your midst the conceited and arrogant; and my holy mountain will no longer be for you, a pretext for boasting.

I will leave within you a poor and meek people who seek refuge in God. The remnant of Israel will not act unjustly nor will they speak falsely, nor will deceitful words be found in their mouths. They will eat and rest, with none to threaten them.

Gospel: Mt 21:28–32

Jesus went on to say, "What do you think of this? A man had two sons. He went to the first and said to him, 'Son, go and work today in my vineyard.' And the son answered, 'I don't want to.' But later he thought better of it and went. Then the father went to his other son and said the same thing to him. This son replied, 'I will go, sir,' but he did not go.

Which of the two did what the father wanted?" They answered, "The first." And Jesus said to them, "Truly, I say to you: the publicans and the prostitutes are ahead of you on the way to the kingdom of heaven. For John came, to show you the way of goodness, and you did not believe him; but the publicans and the prostitutes did. You were witnesses of this, but you neither repented nor believed him.

Is it better to say yes to a command and disobey later on, or to say no and have a change of heart and obey later? The gospel today presents us two sets of response. None of the two seemed to be an ideal response but taking into account human frailty, repentance seemed to be the better response rather than false obedience. That is why the publicans and sinners who initially rejected God but later repented when they heard the preaching of John and, later, that of Jesus, had a head start in God's kingdom. They obeyed when the moment to do so came. Whereas the heirs of Abraham became hard headed, proud and haughty in their privilege, set in their ways, unrepentant and unwilling to change. Bad for them, such pedigree will do them no good when they enter heaven. The doors will be slammed shut on them.

17
DECEMBER

Wednesday

Ps 72:1–2, 3–4ab, 7–8, 17
Justice shall flourish in his time,
and fullness of peace for ever.

3RD WEEK OF ADVENT
Psalter: Week 3 / (Violet)

1st Reading: Gen 49:2, 8–10

"Gather around, sons of Jacob. And listen to your father Israel! Judah, your brothers will praise you! You shall seize your enemies by the neck! Your father's sons shall bow before you.

Judah, a young lion! You return from the prey, my son! Like a lion he stoops and crouches, and like a lioness, who dares to rouse him?

The scepter shall not be taken from Judah, nor the ruler's staff from between his feet, until he comes to whom it belongs, and who has the obedience of the nations.

Gospel: Mt 1:1–17

This is the account of the genealogy of Jesus Christ, son of David, son of Abraham.

Abraham was the father of Isaac, Isaac the father of Jacob, Jacob the father of Judah and his brothers.

Judah was the father of Perez and Zerah (their mother was Tamar), Perez was the father of Hezron, and Hezron of Aram. Aram was the father of Aminadab, Aminadab of Nahshon, Nahshon of Salmon.

Salmon was the father of Boaz. His mother was Rahab. Boaz was the father of Obed. His mother was Ruth. Obed was the father of Jesse.

Jesse was the father of David, the king. David was the father of Solomon. His mother had been Uriah's wife.

Solomon was the father of Rehoboam. Then came the kings: Abijah, Asaph, Jehoshaphat, Joram, Uzziah, Jotham, Ahaz, Hezekiah, Manasseh, Amon, Josiah.

Josiah was the father of Jechoniah and his brothers at the time of the deportation to Babylon.

After the deportation to Babylon, Jechoniah was the father of Salathiel and Salathiel of Zerubbabel.

Zerubbabel was the father of Abiud, Abiud of Eliakim, and Eliakim of Azor. Azor was the father of Zadok, Zadok the father of Akim, and Akim the father of Eliud. Eliud was the father of Eleazar, Eleazar of Matthan, and Matthan of Jacob.

Jacob was the father of Joseph, the husband of Mary, and from her came Jesus who is called the Christ —the Messiah.

There were then fourteen generations from Abraham to David, and fourteen generations from David to the deportation to Babylon, and fourteen generations from the deportation to Babylon to the birth of Christ.

The humanity of Jesus is strongly emphasized in no other passage of the Gospels than in our Gospel today. The long procession of ancestors seemed to hammer the fact that God inserted Himself in our history; therefore, His commitment to humanity is irrevocable. The humanity of the Lord is highlighted by His own share of colorful kin. God does not reserve for Himself only the best of humanity but also embraces our fallen and fallible nature. God is not scared by our inadequacy. Neither should we be scared of God's plenitude that spills constantly.

Thursday

Ps 72:1-2, 12-13, 18-19
Justice shall flourish in his time,
and fullness of peace forever.

18
DECEMBER

1st Reading: Jer 23:5-8

*Y*ahweh further says, "The day is coming when I will raise up a king who is David's righteous successor. He will rule wisely and govern with justice and righteousness. That will be a grandiose era when Judah will enjoy peace and Israel will live in safety. He will be called Yahweh-our-justice!"

"The days are coming," says Yahweh, "when people shall no longer swear by Yahweh as the living God who freed the people of Israel from the land of Egypt. Rather, they will swear by Yahweh as the living God who restored the descendants of Israel from the northern empire and from all the lands where he had driven them, to live again in their own land!"

Gospel: Mt 1:18-25

*T*his is how Jesus Christ was born: Mary his mother had been given to Joseph in marriage, but before they lived together, she was found to be pregnant through the Holy Spirit.

Then Joseph, her husband, made plans to divorce her in all secrecy. He was an upright man, and in no way did he want to disgrace her.

While he was pondering over this, an angel of the Lord appeared to him in a dream and said, "Joseph, descendant of David, do not be afraid to take Mary as your wife. She has conceived by the Holy Spirit, and now she will bear a son. You shall call him 'Jesus' for he will save his people from their sins."

All this happened in order to fulfill what the Lord had said through the prophet: *The virgin will conceive and bear a son, and he will be called Emmanuel*, which means: God-with-us. When Joseph awoke, he did what the angel of the Lord had told him to do, and he took his wife to his home. He did not have any marital relations with her. When she gave birth to a son, Joseph gave him the name Jesus.

Traditional homilies tend to accept the fact that Joseph suspected Mary's fidelity to him. This prompted Joseph accordingly to contemplate divorcing his betrothed quietly to spare her from possible death as prescribed by the Law. But few speak of the possibility that Joseph knew of the mysterious circumstances surrounding Mary's pregnancy. And being a simple God-fearing Jew, he thought himself not worthy of protecting the Son of God as an earthly father. This was beyond his competence. He decided to give way. And so God has to step in and confirm that indeed Mary is pregnant according to the plan of God. And he will name the child to signify his earthly fatherhood. Obedient and trusting, Joseph, like Mary, obeyed God faithfully.

19
DECEMBER

Friday

Ps 71:3–4a, 5–6ab, 16–17
My mouth shall be filled with your
praise, and I will sing your glory!

3RD WEEK OF ADVENT
Psalter: Week 3 / (Violet)

1st Reading: Jdg 13:2-7, 24-25a

Gospel: Lk 1:5-25

In the days of Herod, king of Judea, there lived a priest named Zechariah, belonging to the priestly clan of Abiah. Elizabeth, Zechariah's wife, also belonged to a priestly family. Both of them were upright in the eyes of God, and lived blamelessly, in accordance with all the laws and commands of the Lord, but they had no child. Elizabeth could not have any and now they were both very old.

Now, while Zechariah and those with him were fulfilling their office, it fell to him by lot, according to the custom of the priests, to enter the Sanctuary of the Lord and burn incense. At the time of offering incense, all the people were praying outside; it was then, that an angel of the Lord appeared to him, standing on the right side of the altar of incense. On seeing the angel, Zechariah was deeply troubled and fear took hold of him.

But the angel said to him, "Don't be afraid, Zechariah, be assured that your prayer has been heard. Your wife Elizabeth will bear you a son and you shall name him John. He will bring joy and gladness to you, and many will rejoice at his birth.

This son of yours will be great in the eyes of the Lord. Listen: he shall never drink wine or strong drink; but he will be filled with the Holy Spirit even from his mother's womb. Through him, many of the people of Israel will turn to the Lord their God. He, himself, will open the way to the Lord, with the spirit and power of the prophet Elijah; he will reconcile fathers and children; and lead the disobedient to wisdom and righteousness, in order to make ready a people prepared for the Lord."

Zechariah said to the angel, "How can I believe this? I am an old man and my wife is elderly, too." The angel replied, "I am Gabriel, who stands before God; and I am the one sent to speak to you, and to bring you this good news! My words will come true in their time. But you would not believe; and now, you will be silent and unable to speak until this has happened."

Meanwhile, the people waited for Zechariah; and they were surprised that he delayed so long in the Sanctuary. When he finally appeared, he could not speak to them; and they realized that he had seen a vision in the Sanctuary. He remained dumb and made signs to them.

When his time of service was completed, Zechariah returned home; and, some time later, Elizabeth became pregnant. For five months she kept to herself, remaining at home, and thinking, "This, for me, is the Lord's doing! This is his time for mercy, and for taking away my public disgrace."

God set in motion His plan of salvation when He sent the angel Gabriel to old Zechariah to take away his shame as a childless man. With the conception of the precursor, the Messiah will not be far behind. The opportune time has come. Not even the skepticism of Zechariah can put on hold the project of God. He will be silenced for a while. There is no use listening to doubts and fears when what has been planned will now be set in motion. The silence of Zechariah will be strategic in not preempting prematurely the dawn of salvation arriving at last.

Saturday

Ps 24:1-2, 3-4ab, 5-6
Let the Lord enter;
he is the king of glory.

20
DECEMBER

1st Reading: Is 7:10-14

Once again Yahweh addressed Ahaz, "Ask for a sign from Yahweh your God, let it come either from the deepest depths or from the heights of heaven."

But Ahaz answered, "I will not ask, I will not put Yahweh to the test."

Then Isaiah said, "Now listen, descendants of David. Have you not been satisfied trying the patience of people, that you also try the patience of my God? Therefore the Lord himself will give you a sign: The Virgin is with child and bears a son and calls his name Immanuel."

Gospel: Lk 1:26-38

In the sixth month, the angel Gabriel was sent from God, to a town of Galilee called Nazareth. He was sent to a virgin, who was betrothed to a man named Joseph, of the family of David; and the virgin's name was Mary.

The angel came to her and said, "Rejoice, full of grace, the Lord is with you!" Mary was troubled at these words, wondering what this greeting could mean.

But the angel said, "Do not fear, Mary, for God has looked kindly on you. You shall conceive and bear a son; and you shall call him Jesus. He will be great, and shall rightly be called Son of the Most High. The Lord God will give him the kingdom of David, his ancestor; he will rule over the people of Jacob forever; and his reign shall have no end."

Then Mary said to the angel, "How can this be, since I am a virgin?" And the angel said to her, "The Holy Spirit will come upon you and the power of the Most High will overshadow you; therefore, the holy child to be born of you shall be called Son of God. Even your relative, Elizabeth, is expecting a son in her old age, although she was unable to have a child; and she is now in her sixth month. With God nothing is impossible."

Then Mary said, "I am the handmaid of the Lord, let it be done to me as you have said." And the angel left her.

This time, God visited a young virgin in an insignificant town in the land of Israel. We expect a far more cautious and fearful reception of the divine ambassador from Mary but what transpired was mind blowing. She did not fret nor show excessive feelings. She simply asked, "How can this be?" Her acceptance and obedience is in stark contrast to Zechariah's doubts and hesitation. Clearly age is not a guarantor of courage. Nevertheless, both fulfilled a role in the greater scheme of God by their humble submission to God's will.

1st Reading: 2 S 7:1-5, 8b-12, 14a, 16

When King David had settled in his palace and Yahweh had rid him of all his surrounding enemies, he said to Nathan the prophet, "Look, I live in a house of cedar but the Ark of God is housed in a tent." Nathan replied, "Do as it seems fit to you for Yahweh is with you."

But that very night, Yahweh's word came to Nathan, "Go and tell my servant David, this is what Yahweh says: Are you able to build a house for me to live in?

I took you from the pasture, from tending the sheep, to make you commander of my people Israel. I have been with you wherever you went, cutting down all your enemies before you. Now I will make your name great, as the name of the great ones on earth. I will provide a place for my people Israel and plant them that they may live there in peace. They shall no longer be harassed, nor shall wicked men oppress them as before. From the time when I appointed judges over my people Israel it is only to you that I have given rest from all your enemies. Yahweh also tells you that he will build you a house.

"When the time comes for you to rest with your ancestors, I will raise up your son after you, the one born of you; and I will make his reign secure. I will be a father to him and he shall be my son. Your house and your reign shall last forever before me, and your throne shall be forever firm."

2nd Reading: Rom 16:25-27

Brothers and sisters: Glory be to God! He is able to give you strength, according to the Good News I proclaim, announcing Christ Jesus. Now is revealed the mysterious plan, kept hidden for long ages in the past. By the will of the eternal God it is brought to light, through the prophetic books, and all nations shall believe the faith proclaimed to them.

Glory to God, who alone is wise, through Christ Jesus, forever! Amen.

Gospel: Lk 1:26-38

On the sixth month, the angel Gabriel was sent from God, to a town of Galilee called Nazareth. He was sent to a virgin, who was betrothed to a man named Joseph, of the family of David; and the virgin's name was Mary.

The angel came to her and said, "Rejoice, full of grace, the Lord is with you!" Mary was troubled at these words, wondering what this greeting could mean.

But the angel said, "Do not fear, Mary, for God has looked kindly on you. You shall conceive and bear a son; and you shall call him Jesus. He will be great, and shall rightly be called Son of the Most High. The Lord God will give him the kingdom of David, his ancestor; he will rule over the people of Jacob forever; and his reign shall have no end."

Then Mary said to the angel, "How can this be, since I am a virgin?" And the angel said to her, "The Holy Spirit will come upon you and the power of the Most High will overshadow you; therefore, the holy child to be born of you shall be called Son of God. Even your relative, Elizabeth, is expecting a son in her old age, although she was unable to have a child; and she is now in her sixth month. With God nothing is impossible."

Then Mary said, "I am the hand-maid of the Lord, let it be done to me as you have said." And the angel left her.

Reading: The Gospel today introduces us to the miraculous conception of the Son of God in the Annunciation scene. The protagonists are Mary and the Angel Gabriel. The exchange between the young virgin and God's messenger discloses that it is by the power of the Holy Spirit that the Son of the Most High will become human in the womb of Mary.

Reflection: There is only one Annunciation that has changed the course of salvation history: that which is recorded in our Gospel today. However, there are countless annunciations that take place every day. Perhaps we too have been given a message from heaven. The central question is: are we as courageous as the young virgin in our generosity to respond to God's invitation to serve? If we resist and reject, our ordinary life will continue. But we lose an opportunity to be bigger than ourselves. Greatness passes us by, the doors will close and the roads will vanish. Mary was blessed among women not merely because she was docile. It was her courage that made her great in heaven and on earth.

Response: When was the nth time when I postponed my plan to do something to help my church or the charitable organization that I vowed to support? Today is a good day to actualize that plan and not postpone it again.

22
DECEMBER

Monday

1S 2:1, 4–5, 6–7, 8abcd
My heart exults in the Lord,
my Savior.

4TH WEEK OF ADVENT
Psalter: Week 4 / (Violet)

1st Reading: 1 S 1:24–28

When the child was weaned, Hannah took him with her along with a three-year-old bull, a measure of flour and a flask of wine, and she brought him to Yahweh's house at Shiloh. The child was still young.

After they had slain the bull, they brought the child to Eli. Hannah exclaimed: "Oh, my lord, look! I am the woman who was standing here in your presence, praying to Yahweh. I asked for this child and Yahweh granted me the favor I begged of him. I think Yahweh is now asking for this child. As long as he lives, he belongs to Yahweh."

And they worshiped Yahweh there.

Gospel: Lk 1:46–56

And Mary said,
"My soul proclaims the greatness of the Lord, my spirit exults in God, my savior!

"He has looked upon his servant, in her lowliness, and people, forever, will call me blessed.

"The Mighty One has done great things for me, Holy is his Name. From age to age, his mercy extends to those who live in his presence.

"He has acted with power and done wonders, and scattered the proud with their plans.

"He has put down the mighty from their thrones, and lifted up those who are downtrodden.

"He has filled the hungry with good things, but has sent the rich away empty.

"He held out his hand to Israel, his servant, for he remembered his mercy, even as he promised to our fathers, to Abraham and his descendants forever."

Mary remained with Elizabeth about three months, and then returned home.

When one is so blessed, spontaneous joyful praise streams forth from one's heart. Mary could not contain the joy of her blessings. Praised as blessed among women, she did not deny it. She acknowledged her blessing but pointed in thanksgiving to the author of her privileges. It is not her but God all along Who is to be praised. After two lines of her Magnificat that referred to herself, the rest of her hymn belongs exclusively to the generous God Almighty.

4TH WEEK OF ADVENT
St. John of Kanty, priest
Psalter: Week 4 / (Violet)

Tuesday

Ps 25:4–5ab, 8–9, 10 & 14
Lift up your heads and see;
your redemption is near at hand.

23
DECEMBER

St. John of Kanty

Did you know that: St. John of Kanty, Patron Saint of teachers, spent many of his free hours hand copying manuscripts of the Holy Scriptures, theological tracts and other scholarly works.

_____
_____
_____
_____
_____
_____
_____
_____
_____
_____
_____
_____
_____
_____
_____
_____

The time of God's visitation to His people is finally made sure by the birth of the precursor. With John's birth, there is no turning back on the part of God. One event will lead to another culminating in humanity's redemption. The neighbors of Elizabeth and Zechariah have all the reason to rejoice. Despite not knowing that John heralded the coming of the Messiah, still they knew that something big was coming, the magnitude of which they had no idea at all. They only knew that God's finger was working overdrive. It would be a long time before they could connect the dots between John and Jesus in the future.

1st Reading: Mal 3:1–4, 23–24

Thus says Yahweh: Now I am sending my messenger ahead of me, to clear the way; then, suddenly, the Lord, for whom you long, will enter the Sanctuary. The envoy of the Covenant which you so greatly desire, already comes, says Yahweh of hosts. Who can bear the day of his coming and remain standing when he appears? For he will be like fire in the foundry and like the lye used for bleaching.

He will be as a refiner or a fuller. He will purify the sons of Levi and refine them, like gold and silver. So Yahweh will have priests who will present the offering as it should be. Then Yahweh will accept with pleasure the offering of Judah and Jerusalem, as in former days. I am going to send you the prophet Elijah before the day of Yahweh comes, for it will be a great and terrible day. He will reconcile parents with their children, and the children with their parents, so that I may not have to curse this land when I come."

Gospel: Lk 1:57–66

When the time came for Elizabeth, she gave birth to a son. Her neighbors and relatives heard that the merciful Lord had done a wonderful thing for her, and they rejoiced with her.

When, on the eighth day, they came to attend the circumcision of the child, they wanted to name him Zechariah after his father. But his mother said, "Not so; he shall be called John." They said to her, "But no one in your family has that name!" and they made signs to his father for the name he wanted to give him. Zechariah asked for a writing tablet, and wrote on it, "His name is John;" and they were very surprised. Immediately, Zechariah could speak again, and his first words were in praise of God.

A holy fear came on all in the neighborhood, and throughout the hill country of Judea the people talked about these events. All who heard of it, pondered in their minds, and wondered, "What will this child be?" For they understood that the hand of the Lord was with him.

24
DECEMBER

Wednesday
Ps 89:2–3, 4–5, 27 & 29
For ever I will sing
the goodness of the Lord.

4TH WEEK OF ADVENT
Psalter: Week 4 / (Violet)

1st Reading: 2 S 7:1–5, 8b–12, 14a, 16*

When the King David had settled in his palace and Yahweh had rid him of all his surrounding enemies, he said to Nathan the prophet, "Look, I live in a house of cedar but the Ark of God is housed in a tent." Nathan replied, "Do as it seems fit to you for Yahweh is with you."

But that very night, Yahweh's word came to Nathan, "Go and tell my servant David, this is what Yahweh says: (…) I took you from the pasture, from tending the sheep, to make you commander of my people Israel. I have been with you wherever you went, cutting down all your enemies before you. Now I will make your name great, as the name of the great ones on earth. I will provide a place for my people Israel and plant them that they may live there in peace. (…) Yahweh also tells you that he will build you a house.

When the time comes for you to rest with your ancestors, I will raise up your son after you, the one born of you; and I will make his reign secure. I will be a father to him and he shall be my son. If he does wrong, I will punish him with the rod, as men do. Your house and your reign shall last forever before me, and your throne shall be forever firm."

Gospel: Lk 1:67–79

Zechariah, filled with the Holy Spirit, sang this canticle: "Blessed be the Lord God of Israel, for he has come and redeemed his people.

"In the house of David his servant, he has raised up for us a victorious Savior; as he promised through his prophets of old, salvation from our enemies and from the hand of our foes.

"He has shown mercy to our fathers; and remembered his holy Covenant, the oath he swore to Abraham, our father, to deliver us from the enemy, that we might serve him fearlessly, as a holy and righteous people, all the days of our lives.

"And you, my child, shall be called Prophet of the Most High, for you shall go before the Lord, to prepare the way for him, and to enable his people to know of their salvation, when he comes to forgive their sins.

"This is the work of the mercy of our God, who comes from on high, as a rising sun, shining on those who live in darkness and in the shadow of death, and guiding our feet into the way of peace."

Christmas is a season of songs. Carols permeate the air. No surprise there for many of those biblical characters associated with the season burst into songs of praise and thanksgiving. We have Mary, Zechariah, Simeon and the angelic hosts on that first Christmas night. Songs of praise and thanksgiving is a fitting reception to the newborn king. Heaven and earth are united in joyful praise in this one singular moment in time when divinity dwelt between two realms. We have no reason to be annoyed with Christmas carolers who pop up everywhere. They are in line with the spirit of this beautiful time.

SOLEMNITY OF THE NATIVITY OF THE LORD (CHRISTMAS)
Psalter: Proper / (White)

Thursday

Ps 98:1, 2-3, 3-4, 5-6
All the ends of the earth have seen the saving power of God.

25
DECEMBER

1st Reading: Is 52:7–10

*H*ow beautiful on the mountains are the feet of those who bring good news, who herald peace and happiness, who proclaim salvation and announce to Zion: "Your God is King!"

Together your watchmen raise their voices in praise and song; they see Yahweh face to face returning to Zion.

Break into shouts of joy, O ruins of Jerusalem, for Yahweh consoles his people and redeems Jerusalem.

Yahweh has bared his holy arm in the eyes of the nations; all the ends of the earth, in alarm, will witness God's salvation.

2nd Reading: Heb 1:1–6

Gospel: Jn 1:1–18 (or Jn 1:1-5, 9-14)

*I*n the beginning was the Word. And the Word was with God and the Word was God; he was in the beginning with God.

All things were made through him, and without him nothing came to be. Whatever has come to be, found life in him; life, which for human beings, was also light, light that shines in darkness, light that darkness could not overcome. A man came, sent by God; his name was John. He came to bear witness, as a witness to introduce the Light, so that all might believe through him. He was not the Light, but a witness to introduce the Light.

For the Light was coming into the world, the true Light that enlightens everyone. He was in the world, and through him the world was made, the very world that did not know him. He came to his own, yet his own people did not receive him; but to all who received him, he empowers to become children of God, for they believe in his name.

These are born, but not by seed, or carnal desire, nor by the will of man: they are born of God. And the Word was made flesh and dwelt among us; and we have seen his glory, the glory of the only Son of the Father: fullness of truth and loving-kindness.

John bore witness to him openly, saying, "This is the one who comes after me, but he is already ahead of me, for he was before me." From his fullness we have all received, favor upon favor. For God had given us the law through Moses, but Truth and Loving-kindness came through Jesus Christ. No one has ever seen God, but God-the-only-Son made him known: the one, who is in and with the Father.

This reading is a creative introduction of who Jesus is. This Johannine ode to Jesus gives us a lot to ponder on the nature of Jesus and His purpose for coming here on earth. After a night of revelry that spilled into the wee hours of the morning, John confronts us with a serious reading that demands utmost concentration today. Perhaps this is to remind us that Christmas is not only about happy thoughts and feelings. It is also about a serious God who fulfills His promise today. When feelings subside and reality steps in, we have to grapple with the enormity of the Incarnation in our life.

26
DECEMBER

Friday

Ps 31:3cd–4, 6 & 8ab, 16bc & 17
Into your hands, O Lord,
I commend my spirit.

**FEAST OF ST. STEPHEN,
THE FIRST MARTYR**
Psalter: Proper / (Red)

1st Reading: Acts 6:8–10; 7:54–59

Stephen, full of grace and power, did great wonders and miraculous signs among the people. Some persons then came forward, who belonged to the so-called Synagogue of Freedmen, from Cyrene, Alexandria, Cilicia and Asia. They argued with Stephen. But they could not match the wisdom and the spirit with which he spoke.

When they heard this reproach, they were enraged; and they gnashed their teeth against Stephen. But he, full of the Holy Spirit, fixed his eyes on heaven and saw the glory of God, and Jesus at God's right hand; so he declared: "I see the heavens open, and the Son of Man at the right hand of God."

But they shouted and covered their ears with their hands, and rushed together upon him. They brought him out of the city and stoned him; and the witnesses laid down their cloaks at the feet of a young man named Saul. As they were stoning him, Stephen prayed saying: "Lord Jesus, receive my spirit."

Gospel: Mt 10:17–22

Jesus said to his disciples, "Be on your guard with people, for they will hand you over to their courts, and they will flog you in their synagogues. You will be brought to trial before rulers and kings because of me, so that you may witness to them and the pagans.

"But when you are arrested, do not worry about what you are to say, or how you are to say it; when the hour comes, you will be given what you are to say. For it will not be you who speak, but the Spirit of your Father, speaking through you.

"Brother will hand over his brother to death, and a father his child; children will turn against their parents and have them put to death. Everyone will hate you because of me, but whoever stands firm to the end will be saved."

Just when we are still basking in the afterglow of the Nativity, Stephen enters the scene to remind us of some serious business. Being a follower of Jesus is not only about stars and kings and heavenly hosts making a galactic show for the lowly shepherds. It is also about following Jesus even to the point of death. We may abhor this spoiler during this happy time but the joy of Christmas and the pain of discipleship is closer than what we think. Jesus came not to be happy with us but to suffer for us unto death. And so we take whatever joy that comes our way this season to help us navigate the hardships ahead of following Jesus with courage and faith.

FEAST OF ST. JOHN, APOSTLE AND EVANGELIST
Psalter: Proper / (White)

Saturday
Ps 97:1-2, 5-6, 11-12
Rejoice in the Lord,
you just!

27
DECEMBER

1st Reading: 1 Jn 1:1-4

*T*his is what has been, from the beginning, and what we have heard, and have seen with our own eyes, what we have looked at, and touched with our hands, I mean the Word who is Life.

The *Life* made *itself* known. We have seen Eternal Life and we bear witness; and we are telling you of it. It was with the Father and made himself known to us.

So, we tell you, what we have seen and heard, that you may be in fellowship with us, and us, with the Father, and with his Son, Jesus Christ.

And we write this, that our joy may be complete.

Gospel: Jn 20:1a and 2-8

*O*n the first day after the Sabbath, Mary of Magdala came to the tomb early in the morning while it was still dark, and she saw that the stone blocking the tomb had been moved away. She ran to Peter, and the other disciple whom Jesus loved, and she said to them, "They have taken the Lord out of the tomb and we don't know where they have laid him."

Peter then set out with the other disciple to go to the tomb. They ran together, but the other disciple outran Peter and reached the tomb first. He bent down and saw the linen cloths lying flat, but he did not enter.

Then Simon Peter came, following him, and entered the tomb; he, too, saw the linen cloths lying flat. The napkin, which had been around his head, was not lying flat like the other linen cloths, but lay rolled up in its place. Then the other disciple, who had reached the tomb first, also went in; he saw and believed.

This reading does not seem to be in line with the spirit of the season. We still wallow in the joy of the Incarnation but now we have to go fast forward to the Holy Week scene. Perhaps this out-of-place Gospel is not that off center at all. For the wood of the crib is also the wood of the cross. The baby born in the manger during the first Christmas was really born to die. That Christmas and the Holy Week are intimately connected and shed meaning to one another in ways that otherwise will be overlooked if we treat these two great feasts of our church separately and exclusively. This reading reminds us that joy and pain, triumph and loss, life and death lose the force of their meanings if they are separated from one another.

28
DECEMBER

Sunday

Ps 105:1-2, 3-4, 5-6, 8-9
The Lord remembers his covenant forever.

1st Reading: Gen 15:1-6; 21:1-3

The word of Yahweh was spoken to Abram in a vision: "Do not be afraid, Abram, I am your shield; your reward will be very great!"

Abram said, "My Lord Yahweh, where are your promises? I am still childless and all I have will go to Eliezer of Damascus. You have given me no children, so a slave of mine will be my heir."

Then the word of Yahweh was spoken to him again, "Eliezer will not be your heir, but a child born of you (your own flesh and blood) will be your heir." Then Yahweh brought him outside and said to him, "Look up at the sky and count the stars if you can. Your descendants will be like that."

Abram believed Yahweh who, be cause of this, held him to be an upright man. And he said, "I am Yahweh who brought you from Ur of the Chaldeans to give you this land as your possession."

Yahweh was kind to Sarah as he had said, *and fulfilled his promise to her.* Sarah became pregnant and bore a son to Abraham *in his old age, at the very time Yahweh had promised. Abraham gave the name Isaac to the son that Sarah bore him.*

2nd Reading: Heb 11:8, 11-12, 17-19

It was by faith, that Abraham, called by God, set out for a country that would be given to him as an inheritance; for he parted without knowing where he was going.

By faith, Sarah, herself, received power to become a mother, in spite of her advanced age; since she believed that, he, who had made the promise, would be faithful. Therefore, from an almost impotent man, were born descendants, as numerous as the stars of heaven, as many as the grains of sand on the seashore.

By faith, Abraham went to offer Isaac, when God tested him. And so, he, who had received the promise of God, offered his only son, although God had told him: *Isaac's descendants will bear your name.* Abraham reasoned, that God is capable even of raising the dead, and he received back his son, which has a figurative meaning.

Gospel: Lk 2:22-40 (or Lk 2:22, 39-40)

When the day came for the purification according to the law of Moses, they brought the baby up to Jerusalem, to present him to the Lord, as it is written in the law of the Lord: *Every firstborn male shall be consecrated to God.* And they offered a sacrifice, as ordered in the law of the Lord: *a pair of turtledoves or two young pigeons.*

There lived in Jerusalem, at this time, a very upright and devout man named Simeon; the Holy Spirit was in him. He looked forward to the time when the Lord would comfort Israel; and he had been assured, by the Holy Spirit, that he would not die before seeing the Messiah of the Lord. So, he was led into the temple by the Holy Spirit at the time the parents brought the child Jesus, to do for him according to the custom of the law.

Simeon took the child in his arms, and blessed God, saying, "Now, O Lord, you can dismiss your servant in peace, for you have fulfilled your word and my eyes have seen your salvation, which you display for all the people to see. Here is the light you will reveal to the nations, and the glory of your people Israel."

His father and mother wondered at what was said about the child. Simeon blessed them, and said to Mary, his mother, "Know this: your son is a sign; a sign established for the falling and rising of many in Israel, a sign of contradiction; and a sword will pierce your own soul, so that, out of many hearts, thoughts may be revealed."

There was also a prophetess named Anna, daughter of Phanuel, of the tribe of Asher. After leaving her father's home, she had been seven years with her husband; and since then, she had been continually about the temple, serving God, as a widow, night and day, in fasting and prayer. She was now eighty-four. Coming up at that time, she gave praise to God, and spoke of the child to all who looked forward to the deliverance of Jerusalem.

When the parents had fulfilled all that was required by the law of the Lord, they returned to their town, Nazareth in Galilee. There, the child grew in stature and strength, and was filled with wisdom: the grace of God was upon him.

Reading: Joseph and Mary did the prescribed ritual of offering the firstborn male in the Temple during the purification rite. There they met two extraordinary persons, Simeon and Anna. The prophecies these two holy people spoke regarding the child baffled the couple. After the religious prescription had been fulfilled the Holy Family returned to Nazareth where the child grew in obscurity.

baby who will be the light and glory of Israel. Yet these two personages are not themselves ordinary as they appear. They may be bereft of signs of power and wealth but their spirit is great. They were able to see beyond the plain appearances of the Holy Family. They saw Him of whom others had waited for a long time to recognize. Thus they deserve the joy and happiness that they felt that day. They were ready when the rest of humanity was not.

Reflection: Wonder happens even in the most ordinary setting. Simeon and Anna encountered the greatest wonder of their life when in the Temple they chanced upon a poor and simple couple from the backwater town of Nazareth. Their simplicity belies the treasure beyond price that they carry, the

Response: When was the last time I visited a temple, a sacred place or a pilgrimage site other than the church that I usually go for masses and personal prayer? Today might be a good day for planning a visitation to that holy place I dreamed of visiting and set the date to do so.

_____

_____

_____

_____

_____

29
DECEMBER

Monday

Ps 96:1–2a, 2b–3, 5b–6
Let the heavens be glad
and the earth rejoice!

5TH DAY IN THE OCTAVE OF CHRISTMAS
St. Thomas Becket, bishop & martyr
Psalter: Proper / (White)

1st Reading: 1 Jn 2:3–11*

*M*y dear friends, I am not writing you a new commandment, but reminding you of an old one, one you had from the beginning. This old commandment is the word you have heard.

But, in a way, I give it as a new commandment, that is true in him, and in you, because the darkness is passing away, and the true light already shines.

If you claim to be in the light, but hate your brother, you are still in darkness.

If you love your brothers and sisters, you remain in the light, and nothing in you will make you fall. But if you hate your brother, you are in the dark, and walk in darkness, without knowing where you go, for the darkness has blinded you.

Gospel: Lk 2:22–35

*W*hen the day came for the purification according to the law of Moses, they brought the baby up to Jerusalem, to present him to the Lord, as it is written in the law of the Lord: *Every firstborn male shall be consecrated to God.* And they offered a sacrifice, as ordered in the law of the Lord: *a pair of turtledoves or two young pigeons.*

There lived in Jerusalem, at this time, a very upright and devout man named Simeon; the Holy Spirit was in him. He looked forward to the time when the Lord would comfort Israel; and he had been assured, by the Holy Spirit, that he would not die before seeing the Messiah of the Lord. So, he was led into the temple by the Holy Spirit at the time the parents brought the child Jesus, to do for him according to the custom of the law.

Simeon took the child in his arms, and blessed God, saying, "Now, O Lord, you can dismiss your servant in peace, for you have fulfilled your word and my eyes have seen your salvation, which you display for all the people to see. Here is the light you will reveal to the nations, and the glory of your people Israel."

His father and mother wondered at what was said about the child. Simeon blessed them, and said to Mary, his mother, "Know this: your son is a sign; a sign established for the falling and rising of many in Israel, a sign of contradiction; and a sword will pierce your own soul, so that, out of many hearts, thoughts may be revealed."

St. Thomas Becket
Did you know that: After the canonization of St. Thomas Becket, Canterbury quickly grew to be the most important pilgrim center in England and one of the four greatest in Europe.

Of all the people who looked forward to the Lord's coming, Simeon was chosen by God to witness His Son taking on the helpless fragile state of man. But old Simeon was not fooled. He saw what other people in the Temple at that time overlooked. The love of God is now made concrete among us. Thus he sang his song of thanksgiving grateful for the privilege that was denied from the great men and women who walked the land of Israel at that time. To see the face of the Lord and live is a fitting conclusion to a life of faithfulness to God.

6TH DAY IN THE OCTAVE OF CHRISTMAS
Psalter: Proper / (White)

Tuesday

Ps 96:7–8a, 8b–9, 10
Let the heavens be glad
and the earth rejoice!

30
DECEMBER

1st Reading: 1 Jn 2:12–17

*M*y dear children, I write this to you: you have already received the forgiveness of your sins, through the name of Jesus. Fathers, I write this to you: you know him, who is from the beginning. Young men, I write this to you: you have overcome the evil one. My dear children, I write to you, because you already know the Father.

Fathers, I write to you, because you know him, who is from the beginning. Young men, I write to you, because you are strong, and the word of God lives in you, who have, indeed, overcome the evil one.

Do not love the world, or what is in it. If anyone loves the world, the love of the Father is not in him.

For everything in the world—the craving of the flesh, the greed of eyes and people boasting of their superiority—all this, belongs to the world, not to the Father.

The world passes away, with all its craving, but those who do the will of God remain for ever.

Gospel: Lk 2:36–40

*T*here was also a prophetess named Anna, daughter of Phanuel, of the tribe of Asher. After leaving her father's home, she had been seven years with her husband; and since then, she had been continually about the temple, serving God, as a widow, night and day, in fasting and prayer. She was now eighty-four. Coming up at that time, she gave praise to God, and spoke of the child to all who looked forward to the deliverance of Jerusalem.

When the parents had fulfilled all that was required by the law of the Lord, they returned to their town, Nazareth in Galilee. There, the child grew in stature and strength, and was filled with wisdom: the grace of God was upon him.

Old people are more sensitive to the changes that usually happen around them, Probably it's because they are more attuned to the now, having their mortality firmly fixed in their mind. They savor the present unlike others who still have the time to focus on something else. Thus Anna was with an equally old man Simeon at the Temple when the baby Jesus was presented as was the custom. They thanked God for their good fortune. The hopes and fears of ages past was now right before their eyes. They die assured that God was and is true to His word.

31
DECEMBER

Wednesday

Ps 96:1-2, 11-12, 13
Let the heavens be glad
and the earth rejoice!

7TH DAY IN THE OCTAVE OF CHRISTMAS
St. Sylvester I, pope
Psalter: Proper / (White)

1st Reading: 1 Jn 2:18–21

Gospel: Jn 1:1–18

In the beginning was the Word. And the Word was with God and the Word was God; he was in the beginning with God.

All things were made through him, and without him nothing came to be. Whatever has come to be, found life in him; life, which for human beings was also light, light that shines in darkness, light that darkness could not overcome. A man came, sent by God; his name was John. He came to bear witness, as a witness to introduce the Light, so that all might believe through him. He was not the Light, but a witness to introduce the Light.

For the Light was coming into the world, the true Light that enlightens everyone. He was in the world, and through him the world was made, the very world that did not know him. He came to his own, yet his own people did not receive him; but to all who received him, he empowers to become children of God, for they believe in his name.

These are born, but not by seed, or carnal desire, nor by the will of man: they are born of God. And the Word was made flesh and dwelt among us; and we have seen his glory, the glory of the only Son of the Father: fullness of truth and loving-kindness.

John bore witness to him openly, saying, "This is the one who comes after me, but he is already ahead of me, for he was before me." From his fullness we have all received, favor upon favor. For God had given us the law through Moses, but Truth and Loving-kindness came through Jesus Christ. No one has ever seen God, but God-the-only-Son made him known: the one, who is in and with the Father.

St. Sylvester

Did you know that: Every year in Brazil, the Saint Sylvester Road Race (Corrida Internacional de São Silvestre), a long-distance running event, the oldest and most prestigious street race in Brazil, is held this day which happens to be the feast day of St. Sylvester I, pope.

The majestic hymn of John's Gospel regarding the provenance of Jesus is a fitting goodbye to the year. It gives us a trajectory on how to spend the coming New Year; that is, to contemplate the wondrous commerce that took place between heaven and earth. The Son of God became Son of Man, and how this could take place is more than a lifetime's worth of contemplation. John begins from the very beginning, at a time when there was no time yet. There was the Word. Now He is being revealed through human words that strive mightily to convey His mystery. May we start the year with the Word as our companion. May He light our path to ways that are level and smooth.

ROMAN MISSAL

About the New Translation

In 2001, the Holy See released a new set of guidelines for the translation of liturgical books which requires a word-for-word translation that is closer to the original Latin in content and syntax. In 2002, the Holy See promulgated the 3rd typical edition of the Roman Missal. In 2010, the Pope approved the new English translation produced by the International Committee on English in the Liturgy and the Holy See's Vox Clara Commission. This new translation replaces the second edition in use since 1975.

In July 2011, the CBCP voted to implement this new translation for the whole Philippines on the First Sunday of Advent of 2012 which falls on 2 December 2011 by which time, Masses celebrated in English will have to use the new translation.

About the Eucharist

The Eucharist (also called the Mass) is the memorial of the Lord's paschal mystery – his passion, death, and resurrection through which he redeemed, saved, restored and sanctified humankind. This memorial of the Lord's sacrifice is celebrated by the community of the baptized, the Church, in the form of a ritual meal. In the Mass, Christ comes to us in the sacrament of his body and blood, in the ritual proclamation of God's Word, in the ministry of priests, and in our gathering as a worshipping assembly.

Catholics, by virtue of their Christian baptism, have the right and duty to take part in the Eucharist. Sunday is the Lord's day, the day of the Eucharist, and the day of the Church. We should always participate actively and worthily in the Sunday Eucharist with proper disposition. We should come to church on time and be present from the entrance rite until the dismissal. We should be in our Sunday best.

The Eucharist ought to strengthen individuals in their Christian commitment, in living their baptismal dignity and mission, and in their participation in the life and mission of Christ and His Church.

INTRODUCTORY RITES

Entrance
Celebrant: In the name of the Father, and of the Son, and of the Holy Spirit.
People: Amen.

Greeting
Celebrant: The grace and ... /The Lord/ Peace be with you.
People: And with your spirit.

Penitential Act

FORM A
(Confiteor)
I confess to almighty God
and to you, my brothers and sisters,
that I have greatly sinned,
in my thoughts and in my words,
in what I have done
and in what I have failed to do,
(and, striking their breast, they say)
through my fault,
through my fault,
through my most grievous fault.
(Then, we continue)
Therefore I ask blessed
Mary ever-Virgin,
all the Angels and Saints,
and you, my brothers and sisters,
to pray for me to the Lord our God.

FORM B
Celebrant: Have mercy on us, O Lord.
People: For we have sinned against you.
Celebrant: Show us, O Lord, your mercy.
People: And grant us your salvation.

FORM C
Celebrant: (Invocation)
            Lord, have mercy.
People: Lord, have mercy.
Celebrant: (Invocation)
            Christ, have mercy.
People: Christ, have mercy.
Celebrant: (Invocation)
            Lord, have mercy.
People: Lord, have mercy.
*Kyrie/ Christe, eleison may also be used

Kyrie
When Form A or Form B is used, the Kyrie follows the absolution.

V/. Lord, have mercy.
R/. Lord, have mercy.
V/. Christ, have mercy.
R/. Christ, have mercy.
V/. Lord, have mercy.
R/. Lord, have mercy.
or:
V/. Kyrie, eleison.
R/. Kyrie, eleison.
V/. Christe, eleison.
R/. Christe, eleison.
V/. Kyrie, eleison.
R/. Kyrie, eleison.

From time to time on Sundays, especially in Easter time, instead of the customary Penitential Act, the BLESSING AND SPRINKLING OF WATER may take place as a reminder of Baptism.

Gloria
Glory to God in the highest, and on earth peace to people of good will.
We praise you, we bless you, we adore you, we glorify you, we give you thanks for your great glory,
Lord God, heavenly King, O God, almighty Father. Lord Jesus Christ, Only Begotten Son, Lord God, Lamb of God, Son of the Father, you take away the sins of the world, have mercy on us; you take away the sins of the world, receive our prayer; you are seated at the right hand of the Father, have mercy on us.
For you alone are the Holy One, you alone are the Lord, you alone are the Most High, Jesus Christ, with the Holy Spirit, in the glory of God the Father. Amen.

Collect Prayer
Priest: Let us pray.
[Collect Prayer] ... for ever and ever.
People: Amen.

LITURGY OF THE WORD

First/ Second Reading

Lector: The Word of the Lord.
People: Thanks be to God.

Gospel
Deacon/Priest: The Lord be with you.
People: And with your spirit
Deacon/Priest: A reading from the holy Gospel...
People: Glory to you, O Lord.

Profession of Faith
I believe in God,
the Father almighty,
Creator of heaven and earth,
and in Jesus Christ, his only Son, our Lord,
At the words that follow, up to and including the
Virgin Mary, all bow.
who was conceived by the Holy Spirit,
born of the Virgin Mary,
suffered under Pontius Pilate,
was crucified,
died and was buried;
he descended into hell;
on the third day he rose again from the dead;
he ascended into heaven;
is seated at the right hand of
God the Father almighty;
I believe in the Holy Spirit,
the holy Catholic Church,
the communion of saints,
the forgiveness of sins,
the resurrection of the body,
and life everlasting. Amen

Niceno-Constantinopolitan Creed
I believe in one God, the Father almighty,
maker of heaven and earth,
of all things visible and invisible.
I believe in one Lord Jesus Christ,
the Only Begotten Son of God,
born of the Father before all ages.
God from God, Light from Light,
true God from true God,
begotten, not made,
consubstantial with the Father;
through him all things were made.
For us men and for our salvation
he came down from heaven,
At the words that follow up to and including and
became man, all bow.

and by the Holy Spirit was
incarnate of the Virgin Mary,
and became man.
For our sake he was crucified
under Pontius Pilate,
he suffered death and
was buried,
and rose again on the third day
in accordance with the Scriptures.
He ascended into heaven
and is seated at the right hand
of the Father.
He will come again in glory
to judge the living and
the dead and his kingdom
will have no end.
I believe in the Holy Spirit,
the Lord, the giver of life,
who proceeds from the Father and the Son,
who with the Father and the Son
is adored and glorified,
who has spoken through
the prophets.
I believe in one, holy,
catholic and apostolic Church.
I confess one Baptism
for the forgiveness of sins
and I look forward to the resurrection
of the dead and the life of the
world to come. Amen.

LITURGY OF THE EUCHARIST

Preparation of the Altar and Gifts
When there is no singing
Celebrant: Blessed are you, Lord God of all
creation, for through your goodness we have
received the bread we offer you: fruit of the earth
and work of human hands, it will become for us the
bread of life.

People: Blessed be God for ever.

Priest: Blessed are you, Lord God of all creation, for
through your goodness we have received the wine
we offer you: fruit of the vine and work of human
hands, it will become our spiritual drink.

People: Blessed be God for ever.

Prayer over the Gifts
Priest: Pray, brethren (brothers and sisters), that my
sacrifice and yours may be acceptable to God, the
almighty God and Father.

People: May the Lord accept the sacrifice at your hands for the praise and glory of his name, for our good and the good of all his holy Church.

Eucharistic Prayer

Opening Dialogue
Celebrant: The Lord be with you.
People: And with your spirit.
Celebrant: Lift up your hearts.
People: We lift them up to the Lord.
Celebrant: Let us give thanks to the Lord our God.
People: It is right and just.

Sanctus
Holy, Holy, Holy Lord God of hosts.
Heaven and earth are full
of your glory.
Hosanna in the highest.
Blessed is he who comes in the name of the Lord.
Hosanna in the highest.

Mystery of Faith
Priest: The Mystery of Faith.

We proclaim your Death, O Lord, and profess your Resurrection until you come again.
Or:
When we eat this Bread and drink this Cup, we proclaim your Death, O Lord, until you come again.
Or:
Save us, Savior of the world, for by your Cross and Resurrection you have set us free.

Communion Rite

The Lord's Prayer
Celebrant: At the Savior's command and formed by divine teaching, we dare to say:

All:
Our Father, in heaven,
holy be your name;
your kingdom come,
your will be done on earth
as in heaven.
Give us today our daily bread,
forgive us our sins,
as we forgive
those who sin against us;
do not bring us to the test,
but deliver us from evil.

Sign of Peace
Concelebrant: The peace of the Lord be with you always.
People: And with your spirit.

Communion
Celebrant: Behold the Lamb of God, behold him who takes away the sins of the world. Blessed are those called to the supper of the Lamb.
People: Lord, I am not worthy that you should enter under my roof, but only say the word and my soul shall be healed.

CONCLUDING RITE

Greeting
Celebrant: The Lord be with you.
People: And with your spirit.

Blessing
[Bishop: Blessed be the name of the Lord
People: Now and for ever.
Bishop: Our help is in the name of the Lord.
People: Who made heaven and earth.]

Celebrant: May almighty God bless you, the Father, and the Son, and the Holy Spirit.
People: Amen

Dismissal
Celebrant/Deacon: Go forth, the Mass is ended.
Or:
Go and announce the Gospel of the Lord.
Or:
Go in peace, glorifying the Lord by your life.
Or:
Go in peace.
People: Thanks be to God.

(SOURCE: EPISCOPAL COMMISSION ON LITURGY of the Catholic Bishops' Conference of the Philippines)

Abbreviations

OLD TESTAMENT

Amos	Am	1 Kings	1 K
Baruch	Bar	2 Kings	2 K
1 Chronicles	1 Chr	Lamentations	Lm
2 Chronicles	2 Chr	Leviticus	Lev
Daniel	Dn	1 Maccabees	1 Mac
Deuteronomy	Dt	2 Maccabees	2 Mac
Ecclesiastes	Ecl	Malachi	Mal
Esther	Es	Micah	Mic
Exodus	Ex	Nahum	Nh
Ezekiel	Ezk	Nehemiah	Ne
Ezra	Ezra	Numbers	Num
Genesis	Gen	Obadiah	Ob
Habakkuk	Hb	Proverbs	Pro
Haggai	Hg	Psalms	Ps
Hosea	Hos	Ruth	Ru
Isaiah	Is	1 Samuel	1 S
Jeremiah	Jer	2 Samuel	2 S
Job	Job	Sirach	Sir
Joel	Jl	Song of Songs	Song
Jonah	Jon	Tobit	Tb
Joshua	Jos	Wisdom of Solomon	Wis
Judges	Jdg	Zechariah	Zec
Judith	Jdt	Zephaniah	Zep

NEW TESTAMENT

Acts	Acts	Mark	Mk
Colossians	Col	Matthew	Mt
1 Corinthians	1 Cor	1 Peter	1 P
2 Corinthians	2 Cor	2 Peter	2 P
Ephesians	Eph	Philemon	Phlm
Galatians	Gal	Philippians	Phil
Hebrews	Heb	Revelation	Rev
James	Jas	Romans	Rom
John	Jn	1 Thessalonians	1 Thes
1 John	1 Jn	2 Thessalonians	2 Thes
2 John	2 Jn	1 Timothy	1 Tim
3 John	3 Jn	2 Timothy	2 Tim
Jude	Jd	Titus	Tit
Luke	Lk		

Notes

Notes

Notes

Notes